The Maturing of Multinational Enterprise:

American Business Abroad from 1914 to 1970

Mira Wilkins

Harvard University Press
Cambridge, Massachusetts, and London, England

For more than forty years, volumes published in the Harvard Studies in Business History have contributed to an understanding of the American past. For a long time its editors—Norman S. B. Gras, Henrietta Larson, and Thomas R. Navin—concentrated on publishing books about individual business enterprises and businessmen of the late eighteenth- and nineteenth-century America. Of the first twenty volumes published in the Studies, all but three were this type of case study. Under the able editorship of Ralph W. Hidy, the focus of the series broadened. While topics in nineteenth-century American business continued to be central, both Arthur M. Johnson's *Petroleum Pipelines and Public Policy* and Vincent P. Carosso's *Investment Banking in America* concerned themselves with twentieth-century business, and Raymond de Roover's study of the Medici bank was the first and still the only book in the series on a non-American topic. My hope is to broaden still further the scope of the series. While in no sense intending to exclude books on eighteenth- and nineteenth-century American business history, I would like it to include more studies on the twentieth century, on the business history of other nations, and particularly on topics that cut across national boundaries and include more than a single enterprise or even a single industry.

Mira Wilkins's *The Maturing of Multinational Enterprise* thus provides an admirable volume with which to embark on a policy of expanding the scope of the series. Although it still deals with American business enterprises, it considers the history of many firms operating in many industries and doing so in an international and twentieth-century setting. For this reason the story she tells is central to the understanding of the development of modern, large-scale business enterprise and of its changing role in the international economy.

Indeed the enterprises that Dr. Wilkins examines are among the most powerful private economic organizations the world has yet seen. These multinational corporations are the largest and most complex of the giant, integrated, and diversified business enterprises that have come to dominate major sectors of nearly all technologically advanced industrial economies. These enterprises have become responsible for handling a significant share of the flow of funds and of goods—raw and semifinished materials and finished products—across international boundaries and for making long-term investments in plant and personnel in many different nations. The centralization of this supra-national economic power, both as to the control of short-term flows and the determination of long-term capital investment, is suggested by the fundamental shift that has occurred since World War I in the method of overseas investment. Although by 1914 United States direct investments abroad far exceeded its portfolio stakes, the much larger European investments were predominately indirect in the form of stocks, bonds and other securities. By 1970 close to 75 per cent of all foreign investment had become direct stakes in enterprises controlled by multinational companies.

In nearly all nonsocialist advanced economies, large private enterprises have come to make direct investments overseas. The American multinationals are, however, far more numerous and on the whole larger than those of other nations. Their history, therefore, is of particular importance for the understanding of the growth and activities of this relatively new economic institution.

In relating their story, Dr. Wilkins has concentrated on the historian's basic task of getting the chronological record straight. By careful and painstaking research she has indicated what happened, when, and how. Nor does she neglect the why. Others may have different reasons as to why these developments occurred, but they, and indeed all scholars analyzing the experience of the multinational enterprise, will have to rely heavily on the record Dr. Wilkins presents here. Her history must long remain a basic source for historians, economists, and political scientists who wish to explain the rise and continuing domination of large-scale business enterprises in modern market economies, to understand the growth and changes in international and national economies since World War I, and to study the interrelationships between national economic policies and priorities and a changing international economic order.

Alfred D. Chandler, Jr.

Today the multinational corporation is an important economic institution. Most of the major American corporations do not confine themselves to domestic operations but participate widely in business beyond the national frontiers, having direct investments in many countries. Through the multinational corporation, men, capital, goods, management methods, technology, marketing techniques, and general skills cross over national boundaries. The American multinational corporation has influence on the United States and on foreign economies. Its impact has become vast.

Such a formidable institution did not suddenly spring into existence. Contrary to what has often been maintained, U.S. corporations with interrelated direct investments abroad are *not* unique to the 1950s, 1960s, and 1970s. Rather, the multinational corporation has emerged, grown, and changed over many decades, altering its strategies to respond to challenges and sometimes facing defeat when the challenges have been too great. Companies in certain industries and sectors have fared better than others. The development of multinational enterprise has been an uneven, complex, multifaceted process.

The present study is the second of two books designed to provide the first comprehensive history of U.S.-controlled multinational business. The story, begun in *The Emergence of Multinational Enterprise: American Business Abroad from the Colonial Era to 1914,* published by Harvard University Press (1970), is here carried to 1970. In both books I have been concerned with when, which, why, how, and where American businesses went abroad and in the present volume, especially, with how U.S. enterprises got along once in alien lands. Thus, I am interested in the *entry* of U.S. companies into new direct investments outside the United States and in the *experiences* of existing branches, subsidiaries, and affiliates of those businesses in foreign countries. Throughout, I have sought to appraise the influence of economic, technological, political, military, and social considerations in the United States and abroad on the internationalization of American business.

In 1914, the roots of present-day American multinational enterprise were practically all evident. Worldwide, U.S. direct investments existed. Already, certain companies had developed multinational strategies. Yet, it is after 1914 that the blossoming and vast influence of the U.S.-headquartered multinational corporation came of age. World War I represents a watershed in the history of multinational enterprise and accordingly provides a fine place to begin the present volume.

Part One herein includes the impact of the First World War and the Mexican and Russian revolutions on American business abroad. In Part Two I document the growing U.S. corporations' surge of commitment to foreign operations during the prosperous years of the 1920s. Part Three covers the lessening of the commitment with the Great Depression and the muted concern of most but not all U.S. enterprises in international business in the 1930s; the exceptions are also revealed. Part Four deals with the changed circumstances that faced U.S. business abroad during World War II and in its immediate aftermath. Part Five turns to U.S. corporations' greatly revived enthusiasm for multinational ventures in the late 1950s and 1960s. Although Part Five is devoted to current events (1955–1970), I make no claim to probe in depth into the contemporary experiences of multinational enterprises. Rather, this study's originality and its contribution should lie in its putting today's U.S.-headquartered multinational enterprise in the perspective of American international business history and in its indication of what elements appear to be new and which do not. In the concluding part of the book (Part Six), I have sought to combine the findings of this and the first study to seek a tentative "evolutionary" model of the development of U.S. multinational enterprise—one helpful to our understanding of the course of direct foreign investments by manufacturing, petroleum, mining, and other U.S. companies; I have then attempted to apply the model to U.S. business in the various sectors.

One of the most striking overall features to surface from my inquiry into American business abroad 1914–1970 has been the dramatic U.S. corporate challenge to European enterprise worldwide. In 1914, only in nearby Mexico, Cuba, Panama, and perhaps parts of Central America did the amount of U.S. business exceed the contribution of British investors. The decades after 1914 saw U.S. capital triumph over European throughout the western hemisphere and as far away from home as Liberia and Saudi Arabia. Hopefully, this book will give the reader a sense of the reasons behind and the pace of that accomplishment.

A second striking feature to emerge from this study is the variety of positive, negative, and mixed responses of the United States and foreign governments to the spread of U.S. private enterprise abroad. This book seeks to evaluate and to define some of the divergent foreign and domestic governmental policies that shaped the course of U.S. business outside this country. I have tried to indicate when, which, and whether specific government policies influenced the development of U.S. business abroad.

Third, this book should demonstrate the *cumulative* nature of the activities of American business abroad. What I am writing about is the process of business growth. For U.S. business, integration, diversification, and direct foreign investment, as we will see, are all part of the same process.

It is difficult to record, to synthesize, and to present the history of American business abroad from 1914 to 1970 because the materials available are so immense, the ways of approaching the subject so many, and the implications so profound. Yet, this is what I have attempted. For sources of information, I have used company records, letters and reports in the National Archives, university and financial collections, "oral history" files, and the abundant published data (both governmental and private). My research abroad has been assisted by interviews with U.S. embassy officials and representatives of foreign governments (including one head of state, the president of Liberia). Of vital importance in enriching my understanding of international business have been my interviews and discussions with literally hundreds of businessmen; these took place in air conditioned offices, but also in plush restaurants, in desert sand storms, in 112° heat, in snow blizzards, and at altitudes of almost 15,000 feet; in important world capitals and urban centers, but also in spots such as Ahmadi, Awali, Calama, Chihuahua, Golfito, Ndola, Nsuta, Paramonga, Ras Tanura, and Selukwe. Even the most talented geography student may feel the need to consult his maps to discover these cities or towns in Kuwait, Bahrain, Chile, Mexico, Costa Rica, Zambia, Ghana, Peru, Saudi Arabia, and Rhodesia where enterprising Americans had operations.

I am concerned herein not simply with U.S. businesses that exported to foreign markets or with those that purchased goods abroad. The enterprises that this study deals with all embarked on *operations* abroad. This also means that I am not concerned with U.S. portfolio investments (investments in bonds or stocks that did not carry the power to influence decisions). Rather, my interest is in U.S. *direct* investments abroad—that is with foreign investments by U.S. companies involving management responsibility, the possibility of a voice in management, and direct business purpose.* My research has covered both market-oriented stakes abroad (U.S. investments designed to supply foreign markets, including those in selling, manufacturing, petroleum refining, public utilities, and other services) and supply-oriented stakes abroad (U.S. investments made for export from the host country, designed to fill the needs of the United States or third-country markets—including those investments in purchasing, certain types of manufacturing and processing, oil producing and refining, mining and smelting, and agriculture).

For the years covered by this book, 1914–1970, statistics exist on the book value of U.S. direct investments abroad—by region and sectors.† The best figures for my purpose have been compiled by Cleona Lewis (assisted by Karl T. Schlotterbeck) and by the U.S. Department of Commerce. Their data are included throughout. The reader is, however, cautioned to be wary. The compilers encountered many difficulties in making their estimates, and thus their figures are subject to error. Others have made estimates that do not coincide (some of these estimates are also introduced, when relevant). The figures presented herein are generally satisfactory only as rough *guidelines*. I have not developed new statistical data; instead, I have employed these earlier valiant efforts of others—efforts which I have truly appreciated.

I hope the reader will have patience with the detail and in the process of reading this book will become acquainted with and fascinated by the extent, the nature, and the growth of the participation of U.S. business around the world.

---

*For more on my selective mechanism, see my *The Emergence of Multinational Enterprise: American Business Abroad from the Colonial Era to 1914*, pp. x–xi. Note that from 1914 to 1970, with the possible exception of 1929 (estimates issued by the U.S. Department of Commerce differ), private U.S. investors have always had greater long-term direct than portfolio investments abroad.

† Not for every year, but there are enough numbers to indicate general trends.

Acknowledgments

Courtney Brown, then dean of the Graduate School of Business at Columbia University, made available to me Ford Foundation funds for studies in international business. The initial research on this volume was done under the auspices of the Graduate School of Business at Columbia. Dean Brown also provided me with introductions to businessmen and corporations; his far-reaching contacts proved an invaluable aid in my research.

Raymond Vernon—now director of the Center for International Affairs at Harvard University—read this manuscript at several stages in its creation, each time offering excellent advice. I am indebted to him for his comments on my work and for his prolific and stimulating writings on the multinational corporation. His aide, Joan Curhan, kindly furnished me with data developed at the Harvard Business School on multinational enterprise that helped advance my own studies. I am most grateful to Alfred D. Chandler, Jr., editor of the Harvard Series on Business History and Isidor Straus Professor of Business History at the Graduate School of Business Administration, Harvard University; Professor Chandler had outstanding ideas on how I could improve this manuscript; in addition, his work in the field of business history has immensely influenced my own thinking. Arthur M. Johnson, when he was teaching business history at Harvard, read the first draft of this manuscript and made splendid suggestions. Likewise, I want to express my appreciation to the editors at Harvard University Press who had confidence in this work and guided it to publication.

I owe a debt to numerous other scholars, who have given me valuable pointers, often leading me to specialized volumes in their areas of expertise: Roy Blough (on international business in general), Emile Benoit (on U.S. business in Europe), William A. Hance and Walter Chudson (on Africa), Ronald Schneider, A. O. Hirschman, and the late Frank Tannenbaum (on Latin America), Charles Stewart (on oil in the Middle East), and Nina M. Galston (on law and international business). Dorothy Borg provoked me to penetrate deeper into the history of U.S. direct investments in the Far East.

Librarians and archivists gave me much essential guidance. To Dr. Richmond D. Williams, Director of the Eleutherian Mills Historical Library, particular thanks are due.

Worldwide, literally hundreds of businessmen have answered my queries and directed me to materials on the history of multinational enterprise. Of these W. Rogers Herod (formerly head of International General Electric), Charles M. Brinckerhoff (then president of Anaconda), Henry W. Balgooyen (then executive vice president of American & Foreign Power Company), and the late Lansdell Christie (founder of the Liberian Mining Company) were extraordinarily helpful. In fact, every one of the hundreds of businessmen, whom I interviewed, conversed with, wrote to, and who sent letters on my behalf, contributed generously his time and knowledge. Interviews (confirmed by documents) are invaluable in writing twentieth-century history. The assistance of all the businessmen in talking with me and producing documents was truly welcomed.

In several cities (notably in Tokyo, Caracas, and Buenos Aires), representatives of the U.S. Chamber of Commerce provided information. Likewise, U.S. embassy personnel (particularly the economic officers) made useful suggestions. In Japan, the Ministry of International Trade and Industry found statistical data for me on the history of U.S. business in that country, while in Liberia officials of that government enhanced my understanding of the growth of U.S. investment there.

My husband, George B. Simmons, has been of supreme importance, assisting in a multitude of ways. His encouragement has been incomparable; I have always prized his wise and judicious advice.

The literature on *contemporary* international business is awesome and becomes more so daily. As this book goes to press, new works are appearing, new theses are being completed, new seminars and projects are being undertaken, and the data from Washington on the multinational enterprise proliferate. My bibliography and notes reveal my obligations to many authors.

My special thanks extend to Mrs. Esther Lanzello, a remarkable typist, who was just perfect.

Contents

Tables

One

War and Crisis

"This assemblage of representative businessmen is held with the highest purpose. By gathering and concentrating at this National Foreign Trade Convention the opinion of leading men in commercial affairs in our country, it is hoped to further develop foreign trade opportunity. . . . No issue is of more vital importance." Thus spoke James A. Farrell, president of U.S. Steel (America's largest corporation), at the inaugural meeting of the National Foreign Trade Council in Washington, D.C., in May 1914. A month later, the newly organized International Congress of Chambers of Commerce met in Paris. Americans attended. At both conferences, U.S. businessmen spoke optimistically about the outlook for greater overseas trade. They took for granted world peace. Many of the U.S. corporations participating in these sessions already had direct investments outside their own nation, U.S. Steel included.[1]

2

Indeed, in 1914, when our story begins, American companies already had far-flung operations around the world. Their foreign business activities had developed over time. From the colonial era to 1914, American enterprises had made direct foreign investments. As early as the 1850s, U.S. industrial concerns had opened "branch" factories in England, and by the 1880s and 1890s, there began on a substantial scale the emergence of modern multinational enterprises, enterprises with interrelated marketing and manufacturing facilities in several nations. It was in general the technologically advanced U.S. corporation with new products that had invested to sell abroad. These corporations had opened sales outlets around the world; some built or acquired foreign manufacturing plants, mainly in Canada and Europe—plants to serve foreign markets. At the same time, some U.S. companies invested abroad to obtain raw materials. These went at first principally to nearby areas (Mexico and Canada), and by 1914, they were penetrating deeper into Latin America. Far fewer enterprises had such operations in two or more countries. By 1914, certain large businesses had both market- and supply-oriented stakes beyond the frontiers of the United States. Thus, when our story starts in 1914, there prevailed a network of U.S. corporations' foreign operations. There was a foundation to be built upon. In 1914, the book value of U.S. direct foreign investment was $2.65 billion, a sum equal to slightly over 7 per cent of the existing gross national product.[2]

3

The businessmen who gathered in 1914 at the National Foreign Trade Council and the International Congress of Chambers of Commerce meetings believed that U.S. foreign trade and investment would continue to grow. Their assumption, however, that a peaceful world would persist in which their businesses would flourish was soon shattered. What would the effect of war be on the investments abroad that they had established over the years and now planned to augment? The World War I years would mark a major break in the history of multinational enterprise, influencing the growth and direction of that development.

At the end of July 1914, German tanks crashed across the Belgian frontier. Mobilized armies of Russia, England, Italy, France, Austria-Hungary, and Germany stood in readiness. U.S. businessmen in Europe in late July and early August 1914—either at work or on vacation—rushed to leave. Chaos prevailed. Stock exchanges closed, as individuals and corporations sold securities. Banks shut. In each country, the military commandeered transportation. "Cornelius Vanderbilt was said to have left his hotel without being able to pay his bill; Alfred Vanderbilt was forced to borrow two shillings from the hall porter to get a shave; Chauncey Depew rode a cattle car in France; and Alfred McCormick unsuccessfully tried to buy a yacht when other means of transportation failed." American Express, U.S. consular agents, and a newly organized American citizens' committee sought to assist their stranded compatriots. Many U.S. businessmen left Europe early in August 1914 aware that their corporations' branches, subsidiaries, and affiliates were in the territories of both sets of combatants and that they would have to face the dilemma of dual loyalty. American Radiator, United Shoe Machinery, Eastman Kodak, International Harvester, General Electric, Singer, Standard Oil of New Jersey, and American Express were among the U.S. enterprises with direct investments in lands under control of *both* the Allies and the Central Powers.* [3]

Clarence Woolley, president of American Radiator Company, had reported to his board of directors for years that only a war could halt the successful course of his firm's European business. On July 27, the day after the Austrians sent their note to Serbia, Woolley attended a Paris management meeting involving managers from American Radiator's subsidiaries in England, Italy, France, Germany, and Austria; no participant realized that war was imminent; each manager returned to his respective country on July 28. Woolley remained in Europe. When war began, Woolley tried first to remit as much money as possible from Europe to the United States. With the newly imposed restraints he had only mixed success. Then, he took a ship to New York. As he left Europe, his company's personnel were being recruited into the military. Sixty-seven men were called up from his firm's Paris office. Of the 689 men employed at his company's French plant, all but 28 were mobilized. In Germany, practically the entire staff of American Radiator's subsidiary was drafted. Next came host government intervention and contracts. The French state requisitioned the radiator company's factory at Dôle as a temporary barracks; it ordered the French radiator subsidiary to produce shells for that nation's military needs. National Radiator Company, Ltd. (the English subsidiary of American Radiator Company), agreed to supply the Belgians with hand grenades and closed other contracts with British authorities; later, under the British Munitions Act, 1915/1916, that subsidiary became a "controlled establishment." In Italy, the radiator company's unit pledged to sell that government semicast steel shells. Meanwhile, the two plants of American Radiator Company in Germany made cast iron shells for the imperial regime, and the company's Austrian subsidiary manufactured munitions. The war orders were filled virtually under compulsion. At the start, Woolley expressed concern whether the costs of each subsidiary had been carefully calculated; he was not sure the war

* Other U.S. companies with assets on both sides included Diamond Match, International Steam Pump (later Worthington Pump), Otis Elevator, Texas Company, Vacuum Oil, Western Electric, Westinghouse Electric, and the major U.S. life insurance firms.

business would be profitable. His apprehensions notwithstanding, the profits of the subsidiaries on *both* sides of the battle mounted (despite new, burdensome wartime taxes).[4]

By October 1914 United Shoe Machinery Company's factory in Leicester, England, had sharply reduced production since seven hundred of its sixteen hundred employees had been mobilized. United Shoe's factory in Paris was converted into military barracks. Its plant in Frankfort stopped operating. Unlike American Radiator Company, United Shoe Machinery Company did not prosper.

Eastman Kodak had to reorganize its continental business when the fighting began. Before August 1914, Eastman Kodak's London operation had both managed and supplied Kodak's European trade. Now this was impossible. Accordingly, on August 25, 1914, George Eastman wrote the Berlin manager of Kodak, G.m.b.H.: "In regard to future supplies of goods, you may order them direct from Rochester [the American headquarters of Eastman Kodak]. We rely upon you to manage the affairs of the German Company with the same care and interest that you would if you owned the whole thing yourself." During 1914, George Eastman remained impartial in his dealings with his executives located in the territories of the Allies and the Central Powers. He was, however, concerned over the possible confiscation of the company's properties in Germany and Austria-Hungary (since these had been administered by Kodak's British subsidiary). Eastman appealed to the U.S. Department of State for assistance to "our" companies in these countries. Apparently no assistance was required, for while the United States remained neutral, the Germans did no harm to these enterprises. Meanwhile, in each European nation, the local Kodak subsidiary contributed to relief funds. By mid-1915, George Eastman had become pro-Allies. He rejected the suggestion that his German subsidiary buy German war loan securities, although Kodak units in England and Russia purchased British and Russian war bonds. In January 1916, the parent Eastman Kodak, its foreign subsidiaries, and Eastman personally had $4 million invested in British, French, Russian, and Italian war loans and treasury bills.[5]

When German forces overran an area, that did not mean U.S. manufacturing ceased. The Germans on October 13, 1914, for example, took possession of International Harvester Company's plant at Croix, France. The factory continued to operate, meeting German needs.[6]

Those U.S. companies that did business on the continent in large part through patent and division of territories agreements (General Electric, for example) found the war made such accords temporarily inoperative. Yet, the factories of General Electric's affiliates in England and France prospered. In England, for instance, the G.E. affiliate made shells, high tension magnetos for aircraft, and parts for guns, tanks, submarines, and battleships. In Germany, the G.E.-associated company aided that nation.[7]

The British government took over the operations of Singer's huge sewing machine plant in Scotland, where it manufactured airplane parts and munitions (sewing machine production ceased). By contrast, Singer's German factory—which at the beginning of the war employed two thousand workmen—continued to make sewing machines; it assisted the German war effort, although its work force was depleted by the mobilization.[8]

Some of Standard Oil of New Jersey's European operations suffered as the war progressed. Belgian forces destroyed the company's facilities in that nation rather than have them fall in German hands. In 1915 and 1916, the output of Jersey Standard's Rumanian enterprise declined. On December 2, 1916, anticipating German advances into Rumania, the Anglo-Rumanian Destruction Commission instructed British and American oil companies in Rumania to blow up their properties; Jersey Standard complied, and its manager cabled New York, "Fields and refinery totally destroyed. Compensation guaranteed by allied powers. All important books saved." Yet, even while Jersey Standard was thus acting on behalf of the Allied cause, it retained business relationships with its Deutschland affiliate. Not until February 1917, when U.S. entry into the war seemed imminent, did Jersey Standard sell its shares in its German marketing and refining affiliate—Deutsch-Amerikanische Petroleum Gesellschaft. The shares were sold to Jersey Standard's German partner. The U.S. company received as collateral securities held by the German partner in the United States. It hoped this would protect its properties.[9]

American Express's position, as explained by its historian, was that as long as the United States was neutral, so was American Express—in action if not in thought. American Express representatives moved in and out of Berlin, aiding Americans who for official or business reasons remained.[10]

Indeed, as these cases indicate, between August 1914 and early 1917, American businesses with stakes in Europe saw mobilization of their personnel, encountered host government intervention, and obtained state contracts. Some American units stopped functioning, but most went into war production to fill the host nation's (or the occupying power's) needs. If necessary, the U.S. company reorganized its managerial and/or stock ownership relationships between and among its European subsidiaries and affiliates. The destruction of Standard Oil of New Jersey's properties in Belgium and Rumania was atypical. In general, prior to U.S. entry into the war, little damage was done. In fact, from the summer of 1914 to the spring of 1917, U.S. parent corporations retained direct communications with their subsidiaries and affiliates in Europe—*on both sides of the war*—even though the patriotically inclined European units usually had no contacts with one another.

4

As Europeans fought, Americans had the opportunity to make new direct foreign investments *outside* Europe—in areas where European stakes had been supreme (in Central and South America, Canada, and to a lesser extent east of Suez). Canada excepted, new U.S. direct investments between 1914 and 1917 were in less developed regions. The new foreign investments were made in agriculture, processing of agricultural products, mining and processing of ores, oil production, utilities, manufacturing (including oil refining), and distribution. Many investments were in response to conditions created by the war.

The war in Europe meant, for instance, a giant demand for motor transport, which in turn stimulated demands for rubber tires. The U.S. rubber tire makers anticipated a sharp rise in the price of raw rubber. To protect their source of supply (all rubber came from abroad) and to fill their requirements, U.S. rubber companies integrated backward. They did not follow the route of earlier U.S. speculative enterprises, which had sought rubber in Mexico; political conditions in that country (see Chapter II) seemed to preclude such new entries. Likewise, they ignored Brazil (once a major source of rubber)—in part because of U.S. Rubber's earlier unfortunate experience there.* Instead, U.S. Rubber Company, which in 1910 had acquired an 80,000 acre estate in Sumatra, extended this land holding and found its plantations were filling its "most sanguine expectations." Goodyear opened a buying office in Singapore, and in 1917 that firm acquired a 20,000 acre plantation in Sumatra, its first investment in the Dutch East Indies. Firestone also started a purchasing office in Singa-

---

* U.S. Rubber's frustrations with the "Acre" concession in 1903 are noted in Wilkins, *Emergence of Multinational Enterprise,* p. 188.

pore and contemplated investments in plantations (but did not make them at this time). The backward integration of the three major U.S. rubber tire companies into growing and buying rubber meant that these firms obtained their crude rubber more often directly from the Far East instead of purchasing the commodity in London. These U.S. businesses went to what were formerly British-Dutch sources of supply and circumvented the Europeans.

War brought destruction to the sugar-producing properties in northern France, Belgium, and southwestern Russia as well as the end to sugar exports from Germany and Austria-Hungary. To meet the demands of the Allied powers and to fill U.S. requirements, Americans increased their investments in Cuban cane sugar. New firms proliferated; they, along with the existing enterprises, cleared land, planted cane, constructed mills, and built railway connections. Prices rose, and investors prospered.[11]

Processing agricultural output, likewise, attracted new U.S. foreign direct investment. European armies required vast quantities of meat. Chicago meat packers could not fill the heavy overseas demand from their domestic supplies; thus, Swift, Armour, Morris, and Wilson enlarged their already established meat-packing plants in South America and opened new ones in the southern part of the western hemisphere. Swift also raised the output of its Australian facility, which had opened early in 1914; Australian exports went to Europe.[12]

Nineteen-fifteen saw a war boom in the United States, bringing inflation. U.S. paper and pulp makers found it cheaper to manufacture in Canada than at home.* American newsprint makers recognized the Dominion had inexpensive timber, good water power, and relatively cheap labor; they noted the growth of competitive mills across the border. Since 1911 no duties barred Canadian newsprint from the United States. Thus, from 1914 to 1916 at least four new, giant American paper and pulp mills were constructed across the northern border. The paper and pulp makers planned to export their output to the United States.[13]

American corporations in addition made new direct foreign investments in buying, mining, and processing ores. U.S. businessmen for the first time purchased tin directly from Bolivia, rather than through London; this was possible only after the erection of facilities in the United

---

* In 1915 the average cost of manufacture of a ton of newsprint was $30.52 in the United States and $26.38 in Canada.

States to smelt and to refine the tin.* Processing no longer had to be done in Britain. W. R. Grace & Co.—for years established in trade and investment on the west coast of South America—now organized the International Mining Company, which became a large producer of Bolivian tungsten and a smaller miner of tin.[14] In the direct purchasing and in the investments, here again, as in the case of U.S. stakes in purchasing and growing foreign rubber, Americans were bypassing the British. Also, as in the cases of rubber and paper and pulp, Americans invested to fill the needs of U.S. domestic enterprises.

The war meant new large demands for nitrates (used for explosives and fertilizers). America produced no nitrates, importing its requirements from Chile. Prior to 1914, little American capital had participated in this Chilean industry.† W. R. Grace & Co. had earlier handled the nitrate *trade;* for the first time, in 1916, it integrated backward into ownership of nitrate *oficinas,* buying the Tarapaca & Tocopilla Nitrate Company from British owners (at a price of $3 million). By 1917, Grace's *oficinas* were employing 15,000 men.[15]

Wartime demands for copper rose. Early in 1914, John D. Ryan, president of Amalgamated Copper Company, told the House Judiciary Committee that "from the total known copper resources of this country [the United States] . . . it would seem that copper in this country will be exhausted in 15 years." Thus, U.S. copper companies looked abroad. In 1916, the new Kennecott Copper Company—controlled by the Guggenheims ‡—purchased most of the stock of the American-owned Braden Copper Company in Chile (the cost of the property was estimated at $57 million). This acquisition gave Kennecott an important stake in Chile. The Guggenheims also put added funds into developing their huge open pit mine at Chuquicamata, in northern Chile. In 1916, Ana-

---

* American Smelting and Refining Company built a tin refinery at Perth Amboy, New Jersey, 1915–1916. In 1917, National Lead in a joint venture with Williams, Harvey & Company, Ltd. (the largest British tin smelting company), and Simon I. Patiño (the largest owner of Bolivian mines) constructed a smelter and refinery at Jamaica Bay, New York. Williams Haynes, *American Chemical Industry*, III, 86, and National Lead, *Annual Reports,* 1916–1917.

† Du Pont had a small investment. Wilkins, *Emergence of Multinational Enterprise*, p. 183.

‡ Kennecott Copper Company was incorporated April 29, 1915. In 1915–1916 it acquired certain copper properties in which the Guggenheims already had an interest: in Alaska, Utah, Nevada, Arizona, New Mexico, as well as Chile (F.T.C., *Report on the Copper Industry*, p. 137).

conda Copper Company * made its first acquisitions of Chilean copper properties—at Potrerillos and at a location near Santiago. These investments were all in response to potential shortage and to wartime requirements. Similarly, Bethlehem Steel invested new monies in its Chilean iron ore property (leased in 1913).[16]

By 1915–1916 so significant had U.S. stakes in Chilean nitrates, copper, and iron ore become that the Chilean public and government became anxious. The Chilean press asked: Should Chile conserve its resources? † Were the Yankees taking the wealth out of the country? What legislation ought Chile to pass? How should the country safeguard its legitimate interests? Was it only the Chilean owners of small mines who resented the entry of U.S. capital? "What the country really needs," declared a number of Chilean newspapers, "is better education in mining and geology, plus the development of railroads and highways to open up more mining districts." Many articles urged the encouragement of mining. American businessmen took note of the Chilean response,‡ and they persisted in their investments. In no country in South America were the new U.S. direct investments greater than in Chile.[17]

The war in Europe also prompted new calls for aluminum. To assure itself of adequate supplies of its basic raw material, Aluminum Company of America (Alcoa) increased its bauxite holdings in British Guiana and made investments for the first time in Dutch Guiana. Like U.S. Rubber, Goodyear, and Bethlehem, Alcoa was integrating backward.[18]

Requirements for nickel also rose rapidly. America had no nickel. Already by 1914 U.S. capital, represented by International Nickel Company, controlled the bulk of Canadian nickel mining. International

---

* In May 1915, Amalgamated Copper Company was dissolved, and its former subsidiary, Anaconda, took over all the properties once held by Amalgamated. Anaconda then proceeded to expand.

† "Our rich ground, filled with treasures, is passing slowly into the hands of strangers. The great deposits of copper, iron, nitrate that constitute incalculable fortunes are taken year after year by the capital and by the industry of strangers while we, eyes open with astonishment, slow-witted, dedicate ourselves to discussing the merits of unimportant personalities of people who are of no significance for the resurrection and grandeur of this country." Translation of a passage from an article in *El Coquimbo*, Aug. 17, 1915. The article was headed "Una montaña de Coquimbo transforma en rasoacielos yanquis, en dreadnoughts y balas europeas" ("A mountain of Coquimbo [Bethlehem's operation at El Tofo] transformed into Yankee skyscrapers, into dreadnoughts, and European bullets").

‡ One company kept a scrapbook of articles.

Nickel expanded its production, exporting nickel matte to the United States, as it had in earlier years. The refining was done by a subsidiary of International Nickel at Bayonne, New Jersey. Canadian patriots protested the Dominion's lack of control over its own resources. Refining, they declared, should be done at home. Canadian nickel, they proclaimed, is being shipped from the United States to Krupps to be made into bullets for British soldiers. The United States continued trading with the Central Powers while it was not engaged in the war; in 1914 Canada had joined the side of its mother country. Under intense pressures from Canadian public opinion and from the Dominion and provincial governments (and even threats of expropriation), International Nickel agreed reluctantly in 1916 to build a refinery in Ontario. It could not afford to lose its mining investment and thus was forced to expand into refining in Canada.[19] A new (voluntary) investor in the Dominion in 1917 was the American firm Mutual Chemical Company, which purchased a mine in eastern Quebec, built a concentrating mill, and became one of the nation's two largest shippers of chrome—another metal useful in wartime.[20]

Clearly, the European war prompted U.S. investments in mining and ore processing in the western hemisphere. Note, however, that Mexico (which in 1914 had larger U.S. stakes in mining and ore processing than all the South American nations combined and far larger stakes in mining than Canada) had a decline in direct investments in mining.* This was because of the political situation in Mexico, as will become evident in Chapter II. In sum, the U.S. direct investments in mining and ore processing in the western hemisphere were encouraged by wartime demands, rising prices, absence of certain commodities at home, and anticipated shortages of raw materials. International Nickel's start in Dominion refining had been forced by the host nation. All these ventures were undertaken at the initiative of the American companies.

By contrast, in other instances, the U.S. government was directly responsible for spurring concern with new stakes in mining. Early in 1915, the Department of Commerce attempted to interest U.S. business leaders in Chinese mining. The Chief of the Bureau of Foreign and Domestic

* Howe Sound Company was exceptional when in 1915 it purchased a majority interest in El Potosí Mining Company with mines in Santa Eulalia, Chihuahua. U.S. Dept. of Interior, Bureau of Mines, "Materials Survey Copper," An II–26.

Commerce, E. E. Platt, circularized selected American executives * to inquire whether they might want to invest in Changsha—to "take the place which German capital is forced to relinquish to others." To most of these men, China seemed a distant land, but many took the suggestion seriously. James A. Farrell replied that U.S. Steel had already studied the investment opportunities in the Provinces of Hunan, Yunnan, and Szechuan. R. P. Rowe of National Lead responded, "It is a pretty long way from home but if the Germans and English can do things of this kind there is no reason why the Americans cannot. It will have the most careful consideration from us." By July 1915, Willard Straight of J. P. Morgan & Co. was writing to Platt, "I personally have become interested in a company doing business in Shanghai, which may, I believe, take up mining enterprises." He referred to Andersen, Meyer & Co., headed by the Dane Vilhelm Meyer, which sent American mining experts to China. This trading firm appears to have invested in Changsha. It was exceptional, and its stakes in mining were short-lived. Even though Americans learned the Chinese were "very desirous . . . to do everything possible to encourage American investments" to offset *Japanese* (!) influence, still, U.S. companies did not act in a significant manner. Profit prospects did not seem promising. The Department of Commerce's suggestions were thus not adopted; the western hemisphere remained most attractive to the concerns mining and processing ore.[21]

Petroleum—even more than metals—was in new high demand as wartime requirements for oil-burning ships,† tanks, and cars soared. U.S. oil companies intensified their search abroad to supplement American supplies. They went to Canada, but found no oil. Unlike the U.S. agricultural and mining companies, oil enterprises did not hesitate to invest in Mexico, for Mexico's oil resources appeared so plentiful, demand was so fantastic, and profits were so immediate that the oil companies felt they could afford to discount the political hazards.

Elsewhere, oil and politics became intermixed—U.S. and host nation

* Including William Loeb, Jr., American Smelting and Refining; James A. Farrell, U.S. Steel; Willard Straight, J. P. Morgan & Co.; W. S. Kies, National City Bank; R. P. Rowe, National Lead; Edgar Palmer, New York Zinc; W. G. Sharp, U.S. Smelting, Refining and Mining; and H. S. Kimball, American Zinc, Lead, and Smelting.

† Just before the war, the United States as well as Great Britain had begun to convert their fleets from coal to oil. John A. DeNovo, "The Movement for an Aggressive American Oil Policy Abroad, 1918–1920," *American Historical Review* 41:854 (July 1956).

politics. "The question of oil concessions in Costa Rica is conceived to be of unusual interest because of its relation to naval bases and the proximity of Costa Rica to the Panama Canal," U.S. Secretary of State William Jennings Bryan had written in December 1913. Less than two years later, Dr. L. J. Greulich of New York acquired an oil concession of nine million acres in Costa Rica. The State Department suspected he was working for the Germans and became alarmed. Then, in December 1916, a subsidiary of Sinclair Oil Company bought Greulich's concession. Early in 1917, Sinclair also obtained an oil concession of ten million acres in Panama. These first foreign investments by Sinclair were undertaken independently of State Department approval or disapproval, but documents indicate that the State Department was relieved to have the properties in American hands.[22]

In Colombia one U.S. oil company * had by early 1916 spent $1.75 million and then, according to State Department records, discontinued its investments, unable to comply with national regulations. But independent oil men were not deterred. In 1916, an American group—made up of the wildcatters M. L. Benedum and J. C. Trees—formed the Tropical Oil Company, which obtained an option on the French-held De Mares concession (2,061 square miles). Whereas earlier in the Woodrow Wilson administration, the State Department had emphasized its opposition to "monopolistic concessions" by U.S. business in Colombia, by late 1916, when it was clear America would require foreign oil for national defense, the State Department changed its tone: "the Department knows of no reason why American capital should not be invested in legitimate enterprise in Colombia. On the contrary, it views with approbation the participation of capitalists of the United States in the development of natural resources of South America." [23]

Although Shell in February 1914 had become a commercial producer of oil in Venezuela, adverse government regulations in that country temporarily discouraged U.S. oil companies from making investments.† [24] In Peru, Jersey Standard's affiliate, International Petroleum Company— already a producer of oil—was under attack. The Peruvian government

---

* Standard Oil of New Jersey or Standard Oil of New York (probably the former).

† General Juan Vicente Gómez was friendly to foreign capital, but the mining laws of Venezuela had not been revised to meet the requirements of the American oil companies. Unsure of how much oil was there and aware of the recent past history of political instability in Venezuela, U.S. corporations went first to places where there seemed to be the greatest opportunities.

felt the company's oil lands at La Brea y Pariñas should be taxed on the basis of 41,614 instead of 10 pertenancias (one pertenancia equals about ten acres). In addition, the Peruvian government proposed to raise the export levies on petroleum. I.P.C. protested.[25]

Meanwhile, Standard Oil of New York was surveying the province of Chihli in China and not finding oil; next it concentrated on the province of Shensi and opened talks in the spring of 1915 with the Chinese government for the formation of a joint Standard Oil of New York–Chinese government company, as projected in an agreement made by the two parties in February 1914. The negotiations floundered as the president of China, Yuan Shih-Kai, concluded he didn't want to work with an American company. He explained his reasons by referring to the earlier Canton-Hankow railway fiasco and also to the withdrawal in 1913 of U.S. government support of the so-called American Group.* More important, Yuan Shih-Kai was indignant because Standard Oil of New York had not raised a desired loan for China in New York. By August 1915, talks between the Chinese and the American firm terminated.† Less than two years later, when Yuan Shih-Kai was no longer president,‡ Standard Oil of New York declared itself convinced that neither the Chihli nor the Shensi field had sufficient quantities of oil to warrant the execution of its 1914 plans; thus, in February 1917 the company informed the Chinese

* The American China Development Company (organized in 1895) obtained a contract to build the Hankow-Canton Railway (April 1898); the U.S. investors, contrary to the provisions of the contract, sold out to a Belgian syndicate. In 1905 the House of Morgan acquired control of the American China Development Company. The Chinese were dissatisfied and bought all the assets of the company in China for $6,700,000. The incident was closed when the Sino–Standard Oil of New York agreement was signed in 1914, or so it had seemed. In June 1909, leading American bankers, encouraged by the Taft administration to invest in China, had formed the so-called American Group. When Woodrow Wilson gave the group no support, it was dissolved in 1913, with no accomplishments to its credit.

† The American Charge d'Affaires reported to Washington the discussions in as much detail as he could, but only with secondhand information, for the Standard Oil of New York representative, W. E. Bemis, handled everything himself directly with the Chinese government. When negotiations seemed stymied, Bemis decided to hold a dinner. The Chinese Minister of Agriculture and Commerce said he could not come; Bemis interpreted this as an "excuse," and told the Charge d'Affaires, "And they won't even eat with me." The latter reported to Washington, "It seemed that Mr. Chou would not eat Mr. Bemis's dinner because Mr. Bemis would not do business and Mr. Bemis would not do business because Mr. Chou would not eat his dinner. And so the project fell into abeyance, as solemnly as though this incident of Mr. Bemis's business in China were an adventure of Alice in Wonderland." RG 59, 893.6363/9–27, National Archives.

‡ Yuan Shih-Kai died in 1916.

government that it had no desire to proceed further; in a settlement, the Chinese government paid Standard Oil of New York $543,703 (U.S.) to reimburse part of the company's development expenditures; the Sino-American Agreement of February 1914 was cancelled.* [26] Jersey Standard also looked in vain for oil east of Suez—in the Dutch East Indies (on a concession it had acquired before the war). While U.S. petroleum companies were in 1914–1917 prepared to seek their raw material on a global basis, their main stakes remained in the western hemisphere.[27]

In utilities, also U.S. companies demonstrated new interest in foreign investment, again in the western hemisphere. New stakes in this sector were at the behest of the U.S. government, which asked General Electric's subsidiary, Electric Bond and Share Company (EBASCO), to acquire and develop the electrical systems serving Panama City and Colon. In 1916 EBASCO, accordingly, purchased holdings in existing electric light, power, and ice businesses and in the electric railway service in Panama, as well as in electric light and power services in Colon (the sale was consummated in 1917). Thus, began what would become in the 1920s giant U.S. investments in electric light and power in Latin America.[28]

As for new U.S. direct foreign investments in manufacturing between August 1914 and April 1917, these, too, were mainly in the western hemisphere. American firms desired to take advantage of cheap Canadian water power. This was not only true of the paper and pulp industry, as we have seen, but also of the U.S. abrasives industry. In 1914, U.S. imports from Europe of aluminum oxide, emery, and corundum—essential for grinding wheels and other abrasives—stopped. U.S. supplies were inadequate. Man-made abrasives required cheap water power, and so U.S. investors went to Canada. Table I.1 indicates some of the investments.[29]

In the chemical industry, Aetna Explosives Company built in 1915 a $3 million powder plant, while Nichols Chemical Company † started sulphuric contact units in Canada. Both involved war associated activities.[30] Additional U.S. direct foreign investment in manufacturing in the Dominion included a $1 million plant announced by Procter & Gamble in September 1914 and completed in 1915. The company's historian explains that this first foreign plant was built to protect Procter & Gam-

---

* According to the *China Year Book 1926,* Standard Oil of New York spent more than $2 million prospecting in 1914 alone.

† A General Chemical Company subsidiary. General Chemical became a subsidiary of Allied Chemical & Dye Corp. in 1920.

ble's "Canadian market against [the British firm] Lever, which had recently combined the Canadian soap firms in which Lever had controlling interest into a single company, for virtual domination of the Dominion." Procter & Gamble would strike back while the British were preoccupied in war. In 1916 Carnation Milk bought a creamery in the Dominion—to meet demands there.[31]

Two new U.S. entries into the Canadian automobile industry in 1916 were the Chalmers Motor Corp. (a predecessor of Chrysler), which acquired an assembly plant in Walkerville, Ontario, and Willys-Overland, which bought the business and plant of an existing Canadian auto maker

Table I.1.   The U.S. abrasives industry in Canada, 1914–1916

Company	Place	Product	Date
Exolon Co.	Thorold, Ont.	Silicon carbide	Late 1914
Carborundum Co.	Shawinigan Falls, Que.	Silicon carbide	1916
Exolon Co.	Thorold, Ont.	Aluminum oxide	1915
International Abrasives Co.	Niagara Falls, Ont.	Aluminum oxide	1916
D. A. Brebner Co.	Hamilton, Ont.	Aluminum oxide	1916

Source: Muriel F. Collie, The Saga of the Abrasives Industry (Greendale, Mass. 1951), pp. 212–213, 132, 219.

(Russell Motor Car Company). These firms likewise participated in the Dominion war effort.[32]

More important than the new entries into Canadian manufacturing was the growth of already existing U.S. factories in the Dominion. A few examples are illustrative. Canadian Explosives Ltd. (the du Pont affiliate) expanded, making gun cotton, cordite, and TNT. Ford Motor Company of Canada's production rose more than threefold—from 15,657 units in 1914 to 50,173 units in 1917. Imperial Oil Company, Ltd. (the Standard Oil of New Jersey affiliate), which had one refinery at Sarnia in 1914, constructed new refineries in Vancouver, Regina, and Montreal. By 1917, Imperial Oil's four refineries processed 13,700 barrels daily, compared with the Sarnia refinery's lone production of 5,000 barrels daily in 1914.[33]

New stakes by U.S. companies in Latin American manufacturing were far smaller than those in Canadian industry. The Argentine government, seeking to reduce its dependence on imports, did try to promote industrial development by granting tax exemptions and removing customs duties on machinery and equipment used in industry. A group of U.S. financiers organized the Compañía Argentina de Cemento Portland * in 1915 and took advantage of the favorable treatment. In 1917 it started to build the first modern Portland cement factory in Argentina (some 312 kilometers south of Buenos Aires). In 1914 Ford Motor Company had opened a sales branch in Buenos Aires. Finding its exports to Argentina rising, the company started in the Argentine capital in 1916 the first automobile assembly plant in all Latin America. About the same time, Studebaker, which in September 1915 established a branch in Buenos Aires, opened a sales room, a repair shop, a stock room, and an assembly room.† These were the major new stakes by U.S. enterprises in South American industry from August 1914 to April 1917 (excluding, of course, the earlier mentioned meat packers). Such interests were by no means gigantic, although they did form a basis for later expansion and did stimulate others to look toward opportunities in South America. It was no accident, for instance, that with the automobile companies' small investments in Argentina, Goodyear Tire and Rubber Company in 1915 and U.S. Rubber Company in 1916 opened *sales* branches in Buenos Aires.

Nearer home, in Cuba, a new company, Cuban Portland Cement Company,‡ prepared in 1916 to manufacture and to sell Portland cement in Cuba; the company realized that it could produce and deliver cement in Cuba at a price substantially lower than that of cement imported into Cuba from the United States. The company's organizers forecast that consumption of cement in Cuba would rise rapidly because of the prosperity of the sugar planters.[34]

In short, in the years August 1914 to April 1917, most of the new U.S. direct investments abroad were in the western hemisphere. The bulk of them were in export-oriented industries, although there were exceptions.

* This company became a subsidiary of International Cement Corp., which later changed its name to Lone Star Cement Co. Hughlett, *Industrialization of Latin America*, p. 56.

† This was probably partial assembly of single units: adding wheels, and so forth.

‡ This company became a subsidiary of International Cement Corp. Jenks, *Our Cuban Colony*, p. 296.

Most new U.S. investments were in countries where European money predominated. To American business, the opportunities seemed without limit.

5

National City Bank's activities offer a valuable gauge of U.S. business's concern with direct foreign investment before American entry into the war. "Financially, we have been a provincial people," Frank A. Vanderlip, president of the National City Bank, declared in 1915. Vanderlip did not refer to himself; for years he had been *au courant* with international business; in 1901, he had traveled through Europe, going as far east as Russia, seeking to encourage American banking. In 1902 he published *The American Commercial Invasion of Europe,* in which he predicted, "America will sooner or later enter the European security markets . . . the tables in international investments are to be completely turned."

Since 1897 the National City Bank had the Foreign Department that dealt in foreign exchange, solicited accounts from foreigners, and offered a variety of commercial services to foreign banks and businesses.* The bank had participated in foreign loans. In 1912 Vanderlip had sent a financial emissary from the bank to South America, to investigate the banking and business possibilities there. Directly after the Federal Reserve Act passed in December 1913 (permitting national banks to open foreign branches), the National City Bank began operations in Argentina. "The decision [to open branches in South America] was reached," reported a bank official, "not upon a basis of estimated outlay and return, but upon a basis of whether or not American business interests would find these banking facilities . . . of great help and value in extending business relations." In New York in August 1914, the bank established the Foreign Trade Department to provide services for American firms.

With war in Europe, the National City Bank extended its plans. England, France, Germany, and Holland had been supplying roughly $1.5 billion per annum of new capital for other countries. With the Europeans in conflict, new funds would be curtailed. "If they are not forthcoming, trade will not be very good in Canada, South America and other

---

* The net profits (after deduction of administrative expenses) for the Foreign Department of the National City Bank, 1904–1913, had been $1,032,770.81. John Gardin to Vanderlip, Jan. 2, 1914, Vanderlip Papers, Special Collections, Columbia University Library.

new countries for anybody," prophesized a National City Bank *Monthly Letter*. If the "new countries" were to continue their development "and build works and buy equipment and employ labor as they have been doing, somebody must supply capital." The United States might help, although American capital was needed at home and Americans were unused to giant overseas investment. "We are clearly," the bank *Letter* continued, "under compulsion [however] to make the most of the present opportunity to enlarge our trade in the markets which Europe is temporarily obliged to surrender . . . there is an opportunity to obtain a permanent foothold in fields that offer great possibilities." The expression was felicitous. Americans did enlarge their trade, and, as we have seen, they also expanded their direct investments in Latin America, Canada, and even the Dutch East Indies, in all of which areas European stakes by far exceeded American.[35]

In October 1915, Vanderlip wrote to National City Bank Chairman of the Board James Stillman about two new projects in the foreign field. The first was the bank's plan to purchase the American-financed International Banking Corporation (founded in 1902), with its present network of seventeen branches in China, India, Japan, Philippines, Malaya, England, and Panama. (Its branches in Mexico had closed—with the revolution there.) I.B.C.'s branches would complement the new branches that the National City Bank was opening in Argentina and elsewhere in South America. By 1915 the International Banking Corporation had a capital of $3,250,000; one National City Bank official likened the acquisition of it late in 1915 to Jefferson's "purchase of Louisiana Territory." In an internal memorandum, this same executive explained that the I.B.C. "was bought not for immediate profit, not to keep it from falling into other hands, but as a part of a policy to establish and contribute to the growth of the City Bank." And he added, on a different note, "the great idea which lay behind it [the purchase of the I.B.C.] was so to spread our organization throughout the world as to make possible a service to American exporters, importers and manufacturers which shall be of prime necessity to them." [36]

The second proposal that Vanderlip outlined in his October 1915 letter to Stillman was for a new international company. "I am aiming to unite as far as possible," declared Vanderlip, "all the interests that are looking toward foreign development." With this goal, in November 1915, Vanderlip organized the American International Corporation; he was its first chairman of the board. More than any other event of these years, the A.I.C. symbolized the commitment of key American businessmen to a world role. The new corporation was 50 per cent owned by the stockholders of National City Bank, and 50 per cent of the stock was sold to "interests" in a position to assist it in its work. The files of Vanderlip indicate that all its board members were given the opportunity to subscribe. A.I.C.'s board of directors included prominent international businessmen of that era. Listed were:

J. Ogden Armour	Chief executive of Armour & Company; son of the company's founder. This meatpacking concern had investments in South America in packing houses and in Europe in distribution.
Charles A. Coffin	Chairman of the board of General Electric, which company was already committed to international business.
James J. Hill	Chief executive of Great Northern Railway (who saw in increased far eastern trade more business for his railways; Hill had earlier advocated American acquisition of Canada to increase business there). Hill was the oldest of the directors and died in 1916.
Joseph P. Grace	President of W. R. Grace & Co.; son of W. R. Grace, the company's founder. W. R. Grace had diversified business interests on the West Coast of South America.
Ambrose Monell	President of International Nickel.
Percy A. Rockefeller	A nephew of John D., who had married a daughter of James Stillman (chairman of the board of National City Bank) and who represented Standard Oil of New Jersey on this board.
John D. Ryan	President of Anaconda.
Guy E. Tripp	Chairman of the board of Westinghouse Electric. In 1915 Westinghouse still had its own factories throughout Europe.

Theodore N. Vail   President of American Telephone and Telegraph Company. Vail in the 1880s had set up telephone companies in Latin America; in the 1890s he had become involved in power plants and street railroads in Buenos Aires. Western Electric, A.T.T.'s subsidiary, had a vast international organization, manufacturing telephone apparatus.

Leading bankers were also on the board. Vanderlip invited James B. Duke (now chief executive of the American-controlled, international British-American Tobacco Company) and Cyrus McCormick (International Harvester) to become directors, but they declined.

The board members recognized that "new enterprises in foreign countries are now appealing to American capital . . . There is, therefore, a fertile field in international finance, which it is our national duty to study and our financial opportunity to cultivate." The corporation was launched with unmatched excitement.[37]

Meanwhile, in Buenos Aires, the National City Bank's branch had made "commercial investigations" that brought to light in 1915 "the names of at least one thousand North American manufacturers who are either represented here, or have goods on this market." A list was sent to New York to serve as "a basis for further solicitation of accounts in the North." Most of the one thousand manufacturers had in the past sold through trading firms and commission houses which resented bitterly the entry of the branch of the National City Bank into Buenos Aires, since the bank provided many of the same services free of charge. So successful was this bank branch that by February 1917 the National City Bank had started new ones in Montevideo, Rio, São Paulo, Santos, Valparaiso, and Havana. The bank also made some new entries in Europe, war conditions notwithstanding, in Genoa, and in Petrograd. When in 1917 the First National Bank of Boston opened a Buenos Aires branch (its first foreign branch), Vanderlip wrote in a private letter, "I'm on the whole rather glad to see it. We have been a little too exclusively the leaders in this direction." The First National Bank of Boston began its foreign business financing U.S. exports to Argentina and, even more important, financing the export from Argentina of leather hides, sheep skins, and wool. Boston was the center of the American shoe business, and Argentine hides and skins were in demand. Other American banks opened branches in Latin America, aiding U.S. trade and, subsequently, direct investment.

In January 1917 the National City Bank's *Monthly Letter* declared: "Americans are able to enter this field [the foreign field] in a new capacity,* that of an investor and organizer. The United States has become much the richest country in the world." [38]

6

America was a combatant in World War I only about a year and a half—from April 6, 1917 to November 11, 1918. After U.S. entry into the war, American business in the territory of the Central Powers could not function as before. Under the U.S. Trading with the Enemy Act (approved October 6, 1917), U.S. commerce with enemy nations, or countries associated with them, was forbidden; † the president obtained the power to regulate transactions in foreign exchange, impose embargoes on imports from any country, and establish censorship of material passing between the United States and any foreign nation. The act authorized the creation of an Alien Property Custodian to take over enemy property in this country.[39]

Meanwhile (before the Trading with the Enemy Act passed but after America's entry into the war), the German government had already started to move against U.S. business enterprises located in that country. The following German decrees were issued:

> *August 9, 1917:* Prohibited payments or remittances to the United States of money, drafts, or other negotiable instruments, or the export of certain proscribed goods to America.
> *December 13, 1917:* Ordered compulsory administration by a German official of U.S. businesses; upon the appointment of an administrator by the state, the American citizen would lose possession of his property and his rights and powers would be transferred to the administrator.
> *January 3, 1918:* Authorized the imperial chancellor to decree by special orders the abrogation of American-owned patents, trademarks, and copyrights, when it was in the public interest.
> *January 30, 1918:* Required detailed reports on all American property in Germany.

* The word "new" was used, because the investments were seen to be greater than ever before.
† Except with the license of the president.

March 4, 1918: Authorized the liquidation of U.S. concerns in
Germany.

On May 3, 1918, the U.S. Department of State learned through the
Spanish embassy in Berlin that the Germans were determined to carry
out these decrees "only insofar as the authorities of the Government of
the United States execute the laws which have been passed against the
property of German subjects." By this time, according to the German *Official Gazette,* some seventy-four American firms had already been placed
under sequestration—that is under a German administrator.

When the U.S. Alien Property Custodian took strong steps against
German firms in America, the Germans retaliated. By October 21,
1918, the *Official Gazette* published lists of 159 businesses and properties
of American citizens in Germany that had been placed under sequestration. The number 159 sounds large, yet the properties in many cases
were not substantial—often comprising a sales branch, a warehouse,
and a small inventory.

The German plants of American Radiator Company were among
those put under sequestration. Here, the official's supervision was lenient.
American Radiator Company's president, Clarence Woolley, later concluded that the Germans had dealt gently with American firms, since
there was more German property in the United States than vice versa
and German interests would be jeopardized should they act harshly toward American foreign investment.

Steinway & Sons, with an investment of $1.1 million in a German
plant, got a dispatch from its German affiliate: "Urgently request your intervention with American government regarding liquidation German interests [in the United States] to prevent retaliation detrimental to us."
The American firm transmitted the communication to the U.S. State Department with no comments. It seems the Germans tried to use American
property as a diplomatic tool to avoid action by the U.S. government
against German assets in the United States. It did not prove an effective
tool, for the Alien Property Custodian in the United States remained vig-
ilant.[40]

Some U.S. subsidiaries in Germany took dubious means of defending
their properties. Singer's German subsidiary claimed to be a "German
concern." It posted a circular: "We have never spread any news against
the Germans and we have never given anything to the foreign enemy. On

the contrary, we have not only paid important sums for the objects of the war but we also supplied free of charge three thousand sewing machines to the German and Austro-Hungarian army. We have always assisted the families of our employees who were mobilized and have spent for this purpose a sum of Marks 8,180,000." Despite such protestations, the Singer unit in Germany was put under sequestration, and at war's end, the American Singer company would file for war claims damages.[41]

As noted earlier, Jersey Standard had sold *its* shares in its German Affiliate (Deutsch-Amerikanische Petroleum Gessellschaft) to its German partner. During the war the German partner sold the shares to the Stinnes combine and to the Hamburg-American Line.[42]

While the United States and Germany were at war, the U.S. companies' businesses in Germany and in territories under the control of the Central Powers assumed a functional autonomy, operating without home office supervision. In most cases managers in the United States learned little of their enterprises in enemy territory. The historians of Standard Oil of New Jersey report that that company got "scraps of information . . . through roundabout channels"; on the basis of this information, the company was able to piece together "a reasonably accurate picture of events behind enemy lines." But even Standard Oil of New Jersey did not know all the details until after the war.[43]

7

Meanwhile, in Allied and most neutral nations, U.S. enterprises in general flourished. In Great Britain, factories belonging to subsidiaries and affiliates of American Radiator Company, General Electric, Ford, and Singer *—among others—worked at full capacity, governed by British military law. In France, U.S. plants in unoccupied areas produced to meet wartime demands. G.E. even went into a new joint venture in Russia to manufacture lamps (June 1917). So, too, in Canada, U.S. firms raised output to aid the war effort.[44]

---

* In 1905 Singer Manufacturing Company in the United States had organized a wholly owned subsidiary, Singer Manufacturing Company, Ltd., for the purpose of acquiring and operating the Singer plant in Scotland. Singer Manufacturing Company in 1917 distributed three-fourths of the stock it held in the British subsidiary to its shareholders as a dividend. Until the late 1950s, Singer Manufacturing Company held only a minority interest in its British affiliate. The reasons for this 1917 cast-off are not clear. There may well have been tax considerations involved. See Bristol & Willett, "The Singer Manufacturing Co.," Scudder Collection, Columbia University, and Singer, *Annual Reports*, 1950s.

U.S. entry into the conflict did not stem the tide of new U.S. stakes in Cuba and Central and South America, nor did it serve to deter the few U.S. investors who looked toward expansion in the Far East. U.S. involvement in combat simply meant the country required *more* rubber, sugar, meat, tin, tungsten, nitrates, copper, oil, and other vital raw materials. As rubber prices rose, U.S. tire manufacturers paid greater heed to their investments in rubber plantations in Sumatra. U.S. stakes in Cuban sugar soared to $315 million in 1919 (from a mere $95 million in 1914). The Chicago meat packers expanded their South American and Australian plants to fill Allied demand.* W. R. Grace & Co. augmented its tungsten and tin output in Bolivia. More U.S. funds went into Chilean nitrates. At home, Americans attempted to make synthetic nitrates, so this country would not have to depend on imports, but until this was accomplished investments in the Chilean raw material seemed important. U.S. copper and iron ore firms in Chile and the U.S. copper company in Peru (Cerro de Pasco) recorded record production. Cerro de Pasco operated twenty-four hours a day. In 1917 Brazil supplied some 80 per cent of the manganese required for the U.S. steel industry. No U.S. investments had been made in mining Brazilian manganese up to this point; that year, Companhia de Mineracao, owned by E. J. Lavino interests of Philadelphia (importers of manganese), purchased mines in Bahia. U.S. Steel —which was buying directly from Brazil—considered similar invest-

---

* In 1918 the shareholders of Swift & Co. were given the opportunity to exchange a portion of their stock in that company for stock in the newly formed (August 16, 1918) Compañía (Swift) Internacional, S.A.C. This new unit, incorporated in Argentina, took over the South American and Australian properties of Swift & Co. Swift & Co. explained that the principal reason for the cast-off of the international business lay in the regulations of the United States Food Administration. Business in foreign countries was not under the United States Food Administration. The *Swift Yearbook 1919* also added, "the inclusion of the South American and Australian business in American accounts might result in a general misunderstanding by the public as to the earnings of the meat business in the United States." The business in South America and Australia was lucrative. In 1918 the new Compañía earned 47 million gold pesos (1 gold peso= 1.026 U.S. dollars) on a capital stock outstanding of 22.5 million gold pesos—or more than 208 per cent! Swift & Co. was then involved in an antitrust suit (settled by a consent decree in 1920); it would not want Americans to believe that its earnings in this country were that dramatic. Likewise, the U.S. excess profits tax may well have been a consideration behind the cast-off. *Swift Yearbook 1919*, pp. 8, 9, and Hughes and Dyer, "Compañía (Swift) Internacional, S.A.C.," May 1920, Scudder Collection, Columbia University Library. It is worth noting that the Argentines were none too happy about the profits of the meat packers. The president of a committee of the Argentine House of Deputies, investigating the industry in July 1917, denounced the "foreign" establishments, which "consider our land as a field for lucrative exploitation and nothing more." F.T.C., *Report on the Meatpacking Industry*, pt. 1, p. 179.

ments, but did not make them yet. Alcoa pressed the development of its bauxite holdings in the Guianas.[45]

Similarly, U.S. petroleum companies accelerated their search for oil in the western hemisphere. Some oil men proposed that the United States occupy the Mexican oil fields in Tampico—to keep this vast source of supply secure. Woodrow Wilson rejected that idea, although Secretary of Navy Josephus Daniels confided in his diary on November 7, 1917, "News from Tampico (it comes often) of danger that oil wells might be endangered . . . Saw Lansing (Secretary of State) who agreed that it would be well if marines were on the Gulf, with transport, so they (might) be rushed to Tampico if necessary." Despite the hazardous operating conditions, oil production in Mexico mounted.* [46]

Sinclair Oil Company explored its new properties in Panama and Costa Rica. In Colombia, Benedum and Trees's Tropical Oil Company undertook explorations of its large De Mares concession. In 1918, a subsidiary of the Colombian Petroleum Company † (organized in 1917) paid $100,000 for the Barco concession in Colombia. The Barco concession covered one and a half million acres on the Colombia-Venezuelan border, and its transfer from Colombian to U.S. ownership occurred despite strong protests of the Colombian president and the minister of public works as well as intrigues by German interests. By 1918, U.S. Secretary of State Robert Lansing was prepared to give Americans in Colombia full support, for he was convinced "only approved Americans should possess oil concessions in the neighbourhood of the Panama Canal" and "that no oil properties in the neighbourhood of the Panama Canal should be owned by other than Americans." ‡ [47]

After forty-nine years of negotiations, in 1917, the American firm Central and South American Telegraph Company § obtained from Brazil

---

* In 1918 Mexican consuls, issuing Mexican visas, made each recipient sign a statement that "he had been warned the Tampico oil region is a dangerous district on account of . . . bandits." The American traveled at his own risk. U.S. Senate, Subcommittee on Foreign Relations, *Investigation of Mexican Affairs*, Hearings, pp. 532–533.

† Colombian Petroleum Company at origin was owned by two U.S. companies: 75 per cent by Henry L. Doherty & Company (Doherty was president of Cities Service Company) and 25 per cent by the Carib Syndicate Ltd. (mainly Seligman banking interests).

‡ Note, however, that at this time, the American government did not consider investing in foreign (or domestic) oil production on its own; by contrast, in 1914, the British government had obtained a majority interest in Anglo-Persian Oil Company to assure its Navy a source of oil.

§ Renamed All America Cables in 1920.

the right to lay two cables from Rio de Janeiro and Santos, respectively, to the Argentine republic. This triumph for American enterprise involved breaking the monopoly that the British firm (Western Telegraph Company) had on the route.[48]

Outside of Europe, U.S. enterprises made scattered investments in Allied and neutral countries in 1917–1918 in manufacturing. Since high duties impeded National Lead's exports, National Lead decided to start a Buenos Aires factory to manufacture lead and tin pipe together with solder. General Electric, facing problems with wartime shipments, began to produce incandescent lamps in Brazil. W. R. Grace & Co. in 1917 purchased a majority holding in the Vitarte cotton mill (the oldest Peruvian textile enterprise) and with it obtained a complete mill town. This was Grace's second investment in Peruvian textiles.[49]

In Japan and China, Americans invested in manufacturing. Japan, which in August 1914 had declared war on Germany, witnessed a war-encouraged surge in industrial activity. When in 1917, Gerard Swope of Western Electric arrived there, he arranged for Mitsui interests to purchase shares in Western Electric's existing manufacturing affiliate (Nippon Electric).* Earlier, Nippon Electric had used the Japanese trading firm Mitsui & Company as its trading agent in China; Swope now planned to expand Western Electric's business in China and felt the ties between Nippon Electric and Mitsui should be closer. Swope's actions created the first financial association between Western Electric and the Japanese *zaibatsu*—the large financial, commercial, and industrial groups. Swope traveled from Japan to China, where he organized a new telephone manufacturing affiliate: China Electric Company, formed in 1918, with a Shanghai factory and a Peking head office. China Electric was a joint venture—half its capital came from the Peking Ministry of Communications, one-quarter from Western Electric, and one-quarter from Western Electric's affiliate in Japan, Nippon Electric. Thus, through Nippon Electric, Mitsui continued to participate in Western Electric's China trade.† [50]

Like Western Electric, the larger General Electric expanded its prewar manufacturing business in Japan and started anew in China. In 1917, G.E. formed a wholly owned subsidiary to manufacture lamps in Shang-

---

* Western Electric's equity interest in this manufacturing firm dated back to 1899. Western Electric Archives, New York.

† This was a rare joint venture in manufacturing in that it involved a foreign government agency and a U.S. corporation.

hai. Other new U.S. manufacturing in the Far East included the joint venture of B. F. Goodrich and Baron Furukawa in 1917 in the Yokohama Rubber Company (51 per cent owned by Goodrich and 49 per cent by Furukawa interests), and in 1918 of Libbey-Owens Glass Company and Sumitomo interests in the American-Japanese Sheet Glass Company (35 per cent owned by Libbey-Owens, in return for patent rights and knowhow, and 65 per cent owned by the Japanese group). The U.S. direct investments in Far Eastern manufacturing were in the main in Japan, where the greatest economic development was in evidence.[51]

By war's end, the new American International Corporation had foreign stakes in shipping, trade, rubber plantations, and meat canning; it had entered U.S. shipbuilding (a major bottleneck in what seemed unlimited possibilities for America's overseas trade). As for the National City Bank itself, its worldwide operations had become extensive and its plans even broader. By the end of 1918, National City Bank and its wholly owned subsidiary International Banking Corporation had thirty-seven foreign outlets, chiefly in less developed countries.[52]

8

Inspired by the opportunities and the temporary cessation of European competition, American enterprise had made important direct investments abroad during the war years. When on the 11th of November 1918 the war ended and the armistice was signed, both U.S. business and America itself emerged in a new international position.

From a debtor nation in 1914 to the extent of $3.7 billion, the country was transformed into a creditor nation in 1919 to the extent of the same $3.7 billion. The drastic reduction in foreign investment in the United States and the new U.S. *portfolio* investments in Europe (America's loans to the European allies) more than the rise of U.S. direct investment abroad were responsible for the change in this nation's international position—although the $1.2 billion increase in U.S. direct foreign investments certainly contributed. (See Tables I.2 and I.3.)

Even though America emerged from World War I in a position of new financial strength, in key respects its economic influence remained limited. European investors still controlled such essential raw materials as rubber, tin, and nitrates. By war's end, the total worldwide stake in rubber plantations was roughly $1.25 billion, of which $1 billion was British capital, $225 million Dutch and other capital, and only the remaining

Table 1.2. The international investment position of the United States, 1914–1919 (in billion U.S. dollars)

	U.S. investments abroad				Foreign investments in the United States			
	Total	Long-term		Short-term	Total	Long-term		Short-term
		Direct	Portfolio			Direct	Portfolio	
1914 (June 30)	3.5	2.7 [1]	0.8 [1]	n.a.	7.2	1.3	5.4	0.5
1919	7.0	3.9	2.6	0.5	3.3	0.9	1.6	0.8

Source: U.S. Department of Commerce, Bureau of the Census, *Historical Statistics of the United States* (Washington, D.C. 1960), p. 565; data on U.S. government obligations are not available.
[1] Other sources give these figures as $2.6 billion for direct and $.9 billion for portfolio investments.

Table I.3. Estimates of U.S. direct foreign investments, 1914, 1919 (book value in million U.S. dollars)

Country or Region	(1) Total [1]		(2) Manufacturing		(3) Sales [2]		(4) Petroleum [3]		(5) Mining [4]		(6) Agriculture		(7) Utilities		(8) Railroads	
	1914	1919	1914	1919	1914	1919	1914	1919	1914	1919	1914	1919	1914	1919	1914	1919
Europe	573	694	200	280	85	95	138	158	5	—	—	5	11	5	—	—
Canada	618	814	221[5]	400[5]	27	30	25	30	159	200	101[6]	50[6]	8	15	69	76
Mexico	587	644[7]	10	8	4	5	85	200[8]	302	222	37	48[7]	33	32	110	123
Cuba and other West Indies	281	567	20	26	9	10	6	15	15	21	144	382	58	59	24	41
Central America	90	112	—	—	1	1	—	3	11	14	37	44	3	6	38	43
South America	323	665	7	50	20	55	42	113	221	404	25	29	4	4	4	4
Asia	120	175	10	15	15	25	40	50	3	4	12	32	16	17	10	10
Africa	13	31	—	—	4	10	5	10	4	11	—	—	—	—	—	—
Oceania	17	53	10	16	5	12	2	25	—	—	—	—	—	—	—	—
Banking	30	125	—	—	—	—	—	—	—	—	—	—	—	—	—	—
TOTAL [9]	2652	3880	478	795	170	243	343	604	720	876	356	587	133	138	255	297

Source: Table developed from figures in Cleona Lewis, assisted by Karl T. Schlotterbeck, America's Stake in International Investments, ©1938 The Brookings Institution, Washington, D.C., pp. 578ff.

[1] Total includes the sum of columns 2–8 plus miscellaneous investments.
[2] Excludes petroleum distribution.
[3] Includes exploration, production, refining, and distribution.
[4] Mining and smelting.
[5] Includes investments in paper and pulp ($74 million in 1914, $100 million in 1919).
[6] The drop (1914–1919) is due to an alteration in accounting; the 1914 figure included speculative investments.
[7] If the losses were anywhere near as great as claimed (see Chap. II below), this figure is truly unrealistic. There was obviously a slowness in writing down investments.
[8] Others put this total at $250 million. Somewhere in between is probably valid.
[9] Total may be off because of rounding.

$25 million U.S. direct investment. U.S. direct investments in tin production were minimal. Similarly, American *oficinas* in Chile produced only 3 per cent of Chilean nitrate output.* [53] In Canada and South America in 1918, European holdings still exceeded those of Americans; this was true in Africa, Asia, and Oceania as well. What was important was that by the end of World War I, U.S. direct investment was challenging European hegemony. East of Suez and in Africa the confrontation was not profound. In Canada, on the other hand, U.S. direct investments were rising rapidly, while British interests remained unchanged; the gap was narrowing; it would not be long before U.S. stakes surpassed those of the British in the Dominion. Likewise, in Latin America, British, French, and German properties were passing into the hands of U.S. corporations. The war years set the stage for U.S. leadership in the western hemisphere. When the fighting ended on November 11, 1918, most American businessmen could look to the promise of international investments.

* All these natural products were far more important in 1918 than they are today, with synthetics and substitutes available.

While in aggregate U.S. direct investments abroad rose during World War I (1914–1918), important U.S. businesses in Mexico and on the European continent faced adversity and losses. U.S. companies had not flourished in Mexico with the civil strife there between 1911 and 1914.[1] Nonetheless, in 1914 Mexico was second only to Canada in having the greatest U.S. investment (see Table I.3). After 1914, the woes of U.S. businessmen grew as Mexican authorities failed to control disorder and at the same time embarked on programs of social and economic reforms that were inimical to U.S. investors. Revolutionary chaos—especially in the Mexican state of Chihuahua—resulted in damage to American-owned estates and cattle ranches. Owners saw their lands trammeled, crops destroyed, livestock stolen, and properties seized. Increasingly, in 1914–1916, they abandoned their holdings—leaving them to Mexican supervision. On January 6, 1915, Mexico's chief executive, Venustiano Carranza, issued a decree ordering the return of land to the villages and imposing new taxes on agricultural estates. American Chicle Company, with giant plantations in Mexico, faced a 400 per cent rise in export taxes and an increase in "exploitation charges" by several hundred per cent, as well as other new imposts. (To protect itself, this company invested in a large concession to grow chicle in Guatemala.)[2]

Mining interests also fared badly. On August 20, 1914, Carranza had canceled all mining titles obtained during the regime of his predecessor (Victoriano Huerta) and declared that all fees on mining claims and titles had to be repaid to his government. In northern Mexico, Carranza's antagonist, Pancho Villa, held power. Villa demanded that U.S. mine managers issue paper money against the gold and silver of their companies. He put some U.S.-owned mines under forced operation to provide bullion for his officers. In vain, U.S. mining executives protested to the U.S. State Department. Then on March 1, 1915, Carranza imposed a new, steep export tax on Mexican gold, silver, copper, lead, and zinc. Villa— nineteen days later—proclaimed his own decree: mining companies must work to uphold their claims, but working or not, taxes must be paid to him—Pancho Villa. The American consul in Chihuahua reported "There are many Americans who have bankrupted themselves by the mere payment of taxes on their mining claims." One U.S. mining company executive wrote plaintively to the U.S. secretary of state to ask if he had to pay taxes under the decree of Carranza, since he was operating in Chihuahua and Carranza had no jurisdiction in that state. The manager explained that since he had already paid taxes to Villa, this would be double taxation. The State Department replied that the U.S. government did not recognize the Carranza decree as having force outside the control of the Mexican leader's authorities. In July 1915, Villa demanded of the mining men in Chihuahua a loan of $300,000; they refused, but feared retaliation. The U.S. Department of State dispatched Chief of Staff General Hugh L. Scott to visit Villa; as a result of Scott's mission, Villa agreed not to enforce his demand and "to let the mining men alone." The mining companies presented Villa with one thousand tons of coal to assist in operating the railroads, which action benefited both the mine owners and the Mexican rebel. When by the autumn of 1915, the United States was prepared to give de facto recognition to the Carranza government in Mexico City, U.S. mine owners in Mexico became alarmed. The mining officials claimed Carranza planned to finance his government through excessive levies on their industry. They called on Secretary of State Robert Lansing to "have some satisfactory understanding on mining taxes with the Carranza Government prior to recognition." Their requests were ignored, and on October 19, 1915, the United States recognized Carranza's government. After recognition, the State Department did protest the tax increases on the mining interests. In December of that year Lansing wrote that the U.S. mining and smelting properties in Mexico had endured great hardship, paying no dividends in the last few years and being a drain on their parent companies. The mines employed, he pointed out, more than 500,000 Mexicans, "affording sustenance to five times that number." The companies desired to resume work. Lansing believed that this would be of great importance to Carranza, "because every laborer earning an honest wage is a factor in the restoration of law and order." He urged Carranza not to curb the mining industry through excessive taxation.[3]

Yet, taxes were not lowered and worst still for the U.S. mining companies, the disorder persisted. Pancho Villa renewed his harrassments. Seventeen American mining engineers (connected with Cusi Mining Company) were shot in cold blood on January 10, 1916, by forces under Villa's control. When Villa's forays extended into New Mexico, Woodrow Wilson countered by dispatching General John J. Pershing and more than six thousand men into Chihuahua in pursuit of the Mexican rebel. Pershing's troops had no success, nor did other American expeditions against Villa. During 1916, the smelters of the largest U.S. mining and smelting company in Mexico, American Smelting and Refining Company, did not operate; the company worked only a few of its mines, and those entirely under Mexican supervision. American Smelting and Refining Company was typical; in fact, the entire mining industry in Mexico lay in a stupor.[4] When direct entry of America into World War I seemed in prospect, in January 1917, Woodrow Wilson withdrew American troops from northern Mexico. Villa remained at large.

Meanwhile, officials of U.S. oil companies in Tampico sought peace with the local authorities and security for their properties. Since the European war meant huge demands for oil, American corporations in this industry made new investments. They made them despite the "forced contributions" imposed on the companies by both Carranza and Villa. Between March and May 1915, the armies of Carranza and Villa had clashed in the battle of Ebano with resulting damages to American oil properties. Between May 1915 and February 1916 Carrancistas occupied the facilities of Edward L. Doheny's Mexican Petroleum Company (Doheny was the largest U.S. oil producer in Mexico); Doheny's employees were recruited into Carranza's service. Then, in 1916, Carranza started to talk about Mexican oil belonging not to the property owners, but to the nation as a whole.[5]

A new Mexican constitution was promulgated on February 5, 1917. For American business in Mexico, Article 27 was most important: "In the Nation is vested direct ownership of all minerals or substances . . . such as . . . solid mineral fuels; petroleum and all hydro-carbons—solid, liquid or gaseous." The ownership of the nation was "inalienable." Article 27 also established a formula for solving "the agrarian problem." Likewise, the same article subjected concessions to new restrictions; foreigners who obtained concessions were required to waive rights of appeal to their home nations for protection (the so-called "Calvo Clause"). Article 123 of the constitution provided the basis for subsequent labor legislation.

One might anticipate—and rightly so—that the 1917 constitution would add to the already existing anxieties of U.S. businessmen in Mexico. Most American enterprise did curtail investments. Few new investments were made in mining or in land. The exception lay in the oil industry: stimulated by wartime demands, U.S. stakes in oil continued to rise rapidly. Despite the statement in the Mexican constitution that the nation had direct ownership of oil resources, U.S. companies continued to invest in this industry that was still open to private enterprise. The businesses entered eagerly and aggressively. On February 19, 1918, Carranza issued a decree reasserting that oil belonged to the nation and requiring the oil concerns to file papers with the government in connection with their holdings. Ninety-five per cent of the companies refused, since to comply, they felt, would be to admit they lacked ownership of their properties. Defiantly, they stated the Mexican government decree was illegal. The government countered by refusing drilling permits to companies that had not filed. The issue was joined. Nonetheless—in 1918—with the giant investments in Mexican oil of earlier years, Mexico became the world's second largest oil producer (after the United States). By 1919 between $200 and $250 million was invested by Americans in Mexican petroleum; practically every sizable U.S. oil company had acquired holdings in that country; Doheny testified in September 1919 that 152 American companies had oil lands there.* [6] Whereas at the start of the Mexican revolution in 1911, U.S. stakes in Mexican mines far exceeded those in petroleum, in 1919 the amounts of investment were similar; and whereas in 1911 revenues from Mexican mines far surpassed those from the oil wells, in the first ten months of 1919 petroleum revenues in Mexico totaled 13 million pesos, or 10 per cent of the country's revenues and 1 million pesos more than the revenues from all the mines combined.[7]

In 1918, the mining companies, which did not claim ownership of the subsoil, were not "under fire." The 1918 *Annual Report* for American

---

* Among the American companies in Mexico in 1919 were Mexican Petroleum Co. (Doheny), Huasteca Petroleum (Doheny), Texas Co., Mexican Gulf Oil Co. (Gulf), Freeport and Tampico Fuel Oil Corp. (Sinclair), Cia. Mex. de Combustible (Waters-Pierce), Panuco Boston Oil Co. (Atlantic Refining), and Transcontinental Oil Co. (Jersey Standard). See U.S. Senate, Special Committee Investigating Petroleum Resources, *American Petroleum Interests in Foreign Countries*, p. 335.

Smelting and Refining Company in fact declared, "There are certainly many reasons at the present time for feeling encouraged with respect to political conditions." Its optimism, however, proved premature. Pancho Villa remained at large in northern Mexico, and in 1919 the output of the Mexican mining industry was once again negligible. Cleona Lewis, who studied the records of 110 American mining companies with properties in Mexico, found that only 14 were able to continue in operation from 1914 to 1919. The *Engineering and Mining Journal,* which in 1912 had opposed American intervention in Mexico, by 1919 had changed its mind; it editorialized "when the Díaz government broke down . . . our Government should at once have stepped in and helped the country to an early adjustment." Like the National City Bank and like most business interests, the *Engineering and Mining Journal* spoke against intervention for conquest, "We do not want Mexico"; instead it favored intervention for "progress with our help." The role should be that of "the Americans in Cuba and the Philippines, acting altruistically as liberators and educators." American holders of land in Mexico felt despair, as talk of agrarian reform ran rampant. No steps were yet taken to deprive them of their land, but measures seemed in the offing.

By 1919 most American businesses in Mexico felt that their government had let them down. It was indeed true.* Woodrow Wilson felt little sympathy with their plight. He told Josephus Daniels, "When an American elected to go into a country like Mexico and buy land and oil cheap because of conditions, he had no right to call upon the country he left to send in Army and Navy to make his property more valuable." [8]

At the peace conference at Paris in 1919, American investors in Mexico sought a hearing. A banking group identified with the National Association for Protection of American Rights in Mexico asked the National City Bank president, Frank A. Vanderlip, to represent its point of view. Three others would also be present at Versailles for this purpose, Cornelius Kelley (mining), Edward L. Doheny (petroleum), and Frederick N. Watriss (agriculture).† Vanderlip declined to represent the group. His secretary cabled him in London "State Department apparently does not

---

* Wilson's sending in troops earlier had been not so much to protect U.S. mining companies as to prevent Villa's forays into New Mexico.

† Kelley was president of Anaconda, which had an interest in copper mining in Mexico; Doheny was president of Mexican Petroleum, the largest U.S. oil producer in Mexico; Frederick N. Watriss, a New York lawyer, was president of Yaqui Delta Land and Water Company.

approve. Know you would not." * 9 The investors got little satisfaction. In 1920 Carranza was assassinated, and General Álvaro Obregón became Mexico's chief executive. The decade of turmoil in Mexico was finally ending, but the Mexican revolution was not completed. There were many matters left ill defined. One question was, would Americans get

Table II.1. Awards made in 1938 by Special Mexican Claims Commission for damages, 1910–1920 [1] (in U.S. dollars)

Name of corporation	Compensation awarded
American Smelting and Refining Company	$674,449
Corralitos (cattle company in Chihuahua, 800,000 acres)	175,000
Mexican Petroleum (losses to petroleum properties, $70,110; losses to ranches, $57,000)	127,110
National Mines and Smelters (owner of Santa Maria del Oro Mines Co. in Durango)	85,500
Southwestern Land and Cattle (in Chihuahua)	79,800
Babicora Development (Hearst's ranch in Chihuahua)	76,950
Rascon Manufacturing & Development (San Luis Potosí and Tamaulipas)	57,000
Shareholders in Compañía Vacuna Piedra Blanca (Coahuila)	57,000
Shareholders in Cananea Cattle Co., S.A. (Sonora)	41,040
Cusi Mining (Chihuahua)	34,200
Intercontinental Rubber for losses suffered by Compañía Ganadera y Textil de Cedros, S.A.	34,200
American Chicle	31,450
Waters-Pierce Oil	31,350

Source: Special Mexican Claims Commission (Washington, D.C. 1940), p. 59 (American Smelting and Refining), p. 130 (Corralitos), pp. 226, 336 (Mexican Petroleum), p. 515 (National Mines), p. 362 (Southwestern), p. 560 (Babicora), p. 142 (Rascon), p. 303 (Piedra Blanca), p. 600 (Cananea), p. 353 (Cusi), p. 330 (Intercontinental Rubber), p. 591 (American Chicle), p. 127 (Waters-Pierce).
[1] Only awards of more than $30,000 are included.

* On February 23, J. P. Morgan & Co. announced that an international committee had been set up for the purpose of protecting the holders of securities of the Mexican Republic, of the railway systems of Mexico, and of other enterprises. This was a group of international bankers, including Stillman, chairman of the board of National City Bank. It had no connection with the National Association for the Protection of American Rights in Mexico. Commercial and Financial Chronicle, Mar. 1, 1919.

compensation for losses they had suffered? In 1920 a U.S. Senate committee (the Fall committee) totaled U.S. losses in Mexico during the preceding nine years at $505 million. By 1931, 2,781 claims by Americans
against Mexico had been filed for $513.6 million, and no awards had
been made. A Special Mexican Claims Commission, established in 1935,
considered and decided 2,833 claims against Mexico equaling $219 mil-
lion, covering damages during the years 1910–1920. Its final awards,
made in 1938, came to a mere $5.2 million! Table II.1 lists the awards
over $30,000 to corporations or their shareholders. Clearly, the final pay-
ments did not approximate the losses. To landowners and mining companies and, to a lesser extent, the oil enterprises, the financial damage
during the revolutionary decade had been severe.[10]

How was the 1917 constitution going to be implemented? Did U.S. investment have a future in Mexico? To what extent would U.S. investors
get support from the U.S. government? In the years to follow answers to
these questions would be forthcoming. In 1920 the outlook was uncertain.

2

Revolutionary conditions tend to discourage investment. This was true
of U.S. investors in Mexico—except for the oil companies that were lured
by fantastic prospects. Revolution in Russia also had sharp adverse consequences on foreign investors—consequences more dramatic and longlived
than those of the Mexican revolution. In March of 1917, Nicholas II of
Russia abdicated; a provisional government was established, which ruled
in Russia until November of that year. During this interim period, most
U.S. investors had little fear for their properties; there were actually some
new investments made by Americans in these months.[11] Then, the Bol-
sheviks took power in November 1917, and they issued decrees declaring
banking a state monopoly, repudiating government loans, abolishing private ownership of land and natural resources, and confiscating the properties of insurance firms, foreign trading companies, and finally industrial
enterprises.

"A study of expropriation as an important problem in the 20th century may really begin with the Communist revolution in Russia in
[November] 1917," a recent United States government report has justly
declared.[12] In Mexico there had been destruction of property, taxes that
seemed tantamount to confiscation, the 1917 constitution, decrees, and

other governmental measures that set the stage for later expropriation, but by 1920 no outright nationalization had occurred.* The Russian actions were unique in their comprehensiveness and their lasting effects. In Russia the most serious damage was to European investors, who had the most at stake, but there were also losses to Americans. Singer Manufacturing Company, probably the largest U.S. investor in Russia, wrote off $84.3 million, representing its stake in an office building in Petrograd, a factory at Podolsk, timber lands, fifty district offices, and three thousand local retail outlets.[13] Other substantial losses were suffered by New York Life Insurance, Equitable Life Assurance,[14] International Harvester,[15] United Shoe Machinery,[16] General Electric,[17] Westinghouse Electric,[18] Westinghouse Air Brake, Parke, Davis,[19] Western Electric,[20] and Vacuum Oil.† [21] Some of these properties—for example those of International Harvester, Westinghouse Air Brake, and Western Electric—were not, however, expropriated until 1924. In all, the losses to American direct investors as a result of the Russian revolution appear to have been in the range of $200 million. After the U.S. government recognized the Soviet government (November 16, 1933), the U.S.S.R. assigned to the American government all amounts due it from American nationals. Under Public Law 285 (approved August 5, 1955), this sum—the so-called Litvinov Assignment—was used by the U.S. Foreign Claims Settlement Commission to pay a small portion of the American claims. For the most part, however, U.S. companies were not reimbursed. In 1918, it was by no means certain that the Communists would remain in power. Until the spring of 1920, Russia was torn with civil war. American businesses watched the events with apprehension and attacked bolshevism with vigor.[22]

3

There was also wartime damage to American assets located on the continent of Europe. The extent is unknown. Reports of the Mixed Claims Commission (United States and Germany) indicate sizable awards to some U.S. direct investors (see Table II.2). These by far exceeded the

---

* Earlier, between 1903 and 1909, Mexico had gained control of its national railroads, but stockholders had been compensated. See Wilkins, *Emergence of Multinational Enterprise*, pp. 119–120.

† Other losers were Victor Talking Machine Co., Eastman Kodak, Otis Elevator, Babcock & Wilcox, several large American-owned trading companies, a few mining enterprises, and some miscellaneous investors (see note 21).

Table II.2. Awards to U.S. companies for damage done to U.S. properties in Germany and certain occupied territories as a result of German military action in World War I [1] (in U.S. dollars)

Docket nos.[2]	Name of company	Claims	Awards [3]
4400	Standard Oil of N.J.	$13,339,006	$6,250,000
229 & 330	Standard Oil of N.J.	$388,259 and $140,945	134,531
2504	Singer Manufacturing Co.	398,238	387,000
4000	Singer Manufacturing Co.	13,500,000	4,000,000 [4]
4001	Singer Manufacturing Co.	449,755	325,000
4002	Singer Manufacturing Co.	700,000	122,500
4404	Singer Manufacturing Co.	50,000	6,635
15	International Harvester	3,465,627	3,316,766
7145	International Harvester	2,594,896	1,625,000
165	United Shoe Machinery Co.	3,073,986	1,600,000
193	United Shoe Machinery Co.	315,911	140,000
3	Western Electric	2,145,603	1,585,089
2	Pittsburgh Plate Glass	1,916,520	990,000
178	Security Eyelet Co.	1,162,521	700,000
34	Texas Co.	901,130	547,845
228	United Cigarette Machine Co.	713,770	400,000
118	Virginia-Carolina Co.	508,321	337,957

Source: Mixed Claims Commission, United States and Germany, *First Report of Marshall Morgan* (Washington, D.C. 1924); Mixed Claims Commission, United States and Germany, *First Report of Robert W. Bonynge* (Washington, D.C. 1925); Mixed Claims Commission, United States and Germany, *Report of Robert W. Bonynge* (Washington, D.C. 1934).

[1] Only companies with awards over $300,000 are listed. This incomplete table does not cover all awards over $300,000 or necessarily all awards to the particular claimant.

[2] Docket numbers indicate claims covered. One company might make claims under a number of docket numbers.

[3] Awards include only those covered by the docket numbers and not any miscellaneous claims that the company may have collected, which did not relate specifically to direct investments. To all the awards was added interest of 5 per cent.

[4] One government report—presumably erroneously—listed this award as $4,000 rather than $4,000,000.

awards given by the Special Mexican Claims Commission, noted above, and were far greater than the compensation later granted for claims on Russian losses. In addition, other claims commissions covering losses in Rumania and in the Austrian Empire made awards to Americans. In total, however, the companies felt the awards did not equal the damages.[23]

When awards were granted to American companies, there was no guaranty that they would be paid. The historians of Standard Oil of New Jersey noted that "the matter of collections on the large outstanding Ger-

Table II.3. German payments of World War I damage claims to U.S. private parties [1] (in U.S. dollars)

Size of award	Number of claims	Principal	Total, including interest to date of payment or if unpaid to Sept. 30, 1940	Paid or in process of payment, Jan. 10, 1941 [2]
Under $100,000	6,165	$17,962,113.40	$28,092,510.92	$28,063,830.47
Over $100,000	317	$117,248,037.89	$220,979,299.52	$126,117,106.83

Source: Mixed Claims Commission, United States and Germany, *Final Report of H. H. Martin* (Washington, D.C. 1941), p. 92.
[1] Many of these claims did not relate specifically to direct investments. This table, however, does exclude claims paid on account of death or personal injury.
[2] In April 1941, an additional $2,222,000 was paid.

man and Rumanian debts was one which in future years was to yield Jersey Standard few satisfactions." [24] The larger the award, the more delinquent the payment; almost all the German awards of less than $100,000 were paid (see Table II.3). Nonetheless, in reviewing the evidence it seems that the losses to American investors as a result of the Mexican and Russian revolutions were far more substantial than those due to actions in enemy territory. The difficulties U.S. companies faced in Europe in the aftermath of war were more those of disruption and disorganization.[25]

4

In fact, most American companies with investments in Europe before World War I survived, reorganized and reunited their fragmented European businesses, and were prepared to expand abroad once more. Only a handful decided during the war years or immediately thereafter to abandon international business. One such was Westinghouse Electric. Before the war, Westinghouse had had extensive operations in Europe, which had been unsuccessful. Westinghouse's giant factory in Manchester, England, had never obtained the predicted orders. The American plant management had proved unpopular and labor relations at the facility had been one endless cause of friction. From its origin at the turn of the century, the Manchester enterprise had been a heavy financial burden on the American parent. A friendly biographer called it "one of George Westinghouse's mistakes." The smaller Westinghouse activity on the continent had, likewise, been unsatisfying. Thus, when in 1917, the Metropolitan Carriage, Wagon and Finance Company, Ltd. (a British firm) offered to purchase Westinghouse's British properties, Westinghouse officials were delighted.* Later Westinghouse sold its French and Italian subsidiaries. The German operation was under enemy control and could not be disposed of immediately; the Russian business was not sold for obvious reasons. In a sense, World War I opened the exit door to Westinghouse's international business. The company became soured on foreign direct investment (although it retained its stakes in Canada). After the war, it turned to licensing independent enterprises abroad rather than toward new foreign direct investments. The sympathetic biographer of George Westinghouse, writing in 1919, considered his subject's prewar dream of developing a vast international business as "visionary." [26]

The war also cut the Gordian knot on another group of international enterprises. Before 1914, the three largest American insurance firms—New York Life Insurance Company, Equitable Assurance Society, and Mutual Life Insurance Company of New York—all participated in business abroad. Equitable and Mutual had begun to retreat from their

---

* In 1919 Vickers Ltd. acquired Metropolitan Carriage and changed the name of the British Westinghouse Electric and Manufacturing Company, Ltd., to Metropolitan-Vickers Electrical Co., Ltd. Edwards and Townsend, *Business Enterprise*, p. 304, and *Annual Reports*.

worldwide involvement even before 1914, but that year New York Life Insurance Company was still fully committed to a global role. The wartime inflation in Europe (the insurance companies' largest foreign market)—far more than the high mortality rates—caused major losses to these enterprises. Many of the policies were in gold. Depreciated currency made the cost of paying them exorbitant. Moreover, premiums were based on prewar currency rates; postwar inflation meant the firms had difficulty covering daily operating expenses. "In some countries," wrote a New York Life Insurance vice-president, "the depreciation . . . was so great that even the cost of postage to send notices and mail receipts was greater than the average premium on the policies, and so it was found necessary to discontinue collecting premiums." When the war ended, New York Life Insurance's European agency force of some three thousand individuals had chosen other occupations. By 1919, all the American life insurance companies were convinced that the time had come to rid themselves of foreign (except Canadian) business. They took steps to transfer and to reinsure the outstanding insurance.[27]

5

The principal adverse effects on U.S. foreign investors in the war years have been noted. Other negative impacts were miscellaneous. That shipping to Latin America was affected reduced the profits of certain U.S. companies. Bethlehem Steel Corporation presented a claim for $22.7 million to the Mixed Claims Commission (United States and Germany), arguing that, (1) it had before the war ordered ships from Swedish and Norwegian firms; because of the war, the ships were not built; a loss was thus sustained; (2) since the ships were not built, there was the higher cost of transporting the ores in other ships; as a result the company had lost money in the operation of its U.S. plant; (3) properties in Chile had been leased on the assumption that the ore could be imported into the United States cheaply; the company claimed that since this was not the case the Germans should pay the royalties on the Chilean leases; and (4) Bethlehem had sustained a loss on account of ore undelivered because of lack of shipping. The claim was eventually withdrawn, but it indicates the kinds of problems that one direct foreign investor had during wartime.[28] Some new direct foreign investments made in the war years had been overambitious: certain of the abrasives companies that entered Canada went bankrupt with the end of wartime demands.[29] In the other hemisphere,

German military authorities in 1914 had occupied the Tsingtao, China, facilities of Standard Oil Company of New York, requisitioned large quantities of oil, and used the plant as part of defense fortifications. While in the charge of the Germans, the plant was damaged by Japanese warships. Standard Oil of New York claimed damages of over $1 million. In 1923, the Mixed Claims Commission awarded the company $900,000 plus interest.[30] Yet, such cases were miscellaneous and exceptional. Most U.S. participants in direct investment abroad outside of Mexico, Russia, and continental Europe emerged in 1918–1919 without damage and with excellent profits; after the war they persisted in international business. Newcomers—those who had no previous investments in Mexico, Russia, or continental Europe—in 1919–1920 saw naught but opportunity.

Two

The Nineteen-Twenties

The Outlook

World War I was to have been a war to end war. Allied propagandists convinced many Americans that the tragedy had been caused by wicked men, that the fault lay with the autocratic leaders of Germany and Austria, that if democracy replaced the old order, war would cease forever. With a League of Nations and a World Court, peace could be preserved. "The day of conquest and aggrandizement is gone by," declared Woodrow Wilson.

But as the American president went to Paris to work out the terms of the peace, as the vindictive settlement was imposed, political sentiment in the United States shifted from involvement into disassociation from world affairs. A Republican Congress had been elected in 1918. Woodrow Wilson had proposed the insertion of the Covenant of the League of Nations, as a preamble to the peace treaty, signed June 28, 1919. Yet, when he presented the treaty to the Republican Senate, it was rejected. The 1920 U.S. election, endorsing Warren Harding, seemed a mandate for political isolation. Thus, although an American conceived the idea of the League of Nations, his country never joined. The United States retreated into a political cocoon.

The postwar maps showed more than a dozen new countries carved out of the mighty Russian, Austro-Hungarian, and Ottoman empires. In the Near East, the British and French obtained mandates. In Africa, the British, French, Belgians, Portuguese, and South Africans acquired former German colonies. One-time German possessions in the Far East passed to Japan. In the territorial revisions, the United States gained nothing.[1] It was a sign of America's political disinterest.

On the other hand, Congress had passed measures to encourage U.S. international trade and investment. The Webb-Pomerene bill, which allowed U.S. businesses to join together to export without fear of prosecution under antitrust legislation, was enacted in 1918. Its congressional advocates saw it as putting U.S. exporters in a position to face European buyers, who combined to lower prices. Foreign tax credits had been included in the 1918 income tax law (a major benefit to foreign investors). On December 24, 1919, the Edge Act became law; it inserted section 25a into the Federal Reserve Act, which provided for federally chartered corporations to engage in foreign banking or investment business. With the Edge Act, Congress sought to spur U.S. exports and to aid in reconstruction of Europe. "We must give cooperation to business; we protect American business at home, and we aid and protect it abroad" became the view of President Harding. Thus, the U.S. government, while shying away from international "political involvement," was prepared to assist U.S. foreign trade, and in the main, U.S. foreign investment.[2]

U.S. manufacturers took steps to regain control over their European operations and also invested anew in England and on the continent.[3] One estimate indicated that in Canada U.S. corporations opened more than 200 "branch" factories in 1919 alone, and "a great number" in 1920.[4] All these new plants were built without specific aid from the U.S. government.

At war's end, government and industry circles feared an oil shortage.[5] Companies rushed into international investments. Jersey Standard at the end of the war faced disorder in Mexico; it was quarreling with the Peruvian government over taxation of its oil lands; its distribution network in Europe was disrupted; its producing properties in Rumania were in ruins; in the Dutch East Indies, its explorations brought forth only the "promise of dry holes." Nonetheless, Jersey Standard was convinced that it must expand abroad. It had the representative response to adversity. In its optimistic folly, it even invested almost $9 million in Russian crude oil—*after* the revolution, on the assumption that the communist revolution would not last! *[6]

U.S. investors in agriculture and mining abroad shared the general business buoyancy. They extended their wartime investments as commodity prices in 1919 remained high. U.S. Rubber acquired its first plan-

---

* Jersey Standard made the seed investments of $160,000 in 1919, when Azerbaijan had its own government. In April 1920, the Soviets overthrew the Azerbaijan government and seized the Baku oil fields. Jersey Standard continued its negotiations with the Nobel group and made added investments of $8.8 million between 1920 and 1925! Gibb and Knowlton, *The Resurgent Years,* pp. 328–335, 356.

tation in Malaya in 1919. Soft drink producer Charles E. Hires Co. purchased the Cardenas-American Sugar Company in Cuba early in 1920. The Guggenheims put additional funds into their copper mining operations at Chuquicamata in Chile; Anaconda acquired a copper mining property in Peru in 1920. These were representative investments.[7]

The American International Corporation (established during World War I—see Chapter I above) shared the pervasive business optimism at war's end. So did other banking groups. Bankers started several companies under the provisions of the new Edge Act. Independent of these, twelve U.S. banks and banking corporations by 1920 had 181 foreign offices, a large percentage of which had been started between 1918 and 1920.[8]

The U.S. business enthusiasm for foreign direct investment of 1919–1920 failed to be sustained. Reconstruction in Europe proved far more difficult than most had anticipated. European currencies continued to depreciate. The German economy remained in the doldrums. Russia was wracked with civil war. France and Britain made slow progress in their desperate pursuit of recovery. By 1921, throughout Europe economic conditions seemed disastrous: In Germany exchange was blocked, import restrictions prevailed, and currency depreciation worsened; in Russia a communist state had emerged; in France and Britain, recovery plans stagnated.* [9]

Most U.S. assembly and manufacturing operations in Europe survived with deficits, although Coca Cola's new French bottling plant recorded such losses that in time it was abandoned; Coca Cola turned to the policy of licensing bottling plants overseas, rather than direct investment. A number of the new ventures that had begun in Canada met with failure, as Canada too experienced a postwar recession.[10]

With world prices declining in 1921, raw material prices declined most drastically. Companies that had made wartime and immediate postwar investments in rubber and sugar plantations and copper mines found such stakes to be an incubus. U.S. Rubber operated at a $10 million deficit in 1921. U.S.-owned Cuban sugar companies suffered severe losses; some went into bankruptcy. The Guggenheim operation at Chuquicamata in 1921–1922 failed to make profits. Anaconda left its Peruvian

* Based on 1913 = 100, in 1921 the index for manufacturing production in Russia was 23, in the United Kingdom was 55, in France 61, and in Germany 75. League of Nations, *Industrialization and Foreign Trade*, p. 134.

property unworked.[11] The American International Corporation curbed its activities in 1921; it dropped all interest in direct investment and became simply a holding company for portfolio investments. The new Edge Act companies ceased functioning and were subsequently dissolved. Banks closed many of their new foreign branches.[12]

Economists despaired at the state of the international economy.[13] At home, in the United States, while the war had ended with America more prosperous than ever before, no plans had been made to cope with the effects of demobilization. By late 1920–1921, the United States plunged into the severe worldwide depression. U.S. companies did the best they could to hold together their domestic organizations. Few looked to new prospects abroad. Thus, there was a time of readjustment. Adversity now tempered the optimism.[14]

2

The feeling of distress did not last. Owing to conditions at home and abroad, there was a revival of U.S. direct foreign investment. After 1923, the U.S. economy began to boom. Except for minor downturns in 1924 and 1927, prosperity characterized the rest of the decade. Corporations grew in size, obtained new capital from the sale of securities, reinvested their profits, and added new facilities through mergers. They enlarged their product lines, expanded their markets, and some integrated backward into raw material production. The era of the "Second Industrial Revolution" was the label historian William E. Leuchtenburg gave to these times.[15]

Republican governments in the United States encouraged businesses at home and, in general, encouraged them to move abroad. Harding's backing of American business was confirmed by Coolidge, who declared, "Our government has usually been too remiss, rather than too active in supporting the lawful rights of its citizens abroad." But as secretary of commerce (1921–1928) and then as president (1928–1932), Herbert Hoover expressed concern over certain business abroad. He worried lest U.S. *factories* in foreign lands give employment to alien labor, export technology, and assist other nations' economies; in a neomercantilist formulation, Hoover felt such plants would be competitive with U.S. exports and should *not* be encouraged. Louis Domeratzky of the Department of Commerce's Bureau of Foreign and Domestic Commerce, reflecting his superior's ideas, went so far as to state in 1925, "it would be an unpatriotic act . . . to promote the sale of foreign products competing with those of the United States, *even when such foreign products are the results of investment of American capital"* (italics mine). Others in the department emphasized the dangers when an alien business purchased an American affiliate abroad, pointing to the experience of Westinghouse in England. Westinghouse, the department spokesman claimed, had sold an important part of its export trade for a "mere song." When the Vickers group had purchased Westinghouse's British enterprise, the buyer acquired not only physical facilities, but valuable designs and goodwill; Metropolitan-Vickers "now confronted the Westinghouse Company in all foreign markets"; as a consequence American exports had suffered. On the other hand, Hoover did urge Americans to invest in raw materials abroad to supply American industry; he wanted to break "foreign monopolies" in raw materials and enhance his nation's strategic position. He also applauded U.S. private investments in foreign utilities that would buy American equipment and thus assist U.S. exports.[16]

The Republican administrations favored U.S. investments in less developed areas, especially in Latin America and China. For the first time in American history, the China Trade Act (1922) singled out a foreign nation for specialized tax treatment; when the act did not prove effective, it was amended in February 1925. Under this legislation, American capital could invest in a China Trade Corporation (a U.S. federal incorporation), exempt from U.S. corporate taxation.*[17] The United States sent gunboats to Nicaragua and to China to protect the lives and properties of Americans.† By May 1928, roughly 1500 U.S. Marines were stationed in Shanghai.[18] The administrations sought an "open door" for U.S. business.[19]

With and without U.S. government aid, as we will see in Chapters IV through VI, U.S. direct investment abroad rose during the 1920s.‡ Table

---

* By the end of 1929, charters for 96 China Trade Act corporations had been granted, of which 15 by that time had already been dissolved. The total capitalization of China Trade Act companies in 1929 was estimated by the Department of Commerce to be between $20 and $30 million, owned mainly by U.S. citizens resident in China. Department of Commerce, Bureau of Foreign and Domestic Commerce, *American Direct Investments Abroad* (1930), p. 27.

† The gunboats in Nicaragua were mainly to protect U.S. business; the armed forces in China were to protect American missionaries, scholars, and government personnel, as well as businessmen.

‡ In the 1920s, both U.S. foreign direct and portfolio private investments grew. Foreign loans and investments in securities that did not carry management clearly rose faster than direct foreign investments. Figures differ on whether in 1929 portfolio or

III.1 (using Cleona Lewis's figures) indicates the overall growth between 1919 and 1929. Tables III.2–4 give Department of Commerce figures on U.S. stakes in 1929, by regions and principal countries.*

direct foreign investments by Americans were larger. Thus, in a 1930 study, the Department of Commerce found direct foreign investments in 1929 equaled "nearly half of the total private long-term American investments abroad," while a 1942 Department of Commerce study indicated that direct investments in 1929 constituted 52 per cent of total U.S. long-term investments in foreign countries. Cleona Lewis estimated that in 1929 U.S. direct investment abroad equaled $7.5 billion while long-term private portfolio investments came to $7.8 billion. See Department of Commerce, Bureau of Foreign and Domestic Commerce, *American Direct Investments in Foreign Countries* (1930), p. ii; Department of Commerce, Bureau of Foreign and Domestic Commerce, *American Direct Investments in Foreign Countries—1940* (1942), p. v; and Lewis, *America's Stake in International Investments* (1938), pp. 605–606. The U.S. government was very much concerned over the portfolio transactions; as noted, however, our interest throughout this book is in direct foreign investments.

*The figures on Tables III.2–4 do not always coincide with the revised ones of Cleona Lewis that are given on Table III.1, but the differences are not sufficient to distort in an important manner the pattern of investment.

Table III.1. U.S. direct foreign investments—estimates, 1919, 1929 (book value in million U.S. dollars)

Country or region	(1) Total[1]		(2) Manufacturing		(3) Sales[2]		(4) Petroleum[3]		(5) Mining[4]		(6) Agriculture		(7) Utilities		(8) Railroads	
	1919	1929	1919	1929	1919	1929	1919	1929	1919	1929	1919	1929	1919	1929	1919	1929
Europe	694	1340	280	637	95	133	158	239	—	37[5]	—	—	5	138	—	—
Canada and Newfoundland	814	1657	400[6]	820[6]	30	38	30	55	200	318[7]	50	30[8]	15	245	76	73
Mexico	644	709	8	6	5	9	200	206	222	248	48	58	32	90	123	82
Cuba and other West Indies	567	1026	26	47	10	15	15	62	21	18	382	652	59	105	41	84
Central America	112	251	—	7	1	1	3	4	14	8	44	130	6	33	43	64
South America	665	1720	50	170	55	94	113	512	404	528	29	44	4	348	4	—
Asia	175	446	15	77	25	34	50	151	4	10	32	63	17	65	10	6
Africa	31	117	—	7	10	16	10	32	11	54	—	8	—	2	—	—
Oceania	53	162	16	50	12	22	25	81	—	6	—	—	—	—	—	—
Banking	125	125[9]	—		—		—		—		—		—		—	
TOTAL[10]	3880	7553	795	1821	243	362	604	1341	876	1227	587	986	138	1025	297	309

Source: Table developed from figures in Cleona Lewis, assisted by Karl T. Schlotterbeck. *America's Stake in International Investments*, © 1938 The Brookings Institution, Washington, D.C., pp. 578ff.
[1] Total includes sums of columns 2–8 plus miscellaneous investments.
[2] Excludes petroleum distribution.
[3] Includes exploration, production, refining, and distribution.
[4] Mining and smelting.
[5] Includes $9.8 in aluminum.
[6] Figures include paper and pulp, estimated by Lewis, p. 595, to be $100 million in 1919 and $279 million in 1929.
[7] Includes $56 million in aluminum.
[8] Excludes timberland held by paper and pulp corporations, which is included with paper and pulp under manufacturing.
[9] That the figure on banking showed no rise over 1919 is probably an error.
[10] Total may be off because of rounding.

Table III.2.   U.S. direct investments in Europe, 1929
(book value in million U.S. dollars)

Country	Manufac-turing	Selling	Petroleum	Public utilities	Misc.	Total [1]
Great Britain	$268.2	$ 66.5	$ 21.0	[2]	$129.6	$ 485.2
Germany	138.9	16.8	35.3	[2]	25.6	216.5
France	90.9	13.8	25.1	5.3	9.8	145.0
Italy	13.2	2.3	25.9	66.5	5.3	113.2
Spain	12.4	4.0	8.5	[2]	47.3	72.2
Belgium	38.3	3.5	19.0	[2]	3.5	64.2
Poland	[2]	1.4	[2]	[2]	49.8	51.2
Other European [3]	[4]	[4]	[4]	[4]	[4]	203.1 [3]
TOTAL [1]	628.9	132.9	231.0	145.4	214.6	1352.8

Source: U.S. Department of Commerce, Bureau of Foreign and Domestic Commerce, *American Direct Investments in Foreign Countries,* Trade Information Bull. 731 (Washington, D.C. 1930), p. 10.

[1] Totals do not sum because of rounding.

[2] Included by the U.S. Department of Commerce under "miscellaneous" to avoid disclosure of the operations of individual firms.

[3] Includes in order of size of total investment (in parenthesis in millions of dollars): Netherlands (43.2); Norway (23.0); Sweden (19.2); Switzerland (16.8); Denmark (15.8); Austria (14.3); Rumania (13.8); Portugal (11.5); Danzig, Estonia, Latvia, and Lithuania (10.1); Turkey (8.5); Hungary (7.8); Yugoslavia (6.9); Greece (5.1); Czechoslovakia (4.8); Irish Free State (2.1); Finland (1); Bulgaria (1). Excludes investments in Soviet Union.

[4] Included in total.

Table III.3. U.S. direct investments in key countries in Latin America, 1929 [1] (book value in million U.S. dollars)

| Country | Agriculture | | Mining and smelting | Manufac- turing | Selling [2] | Petroleum | Public utilities [3] | Misc. | Total [4] |
	Sugar	Other							
Cuba	544.0	31.0	[5]	44.7	14.7	9.0 [6]	214.9	60.6	919.0
Mexico	[7]	58.9	230.4	6.3	8.6	205.9 [8]	164.2	8.3	682.5
Chile	—	—	331.5	6.9	13.0	[5]	66.7	4.6	422.6
Argentina	—	—	[5]	82.0	52.9	29.8 [9]	147.8	19.3	331.8
Venezuela	—	[5]	[5]	[5]	.2	226.2 [10]	[5]	6.2	232.5
Brazil	—	[5]	[5]	45.7	15.8	23.0 [6]	96.9	12.2	193.6
Colombia	[7]	15.8	10.6	3.6	3.7	55.8 [10]	24.9	9.6	124.0
Peru	[5]	—	79.5	3.2	2.5	[5]	11.3	27.2	123.7

Source: U.S. Department of Commerce, Bureau of Foreign and Domestic Commerce, *American Direct Investments in Foreign Countries,* Trade Information Bull. 731 (Washington, D.C. 1930), pp. 18–19.

[1] Includes only Latin American countries with over $100 million in U.S. direct investment. These figures do not fully represent the impact; no Central American country is included, because none had over $100 million in U.S. direct investments, yet in the small countries U.S. impact was dramatic.

[2] Excluding petroleum distribution.

[3] Including railroads.

[4] Totals may not sum because of rounding.

[5] Included by Department of Commerce under "miscellaneous" to avoid disclosure of individual operations.

[6] Exclusively market-oriented investment.

[7] Included with other agriculture.

[8] $201.5 million in producing and refining; $4.4 million in distribution.

[9] Includes producing, refining, and distribution.

[10] Almost exclusively in producing and refining.

Table III.4. U.S. direct investments by country (or region) in Asia, Africa, and Oceania, 1929 [1] (book value in million U.S. dollars)

Country or region	Manufacturing	Selling [2]	Petroleum	Public utilities [3]	Mining [4]	Miscellaneous	Total
Australia and New Zealand [5]	49.8	22.0	68.9 [6]	—	[7]	8.5	149.2
China	10.2	7.0	42.8 [6]	[7]	—	53.7	113.7 [8]
Philippines	3.9	9.0	10.4 [6]	35.7	—	20.8	79.9 [9]
British Africa	4.8	13.6	19.2 [6]	—	38.7	.5	76.8
Netherlands East Indies	[7]	2.0	[7]	—	[7]	64.0 [10]	66.0
Japan	40.3	10.6	8.1 [6]	—	—	1.7	60.7
Other Asia and Africa	[11]	[11]	[11]	[11]	[11]	[11]	99.4 [12]
Grand total	133.9	72.0	214.3	35.7 [13]	53.1 [13]	94.1 [13]	645.9 [14]

Source: U.S. Department of Commerce, Bureau of Foreign and Domestic Commerce, *American Direct Investments in Foreign Countries*, Trade Information Bull. 731 (Washington, D.C. 1930), p. 26.

[1] Only countries or regions where the total investments were over $50 million are included. All these figures must be regarded as suspect since Americans often invested in Asia, Africa, and Oceania through third-country subsidiaries and affiliates; while the Department of Commerce tried to allocate the investments by place of operations, in point of fact how these investments were handled statistically varied considerably.

[2] Excludes petroleum distribution.

[3] Includes small investments in railroads.

[4] Mining and smelting.

[5] Combined by the Department of Commerce to avoid disclosures of individual firms. Note the substantially lower figures of the Department of Commerce from those of Cleona Lewis, given on Table III.1.

[6] Practically entirely in oil distribution.

[7] Included by the Department of Commerce under "miscellaneous" to avoid disclosure of individual firms.

[8] The Department of Commerce excluded investments by U.S. citizens *resident* in China. C. F. Remer, *Foreign Investment in China* (New York, 1933), p. 275, includes U.S. residents and puts the total figure at $155 million.

[9] Excluding the investments of U.S. citizens *resident* in the Philippines. Added in the investment, the total would, according to the Department of Commerce, rise to $145 million.

[10] $23.3 million of this was in rubber. Well over $30 million was probably in Jersey Standard's investment in oil production and refining.

[11] Either not available from the Department of Commerce figures or in the case of miscellaneous not a useful figure.

[12] Includes in order of size of total investment as given by the Department of Commerce (in parenthesis in million U.S. dollars): India (32.7), British Malaya (27.1), Portuguese Africa (9), "Palestine, Syria, and Cyprus" (7), Egypt (6.5), Iraq (6.2), "Other Africa [apparently mainly Liberia?] (5.4), Algeria (3.2), "Other French Africa" (1.2), Persia (1.1). Excludes Turkey (8.5), which the Department of Commerce placed under "Europe"—and appears to exclude investments in the Belgian Congo.

[13] The Department of Commerce did not complete totals for public utilities and mining; instead, to avoid disclosure, it included the omitted totals under miscellaneous.

[14] Total off because of rounding.

IV

The Conquest of Markets

One facet of the expansion of U.S. business abroad in the 1920s involved the search for markets. In this chapter, we will consider the industrial corporations that sought to sell abroad to fill foreign demand and invested abroad in order to sell there.

U.S. companies invested in Europe in response to both opportunities and obstacles. By 1923, the British were taking steps toward economic recovery. That country returned to the gold standard in 1925. Yet, the United Kingdom was no longer the strong, proud bastion of prewar times. The McKenna duties, imposed in 1915, to protect weak industries remained in peacetime. To them had been added the Safeguarding of Industry Act of 1921. The British followed with other actions to curtail imports. The French economy, by contrast, began in the early 1920s to show more vitality, as the French put to use in reconstruction anticipated German reparations; in the early 1920s the French actually had lower tariffs than before the war. As for the German economy, after a period of extraordinary disorganization and currency depreciation, in November 1923 the Germans stabilized their currency at a rate of 1 new mark to 1 trillion old marks. This measure and, subsequently, the Dawes plan of April 1924 (reducing annual German reparation payments) proved helpful in rebuilding the Reich. The return of the Ruhr (which had been occupied by a Franco-Belgian army since January 1923) to the Germans in November 1924 renewed the defeated nation's confidence. In 1924 Germany readopted the gold standard. By 1924–1925, the Russian revolution had—it seemed—become set in its confines; the New Economic Policy (introduced in 1921) seemed to demonstrate a more sane approach. In fact, the European economic outlook by 1924–1925 once more looked promising. In pre-1914 terms, normality appeared to have returned to much of Europe, excluding the Soviet Union. In 1927 a feature article in the *New York Times* began, "Europe has come back. Considering the chaos of even five years ago, the achievement is notable . . . The postwar decade will be known in history as the industrial renaissance in Europe." The comeback was, however, accompanied—especially toward decade's end—by growing nationalism and rising tariffs in Germany, France, Italy, Spain, and Austria. England was no longer a free trade nation.[1] U.S. direct investments in Europe practically doubled during the 1920s (see Table III.1). Table III.2 indicates in rough terms the distribution by European country of these interests, in 1929. Practically all the stakes (including most of those in petroleum) were based on marketing strategy. Much of the investment reflected U.S. companies' vaulting tariff walls and operating plants near their customers.

There was, likewise, a sharp rise in U.S. market-oriented endeavors in Canada. The governments of the Dominion, provinces, and municipalities were stable and friendly. In the United States and Canada, people, institutions, values, and customs were similar. Canadians were perhaps more conservative than Americans, but this proved no hindrance to U.S. investors. The risks for U.S. enterprise in crossing the northern border proved minimal. There had been no physical destruction during wartime. As in the past, Canadians by *not* blocking the movement of men, technology, and capital—and by placing tariff barriers to trade—actually encouraged U.S. investment and further secured the position of U.S. business within the Canadian economy. If we exclude utilities (including railroads), the direct investment in Canada in 1929 was pretty evenly divided between market- and supply-oriented stakes. If we include utilities, the stake was overwhelmingly market-oriented.[2]

Many of the same large U.S. industrial enterprises that went to sell and then to manufacture (or refine oil) in Europe and Canada during the 1920s also invested in Latin America, Asia, Oceania, and occasionally in Africa, but they made far smaller capital commitments in their search for markets. Of the countries in these regions, Australia attracted the largest market-oriented stakes. In Latin America, prosperous Argentina lured the greatest investment of this sort.* In the main, however, on these con-

---

* The manufacturing investment given on Table III.3 was by no means all market-oriented. For an explanation of a sizable part of the manufacturing investment in Argentina, Brazil, and Cuba, see Chapter V below. While information on the profitability of market-oriented stakes is very sketchy, fragmentary data indicate that giant profits were made from those stakes in Argentina in the 1920s. One company on a cash

tinents neither opportunities for sales nor obstacles to export (in the form of tariffs and other trade barriers) proved sufficient to warrant giant investments by U.S. companies seeking foreign markets. Thus, in many instances corporations opened sales outlets and built service, assembly, packaging, and mixing plants rather than full-fledged manufactories. As we will see, there were no market-oriented oil refineries owned by U.S. companies in all Asia, Oceania, and Africa in the 1920s.

Specifically, it is important to consider some of the U.S. enterprises in major American industries that made new and enlarged earlier foreign investments, based on marketing strategy. Which industries and companies took the initiative? Why and how did they expand in alien lands? What impact did particular companies and industries have in foreign countries?

2

Americans in the food and beverage industries with specialized, trade-marked products moved abroad. Leading U.S. firms went to Europe, initially to export with no investment plans, beyond perhaps a small interest in sales offices; their first stakes were in distribution to spur their exports. Then some revised their strategies and invested in factories. They built or acquired plants that could use local ingredients, save transportation costs, get behind tariffs, and be nearer their customers.[3]

They moved over the border into Canada in a similar manner, and in addition, many U.S. concerns that had multiplant operations in the United States (and gained economies by having these scattered facilities) also built multiplant networks in the Dominion. Swift, for example, had only a distribution organization in Europe, but in Canada Swift owned six packing plants and nine produce collecting and processing plants, in-

outlay of $300,000 U.S. dollars remitted to the United States from Argentina, between 1921 and 1929, $90 million (U.S. dollars translated at current rate of exchange)! Another company, on a cash outlay from the parent company of $100,000 (U.S.) remitted to the home office $2 million (U.S.) from Argentina in the 1920s. The best profits were made by the companies in Argentina in the 1920s. (Confidential company records). With rising urbanization, a brisk foreign trade, modernization of agriculture and cattle ranching, and the beginnings of industrialization (beyond simply the processing of farm and ranch products), Argentina in this decade seemed poised for tremendous economic development. By 1930, 38 per cent of the Argentine working population was involved in service industries (commerce, finance, personal services, transport, etc.), 36 per cent were in land and cattle farming, while the remaining 26 per cent were employed in manufacturing (including mining and construction). Ferrer, La Economía Argentina, p. 140.

cluding creameries. Likewise, The Borden Company had a subsidiary in England, while in Canada it had by 1930 manufacturing and sales operations at forty-nine locations.[4]

A few enterprises that manufactured in Europe and/or Canada also constructed plants in Australia, where tastes seemed similar to those in the United States (Kellogg and Kraft-Phenix Cheese are examples).[5] Some extended their operations to Latin America and Asia.[6] Corn Products was exceptional among the food companies in having market-oriented operations on six continents. Although Corn Products had distribution facilities abroad before World War I, all its foreign manufacturing began in the postbellum years.[7]

The firms in the food business went abroad in a variety of ways. Some built their own manufacturing plants; others entered into joint ventures abroad (mainly in Europe); still others acquired foreign manufacturers (generally in Canada and Europe). Carnation Milk Products and Pet Milk had in 1919 taken advantage of the new Webb-Pomerene Law that allowed exporters to join together to sell abroad exempt from antitrust prosecution and had organized the American Milk Products Corporation * to export canned milk. As European nations became self-sustaining after the war in milk products, they bought less from the United States. American Milk Products, to defend its market position, began in 1923 to establish evaporated and sweetened milk plants in France, Holland, and Germany as well as can factories in France and Holland. The framers of the Webb-Pomerene Law had not anticipated that Webb-Pomerene associations would be utilized for the purpose of investing abroad, nor had Carnation Milk and Pet Milk planned in 1919 to make such investments; the decision proved a natural evolution—a response to changed conditions.[8] Other firms—United Fruit, for example, retained and expanded pre–World War I distribution networks in Europe and had no need to manufacture abroad.[9]

The Department of Commerce found thirty-five U.S. manufacturing investments in food and beverage products in Europe in 1929; measured in terms of dominance in any European national market, these firms played only a minor role, since literally thousands of small European businesses operated in the food and beverage industries. The U.S. role in Canada, where the Department of Commerce listed fifty-one American

* Name changed in 1931 to General Milk Company.

manufacturing investments,* was larger. American food products were known and common in Canadian retail outlets. Elsewhere, by 1929, the U.S. food and beverage industry seems to have been of little significance.[10]

3

The U.S. textile and apparel industry did not expand abroad importantly in the 1920s. But when it did invest in market-oriented stakes, it was notably in new products and branded merchandise. Thus, du Pont invested in European and Canadian affiliates to make synthetic fabrics; Julius Kayser & Co. manufactured its branded garments in Canada and Australia and probably in Germany; † Jantzen Knitting Mills produced its distinctive clothing in Canada and Australia.[11] Generally, the U.S. textile and apparel industry was an old industry and had little in the way of new technology to offer foreigners; this may be responsible for the limited market-oriented stakes. In this connection, however, one can note the exceptional, and shortlived, stake in the Soviet Union by members of the Amalgamated Clothing Workers Union, advised by U.S. business (the goal of which was to introduce superior American methods).‡ [12]

---

* The definition of a "manufacturing investment" is not clear. Presumably a multiplant operation abroad of a single U.S. company (such as the Borden operation described above) would be a single manufacturing investment. But, if a U.S. company's business in a particular country was done under several manufacturing subsidiaries, would it be treated as one or several manufacturing investments? The report is not clear on this. Such definitional problems could distort the Canadian data, for in 1929 of the *U.S.* companies merged into the U.S. firm General Foods, at least five had Dominion subsidiaries with manufacturing, processing, and packing plants, marketing products as varied as cereal, chocolate, shredded coconut, jello, and coffee. So, too, of the large merged company, Standard Brands (formed in 1929 in the United States), four of the joined firms already had manufacturing subsidiaries in Canada. Likewise, by 1929, National Biscuit had acquired several subsidiaries manufacturing different products in Canada.

† Julius Kayser & Co. had pre–World War I manufacturing in Germany; in 1922 it formed a subsidiary "to handle the export business in Germany" (it is not clear whether the subsidiary manufactured, but it seems likely).

‡ Sidney Hillman of the Amalgamated Clothing Workers Union traveled to Russia in 1921; he returned home with plans to help the Russians reconstruct their clothing factories. In 1922, accompanied by Earl Dean Howard of Hart Schaffner & Marx, Hillman revisited Russia. Subsequently, the Russian-American Industrial Corporation was formed to provide capital and management for Russian industry; the Soviets guaranteed the capital invested and a minimum dividend of 8 per cent payable in U.S. dollars on all money invested. Between $200,000 and $300,000 was invested, and the R.A.I.C. set up several factories. The Russians, however, decided to take them over; by the summer of 1925, Hillman was en route to Russia to "wind up" the venture (see note 12).

In fashions, Americans had a role abroad. McCall and Company established a branch factory in London making paper dress patterns. Butterick Publishing Company had a branch in London making and/or selling paper patterns. The publishers of *Vogue* ran British and French editions.* [13] While there were more U.S. investments in Canada in the textile and clothing industries than in Europe, in fashion U.S. stakes were larger in Europe than in Canada (a reflection perhaps of the style of life).

4

Far greater and more significant worldwide were U.S. interests in the electrical industry. American electrical manufacturers in the 1920s were dynamic and innovative at home and abroad. America's largest enterprise in this field, General Electric, had already by the 1920s a long history in international business. By 1919, it had plants in Europe, Latin America, and Asia, as well as long-time sales operations in Australia and South Africa. On the other hand, in Canada it had an associated company, Canadian General Electric Company, Ltd., in which it had no equity interest (or if it had a stock interest, the amount was negligible).†

In January 1919, Gerard Swope left Western Electric to join General Electric and in April he had become president of G.E.'s new wholly owned subsidiary, International General Electric Company (I.G.E.C.). I.G.E.C. at origin acquired all G.E.'s foreign holdings. Swope, drawing on his experiences at Western Electric, renegotiated G.E.'s prewar contracts and arranged two sets of accords with I.G.E.C.'s affiliates. The agreements dealt with (1) the exchange of experts, (2) technical assistance in making designs and machinery layouts, (3) training of foreign company employees, (4) patents, royalties, and service charges, and (5) market and territorial divisions. One set included manufacturers of lamps and the second, makers of electrical apparatus.

Everywhere, Swope acted according to the prevailing pattern of doing business. When, for instance, in 1921, the European lamp manufacturers organized a price cartel, I.G.E.C affiliates participated. When the cartel collapsed in 1924, I.G.E.C. representatives worked out a new accord

---

* Professor Juan Linz reminded the author of the international nature of fashion. From magazines to dress patterns to cosmetics, U.S. investment in Europe reflected this.

† See Wilkins, *Emergence of Multinational Enterprise*, p. 93, for early history.

among the foreign lamp producers—designed to stabilize the world's lamp business (the so-called Phoebus Contract). General Electric benefited from such price stabilization moves, for the industry's gain was the company's; through I.G.E.C.'s investments, its royalties, and its service charges, G.E. shared in the success of the foreign lamp makers.* [14]

Participation in cartels † did not curb General Electric's expansion abroad. In 1923, on the death of Frederick Nicholls (the Canadian founder of the Canadian General Electric Company), General Electric (not I.G.E.C.) made an offer to the shareholders of Canadian General Electric Company; 90 per cent of them accepted, and General Electric reacquired the majority control of Canadian General Electric Company —control that it had once held (in the 1890s). Beginning in early 1924, General Electric did business directly with Canadian General Electric Company, instead of through International General Electric Company. When the purchase of stock was made, the General Electric *Annual Report* declared: "It is the intention to preserve essentially the Canadian character of this Company and with the freer interchange of scientific, engineering, and manufacturing experience, and by taking full advantage of the resources and facilities of your Company in the United States, it is hoped that the growth and development of the Canadian Company may be such as to serve more effectively the interests of the people of the Dominion." General Electric's investment in Canadian General Electric in the 1890s had been $1.25 million, representing a 62.5 per cent interest. To reacquire control, G.E. paid $12 million, which gave it 90 per cent of the common stock of the largest electrical manufacturer in Canada. By December 1928 the total assets of Canadian General Electric were $31 million. General Electric had obtained control of Canada's foremost electric company. [15]

---

* Did such arrangements violate American antitrust laws? In the 1920s, G.E. lawyers considered the question; the U.S. attorney general and the Federal Trade Commission reviewed the agreements and did not prosecute (Swope, "Memo," April 14, 1942, Oral History Collection, Columbia University, and *U.S. v. General Electric,* 82 F. Supp. 830). Neither G.E. nor I.G.E.C. took part *directly* in the Phoebus Contract. In 1912, Alcoa officials, after signing a consent decree, had asked the Justice Department whether its Canadian affiliate could do what it was prohibited from doing—that is, enter into agreements with European cartels. The Justice Department had not objected (see Wilkins, *Emergence of Multinational Enterprise,* p. 88). It seemed logical to G.E.'s lawyers that I.G.E.C.'s foreign affiliates could follow the same path.

† In this volume, we will use the word "cartel" to refer to formal restrictive agreements between or among otherwise *independent* enterprises, designed to determine prices, amounts produced, and/or methods of marketing.

Meanwhile, International General Electric Company expanded. By 1927, its worldwide investments (excluding Canada) equaled $24 million; they soared to $111.6 million in 1930. The company added to its manufacturing in Latin America and Asia (Japan and China); it undertook to manufacture in Australia; but by far its greatest interests were in Europe. In 1929, I.G.E.C. took its most important steps. Swope, who had become president of General Electric in 1922, has recorded that in December 1927, Reginald McKenna (former British Chancellor of the Exchequer and in 1927 chairman of the Midland Bank of London) invited him to visit England "to consider taking over from the Vickers Company the Metropolitan-Vickers Electrical Company of Manchester." This enterprise—the reader will recall—had purchased the huge English factory built by George Westinghouse. Swope later remembered he was reluctant: "I said we had enough trouble of our own just then." Nonetheless, he traveled to London; while there he suggested to Sir Hugo Hirst, chief executive of General Electric, Ltd. (an independent British company in which I.G.E.C. had started to buy stock on the open market), that all the major British electrical companies—General Electric, Ltd., Metropolitan-Vickers, and British Thomson-Houston (97 per cent owned by I.G.E.C.)—be merged. Sir Hugo turned down the proposition. Swope, however, found the Vickers Company "named such an attractive price that I couldn't resist." As the result of his investigations, in January 1929 Metropolitan-Vickers, the British Thomson-Houston Company (which G.E. already controlled), together with the smaller Ediswan and Ferguson-Pailin, Ltd.,* merged into a new giant—Associated Electrical Industries, Ltd. (A.E.I.). As a consequence of this merger, I.G.E.C. possessed a significant interest in A.E.I., Britain's leading electrical enterprise. It also maintained a minor stake in General Electric, Ltd., Britain's second largest electrical company.[16]

Similarly, I.G.E.C. invested in prominent German electrical firms. General Electric's prewar connections had been with Allgemeine Elektrizitäts Gesellschaft (A.E.G.), the principal electrical manufacturer in Germany. In 1929 I.G.E.C. acquired a substantial minority holding in A.E.G. and pledged additional purchases in 1930 to bring its interest to roughly 25 per cent of the stock outstanding. (To placate German nationalist sentiment, it promised *not* to try to obtain a majority of the capital.)

---

* In 1926 and 1927 British Thomson-Houston had purchased controlling interest in these two small companies. Edwards and Townsend, *Business Enterprise*, p. 305.

In 1929 I.G.E.C. also purchased $11 million in Siemens debentures. Siemens ranked second among the electrical enterprises in the German republic. One economist concluded in 1930 that with these transactions and those of earlier years, "there remains no single German electrical manufacturing company of importance in which remotely or directly, General Electric influence is not felt." [17]

Swope and Owen Young (G.E.'s chairman of the board) believed their corporation should have a *"tranche* in the electrical industry of the world."* I.G.E.C. should buy into every prominent electrical company worldwide. Its objectives were:

1. To stabilize markets, to concentrate on research, to develop new technology, rather than to engage in cutthroat competition. With a friendly atmosphere, the entire industry would profit.

2. To diversify holdings. Business cycles would be different in each country, and with a *tranche* in all nations, General Electric's shareholders would be protected.

3. To enforce patents. This was difficult for an American company remote from the scene; with national affiliates, enforcement was assured.

4. To meet national feelings. Strong sentiment existed in foreign industrial countries against alien products; with G.E.'s global influence, it would have an advantage.

5. To increase U.S. exports. Friendly foreign manufacturers imported American-made products to supplement their own production, which opened more markets to General Electric.[18]

In 1930, as earlier it had promoted lamp agreements, I.G.E.C. led in seeking to stabilize prices in the electrical equipment field. The company believed U.S. antitrust laws denied it the right to become directly involved and decided to participate through a Webb-Pomerene association.* Accordingly, in 1931, I.G.E.C. and Westinghouse Electric Interna-

---

* Here again (as in the case of the milk producers) a Webb-Pomerene association was used in a manner different from that which its congressional framers intended. In 1924, however, in response to questions from a committee of silver producers, the Federal Trade Commission had issued an informal interpretation of the Webb-Pomerene Law: export associations could enter into a "cooperative relationship with a foreign corporation for the sole purpose of operation in a foreign market" and could make "trade arrangements with non-nationals," provided there were no unlawful effects on the domestic commerce of the United States. Federal Trade Commission, *Report on the Operation of the Export Trade Act,* pp. 125–127. This so-called "silver letter" opened the way to arrangements such as I.G.E.C. made. There is, of course, a difficulty

tional organized the Electrical Apparatus Export Association. Through this association, the two principal U.S. electrical companies joined with the major electrical enterprises in Europe in an "International Notification and Compensation Agreement." Each company was required to "notify" an international secretary of customers in certain specified territories; bids were discussed; and the successful tenderer of the bid had to "compensate" the international secretary as well as the other members who had "notified." The accord was only in part an outgrowth of the depression; it was—far more important—a logical extension of the efforts by Gerard Swope and Owen Young to create price stability in their industry. For G.E. international accords and foreign direct investment continued to accompany one another.[19]

The international activities of Westinghouse Electric were small compared with those of General Electric. Because of its earlier poor experiences, Westinghouse shied away from direct foreign investment, preferring licensing arrangements. Its wholly owned international subsidiary, Westinghouse Electric International Company, made contracts with a different group of foreign firms from those initially linked with I.G.E.C. The agreements appear to have been similar. Some contracts were renewals of ones made with now-divested Westinghouse units. (Only after Metropolitan-Vickers merged into Associated Electrical Industries, Ltd., did Westinghouse's contract lapse.) * [20]

With the Phoebus Contract and later the International Notification and Compensation Agreement and with the generally "friendly connections" among the European electrical enterprises, General Electric and Westinghouse in many foreign markets do not seem to have been highly competitive. They became less so in the late 1920s as Swope and Young's idea of a *tranche* in major foreign enterprises took form. Yet, at times, the two American corporations clearly did not cooperate. Thus, a 1949 court concluded that in 1927, I.G.E.C. acted to block Westinghouse's entry into European business—certainly an "unfriendly" step.[21]

---

in the F.T.C. position of the 1920s. If an export company restricts foreign trade *outside* the United States, remotely or directly, it is apt to be restricting trade with the United States. Stabilization of prices abroad might well affect U.S. trade.

* The statement of the Commerce Department official, cited in Chapter III, that Metropolitan-Vickers confronted Westinghouse in all foreign markets may have been inaccurate, for division-of-market agreements may well have barred Westinghouse from certain markets.

General Electric in addition to the above-mentioned stakes also obtained an indirect interest in foreign manufacturing through the Radio Corporation of America (R.C.A.) Under the prompting of Rear Admiral William Bullock and the Navy Department, in 1919 General Electric purchased the British controlling interest in the American Marconi Company and organized R.C.A.* In 1929, R.C.A. bought Victor Talking Machine Company. This *U.S.* acquisition gave R.C.A. multinational manufacturing operations, for Victor Talking Machine Company had affiliates with manufacturing in six European countries, Argentina and Brazil, Japan and India, as well as Australia. R.C.A.'s expansion at home gave it its first role in foreign manufacturing and indirectly enlarged General Electric's operations abroad.† 22

Western Electric (represented in foreign countries since 1918 by its wholly owned subsidiary International Western Electric Company) had long participated in market-oriented multinational investments. Many nations insisted that telephone equipment be made domestically. By the mid-1920s, Western Electric had factories in London, Antwerp, Milan, Paris, and Barcelona, as well as minority interests in telephone and cable companies with plants in Budapest, Vienna, and Berne; in addition, its affiliates had factories in Canada, Argentina, Australia, Japan, and China. Between December 31, 1919, and September 30, 1925, its worldwide stakes had risen from $16.8 million to $18.9 million, hardly a substantial expansion. Apparently, Western Electric's parent—American Telephone & Telegraph Company—felt little enthusiasm about its subsidiary's multinational activities. Outside of Canada, A.T.T. had no foreign stakes of its own and it wished to have Western Electric concentrate on making telephones in the United States. In the early 1920s, the Federal Trade Commission investigated the relations between General Electric, Radio Corporation of America, United Fruit, and A.T.T. and their control over worldwide telephone and radio communication; the investigation seems to have made A.T.T. sensitive about Western Electric's international business.‡ 23 Thus, in August 1925, A.T.T. and Western Elec-

* Westinghouse, Western Electric Co., American Telephone & Telegraph Co., and United Fruit Co. were brought in to avoid patent problems, but G.E. played the leading role.
† In 1933 G.E. distributed the common stock it held in R.C.A. to its stockholders as a dividend—thus ending G.E.'s interest in R.C.A. Hammond, *Men and Volts,* p. 377.
‡ Moreover, at this time A.T.T. was having to defend its domestic rate increase: A.T.T. pointed to the large interest charges it had to pay on loans. Why, the state

tric sold International Western Electric Company to International Telephone and Telegraph Corporation (I.T.T.). (Canadian business was excluded from the sale.) *

Colonel Sosthenes Behn had organized International Telephone and Telegraph Corporation in 1920. A friend described Behn as a "ball of fire, filled with energy, zeal and expansionist fervor." He dreamed of achieving overseas what A.T.T. had accomplished in the United States— the establishment of telephones everywhere. In 1924 I.T.T. had made a contract with the Spanish government to acquire that nation's entire telephone system. The company planned to install American equipment: thus Behn talked with officials in International Western Electric Company, which would be his supplier. Behn's initial idea was to buy I.W.E.C.'s Barcelona factory. Instead, I.T.T. acquired the whole International Western Electric Company. The press proclaimed the transaction as one of the largest "industrial deals" between U.S. enterprises participating in extensive foreign business. Western Electric received $29.3 million. I.T.T. renamed its acquisition: International Standard Electric Company. From 1925 to 1930, I.S.E.C. greatly enlarged its foreign manufacturing facilities, especially in Europe. By 1929, I.T.T.'s subsidiaries owned twenty-four factories in England and on the European continent employing between 30,000 and 35,000 workers. In Latin America, I.T.T.'s plant facilities were more limited than in Europe; I.T.T.'s joint ventures in Japan and China did substantial manufacturing; while its Australian operation seems to have been confined to assembly.[24]

During the 1920s such consumer durables as Kelvinator refrigerators were produced in England and Canada; Hoover and Premier vacuums were newly made by American subsidiaries and affiliates in the neighboring Dominion.[25]

In sum, in the electrical industry, Americans adopted a variety of approaches to direct investments abroad. While the new foreign stakes in manufacturing of General Electric and International Telephone and Telegraph were dramatic, Westinghouse limited itself to licensing and Western Electric had sold its international telephone manufactories (outside

---

regulatory commissions asked, did the company have the expense of borrowing when it had funds tied up in foreign investment? Was this to the American consumer's advantage? Danielson, *A.T.T.*, p. 335, and interviews with Western Electric executives.

* Western Electric owned 43 per cent of Northern Electric, the largest telephone manufacturing company in Canada. Financial Records, Western Electric Archives, New York.

of Canada). Both Radio Corporation of America and I.T.T. moved into foreign manufacturing through *domestic* transactions—that is by purchasing U.S. corporations with such holdings. A number of producers of consumer durables (refrigerators and vacuums) went to Canada, and to a less extent England. By decade's end, from lamps to heavy equipment, to phonographs to telephones, American subsidiaries and affiliates held prominent positions in Europe. In Canada, by 1932 (figures are not available for 1929), fully 68 per cent of the total output of electrical apparatus was reported to come from American-controlled establishments.[26] In Japan Americans were affiliated with the major producers of electrical equipment.[27] In China, they played an important role in this infant industry. As for Australia, they participated in developing electrical activities. In Latin America, U.S. investors took part in the nascent (almost negligible) industry.* Everywhere, Americans offered the most advanced technology. In Europe, they spurred rationalization of older facilities. Unquestionably, they proved a vital element among electrical producers worldwide.

5

Likewise, American makers of automobiles were outstanding on a global scale. Before World War I, only one U.S. car manufacturer, Ford Motor Co., had foreign factories on two continents (in Canada and Europe). By the end of the 1920s, the three leading automobile companies in the United States (General Motors, Ford, and Chrysler) had become multinational, while other U.S. car producers had also started foreign manufacturing and/or assembly operations.

The 1920s witnessed a remarkable growth in automobile output in the United States and the U.S.-inaugurated techniques of mass production were exported. Ford took the initiative; right after the war Ford had begun to erect assembly units in Europe. In addition, it built new assembly plants in Latin America, Japan, and Turkey. It opened foreign assembly plants primarily because it was cheaper to ship "knocked down" rather than "built up" cars. Sometimes also foreign duties were less on parts than on built-up units.

In 1928, Ford started to construct a major manufacturing facility at

---

* They made fragile products such as lamps, while they imported heavy equipment. Victor Talking Machine Company would make records and import the phonographs. I.T.T. assembled telephone equipment in Argentina, importing all the components.

Dagenham, near London, to supply Great Britain, Ireland, and the European continent with the new Model A. The McKenna duties of 1915 made full manufacture of automobiles in England essential. Ford's Dagenham plant would in time replace the company's first less integrated manufactory at Manchester, England (established before World War I). At Dagenham rose the largest automobile plant in the world outside the United States. In its construction, English capital joined with American.[28]

Ford also enlarged its Canadian manufacturing at Walkerville, Ontario, over the Detroit River from the motor city. Here was located the biggest automobile plant in the Dominion, and in fact, in the entire British empire until the Dagenham complex was completed. In addition to its manufacturing, Ford's Canadian unit operated assembly plants in Montreal, Toronto, Winnipeg, and Vancouver, as well as branch sales offices across the Dominion. Abroad, this Canadian enterprise started in the 1920s five assembly and a body building plant in Australia along with assembly plants in India, Ceylon, Malaya, and South Africa. Controlling ownership of Ford of Canada was held—not by the U.S. Ford Motor Company—but by the shareholders of that enterprise (the Ford family); there were also independent American and Canadian stockholdings. In the 1920s Ford ran the Canadian business entirely separately from its other foreign operations.[29]

General Motors similarly established assembly operations worldwide. In 1925 and 1929 respectively, General Motors acquired control of two existing European car makers: Vauxhall in England and Adam Opel, A.G., in Germany. Vauxhall was a small firm; by contrast, Opel had made automobiles since 1898 and by 1929 had the best-selling car in Germany. When General Motors purchased Opel, Opel ranked among the ten largest industrials in Germany. General Motors introduced the latest U.S. methods, substantially modernizing the German firm's operations. General Motors had its main Canadian manufacturing facility in Oshawa —where the McLaughlin Motor Car Co. had started its business in 1907; in 1918, General Motors had obtained full control of the McLaughlin firm and formed a wholly owned subsidiary, General Motors of Canada, Ltd., which in the 1920s handled all G.M. products in the Dominion. Then, in 1929 General Motors acquired 100 per cent of the McKinnon Industries, Ltd., of St. Catherines, Ontario, which made automobile parts and had been a supplier of General Motors of Canada. Like Ford, G.M.

did not consider its Canadian subsidiary to be a part of "foreign operations." G.M. far more closely than Ford coordinated the activities of its
Dominion enterprise with those of the Detroit firm. While Ford for most
of the 1920s was in first place in the Canadian market, in the Dominion
—as in the United States—at the end of the decade, General Motors surpassed Ford and took first rank.[30]

In the 1920s Chrysler's moves abroad were less impressive than those
of its two most important competitors. When Chrysler was organized in
1925, its predecessor companies already had foreign business (in Canada
and England). In 1928, Chrysler in the United States acquired Dodge
Brothers, which manufactured trucks in England and had a car manufacturing plant in Canada. According to economist Frank Southard, by the
end of the 1920s, Chrysler also assembled in Germany. Perhaps because it
was behind and trying to catch up in the United States, Chrysler confined its investments in manufacturing and assembly to Canada and Europe and did not undertake operations on six continents—as did Ford
and General Motors.* [31]

The output of American automobile plants in foreign countries was
for sale there, not for export to the United States. Cars manufactured or
assembled abroad were not competitive in the United States, since without.
the large-scale output of the American factories, it cost more to produce
the vehicles in foreign countries. This American industry was far superior
to its European counterpart in cost structure, technology, capital, and
marketing methods. In Europe, the U.S. manufacturers provided an
"American challenge." European automobile builders sought to imitate
American methods of mass production. At the University of Berlin, a
professor lectured on "Fordismus." The American automobile industry
became a model.[32]

In sum, in 1929 Ford was building in England the largest automobile
plant in the world outside the United States; G.M.'s German-built Opel
ranked first in the German trade; elsewhere on the continent, U.S. cars
held significant market positions. The American automobile industry was
clearly important in Europe. In Europe, however, there remained independent host-nation car producers—Morris, Austin, Citroen, Renault,
and many others.[33] By contrast, in Canada, the native automobile industry had virtually disappeared as U.S. business expanded. Whereas in 1919

* Other U.S. car makers with foreign investments in manufacturing or assembly by
1929 included Willys-Overland, Studebaker, Durant, Hudson, and Graham-Paige.

U.S. capital was estimated to control about 61 per cent of the Canadian motor car industry, by the end of the 1920s U.S.-controlled corporations produced over 83 per cent of the Dominion's cars, trucks, *and* parts.[34] Elsewhere, worldwide, where there was no indigenous (or only a small native) automobile industry, American car exports—often assembled in U.S.-owned facilities abroad—played a major role. For example, in Japan in the late 1920s, practically all the cars sold were made in the United States by Ford or General Motors, shipped knocked-down, and assembled in their new plants.[35] The American car industry abroad represented a triumph of U.S. technology.

6

Suppliers followed the U.S. automobile makers abroad. Several leading U.S. tire manufacturers built European factories.* In Britain the tariff encouraged this, making tire imports from the United States not competitive with British production.[36] Goodyear, U.S. Rubber, Firestone, Goodrich, and Seiberling enlarged their existing Canadian plants and opened new ones. By 1929, the only significant tire producer in Canada that was not U.S.-owned was Dunlop.† [37] Goodyear and Goodrich developed a global marketing organization, including some manufacturing outside of Canada and Europe. Goodyear, for example, made tires in Australia, while Goodrich had a joint-venture operation in Japan.[38]

In addition, American car body builders trailed after their customers to Europe; so did manufacturers of wheels, batteries, roller bearings, spark plugs, artificial leather (for seat covers), finishes, and window glass.‡ [39] A similar (but not identical) group of suppliers invested in Canada.§ The two U.S. Steel and the two Republic Steel plants in the Dominion apparently sold to the automobile producers, as well as to other firms.[40] Far fewer of these suppliers of the automobile companies

---

* Goodrich (1924), Goodyear (1927), and Firestone (1928) in England. U.S. Rubber had a prewar rubber reclaiming plant in Manchester, sales branches or subsidiaries in England and on the continent, but no tire plants in Europe. By the 1920s Goodrich had plants in France and Germany (the French company was a prewar investment).

† Many of the rubber makers produced more than just tires, having a diversified line of rubber goods.

‡ Among them, Briggs Manufacturing Co., Edward G. Budd Manufacturing Co., Kelsey-Hayes Wheel, Electric Autolite, Electric Storage Battery, Timken Roller Bearing, Champion Spark Plug (sales only), du Pont, Libbey-Owens Sheet Glass.

§ Among them, American Auto Trimming Co., McCord Radiator and Manufacturing Co., Champion Spark Plug, Kelsey-Hayes, and du Pont.

invested in the 1920s in foreign facilities—manufacturing or sales—in Latin America, Asia, or Oceania.[41]

7

The nascent U.S. aircraft industry was little interested in foreign investments; those investments made were in Canada and were part of the industry's U.S. domestic expansion, caused principally by the need to get behind Canadian tariffs and to serve better the Canadian buyer (Table IV.1). The Canadian aircraft industry was dominated by U.S. capital.

Table IV.1. American investments in the Canadian aircraft industry

Canadian company	Established	Function
Canadian Wright	1926	Assembly, distribution, and repair of Wright whirlwind engines
Curtiss-Reid Aircraft	1928–1929	Manufacturing (?)
Canadian Pratt & Whitney Aircraft	1928	Assembly, distribution, and repair of engines
Fairchild	1928	Assembly of planes
Boeing Aircraft of Canada	1929	Manufacture of planes

Source: Canadian Annual Review 1928–1929, p. 216; Leslie Roberts, *Canada's War in the Air* (Montreal, 1943), pp. 11, 55.

Perhaps, the reason these U.S. producers did not expand in Europe was that Americans had no clear technological advantage over Europeans in this industry.

8

By contrast U.S. manufacturers of certain metal products did have technological superiority and did move abroad. Many had started operations in foreign lands before World War I. In the 1920s prewar plants were refurbished, enlarged, and sometimes replaced; certain prewar sales subsidiaries were transformed into manufacturing enterprises. Added sales and manufacturing subsidiaries were inaugurated. The process was continuous and worldwide.

From office equipment to sewing machines, to elevators and radiators, and to harvesters, U.S. manufacturers invested in Europe and Canada; many that did substantial manufacturing in Europe and Canada expanded, or opened, new sales, assembly, or service branches or subsidiaries in Latin America, Asia, and Oceania. Only in Europe and Canada did they do full manufacture.

It would bore the reader to catalogue this expansion. Indeed, it would serve little purpose to detail the specific international moves of such multinational firms as Singer, Otis Elevator, American Radiator, or International Harvester, for example. Yet, the overall growth is significant. U.S. makers of office equipment in Europe reflect the development. National Cash Register Company and Burroughs Adding Machine Company had manufacturing plants in Europe before World War I, which they enlarged in the 1920s. By contrast, before the war, International Business Machines's predecessor firms and Remington Typewriter Company had sold in Europe through direct investments in *sales* outlets, and one of I.B.M.'s predecessors (Tabulating Machine Company) had licensing arrangements. In the 1920s, I.B.M. and Remington-Rand * —to get behind tariff barriers—for the first time built manufactories in Europe, and by 1929 each had plants in Germany, France, and England.† Meanwhile, other U.S. office equipment makers—among them Royal and Underwood-Elliott-Fisher—persisted simply with European sales subsidiaries. All of these plants and sales subsidiaries were established, based on marketing strategies. American office equipment sold well in Europe. The products, superior in quality and price to European wares, were presented to foreign consumers with aggressiveness and skill taught by John H. Patterson, founder of National Cash Register Company,‡ and his pupil Thomas J. Watson of International Business Machines—two great salesmen of all times.[42]

In a number of metal products—office equipment, sewing machines, shoe machinery, elevators, radiators, and certain farm equipment, for instance—U.S. companies held an important share of European markets,

---

* Computing-Tabulating-Recording Company was renamed I.B.M. in 1924. The Remington Typewriter Company merged with Rand Kardex and other smaller firms to become Remington-Rand in 1927.

† I.B.M. in the mid-1920s established modern factories in Germany and France. In England one of I.B.M.'s predecessor companies, Tabulating Machine Company, had in 1908 licensed British Tabulating Machine Company to use its patents; in 1927 Thomas Watson declared, "Our Tabulating Machine Division is served by the British Tabulating Machine factory" in England. Watson, *Men-Minutes-Money*, p. 114. I.B.M. also owned at the end of 1929 a 58 per cent interest in International Time Recording Company, Ltd., which had built a small plant in England. New York Stock Exchange Listing Statement, Nov. 26, 1929, #A-9108.

‡ Patterson died in 1922; his trainees made excellent salesmen.

especially in England and Germany. In Canada, by the decade's end over 40 per cent of the Dominion's production of office, household, industrial, and agricultural equipment came from American owned or controlled plants.[43] Worldwide, the United States was a large exporter of such products, and U.S. subsidiaries and branches abroad assisted the exports by handling the sales, assembling, and finishing of the final product.[44]

9

Most of the U.S. stakes in aluminum facilities in Europe by America's one aluminum company, Aluminum Company of America (Alcoa), were to supply the European market. After World War I, Alcoa feared that European businesses would dump their output on the American market.* While the Fordney-McCumber Tariff of 1922 provided protection, Alcoa's president, A. V. Davis, believed that his enterprise "ought to be in a position to manufacture as cheaply as the principal European producers, because there was no certainty that a tariff would be maintained by the United States which would reflect the difference between the domestic and foreign manufacturing costs." Thus, Alcoa made large investments in Europe.[45]

In Canada, by contrast, most of Alcoa's substantial stakes were supply-oriented and will be discussed in Chapter V; Alcoa did have in the Dominion some semifabricating and fabricating plants to process the less than 10 per cent of its Canadian aluminum output sold there—investments based on Canadian marketing considerations. Elsewhere, Alcoa had a few market-related investments. Alcoa (and after 1928 its associated Aluminium Limited) ranked among the leading aluminum enterprises in the world.[46]

10

Unlike most U.S. companies in "growth" industries, the three principal U.S. chemical producers (du Pont, Union Carbide, and Allied Chemical) were far from audacious in their search for international markets. Du Pont (at decade's end, the largest of the trio) had a European manager by 1922, but when it considered developing business in Europe, British Nobel interests in 1923 warned "the introduction of an active campaign

* Professor Raymond Vernon has pointed out that concern with dumping occurs in the aluminum industry primarily because of the high proportion of fixed costs in this industry (private communication to the author).

in the European market [by du Pont] is a violation of the spirit of the understanding [between us]." Du Pont had then retreated, retaining simply a small minority stake in Nobel Industries. In 1925 Nobel Industries and du Pont established Nobel Chemical Finishes Ltd.—51 per cent owned by the British firm and 49 per cent owned by du Pont. Du Pont and British Nobel also cooperated in Canada, where before the war they had started a joint-venture company, and in South America (in Chile, du Pont and Nobel Industries built an explosives factory in 1923). In 1925, du Pont renewed its prewar ties with the German explosives industry. That year, du Pont, Nobel Industries, and Dynamit A.G. formed a joint-venture company to sell in South America; du Pont also invested $1.75 million in two German explosives concerns (Dynamit A.G. and Köln-Rottweiler). In November 1925, I. G. Farbenindustrie A.G. came into existence—the dominant enterprise in the German chemical industry; the next year it took over Köln-Rottweiler; by consequence du Pont became a small holder of stock in I. G. Farben (under 1 per cent). Then, in 1926, Britain's most important chemical company, Imperial Chemical Industries, was organized; it included Nobel Industries; accordingly, du Pont became a small, minority stockholder in I.C.I. Between 1926 and 1928, du Pont entered into a collection of minority-interest ventures in Europe: in finishes, artificial leather, and fabrics—activities connected with supplying the automobile industry. On July 1, 1929, du Pont and I.C.I. made a comprehensive agreement, covering many of the chemical industries in which the two participated.* Du Pont granted I.C.I. exclusive rights for patents and processes for the British empire (excluding Canada and Newfoundland); I.C.I. gave du Pont the same rights for North America (except Canada and Newfoundland). In Canada, du Pont and I.C.I already had the important, now diversified, joint venture initiated by du Pont and Nobel interests before World War I. For the rest of the world, the two corporations granted each other nonexclusive licenses. The accord provided for an exchange of research and technology. In addition, du Pont made agreements or understandings with I. G. Farben, affecting specifically the cellophane, explosives, celluloid, seed disinfectants, and fungicide industries and also certain patents. By decade's end,

---

* Certain important chemical industries were excluded, either because of prior commitments or because of lack of interest by one of the companies: rayon and cellophane, alkalies, military explosives, photographic film, and hydrogenation of oil and coal.

although its direct foreign investments were small and confined to minority positions, du Pont was closely associated with the two principal European chemical enterprises. Through these connections, it had eliminated foreign competition in the U.S. market.* [47]

The second leading U.S. chemical concern in the 1920s, Union Carbide and Carbon Corporation, was founded in 1917 as a merger of five existing chemical companies. During the 1920s it had a number of foreign business ventures; a few in Canada and elsewhere were market-oriented; the majority appear to have been supply-oriented and will be considered in Chapter V.[48]

Allied Chemical & Dye Corporation (formed in a merger in 1920), the third of the large U.S. chemical firms, sought at origin to liberate itself from European control. Its president, Orlando F. Weber, signed a market-sharing agreement with the British chemical firm Brunner, Mond and the Belgian Solvay & Cie. in 1921 that sharply limited Allied's foreign business.† Although this agreement was canceled in 1926, no evidence exists that Allied Chemical established major operations abroad; only in Canada did Allied Chemical have market-oriented stakes.[49]

In total, the three major U.S. chemical enterprises had not yet made dramatic investments abroad. The reason lay in the historic strength of the German and British producers. By contrast, the chemical industry in the United States had gotten its real push in World War I. In the 1920s its costs were high. While the industry was aggressive and expanding, it had formidable adversaries in I. G. Farben and Imperial Chemical Industries. Rather than compete with these giants (competition in which Americans would be at a disadvantage), in the main, U.S. companies steeled themselves to develop *American* business separate from foreign control; they concentrated on a significant expansion in the States; they gained from cross-licensing arrangements with the Europeans as well as from purchases and sales of patents; they tried to keep abreast of Euro-

---

* An exception to the general minority pattern and the ties with Europeans was a fifty-fifty venture between du Pont and the U.S. company, Hercules Powder, in neighboring Mexico; in 1925, the two acquired the only explosives plant in Mexico. See du Pont, *Annual Report 1925*, and J. K. Jenney to J. E. Crane, Dec. 9, 1936, Eleutherian Mills Historical Library, Acc. 1231, Box 2.

† Allied Chemical absorbed Solvay Process Company in 1920, whereupon Solvay & Cie. and Brunner, Mond became minority shareholders in Allied Chemical, owning 20 per cent of the stock. Weber didn't appreciate these European interests and wanted to act independently in the United States. Brunner, Mond became part of I.C.I. in 1926. Reader, *Imperial Chemical Industries*, I, pp. 293, 318–319, and chap. 19.

pean technological developments and research; and in the process, they arranged that I. G. Farben and Imperial Chemical Industries would learn about American innovations.* [50]

During the decade, the Germans had done research on the process of hydrogenation, a way of obtaining petroleum products from crude oil and coal. The British chemical industry was interested; American chemical producers apparently were not.[51] On the other hand, on September 27, 1927, Standard Oil of New Jersey made a contract with I. G. Farben arranging to learn of the German work on the hydrogenation of crude oil. In 1927 there was worldwide overproduction of oil, which Jersey Standard's president Walter A. Teagle felt deferred "indefinitely the commercial use of the [hydrogenation] process for producing gasoline from crude petroleum." Nonetheless, Teagle wanted the rights to the process for both oil and *coal*.† After complex negotiations, Jersey Standard and I. G. Farben on November 9, 1929, made a new agreement covering hydrogenation of both oil and coal and providing for future "close cooperation" between the two enterprises. Jersey Standard recognized the "preferred position of I. G. in the industries known as chemical," while I. G. Farben accepted the "preferred position of the [Jersey] Company in the industries known as oil and natural gas." The 1927 and 1929 contracts would in later years—as we will see—embarrass Jersey Standard; at the time, the oil company anticipated no political repercussions and looked forward to major technical benefits.[52]

Another branch of the U.S. chemical industry—drugs—also associated closely with European enterprise. After U.S. entry into World War I, George Merck, the chief executive of Merck & Co., had turned over to the Alien Property Custodian 80 per cent of the stock in his firm, representing German interests; ‡ in 1919, the Custodian had sold these securi-

---

* I. G. Farben in 1929, according to its chief executive, Carl Bosch, "did not wish to go into competition in the United States with the U.S. chemical industry." Bosch believed the American chemical industry would reciprocate. U.S., Senate, Committee on Patents, *Hearings, Exhibits*, p. 3442.

† While Germany, England, and France desired to produce gasoline from coal for "national purposes," Teagle in 1927 had other thoughts: "U.S. has 52% of the coal reserves, much of which is in close proximity to oil and gas . . . oil produced from coal could be handled through the same facilities that are now handling crude oil . . . looking into the future coal must be considered along with oil . . . the process can be used to better advantage by the oil industry than the coal industry." (U.S., Senate, Committee on Patents, *Hearings, Exhibits*, p. 3434.

‡ Merck & Co. had been formed in 1891 in the United States by a member of the German Merck family.

ties to an American group friendly to George Merck. In the 1920s, the "all-American" Merck & Co. did not compete with E. Merck, its former parent. In Canada, Merck & Co., which had had a branch since 1911, in 1929 incorporated a Dominion subsidiary and advertised "Made in Canada" pharmaceuticals. E. Merck (the German firm) stayed out of the Dominion.[53]

The Bayer Company of New York, formed in 1906 as a subsidiary of the German Friedrich Bayer & Company, had been seized by the Alien Property Custodian during World War I; on December 12, 1918, the Custodian sold the U.S. Bayer Company to the American Sterling Products, Inc. When Sterling Products began to export to Latin America using the Bayer name, the former German parent sued; in 1920, to resolve the litigation, the German Bayer proposed a division of profits in the Latin American trade; Sterling Products agreed. In 1923, Sterling Products's management decided that to develop ethical drugs would require sizable expenditures in research. The Germans offered an acceptable alternative: German Bayer agreed to provide Sterling Products with its manufacturing information, patents, and technical know-how; in exchange, Sterling Products granted the German firm a half-interest in the profits of a newly formed Sterling Products's American subsidiary, Winthrop Chemical Company, which would sell exclusively in the United States and Canada. In 1926, after German Bayer became part of I. G. Farben, Sterling Products obtained the results of I. G.'s pharmaceutical research; Winthrop Chemical became a half-owned I. G. Farben affiliate. In England, Sterling Products purchased Scott & Turner, Ltd., English manufacturer of Andrew Liver Salt, and also participated in a joint venture with I. G. Farben. It extended its business in Canada. In March 1928, in the United States, Drug Inc. was formed; Sterling Products and its various subsidiaries were merged with United Drug Company (owners of Louis K. Liggett Co.), Life Savers, Inc., and Bristol-Myers. In 1928–1929, Drug Inc. had a variety of market-oriented investments in diverse products in England and Canada and a marketing outlet in Australia. The Drug Inc. group was, however, conspicuously absent from the European continent. Part of the reason may lie in the links between Sterling Products and I. G. Farben, and part may be because Germany—the hub of the world's pharmaceutical industry—dominated the continental trade.[54]

Another giant merged unit in the U.S. drug industry was American

Home Products (formed in 1926); it had no known German connections and immediately moved abroad, acquiring two English companies; * then annually, it expanded anew, purchasing in 1927 the International Chemical Company, Ltd. (London manufacturers of bisurated magnesia), in 1928 the Kolynos Company (American toothpaste maker with a British manufacturing subsidiary), and in 1929 Bisodol, Ltd., of London. By 1930 American Home Products sold trademarked proprietary drugs, household products, cosmetics, and dentifrices throughout the United States, England, continental Europe, and South America.[55] Curiously, it listed no plants in Canada.

Parke, Davis, and Company, a pioneer exporter of American drugs, had manufactured near London since 1902. In the 1920s, it tempered its expansion; having lost its Russian factory, it apparently decided against more extensive business on the European continent. It, however, retained its multinational character with manufacturing or sales stakes on six continents.[56]

For sales in Europe, U.S. firms making cosmetics started to mix their compounds there rather than in the States; the trademarks of Hudnut Perfumery, Pond's Cream, Elizabeth Arden, and Helena Rubinstein † became familiar to European women. In soaps, Colgate-Palmolive-Peet had by decade's end plants in Europe, Canada, Latin America, and Australia. It would export until it had obtained sufficient sales volume; then, it would contract with an independent local soap maker to manufacture according to its formula. It kept its own trademark and continued to do the merchandising. As volume rose, it often purchased the foreign franchised manufacturer.[57] Its expansion then would proceed, primarily through reinvested earnings. By contrast, Colgate-Palmolive's main U.S. competitor, Procter & Gamble, made no foreign investments (outside of Canada) until 1930, when it purchased the important Newcastle soap manufacturer, Thomas Hedley & Sons. It did this in part from a desire to challenge Lever Brothers in England, hoping to turn that British firm away from North American markets.[58]

When U.S. pharmaceutical firms, makers of toilet articles, and producers of soap went to Latin America, like other U.S. manufacturers, their

* W. L. Dodge Ltd. and St. Jacobs Oil Ltd.
† Polish-born Helena Rubinstein had started business in Australia, set up branches in Paris and London, and then in the 1920s established her business headquarters in the United States. See O'Higgins, *Madame*.

market-oriented stakes were small compared with those in Europe and Canada. The Department of Commerce reported fifty-two "manufacturing" investments in Latin America in 1929 by U.S. pharmaceutical and toilet preparations companies—yet the *total* investment came to less than $9 million. Some of the $9 million was in soap making; the rest was simply in mixing and packaging.[59]

Eastman Kodak—sometimes classified as in the chemical industry—had long participated in international business; by 1929, it had sales outlets on every populated continent and manufactured in Europe, Canada, and Australia. Its foreign manufacturing had come in the 1920s to include cameras as well as film. In 1928, at Harrow in England, Kodak's British subsidiary inaugurated perhaps the first American industrial research laboratory abroad. Kodak ranked supreme in its product line worldwide.[60]

11

Petroleum enterprises made some of the most substantial market-related investments abroad. Jersey Standard, the world's largest oil company, had long sold and invested in foreign markets. By the 1920s it had market-oriented stakes in Europe, Canada, and Latin America, but *not* in Asia, Africa, and Oceania; with the Supreme Court dissolution of the Standard Oil Group in 1911 these last regions had gone to other Standard Oil units.[61] So too, the Supreme Court had in 1911 separated the large marketer Anglo-American Oil Company, Ltd., in Britain, from Jersey Standard's control, but the U.S. firm continued to sell to Anglo-American even though it held no investment. In 1926 Jersey Standard reentered the British market directly, purchasing control of Agwi Petroleum Corporation, with its small refinery at Fawley, near Southampton. At the same time, Jersey Standard maintained close ties with Anglo-American. (F. E. Powell, chief executive of Anglo-American, was included as a member of Jersey Standard's European committee, a committee set up in 1924 to coordinate the Jersey Standard's European business).[62] In Germany, Jersey Standard sought to rebuild its marketing and refining affiliate's strong prewar position.[63] In Spain, in 1922, the U.S. oil enterprise purchased control of that nation's largest oil marketing firm; Jersey Standard also acquired a 50 per cent stake in an important Spanish purchasing and transportation company. Then, in 1927, the Spanish government made oil distribution a monopoly of the state; over Jersey Standard's loud protests, the Spanish government expropriated its properties, paying Jersey Standard \$5,720,000 in compensation.[64]

In addition, Jersey Standard attempted to enlarge its distribution network in France. In 1924, the French government acquired a 25 per cent interest *—its first interest—in a private oil company, Compagnie Française des Pétroles. Then in 1927, the French government requested the Jersey company's aid in establishing a national marketing cartel; the U.S. firm refused to participate. Walter Teagle, its president, was wary, for he believed the Russians were spending a lot of money in France and "a number of people were trying to create an oil monopoly which they could turn over to Russia as an outlet for Russian oil." Then, a new threat emerged. In 1927, oil had been discovered in Iraq. The French government hoped to have such oil refined in France, and in 1928 passed two laws: the first made all imports of refined products illegal, except by licensed firms; the second provided for a stiff rise in import duties to revive and to develop the French refining industry.† In April 1929, the French government established a refining company, Compagnie Française de Raffinage (C.F.R.), in which the state held a 10 per cent interest.‡ Jersey Standard, if it wanted to continue doing business in France, would have to invest in a refinery there. It did, as we will see (in Chapter IX).[65]

Elsewhere in Europe, Jersey Standard developed its extensive marketing organization. It had small market-oriented refineries in Poland, Italy, Norway, and Belgium, as well as those in England and Germany. In 1923, the only year in this decade for which the present author can locate figures, Jersey Standard's European marketing and refining affiliates employed over 17,000 persons, the vast majority of them Europeans (the number certainly rose during the 1920s). Jersey Standard was by far the largest U.S. oil enterprise in Europe. Vacuum Oil had interests in marketing and in lubricating oil refineries in England and on the continent. Texaco, Cities Service, Atlantic Refining, Tide Water, and Sun Oil owned smaller European distribution organizations. Standard Oil of New York had offices in Bulgaria, Greece, and Yugoslavia. Until the late 1920s, Gulf seems to have sold in Europe through Jersey Standard affiliates; in 1926, it purchased a 25 per cent interest (raised to 75 per cent in

---

* Later raised to 35 per cent.

† The French had had a refining industry before World War I.

‡ And also an indirect interest through its 25 per cent interest in Compagnie Française des Pétroles, which held 55 per cent of C.F.R. Rondot, *Compagnie Française des Pétroles,* pp. 36, 63.

1928) in the Nobel-Good-Andre marketing group in Europe, which had been primarily involved in the sale of lubricating oil.[66]

In Europe American oilmen fought an uphill battle against Royal Dutch-Shell and Anglo-Persian. By decade's end, in Britain, U.S. investors were important (but not in first place); in Germany, U.S. firms sold about half the refined oil; and in France, Jersey Standard was second to Royal Dutch-Shell in sales (Jersey Standard supplied 19 per cent, while other U.S. companies shared 14 per cent of the French trade).[67]

In Canada, by contrast, Jersey Standard controlled that nation's principal oil company—Imperial Oil, Ltd.* By 1928, Imperial Oil had assets of $223 million, which, using the standard of assets, made it Canada's largest corporation.† Imperial Oil owned a number of refineries, had 1,700 marketing outlets, and operated 251 gasoline stations in the Dominion. By 1929, it employed in Canada over 20,000 people. Throughout the decade, it remained that nation's leading petroleum enterprise, despite formidable competition from Shell.[68] The U.S. oil companies—Sun Oil, Cities Service, Union Oil, The Texas Company, White Star Refining (which became a subsidiary of Vacuum Oil in 1930), Quaker State Refining, and Standard Oil of New York—also had direct investments in selling oil in the Dominion.[69]

Throughout Latin America Jersey Standard led in marketing; because the demand for oil products was smaller, the company employed far fewer individuals in selling in Latin America than in Europe or Canada.[70] Other enterprises, from The Texas Company to Tide Water, also had marketing investments in Latin America.

Table IV.2 indicates the most important U.S. oil companies (Standard Oil of New York, Texaco, and Vacuum Oil) with stakes in distribution in Asia, Africa, and Oceania. In Africa and East of Suez, U.S. enterprises had substantial interests in *selling* oil, but none had market-oriented refineries in the 1920s.[71]

Worldwide, of the U.S. petroleum companies only Jersey Standard ranked with Royal Dutch-Shell and Anglo-Persian in the big three. Jersey

---

* The name was changed from The Imperial Oil Company, Limited to Imperial Oil, Ltd. in 1919. Jersey Standard owned 77 per cent of the stock in 1920 and 72 per cent in 1927. Gibb and Knowlton, *The Resurgent Years*, p. 636. The stock was traded in Canada and the percentage outstanding was widely held.

† The Canadian company Brazilian Traction, Light and Power, with assets of $329 million, was larger, but its assets were all *outside* Canada. *Annual Financial Review Canadian* (July 1929).

Table IV.2. Marketing investments of principal U.S. oil companies in Asia, Africa, Oceania, 1929

| Company | Asia | | | Africa | | Oceania | |
	Japan	China	Other	S. Africa	Other	Austra-lia	New Zealand
Standard Oil of New York	Yes [1]	Yes [1]	Through-out Asia [1]	Yes	No	Yes	Yes
Texaco	No [2]	Yes	Some	Yes	[3]	Yes	Yes
Vacuum Oil	Yes	No	Some Near East	Yes [1]	Through-out Africa [1]	Yes [1]	Yes [1]

Source: Interviews and data provided by Mobil Oil and Caltex officials in New York, Japan, India, South Africa, Ghana, Nigeria, Rhodesia, Kenya, and Egypt, 1965 (Standard Oil of N.Y. and Vacuum Oil in 1931 merged into a company that in time became Mobil Oil; on Caltex, see Chapter IX herein). See also U.S. Senate *Special Committee Investigating Petroleum Resources, Hearings,* 79th Cong., 1st sess. (Washington, D.C. 1946), pp. 403–404.
[1] By far the most important of the *U.S.* oil companies in the country or region.
[2] Texaco had representation in Japan until the earthquake of 1923 destroyed its properties, whereupon it retired from the Japanese market.
[3] In 1929–1930, Texaco was investigating outlets in East Africa.

Standard was the largest of the three giants. Of the total consumption of refined products in 1927 outside America's boundaries, the Jersey organization provided 23 per cent, Royal Dutch-Shell, 16 per cent, and Anglo-Persian, 11.5 per cent; Russian-owned refineries accounted for 6.5 per cent, while the remaining 43 per cent came from other companies (in large part U.S.-controlled enterprises).[72]

During the 1920s, Jersey Standard, Royal Dutch-Shell and Anglo-Persian had occasionally been competitive, but sometimes not. An oilman himself, Calouste S. Gulbenkian used to say, "Oilmen are like cats. One never knows when listening to them whether they are fighting or making love." Yet, when during much of the 1920s the enterprises had fought, Standard Oil of New Jersey—deficient in cheap foreign oil—had been on the defensive. Thus, that company's officials were doubtless pleased when Sir Henri Deterding, head of Royal Dutch-Shell, invited Walter Teagle, president of Jersey Standard, and Sir John Cadman, chairman of Anglo-Persian, for a grouse-shooting session at Achnacarry Castle. The grouse-shooting was designed as and became a trouble-shooting affair. The result was the "Achnacarry accord" of September 17, 1928, which put forth "as is" objectives to eliminate ruinous competition.* The agreement covered the world—except the U.S. market, which (in an attempt to comply with U.S. antitrust policies) was explicitly excluded.[73]

In 1929 U.S. direct investment in the European oil industry has been variously estimated at $231 to $239 million, the bulk of which was market oriented.[74] In Canada, usually reliable sources indicate about $55 million was invested by U.S. companies in oil distribution and refining, but these sources must have miscalculated; this figure surely grossly underestimates the stake.[75] The present author would more than double this number. As for Latin America, market-oriented investments in oil distribution equaled about $79 million.[76] In Asia and Africa they came to roughly $87 million—of which $42.8 million was in oil (mainly kerosene) distribution in China.[77] In Australia and New Zealand, the U.S. oil industry's stake (all in distribution) equaled $68.8 million.[78]

12

Companies with their major U.S. stakes in mining had their largest foreign investments in supply-seeking activities (to be considered in Chapter V); many such enterprises also had market-related investments in sales outlets in Europe and in fabricating in Canada. For example, Anaconda by decade's end had investments in sales subsidiaries in England, Germany, and France. In Canada, Anaconda, through its subsidiary American Brass Company, had in 1922 purchased Brown's Copper and Brass Rolling Mills Ltd., with the only complete brass works in the Dominion; Anaconda's goal was "to better the Canadian trade." In October 1926, a Webb-Pomerene association, Copper Exporters, Inc., was formed, including the world's major producers of copper (United States and foreign); it sought to fix prices on copper. American copper producers were of key importance in world trade in this commodity.[79]

---

* Oil was discovered in Iraq in 1927, as noted earlier; on July 31, 1928, a group of U.S. oil companies, with Standard Oil of New Jersey in the lead, had made an agreement with Royal Dutch-Shell, Anglo-Persian, and Compagnie Française des Pétroles covering oil production in much of the middle east (see Chapter V). A month later, on August 31, 1928, Walter Teagle had stated that he favored the status quo—the "same percentage as now" in the French market. Clearly, Jersey Standard did not have to be convinced that cooperation was desirable. U.S., Senate, Committee on Patents, *Hearings, Exhibits,* p. 3430. Jersey Standard saw cooperation as necessary because of the existence by 1928 of "overproduction" of oil and specifically because it wanted to maintain control over the influx of Russian oil into European markets.

13

The above offers a sample of U.S. companies and industries in the 1920s with investments to serve foreign markets. Hundreds more industrial enterprises could have been included. Market-oriented investors not in manufacturing, petroleum, or mining have been excluded (see Chapter VI). Many other industries could have been added or segregated (among them abrasives, heating and plumbing, window glass, cement, steel, rubber products, and tobacco).* The text should, however, cover the principal U.S. companies in the principal U.S. industries with market-oriented stakes abroad in the decade.

Of the U.S. industries that crossed over America's borders, relatively new rather than older ones tended to lead in undertaking market-oriented investments. Firms with trademarked or branded merchandise widely advertised at home moved outside the country, as did enterprises with distinctive products. U.S. industries with worldwide technological leadership gained abroad through the transfer of techniques in product design, engineering, and organization of production. Companies using advanced marketing methods went to foreign countries with those methods. Big companies far more often than smaller ones became multinational, although some of the automobile suppliers that moved abroad were hardly giant enterprises. More in the 1920s than earlier—reflecting the greater business beyond our boundaries—enterprises that had U.S. customers with foreign investments followed their customers overseas.

Only a few atypical U.S. industrial corporations invested in market-oriented stakes abroad because they worried about foreign competition at home. More typically, foreign investors tended to be large exporters. In general, the reason for market-related investments lay in the opportunities to be met outside the country and in the fact that the best way to

---

* The abrasives manufacturers went to Europe and Canada. Heating and plumbing makers went to Europe and Canada. At least one glass maker (Libbey-Owens-Ford) was multinational. Producers of cement seem to have gone exclusively to Latin America. U.S. investments abroad in steel *plants* were limited to Canada, although American steel enterprises did have foreign sales outlets. Rubber products makers—considered in the text as suppliers of the automobile industry—also produced other goods and some such companies were, as noted, multinational. American Tobacco—ousted from most of its foreign investments by a 1911 Supreme Court decision—attempted a limited reentry into foreign manufacturing when in 1927, in retaliation for the invasion of the U.S. market by British-American Tobacco (B.A.T. was by this time a British firm), American Tobacco purchased J. Wix & Sons, an English cigarette manufacturer; American Tobacco also had some negligible market-oriented stakes in Cuba.

meet those opportunities was through investment. The decisions to expand beyond the foreign sales subsidiary were based on a complex of factors that generally could be reduced to questions of cost (broadly defined)—was it more economical to continue to export, or to build a plant abroad? Cost considerations were sometimes comparable to those decisions on building or acquiring a second, third, or fourth *domestic* factory—that is, those considerations relating to the price of and availability of transportation, raw materials, labor, and so forth, with transportation a major element of cost in international decision-making.* Could a new domestic or foreign plant achieve the same economies of scale as the existing facility? If not, how were costs affected? Frequently in international business, costs included the extra expense imposed by the presence of tariff barriers. Likewise, national preferences for homemade goods— expressed in the marketplace or through legislation—might make manufacture in a foreign country imperative if the corporation were to gain or retain that market.† When studying the reasons for market-oriented stakes in manufacturing abroad, no immediate reason related to U.S. government policy.

One finds some sharp differences in the type of market-oriented stakes that went to particular countries. For example, Australia attracted U.S. prepared food, apparel, film and camera, proprietary medicine, and soap makers, while Japan obtained little of this sort of investment. On the other hand, American electrical, automobile, and rubber tire enterprises invested in Japan about as readily as in Australia. China, because of its geographical expanse and because of its demand for kerosene ("oil for the lamps of China"), attracted far larger investments by oil companies than Japan (see Table III.4). Yet, as in the past, so in the 1920s, the largest market-oriented stakes in foreign lands by U.S concerns tended to go to the most affluent nations of the world, those with industrialized and technologically advanced economies, where the market was greatest.

Within particular industries, companies were distinctive in their methods of making foreign investments. Thus, Carnation and Pet Milk invested abroad through a Webb-Pomerene association; The Borden Company did not. General Electric made large foreign investments;

---

* A common motive for domestic and international investment was being near the customer to provide service, interpret his needs, and the like; this can be thought of in terms of cost.

† There is a cost in *not* meeting national preferences.

Westinghouse preferred the licensing route. Ford built its own manufacturing plants abroad; General Motors bought existing foreign manufactories. Remington-Rand constructed typewriter factories outside the United States, while Royal and Underwood-Elliott-Fisher still sold abroad through marketing subsidiaries. The approaches reflected unique characteristics of the management of each enterprise and particular experiences abroad.

The text has indicated the impact of the market-oriented investments in specified regions and countries. Everywhere Americans invested, they communicated concepts of mass production, standardization, and scientific management. The impact appears to have been greatest in Canada and Europe. We will save for Chapter VII the more general impact of U.S. investment abroad as well as national responses to the U.S. stakes.

V

Supply Strategies

U.S. business went abroad in the 1920s to gain supplies as well as markets. Unlike the market-oriented investors that sold mainly within the host nation, supply-related investors exported from the capital-recipient country. Such stakes have often been called "traditional," yet it was really during the World War I years, and especially in the 1920s, that this tradition apropos U.S. multinational enterprise became deeply rooted.[1] Indeed, as markets expanded in the 1920s, corporations' need for supplies increased. Supply-oriented stakes were in purchasing, manufacturing, agriculture, and extraction. A rough calculation reveals that in 1929, supply-oriented stakes represented slightly more than half the book value of U.S. direct foreign investments, excluding those in public utilities and transportation.[2]

Whereas market-oriented interests of manufacturers, oil, and mining enterprises tended to be largest in industrial nations, investments based on supply strategies, as in times past, predominated in the western hemisphere (Latin America and Canada) and then in less developed nations around the world (they existed, but were not substantial, in Europe). Here we will survey these stakes, why they were made, and by what sorts of companies, how they were made, and what impact they had on the host countries.

2

We need merely mention the interests in purchasing. U.S. companies sent representatives to buy from foreign manufacturers, farmers, miners, and oil producers. The investment in purchasing was usually small. Frequently, such an interest was associated with existing foreign investments: thus, United Fruit bought from independent banana growers and also had its own plantations; American Smelting and Refining Company purchased from local mines and also owned its own mines. When we turn to the oil industry, we will see how purchasing in one instance provided the sole available means of obtaining a raw material. Cleona Lewis estimated U.S. direct investment in purchasing abroad in 1929 at a mere $16.1 million.[3]

3

More important, supply-oriented manufacturing comprised numerous facilities and sometimes a substantial capital commitment. While the bulk of U.S. manufacturing abroad in the 1920s, as in earlier and subsequent years, was market-oriented, supply-oriented manufacturing cannot be ignored. Under this rubric were certain operations that required cheap power—including those of electro-chemical and paper and pulp producers. In the first category, several U.S. firms (notably, Union Carbide and Alcoa) invested in Norway in plants that required cheap power—plants for export. More common were such facilities in Canada. Union Carbide constructed several. American Cyanamid expanded its main plant, built in 1913, on the Dominion side of Niagara Falls. Alcoa's Canadian unit—after 1928 Aluminium Limited—had a pre–World War I facility at Shawinigan Falls and in the 1920s opened a new one at Arvida; together by 1929 the two produced roughly 40,000 tons of aluminum of which 36,400 tons were exported. Aluminium Limited was the sole producer in the Canadian aluminum industry.[4] By 1929, three giant enterprises ranked preeminent in the Canadian paper and pulp industry: International Paper and Power, Abitibi Power and Paper, and Canada Power and Paper. In each, U.S. interests participated, but only the first was U.S. controlled. American investors also had smaller stakes in other Canadian paper and pulp plants that sold their output in the United States. While U.S. holdings in paper and pulp were greater than in any other single type of manufacturing in the Dominion and while they were in a major Canadian activity, U.S. involvement—as measured by percentage of output controlled—was far less than in the Canadian electrical, automobile, rubber products, or aluminum industries. U.S. direct investment in paper and pulp in Canada reached $279 million in 1929.[5]

Paper and pulp makers used cheap raw materials in the Dominion as well as cheap power. Other U.S. manufacturers abroad that exported likewise made their investments based on an available (relatively cheap) resource from the forests, waters, ranches, and farms. Thus, by 1929 Armstrong Cork Company had cork factories in four Spanish cities, processing cork for export. In Canada, U.S. investors fished for, processed, and exported sardines. More important, the sizable U.S. holdings in manufacturing in Cuba, Brazil, and Argentina (see Table III.3) were in great part in agricultural (including livestock) processing for export. The U.S. investment in Cuban manufacturing represented a substantial stake in cigar making and, secondarily, in sugar refining.* Investments in meat packing for export inflated the figures for U.S. interests in manufacturing in Argentina and Brazil (the meat packers also served the host-nation market, but the bulk of their output was exported). In 1926, the "big three" American packers—Swift, Armour, and Wilson—slaughtered more than 67 per cent of the Argentine cattle that went to market. Americans were preeminent in this key Argentine industry. Other U.S. investments made to process foreign agricultural and animal output for export from the host country ranged from those in coconut factories and canning facilities in the Philippines, dried egg processing and pig bristles in China, jute mills in India, to meat packing in Australia. Some such plants were owned by multinational enterprises (Swift Internacional, General Foods, and Borden's); others by small businesses.[6]

Two U.S. mining enterprises, which were engaged in mining and smelting in Mexico, in the 1920s built for the first time lead and silver refineries there—for export. American Metal Company invested in a copper refinery in Canada but did not mine in the Dominion.[7] Petroleum firms erected oil refineries near foreign sources of supply—for export. Thus, the large American-owned oil refinery on the Dutch island of Aruba processed Venezuelan petroleum for sale abroad. Jersey Standard's refineries in Peru, Colombia, Rumania, and the Netherlands East Indies handled host-country crude oil for foreign sale.[8]

Finally, there existed a variety of other small, miscellaneous U.S. stakes in manufacturing for export—investments in carpets, hand-woven tapestries, and textile mills in China, embroidery in the Philippines, carpet manufacture in Turkey, and, to repeat, jute in India.† These various

---

* Only a few U.S. companies refined sugar in Cuba; the largest refinery (Hershey's, built in 1926) was for export; smaller ones served the Cuban market. In the main, the sugar companies had plantations and mills; the refining was done in the United States.

† Jute manufacture in Calcutta was dominated by British and Indian capital. Americans made small investments based both on the available raw material and the cheap labor.

interests in textiles were exceptional among U.S. foreign investments in that they were motivated by the existence of cheap labor with a high degree of skill and dexterity. Most of this investment was made by small U.S. businesses, often resident abroad, rather than by multinational enterprises.[9] In short, then, when we consider the figures on U.S. manufacturing abroad in the 1920s it is erroneous to assume that they represent market-oriented stakes—although market-oriented manufacturing certainly did predominate.*

U.S. businessmen when making these manufacturing investments usually took into account the height of the U.S. tariff on the specific import. From their origin, however, American meat packers in Argentina had exported to Europe; in the 1920s they hoped to sell Argentine beef in the United States, a hope that was frustrated when the United States in 1926 embargoed such beef (owing to alleged hoof-and-mouth disease). In imposing this prohibition, a Republican government in the United States favored ranchers at home at the expense of American packers abroad. Swift, Armour, and Wilson continued to sell their Argentine beef in Europe.

Although, as noted in Chapter III, the United States aided American business in China with the China Trade Act, C. E. Herring, assistant director of the Bureau of Foreign and Domestic Commerce, pointed out in a memorandum to the secretary of commerce: "There may be a good deal of opposition . . . to active encouragement by the Government of American investments in China to the real or supposed detriment of American manufacturers and American labor." "The whole matter of potential competition of Oriental labor" alarmed Herring, who noted the migration of the jute industry from Dundee, Scotland, to India and worried about a similar trend affecting a range of U.S. textiles. Yet no efforts were made by the U.S. government to discourage U.S. stakes in supply-oriented manufacturing in China.[10]

Abroad, host-nation political conditions variously affected supply-oriented manufacturers. Usually in the 1920s the influence was slight: although Argentines chafed at the role of the American "trusts" in their packing industry, so far they failed to take meaningful steps to curb the

---

* Note that the "manufacturing" investments in refining by mining and oil companies are placed in the statistics (in Table III.1) under mining and oil; the stake in aluminum is also classified under mining. On the other hand, paper and pulp, sugar refining, and meat packing are under the rubric "manufacturing."

packers' activities. Positive political effects included the Mexican federal and state government incentives that prompted U.S. mining and smelting companies to construct lead and silver refineries. Negative ones existed when Americans built the oil refinery on the Dutch island of Aruba, because they feared future political instability in Venezuela.[11]

4

Americans also participated in foreign agriculture—for export. In discussing these investments it is frequently essential to look at political considerations that influenced both conditions of entry and operations. For example, because of the attitudes of successive Mexican governments, by the 1920s American businessmen, who had once had large stakes in Mexican agriculture, were wary. As noted, the Mexican revolution had brought losses to investors; in the 1920s, nationalization programs began slowly to be implemented. About 161 moderate-sized properties of U.S. citizens were confiscated, the U.S. government's protests notwithstanding.[12] Since American enterprises in the 1920s got little in the way of satisfactory recompense, no enthusiasm prevailed among such investors in land in Mexico.*

Mexico was the only country to nationalize any U.S. landholdings in the 1920s; elsewhere U.S. stakes in foreign agriculture rose.† Fruit growers and buyers expanded their operations throughout Central America, the Caribbean islands, and Colombia. The largest among them continued to be United Fruit. Its main expansion in the 1920s was from the Caribbean to the Pacific coast of Central America.‡ It purchased vast tracts of land, as Panama disease ravaged its existing holdings. It also acquired land for political reasons: in Guatemala, dictators would give land as gifts to their generals. The generals had no use for the land and offered it for sale to United Fruit. Fearful of offending the generals (anyone of whom might become president), the company bought useless land and left it uncultivated. Over time, the enterprise became a giant landholder.

United Fruit was enormous compared with the countries in which it

---

* The figures on Table III.1 indicating an increase in U.S. stakes in Mexican agriculture would seem to be misleading.

† The figures that indicate a decline in agricultural stakes in Canada (see Table III.1) are simply the result of a change in accounting. See note.

‡ In 1929 United Fruit started regular shipments from the Pacific coast of Panama to western markets in the United States.

operated. Its budget in Costa Rica was larger than the national budget. In Costa Rica, where United Fruit had an investment of roughly $10 million, the government asked the firm for aid in floating a loan in New York. Don Ricardo Jiménez Oreamuno, president of Costa Rica, told an interviewer in 1927, "as long as I have known the affairs of my country, which is a very long time, Americans have never mixed in politics, or had candidates, or sought to influence an election, or attempted to exercise any influence outside of their own business affairs. They have stood up for their rights, but they have asked no favours. They have received no favours." Don Ricardo did not add that *he* had asked favors of the company! [13]

Sumner Welles (acting as a personal representative of President Calvin Coolidge) on a trip to Honduras in May 1924 talked with that nation's provisional president, Dr. Fausta Davila, who advised Welles, "that he was grateful for the material assistance which the United Fruit Company and the fruit company owned by the Vaccaro Brothers [Standard Fruit] had afforded the revolution." Welles was shocked by what he learned in Honduras and concluded a report to the State Department: "It is . . . my intention to bring to the attention of the Department my belief that the disasters which have lately overwhelmed the Republic of Honduras can in large measure be attributed to the direct intervention of certain important American interests located in that Republic . . . the troops of the revolutionary forces were paid in large part with money advanced by the interests referred to. Arms and ammunition, including cannon and machine guns were obtained from the same source."/ In 1929 a writer, sympathetic to U.S. business enterprises, found that in Honduras, "agitation against American companies is continuous; one plank in every political program has to do with taking their land away from them." In Honduras, United Fruit and Standard Fruit generated the bulk of the revenue of the nation.

In Nicaragua, where United Fruit Company's holdings were relatively small, political instability was endemic. In 1926, President Adolfo Díaz requested U.S. intervention to suppress his opposition; the United States sent Marines ashore at Puerto Cabezas, indicating that the action was in response to appeals from Americans "to protect U.S. lives and properties." When the civil war in Nicaragua ended, the Marines remained. It is not clear whether United Fruit Company asked for the assistance, but evidently the United States was prepared to dispatch forces. In general,

United Fruit did not need to rely on U.S. Marines and functioned without calling on assistance from the U.S. government.* [14]

As Americans spread abroad seeking fruit (primarily bananas), they also enlarged their stakes to obtain sugar. By 1929, according to the Department of Commerce, some fifty-seven U.S. companies had invested roughly $544 million in sugar production in Cuba. This was big business. Indeed, in the 1920s, primarily because of the new interests in sugar, Cuba became second only to Canada as the nation attracting the most U.S. direct investment (see Tables III.1–4). Sugar dominated the Cuban economy, and U.S. capital dominated Cuban sugar growing. The investors were, explained a U.S. government report, seeking "to make Americans independent of foreign producers as well as to make greater profits." American growers of sugar in Cuba in vain protested in 1921 and 1922 the rise in U.S. tariffs designed to protect domestic sugar planters (here as with the cattlemen a Republican government supported U.S. business at home at the expense of U.S. business abroad). But the U.S. tariff rise was not sufficient to impede the mounting U.S. investments in Cuban sugar. Investment peaked around 1924, and then with lower sugar prices at decade's end, investment slowed. Elsewhere, on other Caribbean islands (especially in the Dominican Republic), in Central America, Colombia, Peru, and the Philippines, American companies acquired new sugar plantations; † nowhere was the commitment as large or as important to a national economy as in Cuba.[15]

Just as Americans invested in sugar to make themselves independent of foreign producers, so, too, U.S. businessmen looked for foreign rubber. In 1922 the British put forth the Stevenson Rubber Scheme to assist British planters in Ceylon and Malaya by restricting output and thereby raising prices. U.S. Rubber and Goodyear—with their existing rubber plantations in the Far East—had some protection against the anticipated

---

* Department of State, *A Brief History of the Relations Between the United States and Nicaragua 1909–1928* (1928) includes an appendix (pp. 65–70) on the 1926 calls for protection by American companies. There is no plea from United Fruit; there are three requests (pp. 67, 69, 70) from Standard Fruit for aid. Standard Fruit stated that it had $8 million invested and about 1000 Americans employed at Puerto Cabeza (p. 67). The American Consul at Bluefield did at one point telegraph Washington that the boats of the two banana companies were being taken from them and their laborers "being recruited or frightened away" (p. 66). Most of the appeals for U.S. intervention from American companies in Nicaragua came from the small U.S. lumber concerns in the mahogany business.

† Some investments were by small companies; others by multinational enterprises (such as W. R. Grace in Peru). See note 15.

higher prices.* By contrast, Firestone, which had not integrated backward, was exposed. Harvey Firestone's response was to develop rubber
plantations. Henry Ford also resolved to grow his own rubber. The Department of Commerce under Herbert Hoover took up the cudgel
against "foreign monopoly" and in 1923–1925 sent expeditions to the
Amazon, the Caribbean, the Dutch East Indies, and the Philippines to
seek opportunities for rubber growing.[16]

In December 1923, a Firestone representative arrived in Liberia—that
small West African country founded in 1822 by the American Coloniza-
tion Society. A group of freed American slaves had settled in Monrovia,
the capital city (named after the American president). The slaves' descen-
dants became the nucleus for subsequent Liberian governments. Liberia,
a republic since 1847, had remained independent as Europeans had
carved up Africa in the late nineteenth and early twentieth centuries. At
the start of the 1920s, the Liberian government had sought a loan from
the United States to cope with its financial difficulties; the U.S. Senate in
1922 had failed to approve the loan. Harvey Firestone, attracted by the
possibilities of growing rubber in Liberia, proposed (1) to arrange a private loan of $5 million to the Liberians; (2) to lease one million acres to
grow rubber; (3) to improve the harbor in Liberia to aid rubber exports;
and (4) to lease the former British (now abandoned) Mount Barclay Rubber Plantation in Liberia, to be used for experimentation. In June 1924,
in accord with the fourth proposal, the Firestone Company leased for
ninety-nine years the 1,500 acre "experimental" plantation at Mount
Barclay.

Implementation of the first three proposals proved far more complex.
In July of 1924, Amos C. Miller, vice president and general counsel of
the Firestone Company, visited the State Department in Washington to
explain he was concerned with the "question of guaranties which would
be necessary to protect them [Firestone] in making any large investment
in Liberia." The company's proposed giant rubber plantation would be
away from the coast; roads would be required. Some 30,000 laborers
would be employed as well as American engineers and technicians. Expenditures in sanitation would be needed, "as all forms of tropical diseases were rampant." Miller felt that the American government had
failed "to accord what they [Firestone officials] considered adequate pro-

---

* U.S. Rubber's plantation in Malaya had to conform to the British restrictions.

tection to American investment in Mexico." Leland Harrison, assistant secretary of state, pointed out that United Fruit Company flourished in Central America without U.S. government guaranties, but Miller and his Firestone colleagues felt "the necessity of obtaining some definite control over the administration of the Republic of Liberia"—controls such as had been incorporated in the proposed U.S. government loan to Liberia. On another occasion, Firestone representative William D. Hines explained to the State Department the risks involved. Initially, everything would be investment with no revenues forthcoming until after the first five years. Firestone would be gambling with "a heavy capital investment [and] he had no assurance that the Liberian government might not go to pieces within the next few years." Thus, "the political fate of Liberia was of the greatest concern to Mr. Firestone." In Washington, in December 1924, Secretary of State Charles Evans Hughes told Harvey Firestone that he "would not and could not commit his successors to protection and support of the investment," but that "it was the historic policy of the Department to lend proper support of a diplomatic character to the just claims of its citizens."

While Firestone officials continued discussions in Washington and Monrovia, the company contemplated investment prospects in the Philippines, but the laws of that country stipulated that a private investor could buy no more than 2,500 acres, which Firestone thought inadequate; then in 1925, the Firestone Company leased a rubber estate in Mexico, but this was abandoned in one year because of the difficult political situation and the unsuitable labor force; early in 1926, Firestone was offered a concession in Sarawak, but under British government pressure the offer was withdrawn. Thus, Firestone came to look more longingly at Liberia, and vice versa.

Liberians saw in Firestone's entry several advantages. First, they wanted the loan that would accompany the concession and second, the entry of an American corporation they thought had *political* value. As a Liberian explained later, "Firestone wasn't brought here for reasons of economic development; we wanted Firestone for *political* reasons." The Liberians argued that (1) British or French loans—if possible to obtain —would involve infringements on Liberian sovereignty; (2) the British and French were already creating border difficulties; with an American corporation there, the Liberians believed the United States would protect the corporation and thus protect the nation's sovereignty from engulfment by Europeans. These were the arguments of President Charles D. B. King when he supported the concession and of Senator William V. S. Tubman, the Firestone lawyer who defended the proposal in the Liberian legislature; Senator Tubman would later become the president of Liberia. Many years later as president, he emphasized that the reasons for Liberians' wanting Firestone had been political. After Firestone came, "political encroachments" of European powers stopped.

Finally, on November 10, 1926, after almost three years of negotiations, the Liberian legislature ratified three contracts with the Firestone Company. The first gave the American company the right to lease up to a maximum of one million acres for ninety-nine years. Firestone promised to develop at least 20,000 acres within five years and to pay an annual rental of six cents an acre on the leased land together with an export tax of one per cent of New York price on the rubber shipped. The second contract was the loan agreement. Under it, the Liberian government was to issue not more than $5 million in bonds, carrying a 7 per cent interest charge. Firestone's newly formed Finance Corporation of America would purchase half of this issue at 90; the remainder would be purchased after certain conditions had been met. Interest on the loan would be paid out of government revenues from the Firestone plantation. At Firestone's insistence, the loan agreement provided for an American financial adviser, "to be nominated by the President of the United States and appointed by the President of Liberia." Other Americans were also to be given powers over the Liberian finances.* Liberians disliked these last provisions, but nonetheless accepted them. The third agreement involved Firestone's assistance in constructing a deep-water harbor, an agreement that was not consummated. By the Spring of 1928, Firestone had 27,000 acres under cultivation; the Liberian government had been loaned $2.25 million; the company looked forward to a successful future in Liberia.[17] This direct investment was exceptional in the involvement of the U.S. government in the loan arrangements.

Meanwhile, Goodyear purchased a second plantation (40,000 acres) in Sumatra and in 1928 bought 2,500 additional acres in the Philippines, which gave it a sum total of 62,500 acres. U.S. Rubber had by the end of

---

* Harvey Firestone had cabled his representative in Monrovia in May 1925: "Impossible to make loan unless Liberian finances are administered by parties making the loan. Liberia fortunate having our government take responsibility administering the loan." *Foreign Relations of the United States 1925*, II, 429.

1927 increased its plantation acreage in Malaya and Sumatra to 135,053 acres—total. The major American rubber companies (B. F. Goodrich excepted) thus protected themselves against British price manipulation schemes. Henry Ford in 1927–1928 also made substantial investments in planting rubber trees, in Brazil.

The companies that integrated backward into rubber growing were not protected against the *fall* in rubber prices that occurred in 1929. Firestone slowed its developments in the Negro nation. U.S. Rubber, still the largest U.S. producer of rubber, found its once profitable plantations a burden.[18]

U.S. enterprises also integrated backward into other farm products—holding some tobacco lands in Cuba and in the case of International Harvester, having a sisal plantation in Cuba and a new hemp plantation (acquired in 1928) in the Philippines. Additional U.S. stakes in foreign agriculture included those in timberlands in Canada (mainly owned by the paper and pulp producers, although other industrial enterprises, Singer Manufacturing Company, for example, integrated backward),* on Caribbean islands and in Central America (owned by small businessmen), and in the Philippines (often owned by U.S. residents there). International Products Corporation in Paraguay held vast cattle lands and quebracho forests.[19]

5

U.S. corporations invested far more abroad in mining than in agriculture in the 1920s (see Table III.1). During this decade, Americans made substantial investments in mining and smelting in Latin America and Canada, and smaller ones in Europe, the Far East, and Africa.† Their mines included asbestos, bauxite, chrome, coal, copper, diamonds, iron ore, lead, manganese, nickel, nitrates, platinum, potash, tin, tung-

---

* Some of the U.S. holdings of Canadian timberland, leases on crown timber, and "cutting rights" compared in size with the huge tracts of land Americans had once held in Mexico (and that Mexican agrarian reform was seeking to reduce), but the total area covered by Canadian territory was 3,851,809 square miles, compared with Mexico's 758,061 square miles, so from a relative standpoint the U.S. stake in Mexican land seemed much more dramatic.

† There may also have been a small stake in Australian mining (the Department of Commerce gives no figures "to avoid disclosure"—see Table III.4 above). Lewis, in *America's Stake in International Investments*, pp. 251 and 584 (see Table III.1), identified a $6 million U.S. stake in Australia in 1929 by American Smelting and Refining Company (ASARCO). This is a mistake; ASARCO did not invest in Australia until 1930 (see Blainey, *Mines in the Spinifex*, p. 142).

sten, vanadium, and zinc, as well as gold and silver. Investors such as the Guggenheims (directly and through their control of American Smelting and Refining Company and Kennecott), American Metal Company, Anaconda, and Newmont Mining were important multinational enterprises in this decade (all except Kennecott were mining or seeking ore in three or more foreign countries).

In Mexico, long-time U.S. investors—among them American Smelting and Refining Company (ASARCO), American Metal,* and Anaconda —faced political uncertainties. At times, the Mexican government hobbled their operations, insisting they employ Mexican doctors, lawyers, and engineers. ASARCO complained to the U.S. State Department, "We do not know of any Mexican mining engineers that are competent to carry on such large scale operations as ours." C. M. Loeb, president of American Metal, joined in the protest.[20] It was clear, however, that the Mexican government meant to have its way; indeed, as they protested, the U.S. mining companies began hiring and training engineers and employing licensed Mexican doctors and lawyers. Actually, not only in Mexico but throughout Latin America, doctors and lawyers—before engineers—were the first "nationals" to be treated as equals by U.S businessmen; these men had acquired professional qualifications. In 1925, a Mexican government decree sought to force the workings of mines (titles were ordered void if not worked). The Mexican Mining Law of 1926—repealed in August 1929—worried U.S. business; the *Engineering and Mining Journal* described it as an attempt "gradually to force the mineral properties of the country into Mexican ownership." Even with the precarious political situation, U.S. mining companies stayed in Mexico—and some even raised their investments.[21]

During the 1920s the increase in U.S. mining in Latin America was greatest in nitrates and copper in Chile, copper, lead, and zinc in Peru, and tin in Bolivia. Throughout the decade, of all nations worldwide,

---

* American Metal Company, Ltd. (American Metal Climax, Inc. since December 31, 1957), was incorporated in 1887 as a trading company, controlled by three firms that were linked by family interests: Ladenburg, Thalmann & Co. of New York, Metallgesellschaft of Frankfort, Germany, and Henry R. Merton & Co. Ltd. of London. World War I disrupted the relationship between American Metal and the European metal traders. Henry R. Merton went into liquidation; in 1920 Metallgesellschaft's shares in American Metal were sold to American interests. American Metal, thus, became in 1920 an American-controlled company. Bernfeld in collaboration with Hochschild, "A Short History of American Metal Climax, Inc.," in American Metal Climax, Inc., *World Atlas*, pp. 1–16.

Chile attracted the most U.S. investment in mining (see Tables III.1–4 for 1929 comparisons). In 1919–1922, through Kennecott Company, the Guggenheims controlled the Braden Copper Company with its giant copper mine southeast of Santiago, at El Teniente, Chile; the Guggenheims also held majority interest in Chile Copper Company, with the largest copper deposit in the world—the open pit mine at Chuquicamata in northern Chile.* At both mines, the Guggenheims had successfully applied new methods of ore processing. As their engineers—E. A. Cappelan Smith, Pope Yeatman, and Fred Hellman—traveled from the Chilean coast to Chuquicamata (which was inland), they crossed through the nitrate regions. The Americans noted the inefficient, small-scale output of the numerous British and Chilean producers. If management were centralized, the engineers speculated, substantial savings in cost could be introduced. Operations at the nitrate fields could be mechanized. Perhaps, moreover, the new techniques of leaching used on copper ore at Chuquicamata could be applied to nitrates. Why not, they asked, introduce low-cost mass production? After all, nitrates, not copper, were Chile's principal export in the 1920s.

The Guggenheim engineers knew that during World War I synthetic nitrates had been developed in the United States; nonetheless, they believed that with efficient production, new technology, and accompanying lower costs, Chilean nitrates would remain competitive. In 1923, the Guggenheims sold their 51 per cent interest in Chile Copper Company to Anaconda for $77 million. This sum provided the Guggenheims with ample capital to invest in Chilean nitrate properties. In 1924, they formed Anglo-Chilean Consolidated Nitrate Corporation to hold nitrate lands they purchased and also the assets of the successful, British-owned Anglo-Chilean Nitrate and Railway Company (established in 1886). The Guggenheims had begun replacing British capital with American. By the end of 1926 they had in operation a modern plant at María Elena. The Chilean government began to fear American interests were becoming too powerful. Over the government's opposition, the Guggenheims next sought control of the Lautaro Nitrate Company, Ltd., a giant British

* Chile Copper Company was a holding company, which owned Chile Exploration Company, the operator of the Chuquicamata mine. The Chile Copper Company was a giant enterprise. Ranked by assets in 1917, the company was the 29th largest incorporated company *in the United States*—ranking ahead of General Motors which was in 30th place. See 1917 list in *Business History Review* 44:369 (Autumn 1970).

producer.* In 1929 Anglo-Chilean acquired the majority of the stock of the Lautaro company and installed its own management. Through control of the Lautaro unit, the Guggenheim Bros. could name the president and control the Nitrate Producers' Association in Chile! In less than a decade the Guggenheims had achieved leadership in Chile's major industry (employing roughly 100,000 men) and representing in 1929 45.6 per cent of Chilean exports.† [22]

In 1929 Anaconda obtained 100 per cent control of Chile Copper Company, which gave Anaconda complete ownership of Chile's largest copper mine. Anaconda had a second significant mining enterprise at Potrerillos, Chile, the Andes Mining Company, which produced its first copper on January 14, 1927. Anaconda, with its mines and smelters, held first place in the Chilean copper industry. Its two enterprises by 1928 employed 11,000 Chileans. The Guggenheims continued to control Kennecott, which owned the Braden Copper Company. The Braden Company, with 6,400 Chilean employees (in 1928), ranked second in Chilean copper.‡ These American companies handled the bulk of copper exports from Chile, which in 1929 reached a new high—40.4 per cent of Chile's exports.[23] American money, technology, and personnel in the 1920s had become of overwhelming importance in the Chilean economy.

In Peru, the principal U.S. investor in mining continued to be Cerro de Pasco, which mined copper, silver and gold, lead and zinc. In addition, acting through American Smelting and Refining Company, the Guggenheims in 1921 entered Peruvian mining. That year ASARCO had established a subsidiary, Northern Peru Mining and Smelting Company, which bought copper, silver-gold, and coal mines in northern Peru.[24]

During World War I, American dependence on Europeans for tin had caused resentment at home; as we have seen, companies had taken certain steps to break the European monopoly. Now more measures were

---

* The par value of the ordinary shares of the Lautaro Company—£8,000,000—was six times that of its nearest rival. Rippy, *British Investment in Latin America*, p. 62.

† Other U.S. stakes in Chilean nitrates—including those of W. R. Grace & Co.—were small compared with those of the Guggenheims. In the mid-1920s, du Pont sold the Chilean nitrate lands that it had acquired before World War I. These properties eventually went into Guggenheim hands. Miller, "General Resume Guggenheim Nitrate Enterprises," Anglo-Lautaro files, María Elena, Chile.

‡ Together the giant U.S. copper companies in Chile employed 17,400 Chileans—a number far smaller than those employed in nitrates. The modern copper industry was far less labor intensive than the nitrate industry.

in order. Just as in rubber and nitrates, so in tin Americans moved into what were in the past British-controlled raw materials. National Lead was in the early 1920s the world's largest consumer of tin; in 1922 it invested $1.5 million in Bolivian tin, chiefly in the stock of Compañía Estanifera de Llallagua, a Bolivian firm. Two years later this firm merged its properties with the mines and railroads of Simon I. Patiño, the Andrew Carnegie of Bolivian tin. Patiño Mines and Enterprises Consolidated, a new company organized in the United States, was founded with an authorized capital of $50 million. National Lead held a small minority interest in this enterprise which produced 15 per cent of the world's output of tin and 60 per cent of Bolivia's tin. Other American companies (and individuals) made portfolio investments in Patiño Mines.[25]

Also interested in Bolivian tin were the Guggenheims. In 1920 they had purchased the Empresa Miñera Caracoles, for a sum said to be $5 million in gold. Two years later, the Guggenheims had established the $40 million Caracoles Tin Company. By mid-decade Guggenheim Bros. declared they were "actively engaged in mining tin in Bolivia, north of the Argentine border and their Bolivian staff is on the lookout for new tin properties." Other U.S. stakes in Bolivian tin were smaller. Americans did not dominate the tin industry in Bolivia, but in the 1920s, Americans developed some added means of control over what had been a "European monopoly." [26] We will see that the Guggenheims also went farther afield to acquire tin properties.

In addition to the minerals mentioned, U.S. businesses invested in iron ore (in Chile and Brazil *), manganese (Chile and Brazil), vanadium (Peru), tungsten (Bolivia), gold (Colombia and Ecuador), platinum (Colombia), and bauxite (Dutch Guiana and British Guiana).[27] So great had the U.S. stake become by 1929 that two experts on mining could conclude "the bulk of the productive mineral resources of South America are owned by American interests." [28]

In Canada, in 1929 the U.S.-controlled International Nickel Company sold more than 90 per cent of the world's nickel. It was the largest mining company in Canada with assets of $182 million in 1929.[29] By 1929, Americans owned not only most of Canadian nickel mining, but also the bulk of the Dominion's copper, gold, and asbestos output. U.S. enter-

---

* These Brazilian investments were, however, frustrated by Brazilian politics; Americans produced no iron ore in Brazil in the 1920s. The story is well told in Gauld, *The Last Titan*, pp. 281–289.

prises had smaller holdings in Canadian coal, silver, lead, and zinc mining (Canada was not at this time a major producer of any of these minerals).[30]

In Europe, International Agricultural Corporation reacquired its prewar German potash mines but did not expand significantly. Anaconda obtained control of the Silesian-American Company with zinc, lead, and coal interests in Poland.[31] The Hammer group got a concession from the Russians to mine asbestos, while the Soviets granted Averell Harriman a concession to extract manganese. The two Russian stakes were short-lived. Dr. Julius Hammer found his asbestos concession (1921–1924) not very profitable, owing to labor and transportation difficulties as well as to competition from state-owned deposits.[32] Yet, as Hammer was terminating his concession, Harriman received his. In October 1924, prime minister of Great Britain, Ramsay MacDonald, lamented, "The whole of that manganese field in the Caucasus [has] gone to an American firm . . . One of the richest fields in the world . . . Our opportunities go . . . The Americans get in." When MacDonald spoke, Harriman's agreement with the Soviets was still pending. On June 12, 1925, the Soviet government gave Harriman a twenty-year concession—to survey, to extract, and to export manganese and peroxide ores at Tchiatouri in Georgia.

From the start, Harriman had problems. The price of manganese declined; the agreement between Harriman and the Russians had not anticipated a price drop. The principals revised their contract (June 4, 1927). Then, Harriman's exports met competition abroad from the Soviet government's manganese mines. The railroad reconstruction specified in Harriman's contract cost more than forecast. Soviet labor organizations made excessive demands. Local Soviet authorities incessantly interfered with the mining operations. "During one year no less than 127 full working days are said to have been taken up by the visits and inspections of various commissions of control," wrote an informant.

An engineer returning from Russia through Prague declared that when the Harriman group first arrived they had found conditions "indescribably bad." He reported,

> The manganese was being handled by oxcart over frightful roads. The employees were barefooted and in rags, they slept on the ground in stables with the oxen. This was soon changed. The Americans raised wages to the highest level in Russia. Permission was obtained to import clothing. Men in the mines were equipped with boots and

rubber hats and slickers. All laborers were given British army shoes. Then the trouble began. The individual workmen were mostly well satisfied but the professional proletarians were only getting started. Their demands rose constantly with the sky as the limit. And it is interesting to note that the first action of the Soviets after the Americans left was to cut wages 20% and collect all of the imported shoes and clothing. The latter were sold in Tiflis and lined the pockets of several worthy communists.

By March 1928 Harriman had told the Soviets he wanted to terminate the concession. In addition to the previously mentioned irritants, the price of manganese continued to fall; Harriman was not making money. He had some 200 points of differences with the Soviets that he wanted to submit to a board of arbitration (provided for by the contract). But since the arbitration was to be held outside of Russia, the Russians did not want it. The crisis occurred over the exchange of rubles: the Soviets insisted the foreign mining engineers purchase rubles through the Russian bank; Harriman employees were buying rubles from Turks at a better rate of exchange. This conflict proved to be the proverbial "straw that broke the camel's back"; in August 1928, a new agreement was made transferring the Harriman concession back to the Soviets. Harriman had invested $3.45 million, which the Russians promised to repay over a fifteen-year period; in addition, to terminate the contract, he agreed to loan $1 million more to the Russians, to be repaid over that same amount of time. Later, Harriman wrote, "we negotiated a settlement with the Soviet Government under which our investment was recouped with reasonable profit." The statement obscured the difficulties. Harriman had in fact learned the perils of combining private enterprise and socialism.* The Harriman concession was the largest U.S. venture in the Soviet Union. The U.S. State Department observed closely the activities of Hammer and Harriman, but since the United States did not recognize the Soviet Union, it never became involved.[33]

U.S. enterprises mined gold in the Philippines and Korea. Department of Commerce statistics record no U.S. mining in China in 1929, but other evidence indicates that American firms explored in China in the 1920s, and some may actually have started mining.[34] In Indo-China, Siam, and

---

* More than three decades later, in a different capacity—as ambassador-at-large—Harriman was warning American businessmen in Ghana of the difficulties involved in meshing socialism and free enterprise. Based on author's interviews in Accra, Ghana, 1965.

Malaya, the New York Orient Mines (which was also in China) prospected seeking iron ore but found no satisfactory properties. In Turkey, in 1929 American Smelting and Refining Company representatives sought chrome concessions, and Newmont Mining looked into copper mining possibilities; neither company seems to have invested. At least one American company, Krebs Pigment & Color Corporation, apparently joined with British and Indian investors to mine ilemenite in India. In Japan no U.S. mining existed, because of the lack of excellent prospects.[35]

For multinational enterprise, the most significant U.S. stake in mining in Asia was made by the ubiquitous Guggenheims. Their Yukon Gold Company had once mined gold in Alaska (as the company's name implies). By the 1920s its gold mining in Alaska was no longer profitable. The Guggenheims had used expensive dredges (each costing several million dollars) in extracting the gold; they realized these dredges could be employed in mining tin. Accordingly, they moved the dredges from Alaska to Malaya and under the name of Yukon Gold Company began to mine tin in Malaya. The dredges advanced the technology of the tin industry, for these were not simply shovels but had an attached concentrating plant. Yukon Gold became the only American tin-mining operation in Malaya (the rest were British). When asked if it was difficult for an American company to invest in Malaya, Charles Earl, a director of Yukon Gold, replied that it took two or three years for the company to get established. The company sent out "several engineers, and, with the assistance of native engineers, they finally gathered up this territory, the tin-bearing areas, and then they went through a long siege with the government officials to get the necessary licenses and permits and concessions in exchange for agreements on their part concerning supervision, limitation of production when required, rate of development, the disposal of the product to the local smelters, and various other things. They had to make these agreements in order to get the permission to mine the ground." Here once more, after "a long siege," Americans moved into British "territory." [36]

In Africa, too, Americans began to challenge Europeans in mining with mixed success. In 1917, Americans had made investments in Ernest Oppenheimer's Anglo American Corporation of South Africa, Ltd., which started in gold mining and then sought diamonds, copper, coal, and other metals. When on December 8, 1928, Rhodesian Anglo American Limited was incorporated in London to extract copper in Northern

Rhodesia (now Zambia), Anglo American provided the management. Despite its name and the U.S. interest, Anglo American was a British-run enterprise.[37]

In 1925, American Metal Company, Ltd., made its first investment in Northern Rhodesian and then South African copper. In May 1928, when the Rhodesian Selection Trust (R.S.T.) * was formed, American Metal Company obtained a minority interest. R.S.T. and the earlier mentioned Rhodesian Anglo American Limited became the two most important enterprises in the new Northern Rhodesian copper industry.[38] By the end of the 1920s, Americans began to arrive in the "copper belt" in Northern Rhodesia, and American Metal Company tried to raise its holdings. But Ernest Oppenheimer of Anglo American thought that to "enhance the influence of American Metal Company in Northern Rhodesia . . . might be inadvisable in the national [read: British] interest." The British wanted American capital, but not the capitalists. William Thompson's American firm, Newmont Mining Corporation (which had already participated in Anglo American, and in other southern African ventures) agreed to supply funds with no managerial "strings attached." As the historian of Anglo American Corporation has recorded: "during all these negotiations [the British had] no thought whatever of handing over control to American interests." [39]

Meanwhile, on February 27, 1927, British mining promoter Sir Edmund Davis had written to the Guggenheim Bros., explaining the position of two Northern Rhodesian companies (Bwana M'Kubwa and Rhodesia Broken Hill) and inviting the Guggenheims "to come in now . . . with us in the development of such promising territory." The Guggenheims replied that they were "seldom, if ever interested in minority-financing . . . Whereas they are always interested in the possibility of acquiring ownership control of any mine of known merit . . . they are not interested in what may be considered purely as a banking transaction, or in the underwriting or purchase of the securities of a company with whose management they are not connected." Sir Edmund Davis did not like the reply; the British had "at no time contemplated handing over the technical administration of the mining companies to the Guggenheims as a firm"; thus, Sir Edmund terminated these negotiations.[40]

The Guggenheims, however, persisted, and in January 1929, acting

---

* Later renamed Roan Selection Trust.

through American Smelting and Refining Company, which they controlled, they attempted to invest in the N'Changa Copper Mines Ltd. (a part of the Oppenheimer's Rhodesian Anglo American group). The British were alarmed. American Metal Company was active. Should American Smelting and Refining Company enter the field in force, the British anticipated an "inevitable" shift in the balance of power in favor of the Americans. Sir Edmund Davis, allied with British Rothschild interests, thwarted ASARCO's move. [41]

Already, Americans had the large copper mines in the United States, Chile, Canada, Peru, and Mexico. The British sought to keep the new Northern Rhodesian industry free from American control. On August 9, 1929, in an interview in *Metallwerkschaft,* the president of American Metal Company, Ludwig Vogelstein, denied that Americans were trying to take over the African copper industry. He stated that although the ore was rich, production costs in Northern Rhodesia would probably be higher than in the United States and South America.[42] Nonetheless, American Metal Company did desire to enlarge its stake. As we will see in Chapter VIII, it would soon get the chance. By the fall of 1929, Americans were challenging the British in the new copper industry in the British protectorate of Northern Rhodesia.

If the British did not want Northern Rhodesian copper in American hands, neither did they like the idea of other African resources coming under the control of American capital. There did not seem to be any such problem when in 1926, two U.S. companies—Vanadium Corporation of America and Mutual Chemical Company—went into a 50–50 venture in Southern Rhodesia * to mine chrome and to achieve a source of supply for their American enterprises. Theirs was a relatively small operation.[43]

On the other hand, Rhodesia Chrome Mines, Limited (incorporated June 27, 1908) and its subsidiary African Chrome Mines Limited (formed August 4, 1928) were the leading chrome producers in Southern Rhodesia; should these fall to Americans, the problems for the British might be serious. For all apparent purposes, Rhodesia Chrome Mines Limited was one of Sir Edmund Davis's many mining ventures (he was chairman and managing director). In fact, Sir Edmund was known as the "Chrome King." Sir Edmund's mining activities ranged from interests in The Brit-

* Now Rhodesia.

ish South Africa Company, to those in Northern Rhodesian copper mining, to investments in South West Africa, and in manganese mining in the Gold Coast. He had been associated with Cecil Rhodes in the early days of British expansion in Africa; as he grew older, he had floated companies as easily as a child sends up inflated balloons. By 1919 he was a director of fifty-two companies! As we have noted, he acted to curtail the entry of American business in the Northern Rhodesian copper industry, but he also participated in making way for the entry of Union Carbide and Carbon Corporation into African mining. Herein lies a fascinating and involved story.[44]

Back in 1910, a company called Fanti Consolidated Ltd. (managing director, Edmund Davis) obtained a concession in the Gold Coast (now Ghana). Four years later, it discovered manganese, and the Wassaw Exploring Syndicate Ltd. came into being (deputy manager, Edmund Davis). On September 8, 1916, the Wassaw Syndicate shipped its first manganese, and after 1918 its mining activity at Nsuta, the Gold Coast, began in earnest. Meanwhile, just after the war, Union Carbide and Carbon Corporation had built a smelting plant in Norway to process carbide. Not long after the plant was erected, the bottom fell out of the market for carbide, and the smelter stopped operations. A Union Carbide executive proposed that the Norwegian smelter be utilized for ferro-manganese production, which seemed reasonable *if* manganese could be obtained at the right grade and price. Accordingly, Union Carbide officials approached the Wassaw Syndicate and in 1923 signed an agreement under which Union Carbide purchased all the Nsuta leases and mining rights. A new company, the African Manganese Company, Ltd., was incorporated in London; Sir Edmund Davis was chairman of the board.

On the surface, African Manganese Company looked like a British firm; it was run from London; the hiring was done in London; nothing identified it with Union Carbide; a man employed would not know of the American interests. But as a result of Union Carbide's investment, African Manganese Company came to be an important source of supply to the smelting plant in Norway and stimulated further Union Carbide expansion in Norway.

The investment in the Gold Coast also led to further stakes by Union Carbide in Africa. As mentioned, Sir Edmund Davis was chairman and managing director of Rhodesia Chrome Mines, Ltd.; Union Carbide was a consumer of chrome. Who took the initiative is not clear, but at least as early as 1928, when African Chrome Mines (Sir Edmund Davis, director) was established as a subsidiary of Rhodesia Chrome Mines Ltd., Union Carbide was an investor. And, here as in the Gold Coast, the stake of Union Carbide was kept *sub rosa*.* The London office of Sir Edmund Davis ran the chrome business; no Union Carbide officials were directly involved; The Bechuanaland Exploration Company, Ltd. (Edmund Davis, chairman), had a contract to manage African Chrome Mines and Rhodesia Chrome Mines. One can hypothesize that the silence of Union Carbide officials was based: (1) on their feeling that a British management could administer mines in British colonies more effectively than Americans; (2) on suggestions by Sir Edmund Davis that it made sense to operate under a "British cloak"; why raise the British ire? (3) on the management of Union Carbide's inclination that it was poor judgment to advertise the size and degree of integration of their firm; and (4) on a general lingering reticence in parts of American industry against any unnecessary disclosure. In any case, as a result of Union Carbide's investments, by 1929, the company had acquired the largest manganese mine in the Gold Coast and the most extensive chrome properties in Africa! [45]

Other U.S. stakes in African mining existed—the Guggenheims participated in mining diamonds in the Belgian Congo (through Société Internationale Forestière et Minière du Congo) and in Angola (through Companhia de Angola)—but the total interests were not substantial. Europeans had far greater investments in Africa than Americans.[46]

In sum, on every populated continent, Oceania probably excepted, U.S. investors penetrated to mine and to export from the host country.

6

Because of concern over future exhaustion of American oil supplies, U.S. businesses after World War I paid new attention to seeking foreign oil; the search was in part to supply U.S. consumers but more important to supply existing worldwide marketing outlets of U.S. petroleum enterprises. Whereas before World War I, U.S. stakes in oil abroad had been predominantly motivated by marketing considerations, in the 1920s, as demands for oil rose, the new investments became ever more mixed— motivated by supply along with marketing strategies.

Searching for oil, Americans went first to Latin America. In 1919, the

---

* One shrewd New York broker, however, knew about it in June 1929 when he wrote, "Union Carbide is understood . . . to have the bulk of the metal [chrome] in Rhodesian deposits." Jas. H. Oliphant & Co., "Union Carbide and Carbon," *Studies in Securities,* June 1929, Scudder Collection, Columbia University Library.

greatest stakes of U.S. companies in foreign oil production were still in nearby Mexico. Mexican oil output rose to a peak of 193 million barrels in 1921, but then declined. Although in 1921 the worst period of Mexican civil strife was over, banditry persisted in the oil regions. Government decrees on oil nationalization (although no actual nationalization) became regular events. In their earlier rush to obtain properties, the oil companies had not been concerned with verifying titles to their acquisitions; now they worried about the validity of their titles. New Mexican taxes were imposed. When on July 1, 1921, the Mexicans levied an export tax of 10 to 12 per cent, Jersey Standard, Mexican Petroleum (E. L. Doheny's company), Atlantic Refining, Sinclair, and Texas urged the U.S. secretary of state to intervene to settle the tax question.* The question was not immediately settled. Labor was restive. But worst of all, the oil companies began to find salt water in their wells. New drilling would mean substantial capital expenditures. This, along with the political, social, and fiscal considerations, encouraged U.S. oil enterprises at the start of the 1920s to seek their crude oil elsewhere.

The Bucareli conferences in 1923 between the U.S. and Mexican governments temporarily eased political tensions. Then, in 1925, the Mexican congress passed a law that most U.S. oil companies, with the agreement of Secretary of State Frank B. Kellogg, considered a violation of the Bucareli understandings. Foreign petroleum producers representing 75 per cent of oil output in Mexico in 1926 refused to comply with the legislation. The Mexican government retaliated by canceling drilling permits. In time, this storm passed. But, while U.S. oil enterprises retained large investments in Mexico, their managers' enthusiasm continued to wane. New monies went elsewhere. Venezuela offered the greatest promise.[47]

From the early 1920s, there was a transfer of American oil men and money from Mexico to Venezuela. Production figures reflected this. In 1921, when Mexican oil output peaked at 193 million barrels, Venezuela produced a bare 1.4 million barrels. As Mexican production started to decline, there occurred in 1922 the famous "blowout" in the La Rosa camp in Venezuela that turned worldwide attention to Venezuelan oil. Investment soared. By 1928, Venezuela produced 106 million barrels,

---

* Pan American Petroleum & Transport Company (a Doheny company) noted in its *Annual Report 1922* that it had paid $15,434,600 in taxes to the Mexican government —a sum two-and-one-half times the amount of dividends its Mexican interests had paid that year. Mexican Petroleum was a subsidiary of Pan Am Petroleum.

Mexico, 50 million. Venezuela in 1928 ranked second only to the United States in oil production.[48]

Throughout the 1920s the political "climate" in Venezuela proved ideal for this expansion. General Juan Vicente Gómez, dictator since 1908, offered order and stability. Early in 1921, the U.S. minister in Caracas cooperated with Jersey Standard, Sun Oil, and the other oil company officials in suggesting changes in the Venezuelan petroleum law "to make it possible for foreign oil companies to extend their oil operations." The result was Venezuela's Petroleum Law of 1922. This law, together with those of 1925 and 1928 (which made minor revisions), set the terms of concessions, taxes, and royalties. An internal memorandum by a Jersey Standard official referred to the legislation as very fair and equitable; indeed, U.S. oil companies considered the laws the best in Latin America. Thus, under propitious political conditions for the foreign investor, the petroleum resources of Venezuela came on the market.[49]

Despite the excellent political climate, oil men had lingering apprehensions, based on their poor experiences in Mexico. In 1923, representatives of Doheny interests visited Washington to talk about Venezuela and to obtain "some confirmation or rebuttal of their own conclusion that the woods are not full of lions." Keeping in mind Mexico, and probably aware of Venezuela's past history of political instability (before the Gómez regime), Lago Petroleum, 1927–1929, constructed its huge export refinery on the Dutch island of Aruba.* In April 1928 a Lago representative (with years of experience in Mexico) visited the State Department in Washington. He explained, "President Gómez could not live forever, and there was always the danger that a new Government, perhaps with more radical tendencies, might seek to confiscate the oil properties and follow some of the policies which have been adopted in Mexico." The Lago representative wanted to inform the State Department of the situation and added, "In Venezuela, and profiting again from their experience in Mexico, the Lago Corporation had been very careful to see that every legal form and technicality was correctly complied with . . . They were very careful to keep their taxes paid up, and they felt that there was not the slightest weakness in their titles anywhere." [50] By 1929, at least thirty-nine

---

* Lago Petroleum was a subsidiary of Pan American Petroleum & Transport Company, which Standard Oil of Indiana acquired from Doheny interests in 1925 (Giddens, *Standard Oil Company* [*Indiana*], p. 240). Lago Oil & Transport Company, another subsidiary of Pan American Petroleum & Transport Company, held ownership of the Aruba refinery.

U.S. enterprises had investments of over \$226 million in Venezuelan oil.[51] Royal Dutch-Shell (not an American company) remained the largest producer, followed by Gulf Oil and Standard Oil of Indiana (through Lago Petroleum Corporation). Jersey Standard had had bad luck, but in 1928, after drilling and abandoning forty-two wells, a subsidiary found oil in commercial quantities in eastern Venezuela. That year, Jersey Standard also acquired control of the Creole Syndicate, with oil concessions in Venezuela.* By 1929, oil represented 76 per cent of Venezuela's total exports and accounted for about one-half the government revenues.[52]

In 1929, nowhere else in Latin America were U.S. stakes in oil production as large as in Mexico and Venezuela, but American corporations did seek oil in Central America, Colombia, Peru, Argentina, Brazil, Ecuador, and Bolivia. Often, they encountered political enmity. Sinclair and Pure Oil late in 1921 and 1922 respectively withdrew from Colombia, complaining of their inability to operate under the petroleum laws. Later in the decade Gulf Oil engaged in a painful, lengthy dispute with the Colombian government over Gulf's newly acquired Barco concession. Oil companies sought in vain to obtain satisfactory petroleum legislation in Argentina.[53] In Chile, the government in 1926–1928 made future oil production a state monopoly and that barred Americans from acquiring concessions.[54]

Frequently, U.S. oil companies asked Washington for diplomatic assistance, and the State Department readily complied, attempting "to facilitate amiable adjustments."[55] Jersey Standard had a long-standing dispute with the Peruvian government over taxes; its problems were set straight (at least temporarily) by a settlement between the Peruvian and *British* governments made in 1922.† The British rather than the U.S. government participated because the operating company, London & Pacific Petroleum Company, although ultimately controlled by Jersey Standard, was incorporated in England.‡ [56]

Among the U.S. companies, Jersey Standard took the lead in investing in Latin American oil exploration and production.[57] Other U.S. partici-

---

* The Creole Syndicate became on March 20, 1928, the Creole Petroleum Corporation. In 1928, Standard Oil of Venezuela (a Jersey Standard subsidiary) became a subsidiary of Creole Petroleum Corporation. Taylor and Lindeman, *Creole Petroleum Corporation in Venezuela*, pp. 88–89.

† A settlement that was issued in April 1922 by the international court, to which the dispute had been submitted.

‡ After the agreement, in 1924, a Jersey Standard affiliate, International Petroleum Company, took over La Brea y Pariñas properties from the London & Pacific Petroleum Company and no longer operated through the London company.

pants included Gulf, Sinclair, Texaco, Tide Water Oil, Standard Oil of Indiana,* Standard of California,† Sun Oil, Atlantic Refining, Pure Oil, Beacon Oil, Cities Service, and Amerada.[58]

In Canada, American enterprises also looked for oil, but with little success.[59] In Europe, Jersey Standard revived its prewar Rumanian production and drilled for oil in Poland.[60] The main interest in oil supplies in Europe was, however, in the vast Soviet oil resources. We have noted that right after World War I, Jersey Standard invested almost $9 million in Russian oil, on the assumption that the Russian revolution would fail. It lost its investment.[61] In November 1923, Sinclair Oil Company signed a provisional agreement with the Soviets to develop oil in the Caucasus, but the Teapot Dome Scandal in the United States in 1924, which implicated Harry Sinclair in fraud and corruption in relation to naval oil reserves in the United States, occupied that businessman's attention and turned him from overseas investments.[62]

Russian oil was cheap, and Americans wanted access to it. Most however did not want to deal with the Soviets who had expropriated foreign-owned oil properties. Vacuum Oil, which had had its pre–World War I refinery and marketing organization in Russia expropriated, nonetheless concluded that the matter of negotiating compensation was separate from that of buying Soviet oil. In 1927, its president, G. P. Whaley, pointed out the cost of transportation made it difficult to sell U.S. oil in Europe: "it is only common sense to recognize that Russia is the economic source of supply for certain markets." Russian oil would penetrate European markets some way. Thus, Vacuum Oil purchased Russian output. That year, Standard Oil of New York built a kerosene treatment plant for the Soviets at Batum. It turned the plant over to the Soviet Naphtha Syndicate, which leased it to Standard Oil of New York. Standard Oil of New York purchased the output, primarily for sale in India. After much hesitation, in 1929, Jersey Standard made arrangements to buy Soviet oil for its European marketing organization.‡ Although purchasing Russian oil at decade's end, Americans did not make investments in producing that oil. Purchasing was the only effective means of access.[63]

On the other hand, no clash with a socialist system blocked U.S. in-

---

* Both directly and through Pan American Petroleum & Transport Company after 1925.

† Standard Oil of California operated under the name of Richmond Petroleum Company in Mexico, Venezuela, and Colombia.

‡ The purchases were made after the Achnacarry accord of 1928 was arranged (see Chapter IV); in effect, the accord regulated the sale of the oil in European markets.

vestment in Near Eastern oil. U.S. stakes in the Middle East were in fact not obstructed by the host nations' policies, but instead by British and other European governments and companies. At the close of World War I, in all the Middle East, only Iran had oil production; Anglo-Persian Oil Company (a British firm in which the British government held majority interest) was the sole producer. Try as Americans would in the 1920s, they failed to enter the Iranian oil industry.[64]

At San Remo, in April 1920, the British and French governments agreed to cooperate in aiding their nations' oil companies in acquiring Near Eastern oil concessions, especially in Mesopotamia (now Iraq). When American oil men wanted such concessions, the U.S. Department of State, trying to maintain the open door, agreed to back them. Secretary of State Charles Evans Hughes often declared that "the Department is always willing and desirous of giving proper diplomatic support to American interests." And then he would add, "but . . . this Government cannot associate itself with one set of American claims as against another." To Jersey Standard officials, this policy meant that the company should join with other U.S. enterprises. "We should select the associates carefully and keep the list as small as possible. Personally, my suggestion," wrote E. J. Sadler, head of Jersey Standard's foreign department, to the company's president, Walter Teagle, "would be the Standard Oil Company of New York, Sinclair, Doheny, Texas, and it seems to me necessarily the Gulf." This private letter, sent in September 1921, indicated that the grouping would be to "gain the support of the State Department."

Eventually, seven American oil enterprises—Jersey Standard, the above mentioned five,* and Atlantic Refining Company—with U.S. State Department aid, entered into protracted discussions with Anglo-Persian, Royal Dutch-Shell, French interests, and the Armenian promoter Calouste Sarkis Gulbenkian, seeking the U.S. oil companies' participation in the development of Middle Eastern oil. While the negotiations progressed, the Turkish Petroleum Company † struck oil at Kirkuk in northern Iraq (October 15, 1927). Less than nine months later (July 31, 1928), the negotiators came to an agreement under which the U.S. oil

---

* Doheny's company was Pan American Petroleum & Transport Company, which he sold to Standard Oil of Indiana in 1925.

† Owned 47.5 per cent by Anglo-Persian, 22.5 per cent by Royal Dutch-Shell, 25 per cent by a French group, and 5 per cent by Gulbenkian.

companies obtained a 23.75 per cent interest in Turkish Petroleum Company; Anglo-Persian, Royal Dutch-Shell, and Compagnie Française des Pétroles each got 23.75 per cent; the remaining 5 per cent went to Gulbenkian. The U.S. companies (by 1928 five, instead of seven, since Texas and Sinclair decided against participation) put their holdings in the Near East Development Corporation.* All the stockholders in Turkish Petroleum Company (which was renamed Iraq Petroleum Company in 1929) pledged to operate only through that company within an area delineated by a red line, encircling a region including practically all the old Ottoman empire. Based on this July 31, 1928, red line agreement, Americans entered into oil production in Iraq—their first entry into a concession where oil had been discovered in the Middle East.

Meanwhile, on behalf of the Eastern and General Syndicate Ltd. of London, between 1923 and 1925 a New Zealander, Major Frank Holmes, had acquired petroleum concessions from the rulers of Saudi Arabia and Bahrain (an island in the Persian Gulf). Holmes also sought a concession from Kuwait (a tiny British protectorate, bordering Iraq and the Persian Gulf). On November 30, 1927, a wholly owned subsidiary of Gulf Oil Corporation (Eastern Gulf Oil Company) purchased Holmes's option on the Bahrain concession and in a second transaction received his options on the Saudi Arabian concessions in al-Hasa (the eastern province of Saudi Arabia) and in the Neutral Zone (between Saudi Arabia and Kuwait) as well as on Holmes's prospective concession in Kuwait. Eight months later (July 1928), Gulf faced a dilemma. By participating in the Iraq Petroleum Company, its management had agreed not to explore (except through that company) within the "red line" area; its Bahrain, al-Hasa, and Neutral Zone options lay inside that region. Only the Kuwait concession, which Holmes was still seeking, was outside the red line territory. At this time, Gulf's partners in the Iraq Petroleum Company were not interested in looking for oil in Bahrain, al-Hasa, or the Neutral Zone (because of adverse geologists' reports); thus Gulf reluctantly approached Standard Oil of California (which was not involved in I.P.C.).

* Near East Development Corporation was owned as follows:
Standard Oil (N.J.)—25% (SONJ)
Standard Oil (N.Y.)—25% (SONY became in 1931 Socony-Vacuum Oil Co.)
Atlantic Refining—16⅔% (sold to Socony-Vacuum in 1931)
Gulf Oil—16⅔% (sold half to SONJ and half to Socony-Vacuum in 1934)
Pan American Petroleum & Transport—16⅔% (sold to SONJ in 1930)
In short, by the end of 1934, Near East Development Corporation would be owned 50 per cent by Standard Oil of New Jersey and 50 per cent by Socony-Vacuum.

By the end of 1928, Standard Oil of California had already spent during the decade about $50 million seeking foreign oil, with no success. Its management was prepared to keep trying and for $50,000 Standard Oil of California on December 21, 1928 acquired Gulf's Bahrain options.* The British government insisted that any concession in Bahrain (a British protectorate) must be operated by a British company and approved by the Colonial Office in London. Accordingly, in January 1929 Standard Oil of California formed a Canadian ("British") subsidiary—the Bahrein Petroleum Company, Ltd †—and sought with U.S. State Department help Colonial Office approval for the transfer of the Bahrain options to that company (the approval would be forthcoming in August 1930).

At the same time, Gulf Oil executives pushed Holmes to obtain a concession from the Kuwaiti government. But by the end of 1929, although prospects looked promising, no concession had been granted.‡

In sum, in 1929 through the Near East Development Corporation, the Bahrein Petroleum Company, and with the activities of Gulf Oil in Kuwait, U.S. enterprises supported by the State Department were making their initial inroads into Middle Eastern oil—entries that set the foundation for subsequent giant investments. Americans were still newcomers; U.S. companies had not in 1929 obtained crude oil from any of their own properties in the Middle East (Iraqi oil, discovered in 1927, was not shipped until the pipeline was completed in 1934). Nonetheless, the European monopoly had been pierced; British, Dutch, and French concern notwithstanding, American business would henceforth be a factor in the Middle Eastern oil industry.[65]

Further east, Americans also ventured for oil. Sinclair in 1922 had made a contract with the Far Eastern Republic for an oil concession in Northern Sakhalin. The Soviets claimed part of that island and required

---

* Gulf also offered to assign to California Standard its agreements for al-Hasa and for the Neutral Zone (although because of arrears in protection fees, there was reason to believe these options had become invalid). California Standard took only the Bahrain options, and Gulf retained the others; since participation in the red line agreement barred it from activity in al-Hasa and the Neutral Zone, on April 1, 1932, it formally let these options lapse.

† Spelling changed to Bahrain Petroleum Co. on January 1, 1953.

‡ Kuwait in 1899 had entered into a treaty with Great Britain; Great Britain promised the ruler of Kuwait (and his successors) protection from outside aggression and in return, the British were given full charge of the country's foreign affairs. The British representative in Kuwait was, in effect, Minister of Foreign Affairs. By a treaty of 1913 the Shaikh agreed not to grant oil concessions without the approval of the British government. Gulf would have to get British approval.

that the concession be approved by them. Sinclair obtained their endorsement, but Japanese military forces in Northern Sakhalin barred the company's personnel from the area. When Sinclair asked the U.S. State Department for help, the department refused, since the United States had not recognized either the Far Eastern Republic or the Soviet Union. Finally, in 1925, Japan agreed to cede Northern Sakhalin to the U.S.S.R., but Sinclair was still not able to develop the concession which the Soviets finally revoked. (The Japanese obtained the opportunity to seek oil in Sakhalin.) [66]

Americans were more successful in the Dutch East Indies, where Jersey Standard—aided by the U.S. Departments of State and Interior *—was able to overcome the preferential treatment given by the Dutch to Royal Dutch-Shell, to find oil in commercial quantities in 1922 in south Sumatra, and to construct a refinery near Palembang that went on stream in 1926. After having invested $21.5 million between 1912 and 1926 in the Dutch East Indies, Jersey Standard finally in 1926 marketed its first barrel of East Indian refined oil. Then, through its Dutch marketing subsidiary, the Jersey company obtained new concessions in the Dutch East Indies, acquiring in 1928 its most prolific holdings. By 1929 Standard Oil of New Jersey was the only American company with oil properties in the Netherlands East Indies, but the monopoly of Royal Dutch-Shell no longer existed.[67]

In fact, on every populated continent Americans looked for oil. Sinclair even moved as far afield as Portuguese Angola and the Gold Coast in Africa, but found no oil.[68] In 1924 and again in 1929–1930, U.S. companies dispatched geologists to Australia but decided against seeking concessions.[69] Neither colonies nor dominions were exempt from American interest.

In 1929, the ten top-ranking oil producing countries in the world were the United States, Venezuela, U.S.S.R., Mexico, Iran, Dutch East Indies, Rumania, Colombia, Peru, and Argentina.[70] By that year, U.S. investors were producing oil in every one of these countries except the Soviet Union and Iran. As U.S. companies hunted for oil worldwide, they were

---

* In 1920 Congress passed the General Leasing Law, which forbade companies of nations that discriminated against American oil firms from leasing oil fields in the public domain. In retaliation against the Dutch barriers to U.S. capital, Secretary of Interior Albert B. Fall, under this legislation, denied Royal Dutch-Shell permission to lease oil lands in Oklahoma. Wilson, *American Business and Foreign Policy, 1920–1933*, pp. 187, 198, and Federal Trade Commission, *Report on Foreign Ownership*, p. xix.

encountering opposition from host governments,* inability to obtain concessions because of colonial policies,† and failures owing to inability to find oil.‡ By 1927–1929, the assumed post–World War I shortage of oil had disappeared; oilmen now talked of an oil glut. Thus, while U.S. corporations still tried to find diversified sources of oil and still sought as cheap oil as their foreign and domestic competitors, the frenzied enthusiasm for oil development had by decade's end subsided.

7

Supply-oriented investors—especially those in agriculture, mining, and oil production—shared common features. They had a distinctive relationship to the host (national or imperial) government. Certain agricultural concerns had special contracts with host governments that established their position. Some extractive companies had simply mining claims; others had concessions under mining or petroleum laws. Although the extent of their government relations rose over the years, to a one these enterprises had more governmental relationships than did the market-oriented operations discussed in Chapter IV.§ Such state-(foreign) private contracts and negotiations in many cases set the rules for long-term exploitation of natural resources.[71]

Supply-related investors generally made large investments. They often had substantial payrolls. Because they exported from the host country, they obtained their revenues mainly in dollars and pound sterling and not in depreciating local currencies. Because they participated in foreign

* Throughout much of Latin America, and, of course, by the close of the 1920s they were barred from direct investments in the Soviet Union by Soviet policy.

† For example, the British Foreign Office declared on April 21, 1921, of British India, including Burma, "Prospecting or mining leases have been in practice granted only to British subjects or to companies controlled by British subjects." This barred Standard Oil of New York, Federal Trade Commission, *Report on Foreign Ownership,* pp. xvi–xvii. Although Iran was not a colony, British policies contributed to U.S. companies' inability to enter.

‡ For example, Richmond Petroleum Company (a subsidiary of California Standard) spent four years (1920–1924) and $1.25 million exploring in vain for oil in the Philippines (Bain, *Ores and Industry in the Far East,* p. 135). Another company obtained a contract with the provisional government of Szechuan, China, to explore for oil, but it found none (*Foreign Relations of the United States 1925,* II, p. 699n). Some oil prospecting was done in southern Africa by Newmont Mining Corporation with no success (*Annual Reports,* 1920s).

§ An official of one U.S. company that had a branch assembly plant *and* an agricultural investment in Brazil in the 1920s, for example, told the present author, "All our government relations in that decade involved the rubber plantation; none involved the assembly plant." Interview with Humberto Monteiro, São Paulo, 1964.

trade and did not serve the local market, they tended to be isolated from changes occurring within the host country. This separation was frequently reinforced by a physical detachment; most operated in remote regions; they planted bananas in the steaming tropical jungles; they found a mine in the mountains or the desert; they drilled for oil on the advice of a geologist or the hunch of an experienced oil man—in desert or jungle.*

Each company in its isolated spot established a type of extraterritorial sovereignty within the host country. Once the company decided that it had a future, it would create a town. While there were U.S. company towns from Canada to Liberia, nowhere were they more numerous than in Latin America, and it is, therefore, to Latin America we must turn to examine this phenomenon.

In the 1920s a large number of American-run company towns sprang up in Latin America. Some corporations had not one but several, or even many, towns. Such communities were without a mayor or a town council, but they had a power plant, a water supply, sewage, housing, a hospital, one or more churches, and perhaps several schools. When a company started in an out-of-the-way area, a new town became essential. The enterprise first constructed houses for the American staff, usually built to American middle-class specifications. Then, if there were families with children, an American school was opened. A sports field or a golf course came next, and also a staff club house. The American community had its own life. In many towns, the staff officials from the general manager down would put on a dress suit or dinner jacket every evening. As one man put it, "None of us are inclined to find our way down to the camps in dinner jackets. When you put on the dress of a gentleman you are inclined to act like one." The dinner jacket became a symbol of civilization and a morale builder.

If an existing village of any size was nearby, the investor did not need to provide workers' quarters. But if there was no village, or if village fa-

* Many of these generalizations do not apply to supply-oriented manufacturing, often located in urban areas. As for the other supply-oriented stakes, it is hard to overemphasize the isolation of the places where investments were made. These were the days before air travel became common. A boat trip to Chile from New York took about nineteen days; from there to the mining camps might take another few days by rail. Some oil operations in Venezuela took weeks to reach, even after the man got to the country. Standard Oil of New Jersey's operations in Bolivia were 1,000 miles or forty-eight hours by train from Buenos Aires, the nearest large urban center; La Paz, the capital of Bolivia, was four days away by the fastest possible route other than airplane.

cilities were clearly inadequate, the company constructed homes for the workers and started a "workers' camp." The workers' living quarters were usually set off from the staff's houses. Often the offices or the plant operations would be located in between the workers' housing and the staff quarters. Workers' housing varied according to the region: in Mexico, companies built barracks of adobe, called *cuadrillas;* in Central America, businesses constructed wooden barracks on stilts, called *barracones;* in South America, the barracks or separate houses were generally flat on the ground and were made from corrugated sheet metal, adobe, or wood. In Peru and Chile, they were called *campamentos.* Brick and cylinder block construction for workers' homes came later. Such homes in the 1920s rarely had indoor toilets or running water. Most U.S. firms, however, provided outhouses—with toilets and showers. The most progressive companies had hot water in the bath houses every day of the week; some companies supplied it several days a week; and those in the tropics did not furnish hot water at all. It was the exceptional American employer in the late 1920s that had a workers' camp and also let its workers use the river for washing and toilet needs; yet at least one U.S. company did. The homes provided by the corporation for the workers and their families were far superior to anything existing locally. In some cases, the enterprise introduced its labor for the first time to such fundamentals as toilet paper! In the 1920s some workers' homes had electricity; some did not. Electricity, for lighting, came in practically every case before indoor toilets or running water. The company-built homes were generally rented to the worker at a nominal fee, or, in some cases, the worker occupied them at no charge.

In certain countries—Chile, Peru, Venezuela—there often came to be three rather than two categories of communities within a company town. The American camp, the camp for *empleados* or intermediate staff camp, and the *obreros* camp. The *empleados* were Spanish-speaking white-collar workers or foremen. The company often furnished them with their own club house, sometimes their own schools, and in certain cases a set of facilities that entirely duplicated those of the workers' camp.

By the 1920s, most American agricultural, mining, and oil installations in Latin America had a hospital, clinic, or at least some provision for first aid to the workers. This was an economic necessity. One of the truly pioneering contributions of American business abroad lies in its activity in the medical field. If Americans were to settle in isolated places and were to bring their families, they had to be assured their children would not catch terrible diseases. Thus, American companies were prompt in sponsoring studies to control malaria and other tropical diseases. Their hospitals—for the American staff and for the workers—were the pride of each town. There were hospitals in most company towns long before they were required by law.

While most camps had schools for the children of American personnel (if there was a need), company towns were slower in supplying Spanish-speaking schools. Some did exist. The Guggenheims were especially progressive in this respect. Schools for workers' children became more in evidence in the 1930s. Generally, by the mid-1930s, companies would be required by law to have schools for their *obreros* and *empleados*.

In the 1920s as company towns increased in size and number, they supplied everything for their own needs: machine shops, warehouses, repair shops, and even small foundries. Practically every company town in the 1920s had a company-owned commissary, and maybe more than one. Some companies had cattle ranches, dairies, and vegetable farms to meet their own requirements.

Certain towns were "closed towns." This meant there was a control station at the gates (in the oil camps, cyclone fences separated the American camp, the intermediate camp, and the workers' section). The company knew who lived in which house, who was in the town, and what he was doing there. No unauthorized person could enter or live in such towns, much less do business there. As a result of such restrictions, around some closed towns there grew up parasitical activities. On the outskirts or on the other side of the fences, people would congregate and build shabby shacks. They would tap the company's water and use it for their own. These people would sell to company employees. Houses of prostitution grew up on the perimeters of certain closed towns. The strictly closed town was especially characteristic of the oil company towns, and in the 1920s and for some time thereafter there was no effort to link the parasitical community and the oil camp—in fact, quite the contrary—the companies shunned and disassociated themselves from the outside slums. Every company town would at one time or other have to face the question of how to cope with the outsider: especially the local merchant who came to sell to the employees.

It goes almost without saying that every company town had its own thoroughfares—some paved and some unpaved. But, even more significant, the company would frequently own the means by which it communicated with the outside world: the company might have its own radio facilities; it built, on occasion, its own roads connecting it to outlying areas; it frequently had its own railroad; it might have its own ships.

Owing to the great distance from the United States, few top-level parent company executives visited these operations. The first Americans that went to manage them were a tough and adventurous lot. Many new arrivals were unskilled or semiskilled construction workers; others were well-trained engineers and geologists. The initial crop were all bachelors, but as soon as the town began to take form, married men brought their wives. The personalities of the men varied; there were some who learned Spanish quickly and made Latin American friends; some married Colombians, Venezuelans, Hondurans, or Chileans. Others remained aloof from the host country's environment, creating a world apart. Legends throughout Latin America describe the American manager, who after thirty years abroad had learned no Spanish and complained vigorously of his subordinates, who could speak no English. Stories exist about the American who knew only, *"¿Donde está la señorita?"* The present author met an American who had lived in Latin America for almost forty years and did not know how to order a "boiled egg" in Spanish.

The language barrier and the fact that most companies were slow in promoting Latin Americans, since few were trained as engineers, geologists, and technicians, created a gulf between the North American and Latin American communities. So serious was the problem of finding trained personnel that the U.S. companies at first brought from home, secretaries, clerks, timekeepers, mechanics, and drillers. Such jobs gradually came to be handled by local people. At the lower levels of mechanical skills, the agricultural and extractive companies did an excellent job of training. Already by the end of the twenties, in certain companies, host-country nationals were moving into staff positions, especially in Mexico, where, as noted, the government encouraged this.

In the 1920s most American companies in Latin America paid the going wage—and in many cases more. They offered employment. In a number of companies, laborers used their wages to buy the first pair of shoes they or members of their families had ever had. The companies contributed to a rising standard of living. Their employees in many countries became the elite of the workforce. Most U.S. companies, like most of their parent corporations in the United States, were not unionized in the 1920s. They ware *not* concerned with solving the social problems of the undeveloped areas; they did not pay high taxes; * but in their effort to make a profit and to do business, they made significant contributions in the field of public health, sanitation, transportation, housing, and to a lesser extent, schooling. Even more important, they opened up to the possibility of future taxation and national use many of the most valuable resources in Latin America. Central American bananas, Chilean copper, and Venezuelan oil became valuable resources *only* because foreign companies were ready and able to take large risks, to supply sizable amounts of money, and to offer technical knowledge and skills.[72]

Indeed, the existence of the special relationships between company and government, the size of investments and payrolls, the isolation of most of these activities, along with their often important impacts on the economies of the host nations made the position of the agricultural, mining, and oil enterprises unique.

8

In sum, during the 1920s, supply-oriented stakes abroad by large U.S. corporations were undertaken in the course of horizontal integration (for example, mining enterprises obtained more mining properties) and vertical integration (for instance, candy manufacturers acquired sugar refineries and plantations). A number of stakes were motivated by absence, shortage, or potential shortage of the commodity in the United States or the availability of a cheaper good abroad. All the supply-oriented stakes in manufacturing in the 1920s were prompted by cheap resources abroad (power, raw materials, and less frequently labor). The supply-oriented interests in agriculture and extraction were to a one conditioned by the potentials for raising a crop or the existence or suspected existence of a foreign resource that determined the location of the investment. By 1929, U.S. investors in many countries participated in negotiations (some friendly, some acrimonious) with host governments dealing with their entry or expansion; at times, from Russia to Brazil to Chile, their efforts to develop a resource had been thwarted by host government policies. In addition, in Asia and Africa, the British and to a lesser extent

---

* The basis for taxation varied widely, and it is hard to make meaningful comparisons. United Fruit throughout the decade typically paid one cent per stem exported (regardless of the price of bananas). The copper companies in Chile paid a 12 per cent income tax in 1928. The oil companies in Latin America appear to have paid roughly 10 to 11 per cent royalties (sometimes export taxes).

other European governments tried to limit U.S. stakes. The Japanese had interfered with U.S. direct investments in Soviet-held Northern Sakhalin. The U.S. government often, but not always, tried to assist these U.S. companies in their negotiations. Obstacles notwithstanding, U.S. supply-oriented ventures had risen in number and scale; company towns formed enclaves in foreign lands; by decade's end U.S. supply-related stakes were of major importance in many nations from Canada to Cuba to Venezuela to Chile to Liberia. While in 1929, U.S. investors were concerned about falling prices of crude rubber, sugar, nitrates, manganese, and oil, still they continued to invest. To diversify and to control their sources of supply, prosperous U.S. companies were in 1929 poised for greater foreign involvement.

Public utilities, transportation enterprises, retailers, construction firms, advertising agencies, accounting houses, credit companies, and banks participated in international business in the 1920s. In the main, such U.S. enterprises had market-oriented stakes abroad, yet their investment activities were sufficiently distinctive to consider them apart from the market-related investments examined in Chapter IV.

By far the single greatest growth of U.S. direct foreign investment in the 1920s took place in public utilities (see Table III.1). At home, during the decade a rapid expansion of public utilities occurred. Paralleling the domestic boom, U.S. corporations made substantial new foreign investments in communications and in power and light.

Radio Corporation of America introduced long distance wireless communication between the United States, Europe, and Asia. It invested in high power radio stations from Poland * to Sweden to China to the Philippines to Argentina. R.C.A. also entered joint ventures in communication with British companies in South America and in Canada.[1] As early as 1904 United Fruit Company had established radio communications in Costa Rica; in 1913, it had incorporated a subsidiary, Tropical Radio Telegraph Company; by the end of the 1920s, it had radiotelegraph, ra-

---

* R.C.A. needed a concession from the Polish government to build the station at Warsaw; the concession it sought in 1919 had monopolistic features; at first, for this reason, the U.S. government was wary of supporting the company. Opposition to "monopoly" had been a consistent part of U.S. policy. Then, it became clear that many departments in the U.S. government, but chiefly Navy, favored the establishment of an American-owned high power station in Warsaw, which would be a base from which "messages could be distributed and received from Eastern Europe and Asia"; it also became evident that if the Americans did not obtain the concession, British or German companies would. Accordingly, the State Department reversed itself and gave assistance to R.C.A., which obtained the concession, RG 59, 860c.74/4, 860c.74/7 and 860c.659 In 8/3, National Archives.

diotelephone, and coastal telegraph facilities throughout Central America.[2] Western Union in the early 1920s opened offices in London and Amsterdam (the first one of a private cable company on the continent of Europe). When the French barred Western Union and Commercial Cable Company (another U.S. firm) from inaugurating offices in Paris, the U.S. government intervened on the businesses' behalf, with success. In 1923, the two firms were able to start offices to deal directly with the French public. Western Union's foreign activity was confined to Europe, Canada, and Mexico,* while Commercial Cable expanded on a global scale.[3] America's largest telephone company, American Telephone & Telegraph Company, restricted its foreign stakes to Canada. During the 1920s, A.T.T. reduced its percentage holding in the largest phone company in the Dominion, the Bell Telephone Company of Canada (from 38.31 per cent in 1920 to 25.13 per cent in 1930). This interest remained sufficient to give A.T.T. control; how much control it actually exercised is not clear.[4]

It was International Telephone and Telegraph Corporation that came to take the lead in worldwide communications. It had begun business in 1920, merging two telephone companies in Cuba and Puerto Rico. Then it expanded, so that by decade's end it also operated telephones in Mexico, southern Brazil, Uruguay, and Argentina. In addition, I.T.T., as we have noted, took over the whole Spanish telephone system in 1924, which made it the largest single U.S. investor in Spain. In 1926, it obtained a contract to modernize Italy's long-distance telephone system. At the same time, I.T.T. participated in telegraph, cable, and radio communication, and in 1927 acquired a 91 per cent interest in the American-financed All America Cables, Inc., with its system of 27,000 nautical miles of cables, connecting land lines between North, Central, and South America and the principal West Indian Islands. The next year, it acquired the already mentioned multinational Commercial Cable Company. By 1929 I.T.T.'s global communications systems were vast and burgeoning. I.T.T.'s business was entirely outside the United States and Canada. Nine years after its formation, its worldwide employment (in 1929) came to 95,000. No other American (or foreign) corporation had such huge investments

---

* In 1926, Western Union acquired 60 per cent of Mexican Telegraph Company from All America Cables. On the other hand, in December 1927, it sold certain properties in Canada's Maritime Province (about $1 million worth) owned by its affiliate Montreal Telegraph (*Moody's 1929*).

abroad in communications. No other U.S. corporation had so many employees in foreign lands.[5]

Americans also made immense new investments in power and light. Some of these stakes were in Europe. For example, in 1929, Utilities Power & Light Corporation of Chicago acquired the largest English distributor of power, The Greater London & Counties Trust Company (assets $40 million) and at once announced a $50 million expansion in the next five years.[6] Major new U.S. investments were made in Italy after 1923, stimulated by Mussolini's turning back to private ownership formerly government-owned utilities (see Table III.2 for U.S. stakes by 1929).[7] Likewise, American power and light enterprises went to Canada. Table VI.1 lists the major border crossings.

So, too, companies went to Latin America. By December 31, 1929, Intercontinents Power Company (formed in 1928) had obtained properties in Argentina, Brazil, and Chile and had 46,466 customers in ninety-one communities. On its board of directors were the president and general manager of Westinghouse Electric International.[8]

But by far the most significant U.S. investor in foreign power and light was the American & Foreign Power Company. In 1923, a General Electric subsidiary, the Electric Bond and Share Company, organized American & Foreign Power Company. A year later General Electric distributed the stock of Electric Bond and Share to G.E. shareholders in a spin-off. American & Foreign Power continued as a controlled affiliate of Electric Bond and Share. The chairman of the board of General Electric (Owen Young) remained on the board of directors of American & Foreign Power for over two decades after the financial separation of General Electric and Electric Bond and Share. American & Foreign Power in 1923 obtained from Electric Bond and Share properties in Panama, Guatemala, and Cuba (acquired in 1917, 1919, and 1922) and then expanded. In 1923 electric public utility services throughout Latin America—its principal area of investment—consisted mainly of those for lighting and for operating street cars. The facilities were under British, German, French, Canadian, or in certain cases local ownership and comprised isolated plants with high costs and unreliable service. American & Foreign Power Company aimed to alter this. It purchased the properties. When it found antiquated laws, it negotiated with host governments to change them. Then it entered into contracts with governing authorities. Next, it reorganized each operating unit with an eye to developing a modern system.

Table VI.1. Nine major U.S. public utilities operating in Canada, 1929

1. Associated Gas and Electric Company (1906) [1]
   In 1926 acquired the Maritime Electric Co., Ltd., and through its subsidiaries furnished electric power to towns in Nova Scotia and New Brunswick.
2. Central Public Service Company (1925)
   Supplied electric power to towns in New Brunswick and Quebec.
3. Cities Service Company (1910)
   Its Canadian public utilities subsidiaries included: Alberta Gas & Fuel Company Ltd.; two major suppliers of gas in Ontario and owners of gas wells (Dominion Gas Company and Southern Ontario Gas Company); a supplier of gas to industrial plants in Hamilton, Ontario; and a supplier of gas, light, and power as well as an operator of street railways in St. John, New Brunswick and the vicinity.
4. International Paper and Power Company (1928)
   Supplied power for its own Canadian operations and sold power in New Brunswick and Ontario.
5. International Utilities Corporation (1924)
   Supplied principal Prairie towns with gas and electricity, and the main towns in British Columbia with electricity. In 1928, this corporation had nine Canadian subsidiaries.
6. National Fuel Gas Company (1902)
   Through a subsidiary provided natural gas to Niagara Falls, Welland, Fort Erie, Bridgeburg and Sherkston, Ontario.
7. Niagara-Hudson Power Corporation (1929)
   Sold power wholesale to Ontario hydroelectric commission. Its subsidiaries had hydroelectric plants on both sides of Niagara Falls.
8. North American Gas and Electric Company (1928)
   Canadian subsidiaries operated electric power properties in southern Saskatchewan.
9. North Continent Utilities Corporation (1922)
   Supplied gas to Sault Ste. Marie, Ontario.

Source: Herbert Marshall, Frank A. Southard, Jr., Kenneth W. Taylor, *Canadian-American Industry* (New Haven 1936), pp. 140–145; Federal Trade Commission, *Electric Power Industry* (Washington, D.C. 1927), pp. 218–219, 154; *Moody's 1929* and *1930; Annual Financial Review, Canadian,* July 1929.
[1] Date in parenthesis indicates when the parent U.S. company was incorporated.

It developed plans for financing major improvements, for ample power plant capacity along with up-to-date transmission and distribution, as well as for the introduction of the latest U.S. marketing methods. American & Foreign Power believed it should establish "closer relations between the operating company and its customers, employees and the general public in the territory served," and in many countries it offered preferred stock of the operating company for sale. Table VI.2 indicates the company's major investments. While American & Foreign Power Company did invest in minority positions in companies in Canada, Europe, and Japan, by far its greatest stake was in Latin America. There its subsidiaries sold not only power and light, but ran street cars, furnished telephone service (Sosthenes Behn, chief executive of I.T.T., was a director of American & Foreign Power, 1927–1938), operated ice plants, supplied water, and manufactured gas. In 1929, American & Foreign Power made its first major acquisition in Asia, obtaining control of the power and light facilities formerly provided by the Shanghai Municipal Council for that city. This was the largest power station in all China; in fact, the U.S. consul in Shanghai wrote home that this step would raise the U.S. investment in Shanghai by about 40 per cent. American & Foreign Power

Table VI.2. American & Foreign Power Company abroad, 1925–1929

	Major property acquisitions		Indices of growth of entire system (as of Dec. 31)		
	Initial control in	Subsequent acquisitions in	Population served	Communities served	Consumers served
1925	Ecuador	Cuba	944,000	99	97,939
1926		Ecuador	1,365,000	105	154,908
1927	Colombia Brazil Venezuela		3,069,000	215	258,139
1928	Costa Rica Chile Mexico	Colombia Brazil	8,217,000	643	626,320
1929	Argentina China India	Brazil Venezuela	12,067,000	780	878,494

Source: American & Foreign Power Co., "The Foreign Power System" (booklet), New York 1953, and *Annual Reports,* 1925–1929.

in November 1929 also purchased one-half interest in the Tata Hydro-Electric Agencies Ltd. of Bombay; in addition, it sought to invest in the Calcutta Electric Supply Corporation, a move that was blocked by British opposition.* By decade's end, American & Foreign Power Company's subsidiaries employed worldwide some 47,000 persons. By then, the company was a half-billion dollar corporation, operating exclusively outside the United States.[9]

2

With a few countries in the Caribbean and Central America excepted, U.S. stakes in railroads declined in the 1920s. New investments were primarily for maintenance and were not significant. Table III.1 above gives the U.S. direct investment abroad in railroads.

Far more exciting and innovative were the U.S. foreign investments in air travel. The available statistics do not segregate these foreign stakes. Initially, they were only in Latin America. Aided by U.S. mail subsidies, Pan American Airways started in 1927 to fly the 110-mile route between Key West, Florida, and Havana, Cuba. Further encouraged by the Foreign Air Mail Act (March 8, 1928) that provided generous mail subsidies, Juan Trippe—Pan Am's ambitious leader—expanded. Pan American Airways qualified for routes to Mexico, the Caribbean islands, and then to Central America. In 1928, Trippe purchased 100 per cent control of Compañía Mexicana de Aviación, a line founded by an American oil prospector named George Rihl. Next, Trippe sought a flying permit from Colombia, only to be refused, for three years earlier the U.S. government had not allowed a Colombian airline—SCADTA (founded by Austrian and German fliers)—to operate an air route from that country to Key West over the Canal Zone. Trippe was not foiled, and in 1929 Pan Am secretly bought an 84 per cent interest in the Colombian air line! Earlier that year, W. R. Grace & Co. and Pan Am jointly organized Panagra (Pan American & Grace Airways), which operated on the West Coast of South America. In Peru, in 1929, an American, Elmer Faucett, with some Peruvian capital, formed Compañía de Aviación Faucett; Panagra acquired 20 per cent of the stock. By 1930, Pan Am was flying throughout most of Latin America, delivering mail and passengers. Everywhere Pan Am's representatives—backed by the U.S. State

* When it was blocked, American & Foreign Power turned to the U.S. government for help in entry. See *Foreign Relations of the United States 1930*, III, pp. 164–165.

Department—negotiated with Latin American governments to operate on air routes, to establish terminals, to obtain exclusive mail-carrying contracts, to simplify customs and clearance procedures for passengers and their baggage, and to import both ground and flying equipment from the United States without paying local customs duties. Pan Am negotiators argued in each nation that U.S. postal subsidies provided the service, and the host countries would have naught but benefits.

In these early days, other American airlines also made plans to fly to Latin America,* but by 1930 these airlines were no longer flying, for the policy of the U.S. government favored Pan American Airways and its affiliates. Air routes became political. The U.S. government attempted to use air connections as a tool in diplomacy in order to hold a regional superiority for the United States in Latin America, to encourage U.S. trade, and to serve as a challenge to the air links Europeans were making.† [10]

3

Other U.S. investors abroad included some in retail stores. The new Drug Inc. (formed in 1928) acquired controlling interest in Boots drug stores in England; in 1928, Boots had 800 retail shops. In 1929 Woolworth had 350 stores in England and was expanding in Germany. Over the Canadian border, Liggett drugstores (a subsidiary of Drug Inc.), Woolworth, Montgomery Ward, Piggly Wiggly, A & P, and Safeway Stores started new retail outlets.‡ It was the drugstore, the five-and-ten, and the grocery store that moved northward, rather than Tiffany's (which had branches in London and Paris) or Best's (which headed its 1929 *Annual Report:* "New York, Paris, London, Palm Beach.") Here again, we have a reflection of market requirements, of style consciousness in Europe and Canada. [11]

4

Construction firms were among the U.S. businesses to set up foreign operations in the 1920s. Ulen & Company, J. C. White & Co., Founda-

---

* N.Y.R.B.A. (New York, Rio, and Buenos Aires), Pickwick Airways, Inc. (Mexico and Guatemala), and Safety Airways (United States and Chile). See Lissitzyn, *International Air Transport,* pp. 241–242.

† This policy was a part of the overall U.S. government attitude that encouraged U.S. investment to surpass European capital in Latin America and "to break" *European* monopolies.

‡ On the other hand, in the 1920s Sears, Roebuck does not seem to have had stores in Canada, nor did such large U.S. chains as J. C. Penney or Walgreen's.

tion Company, and Fredrick Snare & Company constructed railways, docks, and buildings and installed water supply and sewage systems, mainly in Latin America. Other companies went to China. The investments of these concerns consisted of funds advanced to move their supplies to location, their establishing a camp for their employees, and their advances in connection with their contracts. Sometimes these firms worked for host governments, sometimes (less often) for U.S. companies that had expanded abroad.[12]

More responsive to the international activities of U.S. industrial enterprises, American advertising agencies, accounting firms, credit companies, and banks inaugurated foreign offices.* [13] National City Bank remained the leader among U.S. banks abroad; by 1929 it had ninety-three branches in principal cities in Central and South America, Europe, and Asia. Its directors included Americans who headed important multinational businesses: Sosthenes Behn (I.T.T.), Gerard Swope (G.E.), E. A. Deed (National Cash Register), J. P. Grace (W. R. Grace & Co.), and C. H. McCormick (International Harvester). American Express—engaged in banking, transport, and travel and long a foreign investor—had by 1926 forty-seven foreign branches.[14]

Instrumental in introducing the American way of life abroad were the movie makers: "There are few American industries that are more dependent upon foreign markets than the motion picture industry; and there are still fewer industries in which American dominance of world markets has in the past been more dramatic and more complete," declared a writer in the *Harvard Business Review* of April 1930. This was not simply an export industry; U.S. film producers established foreign distribution organizations and invested in theater houses in Europe.[15]

5

In sum, numerous nonmanufacturing enterprises went abroad to extend their markets. Of these, the public utilities had by far the greatest stakes. American capital, technology, management, and marketing expertise combined to make these U.S. businesses fully competitive with for-

---

* The move of U.S. banks abroad in the late 1920s was through foreign *branch* offices and an occasional foreign subsidiary. Edge Act corporations were not used with one exception, the First Federal Foreign Investment Trust, authorized to begin business in May 1926. It had a subsidiary in Switzerland; this Edge Act corporation was liquidated beginning in 1933. *Federal Reserve Bulletin* 42:1298 (December 1956) and 9:272 (May 1933).

eign firms. The U.S. government offered strong support. U.S. investors in telephones and power and light, especially, made huge initial investments to establish themselves in foreign countries. Retailers, advertising agencies, and movie makers, which made smaller foreign investments, also communicated U.S. marketing techniques and introduced American methods abroad.

U.S.-owned public utilities, transportation companies, construction firms, and banks tended to have their most substantial direct investments in less developed countries. In Europe, for example, whereas other market-oriented enterprises tended to invest first in the wealthiest nations (England and Germany), the public utilities made important commitments in less developed Spain and Italy. Public utilities and banks did make direct investments in developed nations, but their stakes were larger in less developed ones. On the other hand, retailers, advertising firms, and movie makers—like the market-oriented industrials considered in Chapter IV—had their most extensive interests in industrial countries. The reason for the difference in pattern seems to lie both in foreign demand and in the extent to which the demand could be met by indigenous enterprise. Thus requirements for telephone, light and power, and banking services prevailed worldwide, but autochthonic enterprises in developed countries were available to meet a large part of the demand; in less developed lands, foreign enterprises had to supply the capital and know-how. Less developed countries with small markets for consumer goods had a more limited need for chain stores and advertising agencies than the developed nations that were receptive to novel, imaginative American techniques. The expansion of nonmanufacturing firms across the U.S. borders was one facet of the overall move abroad by U.S. businesses in the 1920s.

VII

An Overview

The growth of U.S. stakes abroad during the 1920s represented not simply an increase in scale. Rather, U.S. companies were (1) going to *more countries,* (2) building *more plants* in a particular foreign country, (3) manufacturing or mining *more end products* in a particular foreign land, (4) investing in a single alien nation in *a greater degree of integration,* and (5) *diversifying* on a worldwide basis.

Thus far in writing of U.S. corporations in the 1920s, we have concentrated in a conventional manner on the United States (the home of the investor) and the single foreign country where the principal operations of the investor took place (the host nation). Yet, by the late 1920s, many individual U.S. investments abroad came to link three or more countries in a multinational relationship;* it is to this multinational complexity that we now must turn.

Sometimes a U.S. enterprise used an existing or new European subsidiary or affiliate to conduct part of the parent firm's foreign business: Eastman Kodak's English subsidiary had affiliates that sold in East and South Africa, Egypt, Turkey, India, Palestine, Java, Straits Settlements, and Syria. A European subsidiary in the process of expansion might merge with an independent firm that already had foreign interests: thus, Westinghouse Air Brake's English affiliate merged with another British business with affiliates in Australia and India. A U.S. corporation that expanded in Chile could acquire stock in a company incorporated in London (the financial transactions were between Americans and Britishers; the operations were exclusively in Chile): the Guggenheims purchased British nitrate companies operating in Chile. In some instances, generally for tax reasons, U.S. firms or their European affiliates estab-

* Three including the United States.

lished holding companies in Switzerland, Luxembourg, or Lichtenstein: Coty Inc. in 1929 set up a Swiss holding company, which consolidated its European interests.[1]

By 1929, among the U.S. corporations using Canadian holding companies for certain overseas business were Union Carbide (for Norway), Kelvinator Company (for England), Ford Motor Company (for the British empire outside of Britain and Ireland), Standard Oil of New Jersey (for Peru and Colombia), and Aluminum Company of America (for the world outside of the United States). In each of these cases, the parent U.S. enterprise operated in the Dominion along with using a Canadian unit for the added foreign business relations; these were not simply devices for getting out from under U.S. law.[*][2]

U.S. direct investments in British empire countries—in Australia, Malaya, India, and South Africa—were often *owned* by English or Canadian corporations affiliated with the U.S. parent.[†] One American company (Sherwin-Williams) had in 1920 a Canadian affiliate that owned an English company that in turn had sales branches in India, China, and South Africa. Another American corporation had an English affiliate that controlled a European holding company, which in turn controlled a French subsidiary, which then had a subsidiary in French Africa to lengthen the chain (Ford Motor Company in 1929 fits this description). U.S. controlled corporations doing business in any European colony were *normally* incorporated in the imperial nation: Jersey Standard, for instance, conducted its activities in the Dutch East Indies through a company incorporated in the Netherlands.[3]

[*] Bermuda holding companies, Liberian registered ships, and Luxembourg companies, for example, fall into this last category.

[†] For example, General Electric's main business in Australia was done through the British Thomson-Houston Company, which until its merger into Associated Electrical Industries was 97 per cent owned by G.E.'s wholly owned subsidiary International General Electric Company (data from General Electric). Ford operated in Australia, Malaya, India, and South Africa through the Ford Motor Company of Canada, which was associated with Ford Motor Company in the United States through certain common shareholders (Ford Motor Company records, Dearborn, Michigan). R.C.A. did business in Australia and India through Gramophone Company, Ltd., an English affiliate of its subsidiary Victor Talking Machine Company (*Moody's 1929*). Westinghouse Air Brake, Otis Elevator, and United Shoe Machinery were among those enterprises that operated in Australia through English affiliates (H. H. Westinghouse to shareholders, Westinghouse Air Brake Company, April 1, 1921, Scudder Collection, Columbia University Library; Otis Elevator records, New York; International Management Association, *Case Studies in Foreign Operations*, p. 78). The British United Shoe also had subsidiaries in New Zealand and South Africa (International Management Association, *Case Studies*, p. 78).

U.S. capital combined on a number of occasions with foreign capital for joint enterprises in a third country: thus, English and Japanese as well as American and Chinese "associates" joined American & Foreign Power Co. in investing in Shanghai.[4]

The reasons behind these often complicated multinational corporate relationships included financial, administrative, commercial, antitrust, political, and/or tax considerations.

Managerial control might or might not be identical with *immediate* ownership lines. Sometimes, to be sure, control and ownership coincided. Ford of Australia, owned by Ford of Canada, was in the 1920s actually controlled by Ford of Canada. In a totally different case, Compania Swift Internacional—an American-owned company (incorporated in Argentina)—held all the stock of Swift's Australian company, but the direct control of the Australian business apparently emanated from Chicago rather than from Buenos Aires. In a not atypical instance, the South African sales subsidiary of National Cash Register—owned by the U.S. parent—was effectively managed from London by N.C.R.'s English subsidiary. The South African National Cash Register Company had as its "territory" southern Africa, including much of east Africa. Thus, in the 1920s, an N.C.R. representative in Kenya, who would typically be an Englishman or a South African, would report to a manager in Johannesburg, who in turn would report to a London official, whose boss then would report to the company's headquarters in the States. Because of the small investment, the distances, and such pyramided international control patterns, there proved to be a large degree of managerial autonomy in such business operations, although how much autonomy varied by company.[5]

To add to the emerging multinational interconnections, lines of trade might vary from lines of ownership and management. While the bulk of the output of market-oriented subsidiaries was for host country consumption, some European subsidiaries exported to nearby nations or to countries within the host nation's empire. Du Pont's affiliate Société Française Fabrikoid, Paris, for example, manufactured in France and sold in French Algeria, Tunisia, and Morocco as well as in France.[6] U.S. plants in Canada that were built chiefly to serve the Dominion market sometimes exported. Their main exports went within the British empire (see Table VII.1), where since 1915 Canadian products enjoyed tariff preferences. On the other hand, Singer Manufacturing Company seems to

Table VII.1. Geographical distribution of some Canadian exports likely to be products of "branch factories" in the fiscal year ended March 31, 1929 [1]

Articles [2]	Total amount exported	British Empire %	Latin America %	Europe and Mediterranean %	Far East %	Africa %	United States %
Adding machines, number	4,056	32	Less than 1	67	—	—	Less than 1
Automobiles, number	103,566	72	15	5	6	1	Less than 1
Tires, number	1,733,300	44	28	17	9	Less than 1	Less than 1
Inner tubes, number	1,559,621	40	29	18	10	Less than 1	Less than 1
Internal-combustion engines, number	1,696	45	16	35	Less than 1	—	—
Rubber boots and shoes, number	2,067,889	88	1	10	Less than 1	—	—
Canvas shoes with rubber soles, number	7,621,156	47	44	7	1	Less than 1	Less than 1
Rubber hose	$268,698	63 *	7 *	2 *	3 *	—	23 *
Rubber belting, number	1,170,700	48	32	15	4	—	—
Sewing machines	$4,333,533	—	98 *	Less than 1 *	—	—	Less than 1 *
Typewriters, number	1,089	19	27	50	—	—	Less than 1
Phonographs, gramophones, and parts	$99,544	48 *	44 *	3 *	Less than 1 *	—	4 *
Cameras	$128,040	61 *	Less than 1 *	33 *	Less than 1 *	—	5 *
Films, including motion-picture films	$4,265,322	49 *	Less than 1 *	9 *	10 *	—	31 *
Batteries	$627,502	58 *	33 *	3 *	1 *	Less than 1 *	3 *
Electric vacuum cleaners, number	39,556	78	—	21	—	—	—
Electrical apparatus (not motors and ignition)	$609,735	50 *	36 *	—	4 *	—	8 *

Source: U.S. Senate, American Branch Factories Abroad, Sen. Doc. 258, 71st Cong., 3d sess. (Washington, D.C., 1931), p. 26.
[1] Percentage calculated on quantity unless indicated by *.
[2] These are articles produced entirely or largely in American "branch" plants.

have filled its British empire sewing machine trade from its Scottish factory; that enterprise's officials explain that their Canadian plant needed added volume to gain economies of scale; thus, Canadian Singer in the 1920s supplied Singer outlets in Latin America, even in the absence of tariff advantage. Often the plants of Canadian subsidiaries of U.S. enterprises sold in foreign markets when the parent company had excessive demands on it; exports from Canada could fill the interstices in supply.[7] Far fewer market-oriented U.S. enterprises in Latin America exported, but du Pont's explosives plant in Calama, Chile, sold in Bolivia as well as Chile.[8]

So, too, the output of supply-oriented investments by U.S. business, as we have had occasion to note, was generally but not necessarily for sale in the United States. Thus, exports from U.S. owned banana plantations in Central America and the Caribbean went to a small extent to Europe as well as to the United States; manganese from U.S. properties in the Gold Coast traveled to Norway; Jersey Standard's affiliate in Peru shipped its oil to other countries on the West Coast of South America and to Canada; the Argentine meat packers, which were controlled by U.S. capital, exported to Europe.[9] Over time, third nations would be ever more involved in the trade.

If our earlier consideration of U.S. business abroad by market- and supply-oriented stakes tended to obscure the multinational intricacies of individual foreign investments, it also blurs recognition of the multinational complexity of individual foreign investors. In fact, by the 1920s many U.S. enterprises had *both* market- and supply-oriented commercial and industrial interests abroad, and some also operated public utilities along with their other businesses.

In *The Emergence of Multinational Enterprise: American Business Abroad from the Colonial Era to 1914,* the present author tried to assemble a list of companies with market- and supply-oriented stakes for 1914.[10] That roster, which was probably incomplete, included nineteen entries. Of these nineteen, sixteen reappear on a similar 1929 list (see Table VII.2; companies marked with asterisk were on the 1914 list). One omission from the 1929 group is due to a changed name—Amalgamated Copper Company, 1914; Anaconda, 1929.[11] The other two omissions are real: British-American Tobacco and Virginia Carolina Chemical. We will have more to say on British-American Tobacco Company shortly. Virginia Carolina Chemical Company went into receivership in 1924 and

Table VII.2. U.S.-owned multinational businesses, 1929 with both market-oriented and supply-oriented direct investments abroad [1]

Company name	Market-oriented investments [2]	Supply-oriented investments [2]
Alcoa * (see also Aluminium Ltd.)	Canada [3]	Dutch Guiana
Allied Chemical	Canada	Canada
Aluminium Ltd.	Europe, Canada, India	British Guiana, Canada, Europe
American Chicle *	England, Canada, Mexico	Mexico, Guatemala, British Honduras
American Cyanamid	Spain, South Africa [4]	Dutch Guiana, Canada, Spain
American Metal	Europe [4]	Cuba, Mexico, Canada,[5] Northern Rhodesia, South Africa
American Smelting and Refining	Europe [4]	Mexico, Honduras, Peru, Canada
American Tobacco *	England, Cuba	Cuba, France, Turkey
Anaconda	Europe,[4] Canada	Chile, Peru,[6] Mexico, Poland
Anderson, Clayton	Europe,[4] Japan,[4] China [4]	Mexico [7]
Armour *	Europe,[4] Cuba	Latin America
Armstrong Cork	Europe,[4] Canada [4]	Europe, North Africa [7]
Atlantic Refining	Europe,[4] Latin America,[4] Africa,[4] Oceania [4]	Latin America, Iraq
Bethlehem Steel	Canada,[4] Latin America,[4] Japan,[4] Philippines [4]	Latin America
Borden's	Europe,[4] Canada	China
California Packing	Europe [4]	Haiti, Philippines
Cities Service	Europe,[4] Canada	Mexico
Corn Products	All six continents	North Korea
Crown Cork & Seal	Europe, Canada, Brazil	Spain
Diamond Match *	England,[8] Canada	Canada [9]
Du Pont *	Europe, Canada, Latin America, Australia, China,[4] Japan, [9,4]	Canada [14]

Table VII.2 (continued)

Company name	Market-oriented investments [2]	Supply-oriented investments [2]
Firestone	Europe, Canada	Liberia
Ford	All six continents	Brazil
General Foods	England, Canada	Philippines
Goodyear	All six continents	Asia
Grace (W.R.)	Latin America	Latin America
Guggenheim Enterprises * [10]	Europe [4]	Latin America, Africa, Malaya, Canada
Gulf Oil	Europe [4]	Latin America, Iraq, Kuwait, Canada (?) [11]
Hires (Charles E.)	Canada	Cuba
International Harvester *	All six continents	Cuba, Philippines
International Nickel *	Canada, Europe	Canada
Kennecott	Europe [4]	Chile
Liggett & Myers	China [4]	Turkey [7]
National Lead	Europe, Canada, Argentina	Latin America
Phelps Dodge	Canada	Mexico
Sinclair [12]	Europe,[4,13] Cuba [4]	Latin America, Angola
Singer *	All six continents	Canada
Standard Oil of California	Mexico	Latin America, Bahrain
Standard Oil of Indiana	Europe [13]	Latin America, Iraq
Standard Oil of New Jersey *	Europe, Canada, Latin America	Europe, Canada,[14] Latin America, Dutch East Indies, Iraq
Standard Oil of New York *	Southeastern Europe,[4] Asia,[4] Africa,[4] Oceania [4]	Iraq, Mexico
Sun Oil	Europe,[4] Canada [4]	Latin America
Swift *	Europe, Canada, Cuba	Latin America,[15] Australia [15]
Texas Oil *	All six continents	Latin America
Tide Water Oil	Europe,[4] Latin America [4]	Mexico
Union Carbide and Carbon	Europe, Canada, India [9]	Europe, Canada, Africa

Table VII.2 (continued)

Company name	Market-oriented investments [2]	Supply-oriented investments [2]
Union Oil of California	Canada,[4] Oceania [4]	Latin America
United Fruit *	Europe [4]	Latin America
U.S. Rubber *	All six continents	Asia, England,[7] Brazil [7]
U.S. Steel	Canada, Latin America,[4] Asia,[4] Africa [4]	Brazil, Cuba (?) [6]

Source: Moody's, Annual Reports, company histories, and text of Chapters III–VI above.

* Included on 1914 list, given in Wilkins, *Emergence of Multinational Enterprise,* 216.

[1] Excluded are companies, such as food enterprises, that purchased their products in the host country (supply-oriented) and packed them and sold them in that *same* country (market-oriented), or cement companies that bought their raw materials in the host country (supply-oriented) and transformed the raw materials and sold the finished product in the *same* host country (market-oriented).

[2] Often a region rather than a country is listed, if a company had direct investments in two or more countries in that region.

[3] Power facilities.

[4] Sales only.

[5] Copper refining.

[6] Property not being worked.

[7] Purchasing only.

[8] Small minority interest.

[9] Not verified, but seems highly probable.

[10] The Guggenheims controlled American Smelting and Refining, Kennecott Copper, as well as numerous other companies in international mining.

[11] According to *Moody's 1930* Gulf had oil fields in Canada; I have seen no evidence of this elsewhere.

[12] This was what was left of the company's foreign holdings *in 1929.*

[13] Minor activity.

[14] Small relative to company's other investments.

[15] Through a company that had a large percentage of shareholders in common with the U.S. company.

on its reemergence as Virginia Carolina Company had shed its international holdings.[12]

The 1929 list contains fifty entries (compared with nineteen in 1914). Like the previous roster, it is undoubtedly incomplete, but that it contains more than two and one-half times the number of companies included in 1914 is significant. Regrettably such a tabulation provides little indication of the size of the foreign stakes. Nor does the table give a measure of the importance of a particular company's investment; from the table, for example, it is impossible to know that by 1929 Anaconda's copper production outside the United States was greater than that in this country or that Jersey Standard and its affiliates had far more employees abroad than in the United States.[13] When we comment shortly on "dropouts," we will see the list shows some enterprises whose stakes in 1914 were more impressive than in 1929. The table also fails to indicate the literally *hundreds* of U.S. corporations that by 1929 had foreign investments in either market- or supply-oriented businesses but not in both. It thus omits mammoth multinational enterprises such as General Motors and General Electric, since their vast international commitments (each had direct investments on six continents) were all based on marketing strategies.

Yet, limitations notwithstanding, the 1929 list does give a sense of the growing scope of American industry abroad. Most striking among the new entries are the oil companies. The 1914 table included only three such enterprises (Standard Oil of New Jersey, Standard Oil of New York, and Texas Company); the 1929 list contains a dozen. As earlier noted, one of the general characteristics of the 1920s was the shift in U.S. oil investments abroad from primarily a market-oriented activity to a mixed marketing and producing stake.

Table VII.2 deals with market- and supply-oriented operations of industrial enterprises. Note should be made that a number of U.S. agricultural, mining, and manufacturing companies abroad had radio connections, power plants, and/or railroads serving as an adjunct to their foreign operations. W. R. Grace was in such various businesses as trade, shipping, air travel, mining, sugar, and textiles. International Telephone and Telegraph Corporation was not only a major public utility abroad, but also an important manufacturer.

In short, by the late 1920s complex multinational corporate ownership, administrative, and marketing patterns had emerged in many U.S. enterprises and a sizable number of such companies participated abroad in a variety of different activities, comprising horizontal and vertical (forward and backward) integration as well as diversification.

2

In the main, a vast expansion of international business meant—as business historian Alfred D. Chandler has pointed out—a company had to alter its overall management structure if it was to be efficient. Back as far as 1884, the Thomson-Houston Electric Company—a predecessor to

General Electric Company—had had an international subsidiary. It was before its time and disappeared when General Electric was organized and reorganized in 1892–1893.[14] Before and during World War I, a few other companies set up international units.[15] In 1918, Western Electric formed a 100 per cent owned international subsidiary, International Western Electric Company, to own and administer its international business (it was this subsidiary that it sold in 1925 to I.T.T., which the latter renamed International Standard Electric).[16] General Electric followed Western Electric and organized in 1919 the wholly owned International General Electric Company.

The reasons General Electric started I.G.E.C. were: (1) special knowledge was required to cope with the complexities of international trade and payments; (2) distinctive policies had to be developed for manufacturing facilities in many different countries and in a multitude of products; and (3) a man, Gerard Swope, was available to direct the new subsidiary. I.G.E.C. was deputized by its parent (G.E.) to handle General Electric's export trade, to coordinate overseas affiliates, to supervise foreign investment plans, and to renegotiate pre–World War I contracts. It held the stock in most of General Electric's foreign affiliates and became G.E.'s exclusive agent in international business. I.G.E.C.'s investment in overseas manufacturing enterprises varied from 100 per cent in Brazil to a small minority interest in some European firms. In the organization of its business, I.G.E.C. pursued a different course in industrial and nonindustrial countries. In the 1920s its foreign manufacturing affiliates in industrial nations in practically every case had national management and a sizable foreign stock participation, since talent and capital were available. In less developed countries, on the other hand, subsidiaries had American managers and were 100 per cent owned by I.G.E.C.[17] Westinghouse in 1919 also established a wholly owned international company—which handled its licensing arrangements and its export trade.[18]

General Motors, which had had General Motors Export Company—a wholly owned subsidiary—since 1911, in 1924 formed an "Export and Overseas Group."[19] Until 1928, during this decade, Ford with its large international business maintained control of the organization from Dearborn (except for operations in the British empire outside Great Britain that were supervised by its associated Canadian enterprise). In 1928, Ford decentralized its foreign operations, and the direction of the European business was undertaken by Ford's British affiliate. Ford did not, however, establish an international company or an international group in the 1920s. Like General Electric, Ford's operations in developed countries were as a rule after 1928 organized into joint ventures, while in less developed nations they were wholly owned by Ford-U.S. or by Ford of Canada.[20]

Standard Oil of New Jersey by the spring of 1927 had been reorganized to have, as Chandler has put it, "autonomous multi-functional operating divisions with managers who were responsible for performance and with a general office of general executives and staff specialists, which planned, appraised, and coordinated the activities of the various units and of the enterprise as a whole." Among the operating divisions were Imperial Oil, Ltd. (which operated in Canada and supervised subsidiaries in Peru and Colombia) and "the European and Latin American group" (the equivalent of other corporations' "international company" or "overseas and export group").[21]

Among the new "international companies" of the 1920s were American & Foreign Power (1923), ARMCO International (1924), International B. F. Goodrich (1924), Crown Cork International (1928), and Aluminium Limited (1928). By 1928, Pond's Extract Co. had an international company, Pond's Extract Co. International Ltd. Some of these international companies were—like the three in the electrical manufacturing industry—wholly owned subsidiaries; others were partly owned; and still others were enterprises wherein the stockholders of the parent firm became stockholders in the new international company.[22] While all three devices appear to have been used to segregate administratively the international business, in the second case there was also an attempt to raise outside funds (in the United States) to aid in the development of business abroad; in the third case, the "cast-off," there may have been tax advantages to major stockholders (the third procedure was generally followed when the parent company was closely held, so control could continue to be exercised).

Crown Cork & Seal Company fits the second case: its international affiliate had parent company stock holdings and also outside shareholders.[23] Following the third pattern, Alcoa established Aluminium Limited. The president of Alcoa, A. V. Davis, explained the reasons for its new "cast-off" enterprise: Alcoa could not give sufficient attention to foreign business; Alcoa's personnel "naturally preferred to sell in large quantities in the United States rather than bother, as they considered it, with smaller quantities abroad. Very few of the Alcoa people could speak foreign languages or were familiar with foreign business customs." Difficulties with foreign exchange "brought home to Alcoa some of its incompetence in dealing with the foreign situation." Thus, Davis created the new administrative unit to give specialized attention to foreign business. As in the case of General Electric, the timing of the decision to form an international company was based in large part on the availability of an individual to direct it. A. V. Davis planned to pass the presidency of Alcoa to Roy A. Hunt, and of the new international company to his brother, E. K. Davis. In 1928, Aluminium Limited was formed, incorporated in Canada.* [24]

Indeed, primarily for reasons of effective management, a number of U.S. companies in the decade after World War I felt the need to segregate "international business." Alcoa was exceptional in including its Canadian operations in its "international company." Most corporations that established international units isolated the "foreign" activities from those in the United States and Canada. They recognized that business outside the United States and Canada required distinctive and specialized talents. The international company (later, in many cases transformed into an international division †) owes its true beginnings to the organizational changes of the post–World War I decade. It can be added, however, that there were U.S. companies with large foreign investments that did not adopt the new structure. Among these were Anaconda, Kennecott, and American Smelting and Refining Company. The reason seemed to lie in the fact that in the 1920s business abroad for these companies *did not* require "distinctive and specialized" talents. They mined and processed minerals in foreign countries—as in the United States. Their marketing problems for the foreign output were essentially the same as for their American output. Their giant foreign business did not provoke the need for adopting this step in a multidivisional structure.‡ [25]

In the 1920s, U.S. companies abroad acted either through branches,§ 100 per cent owned subsidiaries, or with joint ventures (broadly defined

---

* Aluminium Limited acquired all Alcoa's foreign properties except one large power facility in Canada (transferred to it in 1938) and Alcoa's bauxite holdings in Dutch Guiana (which supplied the U.S. business). *U.S. v. Alcoa, Alcoa Brief*, p. 723.

† After World War II—mainly for tax reasons—wholly owned international companies of times past became international divisions. Some partly owned international companies were bought up and so transformed. It was far harder to handle the "cast-offs," which often—but not always—remained separate, independent corporations.

‡ In the case of American Smelting and Refining, its Mexican operations were not even incorporated into a single company.

§ A branch was not incorporated abroad; it was fully controlled by the U.S. parent.

as the sharing of equity interests with others in a foreign venture *). In the main, as we have seen, if they joined with foreign capital abroad (and this was not uncommon), they did so with indigenous capital in Europe, Canada, and Japan or with European (or possibly Canadian or Japanese) capital in third countries. Occasionally, two or more U.S. companies would join in business abroad (sometimes through Webb-Pomerene associations and sometimes directly). Participation by U.S. enterprises in joint ventures with local capital in underdeveloped countries did exist but was rare. So, too, were joint ventures with foreign government agencies. In fact, the present author knows of only one existing joint venture between a U.S. business and a foreign government in *manufacturing* in the 1920s.†

In the 1920s, the motives behind joint ventures with *foreign* capital seem to have been: (1) to move under a national cloak and to acquire national good will (primarily in Europe and Japan); (2) to obtain more capital (Canada and Europe); (3) to acquire and to share skills, know-how, products, and/or existing facilities, often as an aid to market entry (Europe, Canada, and Japan); (4) to cope with competition ‡ (Europe); and (5) to develop a third-country market or natural resource and to share the costs (joint ventures involving U.S. firms primarily with European or in at least two instances, Japanese capital). The motive behind the ventures with *other U.S. firms* seems to have been mainly to spread the cost of the foreign stake.

If a U.S. company participated in a joint venture abroad (that is if it had anything less than 100 per cent ownership) it would typically in the 1920s make agreements with its affiliated companies. This had gone on for decades.[26] The agreements clarified the relationships between the affiliated units abroad. We have seen, for example, that the agreements of General Electric dealt with the exchange of experts, technical assistance, training of personnel, patents, royalties, service

* "Others" could be a single foreign partner (individual), a foreign family group, a foreign corporation, foreign or domestic public shareholders, a foreign government, or a U.S. business.

† That started by Western Electric in 1918: a joint venture to manufacture in China, which involved at its origin, Western Electric, its Japanese affiliate, and the Chinese Ministry of Communications. In *petroleum*, U.S. companies went into the joint venture in Iraq with British and French companies that had government stockholders.

‡ The author has deliberately used the vague formulation "to cope with competition," for the means might be to buy into a competitor and thus eliminate competition or to buy into a foreign firm that could be used to compete more effectively against other enterprises abroad.

charges, as well as with allocating market territories. Timken Roller Bearing Company had, for instance, licensed an independent agent in 1909 to make and to sell its products in Europe and restricted the territory of that agent. In 1927, the American Timken Company had acquired a majority * interest in the formerly independent British manufacturer, British Timken Ltd. Although its basic patents had expired, American Timken had that year licensed its know-how and given its foreign affiliate the right to use its trademark. In 1928, the British managing director of British Timken (Michael B. U. Dewar) and the American Timken Company participated in joint ownership of French and German Timken companies; the American Timken at first held the majority interest in the two continental firms. Each Timken company made and sold the same products—Timken roller bearings. When the 1927–1928 agreements were made, each agreed to sell in a delineated territory and not to compete with one another. Such territorial divisions allowed U.S. companies to share their know-how and yet be protected from competition from their own products made abroad. Such agreements created order and coherence in the business; they were a typical means of acting abroad.[27] If, on the other hand, a company had 100 per cent ownership of the foreign operations it could define territorial limitations without written formal agreement.[28] It could impose its own arrangements.

In order to eliminate intense competition in foreign sales and to raise prices, U.S. and foreign copper producers (mostly owned by U.S. capital) in 1926 formed the Webb-Pomerene association Copper Exporters Inc. We have also noted that the 1928 Achnacarry accord (see p. 88 above) was designed to obtain "as is" conditions in the international oil business.[29]

3

As we have seen, characteristic of the 1920s was the surge of U.S. business worldwide. At the same time, as indicated, there were "dropouts." In the 1920s, insurance—large abroad in 1914—remained confined in its foreign activities to Canada. Tobacco in 1914 was a major American industry in overseas investment; in the 1920s it showed itself abroad in a minor role. Matches—in 1900 a prominent U.S. industry multinationally —was so no longer. U.S. Steel, which in 1914 had forty warehouses around the world and a plant in Canada, by 1928 had only twenty-four

* In 1935 this became a minority interest.

foreign outlets, two plants in Canada, a manganese mine in Brazil, and possibly an iron ore mine in Cuba. Two of the 1914 U.S. leaders abroad in electrical manufacturing—Westinghouse Electric and Western Electric —in 1929 were so no longer, but this did not reflect an industry pattern for General Electric and International Telephone and Telegraph Corporation expanded greatly in foreign countries.

The reasons behind such "dropouts" varied. In the case of insurance, as noted, the heavy losses in Europe, together with the war's destruction of the existing agency force, meant the principal firms had little will to resume their multinational business after World War I; nothing in the 1920s made them newly eager to operate abroad.[30]

As for the tobacco industry, antitrust action in 1911 had forced American Tobacco to sell its controlling interest in the multinational British-American Tobacco Company and its minority interest in the British, Imperial Tobacco Company. Four new U.S. firms were formed after the 1911 decision: a new American Tobacco, R. J. Reynolds, Liggett & Myers, and P. Lorillard.[31] These made a few investments in Turkish and Cuban tobacco; American Tobacco invested in two European factories; there existed some other miscellaneous overseas stakes; * but in sum the four did not appear to have any enthusiastic desire to renew large-scale business abroad. British-American Tobacco, which at the start of the 1920s remained American controlled, was headquartered in London; it maintained global operations; during the course of the 1920s, it passed to British control.[32]

Why, the reader will ask, did not the U.S. tobacco companies move abroad with vigor in the 1920s? The oil enterprises had responded with larger foreign investments after the 1911 antitrust decision that dissolved Standard Oil. The present writer would hypothesize the following reasons for the absence of zeal on the part of U.S. cigarette makers for foreign business in the 1920s: (1) British-American Tobacco was well entrenched abroad, while in Britain, the former affiliate of the old American Tobacco, Imperial Tobacco, ranked supreme; (2) the boom in cigarette demand at home kept the businessmen occupied; (3) much of the overseas demand for U.S.-made cigarettes could be filled by exports; and (4) in the 1890s, when the U.S. cigarette industry had invested overseas in a massive manner, cigarettes were a new product; by the 1920s

---

* Liggett & Myers, for example, incorporated Liggett & Myers (China) in February 1927, which the present author believes was a marketing subsidiary.

they were so no longer; thus, the *need* for investments to introduce the product was not imperative.

The retreat of the American match industry from business abroad was dramatic. Diamond Match Company once had had world leadership in match-making technology; then it had worldwide operations.[33] By the 1920s, it had lost its technological advantage. Faced with competition from Ivar Kreuger's Swedish Match Company, Diamond Match retreated as Swedish Match became a multinational enterprise. Diamond Match still had foreign stakes in 1929, but it no longer held world leadership.[34]

U.S. Steel's lack of attention to giant market-oriented foreign investments can be explained in terms of the competitive position of American steel. By the 1920s, the costs of foreign steel producers were less than those of the U.S. industry. In response to lower costs abroad, in 1928–1929, U.S. Steel did contemplate building a plant in Belgium—a plant which was never erected.[35]

The retreat of Westinghouse Electric and Western Electric from extensive foreign business has to be explained solely in terms of the histories of these particular firms; the poor experiences of Westinghouse Electric before World War I and the attitude of Western Electric's parent company (A.T.T.) toward international activities.

In short, the major dropouts can be understood in terms of the historical experiences of industries (including the degree of technological superiority maintained) and also the experiences of particular enterprises.*

4

Yet, while there were dropouts, the basic direction of U.S. business abroad in the 1920s was toward expansion. New U.S. corporate excitement about international opportunities dwarfed the dropouts. In fact, so great was the growth of U.S. direct foreign investment that governments and individuals around the world expressed concern.

Europeans were troubled. In 1897–1902 alarms had sounded in Europe about the "American invasion." [36] In the late 1920s, anxieties resurfaced.

---

* There were other dropouts for various reasons. For example, in 1928 Timken stopped manufacturing in Canada and formed a sales subsidiary there because changes in the tariff made manufacturing undesirable. Sinclair's operations abroad were far larger in 1923 than in 1929, because after Harry Sinclair's involvement in the Teapot Dome Scandal in the United States (1924), his firm showed less dynamism at home and abroad. E. L. Doheny also retreated from international business after the Teapot Dome Scandal. As we have noted, U.S. holders of concessions in Russia withdrew.

The Nineteen-Twenties

In England, Germany, France, Switzerland, Italy, and Holland, domestically controlled corporations revised their bylaws to avoid selling voting shares to foreigners, to limit foreign stockholdings to a minority, and to prevent foreigners from voting their shares. The words "foreign" and "foreigners" meant, in effect, "American" and "Americans." Whereas in the mid-1920s, the Soviets had tried to encourage foreigners (including Americans) to take concessions (that is to make investments), in 1928–1929 the Russians had changed their policy and sought technical agreements but *not* direct investments.

In Britain and Germany, the European nations where by 1929 U.S. stakes were largest (see Table III.2), the resentment against the "intruders" was the most intense. "Buy British" became a popular phrase in England. *Ueberfremdung*—a newly coined word in the German vocabulary, meaning alien control—described with a bitter edge U.S. purchases of shares in existing German businesses. In France, proposals were made for an 18 per cent extra tax on the profits of U.S. subsidiaries. Europeans complained about the new entries of Americans *and* the takeovers of European firms, with the latter evoking the most uneasiness. To Europeans, the wealthy Americans seemed prepared to pay preposterously inflated prices for their acquisitions. Europeans, once *the* bankers of the world, saw no possibility of resuming this exclusive position; they were not pleased.[37]

Hostility to the giant U.S. oil company, Jersey Standard, proved virulent. The company's historians explain that the enterprise met with an almost "universal suspicion that the great international oil combines were secretly striving to achieve a monopoly which would wring small consumers and nations alike with its iron fingers" [38] (this despite the fact that the Achnacarry accord was not publicly known). While Spain was the only country on the European continent to nationalize its petroleum industry in the 1920s,* the threat existed elsewhere.

In the *Economist,* the London *Herald, European Finance, Berliner Tageblatt, Die Boerse,* and so forth, articles multiplied on the American invasion. J. Bonnefon-Craponne wrote a thesis at the Sorbonne on the penetration of American capital in Europe. An American, Frank A. Southard, started to prepare his excellent volume, *American Industry in Europe.* Ludwell Denny's *America Conquers Britain* (1930) included the ac-

---

* The Russian nationalization was in 1917–1918.

tivities of U.S. direct investors. Britishers, Germans, Frenchmen, and other Europeans had reason to be disquieted. In 1928–1929, especially in the electrical, automobile, rubber tire, office machinery, and oil industries, as well as in public utilities, U.S. direct investment plans burgeoned. By 1929, more than 1,300 companies or organizations in Europe were either owned or controlled by U.S. capital, and the number seemed destined to rise.[39]

While the English worried about U.S. stakes in the United Kingdom, they were also apprehensive about U.S. international business in the western hemisphere. In 1922, *for the first time,* the value of U.S. investment in Canada was greater than that of U.K. investment there.[40] From that date, U.S. stakes in the Dominion would henceforth predominate over British interests. This constituted a dramatic change. Canada was no longer in Britain's economic bailiwick. And, if Canada was lost to the British, so, too, U.S. properties in Latin America seemed to threaten British investments there. In 1919, U.S. investment had already surpassed that of the British in Mexico, Cuba, and parts of Central America. The statistics are not conclusive, but it seems probable that in 1929, *for the first time* in history, U.S. investments exceeded those of the British in Latin America as a whole.[41] This represented a crushing capitulation for the British.*

Elsewhere around the world, the American business challenge to European investors was not as profound as in the western hemisphere nor the victory as decisive. Yet the trend was identical. Before the 1920s, European investors had had larger interests in Liberia than U.S. business; in 1929 this was no longer true.[42] From India to Malaya to the Gold Coast to Northern Rhodesia within the British empire, Americans made some direct investments, despite British reservations. For every time the British blocked Americans, Americans got over the barriers twofold. In the Netherlands East Indies, a U.S. oil company demanded (and got) equal rights with the Dutch. By 1929, in the Middle East, it was apparent that U.S. petroleum enterprises had no intention of leaving the development of this possibly oil-laden region to the British and the French. This, then,

* Note that in comparing U.S. and British investments in Canada and Latin America, we have used total long-term private investments (that is direct and portfolio investments), instead of merely direct investments. Our reasons for this are two: first, there is no breakdown available by direct and portfolio investments of the British interests that is analogous to comparable U.S. breakdowns; second, the bulk of the British stake seems to have been represented by portfolio investments.

was the vital thrust of U.S. business abroad in the 1920s: Americans were pushing into areas where European investment had been supreme. To a large extent, the worldwide confrontation was between U.S. and European (mainly but not exclusively British) investors. But note that it was not all confrontation. Often there was cooperation. Thus, American and English capital joined to operate in Great Britain, Canada, Chile, Australia, China, and Northern Rhodesia. Some American and European businesses entered into cartel agreements, for example in the electrical, chemical, copper, and oil industries. In short, there existed both rivalry *and* association.*

In countries outside of Europe, in addition to the interplay of American and European interests, there was a national reaction to U.S. investors. Many Canadians applauded U.S. investment: "It builds up Canadian industry, gives employment to Canadian workmen, and provides a larger and better market for our farmers." [43] Little friction accompanied the vigorous U.S. business expansion in the Dominion. Even on oil policy, a generally sensitive issue, conflicts were absent.† The Canadian government's view "that the export of hydroelectric power shall be prohibited so that these great reserves of energy may be utilized in building up the Dominion" merely meant that U.S. companies established facilities across the border. Of course, total harmony between the United States and Canada did not prevail. As Samuel Flagg Bemis notes, a whole "murky atmosphere" of grievances simmered within the Dominion— indignation against America's late entry into World War I, against the failure of the United States to accept the League of Nations, against the "greater force of American culture coming from mere power of territory,

---

* In terms of *total* (worldwide) long-term foreign investments (direct and portfolio investments), in 1929–1930, British stakes abroad remained greater than American. In 1930, British foreign investment equaled $18.2 billion, while U.S. private long-term foreign investments (direct and portfolio) have been variously estimated between $14.7 and $15.4 billion. Woodruff, *Impact of Western Man*, pp. 150–151 (for British and two U.S. estimates), and Department of Commerce, Bureau of Foreign and Domestic Commerce, *A New Estimate of American Investments Abroad* (1931), p. 7. Comparisons on the basis of direct investment abroad are not available. However, by 1929–1930, U.S. *direct* foreign investments alone—$7.5–$7.8 billion—exceeded the direct *and* portfolio foreign investments of France, Holland, and Germany combined! Based on data from the Department of Commerce and Woodruff, *Impact of Western Man*, p. 150.

† A Canadian law, passed in March 1920, stated that Dominion lands could be leased only to companies "registered or licensed in Canada, and having their principal place of business within His Majesty's Dominion," but this would not exclude foreign enterprises because no restrictions existed on registration in Canada. Ise, *United States Oil Policy*, p. 459.

natural resources, and infinitely greater population." Canadians felt Americans did not pay sufficient attention to them. The U.S. commercial attaché in Ottawa reported to the Bureau of Foreign and Domestic Commerce in 1927 that "one of the principal functions of the Canadian Trade Commissioners in New York is encouraging certain branch plants in Canada and *to discourage* certain industries which in the opinion of the Canadian Manufacturers' Association (which controls to a large extent the activities of the Canadian Trade Commissioners) would compete with existing factories in the Dominion" (my italics). Frequently Canadians appealed to British capital to offset American influence. A labor member of Parliament might fret about U.S. capital: "I would far sooner have waited a little longer . . . for the development of our resources than see the people of Canada . . . become hewers of wood and drawers of water to American capitalists." But such sentiments were not outstanding. By the end of the 1920s, Canadian newspaper editorials contained assurances that U.S. business did not bring with it the threat of annexation; that old bone of fear and contention was buried, although the notion that economic control would lead inevitably to some kind of political control remained alive.[44]

Whereas in Europe, there had been the revolutionary expropriations (in Russia), nationalization of oil distribution (in Spain), and prohibitions placed on Americans' voting stock in certain corporations (in a number of countries), Canadians took no steps to translate any of their concern into action, except the tepid *words* of discouragement by the trade commissioners. Yet, Canada—of all countries—had the greatest U.S. stakes (see Tables III.1–4 for amounts of U.S. direct investment by country). A. U.S. Senate report, dealing with 1929, concluded "it is difficult to find a major American product that is not manufactured in Canada." More explicitly, according to Canadian government statistics, at the end of 1930, of the $3.9 *billion* employed in the entire manufacturing sector within Canada, 33 per cent was owned by U.S. residents; of the $800 *million* invested in mining, smelting, and petroleum production,* 34 per cent was owned by U.S. residents; and of the $1.7 *billion* invested in utilities (other than railroads), 30 per cent was owned by Americans. Add to these figures the fact that U.S. direct investment was predominant in stra-

---

* In this accounting, investments in petroleum exploration and development by companies that were engaged principally in refining and distributing petroleum products were included as manufacturing.

tegic industries and in the major companies within the economy, and the breadth of the impact is clear.[45] Nonetheless, despite this substantial stake, Canadians were far less agitated than Europeans (where in each individual nation the U.S. impact was far less significant). The marriage of U.S. business and the Canadian economy was secure.

By contrast, U.S. stakes in Latin America more often evoked animosity. Historian Richard Hofstadter, considering the growth of American business *in the United States* from the 1870s onward, wrote,

> The newly rich, the grandiosely or corruptly rich, the masters of great corporations, were bypassing . . . the old gentry, the merchants of long standing, the small manufacturers, the established professional men, the civic leaders of an earlier era . . . In a strictly economic sense these men were not growing poorer as a class but their wealth and power were being dwarfed by comparison with the new eminences of wealth and power. They were less important and they knew it . . . every fortune, every career, every reputation, seemed smaller and less significant because it was measured against the Vanderbilts, Harrimans, Goulds, Carnegies, Rockefellers, and Morgans.[46]

Change the class description and replace the names of the American entrepreneurs with those of large corporations, and this paragraph helps explain the reactions to American business in Europe and Canada, and to a far greater extent the reactions in Latin America, where the contrasts were sharpest. Indeed, in Latin America at the same time as American capital was helping to create a higher standard of living (higher wages and better medical care) and bringing formerly undeveloped resources on to the market, the effect of the American presence in many nations was jarring.[47] U.S. companies were resented for their size, their power (or potential power), their profits (which were assumed to be enormous),* and for their just being alien enterprises.† [48]

---

* The data on profits—especially for the 1920s—are very poor. There were clearly some large profits, but there were also companies that had low returns during the decade.

† The image of one particular company became especially tarnished. Innumerable responsible American businessmen in Latin America told the present author, "At least we have not made the mistakes of United Fruit." Yet, there exists no good history of United Fruit written by an impartial historian *with access to the company's records.* Was the animus that existed toward United Fruit an inevitable consequence of the company's size and position within the host countries, or was it the result of the use or abuse of this size and position? Without company and host-nation records it is impossible to say. United Fruit's attitudes toward politics at different times and in different countries is highly obscure. Reports such as that of Sumner Welles (cited earlier, in Chapter V) offer no substitute for internal records on United Fruit's goals, plans,

No uniform response to U.S. capital existed, however, within Latin America. For example, Mexico meant to control her national destiny by redistributing the land (and nationalizing some foreign holdings), by pressuring investors in mining to employ Mexican professionals and by passing legislation adverse to foreign mining interests, as well as by seeking to muzzle the foreign oil enterprises. Chile made oil production a national monopoly, thus closing off U.S. participation. At the same time, Mexico encouraged U.S. companies to build lead refineries (and thus bring industry to Mexico) and Chile did not discourage U.S. stakes in copper (which would revive this industry). Venezuela opened wide its doors to the U.S. oil concerns, enacting advantageous legislation, while at the close of the 1920s, the president of Costa Rica would praise United Fruit.[49]

Elsewhere around the globe, in independent nations, attitudes toward U.S. investment were equally mixed. By the 1920s, for instance, Australians had developed a strong sense of "Buy Australian." "My Country First—Protect its Industries—Buy its Goods—Be Australian—Buy Australian-Made Goods" was the motto of the Australian Industries Protection League. Tariffs favored import substitution. When Americans jumped the barriers to invest in manufacturing, reports indicate a "less than cordial" attitude toward U.S. investment. Yet no steps were taken to interfere with the investors.[50] In Japan, in the 1920s, U.S. businessmen found their counterparts eager to obtain U.S. technology and thought them to be fine partners; at the same time there was a resentment toward Americans based on the U.S. Exclusion Act of 1924 that barred Japanese immigrants from the United States.[51] As we have noted earlier, Liberia welcomed U.S. investments for political reasons.

5

When Europeans berated or acted adversely toward American investors *in Europe,* sometimes American businesses protested to the Embassy or to Washington. More often they responded directly.[52] They did what U.S. businesses had done in Europe in the past. They disguised their American origins, by using appropriate company designations (the American

---

and activities. Writers that emphasize and applaud the company's contribution do little to explain the rancor that United Fruit generated. Until company records are scrutinized with care, the sharply conflicting points of view must remain unresolved (see note 48).

XYZ Company would, for example, operate under the name of National XYZ Company in England, the Compagnie Nationale XYZ in France). They did not advertise their American parentage; they employed Englishmen, Germans, and Frenchmen at all levels of management as well as using host-nation labor; they sought host-country directors and stockholders. They used local raw materials and encouraged local suppliers. U.S. enterprises that purchased minority, majority, or even 100 per cent interest in long-established foreign businesses acquired their "goodwill" and sought to operate under a "national cloak." When a foreign firm was purchased, the U.S. buyer generally obtained a national product line and trade names, access to national marketing channels, national management and labor, as well as national political contacts. By the end of the 1920s, some American firms were introducing distinctive products for the European market and many modified their goods to meet "foreign" tastes. In short, the more sophisticated corporations became well aware that a major compromise with nationalism was a prerequisite for doing successful business in Europe. In general, they did not respond by curbing investment.[53]

By contrast, when Europeans tried to close India, the Dutch East Indies, or the Middle East to U.S. investors, the latter complained strongly to the U.S. State Department and obtained diplomatic support. As noted, the State Department came to the assistance of American business by urging an "open door" to U.S. interests. Here, too, Americans tried to expand rather than let the Europeans limit U.S. investments.[54]

In Canada, where investors met little opposition, Americans felt no need to modify their procedures in a significant fashion,* nor did they feel any requirement to go to Washington for aid. Even though in the 1920s Canada had the largest U.S. direct investment of any single country, the U.S. Department of State virtually never got involved on matters dealing with this investment. Books on U.S. diplomacy during the 1920s do not mention problems with Canada relating to U.S. investments there; such problems were not important enough to record. Studies on international business in the 1920s from the vantage point of Washington find nothing to say about Canada.[55]

Just as in Canada American business acted as it would in the United

* The one exception this author has discovered was the largest U.S. business in Canada, Imperial Oil, which tried to take on a Canadian appearance and disguise its U.S. parentage.

States, so, too, in Latin America, U.S. companies sought to do the same. Where host country laws or decrees or even political unrest obstructed the companies in Latin America, their managers sometimes protested to the U.S. State Department, which heard their complaints with sympathy and tried to help them solve their problems. Most large U.S. enterprises, however, managed to deal with their everyday problems themselves. Faced with difficulties in Mexico in the mid-1920s, American Smelting and Refining Company (ASARCO) appointed a vice president of "public relations, safety and welfare, labor and personnel problems," William Loeb. When queried in 1928 on how his company managed "to get along" so well with Mexican authorities, Loeb explained,

> We never knowingly break a Mexican law; we never touch a mining property to which the title is not perfectly sound; it is not our policy to defy or ignore public officials, no matter who they are. We may try to, and frequently do, persuade them that they are taking the wrong position. Sometimes we accept things that we feel to be unjust but we are operating in Mexico under Mexican laws, and in the long run we have found it best to do everything in reason to keep on good terms with the Mexican people. Virtually all of our responsible officials are able to talk easily with the Mexicans in their own language, and this has been a big help. Many disputes can be avoided if men can get together and talk matters over at the outset.

The item about "all of our responsible officials" being able to speak Spanish may have been an exaggeration, but the tenor of Loeb's remarks is accurate. This statement, which would be a common comment of the 1950s and 1960s, was an enlightened one for the 1920s.[56] On other occasions ASARCO, concerned about Mexican legislation, did call on diplomatic assistance from Washington.[57] Sometimes the State Department offered aid to U.S. companies that rejected the offer. Thus, faced with a higher tax in Chile, the principal U.S. copper enterprises in that country made their own presentations to the government in Santiago. They kept the U.S. embassy informed but did not want the ambassador to take up the matter with the Chilean government, "even informally."[58]

Elsewhere in the world, when U.S. manufacturers made market-oriented investments, they usually managed without much help from the State Department. In Australia, U.S. firms frequently sought to take on a national guise—to have the " 'man on the street' . . . consider them entirely an Australian organization," a way of coping with Australian nationalism.[59] Similarly, a number of American manufacturers in Japan took on a Japanese veneer, working with large Japanese enterprises (*zaibatus*).[60] On the other hand, State Department files bulged with unadjudicated claims of losses through looting incurred by Standard Oil of New York in China in the 1920s. The State Department was not able to obtain compensation for the company.[61]

In general, it seems clear that oil companies, mining enterprises, agricultural concerns, and utilities requested and obtained far more assistance from the U.S. government in connection with their business abroad in the 1920s than did market-oriented manufacturing firms. The reasons are not hard to find. When market-seeking manufacturers went abroad—in the 1920s—they invested first in the more industrialized nations and only subsequently and on a smaller scale in less developed countries. Standard Oil of New York's large interest in oil marketing in China was exceptional among the market-oriented investors (note, too, that U.S. stakes in oil distribution were greater in Canada and in Australia, more developed countries, than in China). Often when U.S. companies went to search for raw materials and to operate utilities, they made giant investments in less developed countries. In industrial parts of the world, in the main, U.S. enterprises needed little help from the U.S. government. By contrast, in less developed countries, when they vied with European enterprises, negotiated with foreign (host and colonial) governments, and faced disorder, they more frequently called upon and received assistance from Washington. Because raw material and utilities stakes were most often in less developed countries, problems of government relations were complex.* In developed nations, U.S. companies faced industrial systems not dissimilar to what they knew at home. In less developed countries, laws and attitudes had to be changed to make such areas amenable to capitalist enterprise. In addition, the views of the U.S. government toward U.S. stakes abroad, as described in Chapter III, meant that investors in market-oriented industrial plants would receive less support than those investing in foreign raw materials or utilities. In sum, U.S. multinational enterprises responded in various manners when they encountered

---

* Former Secretary of Defense Robert S. McNamara has made the point that underdeveloped countries have a much higher rate of political conflict and disorder than industrial countries (see *New York Times*, May 19, 1966). This proved true in the 1920s as well as the 1960s and helps explain why the U.S. government had a more prominent role in relation to American investment in less developed countries.

opposition abroad, adapting to foreign conditions and/or calling on the State Department for aid in entry and operations.

6

By 1929 U.S. multinational business was extensive and already quite complex. [62] There existed in 1929 among most U.S. corporations that had direct foreign investments and those that contemplated new ones an enthusiasm about opportunities beyond the American frontiers. European monopolies could be broken. European barriers to investment could be downed. From Canada to Latin America, U.S. investors ranked supreme. In 1929 the book value of U.S. direct investment abroad equaled slightly more than 7 per cent of the 1929 U.S. gross national product.[63] This percentage was to be sure the same as the 1914 U.S. direct investment abroad percentage of G.N.P.[64] American enterprise had gone abroad as the U.S. economy expanded. American business abroad had kept pace with the great growth of U.S. business at home.

Three

The Era of Depression

The 1930s were depression years, but when the stock market break of October 1929 occurred, when the decline in stock values followed, few Americans forecast the future correctly. Indeed, in 1929–1930 certain enterprises in manufacturing, mining, and utilities with direct investments outside the United States found their plans had a momentum that the Wall Street Crash did not at once impede.*

Based on earlier commitments, in 1930 General Electric, for example, made substantial investments in Europe, while Goodyear, Firestone, and Parke, Davis erected factories in Argentina. Yet, on the whole, U.S. manufacturers limited their foreign spending, especially in the second half of 1930. In 1930, U.S. companies started 71 new foreign plants, compared with 132 in the preceding year. American manufacturers that had accumulated surpluses abroad brought them home to aid their domestic enterprises.[1]

Mining companies likewise made some new investments in 1930. American Metal Company Ltd., as we have seen, had been seeking to enlarge its stakes in Northern Rhodesia. Rhodesian Selection Trust, in which American Metal Company had an interest, had planned a stock offering for November 1929; the Crash made this impossible. American Metal Company, Lehman Corporation, and the British house, Messrs. Cull & Company advanced £1,500,000 for the development and equipment of Rhodesian Selection Trust's mines at Mufulira, Chambishi, Baluba, and Roan; the largest contribution came from American Metal Company. The British were glad to have the funds, but as Sir Auckland

* Joseph Schumpeter has pointed out that in the United States as well until about the end of June 1930, "business moved along on a but slowly falling level not much below the figures of 1929 in practically all lines." *Business Cycles,* p. 911.

Geddes of Rothschild interests put it, "I am far from taking up an anti-American attitude; on the contrary, I am in favour of American participation in these great enterprises as I am of French and Dutch and German and any other national participation, but I don't think anyone . . . wants to see the whole Northern Rhodesian copper-field in the hands of the American copper companies." Such by now familiar laments notwithstanding, American Metal enlarged its stakes.[2] Similarly, in 1930, elaborating on discussions initiated in the 1920s, American Smelting and Refining Company (ASARCO) expanded for the first time into mining in Australia.* In 1930, Britisher Leslie Urquhart's Mining Trust Ltd. was in financial difficulty; ASARCO could buy a substantial interest in the Australian Mount Isa lead and silver mines—at a bargain price. The Mining Trust's constitution prohibited foreign control; when the stockholders deleted the restrictive clause, ASARCO purchased control of the Mining Trust Ltd. and obtained through it the Australian holdings. Once again British fears of American domination took second place, as the British required American capital.[3] That same year, the U.S.-controlled Hudson Bay Mining and Smelting Company (in which Newmont Mining Corporation played a significant role) started mining in Manitoba, Canada. And so it went. Depression conditions notwithstanding, in 1930 American mining companies continued to invest abroad.

Likewise, it was impossible to abort the momentum of the vast spending programs of the public utilities. American & Foreign Power Company in 1930 acquired important new properties in Brazil, Argentina, Chile, Mexico, and Venezuela, while at home it stopped paying dividends on its common stock. In 1930 International Telephone and Telegraph Corporation obtained controlling interest in the Peruvian telephone system, a concession to operate Chilean telephones, a similar contract from the Rumanian government, a stake in the Constantinople Telephone Company, and a franchise for the telephone system in the International Settlement in Shanghai! For the first time, in 1930, the Insull Group, the Utilities Power & Light Corporation, and Iowa Southern Utilities Company invested in Canada. Pan American Airways also extended its operations in Latin America. To handle its foreign business more efficiently (and apparently with no regard to the depression), Chase National Bank

* In 1928 ASARCO's president, Simon Guggenheim, had talked with Britisher Leslie Urquhart about the possibilities of financing Urquhart's prewar *Russian* mines should they be returned; Urquhart remembered these discussions in 1930 when he wanted financing for his *Australian* business.

in May 1930 organized a wholly owned subsidiary, Chase Bank—an Edge
Act corporation. After Chase and Equitable Trust merged that year, the
Chase Bank acquired Equitable Trust Co.'s Paris office and Equitable
Eastern's offices in Shanghai, Tientsin, and Hong Kong.[4]

This momentum in direct foreign investment and plans for more foreign business occurred even though the depression was spreading
abroad * and despite revolutions in 1930 in Argentina, Bolivia, Brazil,
and Peru that hardly offered an environment conducive to doing
"business-as-usual." [5]

2

In June 1930 the U.S. Congress, seeking to protect domestic industry,
passed the Smoot-Hawley bill, which imposed high duties on imports.
The measure failed to aid American business. During 1931 and 1932 the
depression at home worsened; manufacturing output in the United States
fell 48 per cent between 1929 and 1932.[6] Most American corporations
turned to cope with domestic adversity.

The Smoot-Hawley tariff did, however, provoke European nations and
Canada to retaliate; each foreign country sought to protect its own economy.[7] Protection seemed of great importance abroad, as poor economic
conditions continued to spread worldwide. The largest commercial bank
in Austria—Kreditanstalt—went bankrupt in May 1931. By June 1931
the German financial situation was so precarious that President Herbert
Hoover declared a moratorium on German war debts and reparations.
Britain, deprived of expected reparations and other revenues, on September 21st left the gold standard. Other nations followed, like dominoes, so
that by April 1932, forty-one countries had either abandoned the gold
standard or had made it inoperative (the United States stayed on the
gold standard). With rising tariffs and declining demand, world trade
shrunk. Measured in gold dollars, by 1932 international trade had fallen
nearly 60 per cent compared with 1929. While the economic deterioration in foreign nations was generally not as devastating as in the United
States, it was still significant.† Especially after 1932, to assist indigenous

---

* The depression spread abroad to different countries at various rates, but by mid-
1930 most of the world was beginning to feel its chilling winds. See League of Nations,
Industrialization and Foreign Trade, pp. 134, 135.

† From 1929 to 1932, manufacturing output in Germany dropped 47 per cent, in
Canada 40 per cent, in France 26 per cent, in the United Kingdom 18 per cent, and in
Japan 4 per cent, compared with the U.S. decline of 48 per cent. Based on League of
Nations, *Industrialization and Foreign Trade*, pp. 134–135.

industries, foreign protectionist tariffs came increasingly to incorporate empire preference provisions—arrangements for "bloc trading." The United States found itself ever more excluded.[8]

Global political conditions reflected the universal disequilibria. In 1931 Japan attacked and occupied Manchuria; the world community proved impotent to curb the aggression. That year a new epidemic of revolutions swept over Latin America, touching Peru, Venezuela, Chile, Ecuador, and Paraguay. In 1931 and 1932, in Germany, confidence in the political system evaporated.[9]

In such a decaying economic and political milieu, American business abroad could not prosper. The dollar value of the properties of U.S. enterprises dropped as foreign currencies were devalued. Nations imposed exchange controls: * U.S. companies that received their revenues in host-country currencies found foreign governments would not let them remit their profits. One company's *Annual Report* for 1932 read: "The expression 'funds held in foreign countries' can be taken literally, since a number of such countries have placed embargoes on exchange movements which prevent in whole or part the conversion of moneys accumulated in such countries into other currencies." [10]

Considering the difficulties of American manufacturing companies abroad, by 1932 financial journals in the United States were advising stockholders *not* to invest in businesses with large stakes in foreign factories. *Financial World* compared American Chicle and W. R. Wrigley and noted in November 1932 that the first had followed a conservative course abroad, while the second had been progressive. "Depreciating currencies, uncertain foreign exchange, and new tariff barriers therefore proved to be the greater burden to Wrigley than to American Chicle." [11] Eastman Kodak's *Annual Report of 1932* spelled out its distress: "the total volume of business of all operating companies declined about 20% . . . In normal times, the fact that the activities of your company are extended over a great many countries would be a feature of strength, as unfavorable

---

* Iran and Turkey were the first to put on exchange controls in 1930; this had little effect on American business, since U.S. companies only had small interests in these nations. More important, in 1931, Brazil, Spain, Germany, Hungary, Chile, Colombia, Argentina, and Nicaragua in that order introduced exchange controls, and the effect on U.S. business became more significant. Data in Accession 507, Box 37, Ford Motor Company Archives and in Donald Bailey Marsh, *World Trade and Investment*, p. 79n. In the autumn of 1931, Greece, Italy, Yugoslavia, Austria, Czechoslovakia, and Denmark also imposed exchange controls. International Monetary Fund, *Annual Report on Exchange Restrictions-1950*, pp. 65–86.

conditions in one country are frequently offset by prosperous conditions in another. As the present depression is world-wide, this advantage does not now exist." [12]

In 1931 and 1932 some American companies with plans for foreign plants canceled such projects. Some U.S.-owned foreign facilities stopped operations. Certain U.S. subsidiaries and affiliates abroad changed nationality, that is, the American parent sold them to Australians, Englishmen, or Canadians.[13] An American trade commissioner in Canada told a Department of Commerce official late in 1931, "it was his impression that in 75 per cent of the instances where American factories had opened branches * in Canada management would now greatly prefer to end the whole thing if that were but possible." The Department of Commerce official added, "Unfortunately, it is not possible." [14] U.S. Steel, for example, found that with "bloc" trading, Canadians bought British steel; the American firm's plants in Canada were not competitive, and in 1932 they apparently ceased functioning.[15] To the south, Brunswick-Balke-Callender withdrew from manufacturing phonograph records in Argentina in 1933.[16] In Brazil, Ford Motor Company discontinued assembly at Rio, Pôrto Alegre, and Recife, although it retained its assembly operations at its main Brazilian plant in São Paulo.[17] The British Woolworth Company—once 100 per cent controlled from the United States—was reorganized in 1931 as a public company, and it sold 48 per cent of its stock in England.[18] So, too, Electric and Musical Industries, Ltd., incorporated in Britain, acquired on April 30, 1931, Gramophone Company, Ltd.† (previously 50 per cent owned by R.C.A.'s subsidiary Victor Talking Machine) and Columbia Graphophone Co. Ltd. (a British enterprise); Victor Talking Machine obtained 29.2 per cent of the stock in the new Electric and Musical Industries—holdings that it would sell in the fall of 1935 for $10.2 million in cash.[19] Drug Inc. began in early 1933 negotiations to sell its entire stake in Boots Pure Drug Company, Ltd.[20] And so it went.[21] The withdrawals from England were not so much because of the severity of the depression there; rather they were a consequence of the depth of the depression in the United States; funds were needed at home.

* The word "branches" was used loosely to include subsidiaries and affiliates.

† Gramophone Co. Ltd. had exclusive rights to manufacture and distribute Victor products in Great Britain and other European markets. In 1930 it had plants in England, France, Spain, Czechoslovakia, Germany, Italy, and Australia.

Paradoxically, however, the crisis years of 1931 and 1932 brought a duality of reactions. At the same time as many U.S. enterprises curtailed and retreated from business abroad, some manufacturers felt compelled to expand. This was not the expansion by momentum of 1930, nor the seeking of depression bargains, rather the new investments were a response to actions of host governments. In the United Kingdom, for example, the new higher tariffs in 1932 meant for many American companies that they either manufactured in Britain or relinquished the market. With imperial preference, it often seemed to American managers wise to *expand* in England to supply areas that once had been served by U.S. exports. Throughout the European continent, the story was repeated. So high had tariffs risen that American businesses were literally forced to add to their investments and to move behind the customs walls. The alternative was to abandon the markets. Exports were no longer competitive. Across America's northern border, the Bennett tariffs of 1930–1931, the Ottawa Agreements of 1932 (giving English goods a substantial advantage over U.S. products in Canada), together with the exchange situation meant American companies could not maintain exports to the Dominion. Many that had exported in times past now moved into manufacturing in Canada. So, too, in Australia, rising tariffs prompted new U.S. stakes. In Japan, as a result of trade restrictions and the Japanese government insistence on industrialization, Americans invested. In sum, the restraints on commerce accompanied by other host government policies aiming at autarchy and industrialization forced U.S. enterprises into new investments that they would not otherwise have made. Whereas, as noted, in 1930 American manufacturers opened 71 new foreign factories, in 1931, as the depression deepened, they established 92 such plants, and in the first four months of 1932 alone, 94 such factories, 87 of which were in Canada. This upturn in new U.S.-owned foreign factories proved temporary; many ventures failed, because of the depressed conditions.* 22

As for U.S. corporations in mining and agriculture, in general they reduced foreign investments in 1931 and 1932. In times of depression, in-

* Compare these figures with 98 new foreign factories in 1928 and 132 new ones in 1929. Based on data collected at the start of 1930, Dept. of Comm., Bureau of Foreign and Domestic Commerce, *American Direct Investments in Foreign Countries-1936*, pp. 47–49. The number of foreign "branch" plants established during all of 1932 and *still in existence in 1936* was only 78—a figure that represents roughly 83 per cent of those established in the first four months of 1932. *Ibid.*, p. 30, and Louis Domeratzky to Rep. John L. Cable, July 18, 1932, RG 151, 623:Br. Factories, National Archives.

vestments in raw materials proved a liability. Companies with direct foreign investments in copper, nitrates, tin, bananas, rubber, and sugar typically recorded losses. Often, it was difficult for such enterprises, located in isolated areas, to cut back. All during 1931, Anaconda, for example, maintained its Chilean mines with men "capable of resuming operations whenever conditions warranted so doing." But by the spring of 1932, with copper prices still descending, Anaconda altered its policy, dismissed much of its staff in Chile, and lowered drastically salaries and wages.[23]

In Northern Rhodesia in 1931 the Bwana M'Kubwa mine, in which American Metal Company had made its first African investment, shut down permanently; at Mufulira, a concentrating plant (completed that December) was not started up and mining was suspended. In fact, of all the mines in the Rhodesian Selection Trust group, only the one at Roan remained in operation. Nonetheless, during 1931 and 1932 American Metal Company provided the desperately required funds to bail out the Rhodesian Selection Trust and finally obtained majority control of this important unit. To finance this activity, American Metal sold 32,000 of its 42,000 shares in the Ontario Refining Company in Canada.[24]

American and foreign copper producers cooperated to stem the price decline, but without success. When in 1932 the United States imposed a 4 cent import tax on copper, Anaconda and Kennecott rerouted their Chilean and Mexican output to Europe; they used their foreign sales organizations that had once handled their U.S. exports to market the foreign U.S.-owned copper. Companies, such as Cerro de Pasco in Peru, which had also sold their production in the United States, switched to selling in Europe. American Metal Company's Northern Rhodesian copper went to Europe. Since it was not economical to export copper from British Columbia across the Atlantic, U.S. mining concerns there cut output drastically. Other American-controlled copper companies in Canada sold mainly in Europe.* In short, the strategies of U.S. copper enterprises abroad were altered to meet changing circumstances. The increased competition from U.S.-owned foreign copper in Europe further depressed prices.[25]

American investors in foreign nitrates found themselves in deep trouble. Faced with competition from synthetics, in 1927 nitrate prices had al-

---

* International Nickel, Noranda Mines, and Hudson Bay Mining and Smelting Company were the principal ones.

ready started to drop; by 1930 prices were so low that Chilean nitrate producers (including the Guggenheims) and the Chilean government made a partnership agreement, which involved: (1) the merger of all existing nitrate enterprises in Chile into a single company (the inefficient small producers would shut down); (2) the formation of COSACH—Compañía de Salitre de Chile—to include all nitrate producers and to assume their assets and liabilities (COSACH would be owned 50 per cent by the Chilean government and 50 per cent by the private companies); (3) the abolition of the export tax on nitrates; and (4) the Chilean government contribution to COSACH of land with 150 million tons of nitrates. On July 21, 1930, the new "mixed" enterprise was approved by the Chilean Congress by a large majority. COSACH was no arbitrary imposition on the industry; E. A. Cappelen Smith and S. W. Howland, both representing Guggenheim interests, had cooperated with the government in formulating the plan. While by no means the first joint venture between private American business and a government in a less developed country, COSACH was an early example of such.*

In the early 1930s, nitrate prices continued to tumble; arrangements to finance COSACH floundered and not until March 20, 1931 did the company come into existence. Thirty-five nitrate firms, representing 98 per cent of Chilean output, were merged into the new unit; E. A. Cappelen Smith was chairman of the board. The depression deepened. Chilean governments came and fell. In 1932, as copper replaced nitrates as Chile's major export (a dramatic change from recent times past), COSACH became the scapegoat for Chile's ills. When on January 1, 1933, Arturo Alessandri became president of Chile, his first act (January 2) was to order the dissolution of the mixed enterprise. At this point, the Guggenheim Bros.' records indicate their firm had a direct cash investment of $48,725,657 and indirect investments of $98,500,000 in COSACH. The news of the dissolution came as a "bombshell" to the American firm.[26] More on what happened when we turn to the U.S. mining companies in the years 1933–1939.

---

* Standard Oil of New York had entered into a joint venture with the Chinese Government (1914–1916); Western Electric had a joint venture in China, which included the Ministry of Communications. To this author's knowledge, this was the first such venture in Latin America. Former Argentine president Arturo Frondizi indicates that Argentines knew about the British government and private investors' role in Anglo-Persian Oil Company and had ideas in the 1920s about a "mixed" company that would involve the Argentine government and foreign investors; the plan never materialized, *Petróles y Política*, p. 155.

Meanwhile, the Guggenheims' stakes in tin were proving more profitable. The reader will recall that when the Guggenheims invested in Malayan tin in the 1920s, they had agreed to output controls imposed by the Malayan government. In 1931 a new comprehensive International Control Scheme included the Malayan, Nigerian, Bolivian, and Dutch governments. Its restrictions were effective, and the dollar price of tin actually moved upward.[27]

In other metals that Americans had foreign investments in, there were international agreements to raise prices.* Most were not successful.[28] Indeed, in the early 1930s, U.S. investors in mining properties felt the ugly hand of depression; practically all survived, but generally only after suffering losses.

Americans with foreign agricultural properties were in a similar predicament. They, too, saw prices of their products plummet. United Fruit in 1932 revalued its assets and reduced by almost $51 million the net book value of its property accounts; in addition, it wrote off another $3 million book value of other assets.[29] The large sugar producers in Cuba recorded losses. The Smoot-Hawley Act had raised the U.S. tariff on Cuban sugar. Domestic and insular sugar cut into the U.S. market for Cuban output. The 1931 international accord to restrict sugar production (made by producers associations in Cuba, Java, and the main European exporting nations) failed to stanch the drop in sugar prices or to increase demand.† Accordingly, U.S. sugar planters in Cuba and also elsewhere in the Caribbean revalued their holdings downward.[30] As the price of crude rubber sunk to 3 cents a pound in June 1932, U.S. Rubber, Goodyear, Firestone, and Ford curtailed their rubber-growing activities.[31]

Processors of agricultural products, likewise, had a dismal outlook. While the U.S. meat packers abroad found they could purchase meat cheaply, they in turn obtained low prices for their output. The Argentine government intervened in its national industry to raise meat exports, to obtain more foreign exchange for the country, and to provide larger returns to Argentine cattle owners. That government required packers to purchase and to sell foreign exchange through the local exchange control board; since the official rates were lower than the free market rates, the

* Some involved private businesses; some included governments.
† It included only 45 per cent of the producers and was therefore ineffective in raising prices. Smith, *The United States and Cuba*, p. 70.

The Era of Depression

packers were penalized. U.S. meat packers had their largest foreign investments in Argentina.[32]

U.S. investors in paper and pulp in Canada lost money; some went into receivership.* Yet, in general, they fared better than their Canadian counterparts because many had long-term contracts with newspapers in the United States. In 1933, American-owned mills in Canada actually produced a larger *percentage* of the Canadian newsprint output than in 1929.[33]

The momentum that had characterized the expansion of the American & Foreign Power Company and the International Telephone and Telegraph Corporation in 1930 was dissipated in 1931 and 1932; these enterprises did make foreign investments but primarily to maintain existing rather than to acquire new properties. American & Foreign Power Company paid no dividends on common stock from 1930 through 1932 and that year stopped paying dividends on preferred stock.[34] I.T.T. revalued its assets because of changes in world conditions; in 1932 it wrote off $35.8 million.[35] Both American & Foreign Power Company and International Telephone and Telegraph Corporation received their revenues in depreciated foreign currencies—and with remittances often blocked, they suffered severely. Nonetheless, both survived. Others fell by the wayside: Intercontinents Power Company (incorporated in 1928) stopped paying dividends and interest on its debentures in 1931; by 1934, it was bankrupt. It explained that the reason lay in the sharp decline in the values of currencies of Argentina and Brazil and the prohibitions on the transfer of funds from Chile. The collapse of the Insull empire in the United States in 1932 carried with it the Insull stake in Canada.[36] Thus, the eddies of the depression reached out to engulf American public utilities abroad. An exception was Pan American Airways, which supported by U.S. government mail subsidies, enlarged its business in Latin America.[37]

In sum, while certain U.S. companies made new investments in factories to sell in foreign markets, while some foreign stakes continued in every sector to maintain existing operations, while Pan Am actually expanded abroad, the general pattern for 1931–1932 involved retrenchment and retreat. In fact, in 1932, the net outflow for U.S. direct investment— although still an outflow—was lower than in any previous year in recorded history.† [38]

* For example, in 1931, Minneapolis and Ontario Paper and Great Lakes Paper companies went into receiverships. Marshall et al., *Canadian-American Industry*, pp. 44–45.

† The reconstructed statistics on direct investment flows go back to 1900. See *Historical Statistics of the United States*, p. 564.

3

Between 1933 and 1937, business conditions in the United States improved, and then in 1938 there was a setback. The recovery of 1933 and 1937 had not been wholly satisfactory, and the downturn of 1938 shook confidence. In these years, with the fight against depression the U.S. government assumed a larger role in the national economy than ever before in peacetime.

On March 5, 1933, the *New York Times* had reported the inaugural address of the president of the United States, Franklin Delano Roosevelt. It also reported on the same front page—and rather incredulously—the rise to power in Germany of Adolf Hitler. The juxtaposition of the two events sets the stage for the rest of the decade. Roosevelt was not in 1933 concerned with the ominous rumblings in Germany. His challenge lay in the domestic economic crisis. As for "our international trade relations," the new president declared, "though vastly important . . . in point of time and necessity," they were "secondary to the establishment of a sound economy." [39]

Roosevelt acted promptly and boldly to deal with the economic crisis at home. And during 1933 and 1934, his administration also took steps that directly affected U.S. business abroad—measures, for example, that would aid U.S. exports (including devaluation of the dollar in 1933, the Reciprocal Trade Agreements Act of 1934, and the establishment in 1934 of two Export-Import banks).* The administration also came out in favor of international commodity agreements to raise the price of wheat, copper, and cotton. [40]

With the devaluation of the dollar, automatically the value of U.S. properties abroad in relation to the dollar rose (but this was only a temporary increase, for other countries followed by devaluing and the "value" of American properties abroad in terms of the dollar dropped accordingly). Actions to spur U.S. exports met the approval of American international businesses, which desired a revival of world commerce.† The Second Export-Import Bank lent money to Cuba to help stabilize the situation there, which aided U.S. sugar interests on the island. The administration's support of commodity agreements also got the endorsement of U.S. enterprises with business abroad. [41]

* Later combined into one.
† Although there was by no means consensus of business opinion that the devaluation of the dollar was a proper way of encouraging exports.

Before the end of 1934, the U.S. government had taken three measures that specifically benefited Cuban raw sugar in the American market: (1) passed the Jones-Costigan Act of May 9, 1934, designed to raise sugar prices and to give the U.S. secretary of agriculture the right to set quotas on the importation of Cuban and other sugar, (2) lowered the U.S. duty on Cuban raw sugar (by presidential proclamation May 9, 1934), and (3) entered into the reciprocal trade agreement of August 24, 1934, between the United States and Cuba, further reducing the tariff on Cuban raw sugar to the lowest rate in the twentieth century to that date. American sugar producers in Cuba believed that without the quotas (imposed under the Jones-Costigan Act and continued when the Jones-Costigan Act was replaced by the Sugar Act of 1937), Cuba's share of the market would have been considerably smaller.* [42]

During the rest of the decade, as Washington sought recovery and reform at home, the administration also acted on behalf of international businesses in aiding their acquisition of import quotas from foreign countries, in helping them obtain dollar exchange from nations abroad and in seeking to eliminate discrimination—including discriminatory taxation (that is, taxation applied to U.S. firms but not to locally financed enterprises in foreign countries). Secretary Cordell Hull saw the State Department's role in relation to U.S. business abroad as one of establishing contacts, providing information, and making judicious suggestions. The Export-Import Bank took steps to free blocked currency for certain American companies—especially in Brazil. U.S. businessmen desired this assistance and appreciated the aid.[43]

At the same time, other actions of the Roosevelt administration were viewed by those engaged in international business "with a mixture of pleasure and alarm." [44] The Good Neighbor Policy, introduced in the new president's inaugural address, meant that when Latin American countries acted to the detriment of U.S. enterprise, the United States no longer held a "big stick." In 1934, the United States and Cuba by mutual consent abrogated the 1901 Platt Amendment that had sanctioned U.S.

* Robert F. Smith, in the *United States and Cuba*, pp. 142–143, indicates that from the start, the Roosevelt administration was sympathetic to U.S. investors in Cuba. Roosevelt's secretaries of treasury (William Woodin), commerce (Daniel Roper), and state (Cordell Hull) had each acted on behalf of U.S. investors in Cuba *before* they joined the cabinet. Their efforts had been primarily to get lower tariffs for Cuban sugar. Likewise, members of Roosevelt's brain trust had connections with U.S. investors in Cuba.

intervention in Cuba to preserve independence and to maintain a government to protect life, property, and individual liberty. The United States had not intervened with troops in some years in Cuba, and U.S. investors did not object to the termination of this amendment that so alienated the Cubans. Yet, as the historian Samuel Flagg Bemis later explained, the general outcome of U.S. policies in Latin America was that "diplomatic expostulations [by the United States] became increasingly ineffective after 1933"; they seemed contrary to the Good Neighbor Policy.[45] In an address to the National Foreign Trade Convention in 1941, Curtis E. Calder, president of American & Foreign Power Company, concluded,

> Those of us who look after investments there [in Latin America] have felt that we have had a cross to bear in the underlying hostility arising from the political acts of our Government in years gone by ["gun boat diplomacy"], and we have been pleased with the fundamental change for the better which has been the result of President Roosevelt's policy. Our alarm, on the other hand, has been due to a strange misunderstanding which has crept into the situation in some countries, where there seems to be a feeling that the change in our national policy means that our country has gone soft and that we and our investments are fair prey for any leader who can trump up some sort of excuse to abuse us, however flimsy.[46]

The continuation of the Open Door Policy in China met the approval of most Americans with business interests there, but some felt this policy jeopardized rather than assisted their foreign operations. Thus, in March 1939, Guy Holman, assistant vice president of the National City Bank—which had branches in China *and Japan*—told State Department officers that "vigorous official efforts in defense of foreign—'open door'—interests in China should be suspended and opposing the Japanese should be avoided." National City Bank could conduct business in a China under Japanese control.[47]

New Deal measures that truly disturbed Americans in international business included: (1) the Tennessee Valley Authority (1933), which indicated that "capitalist" United States was prepared to accept public ownership of hydroelectric power and offered an example to other countries; (2) Section 7A of the National Industrial Recovery Act (1933) and the Wagner Act (1935), which gave a mandate to labor at home and inspired labor movements abroad; and (3) from 1938 the strong antimonopoly program of the Roosevelt administration, which put certain multinational businesses on the defensive. Indeed, as New Deal policy evolved, the administration became ever more hostile to "big business." [48]

Perilous conditions for international enterprises in the years 1933 to 1939 were created by foreign governments' responses to the depression and by their nationalistic actions—including numerous import restraints (tariffs, exchange controls, quotas, and sometimes embargoes), restrictions on profit remittances, bars on capital repatriation, extensive state intervention, higher taxes, state companies that competed with private enterprise, and nationalization. Such measures naturally made American businessmen more than ever desirous of support from their own government at the same time as the New Deal administration was reluctant to offer substantial assistance. Thus, no warship was sent to Liberia when that nation defaulted on its obligations to Firestone—Harvey Firestone's requests notwithstanding. Roosevelt's reaction was, "at all times we should remember that Firestone went into Liberia at his own financial risk and it is not the business of the State Department to pull his financial chestnuts out of the fire except as a friend of the Liberian people." Likewise, often a company requesting aid would hear from the Department of State that the "claimant [should] exhaust all means of redress either in the courts of the state complained of or by other means" before the department would take action. Business sentiment is rarely uniform, yet when at the 1940 National Foreign Trade Convention businessmen commented on the U.S. government policy toward their enterprises abroad, many forgot or minimized the aid given and found their government had "done little, if anything [in the 1930s] to encourage and protect direct American investments in foreign countries." * [49]

4

Fascism in Italy, nazism in Germany, militarism in Japan, the civil war in Spain, the fall of Ethiopia to Italian aggression, and Japanese

---

* While the Roosevelt era marked the end to "dollar diplomacy," there is considerable evidence that the Hoover administration was already moving in that direction. In 1929, the Department of State had published the so-called Clark Memorandum, indicating that the United States would no longer use the big stick to make American republics act responsibly toward U.S. citizens. Hoover's secretary of state, Henry L. Stimson, in 1931 had refused to send more Marines to Nicaragua to protect U.S. citizens and in January 1933 removed the last of the Marines that were there. Bemis, *A Diplomatic History of the United States,* p. 538. Likewise, although the United States did break off diplomatic relations with Liberia in 1930, Stimson was as unprepared as Roosevelt to send warships there at Firestone's bidding. *Foreign Relations of the United States, 1933,* II, 886, 925.

actions in China created a world of uncertainty. Depreciating currencies adversely affected U.S. enterprises abroad, especially in Latin America and Asia. Table VIII.1, providing selected exchange rates for Argentina, Brazil, and Chile, reveals some of the problems. Similarly, the Chinese dollar, worth 42 cents in America money in 1929, could command only 6 cents a decade later. As noted, blocked funds often enhanced the difficulties business encountered with currency depreciations. Along with the political and economic adversities, in many nations there emerged organized labor (often backed by governments), strikes, and new social

Table VIII.1. Selected exchange rates in Argentina, Brazil, Chile [1] (in U.S. dollars)

	Argentine paper peso	Brazilian milreis	Chilean peso
1929	$.419	$.118	$.121
1932	.257	.071	.079
1936	.327	.059	.040
1940	.236	.048	.032

Source: Dudley Maynard Phelps, *Migration of Industry to South America* (New York 1936), p. 330 (1929 and 1932 rates); U.S. Department of Commerce, Bureau of Foreign and Domestic Commerce, *American Direct Investment in Foreign Countries—1940* (Washington, D.C. 1942), pp. 42–43 (1936, 1940 values).
[1] 1929 and 1932 rates are average. 1936 and 1940 rates are December rates.

legislation all of which deterred U.S. investors. For the first time in recorded U.S. history (the reconstructed records go back to 1900), in 1933 statistics on *direct* investment indicated a net *inflow*.* From 1933 to 1940, there continued to be a net *inflow* of U.S. direct investments.† [50] By 1940, the book value of U.S. direct foreign investments was lower than in 1929 (see Table VIII.2).

The detailed figures on Table VIII.2 are to be used with great caution, for the table is most unsatisfactory. For 1929 it includes Cleona Lewis's figures (as indicated in Table III.1 above) and one of several sets of U.S. Department of Commerce figures for 1929 (in parenthesis).‡

---

* This can in part be attributed to the devaluation of the dollar in 1933.
† Not in 1934 or 1936, but the net for the eight years showed an inflow.
‡ The Department of Commerce several times revised the 1929 figures.

Table VIII.2. U.S. direct foreign investments—estimates, 1929, 1940 (book value in million U.S. dollars)

Country or region	(1) Total[1]		(2) Manufacturing		(3) Sales[2]		(4) Petroleum[3]		(5) Mining[4]		(6) Agriculture		(7) Utilities[5]	
	1929	1940	1929	1940	1929	1940	1929	1940	1929	1940	1929	1940	1929	1940
Europe	1340 (1353)	1420	637	639	133	245	239	306	37	53	—	—	138	74
Canada and Newfoundland	1657 (2010)	2103	820[6]	943[6]	38	112	55	120	318	187	30	10	318	407
Mexico	709 (682)	357	6	10	9	7	206	42	248	168	58	10	172	116
Cuba and other West Indies	1026 (1054)	674	47	26	15	13	62	65	18	8	652	286	189	243
Central America	251 (234)	189	7	[7]	1	2	4	8	8	7	130	51	97	96
South America	1720 (1548)	1551	170	173	94	60	512	457	528	330	44	12	348	506
Asia	446 (395)	422	77	58	34	49	151	177	10	8	63	63	71	50
Africa	117 (102)	131	7	18	16	24	32	50	54	22[8]	8	n.a.	2	n.a.
Oceania	162 (149)	120	50	50	22	10	81	49	6	n.a.	—	—	—	n.a.

| TOTAL | 7553 [9] | 7000 [9] | 1821 | 1926 [10] | 362 | 522 | 1341 [11] | 1277 [12] | 1227 | 783 [13] | 986 [11] | 432 [14] | 1334 [11] | 1514 |
| | (7528) [11] | | (1813) [15] | | (368) | | (1117) | | (1185) | (880) | | (1610) | |

Source: For 1929, Cleona Lewis's figures have been used (as in Table III.1, but combining columns 7 and 8 to coincide with Department of Commerce figures). The Department of Commerce several times changed its estimates for 1929. In parenthesis, for totals only, are its most recent estimates for 1929, as presented in U.S. Department of Commerce, Office of Business Economics, *U.S. Business Investments in Foreign Countries* (Washington, D.C. 1960), pp. 92–93. The breakdown for Latin America is from U.S. Department of Commerce, Bureau of Foreign and Domestic Commerce, *American Direct Investments in Foreign Countries—1940* (Washington, D.C. 1942), and coincides with the totals in above cited document. The 1940 figures are from *American Direct Investment in Foreign Countries—1940.*

[1] Totals include sum of columns 2–7 plus some miscellaneous investments.

[2] Excluding petroleum.

[3] Exploration, production, some transporting, refining, and distribution.

[4] Mining and smelting.

[5] Railroads and other public utilities.

[6] Includes paper and pulp, 1929, $279 million, 1940 $308 million.

[7] Less than $500 thousand.

[8] The Department of Commerce excluded U.S. investments in the Belgian Congo—to avoid disclosure. Such stakes appear to be under a million dollars. The decline from the 1929 figure came in the main before 1936 and was the "result of adjustments to balance sheet values . . . and of other technical differences in the methods employed." See Department of Commerce, Bureau of Foreign and Domestic Commerce, *American Direct Investments Abroad, 1936* (Washington, D.C. 1938), p. 14.

[9] Totals include some unclassified by area investments in banking and cables as well as other investments that the compilers failed to locate by area.

[10] This figure is $308 million higher than the one given by the Department of Commerce ($1,618), since it includes the stake in paper and pulp in Canada. The figure also includes unallocated "international" investments.

[11] Total is off because of rounding.

[12] Includes some "international" petroleum investments.

[13] Excludes the Belgian Congo and Australia.

[14] Excludes Africa.

[15] The Department of Commerce in 1929 and 1940 used the figure $1,535 million instead of $1,813; this upward revision was made in the postwar period. It appears to be the only substantial revision in the totals.

The 1940 figures are from the Department of Commerce. Numerous statistical inconsistencies entered into the compilations of these data.* The table does, however, reflect the difficulties of U.S. business abroad in the 1930s in a general manner; the data do correspond to the fact that companies wrote down assets, in part because of currency depreciations; they account for certain dropouts (where funds were repatriated or lost); they vividly reveal the declining stakes in mining and agriculture. The figures do not, however, as clearly demonstrate that at the same time as U.S. enterprises retreated from investments, some augmented their foreign stakes. Indeed, one recent study indicates that corporations had a far larger *number* of subsidiaries and affiliates abroad in 1939 than in 1929.[51] Likewise, Table VIII.2 (column 2) does show a small rise in the total U.S. direct investments in foreign manufacturing; if other Department of Commerce figures are employed (see note 15 to the table) a more impressive rise in investment is recorded.

Among the manufacturing enterprises that retreated from direct investments in Europe was du Pont, which in 1935 sold its interests in Nobel Chemical Finishes Ltd. (England) and later in I. G. Farben (Germany). A du Pont official wrote in 1938 that "for a number of years du Pont has felt that investments in Europe are undesirable," because of unsatisfactory returns and because the future was "exceedingly uncertain." [52] Between 1933 and 1939 other American manufacturing enterprises disposed of all or part of their British businesses.† Some companies remained in operation in Britain, but did not invest added capital; to finance necessary expansion there, they turned to British sources. Thus, American Radiator Company decided to sell in England part of the stock in its then 100-per-cent-owned British subsidiary. Accordingly, its British subsidiary, National Radiator Company, Ltd., changed its name to Ideal Boiler and Radiator Company; by 1934, American Radiator Company retained only 54 per cent of the stock. Similarly, that year Monsanto "angli-

---

* The statistics on American business abroad in the 1930s and in 1940 are terrible because they mixed apples and oranges. Most were reported in the foreign currency and translated into dollars annually at the current rate of exchange (which meant they varied sharply owing to fluctuations in the rate of exchange). Some American companies kept records in dollars so the values of fixed assets remained impervious to exchange changes. There was no uniformity in accounting on foreign properties. U.S. Dept. of Comm., Bureau of Foreign and Domestic Commerce, *American Direct Investments in Foreign Countries—1940*, p. 3.

† Among them were Drug Inc., R.C.A., U.S. Rubber, and Budd International Corp. (which in 1930 had acquired Edward Budd's investment in Pressed Steel).

cized" its English enterprise, raising money from public sources in England for expansion.[53] In Spain, when the civil war broke out in 1936, General Motors closed its Barcelona plant.[54] The properties of other companies went into the hands of opposing forces. In France, with currency depreciation and labor problems, U.S. stakes dropped sharply (see Table VIII.3). U.S. Steel had hoped that the U.S.-Canadian reciprocal trade agreement, concluded on January 1, 1936, would mean it could ex-

Table VIII.3. U.S. direct investments in manufacturing in Europe, 1929, 1940 (book value in million U.S. dollars)

Country	1929	1940	% Change
Great Britain	268.2	275.3	2.6
Germany	138.9	206.3 [1]	48.5
France	90.9	46.5	−48.8
Rest of Europe	130.9	111.3	−15.0
TOTAL	628.9	639.4	1.5

Source: Based data in U.S. Department of Commerce, Bureau of Foreign and Domestic Commerce, *American Direct Investments in Foreign Countries,* Trade Information Bull. 731 (Washington, D.C. 1930), p. 10, and U.S. Department of Commerce, Bureau of Foreign and Domestic Commerce, *American Direct Investments in Foreign Countries—1940* (Washington, D.C. 1942), p. 10.
[1] Includes Austria as well. The Austrian figure for 1929 was only $2.6 million.

port semimanufactured steel to Canada to be transformed there at its manufactories into products for sale throughout the Dominion. Since the 1932 Ottawa agreements, U.S. plants in Canada had used mostly British steel. The trade agreement of 1936, while radically lowering U.S. and Canadian tariffs, did not lower them enough to help U.S. Steel. On September 1, 1937, U.S. Steel sold the properties of its Canadian subsidiaries to Dominion Steel and Coal. "The Canadian properties were disposed of," U.S. Steel's *Annual Report* declared, "because their satisfactory operation was dependent largely upon a supply of semi-finished steel from other manufacturers. Because of Canadian import duty handicaps and other disadvantages, it was not conducive to acceptable results to supply such steel from the United States." [55] Once (in the 1890s) American interests had been active in the formation of Dominion Steel and Coal, but also sold out.[56] In Japan, as the military prepared for war, Japanese partners in American joint ventures politely suggested in every corporate capital increase that Americans not take up their options. Control moved in many cases into Japanese hands. There was a striking reduction in the percentage interest of U.S. corporations in Japanese business (Table X.1, below indicates this).[57]

Yet such instances of retreat were more than matched by new entries into manufacturing abroad, 1933–1939. In Britain, U.S. manufacturers' investments did rise slightly—in response to the economic growth and to the protectionist legislation. It was in Germany, however, that the increase was substantial (see Table VIII.3). The reason did not lie in Germany's impressive economic growth after 1933 (although Americans did hope to take advantage of the expanding German market). Far more important, Americans had no choice; with German rearmament, transfers of funds from the Reich were limited; U.S. subsidiaries and affiliates made profits that remained in Germany and added to the investments.

When Hitler came to power, U.S. enterprises at first found themselves under virulent attack. The Associated Press and the *New York Times* representatives were refused permission to take pictures. The Gillette Company, which owned Roth-Buechner Co., was attacked as an "octopus" and a "Jewish" outfit. Burroughs and Remington-Rand were among the many firms asked to sign statements that they were not under "foreign," "Jewish," or "Marxist" control. They were told that they could not sell to municipalities unless they signed such a statement. Only "pure" German companies would be allowed to operate. The American consul in Berlin brought the matter before the German Ministry of Commerce and was assured that the actions against American firms had not been "official." He learned that the interference came "in every single case from German competitors who wish to use the opportunity of the accession of the [National Socialist] party to power to get business which they have not been able to secure in any other way." The Treaty of Friendship, Commerce, and Consular Rights between the United States and Germany guaranteed American firms or American-owned German companies the same rights in Germany as firms that were entirely German owned. The American consul in Berlin took "untiring" steps to stop the movement that threatened the American concerns.* In time, many American companies were able to obtain certificates that they were "pure" German firms—even though they had foreign stockholders. Moreover, by the mid-1930s the hostility toward the American companies seems to have subsided, since many came to terms with the German way of doing business. Ambassador William E. Dodd wrote Roosevelt on October 19, 1936, that more than a hundred American corporations had subsidiaries in Germany or cooperative agreements with German firms. "The International Harvester Company president told me their business here rose 33% a year (arms manufacture, I believe), but they could take nothing out . . . General Motors Company and Ford do enormous businesses here through their subsidiaries and take no profits out." Dodd reported that Standard Oil of New Jersey had invested $2 million in December 1933 and made $500,000 a year helping the Germans make Ersatz gas for war purposes, but they could not take their earnings out. Other enterprises had "cooperative" agreements.† Some managers of American companies in Germany seem to have been surprisingly unperceptive about political and economic conditions there. While a few companies saw the problems and sought to dispose of their holdings in Germany, often these could find no customers. Many company executives just misunderstood. They had thought in the late 1920s and in 1930 that although the free movement of goods was absent, they could vault the tariff walls, invest in manufacturing, and the free movement of *funds* would be readily available. They could not have been more wrong, and yet many failed to doubt. After the early antagonism subsided, managers were lulled into a false security. One experienced international executive declared that investing money in Germany in the 1930s was as safe as putting it in a bank. Henry Ford authorized an increase in investment in Ford of Germany, never having a question about ultimately obtaining a return on the investment. Thomas J. Watson, president of I.B.M., highly sophisticated in international business, had personal conferences with Hjalmar Schacht and was literally be-

---

* All the action was taken by the consulate general. No formal representations were made by the embassy or the State Department to the foreign office. *Foreign Relations of the United States 1933*, II, 437.

† Dodd noted cooperative agreements of du Pont (which he said was aiding the armament business) and of "our airplanes people [who] have secret arrangements with Krupps." Dodd to FDR, October 19, 1936, in *Franklin D. Roosevelt and Foreign Affairs*, edited by Edgar Nixon, III, 456.

witched. George Monroe Moffett, president of Corn Products Refining Company, which had large stakes in Germany, described himself in 1938 as personally opposed to nazism. He would prefer, he said, "no restrictions whatever on his activities." But, Moffett continued, the restrictions of the New Deal were more onerous than those of Germany. A *Fortune* interview reported him as saying: "In Germany . . . there is no uncertainty, no political caprice and no nonsense. You reach an agreement with the government and it sticks. You have a problem and you go to the government and get a clear, immediate answer, whereas in America you may spend weeks trying to find out where you stand with the New Deal and then just as you seem to have reached an understanding there is an overnight change in policy and you are up in the air again." *Fortune* concluded that "All in all, Mr. Moffett prefers the tangible, explicit Nazi interference to the half-defined meddling of democracy."

Pleased by the fact that they were making good profits (even though the German government would not let them remit the profits to the United States) and pleased by the absence of labor problems so evident in the United States, France, and elsewhere, American businessmen conformed with German requirements. They responded to the German pressure that they export from their German plants and that they barter their exports for such commodities as wool and rubber.[58] A number of American companies in Germany, desiring to take on a national coloration and in some case to profit from I. G. Farben's technology became associated or retained associations with the giant German enterprise. I. G. Farben, for example, took a minority interest in the Ford subsidiary and was represented on its board; there is no evidence that I. G. Farben had any major impact on the policies or activities of the German Ford unit; the I. G. board member was for prestige purposes. National Lead had a joint venture with I. G. Farben in Cologne to manufacture titanium oxide pigments. Du Pont had various agreements with I. G. Farben (it sold its minority stake in I. G. Farben, as noted, in the mid-1930s).* Similarly, National Cash Register went into a new joint venture with Krupp in 1934.[59]

The American companies acted irrespective of politics. Yet, the political and economic life in Germany shaped their operations. When the International Chamber of Commerce met in Berlin in 1937, the new presi-

* Standard Oil of New Jersey was also associated with I. G. Farben.

dent, Thomas J. Watson, set the keynote for the meeting: "World Peace through World Trade." Hitler came to the conference, as did Hermann Goering and Hjalmar Schacht. Watson heard them talk—but was blind to German preparations for war. Meanwhile, under the 1936 four-year plan, American companies in Germany were being used for national goals. It was under such circumstances that U.S. stakes in Germany grew.[60]

U.S. investments in Canadian manufacturing also rose. The number of

Table VIII.4.   U.S.-owned or U.S.-controlled manufacturing enterprises in Canada, 1929, 1936, 1940, excluding paper and pulp

Year	Number of enterprises	Size of U.S. direct investment (in million U.S. dollars)
1929	524	$541
1936	816	530
1940	790	636

Source: U.S. Department of Commerce, Bureau of Foreign and Domestic Commerce, American Direct Investments in Foreign Countries, Trade Information Bull. 731 (Washington, D.C. 1930), p. 13; U.S. Department of Commerce, Bureau of Foreign and Domestic Commerce, American Direct Investments Abroad—1936 (Washington, D.C. 1938), p. 7; U.S. Department of Commerce, Bureau of Foreign and Domestic Commerce, American Direct Investments in Foreign Countries—1940 (Washington, D.C. 1942), p. 21.

manufacturing enterprises (excluding paper and pulp) owned by Americans in the Dominion is indicated on Table VIII.4. The upsurge in number of enterprises between 1929 and 1936 was due to the new entries after the tariff increases; the reduction in numbers between 1936 and 1940 was apparently caused mainly by the liberalization of trade under U.S.-Canadian trade agreements that made certain manufacturing activities uneconomical.* Note, however, that the numbers do not indicate the size of the investment, which between 1929 and 1936 declined only to rise

* The U.S. Steel case cited above—wherein the reduction was not steep enough to make the steel company's plants in Canada economical—was atypical. Usually the problem was the opposite.

The Era of Depression

to new heights between 1936 and 1940, reflecting the fact that those U.S. manufacturers that remained in business expanded. This was not a "forced" expansion; profit remittances from Canadian plants were not blocked.

U.S. companies often started new plants in the 1930s in Latin America, Asia, Oceania, and to a lesser extent Africa (almost exclusively South Africa). Thus, Firestone built new tire and tube plants in South Africa (1936), Brazil (1939), and India (1939), while Goodyear started manufacturing tires in Java (1934) and Brazil (1938). Du Pont—at the same time as it retreated from investment in Europe—made major new entries in joint ventures with the British, Imperial Chemical Industries in Argentina (1933) and Brazil (1936). American drug companies undertook foreign expansion in the late 1930s, mainly into Latin America.[61] U.S. Steel considered the possibilities of a Brazilian joint-venture steel plant (with Brazilian capital) in the late 1930s—a project that did not materialize. On the other hand, American Rolling Mills Corporation in 1939 built a mill at Port Kembla in Australia, with an annual capacity of 30,000 tons sheet steel—a joint venture with the British firm, Lysaght's Works Pty, Ltd. International Harvester, long in international business and with assembly facilities in Australia, constructed its first manufactory there in 1937–1938—to get behind the tariff barrier.[62] Even in Japan, where the general policy was to encourage American technology but to discourage U.S. investment, there were new U.S. stakes: * National Cash Register established its first Japanese factory for assembly in 1934 and the next year opened a joint-venture for manufacturing; † National Lead and I. G. Farben participated in a new Japanese company in 1936; I.B.M. in 1937 organized a wholly owned subsidiary and began manufacturing I.B.M. cards in Japan.[63] Such are isolated examples of the many new stakes worldwide. It seems, in fact, that in the 1930s, in great part as a response to nationalistic government actions, American manufacturing firms did extend themselves and initiate manufacturing in many regions often sup-

---

* American scholars have always assumed that the Japanese wanted to keep U.S. direct investment out of Manchuria in the 1930s. Yukio Chō recently has brought forth evidence that after 1937 certain important Japanese officials wanted Japanese capital to be invested *in Japan* and hoped to attract U.S. direct investment in Manchuria to develop that region's industry. They found no Americans to invest. Yukio Chō, "Importing American Capital into Manchuria," pp. 388–391. See also B. Kopf to Crawford, November 2, 1937, Accession 390, Box 85, Ford Motor Company Archives, for some confirmation of this thesis.

† 70 per cent National Cash Register, 30 per cent Fijiyama interests.

plementing the manufacturing facilities they already owned in Europe and Canada.

In sum, from 1933 to 1939, while there were retreats from investments, there were also new stakes. There seems no question, however, that what expansion there was of U.S. manufacturers to foreign lands in the 1930s was far less than in the 1920s.[64]

5

By contrast, U.S. investments in foreign mining and smelting declined sharply in the 1930s (see Table VIII.2). The main reasons were capital distributions, write-downs, and exchange depreciations. The fundamental problem facing the mining companies was that of low commodity prices. Investments in raw materials in depression time were a burden. Other difficulties were to cope with new host government restraints. Governments passed laws limiting the number of aliens that could be employed by foreign mining firms. They put new pressure on mining companies to hire indigenous personnel in responsible positions, to provide schools, and to offer fringe benefits. They also imposed higher taxes.* Such measures meant increased costs to the companies (even the pressure to hire local staff employees temporarily raised costs, since such men had to be trained). They must be considered along with the depression as factors limiting investment.[65]

By mid-decade, American owners of copper properties in Chile, Canada, Northern Rhodesia, Mexico, and Peru began to make modest profits once again. In 1935 the major foreign producers of copper (including those owned and controlled by U.S. capital) participated in an international agreement "to bring about better conditions in production, distribution, and marketing of copper throughout the world." American executives explicitly excluded the United States from the arrangement because of U.S. antitrust laws. Whether owing to the agreement, or to wartime demand, the copper industry by decade's end was finally out of its doldrums. In 1939, American capital remained in a strong position in worldwide copper, but its stake in the total world output was no larger than in 1929.[66]

* For example, in Chile the U.S. copper companies' income tax payments rose from 12 per cent in 1928 to 18 per cent in 1934, to 33 per cent in 1939. 1928 figures from W. S. Culbertson to Secretary of State, RG 59, 825.5123/27, National Archives; 1934 and 1939 figures from Reynolds, "Development Problems of an Export Economy: The Case of Chile and Copper," p. 238.

Americans continued as investors in lead and zinc in Argentina, Mexico, Peru, Canada, Australia, and Poland. In both lead and zinc international agreements existed, and U.S. producers took part. Here again, because of American antitrust legislation, U.S. companies participated in these agreements to raise prices only for their foreign production. But the accords did little to push prices upward; the companies suffered accordingly. Hardest pressed was Anaconda, with its stake in the Silesian-American Company. Poland remained on the gold standard while most nations abandoned it; thus, Polish costs of operations were relatively higher than those of competing output from countries with undervalued currencies (most of the Polish company's zinc, lead, and coal was exported). Then, as if this and low prices were not enough, in 1936, the Polish government imposed restraints on the transfer of funds. With tensions on the German-Polish border in 1938, the Silesian-American Company operated at a loss. Throughout the decade, Silesian-American paid no dividends.[67]

The Guggenheims did not retire from their nitrate investments in Chile when on January 2, 1933, the government of Arturo Alessandri decreed the dissolution of COSACH. Negotiations between the government and the mining companies resulted in the *producing* enterprises being separated from government control; the Guggenheims resumed management of their former nitrate properties. A new government-owned sales corporation was formed in 1934 to trade in nitrate and iodine—Corporación de Ventas de Salitre y Yodo de Chile (The Nitrate and Iodine Sales Corporation). The producers sold to the *Corporación* at cost, which then resold the nitrates at market price, covered the costs of the transaction, and took 25 per cent of the profit. The rest of the profit was prorated back to the mining firms. The sales corporation in time proved a successful cooperation between government and industry and was one of the earliest experiments of its sort. It had a long history and still existed in the 1960s. The problems of the poverty-stricken nitrate industry remained in the 1930s as prices continued low. The industry never regained its position as Chile's principal exporter; the blame lay in the rise of low-cost synthetics rather than in the way the industry was administered.[68]

In tin, as in nitrates, foreign government intervention to raise prices persisted in the years 1933–1939. The International Tin Control Scheme of 1931 was renewed and expanded to include more governments (1933, 1934, 1937, 1938). By 1934, the dollar price of tin was substantially above that of 1929. American investors abroad abided by the restrictive arrangements. There is no indication that American businessmen led in the tin agreements, or, for that matter, that they objected to them. Edward J. Cornish, chairman of the board of National Lead, told a U.S. House Committee in 1935, that the owners of tin properties had met in England, "to reduce production, so that there would not be too much production that would destroy the price. I gather that from the newspapers. I am not party to it. I was invited to sit in as a director without vote, but I concluded I had better not." When asked, however, "In your judgment is the international tin agreement between these countries that produce tin wise . . . ?" Cornish replied, "I believe it is beneficial to the world to have the production of tin, copper, lead, or wheat limited to the demand made by the public for them." [69]

American producers of other minerals joined in international accords attempting to increase prices. Among the other minerals under some form of international control in the 1930s were beryllium, bismuth, coal and coke, cobalt, mercury, nickel, platinum, phosphate, potash, silver, and sulphur. Americans had foreign investments in many of these minerals. In most cases, when U.S. businesses took part in the international agreements it was through their investments in companies that operated abroad or through Webb-Pomerene associations and not directly. [70]

Despite Roosevelt's declared policy to restore commodity price levels, the U.S. government was a party to only one international accord dealing with metals, the silver agreement. American investors at home and abroad (including Canada, Mexico, Peru, and Australia) were pleased when the United States—along with these other governments—became a signatory to the International Silver Agreement of July 22, 1933.* [71]

In times of low metal prices, the only excellent mining investment is gold. During the 1930s, worldwide output of gold climbed, since costs of production were far below the 1934 U.S. fixed price of $35 an ounce. U.S. companies invested abroad in gold mining: American Smelting and Refining Company in Australia, Canada, the Gold Coast,† and Saudi Arabia; Newmont Mining Corporation in Western Ontario (in the Empire State Mines Ltd.). In the Philippines, Americans mined gold. With new

---

* Silver is used as currency, which creates distinctive problems in its control. In discussions of international commodity agreements, the silver accord is usually excluded because it was "more closely related to monetary than to commodity control policies." Yet, the control relationships were important for the producers.

† This was a 51 per cent interest acquired in 1932 and sold in 1935 at a profit.

discoveries of gold, silver, copper, and lead deposits, between December 16, 1934 and March 15, 1935 the Mexican government granted 154 concessions to foreigners (most of which went to Americans). From everywhere, gold imports into the United States grew, and by 1939 economists worried about the "tendency for gold to become concentrated in the United States!" [72]

In sum, gold mining excepted, in the 1930s Americans had difficulties in their mining operations abroad. Low prices on their output proved a far more serious deterrent to investment than the pressures from foreign governments. Americans participated in international commodity agreements to attempt to raise prices. Practically all the U.S. companies remained in operation, although they often suffered losses.

6

From 1933 to 1939 U.S. investors in agricultural properties met adversity. In Mexico, the government's policy of nationalization accelerated. Lázaro Cárdenas, during his six years as president (1935–1940), arranged for the Mexican peasants to obtain twice as much land as had been transferred prior to 1934. American landowners cried out in anguish; they called on Washington for help. The State Department accepted the right of Mexico to expropriate, while protesting the absence of adequate compensation; but its efforts to obtain prompt and sufficient compensation failed to satisfy the Americans whose land was being expropriated.* American stakes in Mexican agriculture shrunk. [73]

United Fruit gradually recovered from its depression nadir, yet its total foreign investment in 1939 did not reach the level of 1929. In the last half of the 1930s, sigatoka struck the company's Central American plantations. This disease was new to Latin America; in time, with expensive sprays it could be controlled; meanwhile it devastated the land. Since United Fruit's Atlantic coast plantations were by the mid-1930s almost exhausted and filled with diseased plants (caused both by sigatoka and the perennial Panama disease), the company turned more attention to

---

* Not until 1938 did Mexico agree to the establishment of a mixed commission to evaluate the claims. While the commission deliberated, the Mexican government agreed to pay $1 million in May 1939, and on subsequent June 30ths at least an additional $1 million until the awards were paid. On November 19, 1941 (after Mexico had paid $3 million), it was agreed that Mexico would pay an additional $37 million compensation over a period of fourteen years. This was to cover expropriations made during the period August 30, 1927 to October 7, 1940. Former property owners felt the payment was inadequate. See note 73.

growing bananas on the Pacific side of Central America. It started new enterprises in western Guatemala, Costa Rica, and Panama. Despite its problems, in the 1930s the United Fruit Company's crucial position in Central America was *not* diminished. On the contrary, as the countries in which it operated were afflicted by the depression, as independent banana owners (unable to operate because of low prices and sigatoka) went bankrupt, and as United Fruit extended its operations to the west coast, the company actually increased its relative importance. Central American governments, deeply in debt, borrowed from the company to a greater extent than in earlier times. They put new pressures on the company for higher taxes.

In the mid-1930s, United Fruit considered building a port on the Pacific coast of Guatemala to ship its west coast bananas. At this point, the International Railway of Central America was having financial problems. A new west coast port would compete with the railroad, for many producers would export from the west coast instead of shipping commodities northeast along the railroad. United Fruit decided to aid the railroad and not to construct the port. In return for its assistance, it obtained 44 per cent of the railroad's stock. The managements remained separate, although the company did the purchasing for the railroad and the railroad hired certain United Fruit Company personnel. Nonetheless, the company's large interest in the railroad, together with its decision not to go ahead with the port, created new public relations difficulties in Guatemala for United Fruit. Many Guatemalans felt the company got preferential treatment on the railroad. Similarly, United Fruit Company's relations to the Northern Railroad in Costa Rica were subject to this interpretation.

In the 1930s as nationalism became evident throughout Latin America, United Fruit found itself under fiery attack. Central American nationalists felt its aid to their countries was totally inadequate. The company pointed to its contribution: in 1938, for instance, it paid $19.7 million in wages, spent $17.2 million in purchases of fruit, sugar cane, cacao, and other products, $4 million in other local purchases, and $4 million in taxes in Central America. The company's net income that year from all operations totaled $10.3 million, a profit figure which was low compared with the profits of the 1920s.

United Fruit Company's expenditures contributed to the Central American economies. Yet, in the 1930s—with profits lower than ever before in United Fruit Company history—there is some evidence that the Company was not as progressive as it had been in earlier years. More important, perhaps, with the nationalism came intense persistent resentment against a large company which *could have* its own towns and hospitals, which *could have* such a substantial impact on the economy of small countries, and which *seemed* to have a type of extraterritoriality. Such resentment appears to have been not so much founded on specific malpractices, as representing a generalized expression of national sovereignty.[74]

If United Fruit became more important in Central America, it also expanded elsewhere; in 1934 it made its first investment in Africa—a response to "bloc trading." United Fruit had supplied the French banana trade with Central American fruit; it had a marketing organization in France. When the French put restrictions on all banana imports except those from French territories, United Fruit sent a ship to Guadeloupe and Martinique to buy fruit; before its ship could reach France, the French had passed legislation requiring that all bananas imported must be on French flag ships. United Fruit, through its French affiliate, then invested in French overseas territory to supply the French trade. Despite the French government's reluctance, United Fruit's French affiliate, Compagnie des Bananes, obtained in 1934 concessions to grow bananas in the French Cameroons—some sixty miles north of Douala. It would use French carriers in this banana trade and would sell the colony's bananas only in the French market.[75]

U.S. investors in rubber plantations also made new foreign investments. In 1934 the British and Dutch governments, with the governments of Siam and Indo-China, introduced an International Rubber Agreement to regulate rubber exports and to raise rubber prices. The reader may recall that in 1922 Harvey Firestone had protested such international restraints; now with his own rubber supply in Liberia, he did not complain. Neither, however, did his company or the Liberian government participate in the accord. Yet, the existence of the new international agreement seems to have made Firestone direct more attention to enlarging his own rubber output in Liberia; he undertook postponed developments and made new plantings; the Firestone company and the Liberian government also entered into a supplementary loan agreement early in 1935. U.S. Rubber and Goodyear, with their Dutch East Indies and Malayan plantations, were required to conform to the British and

Dutch government limitations; Baron van Lynden, a director of U.S. Rubber Plantations (a subsidiary of U.S. Rubber) became a member of the Dutch Committee of Producers and took part in the negotiations on the International Agreement.

U.S. Rubber and Goodyear were not happy with the restraints; * as prices began to move upward, Goodyear experimented to see if "the economies of scientific production found in Sumatra" could be applied in Panama and Costa Rica, starting plantations in those countries in 1935 and 1936 respectively. Ford, not yet in rubber production in Brazil, put new effort into this task; when the first Ford plantation at Fordlandia proved impractical, the company acquired a new Brazilian plantation site at Belterra. By 1940, Ford had invested $9.5 million in Brazilian rubber and had not received a penny return. Just as United Fruit invested in the Cameroons because of French trade restrictions, similarly, much of the U.S. foreign investment in rubber was prompted by actions of the British and the Dutch governments—in this case to raise the price of rubber.[76]

If there were new U.S. direct investments in 1933–1939 in bananas and rubber, this was not true in sugar. American stakes in sugar, as noted earlier, were greatest in Cuba. The 1931 international sugar accord (which lasted until 1935) failed to increase prices. The 1934 measures of the U.S. government (see p. 178) did assist U.S. investors in Cuban sugar. In 1937, a new international sugar agreement was signed (with the United States a participant),† but the world price of sugar remained depressed. To add to the woes of U.S. sugar growers and processors in Cuba, that government imposed minimum wages and maximum hours and limited the employment of non-Cubans. To protect the small farmers (*colonos*) the government set minimum rates for the purchase of their sugar cane and extended the duration of their contracts with the sugar

---

* U.S. Rubber and Goodyear produced special types of rubber—not in oversupply—and asked for exemptions from certain restrictions. The U.S. government refused to request special consideration for these companies. *Foreign Relations of the United States 1934*, I, 632, 641.

† This and the silver pact were the only international commodity agreements during the 1930s in which the U.S. government participated where U.S. foreign investments were significant. In August 1933 the United States had signed the International Wheat Agreement, but this was to aid *exporters* from the United States, and foreign investment was not an issue. In the summer of 1939, the U.S. government took the initiative in convening an international cotton congress, which was terminated because of the outbreak of war. Here again, the aid was to be primarily to the American exporter rather than to the American foreign investor, although at least one cotton trader (Anderson, Clayton, & Co.) had by this time substantial investments abroad.

companies. Taxes on the sugar enterprises rose. Moreover, companies became aware of agitation for measures "to break up or 'take over' mills, lands, or other properties of sugar companies." One U.S. sugar firm's listing application on the New York Curb Exchange (dated December 18, 1939, amended April 22, 1940) indicated, "The Company disclaims any representation whatsoever as to whether the Cuban Government may have or may attempt to exercise any right, power, or claim to expropriate or otherwise acquire any or all of the properties of its subsidiary." Under such circumstances, it is little wonder that U.S. stakes in Cuban sugar declined. Whereas Americans had direct investments in Cuban sugar of $544 million in 1929, by 1936 the amount was down to $240 million, and then between 1936 and 1940, American investors in Cuban sugar wrote down the value of their property an additional $24 million.[77]

The new U.S. foreign investments in bananas and rubber in the late 1930s were insufficient to reverse the trend; as a consequence of the Mexican expropriations, low prices of agricultural commodities, as well as depreciating currency, total U.S. direct foreign investment in agriculture was in 1940 roughly half what it had been in 1929. Once a major sector for U.S. foreign investment, agriculture was so no longer—nor would it ever be in the future.[78]

U.S. foreign investors in agricultural processing for export for the most part also found the years 1933–1939 a time of travail. In October 1933, a National Meat Law put the Argentine government into the meat-packing business. The law provided for the formation of a Junta Nacional de Carnes (a National Meat Board) and set rules regulating existing meat-packing plants. Under this law, the Junta Nacional de Carnes would aid in establishing the C.A.P.—Corporación Argentina de Productores de Carnes—the cattle owners' meat-packing establishment. American meat packers in Argentina were totally opposed to the organization of the National Meat Board and to the government-subsidized C.A.P. Their protests were in vain. Nonetheless, according to a Cia. Swift Internacional Prospectus, during the 1930s, in its price-fixing, the National Meat Board allowed the industry "to make reasonable profits."

The Uruguayan government's packing plant, opened as early as 1928, obtained in 1934 exclusive rights to supply fresh meat, mutton, and "fancy meats" to that nation's only large city, thus barring American meat packers from the Montevideo trade. In Brazil, the city of São Paulo insisted that municipal packing plants supply much of the meat for the city; in 1939 the share of the three foreign-owned plants was reduced to 40 per cent. While the foreign meat-packing plants in Brazil had been started as exporters, they had come to appreciate the domestic trade.[79]

In Canada, the government did not intervene in the activities of paper and pulp producers—and having weathered the worst years of the depression, American enterprises actually expanded; U.S. direct investment in Canadian paper and pulp operations showed an increase over the 1929 figures (see Table VIII.2, note 6).

Texas-based international cotton merchant, Anderson, Clayton & Co. greatly enlarged its foreign agricultural processing business in the 1930s. Anderson, Clayton had for many years marketed American cotton in Europe and Japan through sales offices located in these areas; it had in earlier years a buying office and a cotton lint factory in Mexico. In 1930 it had started a purchasing branch in Egypt. The Smoot-Hawley tariff, which cut exports to the United States, limited the dollars available to foreigners. Thus, Anderson, Clayton inaugurated purchasing branches in Peru (1933), Brazil (1934), Argentina and Paraguay (1935), all to acquire foreign cotton for sale *abroad;* by 1935 its *foreign* cotton totaled 19 per cent of its sales, and the percentage continued to rise. Then, the firm moved into ginning, cottonseed-oil milling and vegetable-oil refining as well as warehousing in foreign countries; it became in the 1930s one of the most prominent U.S. enterprises in Latin America.[80]

7

Currency depreciations in relation to the dollar affected corporate investments and profits in different sectors in different manners. Manufacturers investing abroad in the main obtained their revenues in the host nation's currency; if possible, they remitted their profits home at once, or if that was impossible they reinvested—thus so much of the forced investment to which we have referred. Companies that exported from host nations got their revenues mainly in dollars and pound sterling; sometimes, they were required by host governments to convert this into local currency; most times, only what was needed for local expenditures went back into host nation currency. Thus, the "forced investments" made by manufacturing companies were not made by the mining and agricultural companies. Fundamentally, manufacturing, mining, and agricultural companies made their pricing decisions based on what the market would bear, or in accord with international agreements. Thus, when a manufac-

The Era of Depression

turing enterprise found its dollar revenues in terms of the franc or the milreis declining, it generally raised its prices to compensate and hoped the reduction in sales would not be significant. As noted, mining and agricultural companies sought—often in concert—to lift prices.

U.S.-owned public utilities operating abroad, like the market-oriented manufacturers, obtained their revenues in local currencies. If possible, like the manufacturing companies, they remitted their profits home at once; when this was not possible they reinvested—"forced investment." But unlike the manufacturing enterprises, the public utilities, because they operated under rate structures controlled by host governments, were unable to offset depreciating currencies by increasing prices. Thus, depreciating currencies had the most influence on their returns.

American & Foreign Power Company found in the 1930s that foreign demand for electric power expanded as did its subsidiaries' local currency revenues. But usually when these revenues were translated into dollars, they yielded lower returns.* With government restraints, the company could not raise its rates fast enough to cope with the foreign exchange losses. Table VIII.5 indicates the impact of foreign exchange depreciation on American & Foreign Power Company properties. To make matters more difficult, as the output of American Foreign & Power's system mounted, the company had to make new investments to maintain and to improve the properties; it spent blocked funds but it also had to add new monies. Between 1931 and 1935, American & Foreign Power invested $50 million on property improvements and expansion, over half of which sum involved dollar expenditures on materials and equipment that had to be purchased in the United States.† And all the while the company was in financial straits; it paid no dividends on common stock during the 1930s, and in 1932 it ceased paying dividends on preferred stock for the remainder of the decade. It borrowed from its parent company, Electric Bond and Share; it went to the banks; Electric Bond and Share took over some of its bank loans.

Throughout Latin America, government intervention in the electric power industry mounted. Nations sought to imitate the Tennessee Valley Authority. Everywhere, American & Foreign Power and the host govern-

---

* Venezuelan revenues were the principal exceptions. Venezuelan currency appreciated in value!

† Equipment that American & Foreign Power used was not available in the less developed countries in which it operated.

Table VIII.5.   1939 exchange rates as they affected American & Foreign Power Co. (in U.S. dollars)

Country	Currency	Rate prevailing when American & Foreign Power made major acquisitions	Yearly average rate, 1939 [1]
Argentina	Peso	$ .424	$ .231
Brazil	Milreis	.120	.047
Chile	Peso	.122	.032
China	Chinese dollar	.416	.060
Colombia	Peso	.973	.570
Costa Rica	Colon	.250	.177
Cuba	Peso	1.000	.927
Ecuador	Sucre	.200	.067
Guatemala	Quetzal	1.000	1.000
India	Rupee	.365	.333
Mexico	Peso	.499	.194
Panama	Balboa	1.000	1.000
Venezuela	Bolivar	.193	.313

Source: American & Foreign Power, *Annual Report 1940.*
[1] Rate used by American & Foreign Power for conversion purposes.

ments argued over rate levels. Because of American & Foreign Power's inadequate returns on investments, by mid-decade the company stopped furnishing new capital. Its return on investment was lower than returns would be in the United States and the risks greater. Latin American governments did recognize the necessity of adequate returns to investors, but since rates were a political issue, the governments would not allow private enterprise to increase rates as fast as currency depreciated.

Conflicts between American & Foreign Power Company and host governments were numerous. When a strike occurred at the company's Cuban facilities on January 14, 1934, the Cuban government temporarily took over the operations.* In 1935, the Chilean government accused the company of having for the past three years dealt on the black market to remit its profits and thus having violated the nation's foreign exchange laws. On November 26 of that year, the Chilean finance minister Gustavo

* The properties were returned to the company's management on February 3, 1934.

Ross and Curtis E. Calder, president of American & Foreign Power, signed an agreement providing for the reorganization of the Chilean unit and resolving the dispute—a pact that the Chilean congress approved in February 1936.* Meanwhile, in Brazil, under Getulio Vargas, the Water Code of 1934 regulated hydroelectric power. It stipulated that all government-power company contracts had to be revised. Pending such revision, no rate changes would be granted. The demand for electricity in Brazil rose; the value of the milreis declined; American & Foreign Power Company could not expand, since the contracts were not revised; the power industry stagnated. In 1937, the new Brazilian constitution forbade any company with foreign stockholders from obtaining new hydroelectrical concessions. American & Foreign Power's investment in Brazil in 1931 had been $107.5 million; in 1940 it was $103.8 million; its return on investment, which was 5.3 per cent in 1931, ranged between 1.8 per cent and 3 per cent in the years 1934 to 1939.

Similarly, in Mexico, American & Foreign Power Company faced obstacles. Government and private attacks on the company for its "excessive" rates mounted. The Mexican Expropriation Law of November 1936 alarmed company officials, although the law was not implemented in relation to the electric power industry. By 1937, American & Foreign Power executives were diagnosing the demands of Mexican unions as extremely severe and if made effective would be disastrous. That year, the Mexican government established a Comision Federal de Electricidad to organize and to direct "a national system for electric power generation, transmission, and distribution."

In the eastern hemisphere, American & Foreign Power's huge investment in Shanghai suffered a loss of revenue and minor physical damage with the Japanese invasion in 1937. Nonetheless, by 1938 the Shanghai subsidiary was back to normal business and although its operating costs rose, its business was soon expanding.[81]

International Telephone and Telegraph Corporation likewise encountered difficulties abroad. Demand for telephones grew, which meant more investments were required; yet, rates were fixed, currencies depreciating, and profit remittances often blocked. Although by 1939 every major tele-

---

* The agreement required American & Foreign Power Company to place seven Chileans on the eleven-man board of directors of its Chilean enterprise; profits were to be distributed one-third to the government, one-third to the stockholders, and one-third to subsidize lower rates, Herring, *A History of Latin America*, p. 595.

phone operating company in I.T.T.'s system (except in Spain) was at its historical peak, I.T.T. failed to flourish. During the Spanish civil war, I.T.T. lost control of its important affiliate in that nation. On December 31, 1929, the consolidated assets of I.T.T. and its subsidiaries had been $535.2 million; they had risen in 1930 to $604.4 million, and in 1931, before the company revalued its assets, to $715.2 million. By 1939 I.T.T.'s consolidated assets were only $503.7 million. The statistics sum up the consequences of the decade.[82]

American & Foreign Power and I.T.T. maintained their business abroad. Others did not. For example, the Utilities Power & Light Corporation, which had made giant investments in England in the late 1920s, in July 1936 sold its properties back to British owners for roughly $32 million, representing a sizable loss; it disposed of its Canadian holdings in 1939; and in 1940, pursuant to a court-ordered reorganization, its remaining business (all domestic) was acquired by the newly organized Ogden Corporation.[83] By contrast, in the 1930s Pan American Airways expanded greatly, adding trans-Atlantic and trans-Pacific service to its Latin American business.[84]

Department of Commerce figures reveal a drop in U.S. foreign direct investments in utilities (including transportation) in the 1930s; on the other hand, if we combine Cleona Lewis's data for 1929 with the Department of Commerce figures for 1940, the results show a rise (see Table VIII.2). The present author's reading of the evidence would indicate that in all probability there was the decline.

As for other service activities, there seems little indication of any growth in foreign investment. As the *Federal Reserve Bulletin* put it later, "The depression of the 1930s and widespread systems of exchange and trade control diminished foreign trade and interest in foreign banking." There were some failures, including the large interests of the American Oriental Banking Corporation in China (in 1935). On the whole, however, most banks continued, as Chase National Bank reported, "to assist our customers in overcoming the many difficulties arising out of exchange restrictions and quota systems prevailing overseas." [85]

8

In sum, for most American companies, doing business abroad in the 1930s proved discouraging. The combination of commercial and political risks made the managements of many concerns feel international business was not worth the effort. U.S. businessmen were appalled with the masses of governmental regulations that they encountered abroad; they resented strongly that coping with such regulations had become a *sine qua non* of international business. When executives weighed the time and energy devoted to foreign operations against the results, many concluded that their company's resources could be better used in the United States.

A mood of disenchantment with international business pervaded many (but certainly not all) U.S. companies. Meanwhile, at home, the antimonopoly policies of the later years of the New Deal added one more reason for American managers to be sensitive about their foreign ventures. Alcoa, which had been a target of antitrust action before World War I, once more became vulnerable. In 1937, in *U.S. v. Aluminum Company of America,* Alcoa had to defend itself and Aluminium Limited against charges of monoply practice. In 1939, a federal grand jury returned an indictment against the Chilean Nitrate Sales Corporation,* Allied Chemical and Dye Corporation (and its subsidiaries) and forty-two foreign concerns (including Guggenheim interests) for having conspired to restrain trade in nitrates.[86] Under the prompting of Assistant Attorney General Thurman Arnold, the Temporary National Economic Committee, established in 1938, began to investigate "cartelization," which it loosely seemed to define as the relationships between U.S. businesses and foreign concerns. What had been routine corporate arrangements went under scrutiny.[87] Big business leaders in the United States became defensive. Indeed, by the end of the 1930s, some international businesses were under attack both abroad and at home, which made them ever more cautious in their foreign relationships.

Meanwhile, the world moved closer to the brink of the Second World War. By 1938, U.S. companies were placing reserves on their books to cover possible losses in Europe.[88] By the summer of 1939, conditions worldwide seemed fraught with danger.

Indeed, and in conclusion, American enterprises with stakes abroad in the 1930s operated in a world where nationalism, militarism, autarchy, and political and economic unrest reigned. In the United States, the severity of the depression had swept away businessmen's confidence. At home, corporation executives saw a greater amount of peacetime government intervention than ever in U.S. history; abroad, they met new inter-

* A subsidiary of Corporación de Ventas de Salitre y Yodo de Chile.

ventions by host governments. Whether it was blocked currency in Germany, a government nitrate sales company in Chile, expropriation of agricultural properties in Mexico, competition from a government-subsidized producers' meat-packing plant in Argentina, or the Water Code in 1934 in Brazil, sovereign governments—especially, but not exclusively, in Latin America—were taking measures that eroded the earning power of U.S. businesses with foreign operations. Ever more frequently businessmen's decisions were conditioned by foreign host government measures.

In the 1930s, world business seemed to take place in a "negotiated environment." * Not only did corporations deal with the governments in each particular host country, but many entered into international agreements to stabilize and to raise prices. The relationships were not unique to the 1930s, but became more widespread in this decade. They seemed to offer a way of survival in a depression-ridden world.

In this decade, while particular facilities were shut, relatively few U.S. companies withdrew from international business entirely. Most persisted. Some even started new foreign enterprises. Profits made outside the United States were often reinvested—sometimes involuntarily—and by decade's end reinvested profits came to form a major part of U.S. direct investment abroad.[89] American direct foreign investments survived far better than did the nation's foreign portfolio holdings; thus, whereas according to one estimate in 1929 direct investment abroad equaled 52 per cent of the total U.S. foreign investment, in 1940 the figure was up to 66 per cent.[90] Yet, during the 1930s, with the unfavorable climate for investment worldwide, the exuberance of American businessmen for direct foreign investment so evident in the late 1920s was in the main subdued. From 1933 to 1939, to repeat, there was a net *inflow* in direct investment to the United States.[91] In 1939, no Europeans were writing of the "American invasion" or the "American challenge"; few others dealt with this subject. There were more important topics—as the war clouds gathered.

* The term is H. van der Haas's and means an environment where negotiated agreements take the place of the market. See his *Enterprise in Transition*.

The Paradox of Oil

The oil industry's desire for overseas producing properties did not lessen because of political instability abroad. In the most unpromising political circumstances (for example, Mexico in 1912–1919, Russia in 1919–1921, or more recently, Indonesia in the 1950s), oil companies have invested. The investment seems predicated on the demand for the raw material, the availability of capital, the potentials for profit, and most of all on the realization that competition will enter if a particular oil company does not.

In the 1930s, coal still surpassed oil as the greatest single source of energy in the world, but oil had numerous advantages—in costs of production, transportation, storage, and utilization—and thus was gaining on its rival. U.S. oil enterprises, despite the political uncertainties of the 1930s, still invested abroad. Oil provided the energy for modern industry.

A director of an important American petroleum company has pointed out, "we work on an insurance policy of spreading risks around . . . We're not smart enough to predict the future . . . We can't figure out which area will go bad. Thus, we diversify and take a part in every area." This statement was made in 1965, but it represents well the attitude toward risk that existed in the earlier years of the oil industry.[1]

Another experienced oil industry executive explained, "the whole oil business is risk; we spend $10 million to search for oil, and don't find it; that is a risk. We go in when there is adversity because we can buy in cheap. It may not turn out well, but we are used to taking gambles. It is the nature of the business." [2]

If we combine Cleona Lewis's data on U.S. foreign petroleum investments with those of the Department of Commerce, the figures indicate a drop in total U.S. stakes in oil abroad (1929–1940), primarily because of the sharp reduction in U.S. interests in Mexican oil. On the other hand,

Department of Commerce statistics show a rise in total U.S. foreign investments in oil (despite the decline in Mexico). Table IX.1 gives both sets of figures. Data presented to a U.S. Senate Committe confirm the growth of such investments in the 1930s.[3] Because of the importance of the stakes in oil, because of significant changes in the 1930s, and because the present author finds convincing the evidence that U.S. oil interests in foreign countries did mount in this decade, this chapter singles out the oil industry for specialized attention.

2

In 1928 the major international oil companies had described their industry as in a state of "overproduction"; as earlier noted, they had made the "red line" stabilization arrangements on July 31, and, on a broader scale, they had entered into the Achnacarry accord on September 17. Because of overproduction in the late 1920s, mid-continental and gulf oil producers in the United States had sought tariffs on imported crude oil to protect the domestic price. U.S. investors in Venezuela were introducing cheap crude oil into eastern United States in competition with home production. Then came the depression, and oil prices sank. Late in 1930, the huge East Texas oil field came into production. The U.S. oil industry went into a "near panic." With no prorationing and no production plan, East Texas oilmen let their wells run "full blast." During 1930 the factory price of all commodities declined 12 per cent; the price of petroleum products sank 20 per cent.[4]

The overabundance of oil, the entry of cheap Venezuelan crude on the American market, and low depression prices caused U.S. international oil companies to reorganize their domestic and foreign business. In a few instances, the old Standard Oil companies recombined and shifted properties. Thus, in July 1931 (after the Department of Justice indicated no objection), Standard Oil of New York and Vacuum Oil Company merged and formed Socony-Vacuum Oil Company. Socony-Vacuum at origin was America's second largest oil company (after Standard Oil of New Jersey).* It acquired the complementary and extensive marketing operations of Standard Oil of New York in the Far East and of Vacuum Oil in Europe, Africa, Australia, and New Zealand, but it lacked significant foreign interests in crude oil production.[5]

---

* Socony-Vacuum was later renamed Mobil Oil.

Table IX.1. U.S. direct investments in petroleum,[1] 1929, 1940 (book value in million U.S. dollars)

	Europe	Canada [2]	Cuba and West Indies	Mexico	Central America	South America	Asia	Africa	Oceania	Total
1929	239	55	62	206	4	512	151	32	81	1,341
	(231)	(55)	(35)	(205)	(4)	(373)	(114)	(32)	(68)	(1,117)
1940	306	120	65	42	8	457	177	50	49	1,277 [3]

Source: For 1929, Cleona Lewis's figures have been used (as in table VIII.2). For 1929 (in parenthesis) and for 1940, U.S. Department of Commerce estimates have been used from U.S. Department of Commerce, Bureau of Foreign and Domestic Commerce, American Direct Investments in Foreign Countries—1940 (Washington, D.C. 1942), and U.S. Department of Commerce, Bureau of Foreign and Domestic Commerce, American Direct Investments in Foreign Countries, Trade Information Bull. 731 (Washington, D.C. 1930).

[1] Includes exploration, production, refining, some transportation, and distribution.
[2] Includes Newfoundland.
[3] Includes some "unallocated petroleum" investments.

Standard Oil of New Jersey also recombined with a former Standard Oil unit in 1930, when it reacquired interests in Anglo-American Oil Company, Ltd., the large British marketing firm that had been separated from Standard Oil by the 1911 decree.[6] Then, in a second, even more important move, in 1932 Jersey Standard purchased from Standard Oil Company (Indiana) the foreign properties of Pan American Petroleum & Transport Company, which Standard of Indiana had obtained from Edward L. Doheny in 1925. Standard Oil of Indiana had watched with apprehension the agitation by domestic producers for a U.S. tariff on imported crude oil. Such a tariff would severely penalize it, for Pan American Petroleum & Transport's giant Venezuelan and Mexican output had been sold in the United States. Standard Oil of Indiana had virtually no foreign marketing organization in 1929. Standard Oil of Indiana had taken two actions: it lobbied vigorously against the tariff, and at the same time, recognizing that it might not be successful, it had spent "millions," trying to create "overnight" a foreign marketing structure. In June 1930 it had purchased the Tide Water Export Corporation, a subsidiary of Tide Water Associated Oil Company, that sold in Brazil and Argentina; less than a year later Standard of Indiana had acquired the Petroleum Storage and Finance Company of England, a holding company for a number of British distributors. Standard of Indiana, however, learned that to create an overseas distribution network was not simple.

Despite its efforts, its main market remained in the United States. Thus, when in February 1931 Jersey Standard and Gulf had proposed to Standard of Indiana that all three voluntarily reduce imports into the United States from Venezuela to ward off congressional imposition of a tariff, Standard of Indiana had declined to participate in the arrangement. Its president, Edward G. Seubert, had declared that the matter of curtailing imports was the "most important question that had ever come before the Board." The life blood of Standard of Indiana's subsidiary, Pan American Petroleum & Transport Company, depended on the decision. At this point, President Herbert Hoover had asked Seubert to cooperate in limiting imports; finally, under pressures of the U.S. president, the company late in May 1931 reluctantly had agreed to do so.

Less than two months later, Seubert announced he would sell the *foreign* properties of Pan American Petroleum & Transport Company to Standard Oil of New Jersey. The nub of the matter was that if the threatened tariff were imposed (which seemed likely), Standard of Indiana would be left with foreign producing properties that were "white elephants," since the company, despite its new marketing outlets, did not have an adequate distribution network abroad. With worldwide oil prices low, its heavy investment in producing properties was a liability.

Actually, Standard of Indiana executives saw before them two choices: (1) to spend millions of additional dollars to develop a foreign marketing organization, to spend this money in the midst of the depression, and to spend it when oil prices (and company profits) were low, or alternatively (2) to sell the foreign properties. It selected the second course.

Jersey Standard already had the foreign marketing organization, built up over fifty years. Accordingly, on April 30, 1932, Jersey Standard and Standard of Indiana made a contract that provided for the sale of all Pan-American's foreign assets to Jersey Standard. These properties included Lago Petroleum Corporation in Venezuela (in 1932 the largest American producer there), Lago Oil & Transport Company (with its substantial petroleum refinery on the island of Aruba), the old Doheny businesses in Mexico, comprising Huasteca Oil Company, Mexican Petroleum Company, and other enterprises (together totaling the greatest U.S. oil output in Mexico), as well as the newly acquired foreign marketing facilities, including Tide Water Export Corporation—in sum, a net book value of $161,090,171.92.* In June 1932 the anticipated tariff was imposed.[7]

Domestic customs duties sometimes have an impact on American international business. When in 1930 the Smoot-Hawley tariff became law and foreigners were short dollars, as noted, the firm of Anderson, Clayton, & Co. began to invest outside the United States and sold *foreign* cotton abroad; by the mid-1930s its entire pattern of trade changed. Likewise, U.S. levies on the entry of foreign copper in 1932 had altered the contours of commerce in copper: American producers of copper abroad supplied Europe from their foreign mines rather than by exporting from the United States. Similarly, the effect of the U.S. tariff on oil in June 1932 was a restructuring international trade in that commodity. Prior to June 1932, Jersey Standard had supplied its European distribution organization primarily with refined oil from the United States. Now, Jersey Stan-

---

* According to a National Planning Association study, Jersey Standard allocated $135 million to the acquisition of the properties in Venezuela and Aruba—"considered to be one of the best spent $135 million in corporate history." Taylor and Lindeman, *Creole Petroleum Corporation*, p. 13.

dard, through its purchase of the foreign properties of Pan American Petroleum & Transport Company, had become the largest U.S. oil producer in Venezuela. It shipped its Venezuelan output to Europe,* where cheaper Venezuelan oil replaced U.S. exports. Some thirty years later, a Jersey Standard official could write: "Up to about 1932 the oil needs of Western Europe (the largest area of consumption outside the United States) were met by exports from the United States, largely in the form of finished products. Then Venezuela became the chief source of European supply until 1948 . . . [when] Middle Eastern crude began to displace oil from Venezuela." The U.S. tariff stimulated the first change.[8]

3

In the 1930s when American oil companies went abroad, as in the past, sometimes they invested individually.[9] Often, however, in the 1930s, U.S. enterprises participated in joint ventures in foreign countries. There was nothing new about their doing so: joint ventures to share production costs and to provide outlets for Venezuelan and Colombian oil had existed in the 1920s; [10] under the prompting of the State Department, as we have seen, American enterprises had joined with European firms in the Iraq Petroleum Company.[11] During the 1930s, as U.S. oil companies moved further afield and as depression conditions prevailed, political and commercial risks loomed larger, capital demands grew, and the need for marketing outlets became more imperative. Thus, U.S. oil men entered into added joint enterprises abroad; with one exception, all the principal ones were with other western oil companies. Table IX.2 contains a brief list of significant joint ventures, which the text will consider.

The first two of the important joint ventures came into existence because the host nations desired domestic refining (imports of crude oil were cheaper than imports of refined products; thus, crude oil imports saved scarce foreign exchange). Accordingly, Jersey Standard, Gulf Oil, and Atlantic Refining organized Société Franco-Américaine de Raffinage in 1930 to build a large refinery near Le Havre, France. French petroleum legislation made the facility necessary.[12] The second, Mitsubishi Oil Company, was formed in 1931; it erected a refinery in Japan. Associated Oil (an American company) owned 50 per cent of the Mitsubishi Oil Company, while the other 50 per cent was held by Mitsubishi interests.

* Much of this was refined at Aruba and then shipped to Europe; later with new refineries in Europe, much of it came to be shipped as crude.

Table IX.2. Principal new joint ventures by American oil companies abroad in the 1930s

Name of joint company	Date of formation joint venture	Companies involved	Purpose of joint venture	Area of operation
Société Franco-Américaine de Raffinage	1930	Jersey Standard Gulf Oil Atlantic Refining	Refining	France
Mitsubishi Oil Co.	1931	Associated Oil Co.[1] Mitsubishi	Refining Marketing	Japan—and parts of East Asia
Standard-Vacuum Oil Co. (Stanvac)	1933	Socony-Vacuum Jersey Standard	Producing Refining Marketing	Asian and African countries east and southwest of the Persian Gulf and Oceania
Kuwait Oil Co., Ltd.	1934	Gulf Anglo-Iranian	Production	Kuwait
Bahrein Petroleum Co., Ltd.	1936	Calif.-Standard Texaco	Production	Bahrain
California Texas Oil Co. (Caltex)	1936	Calif.-Standard Texaco	Marketing	Asia, Oceania, South and East Africa
California Arabian Standard Oil Co. (later, 1944, Arabian American Oil Company, or ARAMCO)	1936	Calif.-Standard Texaco	Production	Saudi Arabia
NV Nederlandsche Pacific Petroleum Maatschappij	1936	Calif.-Standard Texaco	Exploration	Sumatra, Java
Colombian Petroleum Co. (Barco Concession)	1936–1937	Texaco Socony-Vacuum	Production	Colombia
Mene Grande Oil Co. (physical assets only)	1937	Gulf, International Petroleum Company (a Jersey Standard affiliate); Royal Dutch-Shell	Production Refining	Venezuela

Source: See notes 12–29.
[1] Tide Water Associated Oil Co. in 1936 took over the properties of its subsidiary Associated Oil Co.

This Japanese enterprise was the exceptional joint venture between an American oil company and nonwestern capital. It was effectively controlled by the Japanese, for of its three officers, the president, vice president, and managing director, the contract specified that only the vice president would be an American. Americans would supply technical assistance and train Japanese to run the operations; they would also furnish crude oil for the new refinery.[13]

Standard-Vacuum Oil Company was a more comprehensive joint venture. As noted, Jersey Standard had producing and refining facilities in the Netherlands East Indies, but no nearby distribution outlets. It sold its refined oil to Standard Oil of New York (Socony-Vacuum after 1931). It was not economical for Jersey Standard to transport this production to more distant markets and after 1928 it would have been contrary to the spirit of the Achnacarry accord for Jersey Standard to have done so. Socony-Vacuum desired the nearby output. Since Jersey Standard's facilities complemented those of Socony-Vacuum, the two U.S. companies in 1933 organized Standard-Vacuum Oil Company (Stanvac) to produce, refine, transport, and market in Oceania and in Asian and African countries east and southwest of the Persian Gulf. The new Stanvac was owned 50-50 by the two leading U.S. oil companies. In the 1930s, it expanded its producing and marketing operations.[14]

Meanwhile, in Kuwait, when the 1930s began, Gulf Oil was still seeking a concession. Anglo-Persian Oil Company (name changed in 1935 to Anglo-Iranian Oil Company) became interested, and after lengthy negotiations, Gulf agreed to share a concession with Anglo-Persian. Gulf realized that to develop oil in Kuwait it would need extra capital (between 1932 and 1936 Gulf Oil paid no dividends, owing to depression conditions), but more important, the British Colonial Office desired the ruler of Kuwait to confine his concessions to British nationals; one way for Gulf to obtain British approval was to cooperate with Anglo-Persian. Thus, in 1934, the Kuwait Oil Company, Ltd., was formed—owned 50 per cent by Gulf, 50 per cent by Anglo-Persian. The Shaikh of Kuwait, by the oil contract of December 23, 1934, granted Kuwait Oil Company, Ltd., an exclusive oil and gas concession covering the entire Kuwait territory for seventy-five years. The company drilled its first oil well in 1936, which showed heavy oil but not sufficient quantity for commercial exploitation. A second well, drilled at Burgan, south of Kuwait Bay, in 1937, was, to quote Lord Cadman of Anglo-Iranian, "successful in striking oil." Gulf reported that the "successful outcome" of the venture in Kuwait "now seems assured." Yet, at the Anglo-Iranian Annual Meeting in 1939 Lord Cadman neglected to mention Kuwait. He was far more interested in oil in Iran and in his company's exploratory work in England! By the start of World War II, no tanker shipments from Kuwait had yet been made.[15]

Elsewhere, in the vicinity of the Persian Gulf, developments proceeded slowly. Standard Oil of California, as noted in Chapter V, had formed the Bahrein Petroleum Company, Ltd. (Bapco), to explore on the island of Bahrain. On August 1, 1930 (in response to U.S. government pressure), the British Colonial Office reluctantly approved the transfer of the oil prospecting rights to Bapco. The company spudded its first well in 1931 and struck oil in 1932. After the British relaxed their opposition, the Shaikh of Bahrain on December 29, 1934, granted the "Original Mining Lease" to Bapco—a concession for fifty-five years, covering an area of roughly 100,000 acres. Bapco shipped its first crude oil from Bahrain that December.[16]

While active in Bahrain, Standard Oil of California turned its attention to Saudi Arabia—the mainland, only some twenty miles away. On May 29, 1933, Standard Oil of California obtained a concession from Saudi Arabia. In return, the company agreed to loan the government of Saudi Arabia £30,000 gold (or its equivalent).* The government would also receive an annual sum of £5,000 in rental, payable in advance, until the discovery of oil. If the agreement were not terminated in eighteen months, the company was to make a second loan, this one of £20,000 gold (or its equivalent). The two loans were to be repaid by deductions from one-half the royalties due the government. In deference to Moslem practice, the loans carried no interest. On the discovery of oil in commercial quantities, Standard Oil of California contracted to advance the gov-

---

* A loan as a reward for the granting of a concession was not a novel practice. China wanted one when negotiating with Standard Oil of New York in 1914 (RG 59, 893.6363/1, National Archives); Guatemala asked it of Electric Bond and Share in 1919 (RG 59, 763.72113/950, NA); Firestone loaned money to Liberia in connection with its concession in 1926 (see Chapter V). There are other examples. Quite often, after companies had concessions, they would loan money to the host governments, the repayments to be made out of the companies' royalties or taxes due the government in the months ahead. Creole did this in Venezuela (interviews with company officials); United Fruit did this in Central America (see Chapter V). Sometimes the loans would be carried by the company involved; other times, the company would guarantee a loan floated through other channels.

ernment an additional £50,000 gold and a similar amount was to be paid one year later, both loans to be repaid by deductions from royalties. On all the oil produced, the Saudi Arabian government would receive a royalty of four shillings gold (or its equivalent) per ton of oil produced and saved. The initial concession was for sixty years and covered roughly 360,000 square miles (the mileage was not specified in the concession, only the boundaries of the area "covered by exclusive rights"). The concession gave the company "preference rights" to acquire an oil concession covering the balance of eastern Saudi Arabia, including such rights as the government had or might acquire in the so-called Neutral Zone, bordering on the Persian Gulf south of Kuwait. A supplementary letter agreement of May 29, 1933, defined the nature of the preference rights. Article 9 of the concession provided that the company would relinquish to the government such portions of its exclusive area as it might not decide to explore further. Standard Oil of California formed an operating company, California Arabian Standard Oil Company to develop its concession.[17]

While in the past, American companies obtained diplomatic support from the U.S. government in entering the Middle East, Standard Oil of California's inroads in Saudi Arabia did not have U.S. government aid. Franklin Delano Roosevelt in his first months in office and Secretary of State Cordell Hull had little interest in aiding the American oil companies abroad, and Standard Oil of California apparently had no need for the assistance.* With Standard Oil of California's activity in Bahrain and in Saudi Arabia, for the first time a 100-per-cent American-owned enterprise had obtained concessions in what had been the British preserve —the Middle East.†

By 1936 Standard Oil of California looked with only partial satisfaction on its venture in Bahrain. The field was in production; the company was constructing a 10,000 barrel refinery and now sought marketing outlets. In Saudi Arabia, oil had been discovered, but Standard-California informed its stockholders that "the full extent of the field has not yet been established." Recalling these early years, one executive remembered that "sometimes there was an open question whether the venture should

* Hull later wrote "The company obtained the concession on its own initiative . . . King Ibn Saud, suspicious of governmental diplomatic processes, had preferred to deal directly with company officials." Hull, *Memoirs*, p. 1511.

† Technically, these were not the first 100-per-cent-owned concessions Americans had gotten in the Middle East, but they were the first that were obtained, *retained*, and successfully developed.

be abandoned and the approximately $10 million spent written off as a total loss." [18]

At this point, Standard Oil of California started to cooperate with The Texas Company. Texaco had an extensive oil marketing network in India, Australia, China, the Philippines, and South Africa that would be useful for the Bahrain production. As a result of a first set of transactions, Texaco and Standard Oil of California came to share 50-50 ownership in Bahrein Petroleum Company, Ltd. (Bapco), which in turn owned a newly formed marketing subsidiary, California Texas Oil Company, Ltd. (or Caltex, as it was called). Caltex acquired Texaco's marketing subsidiaries in Oceania, Asia, and Africa. Subsequently, Caltex and Bapco would work closely with one another.* Second, Texaco in December 1936 obtained from Standard-California one-half interest in California Arabian Standard Oil Company,† with its Saudi Arabian concession, and also one-half interest in N.V. Nederlandsche Pacific Petroleum Maatschappij, with the concessions it had acquired in Sumatra and Java in 1931.‡ From these arrangements, California-Standard obtained a stake in foreign marketing outlets and a partner to share its risks in exploration and production; Texaco acquired its first holdings in eastern hemisphere producing properties. [19]

By the end of the 1930s, production in Bahrain had reached a "stabilized condition"; oil output was in 1939 roughly the same as in 1937 and 1938. It seemed clear that Bahrain offered no bonanzas. [20] Caltex in the late 1930s enlarged its marketing outlets. In China, Texas Co. (China) Ltd. kept its old name, for the Texaco red star had an established reputation throughout the country; the company could take advantage of the star image and the brand name. On the other hand, where English was spoken, the firm came to change its name to Caltex; thus, there was Caltex (Philippines), Caltex (New Zealand), Australia, India, and so forth. In 1940, Caltex Africa Limited was incorporated in South Africa to carry on the former Texaco business. In many cases, Caltex's distribution outlets were supplied by oil refined in Bahrain. [21]

Finally, the Standard-California-Texaco joint venture in Saudi Arabia

---

* In time, Bapco became a subsidiary of Caltex rather than vice versa. As earlier noted, to meet British demands, Bapco was incorporated in Canada; Caltex, for tax reasons, was incorporated in Nassau, in the Bahamas.

† Renamed Arabian American Oil Co. (ARAMCO) in January 1944.

‡ This company, later renamed N.V. Caltex Pacific Petroleum Maatschappij, also had a 20 per cent interest in N.V. Nederlandsche Nieuw Guinee Petroleum Maatschappij with a concession in Dutch New Guinea. Forty per cent of the Dutch New Guinea company was owned by Stanvac and 40 per cent by a subsidiary of Royal Dutch-Shell.

appeared promising when on October 16, 1938, the California Arabian Standard Oil Company announced its discovery of oil in commercial quantities. Now German, Italian, and Japanese enterprises, as well as the Iraq Petroleum Company, rushed to bid for concessions. But California Arabian Standard Oil Company had preference rights—specified in its initial concession and the letter agreement—and on May 31, 1939, acquired a new concession, raising its exclusive area to roughly 440,000 square miles (an area equal to about one-sixth of the United States). The supplemental concession was to last until 1999. In accord with its initial concession obligations, the company in 1940 built a small refinery at Ras Tanura on the Persian Gulf, although much of its oil still went by tank barge to Bahrain for refining there.[22]

As for the joint venture between Standard Oil of California and Texaco in N.V. Nederlandsche Pacific Petroleum Maatschappij, it discovered oil in June 1939 but did not begin production until after World War II.[23]

Meanwhile in Latin America, joint ventures among American companies assumed importance. The Barco concession in Colombia had become in the 1920s a shared activity between two U.S. companies, South American Gulf Oil Company and the Carib Syndicate. By the 1930s, Gulf Oil, having made a significant commitment in Kuwait and straining its resources in Venezuela, decided not to develop the Barco concession. Accordingly, in 1936 Texaco and Socony-Vacuum each acquired 50 per cent of the stock of the South American Gulf Company; the next year Texaco and Socony-Vacuum bought the interest of the Carib Syndicate in Colombian Petroleum, so that by 1937 Colombian Petroleum Company was owned jointly by Texaco and Socony-Vacuum. These two companies completed a 263-mile pipeline in October 1939, and that November the first oil from the Barco concession was marketed commercially. Up to that time over $60 million had been invested in the property; not a penny dividends had yet come to the investors. By 1940 Texaco admitted, "The Barco concession has thus far been disappointing and the management of Colombian Petroleum Company has considered it necessary to reduce materially its estimates of the crude oil reserves thus far developed." The 1940 combined net loss for the Colombian Petroleum Company and the pipeline company was $7.4 million, based mainly on increased depletion and depreciation charges "made necessary by the changed estimates of crude oil reserves."[24]

In 1937, the Gulf subsidiary in Venezuela, Mene Grande Oil Company, in need of extra capital, arranged to sell half interest in its output to an affiliate of Jersey Standard (International Petroleum Company), which in turn sold one-half of its acquisition to Royal Dutch-Shell, thus enlarging the participation in this joint enterprise.[25]

In short, the principal new joint ventures in oil abroad in the 1930s fell into three categories: (1) two were in refining, (2) two saw the integrating of enterprises where marketing facilities and oil supplies complemented one another, and (3) a number involved the sharing of risks and costs of exploration and production. As has been seen, Société Franco-Américaine de Raffinage and Mitsubishi Oil Company were in the first category; Stanvac and Caltex were examples of the second type; and the cooperative efforts in the Middle East, the Dutch East Indies, and Latin America fit under the third rubric. Joint ventures between western oil enterprises had become a significant way of undertaking business abroad. For the participants, they limited the risks taken and provided partial protection against the perils of international business.

4

Worldwide, U.S. oil companies met a wary reception in the 1930s. In the Middle East, Americans encountered an environment totally new to them. They found women with veils, men with strange customs, a difficult language, and completely unfamiliar religious codes. Moreover, the Middle East was by no means homogenous. Bahrain and Kuwait, as British protectorates, had legal systems that bore some resemblance to what Americans knew.* In both countries, Americans ran their oil operations through "British" companies: The Bahrein Petroleum Company, Ltd., incorporated in Canada, employed in large part a British staff; The Kuwait Oil Company, Ltd., half-owned by British capital, likewise, had a preponderance of British managers. In London, the foreign office insisted not only on the British incorporation but also on the primarily British management. Americans complied.[26]

---

* Over many decades a British adviser to the Shaikh in Bahrain built a stable administration. (Belgrave, Welcome to Bahrain, pp. 40–43). In Kuwait in 1925 a "British jurisdiction" had been established; it administered the law, under English practices, for almost all the non-Arabs within the country; a "national jurisdiction" administered the Islamic law to all Arabs and nationals of Iran; Americans were under the "British jurisdiction." Hijazi, "Kuwait," The American Journal of Comparative Law 13:428ff (Summer 1964). In 1928, one observer had noted "British influence in Bahrain both internal [and] external matters is 90 percent while in Kuwait 30 percent." Holmes cable, cited in Ward, Negotiations for Oil Concessions, p. 69; see also pp. 61–63 for more differences.

In Iran, the oil industry in the 1930s continued to be entirely British owned. Anglo-Persian Oil Company (as of 1935, Anglo-Iranian Oil Company) had had difficulties in the 1920s with the Iranian government over determination of net profits; in November 1932 Riza Shah's government canceled the company's concession. The British government (which had a large investment in Anglo-Persian) appealed to the Council of the League of Nations; then on April 29, 1933, Anglo-Persian accepted a new agreement which "eliminated most of the terms which the [Iranian] government found objectionable." This 1932–1933 confrontation was the earliest clash between an oil company and a Middle Eastern government. It was in the Middle Eastern country that had had self-government the longest (Iran had established constitutional government in 1906) and where the oil industry had had its longest history in that region. In the mid-1930s, American firms continued to seek concessions in Iran: The Amiranian Oil Company (controlled by Seaboard Oil Company, which in turn was affiliated with The Texas Company) got a drilling permit for sixty years, but in 1938 the Amiranian company discontinued operations and was placed in liquidation.* The British remained supreme.[27]

Iraq, under British mandate, had established a constitutional government in 1924; in 1932 the League of Nations recognized Iraq as an independent state. King Faisal died in 1933, to be followed by his son, King Ghazi I. King Ghazi was an ineffective ruler and a succession of cabinets ran the government; tribal revolt broke out within the country. Then, General Bakr Sidqi—an admirer of Turkey's Mustafa Kemal Ataturk—took over in a military coup in 1936. Ten months later he was overthrown and then assassinated. Factionalism, political rivalry, and general instability characterized the next four years. As indicated earlier, Americans held 23.75 per cent interest in Iraq Petroleum Company. American drillers worked at the Kirkuk field in the North. The pipeline from Kirkuk to the ports of Tripoli in Lebanon and Haifa in Palestine was constructed by American engineers using American materials. These were the main U.S. impacts. Iraq Petroleum Company's operating management was primarily British. Thus, it was the British executives who sought to steer an even rudder through the Iraqi political intrigue. From the time Iraq Petroleum began to ship oil in 1934, the Iraqi governments

---

* Herbert Feis, economic adviser in the State Department, writes that the Amiranian Oil Company "never sank a drill. The supporters of the venture faltered over the economic and political hazards . . . the concession was returned to Iran." *Seen from E.A.*, p. 176.

—one after the other—expressed dissatisfaction with the royalties paid by the company. Strong anti-British sentiment existed in Iraq. Indeed, many Iraqis viewed the oil industry with suspicion and distrust—owing to its size, to its being foreign, and to the widespread belief that "the offices of Iraq Petroleum and the offices of the British consulates were one the same." Yet there was no specific confrontation.[28]

The British government had in the Treaty of Jiddah, May 20, 1927, recognized the Saudi Arab Kingdom as a sovereign state. King 'Abd al-'Aziz Ibn Sa'ud became the ruler of that nation. Saudi Arabia was the only Middle Eastern country where in the 1930s Americans provided the entire oil company management. There Americans found a land steeped in religious traditionalism. Their oil concession stated, "To avoid any doubt on the point, it is distinctly understood that the Company or anyone connected with it shall have no right to interfere with the administrative, political or religious affairs within Saudi Arabia."

Company officials did not interfere; but as residents in Saudi Arabia they observed the administrative, political and religious affairs of the nation, and they operated in this for them novel context. Their relations with the government were on a personal basis, at first with the king and then with the minister of finance. In the eastern province where the oil existed, the Wahhabis—with their puritanical Moslem religion and their strict, almost literal, adherence to the teaching of the Koran—presented the newcomers with endless problems of tact and adjustment. Here, there had been no "British tradition." The Saudis were suspicious of foreigners. Their religious leaders objected to the introduction of motion pictures, musical instruments, phonographs, dolls for children (considered as effigies), or even art books. The Americans had to make arrangements for five worship periods a day and for the observation of the Ramadan—a period of 29 to 30 days of daytime fasting—for Arab employees. Weekends in the Moslem world came on Thursday and Friday rather than Saturday and Sunday. The company arranged its schedules accordingly. The company never did adopt "Sun Time" (Arab time based on the sun); oil men used their own time within the company installations. But on the whole the adaptation made by the new arrivals was remarkable.

When the company came to Saudi Arabia, that country had virtually no industry, except for the local manufacture of ornamental knives and swords, some rug weaving, and primitive leather fabrication. Most of the population was nomadic. Many lived on the edge of starvation. Company officials had to teach Arab workers the rudiments of industrialization. Workers had no conception of the bolt and nut; most were illiterate (many learned to read English before learning to read Arabic); skills had to be taught. In the 1930s, although oil production was still minimal, the seeds of change had been planted. And since the Americans were there to stay, the oil company officials began to build their own towns for the Americans who would come to live in Saudi Arabia. Dhahran—the American town—would be an American enclave in an Arab land.[29]

During the 1930s in the Middle East only Iran had contemplated nationalizing oil resources, and then with no success. With the exception of Iran and to a lesser extent Iraq, the Middle Eastern oil industry was in its infancy. Oil companies had more difficulties elsewhere.

5

In Latin America nationalist fervor turned its ardor against the large petroleum enterprises. Oil was seen as a precious and exhaustible resource. Politicians, newspapers, men on the street talked of oil's bringing wealth to the foreign intruder and leaving little for the host countries. Most Latin American nations neglected the possibilities of what could be obtained by appropriate government levies on the petroleum companies; royalties and taxes paid by the oil companies remained relatively small. At the same time as the oil enterprises established towns, furnished employment, and introduced a higher standard of living than those countries had known before, the American staffs remained isolated from the indigenous population. The oil companies were often resented. American drillers, roughnecks, pipeline men, and construction foremen who entered the oil industry in Latin America were frequently tough, brash, and insensitive to national feelings. Many Americans in management shared their lack of respect.

And, when in Latin America nationalists insisted the "oil is ours," the petroleum companies seemed to turn a deaf ear. These enterprises historically had been under hostile pressures. In Rumania when Standard Oil had sought a concession in 1900, the opposition argued that the Rumanian people were "selling their heritage for a mess of potage and would give themselves over into the hands of a monopolistic combination which would endanger their economic independence." [30] Despite such flamboyant phrasing, the company got its concession. During World War I, in Peru the International Petroleum Company had been soundly denounced; yet in 1922 an arbitration settlement gave the company satisfactory conditions. In Mexico, during the 1920s, animosity toward the foreign oil producers had been intense, but the enterprises continued to function—albeit on a more limited scale. Perhaps oil executives had come to accept enmity as one of the many factors in doing business. While the antagonism was only verbal, it did not present a major threat to profits.

But in the 1930s, foreign petroleum companies in Latin America came under a new wave of severe criticism. Increasingly, talk was translated into action. The intensification of nationalism that adversely affected all U.S. companies in Latin America had its most profound impact on those enterprises in the oil industry. The oil companies produced, transported, refined, and sold oil on this continent—and in each role, they found themselves "under fire." U.S. oil enterprises were in fact, as we will see, maneuvered, manacled, and mangled. The following brief survey by country presents a sampling of the confrontations.

In Chile, Brazil, and Uruguay, where there was no oil production in the 1930s,* the host governments played an active role in formulating petroleum policies. While oil production since 1926 had been a government monopoly in Chile, a 1932 law gave Chilean capital a complete monopoly over the importation and distribution of oil. This 1932 law, which was never put into effect, hung like the sword of Damocles over the U.S. oil companies that continued to import and sell in Chile. Three years later, the government-supported Compañía de Petróleos de Chile (COPEC) was formed and obtained preferential treatment in securing foreign exchange for imports. U.S. oil companies—according to an industry report—had no choice but to cooperate in their importing and marketing activities with COPEC.[31]

Brazilian government action put Jersey Standard's wholly owned exploration company out of business. Brazil, desiring to industrialize, wanted refineries. Jersey Standard set out in 1937 to build one. Then, a decree law of April 29, 1938, confined refining to Brazilian born nationals; Standard Oil of New Jersey shut its refinery. Americans could, and did, continue to import and to sell oil in Brazil.[32]

A 1931 Uruguayan law gave that nation's government the exclusive right to import and to refine crude oil. The law authorized a new gov-

* Oil was discovered in Chile in the 1930s, but there was still no production; oil was found in Bahia, Brazil, in 1939 by a government agency.

ernment company, Administración Nacional de Combustibles, Alcohol y Portland (ANCAP) to import petroleum products and to market them in competition with private foreign companies. Certain distribution was handled exclusively by ANCAP. As a result, foreign oil companies saw their market share diminish rapidly. In January 1937, ANCAP built a modern refinery—the first in Uruguay. U.S. oil companies, according to their own statement, "to protect themselves . . . were finally obliged to enter into an agreement with ANCAP, which provided for the maintenance of a certain market position and included an arrangement whereby the companies delivered crude to ANCAP which processed for them in order to meet their finished-product requirements." [33] In sum, in Uruguay, as well as in Chile and Brazil, American companies' activities were circumscribed by host government measures.

In oil producing nations, the badgering of foreign oil companies was more extreme. The Argentine government had participated in oil producing since the industry's inception in 1907; government operations had coexisted with private enterprise. Then in 1935, under a new Petroleum Law, the federal and provincial governments reserved for the government oil company, Yacimientos Petrolíferos Fiscales (Y.P.F.), the areas most likely to have petroleum deposits; private foreign companies were confined to their existing concessions, which would serve to limit their production. The next year (1936) the Argentine government forbade oil exports and, far more important, restricted oil imports. "We are being squeezed at both ends," complained a U.S. oil company executive, referring to the curbs on both oil exploration and imports. Inside Argentina, distribution went under strict government regulation. Standard Oil of New Jersey believed conditions were so detrimental that in 1936 it offered to sell its Argentine holdings to Y.P.F. This required the approval of the Argentine Congress, which did not act. The company then withdrew its offer. On June 28, 1937, the foreign oil firms made a marketing agreement with Y.P.F. They explained that they were forced to do so, for otherwise, they would be deprived of licenses to import crude oil and refined products. The agreement did not calm the anti–Standard Oil agitation so prevalent within the nation.[34]

In Colombia, in 1931, business conditions looked promising; [35] then under Alfonso López (1934–1936) new labor legislation made investors fearful. A constitutional amendment in 1936 gave Colombia the right to expropriate property "for motives of public utility and social interest."

The Era of Depression

Colombia did not expropriate, but oil companies viewed the future with apprehension.[36] The settlement of 1922 governing International Petroleum Company's activities in Peru remained in effect in the 1930s, but increasingly that enterprise's executives heard hostile comments. In 1934, Peru organized the Department of Petroleum, the immediate predecessor to the government oil company, Empresa Petrolera Fiscal. Nonetheless, International Petroleum Company still operated.[37]

Until the death of Juan Vicente Gómez in 1935, Venezuela offered the most ideal place for the foreign oil companies. Then, Gómez's successor, Eleazar López Contreras (1935–1940), made popular the expression "Sow the Petroleum," meaning spread the earnings of the oil enterprises throughout the Venezuelan economy, so the nation as well as the foreigners would profit from oil developments. The 1936 Petroleum Law proved less than satisfactory to the international companies, while foreign businessmen felt the 1938 Petroleum Law imposed "odious" conditions. For the first time, the 1938 law expressedly authorized the Venezuelan government to enter the oil industry. According to an internal memorandum of February 24, 1940, in Creole Petroleum Corporation files, it did not "appear probable that any serious operator would undertake the risk of [new] operation[s]" under the 1938 Petroleum Law.[38] To augment the problems of U.S. companies were the new Venezuelan labor laws. One American oil executive recalled that when the 1936 Labor Law passed—when the foreign oil companies were required to provide housing, schools, hospitals, holidays and to follow the rulings on wages, hours, and working conditions—"every one thought it was going to bankrupt us, but the price of crude oil went up and so the situation turned out not to be serious." Most of the American oil companies in Venezuela already provided housing, schools, and hospitals for their workers, but they did not want to be compelled to do so. Indeed the very fact that the companies apparently felt such indignation at the legislation would indicate that all the requirements had not been met voluntarily. Moreover, the 1936 Venezuelan law legalized unions—an action which was reprehensible to the Jersey Standard general manager in Venezuela, Henry E. Linam, who emphatically declared, "It's against my principles to let anybody else run my business." This echoed what many American businessmen were saying in the United States and was not distinctive to Latin America.[39]

Although in the 1930s the greatly enlarged entry of host governments into the oil business (far more than increases in taxes or royalties) hobbled U.S. enterprises in Latin America, until 1937 there were no confiscations. The change came in March 1937. Standard Oil of New Jersey had found oil in southeastern Bolivia in the 1920s. In 1932, with the depression, with the general abundance of oil supplies, with its new acquisitions in Mexico and Venezuela from Standard Oil of Indiana, Jersey Standard stopped drilling new wells in Bolivia. In 1936, it opened negotiations to sell its Bolivian properties to the government. Then on March 13, 1937, the military junta in Bolivia seized Jersey Standard's properties and turned them over to a newly organized government company. The junta claimed the company had committed "fraud," had not paid taxes fully, and was "smuggling" oil out of the country. The company protested its innocence. Its loss, it stated, was $17 million. Jersey Standard believed there was a "principle" involved; if seizure were recognized, Argentina and Peru might follow and "forcibly" expel the company. The U.S. State Department first advocated that the oil company should exhaust all of its own remedies—through the Bolivian courts. This proved of no avail, and by 1940, the Department had come to feel it should make representations, since the company was entitled to compensation.[40]

Meanwhile, in Mexico the foreign oil companies had become enmeshed in a Mexican-government-backed labor dispute. This was one more conflict in the prolonged, intermittent "war" between the oil enterprises and the Mexican government—a war that had been in process since the fall of Porfirio Díaz in 1911 and especially since the Mexican adoption of their 1917 constitution. In this instance, the foreign firms denied the necessity to obey Mexican labor laws that the enterprises felt were inappropriate. U.S. oil men noted with pride that they paid higher wages than other industries in Mexico. Why, they asked, should they be forced to raise compensation?

In Mexico, the oil industry produced during 1937 roughly one-fourth of Venezuela's output that year, but Mexican production equaled more than that of Colombia and Peru combined. By far the largest oil interests in Mexico in 1936–1937 were owned by Royal Dutch-Shell, its subsidiaries producing in 1936 almost 60 per cent of Mexican oil. The Royal Dutch-Shell subsidiaries had expanded their drilling in the 1920s and 1930s, while the U.S. companies—wary about the political uncertainties—had become more cautious. Of the American enterprises, the most substantial holdings were those of *Standard Oil of New Jersey*—with Doheny's old properties; Consolidated Oil Company of New York (a *Sinclair* company) through its affiliates * produced roughly 9 per cent of Mexican oil output in 1936; *Cities Service*—through Southern Fuel Refining Co., Gulf Coast Corp., and Cia. Petrolera del Agwi S.A. and other firms— accounted for almost 6 per cent of Mexican oil. *The Gulf Oil* group's output was more than 4 per cent. These then were the large American companies; they operated through a number of subsidiaries and affiliates.†

In November 1936 the Mexican Petroleum Workers Union made far reaching demands on all the major oil companies, except Gulf. When the demands were not satisfied, the workers went on strike on May 28, 1937. The Federal Labor Board declared the strike legal. The strike ended on June 10th, but the issue was joined. The union insisted on entirely new conditions of employment, which would raise substantially the cost of doing business for the oil companies.

In August 1937 an official Mexican commission concluded that "The principal oil companies operating in Mexico form part of large North American or English economic units . . . The principal oil companies operating in Mexico have never been fully integrated to the country and their interests have always been alien, and at times even opposed, to the national interests. The principal oil companies operating in Mexico have left in the Republic only wages and taxes, without in reality having cooperated in the social progress of Mexico." The oil companies were accused of: (1) having "earned enormous profits in the exploitation of the subsoil . . ." (2) influencing "national as well as international political events," (3) paying lower "real wages" than those earned by the workers in the mines or on the National Railways, (4) charging higher prices in Mexico than they charged for the oil they exported, and (5) making higher profits in Mexico than in the United States.

The commission decided that the American companies in Mexico could *afford* to raise wages and provide social benefits. It proposed the formation of a National Mixed Commission (composed of company and employee representatives) to settle the dispute and recommended the organization of a worker-company committee to plan recreational activities

* Including Sinclair-Pierce (which acquired the older Waters-Pierce holdings).

† Among the other American companies in Mexico were Standard Oil of California and South Penn Oil Company. By 1937, Texaco, Atlantic Refining, and Tide Water Oil Company had disposed of most of their Mexican holdings. U.S. Senate, *American Petroleum Interests in Foreign Countries,* pp. 241–242, 335.

to fill the leisure time of employees. The commission noted that the immense majority of the drillers in Mexico were foreigners and that "it is advisable to oblige the oil companies to utilize the services of Mexican technicians." Companies ought to supply facilities for workers' libraries, day schools for the workers' children, and night schools for the workers themselves, as well as first-class medical services.

The companies protested. The costs of such benefits would mean "confiscation by slow strangulation." The demands, they thought, represented an intrusion by the unions into management. The dispute continued. On December 18, 1937, the Federal Labor Board rendered an award in favor of the unions. The companies appealed to the Mexican Supreme Court. Their properties were at stake; their language was vigorous in the defense of their rights. "A collective labor contract which they have never been willing to accept is illegally imposed on the complainant companies." There was, they claimed, "no precept of law or of reason . . . whereby the privileges that employers grant their workers should be limited solely by the economic capacity of the former." On March 1, 1938, the Mexican Supreme Court found against the companies and gave them six days to acknowledge and enforce the new contract. The companies asked for a respite and got a temporary suspension.* The unions now claimed the enterprises were in default; the Labor Board agreed.

In his message to the Mexican nation on March 18, 1938, President Lázaro Cárdenas announced that the refusal of the oil companies to comply with the verdict of the Supreme Court left him no choice. Should the country be left to "the mercy of the maneuvers of foreign capitalists who forgetful of the fact that they had previously organized themselves into Mexican companies, in accordance with Mexican laws, are now attempting to evade the mandates and responsibilities imposed upon them by the country's authorities?" Cárdenas asked. He continued, "In how many of the villages bordering on the oil fields is there a hospital, or school, or social center, or a sanitary water supply, or an athletic field, or even an electric plant . . . ? Who is not aware of the irritating discrimination governing construction of the company camps? Comfort for the foreign personnel; misery, drabness, and insalubrity [sic] for the Mexicans. Refrigeration and protection against tropical insects for the former; indifference and neglect, medical service and supplies always grudgingly pro-

* By this time, industry circles warned about the possibility of the Mexican government's confiscating the oil companies.

vided, for the latter; lower wages and harder, more exhausting labor for our people." The president went on with his accusations, "The tolerance which the companies have abused was born, it is true, in the shadow of the ignorance, betrayals, and weakness of the country's rulers; but the mechanism was set in motion by investors lacking in the necessary moral resources to give something in exchange for the wealth they have been exploiting." The corporations were charged with spending money to buy arms and munitions and to develop an "anti-patriotic press," while denying funds to give the workers a "just" compensation. In November 1936 the Mexican Republic had passed an Expropriation Act. Now, on March 18, 1938, Cárdenas, under its authority, expropriated most of the foreign oil industry.*

Josephus Daniels, U.S. ambassador to Mexico, described the action as a "bolt from the blue." The American government—devoted to the Good Neighbor Policy—took no immediate action. The oil companies called for help from the State Department and repeated to their shareholders that they paid far higher wages than the average in Mexican industry. The State Department finally protested the seizure—but at the same time, it added that Mexico had the *right* to expropriate but the "power to confiscate carries with it the power to compensate." † Charles Rayner, petroleum adviser to the State Department, later declared that the American interests affected were promptly and energetically protected. The companies felt otherwise. In truth, gone was the business ori-

* Gulf, which had not been involved in the labor dispute, was the only large foreign company excluded from the expropriation. Wendell Gordon feels that Gulf was excluded because of its "relatively small size . . . combined with fairly good working conditions." Gordon, *Expropriation of Foreign-Owned Property in Mexico,* p. 95. Other companies not expropriated included New England Oil, Seaboard Oil, and Globe Petroleum. The expropriation included the properties of Royal Dutch-Shell, Standard Oil of New Jersey, Sinclair, Cities Service, Standard Oil of California, and South Penn Co.

† On March 27, 1938, a misconceived attempt was made to apply economic pressure. Washington announced that the silver purchase agreement with Mexico was to be suspended. Presumably, the Mexican government, which got a silver export tax and dollar exchange from silver exports, would suffer as a result. As Bryce Wood explains it, what the policy forgot was that it penalized the American mining companies in Mexico, from which 70 per cent of the silver came, and moreover, without Treasury purchases of Mexican silver, Mexico would have difficulty compensating the owners of the petroleum and agrarian properties which was what the State Department was demanding. For three weeks the Treasury sharply reduced its purchases of all foreign silver. Then it resumed its earlier volume of silver purchases at world prices, with no formal arrangement but with no discrimination against Mexican silver. "Economic sanctions" had failed. Wood, *Making of Good Neighbor Policy,* pp. 223–227.

entation of the Republicans of 1920s. Some State Department officials—Ambassador Josephus Daniels in the lead—had more sympathy with Cárdenas than with the U.S. oil companies. There is evidence that Daniels softened certain dispatches from Secretary of State Cordell Hull to the Mexican government. Moreover, the Democratic administration in 1938 was viewing business at home, and abroad, with hostility and distrust; there was little reason to believe that with such an approach, the administration would give the oil industry strong support. No consideration was ever given in Washington to the use of force in Mexico, nor did the oil companies suggest it. They did feel that a more vigorous U.S. stand could have been taken. They would have liked to have seen the expropriation voided, because Mexico, they claimed, could not pay prompt, adequate compensation. The U.S. government only advocated "proper" compensation.

And, what was proper compensation? The U.S. oil companies claimed the potential value of their properties at $200 million (U.S.); the U.S. Department of Commerce in 1938 had listed U.S. direct investment in the Mexican petroleum industry at $69 million; on their own books at the close of 1937, the companies stated their Mexican assets at $60.2 million (U.S.); the Mexican government claimed after set-offs and devaluations that the properties were worth only $50 million (U.S.).

While governmental negotiations on reimbursements ran their course, the war broke out in Europe. With war, a new demand for oil developed. Steps that might have been taken by the oil companies to reverse the expropriation proved impossible under wartime conditions.* The United States and Mexico made an initial agreement for settlement in November 1941. In 1943, the conditions and manner of payment were finally agreed upon by all parties involved: the settlement was fixed at $23,995,991 plus $5,141,709.84 interest (U.S.)! † Meanwhile, on April 22, 1942, a settle-

---

* The oil companies had worldwide marketing organizations. The Mexican government did not. By refusing to handle Mexican oil, the oil industry might have kept Mexican oil off the market. The complication was that Germany, Italy, and Japan needed oil. The State Department did not want Germany supporting the Mexican expropriation and using Mexico as a source of supply. With the war in Europe and the outlook for American entry increasingly probable, the United States did not want a friend of the Axis Powers to our south. Moreover, in wartime we also needed Mexican oil. U.S. policy was (1) of being a Good Neighbor, and (2) of not pushing Mexico into the arms of the Axis Powers. The case of the oil companies was secondary to these considerations.

† This figure exempted Sinclair, which broke ranks and settled separately for $8.5 million in May 1940 (*New York Times*, May 8, 16, 19, 1940). The valuation was set in

ment had been made in Bolivia, with that government paying the Standard Oil Company of New Jersey $1,729,375 (U.S.).[41]

In the passion of political oratory, the charges against the oil companies had grown too extreme; they exaggerated and distorted. On the other hand, the oil enterprises had not been perfect, and they learned from the Mexican experience. More than any other event in history—much more than the Russian revolution—the Mexican expropriation taught executives of the principal U.S. oil companies that foreign governments *did* have the power to confiscate, that talk *could* be translated into action, and that they *must* shape the policies of their enterprises in a fashion to mitigate the threat of nationalization. High wages, which they had always paid, were not sufficient. The State Department could not be counted on to act for them in an emergency. Arguments based on "the principles of property rights" and "the principles of international law" might not be adequate. Executives in petroleum companies *began* to realize, probably for the first time, that "careful planning and close cooperation between the local government and the foreign concessionaire are necessary to assure that the new sources of wealth . . . *will result in the maximum social and economic benefits to the inhabitants.*" This just awakening recognition would have a profound effect on the wartime and postwar activities of the major oil companies.[42]

6

When the Japanese moved into Manchuria in 1931, they sought to integrate the Japanese and Manchurian economies. In Japan and Manchuria they aimed to develop new industries, including oil refineries. Mitsubishi Oil (the joint venture involving Associated Oil Company and Mitsubishi interests) had in 1931 erected a Japanese refinery. Other purely Japanese refineries were built, and in 1931, 1932, and 1933, Japanese imports of refined oil from the United States declined. Even so, in these years most oil sold in Japan and all that sold in Manchuria was produced and refined abroad (mainly in the United States or the Dutch East Indies).

On March 27, 1934, the Japanese passed a Petroleum Control Bill, introducing price controls, new conditions on government sales, and the re-

---

April 1942, but Standard Oil of New Jersey did not agree to accept its part of the award until October 1, 1943.

quirement that six months of oil stocks be held in Japan by all importers and refiners (to give the Japanese oil reserves). By mid-1934, in Manchuria, a Japanese-controlled refinery was under construction, and on November 13, 1934, the Cabinet and Privy Council of Manchukuo (the puppet state set up by the Japanese) approved a Petroleum Monopoly Law. Under this legislation, the Manchurian Petroleum Monopoly acquired the new Manchurian oil refinery and sought to import crude oil from abroad.

The operations of Stanvac in Japan (the only U.S. oil company in Japan) * and Stanvac and Texaco in Manchuria were threatened by the Japanese plans and the new legislation. Stanvac believed it could not comply with the Japanese Petroleum Control Law without major expense; moreover, it feared that should Japan build up refining at home and in Manchuria, Japan would re-export the refined oil products and come to dominate the large oil market in China. Stanvac had important investments in selling oil in China as well as in Japan. Stanvac along with Royal Dutch-Shell sought to take steps to secure their own position.

On August 20, 1934, Stanvac officials in Japan suggested to American Ambassador Joseph Grew that perhaps Japanese authorities would treat their company better if the U.S. and British governments proposed restricting or stopping *crude oil* shipments to Japanese and future Manchurian refineries. The Ambassador endorsed such economic sanctions. Two days later, in Washington, representatives of Stanvac and Shell talked with Under Secretary of State William Phillips and the next day with Secretary of Interior Harold Ickes, requesting the U.S. government to consider such an embargo on crude oil shipments. If the Japanese had no crude oil for their refineries, they would have to continue to buy *refined* oil; since the foreign companies would supply the refined oil, the Japanese, it was argued, could not afford to penalize those firms. On August 31, Stanvac, Shell, and Texaco agreed among themselves *not* to supply crude oil to the new Manchurian refinery. But their private boycott proved to be futile, since Standard Oil of California and Union Oil were prepared to sell. Thus, Stanvac and Shell realized that if they were to act effectively against the Japanese and Manchurian refineries, the U.S. gov-

* Associated Oil Company, as noted earlier, did not control the management of Mitsubishi Oil Company, which acted as a Japanese company, conformed to Japanese laws, and had no difficulties. When State Department records deal with the problems of "foreign companies" in Japan, Mitsubishi Oil Company is not included. Shell was a British-Dutch and not a U.S. company.

ernment would have to halt crude oil exports from the *independent* American oil companies. Stanvac and Shell together could control the rest of the world's crude oil supplies, and would do so, *if* the U.S. government controlled the independent American companies! E. L. Neville, counsellor of the U.S. embassy in Tokyo, was a strong supporter of the oil companies' view—"even at the risk that such efforts may bring added irritation to the relations between Japan and the United States."

On the other hand, in Washington the State Department was ready to press the Japanese to give U.S. investors the same rights and privileges as were granted Japanese citizens, to protest restrictions on American kerosene in Manchuria, to deplore the oil monopoly in Manchuria, and to urge the foreign oil companies to act in concert, but Secretary of State Cordell Hull would *not* support an embargo on crude oil shipments, for he did not want a further deterioration in relationships between the United States and Japan.* No U.S. embargo was imposed.

Later, a State Department representative boasted that his Department had succeeded in "inducing" the Japanese government to postpone indefinitely the stockholding provisions of the 1934 Japanese Petroleum Act. But, that individual did not tell the whole story. To maintain their position in Japan, in December 1935, Stanvac and Shell offered to give the Japanese research results on the hydrogenation process for developing oil from coal resources. This offer was not made surreptitiously. The State Department knew of it, and the oil companies and the State Department both were aware that the results would be used for military purposes. The State Department's only action was to warn the American embassy in Japan to make it clear to the Japanese government that the U.S. government was not associated with the transaction. Japan, hoping to gain knowledge of hydrogenation and requiring massive supplies of refined oil (as well as crude), did not expel the foreign companies, even though the companies never conformed to the stockpiling provisions of the 1934 Petroleum Act.† U.S. *refined* oil exports to Japan rose annually from 1933

* Moreover, an embargo would be contrary to Hull's general policy of relaxing trade restrictions.

† The reader will properly ask, why didn't Stanvac and Shell undertake to refine in Japan to meet Japanese desires for industrialization? The companies did consider this, but the Japanese made it clear that they wanted refining under national control. The Japanese proceeded to build their own refineries. In defense of the companies and the State Department, it should perhaps be added that the research on hydrogenation was still at its very preliminary stages. In the near future, Japan would have difficulty using any of the results. Moreover, late in *1938,* when the Japanese pressed for data on

to 1940 (1938 excepted). Despite the fact that the U.S. government refused in the 1930s to embargo crude oil, Jersey Standard officials did tell Department of State officials that they believed the department had been helpful in Japan.

In Manchuria, Texaco sold its distribution network because of the oil monopoly. Stanvac and Shell tried to do so as well, but their demands were greater than those made by Texaco and negotiations dragged on. For a while, Stanvac sought to defeat the Manchurian oil monopoly through private crude oil boycotts (the State Department told Stanvac it had no objection to the company's taking its own actions). The efforts, however, failed; by 1936 Texaco and Standard Oil of California were selling crude oil to the Manchurian oil monopoly.

In 1937, when the Japanese invaded China, Stanvac and Texaco continued to market refined oil products in China. The *Panay* crisis (wherein a U.S. gunboat, the *Panay,* and three Stanvac vessels were bombed by the Japanese on the Yangtze River on December 12, 1937) passed over quickly, and the Japanese compensated Stanvac promptly for the sunken ships. Yet, operations in China for Stanvac and Texaco met with constant restrictions and restraints, stemming from war conditions. In the Dutch East Indies, as early as January 1937, oil men became aware that the Japanese might, in time, invade the islands to fill their oil needs. The companies anticipated difficulties. Indeed, throughout the Far East, in the late 1930s, U.S. oil marketers and producers faced an uncertain future.[43]

7

No less trying were circumstances in Europe. With oil prices declining in the early 1930s, Walter Teagle of Standard Oil of New Jersey, Sir Henri Deterding of Royal Dutch-Shell, and Sir John Cadman of Anglo-Persian continued their discussions on the regulation of oil supplies. On January 20, 1930, these three international enterprises (the world's leading companies and the leading marketers in Europe) prepared a "Memorandum for European Markets." It contained "the main principles" for the conduct of their operations in Europe. The basic principle was the "as is" condition—in keeping with the philosophy of the earlier Achna-

hydrogenation, the State Department recommended that Stanvac "stall," which it did. See Anderson, "The Standard-Vacuum Oil Company and United States Asian Policy, 1933–1941," pp. 129–130.

carry agreement. The memorandum stated that local representatives of the three corporations would consult with one another on prices and selling conditions with an aim to stabilize the petroleum trade.

The three enterprises supplemented the memorandum with the so-called, "Heads of Agreement for Distribution," December 15, 1932. These headings for agreement were formulated after the imposition of the American tariff on oil and the reshifting of the international oil trade, discussed earlier in this chapter. Socony-Vacuum, Gulf Oil, Atlantic Refining, and Texas, as well as the "big three," participated in this agreement. A new Draft Memorandum of Principles was adopted by the three giants in June 1934 to deal with agreements required by host governments. These attempts at cooperation to stabilize the oil markets seem at best to have been a tenuous proposition; early in 1938, Standard Oil of New Jersey indicated a termination of these specific stabilization arrangements.[44]

That U.S. oil companies, especially Standard Oil of New Jersey, accepted agreements with competitors was a defensive step. The agreements —although more comprehensive—were not dissimilar to those being made by other U.S. businesses dealing with other commodities. All attempted to raise and to stabilize prices. Like other American enterprises in the 1930s, Standard Oil of New Jersey was not adopting the strategies of an aggressive business trying to conquer new markets. Instead, it was fighting an uphill battle against low prices, against its own declining market percentage and against European governments' attempts at regulation.

Throughout the European continent, government policies confronted those of the private foreign oil companies—and the scope of the confrontation was unprecedented. U.S. oil companies encountered import quotas, exchange restrictions, price-fixing regulations, enforced use of alcohol and other petroleum substitutes, new taxation, export subsidies that distorted trade patterns, and reciprocal trade agreements between foreign countries that directly affected their operations. They had their profit remittances blocked. The companies found themselves under pressure to participate in national cartels, not of their own choosing. It is little wonder that in a defensive manner they discussed among themselves means of coping with the abnormal conditions of trade.

Everywhere European governments participated in the oil industry. Each European nation sought self-sufficiency in oil; this would mean savings in foreign exchange and for those governments preparing for war, the goal was to provide the country with the needed petroleum stocks. The aims of the *international* oil companies collided with national aspirations, and the latter won.[45]

One means for a nation to obtain self-sufficiency was for it to encourage new petroleum exploration; in response, American companies pushed their search for oil in Austria, Czechoslovakia, Denmark, France, Germany, Great Britain, Greece, Hungary, Italy, Poland, Rumania, and Yugoslavia.* [46] Another means was to economize on oil, by developing synthetics and by introducing compulsory employment of alcohol or other substitutes as motor fuel. Although the use of alcohol was not economical, many nations required it. Thus, in France, Germany, Italy, Austria, and Poland, petroleum companies had to add a definite percentage of alcohol to their oil products; in Czechoslovakia, Latvia, and Hungary compulsory use of alcohol was required under specified circumstances.[47]

The insistence on refineries was another way by which European governments conserved foreign exchange and improved their trade balance. The old method of using a tariff on refined oil to prompt a company to build a refinery was now supplemented by (1) the widespread use of foreign exchange restraints (limited exchange availability and sometimes exchange earmarked for crude oil only), (2) the licensing of imports and refineries (the government would decide which companies might import and refine, and how much), and (3) government participation in refineries (which forced foreign companies to build similar ones or to lose money). In France, Italy, Austria, and Yugoslavia, for example, American companies erected refineries that would not otherwise have been constructed but for the government pressures.[48]

It became the norm rather than the exception in Europe for governments to expect foreign oil companies to participate in national cartel arrangements. Of Czechoslovakia, for example, an American oil executive explained, "While these combinations were theoretically voluntary, no company—certainly no foreign company—could invite the consequences of acting counter to the wishes of the locally owned companies and the urge [sic] of the government." [49] The French government had an investment in the oil industry in Compagnie Française des Pétroles (C.F.P.).† The French state had established the Compagnie Française de Raffinage

* They made new discoveries in Hungary, Austria, and Germany. U.S. Senate, *Petroleum Interests in Foreign Countries*, p. 187.

† Only 25 per cent (later raised to 35 per cent) but C.F.P., when established in 1924, was authorized to act in the "national interest." Rondot, *Compagnie Française des Pétroles*, pp. 11, 32, 36.

(C.F.R.) in April 1929. Over considerable French opposition, on July 30, 1931, the French parliament ratified the relations between the French state and the C.F.P. and in the process approved the C.F.R.* C.F.R. was authorized to refine 25 per cent of French needs. By 1933 memoranda in Standard Oil of New Jersey files referred to the "socialization of the petroleum industry" in France. One Jersey Standard observer by 1935 was ready to recognize, at least for France, "that failure to cooperate with a national commercial endeavor—whatever the sacrifice in dollars or in principles—invariably provoked retaliatory legislation which was more costly to private interests than the original government proposals." This statement was written before the Popular Front government took power in France and before the wave of antibusiness sentiment swelled. The French industry and government wanted to apportion the French market and to force the foreign companies into national-industry cartel relations. As previously noted, French government actions had made the foreign companies erect refineries that were basically uneconomical. In 1929, 94.2 per cent of oil imports into France were *refined* products; by 1936, 83.7 per cent of oil imports were *crude* oil. Clearly, the policies were successful.[50]

Prior to 1934, Italy had structured its tariff to encourage new petroleum refineries; in that year the fascist government took sterner steps to prompt refining and to compel foreign companies to maintain stocks of crude and finished products as reserves for national defense. A royal decree of January 1934 licensed imports and granted special privileges to those companies that refined in Italy. Any marketer that did not have a refinery was put at a sharp competitive disadvantage. Socony-Vacuum "with a lubricating market built up over two decades was forced either to give up that market or to increase its venture capital enormously to comply and build a refinery." Note that this formulation by a Socony-Vacuum vice president is identical with what other corporate managers were writing of "forced" investments in *manufacturing*. Socony-Vacuum constructed a modern refinery at Naples in 1935–1936 to maintain its market. Another company (Jersey Standard?) preferred not to enlarge its two small Italian plants and accepted the penalties—a drastic cut in import licenses. Meanwhile, as the American companies struggled to hold their market, the government-financed Azienda Generale Italiana Petroli

---

* Owned in 1931 56 per cent by C.F.P., 10 per cent by the French state, and 34 per cent by other stockholders. Rondot, *Compagnie Française des Pétroles*, p. 63.

(AGIP)—formed in the mid-1920s—moved in; by 1936 it held one-third of the petroleum products market. The output of AGIP's refinery competed with the private foreign companies, which were forced either to expand their refining or to lose more ground. The passage of the Neutrality Act in 1935 in the United States did not affect American oil company operations. Oil was not on the list of embargoed items. In October 1935, after Italy invaded Ethiopia, Standard Oil of New Jersey was asked by the press to explain its oil sales to Italy. It replied that its subsidiary had been selling oil in Italy for forty years and the company saw no reason to stop—unless of course the U.S. government changed *its* policy and compelled it to terminate its deliveries. The U.S. government did not take such a step and oil shipments continued.[51]

In Germany no government-owned oil company existed, but regulations multiplied. A representative of the Standard Oil Company of New Jersey telephoned the State Department on July 17, 1934 to explain that its officials in Germany had been summoned to Berlin and told to keep large oil reserves in storage; the companies were expected to carry the exchange risk. Shell was ready to accept this; Standard Oil of New Jersey opposed it. The State Department encouraged the international oil companies to act in concert. Germany was short on oil and throughout the decade sought desperately to develop synthetics and to accumulate reserves for war needs. American oil companies in Germany were manipulated—just as the American manufacturing companies were—to meet the German war needs. They were not permitted to remit profits, but were appeased because they made good profits. Standard Oil of New Jersey became sophisticated in dealing with its blocked currency. A company official explained it,

> We constructed a tanker or two and, therefore, took out and put into use something of use in the business, a capital asset, measurable in dollars, dollars' worth. When we did that in a year, we realized a sufficient number of blocked marks, otherwise non-convertible into dollars.
> . . . If we were able to utilize marks in making repairs to ships, we did the same thing. If we were able, through barter arrangements of sufficient size, to convert dividend marks to dollars, we considered that we had established a realization norm.

But the executive admitted that toward the end of the decade there was a "complete blockage." The company did not consider it "as a realization

being forced to purchase German Government bonds, for instance, out of dividends or . . . being forced to capitalize the blocked surplus of the German subsidiary." The complexities of the oil business throughout Europe in the 1930s with the intensification of nationalism made one commentator as early as 1935 declare, "operations . . . are 90 per cent political and 10 per cent oil." [52]

8

After this narrative on the difficulties of the oil companies in the 1930s, it is worth repeating that U.S. oil investments in foreign lands in this decade appear to have risen. In 1939 Standard Oil of New Jersey, through its subsidiaries and affiliates, still held the leading position among the American companies distributing oil in the western hemisphere and in Europe. With the creation of Standard-Vacuum Oil Company (Stanvac) in 1933, Jersey Standard had for the first time become an important marketer east of Suez. Socony-Vacuum, Texaco, Gulf, and Atlantic Refining had by 1939 important stakes in marketing in Europe. California-Texas Oil Company (Caltex), formed in 1936, made firm strides in market penetration in Africa, Asia, and Oceania. Throughout the decade, "as is" agreements notwithstanding, American international oil companies met competition from Royal Dutch-Shell and British Petroleum (the marketing company of Anglo-Iranian Oil Company), especially in the eastern hemisphere.* In the 1930s, U.S. oil companies had become more multinational in their sourcing for their marketing networks. By 1939 Venezuelan crude oil (sometimes refined at Aruba) was used by U.S. enterprises to supply their largest foreign market (Europe), instead of using U.S. ex-

---

* In 1917, Anglo-Persian purchased a small, German-owned company (British Petroleum Company) that had been selling oil products in Great Britain before World War I. In the 1920s, Anglo-Persian marketed in Great Britain under the BP brand name; at the end of the 1920s, Anglo-Persian and Shell made a marketing arrangement to enter eastern Mediterranean and East and South African markets jointly—under the names BP and Shell-Mex. Anglo-Persian in 1931 entered into another joint enterprise with Shell, to market jointly in the United Kingdom—again under the names BP and Shell-Mex. Theirs became the largest oil marketing organization in Britain and in the eastern hemisphere. By 1939 BP's marketing network (independently, or jointly with Shell, or with others) covered a large part of Europe, Africa, the Middle East, India, and Australia. Anglo-Persian, as noted, changed its name to Anglo-Iranian in 1935; in 1954 it adopted the name British Petroleum Company. Royal Dutch-Shell—through subsidiaries—had an extensive marketing organization in these areas as well as in China, Japan, and southeast Asia; unlike B.P., in the 1930s, it had a marketing organization in the western hemisphere as well. Longhurst, *Adventure in Oil: The Story of British Petroleum*, pp. 178–181.

ports of refined oil. Oil from Bahrain and Saudi Arabia was being marketed by Caltex in foreign countries. Stanvac was selling oil from the Dutch East Indies as well as U.S. refined products.[53]

By 1939 American oil companies had invested outside the United States in 58 refineries, of which 39 operated on imported crude (that is were in consumer countries) and 19 were near or at producing fields. The total crude oil processed per annum by the 39 refineries was considerably less than by the 19. Of the 58 refineries, 28 represented investments by Standard Oil of New Jersey, 15 by Socony-Vacuum, 7 by Texaco, and the rest by other American companies. (The only Stanvac refinery—the one processing crude oil in the Dutch East Indies—is counted twice, under Standard Oil of New Jersey and Socony-Vacuum).* Table IX.3 gives the geographical dispersion of the 58 refineries. Note that in the vast areas of

Table IX.3. Geographical dispersion of American refineries in 1939

Area	No. of refineries
Canada	11
The Caribbean (Cuba, 1; Aruba, 1; Trinidad, 2)	4
Latin America (Colombia, 2; Peru, 2; Venezuela, 4; Argentina, 5)	13
Total Western Hemisphere	28
Europe (Austria, 1; Belgium, 2; Bulgaria, 1; Czechoslovakia, 1; France, 4; Germany, 7; Great Britain, 1; Hungary, 1; Italy, 3; Norway, 1; Poland, 2; Rumania, 2; Yugoslavia, 1)	27
Middle East (Bahrain, 1)	1
Asia (Dutch East Indies, 1; Japan, 1)	2
Total Eastern Hemisphere	30
TOTAL	58

Source: Based on U.S. Senate, Special Committee Investigating Petroleum Resources, *American Petroleum Interests in Foreign Countries, Hearings* (Washington, D.C. 1946), pp. 205–207.

* The small joint-venture refineries of Socony-Vacuum and Texaco in Colombia and Argentina are also counted twice in the attributions.

Africa, Asia, and Oceania, at the decade's end, there were still no American refineries in "consuming" countries—with the exception of the one joint-venture enterprise in Japan. U.S. companies sold imported refined oil.[54]

American oil company investments in foreign producing properties became more widespread in the 1930s. In 1929 the big two of the American producers in Venezuela had been Gulf Oil and Standard Oil (Indiana); in 1939 the subsidiaries of Standard Oil of New Jersey held clear preeminence among the U.S. petroleum companies in Venezuela. In 1929, Venezuela ranked second only to the United States in oil production; although its oil output had mounted in the 1930s, because oil output rose faster in the Soviet Union, in 1939 Venezuela ranked third in world oil production, after the United States and Russia. Venezuela, however, remained the most important foreign source of oil in the noncommunist world. In 1929 American oil companies were still a major factor in Mexican oil production; by 1939 they were so no longer. For the most part, the Mexican oil industry had become government enterprise. By 1939 Mexico had dropped to seventh place in world oil production (following the United States, Russia, Venezuela, Iran, the Netherlands East Indies, and Rumania.[55]

American oil companies in 1929 had just entered into Middle Eastern oil. In 1939, while they still had no production in Iran, Standard Oil of New Jersey and Socony-Vacuum (with interests in Iraq Petroleum Company), Standard Oil of California and The Texas Company (with interests in Saudi Arabia and Bahrain), and Gulf (with interests in Kuwait) had important stakes. Although oil output of the Middle East in 1939 equaled only 14 per cent of the oil produced outside the United States, industry executives recognized the region's potential. Writing in the early 1940s, but aptly of 1939 as well, economist Herbert Feis could declare, "there is no longer justification for assertions or imputations that the United States has been unfairly excluded." [56] The same was true of the Netherlands East Indies. By 1929, Jersey Standard had made its entry; in 1939 Stanvac produced 27 per cent of the output in the Netherlands East Indies,[57] and Caltex, while not yet in production, had discovered oil. In 1929, U.S. companies had their principal foreign investments in oil production in the western hemisphere; this was still the case in 1939; but with their new stakes in the Middle East and in the Dutch East Indies, Americans participated in oil exploration and production much farther afield. In 1939, for the first time, U.S. stakes in foreign oil production exceeded those in marketing oil abroad. By the end of the decade, the depression notwithstanding, because of rising energy requirements, world oil production was sharply higher than in 1929. But whereas in 1929 the American oil companies produced 29.7 per cent of all *foreign* output (392,100 barrels daily) and the British-Dutch group (Royal Dutch-Shell subsidiaries and Anglo-Iranian) produced 41 per cent (541,200 barrels daily), in 1939 the American companies' share had been reduced to 24.9 per cent (554,800 barrels daily), while the British-Dutch group produced 35.7 per cent (795,300 barrels daily.* It was not until after World War II that U.S. oil companies would surpass the British-Dutch group in *foreign oil production*. Slowly, the gap was narrowing.[58]

The rise in U.S. refining and production abroad reflected itself in Standard Oil of New Jersey's operations. In 1929 this company refined more and produced more in the United States than abroad. In 1939 it was otherwise; the output of its foreign refineries exceeded that of its domestic refineries by 15 per cent, while the foreign crude oil production of this company was more than double its domestic production.[59]

By the end of the 1930s, ten American oil companies, Atlantic Refining Company, Cities Service, Gulf Oil, Socony-Vacuum, Standard Oil of California, Sinclair Oil, Standard Oil Company of New Jersey, Sun Oil, Texaco, and Tide Water Associated Oil, represented well over 90 per cent of U.S. oil investments abroad.† [60] Five of these stood out as huge integrated multinational enterprises: Jersey Standard, Socony-Vacuum, Gulf, Standard of California, and Texaco. These, along with the British-owned Anglo-Iranian Oil Company and the British-Dutch Royal Dutch-Shell comprised the seven largest oil companies in the world. Whereas in 1929 there had been the "big three" in the world oil industry—Standard Oil of New Jersey, Royal Dutch-Shell and Anglo-Iranian—now there were seven major enterprises in the international oil business. Thus, the hazards of the depression years notwithstanding, American oil companies had become more multinational.

---

* Both *percentages* dropped because of the large rise in Russian oil production under the control of neither western group. The Russian government produced 27.4 per cent of foreign crude oil in 1939, compared with 21.4 per cent in 1929. In the 1930s this Russian oil went mainly to domestic consumption. Fanning, *Foreign Oil and the Free World*, p. 352.

† Other American companies with investments in oil abroad included: Amerada Petroleum, American Maracaibo Co., Barnsdall Oil Co., Compañia de Petróleo Ganso Azul, Maracaibo Oil Exploration Co., Pantepec Petroleum Co., Seaboard Oil Co. of Delaware, and Union Oil Co. of California.

Four

World War II and Its Aftermath

That corporations were multinational neither calmed nor embittered international relations. The idealism of Thomas Watson's "World Peace through World Trade" and the viciousness of Gerald P. Nye's "Merchants of Death" offered polar interpretative slogans that endowed the companies with more power than they actually held.[1] Instead, as will be evident, after 1939—as before 1939—multinational businesses were buffeted by political conditions beyond their control.

2

September 1, 1939, German troops marched over the Polish border. France and Britain honored their pledge to the invaded country. Europe plunged into war. U.S. corporate executives raised the reserves on their businesses' financial statements for 1939 to cover anticipated losses in Germany, Czechoslovakia, and Poland. Corn Products Refining Co. managed to sell the majority of its shares in its German affiliate, to German owners in return for blocked reichsmarks. Frank A. Howard, president of Standard Oil Development Company (a Jersey Standard subsidiary), found the "war introduced quite a number of complications"; in November 1939 he was writing of an agreement on catalytic cracking of petroleum, involving Americans, British, Dutch, and Germans, that had just been completed: "How we are going to make these belligerent parties lie down in the same bed isn't quite clear as yet . . . Technology has to carry on—war or no war—so we must find some solution." But no solution was discovered.[2]

Throughout Europe, government controls became more extensive. Taxes rose. U.S. subsidiaries saw their personnel drafted into national armies. Between September 1939 and April 1940, however, except for fighting between Russia and Finland, there was no warfare in Europe.[3]

Then the blitzkrieg began. In April 1940 the Germans invaded Norway and Denmark; in May they swept over Belgium and Holland; in June they moved into France. Italy entered the war that June on the side of the Germans, and on September 27, the Tripartite Pact was signed, with Japan pledging its allegiance to Germany and Italy. In Rumania, in October a newly installed profascist regime permitted German troops to "protect" the Ploesti oil fields from the Russians. In November, Rumania and Hungary committed themselves to the Rome-Berlin-Tokyo Axis. And, all the while, most U.S. companies tried to continue operations in everyone of these countries, but they also added reserves to their accounts in anticipation of losses.[4] In 1940, James A. Moffett, chairman of the board of California Texas Oil Company Ltd.,* stated, "American companies and American interests will continue to exist in those countries where property rights of private individuals will remain even if there should be a change of their sovereign government through conquest or otherwise." [5]

Stanley C. Allyn, president of National Cash Register Company, liked to tell the following story:

> Our office in Paris was on the line of march when Hitler's Wehrmacht rumbled into the ancient city and along the Champs Elysee. Suddenly, one of the tanks swerved out of line and headed straight for it. The tank came to a halt and disgorged a German soldier, who thundered on the door and made it plain he wanted to come in. Come in he did, and there he stood in enemy uniform, with a gun on his hip and a grim look on his face.
>   Our French employees had a bad moment—until the German soldier suddenly smiled and said: "I'm from the National Cash Register Company in Berlin. I'm sorry I can't stay very long, but I was wondering—did you make your quota last year?" [6]

Despite such comments, business did not go on as usual. In the early days of the invasion of France, the management of Jersey Standard's affiliate destroyed the affiliate's refinery near Le Havre rather than permit it to fall into German hands.[7] Ford Motor Company's German and French national managements engaged in intense personal rivalry. Ford-France's chief executive (a Frenchman) discovered that when forced to cooperate with the Germans, he got a better reception from Nazi government offi-

---

* In the pre–World War II years, California Texas Oil Company did not operate in Europe, but the statement applied as well to Europe as to the Far East where the company did have stakes.

cials in Berlin than from the German management of Ford-Werke, Cologne! [8]

During 1940, the U.S.-headquartered international corporation had begun to fragment. America was not in the war (although the country's loyalties were becoming clear). There remained in 1940 a scattering of Americans in Europe. But, for the most part, in Germany, Italy, and occupied Europe, the management of U.S. direct investments, the majority of which already had had host country executives, passed completely into national hands. Communications between the American parent companies and their subsidiaries in these countries became irregular.

In Germany and occupied Europe, the Germans tried to turn all American-owned factories and installations to wartime purposes. The American parent had no way of protesting. "Our foreign subsidiaries are corporations chartered under the laws of the countries in which they operate," explained W. S. Farish, president of Standard Oil of New Jersey, to the Truman Committee. "They must obey the laws of those countries." [9]

Bulgaria joined the Axis powers in March 1941; Germany invaded and occupied Yugoslavia and Greece in April. In May, the Germans defeated the British at Crete. They were now positioned to move into the Middle East. They were also bombing Britain, where an invasion seemed imminent. Instead, in June 1941, Germany attacked Russia.[10] At this point, most of continental Europe was under German sovereignty.

In bombed Britain, U.S. subsidiaries and affiliates were converting to war work. The American firm E. W. Bliss (makers of metal-working machinery) in 1939 had started to build a British plant "primarily for production of peace-time facilities expected to be sold in England and in English colonies." By March 1940 the management reported that a portion of the plant would be used "temporarily at least, for the production of munitions." At the start of 1941, Harry H. Pinney, president of E. W. Bliss, wrote, "Our English plant is operating largely in the production of war facilities for the English government as a controlled enterprise." This was typical. With the Battle for Britain, American companies turned to war work in Great Britain.[11]

The facilities of U.S. enterprises (which for the most part had been shut down or operated by Spaniards during the Civil War) were in 1939–1941 returned to American management. Some properties had been damaged. On November 24, 1939, a Spanish law required all new issues of shares of companies incorporated in Spain to be 75 per cent owned by Spanish nationals. Subsidiaries and affiliates of American firms that did not have majority control by Spanish capital (and this included most such companies) were not granted certificates as "national producers" and not permitted to supply the Spanish government. That government restricted imports and did not readily give such companies permission to expand. Some U.S. concerns were now convinced they should liquidate their Spanish businesses; the largest U.S. investor in Spain, International Telephone and Telegraph Corporation, wanted to retire from that nation.* [12]

By contrast, to the problems of most companies, the war in Europe turned Pan American Airway's new Atlantic service into what one historian has called a "bonanza." Pan American moved its main European terminal from Southampton, England, to Lisbon, Portugal—to be located in a neutral country. Increasingly, it flew mail, and also refugees from war-torn Europe, occasional businessmen, diplomats, and military men. [13]

In sum, the war in Europe notwithstanding, most American subsidiaries and affiliates in England and on the continent continued to do business in the period September 1939 to December 1941. Despite the difficulties, they conducted business on both sides of the war—and in neutral countries as well.

3

When in the spring of 1941 the Germans invaded the Balkans and Rommel started his offensive in North Africa, Egypt refused to declare war on Germany, a revolt favorable to Germany occurred in Iraq, Syria showed signs of collaborating with the Axis, while Nazi agents swarmed over Iran. Britain, valiantly defending herself at home, moved rapidly in the Middle East—suppressing the uprising in Iraq, removing the pro-Vichy group in Syria, and joining with the Russians to occupy Iran. By mid-1941 British supremacy was secure in much of the Middle East, and the British-owned Anglo-Iranian Oil Company was in a position to raise oil output for Allied use. On the other hand, Britain did not seek to develop oil production from Iraq and Kuwait, and in 1940–1941, U.S. oil interests in those two countries seemed to have deferred to British initiatives.

---

* Finally after years of negotiations, in 1944, I.T.T. managed to sell the telephone system back to the Spanish government for $88 million (cash and Spanish bonds).

Great Britain had never been pleased with the entry of U.S. oil interests in Saudi Arabia; as part of her Middle Eastern policy and with an eye to extending her influence, the British government in 1941 made loans to King Ibn Sa'ud. Meanwhile, on October 19, 1940, the Italian air force had bombed Dhahran in eastern Saudi Arabia (the headquarters of the California Arabian Standard Oil Company—later ARAMCO). Fearful of more devastating attacks and faced with wartime shipping difficulties, the U.S. oil company decided in June 1941 to shut its new small Ras Tanura refinery. It plugged many oil wells and reduced employment. Its operations ground to a near halt.* [14]

With the war, King Ibn Sa'ud's revenues from pilgrims and from customs duties were reduced; while he turned to the British for funds, he also asked the American oil company for a $6 million advance on royalties. Since the company was reducing its operations, it was not inclined to make the new loan; at the same time, it desired to assist the Arab ruler (and certainly not alienate him in any way). In April 1941, James A. Moffett † visited President Roosevelt and proposed that the U.S. government offer aid to Saudi Arabia—to encourage political stability there, to keep open this American-controlled Middle Eastern oil supply, and to supplement British loans. He noted that, if the financing were left to the British, "Britain's prestige and influence in Saudi Arabia would be so enhanced that . . . we might not be able to maintain the American character of our enterprise," or as Senator Owen Brewster put it later, "The fellow who pays the piper is the one who calls the tune." [15]

On June 14, Roosevelt's special assistant Harry Hopkins wrote a "personal and confidential" letter to Jesse Jones, federal loan administrator and secretary of commerce, "The President is anxious to find a way to do something about this matter . . . I am not sure what techniques there are to use. It occurred to me that some of it might be done in the shipment of food under the Lend Lease Bill, although just how we could call that outfit a 'democracy' I don't know. Perhaps instead of using his royalties on oil as collateral we could use his royalties on the tips he will get in the future on the pilgrims to Mecca." Hopkins also suggested that the Reconstruction Finance Corporation might arrange a loan to Saudi Arabia.[16] According to Charles Rayner, later petroleum adviser to the State

---

* Most of the small Saudi Arabian oil output was refined in nearby Bahrain, as it had been in the late 1930s before the Ras Tanura refinery had been built.

† James A. Moffett had been federal housing administrator, 1934–1935. He was now chairman of the board of California Texas Oil Company (Caltex). For the relationship between Caltex and California Arabian Standard Oil Company, see Chapter IX.

Department, the State Department "strongly recommended" aid.[17] Jesse Jones, however, feared opposition from isolationist elements in the Midwest. He penned a note, which he asked Roosevelt to copy, "7/18–41 Jess—Will you tell the British I hope they can take care of the King of Saudi-Arabia—This is a little far afield for us! FDR." Roosevelt complied with Jones's advice, *at this point;* Jones then, with "FDR's note" in hand, proceeded to inform the British that Saudi Arabia was in the "British sphere." [18] Thus, in 1941 Moffett failed to obtain any U.S. government funds for Saudi Arabia, although American Lend Lease to Great Britain was being used in part for loans *from the British* to King Ibn Sa'ud. With the curtailment, by December 1941 oil output in Saudi Arabia was negligible.[19] In fact, in all the Middle East, only in Iran was there substantial oil production—and U.S. oil interests had no stakes in Iran.

4

In 1939–1941, U.S. enterprises continued in business in Japan and China, and throughout the Far East, despite the Sino-Japanese war and mounting restrictions. In Japan, as the military gained ascendancy, we noted U.S. companies reduced their ownership in their Japanese affiliates. The decline of ownership accelerated in 1940 and 1941, so that by 1941 the Japanese controlled many of the U.S. affiliates in their country (see Table X.1). National Cash Register Company, which had opened a joint-venture manufacturing plant in Japan in 1935, because of Japanese governmental restrictions, discontinued manufacturing cash registers and sold its new plant in 1940; it continued limited selling operations.[20] Surprisingly, in 1940, visitors to Shanghai, China, found business booming —war notwithstanding.[21] While in 1941 National City Bank closed several of its branch offices in China, some remained open, as did its Tokyo office. So, too, Standard-Vacuum Oil Company operated in both Japan and China, along with other U.S. industrial enterprises. Late in 1939 and in 1940, the Dutch government made plans for the U.S. and British-Dutch oil companies in the Netherlands East Indies to destroy their wells and refineries—should the Japanese invade.[22]

Australia and New Zealand joined the war against Germany in September 1939; U.S. companies in those commonwealth countries participated in war production when possible. Pan American Airways expanded in the South Pacific in 1939–1941. It obtained landing rights in Australia, New Zealand, and finally in November 1941 in Singapore.[23]

Table X.1. Equity of selected U.S. corporation in Japanese businesses, 1931–1941 (percentage of stock held)

U.S. corporation	Percentage equity in Japanese enterprise	
	1931	1941
Carrier Corp.	50	46
General Electric	56—32 [1]	15
Goodrich (B. F.)	57	9
International Telephone and Telegraph	59	20
Libbey-Owens Glass	30	17
R.C.A. (Victor Talking Machine)	68	0
Tidewater (Associated Oil 1931)	50	25
Westinghouse Electric	9	4

Source: Ministry of International Trade and Industry, Tokyo.
[1] Equity in two Japanese enterprises, which were merged in 1939; thus, only one figure is given for 1941.

5

In the western hemisphere, in the years 1939–1941, U.S. businesses enlarged substantially their foreign operations. September 10, 1939, Canada declared war on Germany. U.S. direct investments in Canada (in 1940) were more than those in Europe, Asia, and Oceania combined—over $2 billion (see Table VIII.2). On the 15th of September 1939, an Order in Council in the Dominion established a Foreign Exchange Control Board to protect Canadian resources for war uses. For the first time in Canadian history, the board introduced foreign exchange controls, licensing of imports, and restraints on essential exports. But, because the board did not "wish to upset any existing arrangements which the Canadian companies have with their parent companies by way of inter-company accounts," permits were provided for Canadian subsidiaries of American firms to carry on as before.[24]

During 1940, U.S. businesses in Canada converted to wartime production.[25] Controversies about "foreign" control over Canadian industries did not arise; nothing equivalent to the incident over International Nickel in World War I occurred now. U.S. businessmen were sympathetic to Canadian needs and had no fears as they expanded in the Dominion. New airline routes connected the two nations, the bulk of them controlled by U.S. interests.[26]

While in 1940 in no single country (or region) within Latin America were U.S. investments as large as in Canada, in Latin America *as a whole* U.S. stakes did exceed those in the Dominion (see Table VIII.2). Such interests now rose. In 1939 (as in 1914) Americans sought to export and invest in Latin American markets that had formerly been supplied from Europe.[27] Europeans had provided roughly 80 per cent of Latin America's drug and toiletry needs in the 1930s.[28] The leading names in the trade were Bayer, Merck, and Schering.[29] Schering was 100 per cent German (even in the United States, Schering Corporation was a wholly owned German subsidiary).[30] The trademark *Merck* in all of Latin America, except Cuba, was German.[31] As for Bayer, the once-German Bayer Company of New York had passed in 1918 to the American firm, Sterling Products, Inc., but in the 1920s, as noted, Sterling Products had made various agreements with I.G. Farbenindustrie.* By the end of the 1930s, Sterling Products and I. G. Farben jointly owned drug manufacturing facilities in Chile and Argentina and shared the overall South American trade.† [32] With war in Europe, the British blacklisted all I. G. Farben's affiliates in Latin America. Nonetheless, W. E. Weiss, chief executive of Sterling Products, felt "even if we can't make any money, we must keep our business alive and going." In November 1940 he pledged to do the best he could. "We are going to do for your [I. G. Farben's] interest, just as we always have," he wrote his German partners. Thus, it seems that the new efforts of Sterling Products in Latin America were not competitive but rather were based on a wish to maintain an existing joint market.[33] On the other hand, when such U.S enterprises as E. R. Squibb & Sons, Lederle (a subsidiary of American Cyanamid), and various subsidiaries of American Home Products pushed into Latin America, they did replace German interests. Such companies started branches and subsidiaries to sell, mix, bottle, and pack their products.[34]

By November 1940, a U.S. Bureau of Foreign and Domestic Commerce

---

* See Chapter IV. Sterling Products had become as noted a subsidiary of Drug Inc., but Drug Inc. did not survive the depression, and in 1933 Sterling Products again became independent. The German Bayer Company had been merged into I. G. Farben in 1925.

† The U.S. and German firms agreed that South American markets for certain products should be supplied by whichever company (Sterling Products or I. G. Farben) could sell more cheaply, although profits for the business were to be divided 75 per cent to I. G. Farben and 25 per cent to Sterling Products. By 1933–1934, the American firm had the lower costs, but I. G. Farben, under pressure from the German government to export, had not surrendered the market.

representative could write, "a number of American concerns are planning to expand their existing branch factories or establish new ones [in Brazil]." The products involved included toilet preparations, fertilizers, ladies dresses, safety razors, and electrical goods.[35] Keeping pace with the new trade and investment activity, Pan American Airways improved its service in Latin America.[36]

6

Meanwhile, numerous U.S. government measures in 1939–1941 began to affect American business abroad. Despite isolationist sentiment, the United States started to prepare for the possibilities of entry into the war.[37] At Havana, Cuba, in July 1940, the United States pledged itself to participate in inter-American defense.[38] On April 20, 1941, the United States and Canada agreed that "each country would provide the other with defense articles . . . [and] production programs should be coordinated to this end.[39] In the interim, on March 11, 1941, the United States adopted the Lend Lease Act, and for the first time in American history, this country entered into a major foreign aid program. Clearly, the U.S. government's international economic involvement was mounting.[40]

Certain measures emanating from Washington specifically required the aid of international business and, in some instances, stimulated U.S. corporate expansion abroad. One such was the Strategic Materials Act of June 7, 1939. Under this act, in June 1940, the newly created Metals Reserve Company (a subsidiary of the Reconstruction Finance Corporation) was authorized to stockpile strategic and critical metals.* It purchased for the stockpile and did "preclusive" buying (to prevent the Axis from obtaining raw materials vital to *their* needs). The Metals Reserve Company was staffed by Americans trained in the U.S.-based international mining firms.† [41]

The Metals Reserve Company asked U.S. business for help in obtaining tin. It negotiated directly with the International Tin Cartel, as well as with individual U.S. companies. Since U.S. firms were not prepared to

* Strategic materials were necessary for the prosecution of the war and had to be obtained wholly or in large part abroad. Critical materials were also necessary but could be obtained in greater quantity in the United States. Walton, *The Miracle of World War II*, p. 45.

† Temple Bridgeman, consulting engineer for Guggenheim Bros., was an expert on tin. David D. Irwin had just returned from Northern Rhodesia where he had managed the Roan Antelope Copper Mining Company; he was an expert on copper. Henry DeWitt Smith came from Newmont Mining Corporation.

World War II and Its Aftermath

build a smelter in this country,* a large U.S.-government-owned smelter was erected in Texas City, Texas. The Reconstruction Finance Corporation in 1941 became the sole importer of tin into the United States—tin from the southwestern Pacific and Bolivia.[42]

By 1941 shortages were evident in copper. The U.S.-owned copper companies in Chile had arranged to sell a large order to Japan. Jesse Jones † later wrote, "I asked the copper people [in 1941] to say to Japan that they would have to *delay* the shipment a few months. At that stage we were not at war with Japan, and I could not ask that the contracts be cancelled. But the delays were arranged—and we got that copper." U.S. enterprises in Latin America—Anaconda, Kennecott, Cerro de Pasco, and American Smelting and Refining—which had sold their foreign copper mainly in Europe in the 1930s, redirected their trade back to the United States, and the Metals Reserve Company became their largest customer. The Metals Reserve Company also bought lead and zinc from Cerro de Pasco and American Smelting and Refining.[43]

Aluminum was essential for U.S. aircraft production. Sixty-five per cent of the United States' total supply of bauxite (the basic raw material) came from Dutch Guiana (Surinam), where the bulk of the mines were owned by Aluminum Company of America. In the fall of 1941, Cordell Hull asked permission from the Dutch government in exile in London for U.S troops to be sent in to protect the raw material; the Dutch agreed, and between November 25 and 30, 1941, one thousand American troops moved into Surinam. Likewise, to safeguard aluminum needs in 1941, the Metals Reserve Company ordered 750 million pounds of aluminum from Aluminum Company of Canada (owned by Aluminium Limited, which in turn was American controlled). In time, the Reconstruction Finance Corporation would loan $68.5 million to the Aluminum Company of Canada for plant expansion.[44]

In 1941, the United States and Japan entered into rival bidding for the tungsten output of Bolivia. The United States won, and on May 21, 1941, the Metals Reserve Company signed contracts with Bolivian tungsten ore producers, guaranteed by the Bolivian government, for the na-

---

* U.S. firms had built smelters in the United States during World War I; these had proved uneconomical and had been shut after the war. In 1940 all tin imported into the United States was smelted abroad—Bolivian tin in Great Britain and southeast Asian tin near the mines.

† Then federal loan administrator and secretary of commerce.

tion's entire production of tungsten ore concentrate. Some but not a substantial amount of U.S. investment was involved; it may well, however, have helped to turn the contracts to the United States.[45]

Nickel, antimony, platinum, and manganese were also stockpiled, and U.S.-owned mining, smelting, and refining companies in foreign countries contributed. Statistics are not available on what percentage of the Metals Reserve Company supplies came from American-controlled enterprises; the government agency did not buy exclusively from U.S.-owned business. Nonetheless, the growing output from U.S.-controlled foreign mining companies did prove important to American defense.

The Rubber Reserve Company (another subsidiary of the Reconstruction Finance Corporation, formed in June 1940) also began to stockpile. In 1940–1941 almost 97 per cent of the world's rubber came from the Far East. The Rubber Reserve Company cooperated with the leading U.S. tire makers that had rubber plantations abroad and also negotiated with the International Rubber Regulation Committee (headquartered in London) to start a stockpile. In 1941 Goodyear (in May), Firestone (in July), and U.S. Rubber (in September) began to build synthetic rubber plants in the United States under government auspices.[46]

Oil was vital to national defense. Although in 1939–1941, the United States was still a net exporter of oil, Washington recognized the need for foreign oil—that is, oil in the western hemisphere—to contribute to the Allied cause. Because of State Department policies, America's friendly relations with Mexico were not harmed by the oil expropriation there. "The broad settlements [of the oil question] reached with Mexico were a large factor in having our neighbor to the south in full accord with us at the moment of Pearl Harbor," Cordell Hull would write at a later date.[47]

To assure the flow of petroleum and to maintain the Good Neighbor Policy, the Department of State wanted U.S. oil companies' relations with Venezuela to remain amicable. Venezuela produced much more oil than Mexico and was the world's largest producer after the United States and the Soviet Union. On May 5, 1941, General Isaías Medina became president of Venezuela and pledged to obtain for his nation higher profits from oil.* The State Department, desiring to avoid a Venezuelan expropriation similar to the one that had occurred in Mexico, sought to guide

---

* Medina's government also sought better conservation of gas and oil, pipelines as common carriers, a method to stabilize the government's income from oil, and greater refining capacity in Venezuela.

the U.S. oil enterprises toward an open-minded approach to Medina's proposals.[48] The oil companies entered into discussions with Medina's government for several months in 1941 and then the negotiations collapsed. Within Standard Oil of New Jersey (subsidiaries of which were the leading producers in Venezuela), there formed two camps. One group of executives felt that Jersey Standard's subsidiaries had valid contracts with the Venezuelan state and that there was no need to alter the contracts to give Venezuela a greater (and the company a lesser) share in the earnings. Technically, this position was defensible. It is reported that a prominent international lawyer, brought in as a consultant, strongly supported this viewpoint before the Jersey company's board of directors. In Venezuela, the company's manager, Henry E. Linam, believed General Medina's proposals should not even be considered. By contrast, the second group within Jersey Standard recognized that such a stance had not served Jersey Standard in Mexico. There existed, they emphasized, the *fact* of the Mexican expropriation. These men warned of the possibility of a "repeat performance" in Venezuela and argued for flexibility. Based on their interpretation of their company's needs, their views corresponded with those of the State Department. The resolution of the division within the oil company would not come until after the United States entered World War II.[49] Meanwhile, despite the breakdown in Venezuelan-oil industry talks, in response to the demand for oil supplies, in 1941 Venezuelan petroleum output reached a new peak.[50] Table X.2 shows the crude oil production by U.S. companies in foreign countries 1939–1941 and reveals the significant role of Venezuela. Note that the 1941 increase was almost exclusively caused by the rise in output in Venezuela.

As a matter of public policy, it would be useful to document the advantages of U.S. corporate ownership of essential foreign commodities. U.S business ownership does seem to have facilitated the obtaining of foreign raw materials for U.S. needs in the period before American entry into the war. At this time the State Department also sought more control for U.S. business over world communications to serve the national interest. Thus, Frank Page of International Telephone and Telegraph Corporation wrote Harry Hopkins on June 18, 1941, that the State Department believed I.T.T.'s holdings in Latin America should be expanded, since the company assisted "a needed part of our export trade and it was necessary to assure the predominance of American interests in the communication field as against any European interests."[51] U.S. government funds

Table X.2. Crude oil production by American companies in foreign countries, 1939–1941 (in thousand barrels daily)

	1939		1940		1941	
Western Hemisphere	442		422		512	
(Venezuela alone)		335		312		404
Europe [1]	20		21		23	
Middle East	50		43		34	
Dutch East Indies	43		42		41	
TOTAL	555		528		610	

Source: U.S. Senate, Special Committee Investigating Petroleum Resources, *American Petroleum Interests in Foreign Countries*, pp. 193, 71, 337.

[1] Mainly Rumania, Germany, and Hungary.

made it possible for Pan American Airways to build new airports in Latin America. In July 1941, Juan Trippe, Pan Am's chief executive, obtained from Roosevelt the assignment of improving and adding to air routes across Africa—from the Atlantic to the Nile. Lend-lease funds were provided.[52] It became under the Democratic administration, as it had under earlier Republican administrations, an integral part of U.S. policy for American business to have control over certain resources and over certain communication channels, especially in the western hemisphere.*

At the same time as the U.S. government was giving aid to and receiving aid from multinational enterprises in obtaining foreign resources and developing foreign communications systems, Washington also *restricted* the operations of U.S. international business. The restrictions, a consequence of wartime conditions, were in their breadth unprecedented. For example, in the late fall of 1939, the U.S. government ordered Pan American Airways to purge its Colombian affiliate of all its German connections. Accordingly, in June 1940, the German fliers for the Colombian affiliate were fired. Having insisted on this, the U.S. government agreed to reimburse Pan Am for its losses and its labor dismissal costs.†

---

* At least not to have the control in European hands. Note the Democratic administration's acceptance of Mexican nationalization and its lack of full support to U.S. oil interests in Mexico.

† The German pilots were paid about one-third the going rate for U.S. pilots.

The Colombian affiliate—Sociedad Colombo-Alemana de Transportes Aéreos (SCADTA)—was reorganized as Aerovias Nacionales de Colombia (AVIANCA), with the Colombian government holding first a minority interest (later to become a majority). Under U.S. government encouragement, Pan Am Grace Airways (PANAGRA) duplicated the routes of German airlines on the west coast of South America; as soon as its service was established, Washington urged U.S. oil companies to cut off supplies to the German airlines.[53]

In April 1940, after the German invasion of Norway and Denmark, the U.S. Department of Treasury introduced foreign fund control.* On July 2, 1940, a law to strengthen national defense authorized the president to prohibit or curtail certain exports.† By spring 1941, U.S. corporations were required to obtain licenses to export specified products, materials, and technical processes; Washington look askance on U.S. companies' dealing with German firms. On July 14, 1941, the president issued a "proclaimed list" of 1,834 companies and individuals, mainly in Latin America, considered pro-Nazi, with whom trade was prohibited. That summer, Vice President Henry Wallace took charge of the newly created Economic Defense Board (later the Board of Economic Warfare) with authority over international economic matters, foreign exchange, and international trade.

Such actions affected U.S. participants in international business. On April 18, 1941, a du Pont vice president cabled I. G. Farben: "AM WRITING YOU TODAY SUGGESTING THAT IN VIEW OF GOVERNMENT RESTRICTIONS OUR TWO COMPANIES MUTUALLY AGREE DISCONTINUE EXCHANGE TECHNICAL INFORMATION PATENT APPPLICATIONS ETC ON ALL EXISTING CONTRACTS UNTIL THE PRESENT EMERGENCY HAS PASSED BUT ALL OTHER OBLIGATIONS IN CONTRACTS TO REMAIN IN FORCE." Du Pont's cable was a direct response to Presidential Proclamation 2465 (effective April 15, 1941) that required

---

*The first controls were (1) to prevent Germany from issuing instructions which would put Norwegian and Danish assets in the United States under German control, and (2) to protect American banking institutions from having to transfer funds which might result in conflicting claims. After the Low Lands and Luxembourg were invaded, on May 10, 1940, the president froze all funds due those countries. France was soon included under the U.S. controls. A year later, June 14, 1941, all European countries under Axis control were put under the American foreign fund controls, and the neutrals (Portugal, Spain, Sweden, and Switzerland) were also included, since they might be used as "cloaks for the carrying out of Axis transactions." In July 1941, Japan and China were subjected to the "freezing controls."

† The goal was to keep critical materials and military equipment within this country for U.S. defense, but the act also provided a means for keeping critical materials out of German and later Japanese hands.

the licensing of such technical information exports. In 1941, International Telephone and Telegraph Corporation sold its telephone concession in Rumania to that government; the U.S. Treasury Department licensed the Rumanian government to use its blocked funds to make the purchase. In most other cases that involved Axis funds, the Treasury Department refused to issue licenses. Thus, in late 1940, I. G. Farben offered to buy Standard Oil of New Jersey's Hungarian subsidiary, Magyar Amerikai Olajipari, R.T. Representatives of Jersey Standard and I. G. Farben met in Rio in July 1941 and agreed on a price of $24 million gold—part to be delivered to Jersey Standard at Lisbon. The Treasury, however, rejected Jersey Standard's application for permission to make the sale, explaining that "to have approved the proposed sale . . . would have been tantamount to an approval of Germany's new economic order in Europe." [54] Similarly, Anaconda had negotiated with several Swiss banks for a loan to pay the debts of its affiliated Silesian-American Corporation. Before the arrangements could be completed, Switzerland was included under the U.S. "freezing controls." Anaconda applied for a license to carry out the transaction, which the Treasury Department refused to grant; as a result the Silesian-American Corporation went into bankruptcy. [55] With the freezing of Japanese assets in the United States and the Japanese retaliatory freezing of U.S. assets in Japan in mid-1941, American business in that country came to a virtual halt, although for the most part U.S. businessmen with direct investments remained there, hoping for better times. [56]

When Roosevelt's crusading assistant attorney general in charge of the antitrust division of the Justice Department, Thurman Arnold, learned of the activities of Sterling Products in Latin America (see p. 252 above), he strongly objected. Dismay prevailed in Washington that an American firm was bypassing the British (and by mid-1941 the American) blacklist and cooperating with the Germans. Under pressures from the Departments of Justice, State, and Treasury, Sterling Products on August 29, 1941, removed its chief executive (W. E. Weiss) and installed a new management. Sterling Products signed a consent decree on September 5, 1941, agreeing to sever all ties with I. G. Farben. The new management declared its company was dedicated to invading the Latin American market independently. [57]

Meanwhile, Standard Oil of New Jersey's marketing subsidiary in Brazil held a contract to supply oil to Condor, a German airline that operated out of Brazil. The Truman Committee reported, "In October

1941 Standard notified the State Department that unless the United States Government was willing to protect and indemnify its subsidiary against a possible lawsuit and fine, the contract would have to be fulfilled. The State Department was forced to threaten to blacklist Standard's Brazilian subsidiary in order to stop the deliveries. Deliveries of gasoline by Standard's Brazilian subsidiary were, however, continued under direction of the American Ambassador to Brazil until a substitute service could be established." The embassy recognized—if the Truman Committee later did not—that to halt deliveries entirely would penalize the Brazilian economy, which was not the aim of the measures. The Truman Committee report did note that, "an overwhelming majority of the companies asked by the State Department to refrain from doing business with German companies in South America had complied immediately and taken whatever losses accrued from it." [58]

The German connections of many American firms prompted the Justice Department to deepen its inquiries into international cartels. It looked into a range of corporate ties that might be thought restrictive. The Truman Committee, beginning its investigation of the national defense program in 1941, started to uncover evidence which it felt showed that the international relationships of U.S. corporations were retarding the U.S. defense efforts.[59] It is paradoxical that at the same time as the hostile scrutiny of cartels progressed, the Metals Reserve Company and the Rubber Reserve Company found it useful to consult with such cartels as the International Tin Cartel and the International Rubber Regulation Committee in order to aid U.S. procurement.

7

In sum, then, before December 7, 1941, U.S. direct investments worldwide were affected by the war abroad. The effects were not of a piece. Certain enterprises grew, while others contracted. Some corporations expanded in one foreign area and cut back in another (for example, Anaconda added to its stakes in Chile but closed its operations in Poland). American businesses met with new host-government or occupying-power interventions in their multinational activities, as well as with new U.S. government involvement. As in World War I, so now, as Europeans fought, Americans moved into European markets. American business's position, in the western hemisphere especially, was being enlarged vis-à-vis European interests.

With the bombing of Pearl Harbor on December 7, 1941, the United States finally entered the war with men as well as materiel. For U.S. corporations abroad, circumstances altered dramatically. Many U.S. businessmen fled from China and Japan to the Philippines, only to be rounded up by the Japanese on January 2, 1942. Remaining American businessmen in Europe left for home as rapidly as possible.[1]

In the six months following Pearl Harbor, the Japanese swept through southeast Asia. In February 1942, under orders from the Dutch military authorities, Standard-Vacuum officials blew up the company's refinery near Palembang, Sumatra, and plugged its oil wells with cement.[2] The rubber plantations of U.S. Rubber and Goodyear in southeast Asia, the Guggenheim stake in Malayan tin, and International Harvester's hemp plantation in the Philippines fell to the Japanese. With these natural resources under enemy control, there was no longer an advantage to the United States in their once having been part of an international business.

Indeed, after U.S. entry into World War II, American multinational enterprise became completely fragmented. A common strategy no longer prevailed. Properties that had been owned by U.S. companies in Axis and occupied countries in Asia and Europe were now totally severed from the control of their parent firms. For the next four years, isolated intelligence on the European units might reach the U.S. parents through the State Department, through Vichy France, or occasionally through Latin American agents, but for all practical purposes the affiliated and subsidiary corporations in Axis territory were no longer parts of multinational enterprises. They provided no revenues to their erstwhile U.S. parents.*

* There is some controversy on just how much fragmentation actually occurred. My research leads me to believe that once America entered the war, the former interna-

World War II and Its Aftermath

In Germany, Italy, and Japan, the enemy assumed control over American properties. In some cases, the businesses were sold, while in other instances the operations remained under the same national management as before the war—except the national managements now more than ever worked for their country's cause rather than splitting allegiance between the nation and the international corporation. In occupied lands, the occupying power took charge. The output of units, formerly controlled by Americans, was used to serve the Axis war effort.* [3]

At the same, time, in England, Canada, India, Australia, Northern Rhodesia, the Gold Coast, Latin America, and elsewhere, U.S. subsidiaries and affiliates produced to fill Allied military and defense requirements. Pan American Airways officials boasted that "nearly all of the overseas routes used by the Air Transport command were first pioneered by Pan American as a commercial enterprise." † In Latin America, U.S. corporations also started new manufactories to meet local needs—needs formerly met by imports.‡ [4]

---

tional corporation in effect ceased to function. On the other hand, Corwin Edwards, writing in 1944, felt that one of the dangers of the international corporation was the "continuance of mutual loyalties and of joint property interests which unite concerns lying on opposite sides of the battle lines." Edwards does *not* seem to me to have proved his contention in connection with the American-based corporation. All his evidence comes from before December 7, 1941; none of it covers the years *after* America entered the war. Edwards, *Economic and Political Aspects of International Cartels*, p. 71.

* Under the Trading with the Enemy Act of 1917 (revived in 1941), American citizens were not allowed any dealings with enemy nations without explicit government approval. This meant not only that direct communication was forbidden; but as one former government official explained it, the law "prevented American subsidiaries abroad, especially in the European neutral countries, from trading with Axis territory except where a particular transaction would definitely benefit the allies." For example, a U.S. subsidiary operating in Sweden could not sell to a Norwegian enterprise. Gordon and Dangerfield, *The Hidden Weapon*, p. 151.

† The U.S. Air Transport command on October 15, 1942, "militarized" the African routes established by Pan Am.

‡ In 1942 for the second time in American history, the Internal Revenue Code gave tax advantages to foreign investment in a particular region. The first case had been the China Trade Act; the new case was the Western Hemisphere Trade Corporation. Congress felt that with the introduction of the Western Hemisphere Trade Corporation in 1942, American companies doing business in Latin America would be in an improved position over foreign enterprises. The provisions were primarily to encourage U.S. foreign investment. To qualify as a W.H.T.C., a domestic company had to do all of its business in the western hemisphere (aside from incidentals), derive more than 95 per cent of its gross income from sources outside the United States, and obtain more than 90 per cent of its gross income from the "active conduct of a trade or business." Dam, "Background Paper on Taxation of Foreign Income," pp. 28, 3.

2

While the enterprises continued to produce abroad for Axis and Allied needs, at home attacks on U.S. international business mounted. Assistant Attorney General Thurman Arnold and the Truman Committee were joined by new opponents of corporate power. In April 1942, Homer T. Bone's Committee on Patents heard testimony that demonstrated (at least to the committee's chairman) that the patent arrangements made by leading international businesses hindered independent U.S. firms from developing new technology and slowed U.S. defense preparations. In interrogating a Standard Oil of New Jersey representative, Senator Bone added as *obiter dicta,* "If it were not for Germany, poor General Electric and Standard Oil and all the rest of the big outfits that guide this country would be babes in the woods . . . Of what avail is all this vast American research if it has left us in the position of being dependent on other countries?" And then, Senator Bone muttered about the perfidious dealings of the "big outfits." [5] Later, beginning in 1943, the Kilgore Committee—the Senate Subcommittee on War Mobilization—heard testimony that international cartel relationships had caused American firms to be dependent on and subject to foreign firms in such strategic materials as synthetic rubber, tungsten carbide, magnesium, military optical supplies, chemicals, and dyestuffs. In a monograph for this committee Corwin Edwards expressed apprehension that the commitments inherent in international business endangered national security. [6]

U.S. antitrust cases multiplied, with civil and criminal actions against the so-called "foreign monopolies." American businesses were accused of restraint of trade in drugs, light metals, chemicals, electrical products, petroleum, glass, plastics, explosives, and aircraft accessories. Most of the U.S. actions sought remedies against the "alleged German control over our industry." I. G. Farben and other German concerns were described as instruments of Nazi policies; American corporations that had dealt with the German firms were charged with having done business with the equivalent of the German state. The United States argued in the court cases that international arrangements made by corporations restrained free competition, restricted exports and imports, divided world markets, curtailed world production, and deprived American independents of the benefits that would "otherwise flow from free vigorous competition." Consumers got higher prices and poorer quality as a result. International concerns (what we now call international business) and international cartels were seen as violations of the Sherman Antitrust Act.* Business relations—some of which went back before World War I, some to the 1920s—underwent penetrating scrutiny. Several court cases were concluded in 1942 with consent decrees; † others were postponed until the war's end. A rash of new cases began in 1944 with that end in sight.[7]

Of all companies, Standard Oil of New Jersey probably got the worst publicity in the hearings and court cases. As noted in Chapter IV, Standard Oil of New Jersey had made contracts with I. G. Farben in 1927 and 1929, dealing with the hydrogenation of oil and coal (oil only in the 1927 contract). The petroleum company was concerned with the technological achievements forthcoming from this process for *its* industry, and, as we have noted, it agreed in 1929 to recognize the "preferred position of I. G. in industries known as chemical"; I. G. in turn recognized the "preferred position of the [Jersey] Company in the industries known as oil

* The word "cartel" was loosely used. The purist defines it as a formal restrictive agreement between or among otherwise *independent* concerns, designed to control prices, amounts produced, and/or major methods of marketing. However, its use in these years was broader. All agreements entered into by firms, whether with independent companies or with affiliates, that could be conceived of as restrictive were labeled "cartels." "International business and cartels are different matters," a colleague of mine said not long ago. On the other hand, a newspaperman, who heard I was writing on international business responded, "Oh, you are writing on cartels." Unquestionably, my colleague is right, at least in theory: international business (one firm as it expands abroad) is different from a collection of otherwise independent firms that join together to achieve monopoly power. A company can be in international business and have nothing to do with cartels, although Justice Department critics of the 1940s would have found this hard to believe. Part of the difficulty in dealing with cartels lies in the questions of what constitutes an independent firm, and, in fact, what constitutes a firm. Sometimes there is no doubt: Company A is owned and managed by a group that is entirely different from the group that owns and manages Company B; Companies A and B are independent firms. But suppose Company A owns 5, 25, 50, 51, 75, 100 per cent of Company B—at what point does Company B cease to be independent? Is independence a matter of ownership or management? Suppose Company A forms Company B and owns 100 per cent of Company B; Company B is clearly not independent and is part of one business. Suppose as a next step, Company A and Company B agree as a matter of convenience that one will supply one market and the other another one. *Then* suppose Company A sells 60 per cent of its ownership in Company B, retaining 40 per cent. If Company A and Company B keep the old agreement are they now participating in a cartel? It is in cases of this sort that the confusion arises between international business and cartels. These distinctions were not clear in the World War II discussions. Subsequently, the courts have had much to say on these questions.

† U.S. v. Alcoa, Civil #18–31 (SDNY 1942), and U.S. v. Standard Oil (N.J.), Civil #2091 (DCNJ 1942), for example.

and natural gas." Unquestionably Jersey Standard gained technical know-how from the Germans in petroleum products. But the Truman, Bone, and Kilgore committees found, "There is considerable evidence that the development of buna-s rubber, which is regarded as the best type of synthetic rubber in the United States, was seriously retarded as a result of the 1929 agreement between I. G. Farben and Standard and the action taken pursuant thereto." I. G. Farben and Standard Oil of New Jersey, the Truman Committee concluded, had by their actions discouraged independent development and production by other companies. There was, the Truman Committee declared, "no question of moral turpitude or of subjective unpatriotic motive on the part of Standard [Oil of New Jersey] or of any of its officials." But the agreements had nonetheless forced Standard Oil of New Jersey into a compromising situation.[8]

The crux of the issue was business policy. Standard Oil of New Jersey had made contracts with I. G. Farben. It had made these contracts in good faith. To be sure, as early as 1935, Standard Oil of New Jersey was aware that I. G. Farben was withholding technical information on buna-s rubber on the grounds that the work was being done for the German government; in 1938 a vice president of Standard Oil of New Jersey "deplored the . . . German government's restrictions on I. G.'s freedom of action," which resulted in I. G.'s not furnishing data useful in the "commercial development of synthetic rubber in the United States." But, Jersey Standard blamed the German government, not I. G. Farben. The American company independently did research on butyl—another synthetic. Jersey Standard also got some information from the Germans. Neither German know-how nor Jersey's own research was made available to the U.S. rubber companies. Under peacetime conditions no one would expect the release of such trade secrets.

A government civil action taken against Standard Oil Company of New Jersey contended that the company had restrained trade in violation of the Sherman Act. Standard Oil of New Jersey entered a plea of *nolo contendere* and accepted a consent decree on March 25, 1942. The company agreed to release *all* its rubber patents, royalty free, for the duration of the war. After the war, the royalty was to be determined. Standard Oil of New Jersey officials told the Truman Committee that the company considered its 1929 understandings with I. G. Farben dissolved and that "Standard has no obligation, moral or otherwise, to resume the relationship." The Company pledged to devote its best efforts to the development of rubber and not to withhold know-how or technical information from the U.S. government.[9]

Throughout the various proceedings Jersey Standard insisted it was not involved in a "worldwide cartel," that it learned more from the Germans than it would have without the agreements, that in 1939 it had encouraged the U.S. government to become interested in synthetic rubber, that it tried to get the rubber companies concerned with synthetic rubber, and that it did not discourage licensing them after American entry in the war. It claimed to have only accepted the consent decree because to have fought its position through the courts would have been time-consuming and would have diverted its top management from the important task of winning the war. It would have preferred complete vindication. Despite the company's defense, the Truman Committee concluded,

> Standard is only one of a group of companies producing critical materials which, by cartel agreements and by subsequent control of patents, have sought to restrict and control production. This has constituted one of the greatest menaces to our war effort . . . [The committee] has found that such arrangements are harmful in peacetime, but disastrous in time of war. They cannot be allowed to flourish and choke the great war machine the United States is building. They must be stamped out quickly and completely . . . The committee believes that future arrangements whereby foreign business interests dominated by hostile governments can create bottlenecks in our industrial machinery can be prevented.[10]

Other companies found to participate in "similar" arrangements included General Electric (tungsten carbide), National Lead (titanium), Alcoa and Dow (magnesium), Allied Chemical (dyestuffs), du Pont (various chemical products), and Rohm & Haas (plexiglass).* The investigations posed important questions on international business relations in peacetime and war, of the loyalties involved in international enterprise, of the gains and losses in the interchange of technological know-how and patents. An important issue was, should domestic antitrust legislation be applied to international transactions? What should be the behavior of subsidiaries and affiliates of American firms abroad when con-

---

* The inquiries focused on contractual relationships rather than on business investment abroad, yet many (although not all) of the companies under scrutiny had foreign investments associated with their agreements.

fronted by foreign business and foreign government endorsement of agreements restraining trade? What was the applicable law—that abroad or that at home? Did or should American legislation extend to subsidiaries or affiliates of the American firm outside of the United States?

A basic matter was, when contracts were made with foreign affiliates or foreign firms, when the Justice Department knew of them and gave them tacit approval, should changes in American antitrust policy render these same contracts illegal? During the war years, with the issue of national security foremost, there seemed to be an implicit assumption underlying most of the litigation that businesses should either have been more isolationist than they were or that businesses ought to have been more *politically* astute than the State Department. The relationships criticized were ones made in time of peace. They had not been subject to litigation in peacetime. Ought businesses to have anticipated the war and not made such ties? Ought businesses to have imposed their own embargo on technical aid to the Germans—and deprived themselves of the research information that they could obtain from the Germans? The answer to this last question in the passion of the war years seemed to be "yes." In retrospect, one wonders. Divorced from the issue of war and peace, it seems clear that many of the most vulnerable agreements substantially aided the development of American corporations—and the American economy.[11]

3

Despite this background of recrimination, investigation, and litigation, U.S. enterprises sought to assist their country's war effort. The War Production Board (established in January 1942) set down the requirements. In the main, U.S. *manufacturers* turned from foreign to domestic operations.[12] In the past, the chief executives of many large manufacturing concerns had paid attention to business abroad. Now, for the most senior executives in manufacturing companies, the prime challenge became that of obtaining output at home for U.S. military needs. Managers who had served with foreign subsidiaries could provide intelligence to Washington on the size and location of Axis plants; but these same managers, once they reported to Washington, went into the military forces, went to work for the government, or returned to New York, Detroit, or Schenectady to plan *domestic* production.* In many instances, the foreign subsidiaries and affiliates of these manufacturing companies assumed a functional autonomy abroad; they reinvested profits, and some expanded.† [13]

Executives of international oil and mining companies and manufacturing enterprises with rubber plantations, likewise, could tell Washington aides about resources in enemy hands. Information provided by the oil companies, especially Standard Oil of New Jersey, proved crucial.‡ But unlike officials in international manufacturing concerns, high-ranking executives of companies with foreign extractive and agricultural investments remained in intimate touch with international business. America required foreign metals, rubber, sugar, hemp, and petroleum.

To obtain needed metals, the U.S. government even entered a joint venture with a U.S. company abroad: Freeport Sulphur owned the common shares of the new Nicaro Nickel Company (operating in Cuba), while the U.S. government owned the preferred shares (purchased for $33 million); the Defense Plants Corporation (a U.S. government agency) built the plant facilities in Cuba. For U.S. and Canadian needs, the American-controlled International Nickel almost doubled its Canadian output—producing copper and platinum as well as nickel.[14] At Chuquicamata in Chile in 1942, at the request of the U.S. government, Anaconda expanded its copper mining and treatment facilities; in Mexico, Anaconda's subsidiary developed a large body of low-grade copper core.§ During the war years, except for a small amount of copper sold in

* Like most generalizations, this is subject to exceptions. Coca-Cola was an exception. During the war years, since the U.S. armed forces were stationed abroad, Coca-Cola established or licensed many foreign bottling plants to serve the army. Atypically for manufacturing companies, the war years, produced a tremendous expansion of Coca-Cola's foreign business under the supervision of U.S. management.

† According to revised figures of the U.S. Department of Commerce, U.S. direct foreign investment in manufacturing rose from $1.9 billion in 1940 to $2.4 billion in 1946. U.S. Dept. of Comm. Office of Business Economics, *U.S. Business Investments in Foreign Countries*, pp. 1, 96. The figures for 1946 are not broken down by region, but it appears that most of the rise was in Canada and Latin America.

‡ Representatives of the War Department spent approximately six months in 1942 studying Standard Oil of New Jersey records to obtain up-to-date maps and other information valuable to the military. Popple, *Standard Oil Company (New Jersey) in World War II*, pp. 289ff.

§ In connection with this expansion in Mexico, there were negotiations between the U.S. and Mexican governments, first at a State Department level and then through the Metals Reserve Company, which handled the financing arrangements. This appears to have been a rare use (to that date) of diplomatic channels for Anaconda's activities abroad. Interview with R. E. Schneider, Anaconda Company, New York, April 4, 1963; see also *Paley Report*, p. 133.

Latin America, the output of Anaconda's subsidiaries in Chile and Mexico was sold to U.S. government agencies.[15] Kennecott similarly reported that practically all its Chilean copper production went to U.S. government agencies.* [16] On November 1, 1942, the Metals Reserve Company agreed to pay the costs of Phelps Dodge's opening the lower levels of its old Mexican copper mine at Nacozari. In July 1943 Phelps Dodge made an additional contract with Metals Reserve Company to develop La Fortuna mine, a new small, Mexican zinc mine.[17] And so it went. Before the war's end, the Metals Reserve Company had spent almost $2.75 billion, acquiring roughly fifty different metals from 51 foreign countries, 38 states, Alaska, and the Philippines. It had financed projects in Latin America and Canada, as well as in the United States. It continued to buy from both American-owned and non-American foreign sources.[18]

When the southeast Asian rubber plantations fell to the Japanese, the Rubber Reserve Company rushed to create a domestic synthetic rubber industry. At home, U.S. companies pooled patents, and remarkably, by 1943 large-scale synthetic rubber production had become practical. Meanwhile, the Rubber Reserve Company, and then its successor, the Rubber Development Corporation, sought natural rubber in seventeen Latin American countries, sponsoring the tapping of wild rubber. Pre–World War I interest in the guayule plant in Mexico revived. Goodyear improved its rubber plantations in Central America (acquired in the 1930s), while Ford's two Brazilian plantations produced small amounts of rubber and United Fruit explored the possibilities of growing rubber.[19]

In Liberia, Americans had an excellent source of natural rubber. As rubber prices had risen after 1934, Firestone had cleared and planted vast acreages. The Firestone company also helped independent Liberians cultivate rubber, promising to buy their output. When the war came, the Firestone company had established the foundation for rapid expansion. Production at its plantation soared from 7,000 tons in 1940 to 20,000 tons in 1945. Liberia could offer the United States an emergency source of

---

* The governments of Chile and the United States in January 1942 had agreed to impose a wartime ceiling price of 12 cents a pound on Chilean copper; the U.S. excise tax of 4 cents a pound was waived (it was finally repealed in 1947). Chile increased the tax on the industry to an effective 65 per cent of profits. There was considerable resentment in Chile against the U.S. price ceiling, which Chile claimed deprived it of greater revenues; in addition, some Chileans disliked the integration of the Chilean economy into the U.S. war effort, although Chile did, finally, in January 1943, declare was against the Axis powers. See Reynolds, "Development Problems," pp. 239–240.

rubber to supplement the new synthetics and the rubber from Latin America.

In the years 1942 through 1945, the United States obtained 153,545 long tons of wild rubber from Latin America and 65,000 long tons of rubber from Liberia (mainly from the Firestone plantation). As for synthetics, U.S. output reached more than 700,000 tons in 1944 and at war's end in 1945 was at a rate in excess of 1,000,000 tons per annum.[20]

Within the Department of Agriculture, the Commodity Credit Corporation arranged for the financing of agricultural products (including sugar) from abroad. The U.S. duty on Cuban sugar—with the trade agreement of January 5, 1942—dropped lower than ever before in the twentieth century. Sugar prices rose, which encouraged U.S. investment.[21] United Fruit planted about 28,000 acres of abaca (Manila hemp) on the Caribbean coast of Central America on behalf of the Defense Supplies Corporation (a Reconstruction Finance Corporation subsidiary) and also experimented with quinine and palm oil production in Central America.[22]

4

Of all international businesses, oil attracted the spotlight. For ships, tanks, and airplanes, the Allies depended on oil—oil from the western hemisphere.[23] But in 1942 Venezuelan oil output declined sharply. Early that year, the Germans shelled the oil refineries at Aruba. More serious, negotiations between the oil companies and the Venezuelan government remained suspended for the first part of 1942. According to a Creole Petroleum Corporation Report to the Shareholders, March 11, 1943,* "Early in the summer of 1942 the Department of State at Washington informed the oil companies that it had been officially advised that the Venezuelan Government was determined to obtain a greater financial return from the operation of its petroleum economy; that it did not intend to expropriate private properties, but that it had other adequate legal means to accomplish its purpose. The Department felt that a real problem was involved and suggested to the companies that it would be wise to re-open negotiations with Venezuelan officials in a cooperative spirit." Over the summer of 1942, as oil production declined, tensions mounted. In August 1942,

* Creole Petroleum Corporation was at this time a holding company, owning stock in Standard Oil Company of Venezuela, which carried on part of Jersey Standard's operations in Venezuela.

Venezuela's president, General Isaías Medina, wrote to Roosevelt and made speeches in Venezuela, in each instance condemning the U.S. oil companies; rumors circulated that Medina's words might be a preface to expropriation. In September the U.S. State Department advised the oil enterprises to replace their officials in Caracas with men who had no connections with the old Gómez regime, for Medina had pledged a total "post-Gómez" reordering of oil policy, By this time, discussions were at last underway in New York and Washington between Venezuela's attorney general and the U.S. oil companies.

Jersey Standard's representative in Caracas, Henry Linam, was thoroughly identified with the "old order." He frequently referred to Venezuelan plans as a "rape of the industry." One report says that Linam quit rather than comply with Jersey Standard's orders that he negotiate with the Venezuelan government. Another account indicates that Jersey Standard "fired" the manager. In any case, Linam left Caracas for good in December 1942.* By this time, within Jersey Standard—and in the industry —the advocates of flexibility and compromise had prevailed. In Linam's stead, Arthur Proudfit went to Venezuela representing Jersey Standard; his instructions were to negotiate with Venezuelan government officials.

General Medina and the oil companies soon agreed *in principle* that the government should obtain from the oil output revenues equal to those of the companies—that is, the profits should be split 50-50, "a concept of taxation that was then revolutionary in the oil industry." † The new law of 1943 superseded earlier legislation and established unified practices. All existing oil concessions were to be replaced by new ones. Taxes and royalties paid by the companies rose. The government stated the new minimum royalty of 16⅔ per cent along with the other taxes would give Venezuela a participation in the profits equal to that of the industry. The companies, while having to accept the higher taxes, got important advantages: (1) all new concessions under the law were recognized as valid; this settled questions on alleged title defects, which worried some companies, (2) concessions under the new law, including old

* Linam became vice president of the Rubber Development Corporation in Washington after leaving Venezuela. Jones, *Fifty Billion Dollars*, p. 428.

† Actually, as early as April 1, 1942, Wallace E. Pratt, a director of Standard Oil of New Jersey, searching for solutions to the *Mexican* dilemma, had told the U.S. State Department that his company "would be willing to see that Mexico received 50% of the profits through royalties, et cetera, and that a working arrangement would be better than a fair or unfair evaluation [of the company's properties]." Cronon, *Josephus Daniels in Mexico*, pp. 269–270.

ones that were converted, would run forty years; this lengthened the time of concessions, some of which were to expire in ten to fifteen years, and (3) the government agreed to simplify its regulations, "in connection with oil shipments, port charges, customs procedures, and stamp taxes."

When the bill became law on March 13, 1943, Arthur Proudfit, the recently arrived representative of Standard Oil of New Jersey, applauded it. The government of Venezuela expressed pleasure. On the other hand, Acción Democrática, the Venezuelan opposition party, condemned the legislation as too conservative. Rómulo Betancourt on behalf of Acción Democrática argued that under the existing costs and prices, the government might get 50 per cent of the profits, but should costs and prices change, the government would not receive its 50 per cent (not until 1948 was the mandatory 50-50 written into the law; thus, although the 1943 legislation established the principle, the 1948 law set the famous 50-50 rule).

Meanwhile, on August 23, 1943, Jersey Standard consolidated all its holdings in Venezuela into a single operating company, the Creole Petroleum Corporation. In 1944 and early 1945, under the new relationship between the oil companies and government, oil output in Venezuela expanded rapidly. U.S. foreign aid entered the country. Euphoria reigned. Companies enlarged their investments; Standard Oil of California, which had left Venezuela in the 1930s, reentered; Phillips Petroleum Company invested for the first time. An oil boom began. By 1945 Creole Petroleum Corporation produced well over half the oil in Venezuela, Shell, roughly one-third, Gulf, less than 10 per cent, and Texas, Socony-Vacuum, Standard Oil of California, and other American companies, the remaining small amount. By 1944 Venezuelan oil output (having surpassed Soviet production) was once more second only to that of the United States.[24]

Venezuelan oil in 1943–1945 made an important contribution to the Allied war effort. It was developed by American private enterprise, backed by the U.S. State Department, which chose the route of intelligent advice rather than direct government investment or the "big stick." Whereas Petroleum Administrator for War Harold Ickes had suggested (in late 1941) that the U.S. government should buy the *Mexican* oil fields, Roosevelt rightly replied that the Mexican government would be unlikely to entertain the "idea of having the oil lands in Mexico owned by our own or any other foreign government."[25] Other than Ickes's suggestion, there never seems to have been any plan during or before

U.S. entry in the war for the U.S. government to invest in Latin American oil. The role of the U.S. government was different elsewhere.

5

"The Canol project, as far as I know, is the first major venture of the United States government in oil production on foreign soil. After our experiences with gasoline rationing and the serious depletion of our own crude-oil reserves, I believe that the American people may favor similar ventures in the future . . . Our participation in oil reserves on foreign soil is necessary to our national welfare and our future defense." Thus spoke Under Secretary of War Robert P. Patterson to the Senate Committee, investigating the national defense program, on November 23, 1943.

The Canol Project had been approved by the War Department on April 29, 1942. During the war years, as in the past, Canada continued to be an importer of oil. Canadian petroleum companies, the largest of which was Standard Oil of New Jersey's affiliate, Imperial Oil, Ltd., had sought oil in the Dominion for decades, but their output remained small. Back in 1919 Imperial Oil had opened several wells near Fort Norman, high in the Canadian Northwest Territories, practically at the Arctic circle. It had discovered oil in 1920 and constructed a small refinery at Norman Wells to meet the requirements of mining and transport work in the remote, snow-bound region. In the early 1940s, with the building of the Alaskan highway and the new U.S. air fields in Alaska, the U.S. War Department wondered how the Alaskan air bases and transport would be supplied with fuel. With the war, sea routes were perilous and tankers in short supply. In 1941 the Arctic explorer Vilhjálmur Stefánsson brought the Norman Wells oil resources to the attention of the War Department, and in April 1942 the department had invited Imperial Oil officials to Washington. That company described the oil field at Norman Wells as untested and inaccessible; while indications of oil were promising, the company had not fully explored.

The War Department brushed aside the reservations; the matter was desperate. The department ignored cost considerations.* It feared the

* War Department officials reiterated many times: "It never was and never will be a commercial project." "The question of cost was something I knew nothing about." "There wouldn't have been any cost too great." "The cost as such was not fully discussed." "This was a military project, not a commercial one." *Truman Committee Hearings*, pt. 22, pp. 9376, 9494, 9495. 9505, 9600.

Japanese might carry their offensive to the western hemisphere; Alaska must be the bastion for defense. "In addition to defending Alaska," Under Secretary of War Robert P. Patterson explained in 1943, "it was then our plan, since consummated, to ferry combat planes to Fairbanks, there to be delivered to the Russians for use against Germany on the Russian front. This is the short Arctic route to Russia."

Without consulting Petroleum Administrator for War Harold L. Ickes (who when he heard of the project opposed it), aware of Imperial Oil's reservations, and lacking information about the general terrain, the War Department nevertheless arranged for contracts in the spring of 1942 involving the U.S. and Canadian governments and Imperial Oil. The "Canol" (Canadian Oil) Project was underway.* Imperial Oil was to explore, to drill, and to produce oil at Norman Wells; it would not participate in laying the projected pipeline, in building the new refinery, or in the subsequent distribution of the petroleum products—all of which would be carried out by the U.S. War Department.

The U.S. Bureau of Budget made an initial requisition of $25 million for the Canol Project; but by June 1943 the estimated cost was $119 million! The expenditure covered the 550-mile road and pipeline through the icy, mountainous region from Norman Wells to Whitehouse (in the Canadian Yukon Territory), the refinery at Whitehouse for the production of aviation gasoline and other petroleum products, and the distribution lines from Whitehouse to Watson Lake in Canada and Skagway and Fairbanks in Alaska.

By mid-1943 Imperial Oil had found considerable oil in the Norman Wells fields, so much, in fact, that the War Department boasted its program had uncovered a "major oil field." By then, however, the original rationale for the project no longer existed: Japan no longer threatened the western hemisphere. Should this project—"a military project, and not

---

* Simultaneously, the War Department sought oil in Australia and New Zealand as part of the strategy to defend the Pacific. Caltex (Australia) Oil Development Pty, Ltd., had obtained permits to explore in Western Australia in 1940; it had started exploration, but on March 10, 1942, had suspended efforts. General Brehon B. Somervell told the Truman Committee that he was advised the prospects of oil in Australia were discouraging, but that on April 29, 1942, on the same day as he issued orders to go "after the oil in Norman Wells," he also authorized drilling of wells in New Zealand. A Houston-headquartered company, Superior Oil Company, "had outlined some prospects there." Two "were taken up by us [the War Department] with the Superior Oil Company, and it was thought best for us to help them with priorities and with materials." Superior Oil Company did not find oil in New Zealand. *Truman Committee Hearings*, pt. 22, pp. 9660, 9663, and *Petroleum Hearings*, p. 381.

a commercial one"—be continued? The War Department answered, "yes." Worldwide oil and tanker shortages "dictated that Alaska be self-sufficient insofar as possible . . . Military necessity then existed for the provision of aviation gas to support a possible air offensive against Japan." The Canol project would assist in the offensive.

By December 1943 roughly $105 million had been spent, and the total cost estimate had risen to $134 million! Within the United States, congressmen questioned this alleged extravagance. Pennsylvania representative Leon H. Gavin objected: "We have just carried on a gigantic W.P.A. project for the benefit of the Canadian people, opening up the Canadian wilderness, and Uncle Sam isn't getting anything out of it." The Truman Committee concluded in January 1944 that it was "definitely of the opinion that the Canol project should not have been undertaken, and that it should have been abandoned when the difficulties were called to the attention of the War Department."

Nevertheless, the $134 million project went forward and was completed in the spring of 1944. The refinery and pipeline served for a year. Then in March 1945 the War Department withdrew. The Canadian government, which had an option to buy the pipeline and the Whitehouse refinery, indicated it was not interested—nor was Imperial Oil. *Business Week* explained, "The project would have little appeal to an oil company as a commercial venture, even as a gift."

The War Department said its withdrawal was because of the anticipated improvement in the tanker situation and the better military outlook. Senator James M. Mead, on the other hand, noted that the operating costs had been excessive and that the output of the 100-octane gasoline refinery was far less than the War Department had predicted. The pipeline had limited capacity and thus no "permanent defense value." The whole operation was dismantled and sold "for junk."

And, what of the "major field" discovered as a result of the War Department's effort? Geologists still believe that there is a major field; the Gordon Report on the Canadian economy in 1957 noted that the "Western Canada sedimentary basin, stretching from Norman Wells in the Northwest Territories to Red Coulee in southern Alberta and from Fort Saint John at the western end of the Peace River district to Virden in Manitoba, contains approximately 750,000 square miles; and that whole area is considered favorable for the discovery of oil." Yet, the wartime efforts had no *immediate* peacetime consequences. Thus sadly ended the "first major venture" by the American government in cooperation with international business to develop oil resources on foreign soil. Oil explorations of Alaska and the Northwest Territories in the 1960s seem to have owed little to these wartime efforts. But, by 1969–1970 there was once more an active search for oil going on in Canada's far north, including the area around Norman Wells.[26]

6

The next efforts of the U.S. government dealing with foreign oil production had more immediate long-range consequences. Fearing a serious worldwide oil shortage, in 1943 Americans turned new attention to the Middle East. In Iran the British were producing oil in quantity. On the other hand, Iraq's output remained low. The management of Kuwait Oil Company in 1942 had plugged its wells with cement, deciding that shortages of equipment and manpower precluded operations; no oil shipments were made from Kuwait during the war.

In the fall of 1942, the British made their influence felt in Saudi Arabia, and on February 8, 1943, the president of The Texas Company, W. S. S. Rodgers wrote to Henry Wallace, Milo Perkins, and E. R. Stettinius, Jr.,* that he and H. D. Colliers (president of Standard Oil of California) would be in Washington on February 10th and 11th to discuss the situation in Saudi Arabia. The oil company executives also made appointments with Harold Ickes (secretary of interior and petroleum administrator for war), Frank Knox (secretary of the navy), Henry L. Stimson (secretary of war), Sumner Welles (under secretary of state), and James Forrestal (under secretary of navy). The two oil men sent out the following memorandum:

> the British government is now insisting that Saudi Arabian financial requirements be met by an internal note issue backed by a British bank and controlled by the British Currency Control Board—the practice followed in British controlled territory.
>
> Concern is felt over the rapidly increasing British economic influence in Arabia because of the bearing it may have on the continuation of purely American enterprise there after the war.
>
> Direct aid from the United States government to the Saudi Arab government instead of indirect aid through the British as at present

---

* Wallace was vice president and head of the Board of Economic Warfare, Perkins was executive director of the Board of Economic Warfare, while Stettinius was lend lease administrator and special assistant to the president.

would check this tendency and give some assurance that the reserve of oil in Saudi Arabia will remain under control of Americans; and consequently remain available to American economy and to American naval and military forces of the future. The Middle East oil reserve is without question the world's greatest oil reserve.

The memorandum advocated that the United States extend Lend Lease aid to Saudi Arabia and also take over Saudi Arabia's obligations to Britain. After the two executives had had their discussions in Washington, Ickes on February 16 met with Roosevelt, who two days later issued an executive order making Saudi Arabia eligible for Lend Lease for the first time.*

In order to protect our sources of oil supply, Stimson, Knox, and Ickes now felt the U.S. government should become a part owner (Ickes felt 100 per cent owner) of the California Arabian Standard Oil Company. Admiral William D. Leahy recommended the U.S. government obtain its own Saudi Arabian concessions to establish naval fuel reserves; Secretary of State Cordell Hull, by contrast, wrote in his *Memoirs* that he opposed the direct entry of the U.S. government into the Middle Eastern oil business.† President Roosevelt leaned toward Ickes's view.

Accordingly, the Reconstruction Finance Corporation established in July 1943 the Petroleum Reserve Corporation, authorized to participate in every aspect of the oil business—domestic or foreign. Ickes became its president. Immediately the Petroleum Reserve Corporation sought ownership of the stock held by Standard Oil of California and Texaco in the California Arabian Standard Oil Company and also in the Bahrein Petroleum Company. The top executives in those companies had pressed the U.S. government to be concerned with issues in the Middle East; they had, as we have seen, advocated the extension of Lend Lease to Saudi Arabia; but they had *never* contemplated the government's becoming a direct participant in their business. Ickes later testified, "I remember distinctly when I suggested to these men with a dead-pan face that the United States ought to have all of their stock interest; they nearly fell off their chairs, and it scared them quite a lot."

* The United States did not, however, go so far as to acquire Saudi Arabia's obligations to Britain, as the oil company executives had desired.

† Herbert Feis, economic adviser in the State Department, wrote that Hull acquiesced in the stock purchase plan, while Under Secretary of Navy Forrestal testified in 1947 that "in principle I joined in the recommendation that was made, first, I think, by the four Secretaries, Mr. Ickes, Mr. Knox, Mr. Stimson, and I think Mr. Hull, and which dealt with an acquisition of the entire concession."

Standard Oil of California and The Texas Company did not want to sell their stock to the U.S. government. So the Petroleum Reserve Corporation made a bid for the half interest held by the Gulf Oil in the Kuwait Oil Company. The British government owned a large percentage of the shares in Anglo-Iranian Oil Company, Ltd. Why should not the American government similarly become involved? Gulf, likewise, did not desire to sell. After much publicity and controversy, the proposal that the Petroleum Reserve Corporation acquire a stock interest in existing U.S. stakes in Middle Eastern oil died stillborn. "Such governmental participation in the field of private industry was not compatible with traditional American concepts," was the later explanation of the *ARAMCO Handbook*. The handbook did not add that in wartime the U.S. government participated in numerous other formerly private businesses.

Thus, under private American ownership, in response to oil demands, Saudi Arabian oil output in late 1943 began to move upward. The War Production Board released steel and other critical materials, as well as technicians, to go to Saudi Arabia so the U.S. company could build a 50,000-barrel-a-day refinery at Ras Tanura (replacing the earlier, small refinery). The California Arabian Standard Oil Company (in 1944 renamed Arabian American Oil Company—ARAMCO) had refinery construction underway by the end of 1944. In the interim, the rising crude oil output went by barge to nearby Bahrain for refining there. (A pipeline between Saudi Arabia and Bahrain was completed in 1945.) Bahrain boomed. Its expansion of oil refining was partly U.S. government-financed: the American-owned Bahrein Petroleum Company, Ltd., got U.S. government loans on equipment; it borrowed funds on U.S. government guarantees. By war's end, its refinery output had risen from 35,000 to over 60,000 barrels a day.[27]

Since Ickes failed to obtain U.S. government control over the major U.S. oil companies in the Middle East, he next tried to obtain government ownership of a projected pipeline from the Arabian oil fields to the Mediterranean. On February 6, 1944, Standard Oil of California, Texaco, Hull, and Ickes announced that the U.S. government would construct, own, and maintain a pipeline system from the Persian Gulf to the Mediterranean to carry Saudi Arabian oil nearer European ports. Here, too, while Standard Oil of California and Texaco reluctantly agreed to this proposal, they preferred private ownership. Then, after much controversy, the plans for a U.S. government-owned pipeline were put aside in mid-1944; in the fall of 1944, when an ARAMCO reconnaissance group surveyed a possible pipeline route, Hull indicated this was "solely an Arabian American Company matter not involving this Government, although we had no objections to the company's plans of which we were fully informed." Construction did not start until after the war was over and then under private ownership.[28]

Meanwhile, the U.S. government's interest spread to other Middle Eastern oil prospects. On October 15, 1943, James F. Byrnes, director of the Office of War Mobilization, wrote a memorandum to the president advocating, "Vigorous negotiations should be pressed with the British for the acquisition of a third interest in the Iranian oil fields now owned wholly by British interests, to be assigned to the United States by Great Britain in consideration of Lend Lease contributions of petroleum during the war and in consideration of the construction of a pipe line from the Iranian oil fields to Haifa at an approximate cost of $200,000,000." This idea came to naught.

Likewise, late in 1943 Standard-Vacuum Oil Company asked the State Department its feeling about that company's seeking petroleum in Iran. Hull gave the "green light;" early in 1944 both Standard-Vacuum Oil Company and Sinclair sent representatives to Teheran. Since the 1920s, U.S. oil companies had attempted in vain to enter the British-controlled Iranian oil industry. Now, once more they tried. Royal Dutch-Shell also sought a concession, as did the Soviets. The Iranians opted to postpone all decisions until war's end. Thus, once more American oil companies in Iran had been thwarted.[29]

With the heightened activities of the U.S. oil companies in Saudi Arabia and Bahrain and their renewed attempts to gain stakes in Iran, relations between the United States and Great Britain showed signs of strain. As early as November 1943, the State Department invited British government representatives to Washington to discuss such "problems of mutual interest." On February 20, 1944, Churchill cabled Roosevelt of British concern that the United States sought to deprive the United Kingdom of Near Eastern oil, to which Roosevelt retorted that he had heard the British were trying to "horn in" on the oil reserves in Saudi Arabia. Negotiations proceeded, and on August 8, 1944, Edward R. Stettinius, Jr., then acting secretary of state, and Lord Beaverbrook signed an Anglo-American Petroleum Agreement, covering the orderly development of oil reserves and dealing with international trade in petroleum. The agreement was submitted to the United States Senate for ratification, but after vigorous opposition from the domestic oil industry, was withdrawn.* On September 24, 1945, a revised agreement was signed, resubmitted to the Senate, pigeonholed, made the subject of hearings in June 1947, but never ratified.[30]

Meanwhile, during 1945 oil production in Saudi Arabia mounted, although throughout the war years it never reached even the low level of the Iraqi output. In fact, little U.S.-owned Middle Eastern oil got into World War II. Nonetheless, the new refinery at Ras Tanura, the wartime expansion of the Bahrain refinery, the plans for the pipeline from the gulf to the Mediterranean, the final decision that the U.S. government would not become a direct investor in Middle Eastern oil provided a solid foundation for fantastic postwar growth. Also important was the aid by the U.S. government to Saudi Arabia during the war years; this helped create a friendly environment in the postwar period and assisted in the retention of U.S. interests in the region. In the war years, American foreign aid to Saudi Arabia totaled $18 million ($5 million in grants and $13 million in credits). Never again would Americans consider Saudi Arabia in the "British sphere." [31]

Thus, the U.S. government had resumed its assistance to U.S. oil companies in the Middle East. The Democratic administration was acting consistent with the policies of the Republican administrations in the 1920s in trying to secure for American capital a permanent stake in the Middle East. The phrase of earlier times—"breaking the British monopoly"—was gone (and so was the "monopoly"). But the same determination that the door not be closed to American capital was present. By the end of the war, the Middle East had become a crucial area for American diplomacy. The petroleum adviser to the State Department in 1945 could tell a Senate committee, "I think our policy, should be to give them [the oil companies] every diplomatic support that is possible, to see that there is no discrimination against them, to insure that their activities abroad are amply protected insofar as it is within the power of the Department to do so." [32]

7

Many of the huge demands for oil were based on a war fought in the air. Air travel during wartime rose. New airports were constructed and

---

* The independent oil men had thought that as worded the agreement could be construed to cover the domestic U.S. industry; this was not its intention.

air routes developed. U.S. airlines other than Pan American Airways got into international business; the exclusive position of Pan Am was shattered. The growth of air travel provided a cornerstone for postwar expansion.[33]

Between 1942 and 1945, whether through the president, the executive departments (state, treasury, war, navy, agriculture), the subsidiaries of the Reconstruction Finance Corporation, or Lend Lease, the United States participated in international economic relations to an unprecedented extent. Numerous other agencies of government took part in international economic affairs. The Board of Economic Warfare, headed by Vice President Henry Wallace, negotiated with foreign governments on economic questions and administered U.S. export controls. The Alien Property Custodian took over enemy properties in the United States. The Office of the Coordinator of Inter-American Affairs—headed by Nelson Rockefeller—provided technical assistance to Latin America. The Export-Import Bank furnished large credits to Latin American countries. The Petroleum Administrator for War had dealings in foreign affairs. In September 1943, a Foreign Economic Administration was established to take charge of export control, foreign supply and procurement, Lend Lease, and economic warfare.

Meanwhile, the tides of war were changing. In the first half of 1942, the Allied forces had been on the defensive. Then Japan's conquests in the Pacific reached their limit in July. The Allies took the initiative in North Africa, and by the fall of 1942, Rommel was retreating. The Germans arrived at Stalingrad that autumn, which battle ended with massive German surrenders on February 1, 1943. During 1943 the Allied counter-offensive gained momentum. In May, the Allies obtained control over North Africa; in July, they established beachheads in Sicily—and by September 3, 1943, the new Italian government of Marshall Badoglio signed an armistice. Russian troops swept westward, recapturing lands under German authority. In the Pacific, the tide had clearly turned.

On June 6, 1944, D-Day, the western Allies landed at Normandy; British and American troops moved across Europe while from the other direction Russian troops advanced. An Allied victory was near, and postwar planning accelerated. At the Bretton Woods Conference of July 1–12, 1944, the International Monetary Fund and the International Bank for Reconstruction and Development (the World Bank) came into existence. The World Bank could be expected to aid private as well as public financing in the future. The Charter for the United Nations, discussed at San Francisco from April to June 1945, was on June 26th ratified by fifty participating countries. As the representatives gathered to form the world body, on May 7, 1945, the German army surrendered. Three months later, the Japanese were defeated, and the long war was finally over.[34]

During the war years, the economic policies of the U.S. government had become international to an unprecedented extent. In the postwar European recovery, in the restructuring of the Japanese economy, in Middle Eastern affairs, America would clearly have a significant role to play. The new scope of the U.S. government's participation would inevitably alter the future relationships between it and U.S. international corporations. Between March 1941 and V-J day, the Lend Lease allocation totaled $47 billion, a sum more than six and a half times the book value of existing U.S. direct foreign investments at war's end.[35]

The Russian victories in eastern Europe would have an important impact on the postwar world—and America's policies would be influenced by Soviet actions. Soviet policies would more than in the past limit the geographical sphere of U.S. direct investment.

The war had given Asians and Africans a dream of freedom. As a result, in the two decades after the war, the great European colonial empires would disintegrate (symbolically, America's one "aspect" of empire, the Philippines, would become independent in 1946). Just as the Russian, Austro-Hungarian, German, and Ottoman empires disappeared after World War I, so after World War II, the English, French, Dutch, and Belgian empires went into oblivion. The change would have impact on U.S. direct investors.

During World War II, the United States had grown closer to Latin America than ever before. All the Latin American nations (including Argentina—at the last moment) joined the war against Germany. In Latin America the desire for industrialization mounted; already in 1945 it seemed evident that the United States would aid Latin American industry—although the nature and scale of America's role was still ill defined.

The activities of the United States in wartime in accumulating strategic and critical metals, rubber, and oil meant that international corporations participating in raw material procurement received far more attention during the war years than manufacturing firms abroad. As a consequence in 1945 when most Americans thought of direct foreign investment, they thought of stakes in raw materials. In many international *manufacturing* companies, there had arisen during the war years a feeling of distrust and disdain for business abroad. These companies had had important operations in Europe. Their plants in many cases had been destroyed by bombing; their marketing channels had been disrupted; their foreign administrative structures were no longer intact; in some cases, their properties in enemy lands had been sold. Many officials in manufacturing companies felt that foreign enterprise (except in Canada) brought frustration abroad and verbal and legal (antitrust) attacks at home and meant far greater risk than domestic enterprise. Was it worth it? A number of chief executives of manufacturing companies that had led in the foreign field now answered this question in the negative. It is important, moreover, that corporate managements change over time; by the close of World War II, the executives who had made the commitments of the halcyon days of the late 1920s were retiring; newcomers in these firms remembered foreign business only through the trials of the depressed 1930s and war-torn 1940s. Although as many as 2,750 American businesses had direct foreign investments, there was little enthusiasm on the part of the vast majority.[36] Domestic investment seemed far more promising.

While U.S. direct investment abroad in 1946 exceeded that in 1940, revised figures indicate it was not much larger (see Table XI.1) and re-

Table XI.1. U.S. direct foreign investments by area 1940–1946 (book value in billion U.S. dollars)

	1940	1946
Area		
Canada	2.1	2.5
Latin America	2.8	3.1
Europe	1.4	1.0
Middle East and Africa	0.2	0.2
Other Areas	0.5	0.4
TOTAL	7.0	7.2

Source: U.S. Department of Commerce, Bureau of Foreign and Domestic Commerce, *American Direct Investment in Foreign Countries—1940* (Washington, D.C. 1942), pp. 4–5 (1940 figures). U.S. Department of Commerce, Office of Business Economics, *U.S. Business Investments in Foreign Countries* (Washington, D.C. 1960), p. 1 (revised 1946 figures).

mained lower than in 1929. Moreover, in the years 1941–1946, U.S. direct investment abroad had lagged relative to the booming domestic economy. If the revised figures on U.S. direct investment abroad are to be trusted, as a percentage of U.S. gross national product, in 1946 direct investment abroad equaled only 3.4 per cent, apparently the lowest percentage during the twentieth century.[37] The revised figures show that all the wartime increase in U.S. international business had come in Canada and Latin America (see Table XI.1).* Petroleum companies, fearing possible shortages of oil and oriented toward risk-taking, were prepared in the immediate postwar years to undertake new giant foreign investments. In their impressive plans, the oil enterprises were alone.

* The revised figures for 1946—as indicated on Table XI.1—were published by the Department of Commerce in 1960. Preliminary figures for 1946 that apparently did not take into account war losses put total U.S. direct investments in Europe at $2.1 billion instead of the revised $1.0 billion, and east of Suez and African investments at $.9 billion instead of $.6 billion. For detailed figures, see *Survey of Current Business* (December 1951), p. 13. All these figures should be used with great caution.

Recovery and Reconsideration, 1945–1954

American business came out of the war no longer bedeviled by depression woes. Reconversion to domestic civilian output captured the attention of top managements. In the first World War, American industry had not fully converted to a wartime economy; after the second, by contrast, reconversion proved extensive since practically all U.S. industry had participated in wartime production.

After World War II, domestic investment opportunities seemed splendid; consumer demands were high. Business expanded, albeit with caution; businessmen did not want to be caught short as in the post–World War I crisis of 1921. U.S. corporations turned to filling market needs at home. When in 1949 there seemed likely to be a depression, businesses curtailed quickly, but the upturn in economic indicators in 1950 wiped away the fears. As in the immediate aftermath of World War I, the expansion at home was accompanied by a move abroad, yet there were differences—as will be evident. One principal difference was that the world had become smaller. Domestic and international airline travel was becoming increasingly common as U.S. and foreign carriers offered improved international service.* Also contributing to a "smaller world" was the presence of nuclear weapons, at first only in American hands and then from 1949 on in Soviet hands as well. This meant the U.S. industry —especially after 1949—would shape its course far more conscious of problems of national security than ever in peacetime history.

2

At war's end, the United States accepted the responsibility to aid in bringing Europe back to at least its prewar standard of living. Should

---

* Pan American Airways never resumed its prewar exclusive position as *the* American carrier outside the United States and Canada. Instead, a number of U.S. firms participated.

European economic chaos be perpetuated, the United States believed democratic systems were in jeopardy. As Soviet power extended through eastern Europe, U.S. policy aimed to contain communism. One means was to offer economic and military aid to the noncommunist west. Initial piecemeal efforts of 1946 were soon supplemented by economic and military assistance to Greece and Turkey in 1947, and then most important in 1948, the European Recovery Program, the Marshall Plan, was adopted.* In 1949, the United States joined Canada and ten western European nations in the North Atlantic Treaty Organization (NATO); the nations pledged mutual assistance. In October of that year, after the Soviets tested their first nuclear weapon (in September), Congress enacted the Mutual Defense Assistance Act to provide military equipment, materials, and services to the participants in NATO. U.S. foreign aid, mainly to Europe, in the first five postwar years totaled $28 billion.[1]

Meanwhile, in January 1949, President Harry S. Truman proposed a "bold new program for making the benefits of our scientific advances and industrial progress available for the improvement and growth of underdeveloped areas." Economic aid would help maintain democratic, friendly systems, it was hoped. On June 5, 1950, the so-called "Point Four" program (point four of Truman's address) began with the approval of the Act for International Development.[2]

So-called "revisionist" historians have seen these measures as an attempt "to restructure the world so American business could trade, operate, and profit without restriction everywhere."[3] By contrast, most historians find such an overall view too narrow—too economically deterministic; they see U.S. policy as more complex, more political, more oriented toward coping with Soviet aggression and maintaining a democratic world. To reduce the aims to economic ones, they argue, fails to accord with the motives of the participants in American postwar policies. The present author accepts the latter view and believes the economic policies of the U.S. government were a facet of broader policy considerations; moreover, as we will see, there was by no means an exact coincidence between U.S. government policies and the desires of international businesses— although often such approaches did coincide. Because we are concerned

---

* Secretary of State George Marshall had proposed such a program in June 1947; an emergency aid bill was passed that December. The Economic Cooperation Act of 1948 was the basic measure.

with U.S. business abroad, we will deal specifically with the aspects of U.S. foreign (and domestic) policy that affected the expansion of such enterprises.

First, "the commercial equivalent to our political objective of 'containment' " (to quote the formulation of Benjamin J. Cohen of Princeton) proved not to encourage but to restrict U.S. business expansion abroad. Its aim was "to minimize our own and our allies' trade with the [communist] bloc in order to deny the Soviet Union and its associates the major benefits of an international division of labor." Thus imbued with the cold war spirit, in 1948 the United States imposed mandatory export licensing controls which were formalized in February 1949 when Congress passed an Export Control Act. The act authorized the president (or a department of the U.S. government to which he delegated the authority) to "prohibit or curtail the exportation from the United States . . . of any article, materials, or supplies, including technical data"— when necessary "to further the foreign policy of the United States." Export controls were to be imposed in the interest of "national security." [4]

U.S. trade policy sought both to penalize communist nations and to serve America's domestic requirements. Accordingly, the Export Control Act of 1949 also declared that the restraints should be used "to protect the domestic economy from the excessive drain of scarce materials and to reduce the inflationary impact of abnormal foreign demand." [5]

Even though the Export Control Act contained potentials for limiting international commerce, America in the postwar years remained committed to the overall policy of freer trade—that is among noncommunist countries. Though trade, assistance could be given to friendly nations and the United States could obtain scarce materials. With other members of the United Nations, the United States joined in preparing the Havana Charter of 1948 that put forth a plan for an International Trade Organization—to promote lower trade barriers, to sponsor aid to less developed countries, and, in addition, to provide a code on foreign investments, controls on cartels, and standards for international commodity agreements.* In January 1948 the General Agreement on Tariffs and Trade (GATT) came into effect, with the United States a participant;

---

* I.T.O. would be a specialized agency of the United Nations, like the International Monetary Fund and the International Bank for Reconstruction and Development, which had been established earlier.

GATT would be a temporary measure, pending the ratification of the Havana Charter.* As the U.S. Senate considered the charter, large international businesses expressed concern. While these enterprises shared the proposed organization's advocacy of freer trade, they objected to the charter's provisions binding member nations to undertake large foreign aid programs, for they believed that "the provision of investment capital for economic development of other countries is a function of private enterprise and not government." More important, in the view of the National Foreign Trade Council (which had become a spokesman for international business), the Havana Charter did not offer adequate safeguards for private foreign investment, while its provisions on restrictive business practices would open the way for "harrassment and interference with American enterprises operating in foreign countries." Finally, in December 1950, the administration dropped its support of the I.T.O., and the Senate never ratified the charter.[6] GATT, however, remained and pursued its objective of reducing barriers to trade.[7] U.S. aid and trade policies would be self-regulating and not guided by an international trade organization, yet the overall U.S. support for freer trade remained.

U.S. government advocacy of greater foreign aid, and, in general, greater international trade, included approval of U.S. private foreign investment—to serve national foreign economic policy objectives. To encourage American business abroad, Washington negotiated treaties to protect the U.S. investor from double taxation and to prevent discrimination against U.S. capital.[8] Specifically, to spur reluctant U.S. businessmen to invest in western Europe, Congress introduced investment guaranties in the Economic Cooperation Act of 1948—the first such guaranties ever offered by the U.S. government. The guaranties initially covered only convertibility of compensation resulting from the sale of foreign property (later they would be extended).[9] Other U.S. government backing for U.S. corporations included new means for financing their foreign ventures. The Economic Cooperation Administration (established in 1948) originated certain financing. The older Export-Import Bank (dating from 1934), with enlarged lending power, and the new World Bank—the International Bank for Reconstruction and Development—made funds available for U.S. pursuits from electric power in Latin America to iron

---

* GATT provided a mechanism for multilateral tariff negotiations, introduced trading rules, and offered a forum for discussions of disputes among nations over violations or interpretations of trading rules.

ore mining in Liberia.* [10] The emergence of these U.S. and U.S.-supported international financial bodies that could assist U.S. private direct investment in foreign lands was a truly distinctive aspect of the postwar years.†

Whereas after World War I, as noted, the U.S. government help to direct foreign investors was to assist those that served (1) to increase U.S. exports, (2) to give Americans control over raw materials, (3) to break "foreign monopolies," and (4) to improve the strategic position of the United States abroad, in the immediate post–World War II years, the U.S. government sought to promote all U.S. private investment abroad in friendly countries, at first especially in Europe and then in the early 1950s in less developed lands. The sentiment of the 1920s in Washington that this nation's businessmen should *not* invest in manufacturing abroad and should not export technology, skills, and management (for to do so would create foreign competition) was gone by the late 1940s. By contrast, the Truman administration felt America would prosper in a prosperous world; private enterprise *ought* to export capital, technology, skills, and management to foster foreign economic growth. Economic growth—industrialization—would provide the foundation for a democratic world.[11] The point of view, international in orientation, represented a significant shift in U.S. policy.

In the immediate postwar years, America had balance-of-payments problems, owing to its dollar *surpluses*. Secretary of State Dean Acheson, addressing the National Foreign Trade Convention in November 1949, noted that means of coping with the payments disequilibrium included (1) economic assistance to other countries, (2) a reduction in exports, (3) an increase in imports, and (4) foreign investments by private U.S. businesses.[12] Actually, no one seriously recommended reducing exports (although the Export Control Act did provide a means to do so), but in granting economic assistance, in stimulating trade (hopefully imports), and spurring U.S. private foreign investment, the United States could and did take far-reaching measures in line with the nation's overall foreign economic policy as well as the more specific balance-of-payments requirements.[13]

* The Export-Import Bank was strictly an American institution, while the World Bank was an international unit, a specialized agency of the United Nations. The United States was a major contributor to the World Bank's resources.

† The Export-Import Bank, although dating back to 1934, had played only a small role in aiding U.S. private investment abroad in the 1930s.

While in 1948–1949 with cold war fervor mounting Americans had become more security conscious, the war in Korea intensified this consciousness. At dawn on June 25, 1950, North Korean communist armies swept southward; America stepped in to defend South Korea. In September 1950 Congress passed the Defense Production Act, a foundation for economic mobilization. Defense spending expanded. The Korean war meant that more private foreign investments were required to meet U.S. needs—investments in mining and oil especially. The United States added to its stockpiles of ores, metals, and other raw materials, drawing on both domestic and foreign sources.[14] Under the Defense Production Act, President Truman established the Petroleum Administration for Defense (P.A.D.). Section 708 of that act gave private companies exemption from U.S. antitrust laws in times of emergency; in 1951 under the authority of that section, the P.A.D. worked out a plan in cooperation with the large U.S. oil companies for pooling U.S.-controlled oil resources at home and abroad to aid the flow of oil to U.S. forces in the Far East.[15] In 1952, with a friendly government in Venezuela, the United States and that country signed a trade agreement, reducing U.S. duties on Venezuelan oil imports. Such measures would serve the national interest in the emergency. That year, 1952, the President's Materials Policy Commission (under William S. Paley) emphasized America's desperate raw materials needs and recommended that the U.S. government should continue to foster private U.S. stakes in foreign mining and oil production to fill America's requirements. "Private [U.S.] investment must be the major instrument for increasing production of materials abroad" for American use, declared the Paley Report.[16] In 1950, and then on a regular basis after 1953, the United States became a net importer of petroleum and petroleum products.

Meanwhile, on October 10, 1951, the Mutual Security Act unified most of the U.S. foreign aid programs under the supervision of the Mutual Security Administration.* Foreign aid became more specifically associated with defense and security objectives. Later that month Congress passed the Mutual Defense Assistance Control Act (the Battle Act) that "embargoes the shipment of arms, ammunition, implements of war, atomic energy materials, petroleum, [and] transportation materials of strategic

---

* The Mutual Security Administration replaced the Economic Cooperation Administration in supervising aid programs; it, in turn, came to be replaced on August 1, 1953, when the Foreign Operations Administration took over the aid programs.

value . . . to any nation or combination of nations threatening the security of the United States, including the U.S.S.R. and all countries under its domination." Under this act, the United States would not give military, economic, or financial assistance to any nation unless that country applied a similar embargo.[17] Whereas the Export Control Act of 1949 had dealt solely with U.S. exports, under this measure, the United States expected governments of countries where U.S. enterprises had subsidiaries and affiliates to stop them from violating our legislation. The Battle Act would prove embarrassing to U.S. businesses with subsidiaries in foreign nations that objected to the extension of U.S. law to their sovereignties. These restraints did not mean that the United States desired to discourage international business; on the contrary, the encouragement of business abroad in "friendly" countries persisted. In fact, out of Washington came recommendations favoring more U.S. direct foreign investment.[18]

3

Although the U.S. government throughout the postwar decade aimed to promote U.S. direct investment abroad, American businessmen were not absolutely convinced that their government's policy achieved this goal. As noted, some U.S. businessmen had reservations about the foreign aid program, fearing public assumption of functions more properly undertaken by private enterprise. Yet, in sum, foreign aid probably served more as a help, a complement, than an impediment to U.S. direct investment abroad. Likewise, even though they created certain difficulties for U.S. business abroad and did curtail East-West commerce, there is no evidence that either the Export Control Act or the Mutual Defense Assistance Control Act retarded the activities of U.S. direct foreign investors in a meaningful manner.

When in December 1952 and January 1953 the Department of Commerce queried 122 U.S. executives on obstacles to foreign investment, fully one-third volunteered statements on U.S. taxation. The alleged hindrances can be divided into those of commission and omission. Included in the first category were: (1) U.S. taxes were too high, which limited capital available for investment; companies invested at home (where it was safer) rather than abroad; high U.S. taxes, in addition, made competition abroad more difficult, since foreign businessmen paid lower taxes and thus obtained a competitive advantage. (2) U.S. taxes counteracted the effect of tax incentives offered by other nations to attract American capital. (3) U.S. tax revenues went to foreign aid, which, as we have noted, some businessmen believed was undesirable. The deterrents by omission were: (1) "Since U.S. tax policy does not recognize the greater risks in investment abroad, companies find domestic expansion all the more to be preferred," and (2) "Government measures of tax relief for U.S. foreign enterprises are inadequate."

U.S. tax policy seems, however, to have been only one among many factors limiting foreign investment and hardly crucial. The U.S. government, through tax treaties, was attempting to assist U.S. businessmen abroad. The earlier Western Hemisphere Trade Corporation had given special tax advantage to certain foreign investors. In addition, U.S. companies could take U.S. tax credit on foreign taxes, which greatly aided them in their multinational business.* What seems important is that in the postwar years, U.S. taxes were higher than ever before in peacetime; accordingly, they became a factor for executives to consider to a greater extent than ever before in their planning of operations abroad.[19]

In net, the rash of antitrust cases in the immediate postwar years may have done more than U.S. foreign aid programs, export legislation, or tax measures to impede foreign investment—at least temporarily. By keeping international business "under fire," the Department of Justice acted at variance with U.S. policies seeking to prompt foreign investment. The postwar antitrust actions disrupted the particular enterprises under attack and served as a warning to other corporations. Yet, as we will see, in certain instances, antitrust litigation did not retard investment but had the opposite impact, opening the way to greater expansion abroad.[20]

In *U.S. v. National Lead,* the district court found in 1945 that the defendant had restrained world trade in titanium pigments. Since the 1920s, National Lead had participated in joint ventures in Europe, Canada, and Japan—making agreements with its affiliates to divide world markets, share technology, and exchange licenses. The court held that under the Sherman Antitrust Act these agreements were illegal. The Supreme Court in 1947 affirmed the lower court's ruling that National Lead Company should either sell its stock in the specified foreign businesses or purchase the interests of the other shareholders in the affiliates. In short, the courts insisted that National Lead should terminate the agreements *and* the joint ventures.

---

* By the Revenue Act of 1951, U.S. foreign tax credits were given more freely to U.S. enterprises abroad. See *Paley Report,* I, 70, for details.

National Lead responded by acquiring 100 per cent control of its Canadian and German affiliates and selling its holdings in its British and Japanese joint ventures. The courts dealt specifically with National Lead's restrictive relationships in titanium pigments and not with the company's other foreign investments. In later years, National Lead expanded abroad in many industries. Although it seems to have been careful not to make restrictive agreements, it did not shy away from joint ventures.[21]

In *U.S. v. Electric Storage Battery Company,* which terminated in a district court with a consent decree in 1947, the court found a conspiracy to divide world markets in batteries and ordered the company to divest itself "of all rights and power . . . to influence, affect or determine the policies" of its English affiliate Chloride Electric Storage Syndicate. The company did so.[22]

Then there was *U.S. v. Timken Roller Bearing Company,* a case that frightened American businessmen. As we have seen, the Timken enterprise, like many others, had arranged for its foreign affiliates to sell in a delineated territory and not to compete with it or with one another. In 1949, the district court found Timken's division-of-markets agreements of 1927–1928 illegal and ordered American Timken to sell its holdings in the English and French Timken companies.* On appeal, the Supreme Court in 1951 failed to sustain the divestiture but did affirm the illegality of the division-of-markets agreements. It ordered the American, British, and French Timken companies to compete with each other. They did so, and the American Timken, deprived of control over the sales and pricing policies of its affiliates, found itself meeting "cutthroat" competition to its own detriment and that of its affiliates;† American Timken reported lower sales at home and lower dividends from abroad.[23]

In 1952, in *U.S. v. Imperial Chemical Industries Ltd.,* a district court found that joint ventures established by I.C.I. and du Pont in Argentina, Brazil, and Canada were "used to accomplish the ends of an illegal agreement and understanding." It ordered divestiture of the joint ownership of three affiliated companies.‡ As a result, du Pont obtained the "Du-

---

* Its German company had by this time stopped operations.

† By 1951, American Timken's main partner (Michael Dewar) had died; it bought his interest; this made American Timken's holdings in British Timken 54 per cent and in French Timken 100 per cent, but with the Supreme Court decision, American Timken was still helpless to exercise control.

‡ Two joint ventures (one in a small explosives plant in Chile and one in Brazil) were exempted. Du Pont had purchased Hercules' interest in the Mexican explosives plant; by 1944, it was wholly owned by du Pont.

cilo" enterprise in Argentina, I.C.I. acquired the bulk of the joint business in Brazil, and the Canadian affiliate was split between du Pont and I.C.I. Du Pont emerged with a substantial stake in Argentina and Canada and a negligible one in Brazil. The case transformed du Pont's strategy abroad: it cleared the way for that company to expand in Europe on a giant scale, which du Pont had not done, in large part because of its ties with I.C.I. This was an exceptional instance, wherein an antitrust action of this period actually seems to have encouraged greater corporate interest in foreign investment.[24]

The opposite was true of General Electric. The cases against General Electric spanned a dozen years and wreaked havoc with that enterprise's international business. General Electric and its wholly owned subsidiary, International General Electric Company,* were found guilty of participating in cartels in lamps and electrical equipment.[25] In the lamp case, begun in 1941 and not concluded until 1953, General Electric and International General Electric were each "enjoined and restrained, so long as it holds stock or any other financial interest in any foreign [lamp] company [excluding subsidiaries, more than 50 per cent owned]" from: (1) making agreements with such a company relating to technical information, (2) acting to influence that company to deprive a third manufacturer of access to patents or technical information, and (3) acting to prevent such a company from competing in the United States. The government had wanted G.E. and I.G.E. to rid themselves of all financial interest in the foreign lamp companies, but the court failed to order this.[26]

By 1953, within General Electric, the top management had become disenchanted with business in Europe and Japan where the company had minority interests in important enterprises. Neither chief executive, C. E. Wilson, nor his successor Ralph Cordiner was especially interested in business in Europe. The company had lost money in its foreign operations during World War II; the antitrust cases proved a headache; the remedy in the lamp case in effect "sterilized" G.E.'s stock holdings. Funds were needed for expansion at home. General Electric's Board of Directors favored repatriating the European investments and reinvesting the funds in the United States, Canada, and underdeveloped countries where G.E. had 100 per cent ownership. Thus, when the company got a favorable

* International General Electric Company became International General Electric Division in 1952—and a part of General Electric.

offer for its stock in what was then the largest British electrical company, Associated Electrical Industries, Ltd., it sold at a profit. It sold its interests in France, its stake in N. V. Philips Gloeilampenfabrieken in Holland, and its holdings in Brown, Boveri in Switzerland. It did not sell its interest (roughly 12 per cent) in Allgemeine Electrizitäts Gesellschaft in Germany, which had been written off during the war (G.E. reacquired it at low cost). Likewise, in Japan it took back its minority holding in Tokyo Shibaura Electric (Toshiba) that it did not seek to enlarge. In Australia, where G.E.'s business had started in the 1890s, in 1930 Associated Electrical Industries Ltd. and G.E. had combined their existing operations into a 50-50 joint venture. In the postwar years General Electric's lawyers thought the arrangement dangerous from an antitrust standpoint. Australia wanted more manufacturing. G.E. was prepared to provide the capital and expand; A.E.I. wanted to continue to export and not enter into full manufacturing in that nation. Because of the incompatibility of viewpoints and even more because of antitrust considerations, G.E. offered to buy A.E.I.'s stock in the Australian affiliate, or, alternatively, to sell its interest to A.E.I. (The reader will recall from the *National Lead* and *I.C.I.* cases that either was an acceptable procedure.) A.E.I. wanted the Australian business, and in 1955 G.E. sold. A General Electric manager in Australia later recalled, "Our antitrust laws killed us on that . . . The company had fine personnel, excellent equipment; it had been built up based on American technology. I almost cried." In sum, as a consequence of wartime losses, exacerbated by the antitrust litigation, top management at General Electric had lost enthusiasm for foreign investment; General Electric's international business empire that had been developed since the 1880s and that Gerard Swope and Owen Young had so carefully constructed during the 1920s had been torn asunder. Only majority-owned subsidiaries (mainly in Latin America and Canada) were left untouched in the aftermath of the court decisions and the subsequent repatriations by General Electric. These were not the heart of the business. The empire was in shambles. When in the early 1960s, General Electric would begin to rebuild, it had to start almost from scratch.[27]

The antitrust cases cited all dealt with U.S. companies and their foreign affiliates (agreements between parent companies and wholly owned foreign subsidiaries were not vulnerable, for 100 per cent owned units were considered part of a single enterprise and a corporation cannot conspire with itself). None of these cases declared in so many words that a joint venture in and of itself was illegal. None was designed to hamper legitimate U.S. direct investment abroad. As law professor (and now president of Yale) Kingman Brewster has pointed out, the *National Lead* case demonstrated that joint ownership of foreign properties to accomplish restrictive purposes was illegal, while the *Electric Storage Battery* case attacked division of markets by affiliated and nonaffiliated companies. The *Timken* case indicated that even though the foreign companies involved were in no sense independent units, even though they had been brought to prosperity by American Timken, and even though they made the same products, used the same trademarks, operated under a license, and had American Timken as a major stockholder, this did not give American Timken legal immunity for explicit, exclusive, or restrictive arrangements. The illegality of the I.C.I.–du Pont joint ventures, as Brewster aptly put it, "turned on the finding that they were forged to supply the missing links in a global cartel chain." So, too, the G.E. lamp case remedy voided the restrictive agreements and not G.E.'s stockholdings. In the past, joint ventures of U.S. companies abroad usually involved relationship agreements between affiliates; if these agreements were to be considered "cartels," numerous corporations would be brought into litigation. Some companies responded by avoiding joint ventures; numerous enterprises rewrote their agreements, eliminating exclusive and restrictive arrangements; in subsequent years, when companies made agreements, most were drafted in order to be nonrestrictive—except for the legitimate restrictions involved in trademark and patent use.* [28] Nonetheless, despite

---

* It seemed that under U.S. antitrust and trademark law, an American company, Company A, could register or have common-law rights to a legitimate trademark (one that it spent time, energy, and money promoting) in Country X (the United States or a foreign country). Company B (a foreign affiliate of Company A or an independent foreign company) would then not be able to use that trademark in Country X. This seemed a legal restriction. *But,* Company A could not prohibit Company B from selling in Country X. That was illegal. Nor could Company A insist that Company B only use that trademark when marketing a particular product (Ebb, *International Business,* pp. 353ff, and Brewster, *Antitrust and American Business Abroad,* pp. 245–246). Yet, even this is not altogether clear, for in *U.S. v. Guerlain, Inc.,* 155 F. Supp. 77 (SDNY 1957), vacated mem. 358 U.S. 915 (1958), the defendant excluded imports into the United States of trademarked perfume produced by its foreign affiliate; the defendant argued that section 526 of the Tariff Act of 1930 allowed a domestic trademark owner to exclude imports of goods manufactured abroad bearing its trademark. The district court ruled that section 526 did not grant protection when the American trademark owner was part of an international business. The government then indicated that it planned to seek legislation dealing with the problem (none has

these cases, there is evidence that some companies did continue to place restrictions on the trading activities of their affiliates.[29]

The *Alcoa case,* unlike those just mentioned, did not deal with relationships between parents and affiliates. In 1928, as we have seen, Aluminum Company of America (Alcoa) had established and "spun-off" Aluminium Limited. Aluminium Limited, incorporated in Canada, had then made agreements with European producers impeding imports into the United States. The Sherman Antitrust Act clearly prohibited contracts that restrained the trade of the United States with foreign nations, but could Alcoa be found guilty of the proscribed behavior if the actions were undertaken by Aluminium Limited, a Canadian corporation? How independent was Aluminium Limited? While it was not a subsidiary or affiliate of Alcoa, it did share with that company key American shareholders. Would this link be enough to implicate Alcoa? Moreover, since Aluminium Limited had a New York business headquarters and U.S. stockholders that exercised control, was it "primarily American in all respects save form" and thus subject to U.S. law? Judge Learned Hand in his ruling stated the highly debatable proposition, "it is settled law . . . that any state may impose liabilities even upon persons not within its allegiance, for conduct outside its borders which has consequences within its borders which the state reprehends." In short, Judge Hand believed the acts of the Canadian-incorporated Aluminium Limited that were contrary to the Sherman Act fell within the jurisdiction of the American courts, since the effects were on U.S. commerce and the intent to accomplish such effects was proven. In 1950, nine individuals (members of the Mellon and Davis families) held 46.3 per cent of the stock in Alcoa and 44.65 per cent of the stock in Aluminium Limited. That year, the court required the shareholders of Alcoa to dispose of their stock holdings in either Aluminium Limited or Alcoa. Thus, the 1950 ruling completely severed the two companies from one another. (Aluminium Limited, however, continued to have the majority of its stockholders in the United States.) [30]

The Department of Justice and the Federal Trade Commission also scrutinized Webb-Pomerene associations. The reader will recall that the

---

been passed) and, prior to the argument before the Supreme Court, moved to void the judgment; the decree was dissolved. Likewise, there have been a number of consent decrees where the defendants were ordered to grant patent licenses to all applicants. See American Bar Association, *Antitrust Developments 1955–1968,* p. 58.

Webb-Pomerene Law of 1918 had allowed U.S. exporters to join in *selling* abroad, exempt from U.S. antitrust prosecution. As noted, some American companies had used Webb-Pomerene associations not only for export but for international accords and foreign investments.[31] One of the cases against General Electric dealt with the Electrical Apparatus Export Association (a Webb-Pomerene association); G.E. was "enjoined and restrained" by the court from acting through this or any Webb-Pomerene association to enter "into any contract, agreement, or understanding with any foreign company or companies in competition with the defendants to fix prices, allocate orders, or divide sales territories." In 1947 the court ordered the Electrical Apparatus Export Association dissolved.[32]

That same year, 1947, in a Federal Trade Commission case, the employment by Pet Milk and Carnation Milk Products of a Webb-Pomerene association (General Milk Company Inc.) for their joint ventures abroad was held to be improper. The F.T.C. ordered the General Milk Company to abandon its foreign affiliates or to dissolve itself as a Webb-Pomerene association. It chose the second course. General Milk Company kept its ownership of the foreign affiliates. Its parent companies then incorporated a *new* General Milk Sales Inc.—a Webb-Pomerene association for joint exporting.[33]

In the *Minnesota Mining* case (1950) the joint ownership of the foreign subsidiaries was not by the export association but by the stockholders of the export company. Despite the *General Milk* case, the defendants claimed the Webb-Pomerene Act offered protection to joint-capital export. The district court disagreed and ordered the U.S. companies to divest themselves of their foreign joint subsidiaries. The court maintained that joint ownership abroad by the U.S. companies restrained each firm's freedom of export. Clearly, concluded Kingman Brewster, "Webb association projection into foreign manufacturing is unauthorized, and joint ownership of foreign subsidiaries will not gain any special immunity from Sherman Act risks because the American parent is a Webb association or member of such an association." In the *Minnesota Mining* case, the defendants had claimed the decline in exports from the United States was due to foreign restrictions; they argued they had "no motive or purpose to affect American foreign commerce"; they had established foreign factories to preserve and to expand their foreign markets, which were disappearing in the face of foreign countries' tariffs, quotas, import controls, dollar shortages, exchange restrictions, local preference campaigns, and similar nationalistic measures. Their statement was important, for literally hundreds of manufacturing companies could have explained their rationale for foreign manufacturing in the same terms. But this did not satisfy Judge Charles E. Wyzanski. The basic question, he maintained, was, could the defendants have continued to export from the United States at a profit a substantial volume of coated abrasives into the areas where they built foreign factories? The judge found that the "defendants' decline in exports to the United Kingdom [and Canada] is attributable less to import and currency restrictions . . . than to defendants' desire to sell their British-made goods at a large profit rather than their American goods at a smaller profit and in a somewhat (but not drastically) reduced volume." He ruled this constituted a restraint of trade. "It is no excuse for the violation of the Sherman Act that to supply foreign customers from foreign factories is more profitable and in that sense is, as defendants argue, 'in the interest of American enterprise.' Financial advantage is a legitimate consideration for an individual non-monopolistic enterprise. It is irrelevant where the action is taken by a combination and the effect, while it may redound to the advantage of American finance, restricts American commerce." Judge Wyzanski stressed that "nothing in this opinion can properly be read as a prohibition against an American manufacturer seeking to make larger profits through the mere ownership operation of a branch factory abroad, which is not conducted as part of a combination, conspiracy or monopoly." His decision seemed to say that international business by one firm as it operated abroad was perfectly legitimate; foreign joint enterprises by competitive American firms were by contrast vulnerable. As a consequence, the joint ventures of the abrasives companies in Canada, Australia, Europe, and Latin America were divided among the participating U.S. businesses.[34]

In 1952 a staff report to the Federal Trade Commission was entitled the *International Petroleum Cartel* and in 1953 a civil antitrust suit was filed against the five largest American international oil companies.[35]

All these cases in the postwar decade indicated to U.S. corporation executives that their nation's courts were concerned with the practices of multinational enterprises, that the Sherman Antitrust Act clearly applied to international business, that restrictive agreements affecting or having an intent to affect U.S. foreign commerce were contrary to the Sherman

Act, that while joint ventures outside the United States were not illegal per se, relationships up to then accepted as inherent in a joint venture might well be subject to investigation, and that Webb-Pomerene associations should be confined to joint exporting. The arguments of defense attorneys that restrictive agreements were a legitimate part of doing business abroad, that such agreements were incidental to otherwise valid joint ventures, and that corporations were adapting to the facts of foreign business life and functioning in a manner to enhance rather than to retard business operations failed to have any impact on the court rulings.[36] The dissolution of a joint venture did not bar a U.S. enterprise from a particular locale, but instead required it to act independently, which meant in some instances that a company had to start from scratch and with existing barriers to entry, existing competition, this might be difficult.

In the long run, the antitrust actions appear to have had no serious effect on the volume of U.S. direct foreign investment.[37] Most businesses came to "lick their wounds" and resume operations abroad. Even General Electric, on which the immediate impact was devastating, by the 1960s had once more launched a formidable overseas expansion program. Nonetheless, it seems very clear to the present author that in the years 1945–1955, the litigation did make U.S. executives wary. Large European companies shied away from participation with Americans lest they be dragged into the U.S. courts. Companies delayed reentry into markets that they had abandoned because of antitrust action. Yet, to some extent, the antitrust cases may have in the short run, as well as in the long run, contributed to the development of multinational business of certain U.S. corporations, since these firms could no longer depend on the crutch of international agreements. Moreover, giant U.S. enterprises, aware of the court decisions, were in the future more apt to consider exporting or enlarging exports from their foreign subsidiaries and affiliates. Since explicit territorial limitations seemed taboo, the way was open to more complex multinational organization. The heyday of private international agreements regulating trade was past.[38]

4

Domestic considerations notwithstanding, in the immediate aftermath of World War II, political, economic, and military uncertainties *abroad* proved by far the most significant deterrents to U.S. foreign investment.[39]

Wartime destruction had left much of Europe and Japan in ruins. Dollar shortages delayed trade recovery. Governmental restraints on commerce and exchange transactions were the norm,[40] as were currency deprecia- tions in relation to the dollar. U.S. investors feared the spread of commu- nism as well as the general rise of public sector activities abroad. Still suf- fering from wartime dislocation, U.S. businesses in foreign lands experienced further sizable losses as a consequence of expropriation in communist and noncommunist countries.[41]

These factors made U.S. executives cautious about new foreign stakes. That U.S. investment abroad rose as much as it did was remarkable. Ac- tually, in the immediate postwar years, only U.S. stakes abroad in oil soared. The growth of U.S. foreign direct investment in manufacturing was, however, also significant. Toward the end of the 1940s (and espe- cially at the start of the 1950s with the Korean war), there were new large mining ventures, mainly in Canada and Latin America. As for utilities, the rise in U.S. international business from 1946 to 1954 proved relatively small (see Table XII.1). By 1950, while higher than in 1940, total U.S. direct investments abroad in agriculture equaled only $589 million.* [42]

Table XII.1. U.S. direct foreign investments, 1946, 1950, and 1954, by sectors (book value in billion U.S. dollars and percentage increase)

	1946	1950	1954	Increase 1946–1950	Increase 1950–1954
Petroleum	1.4	3.4	5.3	143%	56%
Manufacturing	2.4	3.8	5.7	58%	50%
Mining	.8	1.1	2.1	38%	91%
Utilities	1.3	1.4	1.5	8%	7%

Source: Adapted from the revised figures given in U.S. Department of Commerce Office of Business Economics, *U.S. Business Investments in For- eign Countries* (Washington, D.C. 1960), p. 1, and *Survey of Current Busi- ness*, August 1956, p. 19.

* Sixty per cent of this amount was in sugar, mainly in Cuba and the West Indies; another 26 per cent was in fruit (principally bananas) in Central America. U.S. De- partment of Commerce, Office of Business Economics, *Foreign Investments of the United States, 1950*, p. 15. In 1945, Ford Motor Company sold its rubber plantations in Brazil to the Brazilian government at a substantial loss. Wilkins and Hill, *American Business Abroad*, p. 183. In 1947, the International Basic Economy Corporation was

In the years 1946–1954 there was no marked increase in direct investments in trade or banking abroad. Direct foreign investment in manufacturing remained, as it had been since the mid-1920s, the largest single industrial group in direct foreign investment. A review of the activities of U.S. direct investors abroad in utilities, mining, manufacturing, and oil reveals their foreign investment experiences.

5

In 1946 and in 1950, U.S. stakes in utilities abroad were less than in 1940; by 1954, they had barely exceeded the 1940 stakes ($1.54 billion versus $1.51 billion). Foreign demand for electric power and for the telephone systems mounted, but U.S. companies hesitated to make substantial investments. For one large investor, American & Foreign Power Company, the postwar years seemed a nightmare. In 1940 this company's subsidiary in China had operating revenues of almost $7 million; between 1942 and 1945, the facility provided no revenues to the American company; it was reacquired by the U.S. parent in 1945, only to be expropriated in 1949 by the Chinese communists—with no compensation forthcoming. In 1947, under pressure from the Indian government (India became independent that year), American & Foreign Power Company relinquished control of its Indian properties. More threatening were the expropriations in Latin America. In 1947, the municipal authorities of Cali, Colombia, expropriated the company's facilities.* Under Juan Perón (president of Argentina, 1946–1955), assets representing 38 per cent of the book value of American & Foreign Power Company's Argentine properties were confiscated. In 1950, the company offered to sell its properties in Argentina to that nation's government—a proposal not acted on during the Perón era. In Mexico, while American & Foreign Power Company expanded, by 1953 its capacity for generating electric power was considerably less than half that of the rival Mexican government facilities.

Throughout Latin America, electric power rates remained a political issue. Rising wages, costs of materials, and taxes increased the company's

---

formed and embarked on a number of agricultural ventures in Venezuela and Brazil, most of which it had written off as failures by 1955. Broehl, *The International Basic Economy Corporation,* pp. xvi, 45, 58. Figures are not available on the percentage change 1946–1954.

* Later the company was compensated.

operating expenses; most Latin American currencies depreciated, causing declines in the value of the properties and in dollar profits (see Table XII.2). Governments resisted giving the company permission to raise rates. Blocked profit remittances and multiple exchange rates, which acted to the company's disadvantage, added to the difficulties of American & Foreign Power Company in Latin America. The postwar inflation in the United States compounded the problems, making "the cost of the imported materials and equipment required by the public utility industry in Latin America, as well as the costs of transporting these goods to their destinations" ever more expensive. So serious was the situation that in 1952 American & Foreign Power Company underwent a corporate reorganization. After simplifying its capital structure, it sought a new basis for expansion. It sold common stock of its foreign subsidiaries in Brazil, Cuba, Costa Rica, Panama, and Guatemala. It obtained funds from the Export-Import Bank, national development banks, and local banks to initiate needed expansion. At the same time, its management began to

Table XII.2. **Comparative exchange rates as they affected American & Foreign Power Company, 1945–1954 (in U.S. dollars)**

| Country | Currency | Rate prevailing when American & Foreign Power made major acquisitions | Yearly average rate [1] | |
			1945	1954
Argentina	Peso	$ .424	$ .248	$ .071
Brazil	Cruzeiro [2]	.120	.050	.036
Chile	Peso	.122	.032	.009
Colombia	Peso	.973	.571	.398
Costa Rica	Colon	.250	.178	.176
Cuba	Peso	1.000	1.000	1.000
Ecuador	Sucre	.200	.074	.066
Guatemala	Quetzal	1.000	1.000	1.000
Mexico	Peso	.499	.206	.089
Panama	Balboa	1.000	1.000	1.000
Venezuela	Bolivar	.193	.299	.299

Source: American & Foreign Power Company, *Annual Report 1954.*

[1] Rate used by American & Foreign Power for conversion purposes.

[2] In 1942, the Brazilians changed their currency from the milreis to the cruzeiro; one cruzeiro was the equivalent of the old milreis.

doubt the wisdom of operating utilities in Latin America. Alternative investments seemed far safer and more profitable. In 1952, the company suggested to the Mexican and Chilean governments that they might want to purchase the company's properties "on a fair basis," suggestions not acted on at the time. For a while, despite the adversity, American & Foreign Power Company expanded, but not dramatically.[43]

International Telephone and Telegraph Corporation—the other giant of earlier years—had similar problems and reservations. In 1944, as noted earlier, I.T.T. had sold its Spanish telephone system for $88 million; in 1945 it sold its Argentine telephone subsidiary to that government for approximately $95 million. Its Shanghai telephone company was expropriated by the communists in 1949, as was its telephone manufacturing plant there. I.T.T. retained and reacquired its European manufacturing plants, while it shed investments in utilities. At the same time, Sosthenes Behn, still the ambitious, enthusiastic chief executive in I.T.T., tried to make *domestic* investments for I.T.T. to offset the hazardous foreign stakes. In June 1952 he told his shareholders, "As to expansion of our activities in the United States, I can only repeat that because of changed world conditions particularly in the early thirties and substantial depreciation of foreign currencies coupled with limitations and control of dividends and exchange transfers, we unhesitatingly decided to meet such changed conditions by developing our strictly dollar revenues. This has since been our firm policy." Nonetheless, I.T.T., like American & Foreign Power Company, found its established enterprises abroad required supporting investments, which it made. I.T.T. remained a giant in foreign business.[44]

6

World War II placed heavy demands on America's mineral resources; after the war, forecasts of shortages were frequent. Direct foreign investments in mining were made to cope with potential domestic shortages. American iron ore resources seemed particularly inadequate. The great Mesabi iron ore range appeared near exhaustion. Thus, large U.S. steel companies, iron ore firms, diversified mining enterprises, and individual entrepreneurs sought foreign iron ore to supply American steel makers. Brazil's large iron ore resources had long been known, but Brazilian politics combined with high-cost rail and ocean transport militated against their immediate development. In 1945 Republic Steel acquired iron ore reserves in Mexico, while Jones & Laughlin purchased properties in Cuba. In the next few years, Bethlehem Steel extended its mining of Chilean iron ore and began to develop deposits at Romeral.* It was Venezuela, however, more than any other Latin American republic, that attracted huge new U.S. stakes in this industry. As early as 1933, Bethlehem Steel and U.S. Steel had acquired iron ore properties in Venezuela; only in the postwar years did they develop these properties. In 1949 U.S. Steel announced the discovery of the giant Cerro Bolivar iron ore body; after extensive development efforts, in 1954 U.S. Steel finally made its first ore shipment from this Venezuelan property. By that year an important Venezuelan industry had been inaugurated, and the total U.S. investment in Venezuelan iron ore (made by Bethlehem Steel and U.S. Steel) reached $269 million. Compared with the $2 billion invested by U.S. enterprises in Venezuelan oil in 1954, this figure seemed small, but the oil investments had been made over several decades, while the iron ore investment was virtually all postwar.[45]

Practically every principal U.S. steel company participated in mining Canadian iron ore. Many of the new stakes were in the Quebec-Labrador region, where in 1942–1943 M. A. Hanna Ore Mining Company (an American firm with domestic iron ore resources) had begun to invest in Hollinger North Shore Exploration and Labrador Mining and Exploration companies—two Canadian enterprises. In November 1949, five U.S. steel companies † formed, in connection with Hollinger and Hanna interests, the Iron Ore Company of Canada to develop iron ore in the Labrador-Quebec region. Before the first shipment was made in 1954, expenditures reached $258.6 million. Likewise, in Canada, Kennecott Copper Company and New Jersey Zinc Corporation jointly carried on exploration for iron ore in eastern Quebec, in the Allard Lake region, where in 1948 they found a large reserve of iron and titanium ore; the two U.S. companies organized the Quebec Iron and Titanium Corporation. Such investments were only a start. U.S. Steel's subsidiary (Cartier Mining Company Ltd.) began exploring in New Quebec in 1951.[46]

Across the Atlantic, Americans turned to French West Africa but decided not to develop known iron deposits, since the French insisted on

* Part of the iron mined at Romeral was for export; part was sold to Compañía de Acero del Pacifico—the Chilean steel enterprise.
† Republic Steel, National Steel, Armco Steel, Youngstown Sheet & Tube, and Wheeling Steel.

majority ownership and managerial control. In Liberia, where no colonial power impeded U.S. investment, the American entrepreneur Lansdell Christie obtained a concession in 1946 to mine iron ore; by 1949 he had interested Republic Steel in investing. Other companies would follow. A new Liberian industry had begun.[47] By the 1960s, iron ore exports would exceed rubber exports from Liberia.

Investments in mining iron ore were the most significant new stakes by Americans in foreign mining in the immediate postwar years. While there had been U.S. investments in mining iron ore abroad in the past, prior to World War II (Bethlehem excepted) none of the principal U.S. steel companies mined iron ore outside the United States. U.S. Steel, for example, had had foreign investments in distribution for decades. It had had a manganese mine in Brazil since 1920; according to the historian Leland Jenks it had an undeveloped Cuban iron ore mine in the 1920s; * and it acquired mining properties in the 1930s. But only when America's domestic resources appeared inadequate did U.S. Steel and the other major U.S. steel makers move into large investments in mining their basic raw materials abroad. While Bethlehem Steel was atypical in having mined iron ore in foreign countries since before World War I, its post–World War II expansion was similarly predicated on anticipated shortages.[48]

Another truly *new* surge in investment was in uranium. Overnight, with developments in atomic energy, uranium mining became important. U.S. companies inaugurated this Canadian industry. In addition, U.S. mining firms added to their existing foreign stakes in other minerals. America, once an exporter of copper, lead, and zinc, was so no longer and would have to develop imports.[49]

In the immediate postwar period, whereas the utilities had been confronted with expropriation abroad, U.S. mining companies were not.† But the phrase "creeping" or "nibbling" expropriation came into the vocabulary of the mining men: nations, through fiscal policies, social legis-

---

* The *Annual Reports* of U.S. Steel make no mention of this mine.

† In 1952 the Bolivian expropriation of the major tin mines involved large U.S. *portfolio* investments, but not direct investments. National Lead had sold its interests in Bolivia's Patiño mines in 1944 (Eastman, Dillon & Co., "National Lead," Nov. 9, 1950, Scudder Collection). The Guggenheims were apparently no longer direct investors in Bolivian tin at the time of the expropriation (interviews, Guggenheim Bros., New York). W. R. Grace & Co. had a tin and tungsten mine that was not expropriated, but it was small compared with the Patiño, Hochschild, and Aramayo enterprises that the Bolivians took over (interviews, W. R. Grace & Co., New York).

lation, encouragement of unions, local purchasing requirements, adverse dollar conversion rates, and trade restraints acted to make business difficult and to erode substantially a company's profits without any actual confiscation. Fearing such "creeping expropriation," many mining firms were shy about new investments in underdeveloped countries, although the caution was always balanced by the potentials for profit and the keen need for raw materials—a need that accelerated with the Korean War.* Likewise, if a company had an established investment, retreat might mean greater loss than continuance (with supporting investments) on the unfavorable terms.[50]

Because of the difficulties in less developed countries, for new ventures, Canada seemed especially attractive. A Canadian government report later explained,

> Canada was in a uniquely favourable position to take advantage of the . . . post-war surge in the market for metals and minerals. We had an already well-established and advanced mining industry, proven mineral resources, ample supplies of available or accessible power, and an economy capable of supplying the trained manpower and often complex goods, transport facilities and engineering and other services basic to successful resource development. Our geographical position, the close corporate or other links [managerial and financial] of many Canadian mining firms with mining and mineral processing companies elsewhere (primarily in the United States), a favourable tax structure, and a political climate conducive to investment were other factors tending especially to stimulate our post-war mining development. Moreover, the country had a practically untapped geological potential which promised well for future discoveries; with the aid of new prospecting techniques like the geiger counter and the airborne magnetometer large new ore-bodies like the nickel find at Mystery Lake [Manitoba] were located. At the same time, new extractive and refining processes favoured the exploitation of newly discovered or previously known deposits.

Thus, not only did Americans move in numbers to develop Canadian iron ore and uranium, but Canada became for the first time a major pro-

---

* In June 1950, with the Korean war, the U.S. copper companies in Chile made a pact with the U.S. Office of Economic Mobilization that provided for a fixed price of 24.5 cents a pound on Chilean copper for the duration of the war. The Chilean government was furious that it had not been consulted (it, after all, depended on copper revenues). Attempts were made in 1951 to assuage the antagonism, but in 1952, the Chilean congress put extraordinary new controls on the industry. Reynolds, "Development Problems," pp. 245–246.

ducer of titanium dioxide, lithium, potash, and sulphur. U.S. investors also expanded in Canada in copper, nickel, lead, zinc, asbestos, and gold. Americans unquestionably took the lead in the growth of mining and mineral processing that occurred in Canada.[51]

7

The rise of U.S. stakes in foreign manufacturing in the immediate post-war years came almost entirely from reinvested earnings of established foreign subsidiaries and affiliates. Sometimes companies reinvested because of blocked profit remittances and the need of foreign subsidiaries to reinvest before the funds depreciated in value. Likewise, in these years (as in earlier ones) profits of foreign subsidiaries and affiliates retained abroad and reinvested there were not subject to U.S. tax.* If the foreign subsidiary or affiliate of an American manufacturing company required the funds or even could use the monies in a profitable fashion, the parent company was wise to have the foreign unit reinvest its profits rather than have the profits returned to the parent as dividends (on which the parent firm would pay U.S. taxes) and then have the parent invest new funds later. Moreover, there seems to have been an aspect of convenience—or perhaps corporate bureaucratic inertia—involved: monies earned abroad were there and available for use abroad. More positively, managers abroad held on to these funds, considering them to be for their use. As in earlier years, reinvested profits were a typical means of financing normal expansion of American manufacturing enterprises outside the United States.† [52]

The end of the war was a watershed in the history of U.S. enterprises manufacturing in Europe. In England, where a labor government had been elected, American companies reconverted to peacetime production, facing state intervention unprecedented in peacetime Britain. On the continent, the war had disrupted operations. Properties had to be reacquired, rebuilt or repaired, and provided with new managements; dealer and supplier relationships had to be re-created. No one could predict the

---

* Prior to the 1962 Revenue Act, a U.S. company did not pay U.S. taxes on any profits of foreign subsidiaries and affiliates until the profits were returned to the United States. The 1962 act taxed the profits of foreign tax havens even if they were not returned to the United States, but that change applied only to a limited amount of foreign income, so even after 1962 the basic tax rule was unaltered.

† I use the word "normal," for with large expansion programs, new capital was always added. There were, however, few "big" expansion programs in the immediate postwar years by American manufacturing companies abroad.

fate of postwar Germany, a divided, occupied country; U.S. investors feared for their prewar holdings in west as well as east Germany. Strong communist parties in France and Italy meant a poor investment outlook. Soviet forces that liberated eastern Europe helped themselves to American properties; and then east European governments expropriated remaining assets.*

Not until 1947–1948 did the prospects for European recovery seem at all promising. By then it had become clear that the Allies would permit West Germany to rebuild its industry. The West German mark was stabilized in June 1948. Even though cold war anxieties were accentuated in 1948 by the Berlin blockade, still it looked as though West Germany had the will and ability to surmount the crisis and to develop with U.S. help. Under the Monnet plan in France, that nation was en route to recovery. Britain—restrictions remaining—was seeking a viable basis for reconstruction; then, the 1949 devaluation of the pound sterling put the value of British currency on a more realistic basis. With the Truman Doctrine (1947) that committed the United States to defend Greece and Turkey and the European Recovery Program (1947–1948), with the formation in 1948 of the Organization for European Economic Cooperation (O.E.E.C.) and in 1949 of the Council of Europe,† and with the establishment of the North Atlantic Treaty Organization in 1949, it became clear that not only would the United States furnish political, military, and economic aid to Europe, but that Europe was going to help itself. The events seemed harbingers of a possible future western European unity, in a western Europe secure from communism.

Nonetheless, cold war anxieties, restrictions on foreign remittances and

---

*Eastman Kodak, for example, reported that they lost "our film manufacturing plant in Copenick, East Germany; our paper producing plant in Vacz, Hungary, and of course our distribution houses in Rumania, Poland, Czechoslovakia, Yugoslavia, Hungary." Fenn, *Management Guide to Overseas Operations*, p. 103. *Claims* for losses to U.S. properties—not simply to manufacturing companies—ran well over $1 billion. Based on data in U.S. Legislative Reference Service, *Expropriation of American Owned Property*, pp. 13–16.

† The O.E.E.C. involved the commanders in chief of the western zones of occupation in Germany (later the government of the Federal Republic of Germany) and Austria, Belgium, Denmark, France, Greece, Iceland, Ireland, Italy, Luxembourg, the Netherlands, Norway, Portugal, Sweden, Switzerland, Turkey, and the United Kingdom. It worked with the American, Economic Cooperation Administration (E.C.A.) to develop programs to benefit western Europe as a whole. The Council of Europe initially brought together Belgium, Denmark, France, Ireland, Italy, Luxembourg, the Netherlands, Norway, Sweden, and the United Kingdom for debates on future strategies. In 1950, the European Payments Union was created under the auspices of the O.E.E.C., it provided a first step in monetary cooperation.

trade, along with governmental attempts at planning, persisted and remained factors hindering U.S. direct investment in European manufacturing. Some U.S. companies with sales subsidiaries and the "desire to keep, renew, or establish markets in soft currency areas" did establish new production facilities in Europe. Minneapolis Honeywell, for example, before the war had been an exporter to Europe, with sales subsidiaries in England, Sweden, and Holland. When its U.S. and Canadian plants could no longer fill English needs (owing to exchange difficulties), it started a small manufactory in the United Kingdom in 1948—a typical "defensive" investment.* On the other hand, with blocked currency, liquidation of existing stakes proved difficult. While some companies managed to sell out, the vast majority of U.S. enterprises with European manufacturing operations neither added much in the way of new funds nor liquidated; left alone, so to speak, most reinvested their profits and grew —pacing the European recovery.

Adversity in the form of dollar shortages, import licensing, restrictions of remittances, and similar obstacles to foreign trade in the immediate postwar years paradoxically contributed to some U.S. corporations becoming more multinational. European factories owned by U.S. subsidiaries supplied customers in countries that lacked dollars to buy American goods. The British government urged American firms in the United Kingdom to export, and they complied. There were more exports to third-country markets from British and certain European units of U.S. international businesses than ever before.

In Britain, the 1949 devaluation of the pound sterling seemed to have eliminated the need for further devaluations (at least in the immediate future). From January 1950, "approved" U.S. investments in the United Kingdom could be repatriated on demand. Then in 1951 a conservative government replaced the socialists there. By 1951, French industry was producing practically double its prewar output. By 1952, an "economic miracle" had occurred in West Germany, where production was 145 per cent above the prewar level. The three successors to the partner of so

---

* U.S. guarantees did little to spur investment; in fact only about two dozen companies took advantage of the Economic Cooperation Administration guaranty before they made investments. In 1949, the guaranty was extended to cover convertibility of earnings and profits as well as the capital originally invested. The extended program was not particularly popular. On December 31, 1951, with the end of the E.C.A., the Investment Guaranty Program was shifted to the Mutual Security Agency. See Gaston, *Obstacles to Direct Foreign Investment*, p. 297, and Whitman, *Government Risk-Sharing in Foreign Investment*, p. 91.

many U.S. businesses (I. G. Farben)—Farbenfabriken Bayer, Farben-werke Hoechst, and Badische Anilin-und-Soda Fabrik—were on route to recovery.* Already the German Volkswagen was outproducing General Motor's Opel, the pre–World War II leader in Germany. In 1952, the treaty establishing the European Coal and Steel Community led to a common market among France, Belgium, Italy, Luxembourg, Holland, and West Germany for coal and steel. By 1951–1952 America was totally committed to aid and defend western Europe and "contain communism." † At this point, 1951–1952, U.S. businessmen renewed their interest in the possibilities of investment in manufacturing in western Europe to fill the demands of these markets—demands that exports from the United States failed to fill.[53]

Meanwhile, in Canada, the U.S. subsidiaries and affiliates that had manufactured for war reconverted to peacetime operations, paralleling the activities of their parent firms across the border. U.S. enterprises that were shy about other foreign stakes had no worries about their holdings in the Dominion. "Personally, I am afraid of foreign investments," wrote the treasurer of a large U.S. company in 1946. He continued the internal memorandum, "The record does not show that our foreign investments to date have been very profitable, except for those in Canada, which I do not regard as a foreign country." The response was typical. U.S. companies knew that their factories in the Dominion had not suffered physical damage during the war, and more important, their business would not be troubled by the political and economic stresses so evident elsewhere. Accordingly, between 1943 and 1950, U.S. direct investments in manufacturing in Canada doubled; from 1950 to 1954 they rose from $1.9 billion to $2.6 billion.[54]

U.S. stakes in manufacturing in Latin America had historically been far less than in Europe or Canada. The postwar years represented no exception. Expansion programs of U.S. manufacturers in Latin America during World War II continued into peacetime; U.S. direct investments in manufacturing in Latin America more than doubled between 1943 and 1950, and between 1950 and 1954 they increased from $780 million to $1.24 billion. The growth was greatest where the market appeared to

---

* I. G. Farben had been broken up after the war.

† NATO members established a Consultation Group Coordination Committee (COCOM as it was called) whose members drew up a list of strategic goods barred from communist countries. COCOM met regularly to discuss what goods should be listed.

be largest and where political and economic conditions seemed advantageous—namely in Brazil and Mexico.* The investment was in market-oriented manufacturing. In Brazil, U.S. manufacturing firms reinvested blocked profits; because of restraints on imports (licensing, foreign exchange controls, as well as tariffs), they changed sales outlets into manufacturing facilities. In Mexico, where there were no limits on profit remittances but where the government was protectionist and encouraged import-substitution, manufacturing firms reinvested profits and expanded to meet growing demand.† A number of U.S. manufacturing companies in Brazil and in Mexico, hoping to meet national wishes, went into joint ventures with local businesses, obtaining stock in exchange for licenses and know-how.

During the Perón era in Argentina, U.S. companies faced multiple exchange rates, controls over profit remittances (at times complete blockage of dividends), no licenses for imports, controls over exports, monumental labor problems, new taxes, and, in general, excessive government controls. Despite such adversity, some firms expanded. "We had expansion programs in mind; we used blocked profits, whenever they were blocked," explained one American executive of his company's operations in Argentina, and, he added, "we did well." Another executive (in a chemical company) later recollected, "Had we been able to remit profits, our parent company would have had us do so; not being able to do so, we reinvested the funds. By the end of the Perón era, we had a healthy, important enterprise." On the other hand, operations of some U.S. manufacturers in Argentina were suspended. The meat packers faced special difficulties. Cheap meat remained a political issue. The industry began to fear expropriation. Executives in U.S. meatpacking companies spent half their time arguing with government officials. As one general manager put it: "We were told what to pay for cattle, what to pay labor, what price our meat could be sold for; there was strict government control of costs; free enterprise was curtailed; they didn't allow reasonable profits and since we had no prospect for profits, we made no investments. When

---

* Through all the difficulties that U.S. investors had had in Mexico from 1910 through the 1930s, the small investments of U.S. manufacturers had never been expropriated.
    † *Total* U.S. direct investment in Mexico was higher in 1929 than in 1954, but U.S. direct investment in *manufacturing*, by contrast, showed a steady rise: 1929, $6.3 million; 1940, $10.5 million; 1943, $22.3 million; 1950, $133.0 million; 1954, $217.0 million! U.S. Dept of Comm., Bureau of Foreign Commerce, *Investment in Mexico*, p. 16.

Perón was out in 1955, the industry was in a state of despair. No one had closed up, but the plants were rundown."

Throughout Latin America, U.S. pharmaceutical companies continued to take advantage of the temporary German withdrawal to establish themselves securely. Food processors (other than meat packers) entered and expanded. Some new investments were made by chemical companies. By 1950 U.S. stakes in manufacturing—primarily market-oriented manufacturing—in Latin America already exceeded those in mining (see Table XIII.2).[55]

U.S. investors in manufacturing in the Far East tried to reestablish themselves. Properties in China were reacquired. Then the communists took over mainland China in 1949. U.S. firms went out of business, owing to restrictions, onerous taxes, and finally expropriation; by decree, December 29, 1950, the Chinese communist government officially took control of all U.S. property in that country.* In Japan, during the occupation, American businessmen sought to reclaim their properties. They found the Japanese had been scrupulous in keeping accounts; the books were all in order, but the restoration of the properties proved tardy. Not until 1950, under the "Law Concerning Foreign Investment," could most U.S. manufacturing companies resume their prewar Japanese business, although some U.S. enterprises did undertake operations supplying the allied forces during the occupation. As in Germany, so in Japan the occupation adopted an antimonopoly policy. The *zaibatsu* groups were to be torn asunder. Yet, the policy had limited success in Japan. When in the early 1950s American companies reestablished themselves there, most found it desirable to enter into joint ventures with Japanese capital, and they generally joined with the same groups with which they had been associated before the war.† International Business Machines, which in the

---

* An American, employed by a General Electric subsidiary, Andersen, Meyers & Co., recalls that when he returned to Shanghai after the war, "we found a better factory than we left; the Japanese had improved our manufacturing." Then in 1949, the Chinese communists took over the facilities. Not until 1951 was the last company representative permitted to leave. Interview, P. M. Markert, Johannesburg, South Africa, Aug. 3, 1965.

† Although the evidence is not all in, it seems that in Japan (far more than in Germany), U.S. companies soon after the war reestablished prewar relationships with Japanese firms. One can speculate on the reasons: (1) U.S. business relationships in prewar Germany had been, as noted, under attack in the United States; U.S. investments and agreements in Japan had not undergone the same hostile scrutiny (probably because they were less important and also because no one found evidence that such *investments or agreements* had retarded the U.S. defense program; prewar exporters to

1930s had entered Japan on a 100 per cent basis, was exceptional in that it returned on those terms; it resumed operations, using blocked yen—at first only manufacturing cards and then expanding.[56]

The Australian government during World War II had realized how vulnerable its land was to attack; thus, it sought new foreign investment to aid industrialization. Many U.S. citizens were stationed in Australia during the war; air travel shortened the distances between the two countries; the Anglo-Saxon tradition within the commonwealth made it a nation that U.S. businessmen could understand. A high standard of living prevailed. These factors, combined with tariffs and licensing of imports, turned U.S. executives to consider building new factories to serve the Australian market. General Motors, which had assembled in Australia since the 1920s and had in 1931 purchased the Holden Motor Company, Ltd., makers of automobile bodies, took the initiative among U.S. investors in Australia. Between 1943 and 1950 U.S. direct investment in manufacturing in Australia more than doubled; by 1954, it had again more than doubled. The sum was still, however, relatively small.[57]

8

The only truly aggressive U.S. investors abroad in the immediate postwar years were the oil companies. They encountered every problem of other investors, as well as additional ones. At home, they had antitrust difficulties. Abroad, they faced expropriation (in Poland, Czechoslovakia, Yugoslavia, Rumania, Hungary, East Germany, and China), "creeping expropriation" (in many countries), political instability, labor difficulties, dollar shortages, restraints on trade and payments, investment control laws, legislation excluding their participation, foreign government intervention in their business, and so forth. They had a backlog of harrowing memories of experiences in the 1930s, including the expropriations in Bolivia and Mexico, and of property losses in Europe and Asia during the war years. Yet, such obvious deterrents to foreign investments notwith-

Japan had been maligned, but not investors per se); thus, the early resumption of ties with I. G. Farben's successors might well be seen by U.S. businessmen as a more tenuous proposition than the resumption of joint enterprises with Mitsui, Mitsubishi, or Sumitomo firms. (2) Germany provided a more familiar investment arena than Japan (Americans could find U.S. managers who spoke German; many Germans spoke English); in Japan, because of Americans' lack of knowledge, operations not in a joint venture were difficult. It was also helpful to obtain Japanese aid in marketing. (3) The Japanese government virtually required joint ventures; the German government did not.

standing, the major oil companies expanded abroad in every single facet of their business. Energy requirements were rising; profits were to be made; despite the obstacles, the U.S. oil enterprises hoped to take advantage of the opportunities.[58]

Jersey Standard and other U.S. oil companies reconstructed their marketing organizations and rebuilt their damaged refineries in western Europe. With dollar shortages and controls on trade and foreign exchange, European governments insisted ever more vigorously that companies refine within the nation. The motives were the same as before the war: Each country desired to devote limited foreign exchange to importing the cheaper crude oil rather than refined products. With the opening up of new Middle Eastern oil production (much of it U.S. owned), it proved economical for U.S. companies to ship crude and to refine in the large European markets. After 1948, Middle Eastern oil increasingly substituted for Venezuelan and U.S. oil in Europe. The European Recovery Program required vast quantities of petroleum products. Already by 1948, Standard Oil of New Jersey's prewar French refinery was operating 35 per cent *above* its prewar rate; in Italy Jersey Standard planned to acquire an interest in an existing refinery; in Germany, it would rebuild its Hamburg refinery. As for England, it replaced its small refinery with a giant one at Fawley, completed in September 1951. Jersey Standard was not alone. Socony-Vacuum likewise rehabilitated its prewar refineries in France and Italy, and by 1950 it had refineries in Germany and Austria as well. It built a large refinery at Coryton in England, a joint venture with the British firm Powell Duffryn Ltd. Before the war, Texaco had given Caltex the option to purchase its European distribution organization, and in 1947 Caltex made the acquisition. As a start, between 1947 and 1949, Caltex (jointly owned by Texaco and Standard Oil of California) built refineries in Holland, France, Italy, and Spain—and then continued to expand.[59]

Across the world, in Japan, Americans also invested in refineries. Before the war, the only refinery that had had U.S. interests had been that of Mitsubishi Oil Company. Supreme Commander for the Allied Powers, General Douglas MacArthur, in November 1945 established a Petroleum Advisory Group (composed of leading U.S. and foreign oil men) to regulate and to control the supply and distribution of petroleum and ultimately to return the oil business to private ownership, which occurred in 1951. By then, Stanvac and Caltex had established joint ventures with

Japanese firms and participated in refining. Stanvac came to be connected with Toa Nenryo Kogyo, K.K., while Caltex went into joint ventures with Nippon Oil Company and Koa Oil Company. Tide Water resumed its prewar ties with Mitsubishi Oil Company. To the Japanese, Americans offered some capital, arrangements for financing, equipment, advanced technology, and an assured supply of crude oil. For Japan, as for Europe, Americans would ship crude oil mainly from the new, expanding Middle Eastern sources. Before World War II, Japan had been an important purchaser of refined oil from the United States; it was so no longer. The entire role in trade and investment of the American oil companies in Japan was altered.[60]

Worldwide, in countries where U.S. firms had never refined, governments desired refineries. In response, as a start, Stanvac in 1949 and Caltex in the early 1950s built refineries in Australia; both companies also erected refineries in India.[61]

While the American oil companies' new stakes in distribution and in consumer-nation refining grew, they were more than equaled by giant new investments in production and transportation—especially in Canada, Latin America, and the Middle East. In 1947, Jersey Standard's affiliate Imperial Oil, Ltd. discovered oil at Le Duc, a small town south of Edmonton, Alberta, Canada. Overnight, the Dominion attracted wildcatters, prospectors, and major oil enterprises. Oil discoveries continued. Pipelines, financed by American and Canadian oil companies, improved transportation from the remote fields. Canada's natural gas industry grew, following on the heels of the oil industry.[62]

In Latin America, U.S. companies continued to produce oil, mainly in Venezuela but also in Argentina, Colombia, and Peru.* In October 1945, Acción Democrática (headed by the longtime foe of the foreign petroleum companies, Rómulo Betancourt) overthrew Venezuelan president General Isaías Medina and in December imposed a new income tax on the oil industry. Labor agitation mounted, with Betancourt expressing sympathy for the workers' demands. On June 14, 1946, for the first time, the foreign oil firms signed contracts with labor unions in Venezuela.

---

* In Brazil and Chile, government oil companies produced the limited output, while in Mexico and Bolivia, government companies operated the expropriated industries. In 1951, Bolivia ended its monopoly of oil exploration and adopted "an open door policy toward private capital." At first, the major U.S. companies were not interested, because of Standard Oil of New Jersey's experience with expropriation. A small Texas concern did, however, take a concession in 1954. See *Petroleum Press Service* 23:260 (July 1955). Later Gulf Oil would invest in Bolivia.

The companies recalled the Mexican expropriation that served as a dire warning of the sensitive relationship between labor, government, and industry. The 1938 experiences in Mexico were not repeated in Venezuela. The companies in their 1946 contracts conceded large wage increases, vacations with pay, along with numerous other fringe benefits. The industry declared the settlement raised wages 35 to 50 per cent for Venezuela's 25,000 oil workers. In February 1948 new contracts even more favorable to the unions were signed. The fringe benefits added more than one-fourth to the basic payrolls. After discussions between the Venezuelan government and the oil companies, on November 12, 1948, a revised income tax law introduced a mandatory 50-50 split of profits. Jersey Standard's subsidiary Creole Petroleum Corporation (by far the largest corporation in Venezuela) agreed to pay "back taxes" that "equalized the government's income from Creole with the Company's profits since 1946." The 50-50 profit split provided the example for the worldwide petroleum industry. In the years 1945 to 1948, under the administration of the feared Acción Democrática party, the oil industry not only weathered the threat of expropriation, but flourished. Production of oil swelled from the new high of 886,000 barrels per day in 1945 to 1,339,000 barrels per day in 1948. Creole's net income (after taxes) alone soared from $64.6 million in 1945 to $198.7 million in 1948. It could afford to play a major role in the nation's social welfare and did so. By 1948 the oil industry as a whole was paying $374.8 million (U.S. dollars) in taxes to the Venezuelan government. The companies had the best wages in the nation and were furnishing major benefits.

On November 24, 1948, a dozen days after the landmark income tax legislation establishing the mandatory 50-50 profit-sharing, a military junta overthrew the Acción Democrática party. The oil industry tried to remain aloof from, but well informed on, the political struggles; the industry accepted and adapted to the change in government. No alterations were made in the 50-50 provisions. While the army junta held power (1948–1952), the oil industry got full cooperation; it expanded and contributed giant sums to the Venezuelan treasury (see Table XII.3).* In 1952, Marcos Pérez Jiménez took power and also provided the industry

---

* The sums included income tax, royalty, surface tax, import duties, and other miscellaneous taxes, which meant the government share of oil industry net income before taxes was more than 50 per cent (55 per cent, 1948; 60 per cent, 1949; 51 per cent, 1950; 55 per cent, 1951 and 1952). Data from Creole Petroleum Corporation. In the 1950s, Venezuela was second only to Canada in the book value of U.S. direct investment. Data from U.S. Department of Commerce.

Table XII.3. Venezuelan government income and oil industry's contribution (in million U.S. dollars)

(1) Year	(2) Total Venezuelan government income [1]	(3) Total Venezuelan oil industry taxes [2]
1948	533.5	374.8
1949	594.5	410.7
1950	575.7	291.6
1951	680.6	426.2
1952	723.0	477.6
1953	760.8	514.2
1954	790.3	484.7

Source: Creole Petroleum Corporation, Caracas.

[1] The rate of exchange in column 2 is Bs. 3.33 per U.S. dollar (the official rate of exchange).

[2] The rate of exchange in column 3 is Bs. 3.09 per U.S. dollar (the rate of exchange applicable to the petroleum industry).

with a friendly environment. With Creole in the lead, foreign oil companies sought to become "model citizens." Creole became concerned not only with its own employees, but with the community as a whole. It enlarged its training of Venezuelans, although in 1952 it still had 1,176 Americans working for the company in that country. By the early 1950s, oil industry executives in Venezuela, especially those in Creole, talked of statesmanship, participation in economic growth, industry-government agreement, rather than, as in prewar years, placing major emphasis on the company's "legal rights." * [63]

In Argentina, Yacimientos Petrolíferos Fiscales, the government oil company, raised its output; private companies, which by law were confined to their existing concession, annually saw their output decline. In Colombia, the de Mares concession of the Jersey Standard affiliate (Tropical Oil Company) expired in 1951 and was not renewed. The Colombian government oil company Empresa Colombiana de Petróleos, in

---

* Some of the smaller American companies felt that Creole Petroleum Corporation went too far in its aid to Venezuela; they maintained that Creole had high profits so that it could afford to be generous and argued that it was far more difficult for them to be such "good citizens." Interviews in Venezuela.

accord with the terms of the concession, repossessed it along with the installations of Tropical Oil. Nonetheless, other U.S. companies, in an adverse environment (poor management-labor relations and discriminatory laws), maintained their search for and production of oil in Colombia. In Peru, where operating conditions were temporarily more favorable than those in Argentina or Colombia, International Petroleum Company (a Jersey Standard affiliate) developed new properties.* [64]

In these postwar years, U.S. stakes in Middle Eastern oil burgeoned. To gain extra capital and to share their risk, as well as to find marketing outlets for the potential output, Standard Oil of California and Texaco in December 1946 agreed in principle that Standard Oil of New Jersey and Socony-Vacuum would participate in both the Arabian American Oil Company (ARAMCO) in Saudi Arabia and in the new Trans-Arabian Pipeline Company (Tapline). Documents were signed on March 12, 1947, the same day President Truman announced the policy of granting U.S. economic and military aid to Greece and Turkey. William S. S. Rodgers, chairman of the board of The Texas Company, told a Senate Committee that this was "absolutely coincidental . . . We were amazed . . . when we heard it. If I had known about it, I think we would have probably held up our arrangements with Standard Oil of New Jersey and Socony-Vacuum." The U.S. government's commitment to contain communism in Greece and Turkey proved reassuring to U.S. investors in the Middle East.

Standard Oil of New Jersey and Socony-Vacuum, with marketing facilities to sell Saudi Arabian oil, were prepared to pay $102 million for a 40 per cent stock interest in ARAMCO.† But before they could do so they had to terminate their arrangements under the 1928 red line agreement that bound them not to operate within the "red line area" (which included Saudi Arabia) except in connection with their partners in the Iraq Petroleum Company. The two U.S. companies told their partners in I.P.C., quite correctly, that the restrictive agreement was not valid under the new interpretations of American antitrust law. (Here, American antitrust law served the purposes of American companies abroad.) The French participant in Iraq Petroleum Company (Compagnie Française

---

* In 1948 Jersey Standard purchased Imperial Oil's interests in International Petroleum.

† Thirty per cent to Jersey Standard and 10 per cent to Socony-Vacuum, leaving Standard Oil of California and The Texas Company each with a 30 per cent interest.

des Pétroles) and C. S. Gulbenkian sued for breach of contract; not until 1948 did the U.S. companies settle the litigation; then they were free to join with Standard Oil of California and The Texas Company in ARAMCO and Tapline. By that time, ARAMCO's output was mounting, and the pipeline was under construction.[65]

The pipeline from eastern Saudi Arabia to the Mediterranean would run 1,068 miles, spanning some territory on which no westerners had ever before set foot. It cost over $200 million and was built by 1,550 Americans and 14,560 men of other nationalities (mainly Arabs). Construction engineers met technical difficulties. Roads had to be built, new towns created, and water wells drilled along the route. An outbreak of cholera in Syria and a smallpox epidemic in Lebanon temporarily halted work. Political complications were multiple, since the company had to negotiate with the governments of Palestine, Jordan, Syria, and Lebanon, as well as Saudi Arabia, for right-of-way concessions. The initial plan was to terminate the pipeline in Palestine, but late in 1947, with the United Nations vote to partition that country and tensions mounting between Jews and Arabs, Tapline officials had second thoughts. Then on May 14, 1948, the British ended their mandate in Palestine and the Jews proclaimed the state of Israel. The armies of the Arab League (including Egypt, Syria, Lebanon, Transjordan, Iraq, Saudi Arabia, and Yemen) invaded. Many Arabs fled their homeland, presuming they were leaving for a week or two. The state of Israel remained. Under U.N. guidance, a truce was arranged in the summer of 1948, and in 1949 armistice settlements were made with the various Arab states. The Arab world—made up of nations that had little in common—was united in its hatred of Israel. Now there was no question: the Trans-Arabian Pipe Line would have to bypass Israel.* Finally, in November 1950, oil flowed through the new pipeline from eastern Saudi Arabia to the outlet at Sidon, Lebanon. By this time, ARAMCO's production in Saudi Arabia was second only to Iran's in the Middle East.[66]

Meanwhile, directly after World War II the Kuwait Oil Company, Ltd. (jointly owned by Gulf Oil and Anglo-Iranian Oil) embarked on a large development program. Commercial shipments of crude oil from Kuwait began in June 1946, and by 1950, that tiny Shaikhdom had

---

* Likewise, the Iraq Petroleum Company had its pipeline terminating at Haifa; this terminus was closed, and its pipeline was rerouted through Lebanon to conform to political realities. A new pipeline to Banias, Syria, was added in 1952.

achieved sixth place in world production, after the United States, Venezuela, U.S.S.R., Iran, and Saudi Arabia.[67]

New U.S. oil companies in the Middle East in the immediate postwar years included the American Independent Oil Company (AMINOIL) * and J. Paul Getty's Pacific Western Oil Company (later Getty Oil). These two companies obtained concessions from Kuwait (1948) and Saudi Arabia (1949) respectively for each of these country's undivided half-interest in the mineral resources of the Saudi Arabia-Kuwait Neutral Zone.[68]

With oil production and profits mounting in the Middle East, Middle Eastern governments desired a greater share of the industry's earnings. Saudi Arabia had obtained advantageous terms in the new Getty concession, and this stimulated Middle Eastern states to press established enterprises for higher revenues. Under U.S. tax law, U.S. companies could obtain tax credits on practically all their foreign taxes; they would not have a much greater tax liability if the 50-50 profit-sharing arrangement adopted in Venezuela in 1948 was introduced in the Middle East. Standard Oil of New Jersey's subsidiary, Creole Petroleum Corporation, had been closely involved in the Venezuelan arrangements; it seems likely that Standard Oil of New Jersey played a major role in the transfer of the 50-50 concept to the Middle East. In 1950 ARAMCO and the Saudi Arabian government were the first in the Middle East to agree to the 50-50 arrangement, followed by Kuwait Oil Company and Kuwait (1951), Iraq Petroleum Company (and its associated companies) and Iraq and its new operations in Qatar (1952), and then the Bahrein Petroleum Company and Bahrain (1952). Expert on the petroleum industry Henry Cattan estimates that the 50-50 profit division in the Middle East yielded about a threefold to fourfold rise in host government revenues.[69]

Iran chose an alternative path. For years, Iran (the largest oil producer in the Middle East) had sought revisions in the concession agreement with Anglo-Iranian Oil Company and had rejected various offers made by that company. On April 30, 1951, the Iranian parliament voted to nationalize the nation's oil industry. After nationalization, Iranian oil output plunged downward. The international oil companies boycotted Iranian oil, and the government had no distribution channels to sell its oil

---

* AMINOIL was an independent company; its stockholders were Phillips Petroleum, Signal Oil and Gas, Ashland Oil & Refining, J. S. Abercrombie, Crescent (stock sold in 1962), Sunray Mid-Continental, Globe Oil & Refining, Lario Oil and Gas, and Pauley Petroleum.

World War II and Its Aftermath

abroad (practically all Iranian oil was exported). To fill the demand for Middle Eastern oil, oil production in Saudi Arabia, Kuwait, and Iraq surged to record levels.* For the first time in history, in 1951, America's share in Middle Eastern oil output surpassed the British and British-Dutch portion, reaching 58 per cent. Henceforth, U.S. oil companies would retain their first place standing in the Middle Eastern oil industry. The Iranian nationalization seemed so to threaten free world oil supplies that the U.S. Petroleum Administration for Defense urged the cooperation of U.S. oil enterprises to see to it that U.S. troops in the Far East got adequate oil.

Iran could not sustain its oil expropriation. Deprived of most of its oil revenues for almost two years, the nation felt the financial pinch. The government of Muhammad Mossadegh, initiator of the nationalization, fell on August 19, 1953. His successor, General Fazlollah Zahedi, was ready to negotiate. Iran, however, refused to let a purely British company return (the British had occupied Iran during the war and anti-British feeling was intense). Anglo-Iranian Oil Company recognized it must bring in other petroleum companies.

Since the end of World War I, American oil enterprises had made efforts to invest in Iran. By the mid-1950s, for some companies (Socony-Vacuum, for instance), the extra oil would be of positive advantage. For Standard Oil of New Jersey, it was otherwise. Its decision to invest in Iran in 1954 was "political." The Company had a 30 per cent interest in ARAMCO—and from Saudi Arabia it could get far cheaper oil than from Iran. "We would have made more money if we had done added drilling in Saudi Arabia; we had plenty of oil there. We were pushed into the consortium [in Iran] by the United States government," declared a Standard Oil of New Jersey director at a later date. "We recognized the dangers if Russia got in; we had a real interest in seeing to it that the problem was solved. We didn't balk at participation. Had the Russians gotten Iranian oil, and dumped it on world markets, that would have been serious." Moreover, if the Iranian nationalization had been sustained, it would have created a bad precedent. Standard Oil of New Jersey entered the Iranian industry not in order to get more oil, but because of the political and economic consequences of *nonparticipation.*

* By 1953–1954, Kuwait oil production ran practically even with Saudi Arabian production, competing for first place in the Middle East, and fourth place in the world, after the United States, Venezuela, and the U.S.S.R.

Here was a vivid illustration of the mixture of economics and politics in the oil industry.*

The resolution of the Iranian crisis involved recognition of the Iranian government's nationalization of the oil industry. The Iranians paid the Anglo-Iranian Oil Company compensation. A consortium—made up of British, American, French, and British-Dutch companies †—was organized. On August 5, 1954, the Iranian government and the consortium signed a twenty-five year contract (with a fifteen-year extension clause), under which the consortium would *operate* the Iranian oil industry in a specified area in southwestern Iran, paying Iran 50 per cent of its earnings. Thus, Iran also adopted the 50-50 principle. Production at the oil fields revived. The U.S. oil companies' participation in the new consortium meant that after decades of exclusion from Iran, they had finally penetrated the last country in the Middle East that was an exclusively British source of oil. Accordingly, in every Middle Eastern nation where oil was produced, there were by 1954 U.S. interests, either involved in all-American companies or in joint enterprises with British Petroleum Company (the old Anglo-Iranian Oil Company now renamed) and/or Royal Dutch-Shell.[70]

In the Dutch East Indies, disturbed political conditions in the aftermath of the Japanese occupation notwithstanding, U.S. oil companies rehabilitated their fields. The Japanese had started drilling on the Caltex properties, and their wells served as a foundation for Caltex's expansion. On December 27, 1949, the Dutch recognized Indonesia's independence; Sukarno became the chief executive of what had been the Netherlands East Indies (excluding West Irian, which became part of Indonesia in

---

* Professor Raymond Vernon has suggested his doubts about this interpretation, writing the present author, "In my opinion, Jersey's main motivation in going into Iran was the usual oligopoly motivation: to make partnerships with other members of the oligopoly at every possible stage, in order to ensure that unanticipated initiatives would not occur." Perhaps the motivations were mixed.

† The companies in the consortium were British Petroleum Company (formerly Anglo-Iranian Oil Company), 40 per cent; Royal Dutch-Shell Group, 14 per cent; Compagnie Française des Pétroles, 6 per cent; Standard Oil (New Jersey), 8 per cent; Standard Oil of California, 8 per cent; Gulf Oil Corp., 8 per cent; Texaco, 8 per cent; Socony-Vacuum Oil, 8 per cent. In 1955, each of the American companies assigned an eighth of its holdings to the Iricon Agency, which gave Iricon 5 per cent and reduced the share of each of the large U.S. companies to 7 per cent. Iricon Agency was made up of eight independent American oil companies: Richfield Oil, Signal Oil and Gas, Tidewater, Getty Oil, American Independent Oil, San Jacinto Petroleum, Standard Oil (Ohio), and Atlantic Refining.

1963). Despite the uncertainties under Sukarno, Caltex invested sizable sums in oil production; Stanvac also expanded.[71]

9

In sum, in the first postwar decade, U.S. businesses moved abroad. Slowly, in most sectors (agriculture and utilities excluded), the hesitation of the early postwar years was replaced by renewed corporate interest in direct foreign investment. The end of the Korean war in 1953 seems to have had no impact on the new plans. The realization remained that the American nation was short (in terms of future needs) of mineral resources, including oil. More important there was evidence of the potentials for U.S. products abroad and the knowledge that foreign stakes in market-oriented manufacturing were required to meet foreign demand. Short memories soon forgot the expropriations in eastern Europe and in communist China of the not-so-distant past.* The stage was set for a substantial growth of U.S. direct investment abroad.

* A file in the general counsel's office dealing with the losses and the claims was often the sole reminder.

Five

The Contemporary Scene

The Environment for Multinational Business, 1955–1970

The years 1955–1970 proved prosperous ones for U.S. business at home. Corporations grew in size, diversified their products, and moved into additional industries. In the 1960s, mergers accelerated, with the number reaching new peaks. Many companies became conglomerates—that is, they produced a range of often unrelated products.

The era saw unparalleled expenditures for research and development by both U.S. corporations and the U.S. government. Because of the cold war (and the hot war in Vietnam), American defense expenditures remained high; corporations committed resources to defense activities. Technological change was rapid, especially in the fields of electronics (including the computer) and chemicals (including pharmaceuticals). Research in atomic energy and space age sciences took on significance.

Stockholders became more numerous; often they were represented by institutions or mutual funds. To cope with the needs of giant corporations, American business leaders became ever more conscious of the requirements for management. From the fundamentals of planning, organizing, motivating, and controlling to systems analysis, operations research, and financial projections, U.S. executives in large enterprises became more professional.

With new wealth, with frequent dealings with government agencies, with the profusion of technological innovation, with large numbers of stockholders, more than in the past U.S. corporations acknowledged social responsibility—to shareholders, employees, customers, and community. Gone forever were the days when a big business could justify any act, so long as it was profitable. All these aspects of enterprise had, as will be evident, implications apropos multinational business.[1]

In the late 1950s and 1960s a revolution in transportation and communication occurred. In 1958, the first commercial jet made an Atlantic crossing. The effect was dramatic: the jet capsuled distances. Americans could move with unprecedented speed and in unprecedented comfort. Travel by jet broadened the vision and knowledge of U.S. businessmen and facilitated the translation of prospects into actual foreign investments. So, too, the telex, far more than international telephones, opened the way for rapid, ungarbled international communication and coordination of multinational business. The television set brought to Americans immediate visual perceptions of foreign lands and cultures, and undoubtedly acted as one more stimulus—albeit indirect—to open the minds of U.S. executives to more extensive foreign investments. Tables XIII.1, XIII.2, and XIII.3 reveal the spectacular growth of U.S. direct investment abroad.

2

Washington's full commitment to participate in international economic affairs persisted. But from their earlier orientation toward Europe, U.S. foreign assistance programs now turned to less developed countries to raise their standards of living and to maintain their friendship. By the mid-1950s in the United States, opponents of foreign aid had become more articulate. Foreign aid programs remained linked with U.S. security objectives and now more often with assisting the well-being of *U.S.* enterprise.* [2] The United States came to rely increasingly on U.S. private rather than public investments in less developed lands.

While, to be sure, Washington continued to give general support for U.S. private stakes abroad, while treaties of friendship, commerce, and navigation with developed and less developed nations were negotiated with clauses protecting private property,† [3] while tax treaties to avoid

---

* A slackening of interest in foreign aid occurred during the Eisenhower years; concern with aid programs revived under Kennedy and, to a far lesser extent, under Johnson. In fact, by the end of the 1960s, public aid was being cut and being ever more specifically molded to *U.S.* national requirements. In June 1968, William S. Gaud, administrator of the Agency for International Development, could report, "The biggest single misconception about the foreign aid program is that we send money abroad. We don't. Foreign aid consists of American equipment, raw materials, expert services, and food . . . Ninety-six per cent of A.I.D. funds are spent directly in the United States." Address to National Foreign Policy Conference for Education Leaders, June 20, 1968, A.I.D. Press Release. In 1969–1970, under Nixon, aid programs were further reduced.

† By 1963, the United States had such bilateral treaties with forty-one different countries.

Table XIII.1. U.S. direct foreign investments by sectors, 1946–1970 (in billion U.S. dollars)

Year	U.S. capital net outflow for direct investment	Book value of direct investments abroad by sector [1]					
		(1) Total [2]	(2) Manufacturing	(3) Petroleum	(4) Trade	(5) Mining [3]	(6) Public utilities [4]
1946	.23	7.20	2.40 *	1.40	n.a.	.80	1.30
1947	.75	5	5	5	5	5	5
1948	.72	5	5	5	5	5	5
1949	.66	5	5	5	5	5	5
1950	.62	11.79	3.83 *	3.39	.76	1.13	1.42
1951	.51	13.09	4.35 *	3.70	.88	1.32	1.43
1952	.85	14.81	4.92 *	4.29	.97	1.64	1.47
1953	.73	16.29	5.24 *	4.93	1.05	1.93	1.50
1954	.67	17.63	5.71 *	5.27	1.16	2.08	1.54
1955	.82	19.31	6.35 *	5.85	1.28	2.21	1.61
1956	1.95	22.18	7.15	7.28 *	1.44	2.40	1.70
1957	2.44	25.26	8.01	9.05 *	1.67	2.36 [6]	2.14
1958	1.18	27.26	8.67	9.82 *	1.78	2.56	2.27
1959	1.37	29.74	9.69	10.42 *	2.04	2.86	2.41
1960	1.67	31.82	11.05 *	10.81	2.40 [7]	2.95	2.55 [7]
1961	1.60	34.67	12.00	12.19 *	2.65 [7]	3.04	2.17 [7]
1962	1.65	37.23	13.25 *	12.72	3.02 [7]	3.19	2.04 [7]
1963	1.98	40.69	14.94 *	13.65	3.31	3.37	2.06
1964	2.33	44.38	16.94 *	14.33	3.69	3.57	2.02
1965	3.47	49.33	19.34 *	15.30	4.22	3.78	2.14
1966	3.66	54.71	22.06 *	16.22	4.72	4.32	2.28
1967	3.14	59.49	24.17 *	17.40	5.01	4.88	2.39
1968	3.21	64.98	26.41 *	18.89	5.28	5.44	2.67
1969	3.25	71.02	29.53 *	19.88	5.83 [7]	5.66	2.68 [7]
1970	4.40	78.18	32.26 *	21.71	6.55	6.17	2.87

Source: Figures on capital outflow are from *Survey of Current Business*, June 1969, pp. 26–27, and November 1972, p. 24. The book value figures are whenever possible the most recently revised figures from annual issues of *Survey of Current Business;* U.S. Department of Commerce, Office of Business Economics, *U.S. Business Investments in Foreign Countries*, Washington, D.C. 1960; *Survey of Current Business*, September 1967, p. 45; and Bureau of Economic Analysis, U.S. Department of Commerce.

* Leading sector for investments.

[1] Includes reinvested earnings and adjustments.

[2] Equals the sum of columns 2 through 6 plus "other" investments.

[3] Includes smelting.

[4] Includes transportation.

[5] Available published figures (see *Survey of Current Business*, January 1951, p. 28 and December 1951, p. 13) are *not revised* and do not correspond with those in the revised series that are included herein.

[6] This decline appears to be due to a change in recording procedures rather than any actual drop.

[7] Preliminary figures (this author cannot locate published revised figures).

Table XIII.2. U.S. direct foreign investments, 1950, 1960, and 1970 (book value in billion U.S. dollars)

Country or region	(1) Total[1]			(2) Manufacturing			(3) Petroleum			(4) Trade			(5) Mining[2]			(6) Public utilities[3]		
	1950	1960	1970	1950	1960	1970	1950	1960	1970	1950	1960[4]	1970	1950	1960	1970	1950	1960[4]	1970
Europe	1.73	6.69	24.52	.93	3.80	13.71	.43	1.76	5.47	.19	.74	2.79	.03	.05	.08	.03	.04	.11
Canada	3.58	11.18	22.79	1.90	4.83	10.06	.42	2.66	4.81	.24	.63	1.32	.33	1.32	2.99	.28	.64	.68
Latin America[5]	4.59	8.32	14.76	.78	1.52	4.62	1.31	3.12	3.94	.24	.78	1.54	.67	1.27	2.07	.94	1.18	.61
Asia	1.00	2.48	5.56	.06	.29[4]	1.52	.78	1.66[4]	3.02	.05	.14	.46	.02	.02[4]	.09	.05[6]	.10	.14
Africa	.29	1.07	3.48	.06	.12[4]	.54	.12	.41[4]	2.09	.02	.05	.21	.06	.25[4]	.45	[7]	.01	.01
Oceania	.26	1.01	3.49	.01	.49[4]	1.81	.11	.37[4]	.74	.02	.06	.23	.01	.03[4]	.49	[8]	[8]	.01
TOTAL[9]	11.79	31.82	78.18	3.83	11.05	32.26	3.39	10.81	21.71	.76	2.40	6.55	1.13	2.95	6.17	1.42	2.55	2.87

Source: See source for Table XIII.1.
[1] Total is the sum of columns 2-6 plus miscellaneous investments.
[2] Including smelting.
[3] Includes transportation.
[4] Preliminary figures (this author cannot locate revised figures)
[5] Includes European and former European dependencies.
[6] Practically all in the Philippines.
[7] Less than $5 million.
[8] $1 million or less.
[9] Includes unallocated international.

Table XIII.3. U.S. direct investment in manufacturing, 1950, 1955–1970
(book value in million dollars)

Year	Europe Total	U.K.	EEC [5]	Canada	Latin America [1]	Asia	Africa [2]	Oceania [3]	Total [4]
1950	932	542	317	1,897	781	60	55	107	3,831
1955	1,640	946	563	2,841	1,372	94 [6]	86 [7]	258	6,349
1956	1,816	1,052	659	3,196	1,543	113 [6]	94 [7]	285	7,152
1957	2,195	1,238	831	3,924	1,280 [8]	190	106	314	8,009
1958	2,475	1,361	970	4,164	1,334	217	117	365	8,673
1959	2,927	1,607	1,135	4,558	1,425	248	120	412	9,692
1960	3,804	2,164 [9]	1,436 [9]	4,827	1,521	286 [9]	118 [9]	494 [9]	11,051
1961	4,255	2,305 [9]	1,659 [9]	5,076	1,707	321 [9]	113 [9]	423 [9]	11,997
1962	4,883	2,512 [9]	2,063 [9]	5,312	1,944	348 [9]	141 [9]	618 [9]	13,250
1963	5,634	2,739	2,528	5,761	2,213	430	177	723	14,937
1964	6,587	3,010	3,139	6,197	2,507	556	227	860	16,935
1965	7,606	3,306	3,725	6,872	2,945	676	292	948	19,339
1966	8,876	3,716	4,401	7,675	3,317	796	333	1,061	22,058
1967	9,798	3,878	4,976	8,095	3,586	988	370	1,336	24,172
1968	10,796	4,243	5,399	8,568	4,005	1,144	403	1,497	26,414
1969	12,280	4,567	6,382	9,406	4,347	1,378	453	1,661	29,527
1970	13,706	4,977	7,177	10,059	4,621	1,524	538	1,814	32,261

Source: See source for Table XIII.1.
[1] Includes European and former European dependencies (except 1955–1956).
[2] The largest part of this is in South Africa.
[3] The greatest part of this is in Australia.
[4] Includes some unallocated international investments.
[5] Germany, France, Italy, Belgium, Netherlands, Luxembourg—countries that joined in the European Economic Community in 1957. Data before 1957 excludes Luxembourg, but investment there in manufacturing was small (exclusion is because figures are not available.)
[6] Includes only India, Indonesia, Japan, and the Philippines.
[7] South Africa only.
[8] Drop may be because of change in series.
[9] Preliminary figures (this author cannot locate published revised figures).

double taxation aided investors in both developed and underdeveloped lands,[4] U.S. policies in the late 1950s and 1960s tended to seek to foster private U.S. direct investment in less developed and *not* in developed countries. Thus, the U.S. government guaranty program for new investments (initiated with the European recovery plans) was in the late 1950s and 1960s applied exclusively to underdeveloped nations.* At first,

* The government of the host country had to agree to the guaranty program and the specific project before the U.S. government would issue guaranties. A.I.D., *Aids to*

most U.S. businessmen felt the guaranties were both unnecessary and expensive; few bothered with the insurance. Then came the rude shock of the Cuban expropriations of 1959–1960, and guaranties became more popular.* By the 1960s extended risk guaranties applied to all losses, except by fraud and misconduct of investors, of up to 75 per cent of the investment,† while specific risk guaranties covered losses due to (1) war, revolution, and insurrection, (2) expropriation, and (3) convertibility of foreign currencies. By 1967, U.S. guaranties on new investments were available for seventy-eight developing countries, and managers of U.S. corporations had no reservations about the program. By 1970, the government had provided coverage for 3,500 new private investments, equaling $7.3 billion.‡ [5]

Meanwhile, in August 1957, Congress passed the Cooley Amendment to the Agricultural Trade and Development Act of 1954 (P.L. 480), which stated that a portion of the foreign currencies received by the United States for surplus agricultural commodities might be lent to U.S. investors abroad—an added assistance to U.S. enterprise operating in less developed countries. [6]

During the 1960s, the guaranty program and P.L. 480 funds came to be administered by the Agency for International Development, established in 1961.§ A.I.D. acquired other functions to encourage U.S. direct investment in less developed lands, among them making dollar loans to private U.S. investors abroad, conducting foreign investment surveys, and giving information on investment prospects. [7] Under the Foreign Assistance Act of 1969, the Overseas Private Investment Corporation was created and in time it assumed A.I.D.'s responsibilities in promoting U.S. private investments "in less developed friendly countries." [8]

Likewise, assisting U.S. enterprises in the poorer regions of the world were the U.S. Export-Import Bank and the international bodies in which the United States played a significant role, among them the International Bank for Reconstruction and Development, the International Finance

---

Business (1966), pp. 14–15. The Mutual Security Act of 1959 excluded new U.S. investments in developed countries from the guaranty program.

* Guaranties had been available for Cuba, but U.S. businessmen had not purchased them.

† There were also extended risk guaranties up to 100 per cent on certain housing projects.

‡ The vast majority were specific risk guaranties.

§ A.I.D. was the direct successor of the International Cooperation Administration, which had come into existence on June 30, 1955, and had taken over the functions of the Foreign Operations Administration.

Corporation (organized in 1956 as an affiliate of the I.B.R.D.), and the Inter-American Development Bank (started in 1960).[9]

In 1962, Congress, over the objection of the State Department that desired flexibility in the foreign aid program, passed the Hickenlooper Amendment to the Foreign Assistance Act. The Amendment stated that foreign aid to a particular nation would be withdrawn should any expropriation of U.S. properties after January 1, 1962, not be followed by prompt and adequate compensation. The United States recognized the right of a foreign country to confiscate private property, but not without speedy and just recompense.* The Hickenlooper Amendment, its sponsors hoped, would make host governments think twice about expropriation. For a while, it seemed successful. After its passage, International Telephone and Telegraph Corporation obtained an early settlement of its claims against the State of Rio Grande do Sul in Brazil, which had expropriated that company's facility. One executive in another utility remarked of the Hickenlooper Amendment, "it became implicit in discussions between us and foreign governments." Yet when, in 1968, Peru expropriated the assets of International Petroleum Company (a Standard Oil of New Jersey affiliate), the threat of termination of U.S. aid proved of no help to the U.S. enterprise.[10] In fact, as U.S. aid programs were reduced in scale, the warning about cutting off aid became less meaningful.

Such governmental measures to spur U.S. direct investment *in less developed countries,* whether through guaranties, soft and hard currency loans, or the "club" of the Hickenlooper Amendment, were in their breadth unique in American history. To be sure, in the 1920s (and earlier), the U.S. government might have sent Marines to protect endangered U.S. properties; government loans had aided U.S. business abroad before World War II; † over the years the U.S. government had participated in diplomatic discussions on behalf of U.S. business and acted on claims commissions to try to recoup losses; the Department of Commerce

---

* The U.S. Constitution (article 5 of the Bill of Rights) states that within the United States private property could be taken for public use, but only with just compensation. The United States came to accept this point of view internationally (note Washington's acceptance of the Mexican expropriation of the oil companies in 1938). Expert on international law Wolfgang Friedmann wrote in 1964 that no government or responsible writer would deny that "international law grants any state the legal power, in the exercise of its sovereignty, to nationalize . . . resources, industries, or utilities to any extent it considers proper." Friedmann, *Changing Structure of International Law,* p. 180. The United States insisted that the compensation must not only be just (i.e., full and adequate), but also be prompt.

† Export-Import Bank loans to Brazil in the 1930s had, for example, freed U.S. blocked currency.

had surveyed foreign investment opportunities (mainly in raw materials). Yet the specific measures taken in the late 1950s and 1960s to promote private direct investment in less developed countries and *to cope in advance with the uncertainties* (with the guaranties) were unquestionably new. At the same time, by the 1950s and 1960s, the dispatching of U.S. armed forces for the specific reason of protecting U.S. investments abroad had become unacceptable.*

While the U.S. government was encouraging U.S. business to invest in less developed countries, in the 1950s the U.S. balance-of-payments surplus was changing to a deficit. Washington hoped to deal with this problem—without jeopardizing economic aid to less developed countries. The 1960s saw the deficit increase. The 1962 Revenue Act ended deferral of U.S. taxes on income from tax havens abroad (this represented only a small portion of overseas income); at the same time, the act gave special tax advantage under particular circumstances to U.S. investors in less developed countries.† Some government officials believed the legislation would cut U.S. direct investment abroad.[11] Business leaders described the law as "a deterrent to American business entering the world market." [12] Nonetheless, U.S. stakes abroad, especially in industrial nations, continued to rise.

Presidential adviser Theodore Sorensen writes of 1963 that "Every time General De Gaulle and his aides talked menacingly about keeping American investments out of Europe, Kennedy [with his eye on the U.S. balance of payments] secretly wished they would." [13] Indeed, it is reported that the U.S. government never protested the French attempts to limit U.S. direct investment, although, as one writer on U.S. investments in Europe, Christopher Layton, has pointed out, there were ample grounds for so doing.‡ [14]

---

* It can be argued, that the U.S. use of force against procommunist regimes in Guatemala (1954) and Cuba (1961) and against a possibly communist-dominated revolutionary movement in the Dominican Republic (1965) had as a by-product the protection of U.S. business abroad. In Guatemala an expropriation decree of Jacobo Arbenz directed against United Fruit was withdrawn after the change of government; in the Dominican Republic, an administration not hostile to U.S. enterprise resulted; in Cuba the attempted intervention failed.

† When a foreign investment was liquidated or when capital distributions were made, under the 1962 Revenue Act, the U.S. shareholder or parent company had to pay tax on the gains at income rather than capital gains tax rates, *except* for gains from certain operations in less developed countries. Harberger, "Tax Aspects of Foreign Economic Policy," p. 67.

‡ Inconsistently, the U.S. government did protest Japanese obstacles to U.S. direct investment, although apparently the protests lacked vigor during the Kennedy administration (interviews in Tokyo). Later, the protests in Tokyo increased.

In February 1965, President Lyndon B. Johnson announced a "voluntary balance of payments" program. He urged some five hundred large corporations (four hundred more were added in 1966) to improve their *individual* balance of payments by raising exports, bringing home more income from abroad, repatriating short-term assets, and borrowing in industrial countries instead of exporting U.S. funds or reinvesting monies earned overseas. Initially, Johnson's guidelines applied to industrial nations excluding Canada, although in 1966 they were extended to Canada and the less developed oil producing countries.* [15]

The program did not cope with the U.S. balance of payments deficits.† Thus, on January 1, 1968, President Johnson imposed for the first time in American history mandatory controls on the outflow of all U.S. direct investments as well as controls over the reinvestment of U.S. business profits earned abroad. Three schedules were established—Schedule A, covering less developed countries; Schedule B, initially covering Canada, United Kingdom, Australia, Japan, and the Middle-Eastern oil producing countries; and Schedule C, applying to industrial Europe. [16] In June 1968, Canada was given special treatment: U.S. companies were allowed unlimited direct investments there although they still had to report their Canadian transactions. [17] The plan was that in less developed countries, U.S. corporations could raise their direct investments (outflow from the United States and reinvested profits); in Schedule B nations such investments would be curtailed; and in Schedule C countries no new capital would be allowed to flow from the United States, but a specified percentage of profits earned abroad could be reinvested. [18] The aim was not to limit U.S. private foreign investment as such, but to limit the negative balance of payments effect of U.S. direct investments abroad. U.S. business could and did borrow abroad to finance their foreign operations—especially in industrial countries. Whereas from 1961 to 1966

---

* Canada was, however, treated in a distinctive manner. See Department of Commerce press release, Dec. 6, 1965.

† In fact, in 1965 and 1966, the net outflow of U.S. capital for direct investment reached new peaks (see Table XIII.1). For the first time in the entire postwar period, this outflow in 1965 and 1966 exceeded the new outflow for all U.S. *government* grants and capital (data from Department of Commerce, Office of Business Economics). In 1967, the outflow for direct investment was cut back, and U.S. government outflow increased, again exceeding the private sector figure. On November 18, 1967, Britain devaluated the pound from $2.80 to $2.40. Other countries followed with devaluations. (See *International Financial News Survey* 19:381–382 [Nov. 24, 1967]). This would put a further strain on the U.S. balance of payments, for U.S. exports would meet greater competition abroad. U.S. imports would probably increase, and U.S. businessmen would presumably add to their foreign investments.

the capital outflow from the United States for direct investments rose annually, in 1967, 1968, and 1969 the rise was halted and there was some reduction in the outflow. Under Nixon the controls were liberalized, and in 1970 the outflow exceeded that of 1966, reaching a new peak (see Table XIII.1).[19] Corporate leaders in the United States had numerous reservations about the mandatory measures.[20]

U.S. trade as well as aid and payments policies influenced U.S. investors abroad. Throughout most of these years, America remained committed to freer trade—and corporations in international business applauded U.S. efforts to lower barriers worldwide. The country continued to participate in the General Agreement on Tariffs and Trade (GATT) and in its attempt to remove restraints on international commerce. The Trade Expansion Act of 1962 represented a landmark toward trade liberalization. New measures contrary to a freer trade policy (such as the lead and zinc import quotas of 1958, and the oil import quotas of 1959, designed to protect domestic producers in the interests of national security) were few and far between. In the late 1960s, however, protectionist sentiment rose in the United States, *not* among businesses with market-oriented investments worldwide, but rather among firms in textiles (which had few foreign stakes), in steel (the foreign holdings of which were in large part confined to obtaining resources),* and in boots and shoes. In the 1960s, Japan and the United States agreed on voluntary limitations on Japanese cotton textile exports to the United States; so, too, in 1968, Europe and Japan accepted voluntary restraints on steel shipments to the United States, but when in late 1969 the Japanese and the United States could not agree on voluntary restrictions of Japanese wool and synthetic textile exports to the United States, Congress considered imposing restrictions. As the 1970s started, the commitment of Americans to reducing trade barriers had been shaken. Multinational businesses expressed concern, for the powers of foreign governments to retaliate against U.S. products and investors were immense.[21]

America's general foreign policy, as in the past, affected enterprise abroad with positive, mixed, and negative impacts. For example, U.S. fears of Soviet influence in less developed countries coincided with the desires of U.S. oil companies to hold certain markets for American-owned

---

* The steel industry, while advocating limitations on imports of finished steel products, never favored limitations on imports of iron ore, manganese, nickel, vanadium, and so forth.

foreign oil—markets threatened by Russian oil.[22] Kennedy's Alliance for Progress in its idealism (its long-run ineffectiveness notwithstanding) may well have helped U.S. companies in Latin America in much the same manner as did the Good Neighbor Policy of the 1930s; it, likewise, may have had the same type of detrimental effects.[23] The politically motivated U.S. controls on trade with communist countries continued to curtail the business of U.S.-owned international corporations. But in the late 1950s and especially in the 1960s, as our policy toward communism in eastern Europe moved from containment to peaceful coexistence, commerce emerged as a means to this end. On October 7, 1966, President Johnson announced the United States would reduce its controls on about one hundred nonstrategic items, and by 1970 trade in nonstrategic goods with eastern Europe was finally being encouraged. By this time, American firms with subsidiaries and affiliates in Europe were selling their Western-European-made products in eastern Europe.* [24] On the other hand, the United States imposed a nearly complete trade embargo on Cuba, North Korea, North Vietnam, and communist China during the 1960s. Under the Mutual Defense Assistance Control Act, the United States had a means of controlling its allies' trade in strategic goods, and under the Trading with the Enemy Act, the United States asserted its authority to file criminal liability charges against the directors and shareholders of a U.S. parent corporation *if* its foreign subsidiary or affiliate exported anything to these communist countries. Such strictures proved embarrassing to U.S. enterprises with affiliates in nations that desired such commerce.[25] Finally, on December 19, 1969, the State Department lifted the ban on U.S. foreign affiliates' trading with communist China in nonstrategic materials, effective December 22. It was a first step in opening the way for U.S. trade with China.[26]

As for private investment in communist China and Cuba, U.S. policy (leaving aside host nation policy) made it impossible for any American corporation. In the 1920s, after the Russian revolution and expropriations, certain Americans made new direct investments in the Soviet Union irrespective of the U.S. policy of nonrecognition; this did not occur in communist China in the 1950s and 1960s, nor in Cuba in the 1960s.

Moving to a different facet of U.S. foreign policy, the U.S. government

---

* The trade was carried on by European subsidiaries and affiliates, because of both cost and political considerations. European governments desired the trade.

boycotts of Rhodesia (imposed in 1966 and 1967 after that nation's 1965 declaration of unilateral independence) proved detrimental to U.S. corporations with properties there. At least one U.S. company sold its investment in Rhodesia as a consequence.[27] U.S. policies that expressed sympathies with Israel in the Arab-Israeli conflicts made conditions of business for U.S. oil companies in the Middle East precarious. U.S. participation in the Vietnam war affected U.S. multinational enterprise, as it did all other segments of American society. The unpopular war was not a businessman's war. There were—before and during the war—only minor U.S. investments in Vietnam. It seemed unlikely the war would open the way to major investment opportunities; in fact, in that the war acted to retard the recommencing of commercial relations with the Chinese mainland, it proved an obstacle to the enlargement of world trade and investment.[28]

In short, as these examples indicate, certain facets of U.S. foreign policy proved helpful to U.S. international businesses; in other cases, foreign policy considerations clashed with the interests of American business in particular countries. Only when corporate and Department of State archives are open for the late 1950s and 1960s will we be able to evaluate the full impact of U.S. foreign policies on U.S. private enterprise abroad.

On a domestic basis, the U.S. government, on the one hand, aided its corporations, providing defense contracts and underwriting much basic research. The aid in research and development gave American corporations and their foreign subsidiaries a competitive advantage worldwide.* [29] The extent of this assistance was unique. On the other hand, Washington continued to look for abuses of antitrust laws. United Fruit was forced in a consent decree of 1958 to sell important foreign properties that it had held for years; Standard Oil of New Jersey, after a consent decree in 1960, broke up almost entirely its partnership with Socony Mobil in Standard-Vacuum Oil Company (Stanvac).† These are but examples.

---

* It can be argued that without the cold war and the Vietnam war, such large support of research and development would not have been forthcoming, and therefore the tensions (at least in this one respect) aided U.S. business in multinational activities. Others argue that defense-related research and development has little peacetime spin-off, and the research that gave American business its competitive advantage had little to do with the war. See, for example, Clayton, *Economic Impact of the Cold War,* for discussion of domestic implications.

† Not entirely; Stanvac still operated in Indonesia, where the management was exclusively in the hands of Standard Oil of New Jersey. Socony Mobil was the old Socony-Vacuum, renamed in 1955; the name would again be changed—to Mobil Oil—in 1966.

In 1955–1970, U.S. antitrust policies remained applicable to international business—agreements, joint ventures, and acquisitions that had "substantial anticompetitive effects" on U.S. commerce.[30]

In the late 1950s and 1960s, as in the past, U.S. government policies toward American direct foreign investment were not homogenous. The Departments of State and Justice continued to find their foreign economic and antitrust policies not entirely at one.* The Department of Defense's desire to have U.S. international businesses cooperate in supplying the nation's defense needs on occasion clashed with the Department of Justice's antitrust policies.† The Department of State's encouragement of U.S. stakes in less developed countries to assist their economic development collided with the Department of Treasury's wish to curb dollar flows to redress the balance of payments deficit. Professor Jack Behrman has pointed out that whereas the Department of Justice's antitrust policy might look askance at a company's "tied sales" to licensed foreign affiliates, the Departments of Commerce and Treasury were delighted with the resulting rise in U.S. exports.[31] So, too, State Department and White House attitudes on trade with communist countries that stimulated commerce by U.S. affiliates *abroad* but not U.S. exports were obviously contrary to the goal of the Departments of Commerce and Treasury of increasing the foreign sales of the United States.

For participants in international business, the effectiveness of the U.S. government in defending foreign direct investment remained an issue. American businessmen appeared to agree that their government should support U.S. companies as they invested abroad. Some felt the assistance should be essentially negative: "What business really needs from Government is not help, not subsidy, but the removal of hindrance, the removal of barriers that thwart and pervert trade." [32] Some argued the aid should

---

* Seymour Rubin, former general counsel for the Agency for International Development, reported, however, a "continuing practice of consultation" between the Departments of State and Justice "to mitigate the force of the conflict." See his testimony before the Subcommittee on Foreign Economic Policy, 1970, p. 919.

† Under the Defense Production Act of 1955, companies got limited exemptions from the antitrust laws to meet defense needs. With the Suez Crisis of 1956, U.S. international oil companies—and the new Petroleum Security Subcommittee (organized under the Defense Production Act)—cooperated to meet the oil crisis. Subcommittee of Antitrust and Monopoly, *Hearings*, 1966, p. 506. According to a later *New York Times* article (Jan. 17, 1971), in 1956 U.S. oil companies obtained permission from the Justice Department to act together in the international negotiations—negotiations that the State Department (and presumably the Defense Department) approved, but that the companies felt might make them vulnerable under antitrust law.

be comprehensive: "Let our government develop a foreign policy . . . [based on] the tenet that 'American business is a facet of American foreign policy.' " [33]   A very few wanted the revival of "gunboat diplomacy." [34]

Certain business leaders believed U.S. government representatives in the United States and abroad in the years 1955–1970 were not helpful to them in their pursuit of foreign opportunities. On the other hand, one executive in a company with large stakes in utilities declared in the mid-1960s, "We have always kept the State Department and the American embassy informed on what we are doing, and unlike many other business friends of mine, we can say that we have always gotten very good results from our dealings with the State Department. If you're put on, the U.S. government will help you. We are faced with expropriation, and many problems. We have consistently found the State Department will do its best to aid American business abroad." This executive declared his company probably got more support under Democratic than under the Republican administrations—because the former were less fearful of being accused of being probusiness.[35]

Multinational corporations sometimes discovered in the late 1950s and 1960s that their approach to facets of U.S. policies were split between the interests of their own domestic business and particular foreign subsidiaries. Thus, the oil import quotas of 1959 found at least one international oil company divided (the domestic operations desiring the quota, the Venezuelan affiliate opposing it); [36] so, too, sentiment in the United States that was "anticommunist" or "pro-Israel," or concerned with the "Negro market" might cause rifts in a multinational corporation (with domestic operations worrying about an affiliate's participation in East-West trade, while the European affiliate favored it; or with the domestic operations' endorsing a new Israeli plant, while affiliates in Arab countries denounced it; or with the domestic operations' approving the U.S. boycott of Rhodesia, while the Rhodesian affiliate disapproved).*

Moreover, sometimes U.S. corporations realized particular U.S. policies were desirable for one facet of their *foreign* business, but not for another. Multinational firms with interests in *both* Arab countries and Israel were

* Similarly, those managers involved exclusively in domestic operations might like to see the United States take a strong stand against South African policies, while affiliates in South Africa and top management in the United States would wish the United States would "leave well enough alone."

internally split on U.S. sympathies toward Israel. So, too, while U.S. investors in Rhodesia suffered by the U.S. boycott, the same enterprises often had stakes in black Africa where the boycott was widely approved and where subsidiaries and affiliates applauded the policy.

Nonetheless, patriotism aside, as Seymour Rubin has perceptively pointed out, U.S. international corporations generally desired to abide by the American government's policies and wishes, for the U.S. government as an important consumer of corporate products and with substantial power could retaliate severely against a defiant corporation.[37]

In sum, in the late 1950s and 1960s (as in times past), U.S. government policies had both positive and negative effects on the operations of U.S. multinational business. On the surface—and the historian is stymied because the archival material is not yet available—the impact of U.S. governmental activities in recent years appears to have been greater than in earlier periods of American history—reflecting the generally enlarged role of the U.S. government and U.S. business in both the international and domestic economies.

3

In the past, however, *foreign* conditions and the actions of *foreign* governments far more than the policies of the U.S. government influenced the decisions of American investors abroad. Recent years—1955–1970— offer no exception. Indeed, the places U.S. investors went in greatest numbers were, in general, those where there was a high standard of living, healthy economic growth, resources desired by the investor, and, of great importance, a favorable political environment for investment.

In the late 1950s and 1960s, as in earlier years, of all European nations, Great Britain had the most U.S. direct investment. In 1960, the United Kingdom attained second place (after Canada) as the country with the greatest U.S. stakes. This was despite Britain's phlegmatic economic growth. Rather the reason was that, as in the past, it remained relatively easy for Americans to do business in Britain, where there were no language barriers; while unfamiliar rules, regulations, and legislation existed, while the public sector had become larger in the United Kingdom than in the United States, while companies had unique (often difficult) relations with labor unions, essentially the social and cultural patterns in Britain still were not alien to Americans; as U.S. enterprises invested, they continued to stimulate their compatriots to follow and so created a more conducive climate for greater penetration. Americans operating in Britain had often used their British base as an outlet for exports to commonwealth countries or to Europe. In the late 1950s and into the 1960s, there existed the possibility that Britain might join the European common market; American companies would be in a splendid position to take advantage of such a step—if *Britain* should join. Many businesses increased their stakes on that assumption, which for that period turned out to be mistaken.[38]

The British government screened all new foreign investment, but it did not exclude such stakes. On December 27, 1958, Britain announced the immediate convertibility of the pound sterling by residents of countries outside the sterling area. Thereafter, earnings could be freely converted. This encouraged new U.S. investment. Businessmen, including foreign investors, who exported, raised industrial productivity, and provided jobs in regions of high unemployment were given special rewards by the British state.[39] By the late 1950s and 1960s, as one commentator put it, "Britain's historic commitment to the free flow of capital internationally and the hope that foreign business will provide a much needed stimulus to economic growth preclude[d] serious interference [with U.S. investment]." * [40] And, thus, the stakes grew. By 1970 the book value of U.S. direct investment in the United Kingdom reached almost $8 billion.[41]

On March 25, 1957, the governments of Belgium, Luxembourg, the Netherlands, West Germany, Italy, and France signed the Treaty of Rome, creating the European Economic Community (E.E.C.)—the common market. By July 1, 1968, free trade in goods, services, and men among the six participants had been achieved. During the 1960s, full membership in the common market was confined to the six founders. In 1959, seven European nations (none of which participated in the European Economic Community) † bound themselves into the European Free Trade Area, committed to tariff reductions, although not to a common external tariff.[42]

In response to these moves toward freer trade and economic integra-

---

* In the interest of national security, there were *minor* interferences. For example, in 1968 the British government acquired an equity interest in the British firm International Computers, in the process making less attractive take over bids by U.S. investors. See Friedmann and Garner, *Government Enterprise*, pp. 60–61.

† Great Britain, Sweden, Norway, Denmark, Switzerland, Austria, and Portugal.

tion, to the fact that in 1958 the currencies of many European countries became convertible for the first time since the war,* and to the emerging prosperity on the continent, from the late 1950s there occurred a fantastic acceleration of U.S. direct investments; E.E.C. countries—with the large market—became especially attractive to U.S. investors.† [43] The temporary heightening of cold war tensions, with the Berlin Wall (erected in the summer of 1961), did not abate U.S. direct investment in Europe. Likewise, when negotiations for Great Britain's entry into the common market collapsed in January 1963, U.S. businesses that had expected to export from British plants to the continent turned to make new investments within the European Economic Community. In western Europe there developed a Eurodollar market for lending and borrowing mainly dollars, but also other currencies; by the late 1960s, it had become one of the world's largest for short-term funds. There also developed a Eurodollar bond market. U.S. companies employed effectively the resources of these markets. Dollar shortages in Europe had turned into dollar surpluses. When U.S. government balance-of-payments-motivated restrictions were imposed on U.S. direct investments in western Europe, U.S. business there could continue to grow using funds borrowed in Europe.‡ [44]

In West Germany and Belgium, especially, U.S. investors were welcomed; these two countries placed few restrictions on the foreigners' activities—although the German derogatory word, *uberfremdung*, meaning alien control, once more became part of that nation's vocabulary, and Belgium did block the takeover by a U.S. company of the oil enterprise, Petrofina, the country's largest firm.§ [45] The sizable West German market and the high per capita income, along with the national acceptance

* Britain's Dec. 27, 1958, announcement of convertibility of the pound sterling was followed by similar announcements by Austria, Belgium, Denmark, Finland, France, West Germany, Ireland, Italy, Luxembourg, the Netherlands, Norway, Portugal, and Sweden. Most countries exempted capital from the convertibility provisions, but earnings were freely convertible.

† U.S. direct investments in the European Economic Community grew faster than those in Britain. The growth in stakes in manufacturing reflects this. See Table XIII.3.

‡ In anticipation of U.S. government controls over capital movements, some U.S. companies with business in Europe had sent money there, borrowed in Europe, and sold bonds in Europe to cover future needs and to hedge against the day when funds from the states would not be available. Kindleberger, *Power and Money*, p. 174.

§ By 1969–1970, Germany, too, had become sensitive to foreign takeovers in its oil industry and was acting to curb them. See Hellmann, *Challenge to U.S. Dominance*, p. 56, and Turner, *Invisible Empires*, p. 175.

of free enterprise, proved most attractive to U.S. investors.* The small nation, Belgium, offered lures to foreign investors, such as tax concessions, subsidized interest rates on loans, and good prices for land purchases.† [46] Italy, despite its large public sector, spurned neither domestic nor foreign private enterprise and sought to attract U.S. investors, especially to the less developed southern regions.‡ [47] By contrast, the French were more wary.§ In the early 1960s, with new U.S. investments mounting, the French authorities carefully screened the new stakes, apprehensive lest foreign control in the principal sectors endanger national security, planning, and research. The French government feared U.S. multinational enterprise could elude its controls. When in the early 1960s, the U.S. government forbade the selling by I.B.M.'s French subsidiary of a large computer for the French nuclear program, French alarm and concern for national sovereignty reached new heights. [48] After a commotion in the French press and within the government over U.S. influence and the imposition of some restraints on U.S. investors, the French by the mid-1960s seemed to have concluded that if Americans were going to invest in a common market country if might as well be in France. The French did, however, take steps when, for instance, General Electric invested in Cie. Machines Bull to reserve for domestic interests control over basic research and development. A separate company, entirely French owned, was carved from Machines Bull to undertake classified defense work. [49] Likewise, even while there was talk of liberalization of French investment policy, by early 1970 American businessmen were aware that the French government had vetoed Westinghouse Electric's bid to acquire the important French electrical equipment manufacturer (Jeumont-Schneider) and also International Telephone and Telegraph Corporation's plan to buy a French pump manufacturer. The French had indicated as early as the summer of 1965 that they opposed U.S. "takeovers" of large French-

* In 1964, West Germany had a population of 58.3 million and a G.N.P. per capita of $1,500. (Mid-decade figures, rather than late, are given to indicate the conditions under which the U.S. stakes grew.) By 1970, U.S. direct investment in Germany reached $4.60 billion, *Survey of Current Business,* November 1971.

† While these lures did attract investors, the fact that Belgium had a small population (9.3 million in 1964) and that goods would have to be shipped to major markets served as deterrent to direct investment. By 1970, U.S. companies had invested $1.53 billion in Belgium and Luxembourg (the bulk of it in Belgium).

‡ Italy had a large population (51 million in 1964), but the G.N.P. per capita of $850 reduced the market. By 1970, U.S. companies had invested $1.55 billion in Italy.

§ France had a large population (48.4 million in 1964) and a high G.N.P. per capita ($1,540 in 1964). On this basis, it would be expected to attract U.S. investors.

owned concerns, while favoring "creative" new stakes. De Gaulle's exit from the government notwithstanding, the policy had not changed. By 1970, while the book value of U.S. direct investments in Germany equaled $4.60 billion, it was only $2.59 billion in France—a reflection in great part of the differences in government policies toward foreign investors.* [50]

In Great Britain and much of western Europe (excluding Germany, Belgium, and Switzerland), the rise of direct state participation in the national economies offered a challenge to U.S. business. The British, French, and Italian governments, especially, owned basic industrial operations. In oil, the British government had been an important stockholder since 1914; the French and Italian governments had been direct participants since the 1920s; yet for France and Italy, the extent of state involvement and competition with the private sector in the oil industry lacked precedent.† U.S. companies had to learn (and did learn) to coexist with the enlarged government role; in fact, some American firms even entered into joint ventures in Europe with host government agencies. [51]

In the 1960s the rash of books with titles such as *The Americanization of Europe* (Edward A. McCreary), [52] *The American Invasion* (Francis Williams), [53] *The American Challenge* (J. J. Servan-Schreiber), [54] and *The American Take-Over of Britain* (J. McMillan and B. Harris) [55] reflected the growth of U.S. stakes in Europe. Despite the rise in national government participation and despite the general concern over the expanding U.S. interests, as we have seen, little concrete action was taken by the governments in the United Kingdom or on the continent (except in France)

---

* This difference was not completely a consequence of *government* policies. Part of it resulted from a feeling among many American managers that German business practices were more congenial than those in France. Germans were seen as more efficient, more amenable to mass-production technology, and more used to "big business" than were the French. Note that in the early 1960s, not one French-owned firm had sales of over $1 billion, while five German-owned firms were that large (*Fortune*, August 1964, p. 152). In 1969, one French firm had sales over $2 billion (and it—Renault—was government owned), while six German firms exceeded that figure and all were private (*Fortune*, August 1970, p. 143).

† The French government continued to participate in Compagnie Française des Pétroles (with interests in Iraq Petroleum Company) and was anew involved in the Bureau de Recherches de Pétrole and Régie Autonome des Pétroles—which two combined in 1965 into Entreprise de Recherches et d'Activities Pétrolières, ERAP, a company with widespread producing interests abroad. The French government participated in refining in France. Both CFP and ERAP marketed in France. Early in 1968, ERAP became ELF-ERAP. In Italy, Ente Nazionale Idrocarburi (ENI) and its subsidiary Azienda Generale Italiana Petroli (AGIP) produced abroad and marketed domestically.

to exclude the investors. In fact, quite the contrary, Europeans compared their enterprises with those of Americans and found their own wanting. They desired U.S. business for its technology and management and its contribution to their nations' economic well-being.[56] In many ways, although there were important differences, the climate for direct investment in Europe in the late 1950s and 1960s seemed slightly reminiscent of the late 1920s, where there was also a body of literature concerned with the American invasion, when Europeans took steps to restrain such stakes, and when at the same time, a fascination existed in Europe with the methods of U.S. enterprises.* Unlike the late 1920s, however, in 1969 for the first time in history total U.S. direct investment in Europe— responding to the generally favorable environment for investors— surpassed the level of direct investment in Canada.[57]

Meanwhile, in the late 1950s and 1960s, U.S. companies did not cease their expansion in Canada, filling the needs of growing Canadian markets and developing Canada's newly discovered mineral and oil resources (see Table XIII.2 for investments by sector). While reports indicated extraordinary and mounting U.S. economic control over the Canadian economy, while Canadians talked of the rising wave of nationalism in their country, while their government endorsed a goal of national independence, and while "continentalism" (the integration of the U.S. and Canadian economies) became a suspect word in certain circles in Canada, nonetheless, restrictions on U.S. stakes remained few.[58] The principal restrictions were in the 1950s on U.S. investments in television stations and insurance firms and in the 1960s on new U.S. interests in newspapers and banks.[59] The sectors where U.S. holdings were largest were not hobbled.†
The government provided certain tax incentives to foster Canadian eq-

* Of course, the European Economic Community did not exist in the late 1920s, nor did the Eurodollar markets or formal national screening procedures. To this writer's knowledge, there were no cases in the 1920s where a European government actually closed the doors to a U.S. *manufacturer* (as for example in the Westinghouse case cited above), although the French government did bar the U.S. cable companies, a bar removed after U.S. government protests, and Spain did nationalize the holdings of Jersey Standard; likewise, private European companies acted to protect themselves from takeovers by U.S. manufacturers. See Chapter VII above.

† Moreover, when in 1965, Canada passed a bill denying tax deductibility for advertising to any foreign-owned publication aimed at the Canadian market, the two existing U.S. giants in Canada, *Time* and *Reader's Digest*, were exempted from the legislation (Levitt, *Silent Surrender*, p. 8). In 1970, the Canadian government (acting under the Atomic Energy Control Act) did, however, block the sale of a Canadian uranium company to the U.S.-controlled Hudson Bay Oil & Gas Co.—an action it probably would not have taken in the 1960s, *New York Times*, Feb. 3, 1971.

uity participation in U.S. subsidiaries and issued guidelines on proper behavior for foreign investors, yet such measures did not curtail U.S. investment. Actually, that government—like most in West Europe—desired
U.S. direct investment to maintain the rising standard of living. As one
report put it, "it has in general been the policy of all levels of the Canadian government not only to permit, but to actively encourage foreign investment." Indeed, Canadians correctly saw their policies toward U.S.
capital as among the most liberal in the world.[60] In the 1960s and at the
start of the 1970s, Canada continued its practice of subsidizing selected
U.S. corporations. Thus, in 1970, the government pledged to help the
U.S. computer company, Control Data, provide research, development,
and manufacturing facilities in Toronto and Quebec City.[61] It was little
wonder that under such propitious circumstances U.S. stakes rose.

To be sure, there existed conflicts; in the late 1950s and 1960s, U.S. enterprises in the Dominion were occasionally caught between U.S. and Canadian policies and expected to conform to both. Canadians resented the
fact that under U.S. law, American subsidiaries (until December 1969)
were not permitted to trade with communist China. To calm antago-
nisms, President Eisenhower and Prime Minister John Diefenbaker on
July 9, 1958, declared both national governments would consult when export policies and laws were not in accord.* [62] When the U.S. government
imposed oil quotas in 1959, Canadian crude oil exports were exempted
from them.† [63] Consultation procedures were established in 1960 in relation to antitrust enforcement—when U.S. laws were extended to American enterprises in Canada.[64] Canadians feared that U.S. balance-of-payments policies would have adverse effects on their nation's balance of
payments; as noted, when in 1968 mandatory controls were imposed on
U.S. direct investors, the U.S. government soon excluded Canada from
the restraints.[65] Such compromises of U.S. and foreign national policies
apropos multinational corporations appear to have been far more com-

* While U.S. policy forbade Ford of Canada from selling trucks to mainland China,
some U.S.-owned flour mills in the Dominion from selling to Cuba, and some U.S.-con-
trolled Canadian drug companies from shipping to North Vietnam, American subsidiaries in the potash industry in Saskatchewan did obtain exemptions from U.S. prosecution and did fill orders from communist China, Levitt, *Silent Surrender*, pp. 5–6.

† As a result, Canadian crude oil exports (a large percentage of which were by U.S.
companies in Canada) expanded from 33.7 million barrels in 1959 to 214.7 million bar-
rels in 1969. See *Petroleum Press Service* 37:216 (June 1970). According to the *New
York Times* (Nov. 28, 1970), President Nixon in March 1970 imposed import quotas on
Canadian oil east of the Rockies, but these were reversed after discussions between the
United States and Canada in November 1970.

mon between the United States and Canada than between the United States and any European country. They were by no means unprecedented or distinctive to U.S.-Canadian relationships. In a sense, in late 1941, when under the direction of the U.S. ambassador to Brazil, Standard Oil of New Jersey's subsidiary in Brazil supplied oil to a German airline in the interest of the Brazilian economy, but in violation of general U.S. policies, a similar compromise was worked out. Other cases could be given. Moreover, beyond the compromises there was one outstanding attempt to develop a joint industry to benefit both Canada and the United States. The automobile agreement between the United States and Canada (1965) sought to give the industries of both countries the opportunity to profit from economies of scale, international division of labor, and international trade. Multinational corporations were active in the discussions leading to the accord.[66] In the main, the compromises and the trade accord proved successful. While Canadian governmental and private alarm over U.S. direct investment failed to subside, the alarm did not retard U.S. direct investments since it was not translated into hostile measures directed at the main investors.* Canada remained the single foreign *nation* with the greatest U.S. direct investment—a position it had held since 1914.

In the British commonwealth countries, South Africa and Australia, where U.S. direct investment was rising, the governments took conventional measures (tariffs and other import restrictions) to prompt U.S. corporations to manufacture within their boundaries. In South Africa, U.S. businessmen felt they should operate under that nation's laws, while the U.S. government, opposing apartheid, urged American enterprises to take leadership in lowering racial barriers. The corporations, however, had no desire to be pioneers in breaking South African law.[67] In Australia, where U.S. stakes were far larger than in South Africa, American enterprises also participated in industrialization. While the Australian government sought foreign capital and management to aid the nation's economic growth, as in Europe and Canada, it also expressed fears of excessive U.S. stakes.[68] No steps, however, were taken to limit the expanding investment. On September 16, 1969, Prime Minister of Australia

---

* It is a mistake to assume Canadian alarm was new. It had ebbed and flowed. On earlier manifestations see Wilkins, *Emergence of Multinational Enterprise,* pp. 139–140 (on Canadian worry over U.S. influence on Bell Telephone Co. of Canada) and the present volume for concern over International Nickel during World War I and general concern in the 1920s.

John Gorton announced new guidelines for overseas investments in his country; his proposals preserved the "open door" philosophy, while encouraging foreign enterprises to offer equity interests to Australian residents.[69]

American companies wished to invest in fast-growing Japan; here they were often thwarted. Japan's fantastic economic expansion in the late 1950s and 1960s was masterminded by a remarkable interaction of Japanese private and governmental activity.[70] The Japanese anticipated the problems of Canada, France, and other countries; they argued that they would not permit American corporations to play a large role and thus would have no basis for subsequent concern. The Japanese, in these recent years, as in the 1930s, desired American technology; they wanted to learn about U.S. management methods; nonetheless the *control* of major industries, they insisted, must be vested in Japanese hands. Japanese enterprises found they could purchase American technology and were ready to pay a good price ("it is worth paying a good price for it," a Japanese businessman explained; "the American government subsidizes American corporations to do research; we do not need to repeat that research; all we do is buy it.") [71] At the same time, the Japanese innovated in many basic industries. While they studied American management methods, they did not adopt them. Rather they developed business organizations compatible with Japanese conditions. Important to Japanese success has been the effective mixture of innovation and imitation, along with governmental control on foreign business entry. In this complex, American multinational corporations have been effectively used by Japanese private industry and government in that nation's economic growth.

Although in the late 1960s, the Japanese felt secure enough to liberalize their rules on the influx of foreign capital,* although there would in the future be more joint ventures between U.S. and Japanese capital, it remained evident that the Japanese had no intention of allowing U.S. business to assume leadership in any basic Japanese industry.[72]

In sum, the industrial nations in the late 1950s and 1960s have been concerned over the entry of giant U.S. multinational enterprises and prepared to impose certain controls. Yet despite enhanced governmental ac-

---

* The actual liberalization was a response to considerable pressure from the United States and from the Organization for Economic Cooperation and Development (the successor to the Organization for European Economic Cooperation), which Japan joined in 1964.

tivities, Japan excepted, few important foreign governmental restraints on the entry or growth of U.S. business investment actually emerged in industrial countries in the free world. A U.S. company might, to be sure, have had difficulty entering France, but it could always invest in another nation in the European Economic Community and thereby achieve entry into the French market. As a result, and here again Japan excluded, American manufacturing, petroleum, and various service companies could and did take full advantage of the growing markets. In Canada and Australia, mining and oil companies ventured to uncover raw materials under conditions of political stability. By 1970, the book value of U.S. direct investments in developed nations was almost two and one-half times that in less developed countries ($53.1 billion v. $21.4 billion).[73] Such figures demonstrate clearly that the environment abroad is more important than U.S. policy in stimulating investment, for, the reader will recall, in these years (1955–1970) practically all the U.S. encouragement to direct foreign investment was to American enterprises in *less developed* lands.

4

The lower U.S. investment in less developed nations was a direct consequence of conditions in those countries. Most less developed countries in the late 1950s and 1960s shared characteristics: (1) by definition they were poor—that is, they had a low gross national product per capita and a large proportion of their population lived in poverty; (2) most were politically instable; many of their governments lacked, in Samuel P. Huntington's terms, political institutionalization, adaptability, complexity, autonomy, and coherence in organization;[74] (3) in many, inflation was rampant and currency depreciated rapidly; (4) in most, there existed strong anti-American feeling; (5) in most, there was strong nationalistic sentiment, accompanied by the desire for industrialization; (6) in many, there was ambivalence involving a want for U.S. investment (to raise national income) and a fear that such investment would be costly and might impair independence; and (7) in most, there was a recognition that the government had to play a crucial role in the national economy; private enterprise (domestic or foreign) could not accomplish the gigantic tasks at hand. (Obviously, the last three were not unique to less developed lands.)

Such conditions keenly affected U.S. investors. Taken in order, first, poverty meant, as in the past, markets would be small.* Second, political instability implied difficulties: one day, U.S. investors would be optimistic (in Venezuela under Pérez Jiménez, in Brazil under Kubischek, or just before independence in the Congo),[75] and the next day, U.S. investors would be frightened (in Venezuela under Betancourt, in Brazil under Goulart, in the Congo when civil strife erupted). Similarly, one day a nation would be an unsatisfactory place for U.S. investment (Indonesia under Sukarno, for example), and the next day it would be successfully wooing investors (Indonesia under Suharto). Nowhere was this unpredictability more in evidence than in Cuba—that nearby island that once seemed practically part of the United States. "There is little xenophobia in Cuba and Americans are particularly welcome," declared a Columbia University report on investments in Cuba as late as 1958.[76] Fidel Castro's expropriations in 1959–1960 shattered the euphoria. The U.S. State Department estimated that the loss to American investors was $1.375 billion.[77] Actually, such uncertainty in operations in less developed countries should have been no surprise to investors who knew their history. But managements of corporations change. Many investors were new. Few companies had studied the history of foreign investments in less developed countries.[78]

Third, currency depreciation continued in many less developed countries, especially in Latin America. Businesses constantly had to raise prices, because profits earned through local sales, when expressed in dollars, evaporated as currencies fell in value.[79] Fourth, anti-Americanism in less developed countries cropped up sporadically. In the late 1950s and 1960s, it often manifested itself in physical attacks on the properties of U.S. firms. Some anti-Americanism was government sponsored; some of it, host governments were unable or unwilling to control. Anti-British sentiment occasionally resulted in destruction of properties jointly owned by American and British concerns. Thus, with the Suez Crisis of 1956, pipelines of the Iraq Petroleum Company were blown up as was a well in Kuwait.[80] During and after the Arab-Israeli six-day war of June 1967, anti-Americanism in the Middle East reached epidemic proportions.[81] In 1969, the Iraq Petroleum Company attributed its decline in production to sabotage.[82] In May of that year, a splinter Arab commando group blasted the Trans-Arabian pipeline where it crossed Israeli-occupied

---

* A market is defined by the number of people who will buy a product, not by the number of people.

Syria; the line was shut for one hundred days.[83] The next May (1970), telephone engineers ran a bulldozer into the same pipeline in Syrian territory, and the line was out of operation for nine months.* [84] In 1964, the present author was in Venezuela, visiting a U.S. oil company building in Caracas and was asked as a routine to open her purse to prove that she was not armed. Near Lake Maracaibo, she passed a road covered by wire tenting, apparently to keep men in moving trucks from throwing hand grenades at the nearby power station. Nowhere else in Latin America was there such extreme tension, but concern prevailed for the properties of American companies. When in June 1969, Governor Nelson Rockefeller visited Latin America on President Nixon's behalf, nine supermarkets in Buenos Aires owned by the International Basic Economy Corporation, a Rockefeller enterprise, were demolished by time bombs.[85]

Fifth, often the anti-Americanism that U.S. businessmen encountered in less developed countries was associated with nationalism and with a condemnation of imperialism and neocolonialism. It is hard to overestimate how much less developed countries desired *economic and political* independence from all great powers.† These nations wanted to build their own industrial states.[86] The intensity of the nationalism was at times self-defeating. Attempts at regional integration that might provide a viable basis for development floundered on the rocks of nationalism. The Latin American Free Trade Area (initiated in 1961) made only modest progress. The Central American Common Market (started that same year) showed early promise, only to be in difficulty when Honduras and El Salvador went to war in 1969. Various attempts at African integration conflicted with nationalism and were accordingly impaired.‡ Years earlier, western European nations had gone through periods of "economic nationalism"; Canada (to some degree), Australia, South Africa, as well as the less developed countries were doing so now. For most U.S. investors in manufacturing, nationalism meant constraints on operations and the limited success of regional integration among poorer countries meant the perpetuation of small markets.§

---

* Political not repair considerations kept it shut; once the political questions were negotiated the line reopened in two or three days.
 † The U.S. company in this context became the symbol for the United States itself.
 ‡ In Africa tribal conflicts in turn vied with nationalism.
 § In wealthy nations with large markets, U.S. manufacturers invested to come to terms with nationalism; in poorer nations with small markets, such investments often were not warranted.

Sixth, U.S. direct investment could be an aid to economic growth, yet as in industrial nations, so, too, in less developed ones, countries feared the U.S. stake might retard indigenous development (leaving the nation exploited and dependent). Thus, in less developed countries, as in wealthier nations, there existed an ambivalence toward the foreign stake.[87]

Seventh, despite political instability, there was the pronounced inclination in less developed countries to have the government participate directly in the process of economic development and in controlling foreign investors. Far more than in most industrial nations, in the late 1950s and 1960s less developed countries adopted regulations and legislation that established conditions for direct foreign investment. Practically everywhere taxes rose, so that the foreign investors would contribute more to the economy. Social legislation was commonplace. Sometimes foreign investors were encouraged and sometimes compelled to enter into joint ventures in the host country with the public, private businesses, or government companies. Sometimes, government activity precluded U.S. direct foreign investment. The rise in the economic power of host governments in underdeveloped countries was ubiquitous. It was so significant that it deserves specialized attention. It proved to be the crucial element in the investment climate in less developed countries in the late 1950s and 1960s.[88]

In Latin America, where independent governments had a long history and where state intervention in the national economies was no novelty, government action was directed toward import substitution, that is, industrialization. In the late 1950s and early 1960s in Brazil and Argentina, government decrees requiring local manufacture proved successful in prompting large U.S. direct investments in factories. Punitive restrictions on imports meant that in many Latin American countries, U.S. companies either manufactured or relinquished the market. Forced by government measures, U.S. businesses that had had substantial European and Canadian manufacturing enterprises for decades transformed their long-time Latin American *sales, service, and assembly* operations into full-fledged manufacturing facilities.* During the late 1950s, new American-owned manufacturing complexes began to rise in food processing, chemicals and pharmaceuticals, electrical supplies, and rubber, as well as in automobiles, machinery, office equipment, and household goods indus-

* Singer, Remington-Rand (now Sperry-Rand), Ford, and General Motors are excellent examples.

tries. U.S. direct investments in Latin American manufacturing increased from $1.4 billion in 1955 to $4.6 billion in 1970. These figures underestimate the real development, since net working assets were written down to account for currency depreciations. By 1970, the U.S. direct investment in manufacturing in Brazil equaled $1,247 million, in Mexico $1,199 million,* and in Argentina $771 million. Despite the growth of public sector activities throughout Latin America, except for the Cuban expropriation, U.S. *manufacturers* in the years 1955–1970 remained exempt from government takeovers. For the first time in history in 1966, U.S. direct investment in manufacturing became the leading sector for U.S. stakes on that continent (when such investments surpassed the U.S. interests in petroleum). Host government action in Latin America to encourage industrialization had "forced" U.S. manufacturers to invest, for the only way American companies could gain and maintain markets was through such investment (in 1968 U.S. manufacturing companies in Latin America sold roughly 89 per cent of their output in the host country).† [89]

Yet, as Table XIII.3 indicates, by 1970 the book value of U.S. direct investments in manufacturing in Latin America *as a whole* remained less than such stakes in either Canada or the United Kingdom. The reason lay in currency depreciations,‡ smaller markets (because of low per capita income), and political uncertainty. But even if the rise in U.S. direct investments in manufacturing in Latin America was not as dramatic as that in Europe, the additions to U.S. stakes in Latin American manufacturing in response to host government pressures were unquestionably important. Indeed, the very import-substitution by direct foreign investors that took place *because* of governments' nationalistic measures came to be regarded by Latin American nationalists as a new cause for alarm over foreign domination.[90]

---

* Between 1954 and 1970 the currency was stable in Mexico.

† The analysis above describes the bulk of new U.S. stakes in Latin American manufacturing; they were market-oriented. Mention, however, should be made of the border industrialization program inaugurated by the Mexican government in 1965 to cope with unemployment on the Mexican-U.S. border. The Mexican government created incentives for U.S. firms to establish manufacturing plants over the Mexican border, obtain cheap labor, and then export their output to the United States. By mid-1970, more than two hundred U.S. enterprises (most in electronics, toys and dolls, and wearing apparel) were participating in the new program. See Baerresen, *Border Industrialization Program*, pp. 3, 6.

‡ While Mexico, Venezuela, Guatemala, and Panama had stable currencies, currency depreciations in Brazil, Chile, and Bolivia were rampant; Argentine currency also depreciated sharply in relation to the dollar. See *International Financial Statistics*.

Even more than manufacturing enterprises, U.S. oil companies in Latin America found their activities shaped by host government actions. National governments required the oil producers, refiners, and marketers to pay higher taxes, to buy more locally, to encourage ancillary industries, to train indigenous personnel, and to supply fringe benefits of various sorts. In Venezuela, with the largest U.S. oil stakes, under the administration of Marcos Pérez Jiménez in 1956–1957 many oil concessions were granted. Then in January 1958, Pérez Jiménez was overthrown. A provisional government in December 1958 decreed a change in the tax on the oil companies (without consulting them); * technically the 50–50 profit-sharing law remained, but after 1958 the Venezuelan government's take grew greater. The first jump was to 65–35 in favor of the government. That December Rómulo Betancourt was elected president of Venezuela (he took office in February 1959). The companies made good profits, despite a president who was antagonistic to them † and despite the new tax levies. U.S. companies conformed to the new tax requirements; there was too much at stake not to do so.‡ 91

Then, in Cuba, where the holdings of U.S. oil companies were far smaller than in Venezuela, in 1960 ESSO and Texaco refused that government's request to process Russian crude oil in their Cuban refineries and Fidel Castro expropriated the U.S. firms' facilities. The loss was important, but what the U.S. companies even more feared was that Castro's action would stimulate Venezuela to follow suit.

Distrusting Venezuela's Betancourt, in 1960 U.S. oil companies repatriated large amounts of capital from that country. Yet, no expropriation took place there. There were, however, higher taxes under Betancourt (1959–1964) and Raul Leoni (1964–1969),§ and no new concessions were

* The companies had become accustomed in Venezuela to negotiations on changes that affected them.

† In 1956, Betancourt, who was then in exile, published in Mexico his *Venezuela: Política y Petróleo*, a stinging attack on the foreign oil companies.

‡ Judiciously, Jersey Standard sent Arthur Proudfit (then a board member of the parent company) back to Venezuela to assume the presidency of its subsidiary, Creole. Proudfit cooperated with the government. See Standard Oil Company (New Jersey), "Proceedings of 77th Annual Meeting," (May 27, 1959), p. 11. The reader will recall that Proudfit had acted on Jersey Standard's behalf in the delicate negotiations on the 1943 Venezuelan legislation. Venezuela from 1944 through 1960 ranked second only to the United States in world oil output; after 1961, it ranked third (after the United States and the U.S.S.R.). See U.N., *Statistical Yearbook 1966*, p. 202, and *Petroleum Press Service* 37:6 (January 1970).

§ In 1966, Venezuela adopted a "tax reference" price similar to the posted price in the Middle East, one important action to raise the levy. Hartshorn, *Oil Companies and Governments*, p. 197.

granted. By 1969–1970, Venezuela's share of the foreign oil companies' profits was reaching as high as 80–85 per cent. U.S. petroleum companies were limiting investment.[92]

In Peru, the leading U.S. producer—International Petroleum Company (a Jersey Standard affiliate)—tried to conform to government wishes, by building a superior company town and promoting Peruvians, but it never resolved the question of its tax basis. Successive Peruvian governments had been discontent with the accord of 1922. Finally, in October 1968, a newly installed Peruvian government expropriated International Petroleum Company's properties and proclaimed this the "DIA DE LA DIGNIDAD NACIONAL." *[93] Meanwhile, in Bolivia, where in 1937 the oil industry had been nationalized, in 1956, Gulf Oil Corporation broke ranks with the other major U.S. oil companies and signed a forty-year agreement with the Bolivian government to develop oil production. Gulf discovered oil, built a pipeline, and by 1969 claimed to have invested nearly $150 million.[94] In October 1969, the military government of General Alfredo Ovando Candia nationalized Gulf's holdings, but less than a year later (September 1970) the press reported Bolivian plans to indemnify Gulf with "more than $100 million." [95] Whether this plan would be altered by the Bolivian revolution in October 1970 was not clear.

By the end of the 1960s, government oil companies existed throughout Latin America. Some were new; most were not.† Some competed with foreign enterprise.‡ Some held a monopoly over one or more facets of the oil business, permitting private foreign companies to operate in one or more other branches.§ Four government companies administered properties that had been expropriated from private foreign companies

---

* Professor Robert Stobaugh has perceptively pointed out that by 1968, Peru had the technology to run the oil industry and the domestic market for its output. A foreign company was no longer needed. See his testimony before the Subcommittee on Foreign Economic Policy (1970), p. 880.

† The Argentine government after all had been involved in the oil industry since 1907. Government oil units had been established in Chile in the 1920s, in Peru, Mexico, Bolivia, Brazil, and Uruguay in the 1930s, in Colombia in the early 1950s, and in Cuba, Venezuela, and Paraguay in the 1960s.

‡ In Argentina, Uruguay, and Venezuela, for example, both government and private foreign oil companies *distributed* oil. In Argentina and Colombia, both government and private foreign companies produced oil. Grunwald and Musgrove, *Natural Resources in Latin American Development*, p. 288.

§ In both Chile and Brazil, oil production remained a government monopoly—as it had been for years—while U.S. companies could continue to distribute oil.

(expropriated in Bolivia in 1937 and 1969, Mexico in 1938, Cuba in 1960, and Peru in 1968).

A new device that involved cooperation between U.S. and state oil agencies was the service contract; it gave the nation a "moral victory." The nation *owned* the resources and the assets of the industry. In Colombia, when in 1951 Standard Oil of New Jersey's oil concession had run its time and reverted to the government, the company obtained a service contract. In Argentina, under President Arturo Frondizi in 1958–1961, U.S. corporations got exploration and development contracts. President Arturo Illía by decree in 1963 canceled the contracts. Then, after June 1966, when General Juan Carlos Onganía took power in Argentina, all the U.S. oil companies were compensated; by 1967, the government was again encouraging new contracts.* [96] In 1961, after Betancourt announced that all unassigned oil reserves in his country would go to the state-owned Venezuelan Petroleum Corporation, U.S. oil companies began to negotiate service contracts; in November 1970, the first exploration and development contracts were signed.[97] The service or operating contract concept was new to Latin America in the 1950s and 1960s. Whether it will be an effective means of accomplishing the purposes of the less developed countries remains to be seen. It is significant, however, as a symbol of the rising role of national governments in the Latin American oil industry.

Oil—an energy source akin to public utilities—for a long time seemed more open to state involvement than mining. Indeed, in Latin America host government companies in the oil industry everywhere had a substantial headstart over those in mining.† By the late 1950s, most U.S.-owned mining companies in Latin America expressed concern over higher taxes, regulatory legislation, and increased labor costs but not over outright expropriation or nationalization, nor often over competition from state-owned companies. While some mining firms (such as Hanna in Brazil) ‡ had difficulty obtaining permission to function, others made sizable new

---

* The June 1967 legislation also opened the door to new concessions. See Odell, in Penrose, *Large International Firm in Developing Countries*, p. 288n, and *Petroleum Press Service* 3:11 (January 1970).

† Even where there were important government-controlled mining companies, such as Corporacion Minera de Bolivia in tin mining in Bolivia (formed in 1952) and Companhia Vale do Rio Doce, S.A., in iron ore mining in Brazil (formed in 1942), government-owned *oil* companies in these countries had been organized earlier.

‡ Hanna did meet competition from a state-owned company.

investments (for example, Southern Peru Copper, owned by leading U.S. mining enterprises, worked important undeveloped Peruvian copper deposits, while in neighboring Chile, under Law 11,828 of May 6, 1955, Anaconda especially made large new investments).[98]

Then, in 1960 conditions changed. For the first time since the beginning of the century,* U.S.-controlled mining properties in Latin America were expropriated—in Cuba. In the 1960s, Latin American governments pressed hard for national participation in mining and urged foreign companies to offer stock to host-country shareholders, which few had done in the past. Under the 1961 Mining Law, Mexico gave significant tax advantages to firms 51 per cent Mexican owned. Accordingly, American Smelting and Refining Company for the first time consolidated its Mexican properties under a Mexican company; in July 1965 it arranged to sell 51 per cent of the subsidiary's stock to a Mexican group.[99] Hanna Mining, after seven frustrating years of trying to develop Brazilian iron ore properties on its own, finally agreed in December 1965 to a joint venture with the Brazilian Antunes group.† [100] In Chile, apparently on the initiative of Kennecott's management, after the 1964 election plans were made for the "Chileanization" of the copper industry.‡ Legislation passed in 1966 by the Chilean congress provided for joint ventures between that government and certain U.S. copper producers; in

* In the late nineteenth, early twentieth century, Venezuela terminated the New York & Bermudez Asphalt Company's concession, canceled The Orinoco Company's concession, and declared the United States & Venezuela Company's contract null. In each case, either compensation or restitution was made. See Wilkins, *Emergence of Multinational Enterprise*, pp. 163–164. As noted, when in 1952 Bolivia took over the three major companies in its tin industry, U.S. *direct* investment was not affected.

† Bethlehem Steel, an exceptional company, had after World War II entered into a joint venture in manganese ore mining with the Antunes family. It had encountered none of the hostility Hanna faced. Bethlehem owned 49 per cent of Brazilian enterprise, which mined manganese in Amapá, in northern Brazil. U.S. Dept. of Comm. Bureau of International Programs, *Brazil*, p. 100.

‡ Kennecott suggested the mixed venture because its management believed that in partnership with the Chilean state, it would make higher profits than under existing conditions. The company felt that if the Chilean government held 51 per cent of the Chilean venture, labor relations would improve and taxation would be less onerous. Kennecott in 1962 paid 83 per cent of its Chilean profits in Chilean taxes, and in 1963, 86 per cent. Our source for the Kennecott initiative in these negotiations is Charles D. Michaelson, vice president of mining and director of Kennecott Copper Company (Comments at American Management Association Meeting, New York, April 1965). The tax levels are given in Kennecott, *Annual Reports 1962, 1963*. It is worth recalling that an early (short-lived) joint enterprise between the Chilean government and the Guggenheim interests, COSACH, had the industry playing a major role in its formulation.

compliance, Kennecott arranged in 1967 for the Chilean government to obtain a 51 per cent interest in the mine of its subsidiary, Braden Copper Company; a new joint enterprise was started. Henceforth, new mines in Chile were to be developed as "mixed enterprises" with the Chilean state. In 1966–1967, Anaconda's huge copper mine at Chuquicamata and its newer, El Salvador mining operation * remained 100 per cent owned by the U.S. parent. Finally, on June 2, 1969, Anaconda agreed reluctantly to sell the Chilean government 51 per cent of these two major Chilean mining operations.† The step came after the October 1968 expropriation of International Petroleum Company in Peru, after the long-term pressure from the Chilean left on that government to take over Anaconda's mines, and after years of negotiations. With threats of nationalization, by June 1969 Anaconda was prepared to give in while it was still ahead. It agreed to sell the 51 per cent and also offered Chile the opportunity to buy the remaining 49 per cent over a period of years. An agreement was reached; two new companies (incorporated in Chile) ‡ were formed, and on December 31, 1969, Chile's state copper company received 51 per cent of the stock in each enterprise. For Anaconda, clearly the decision was painful. A large portion of Anaconda's assets were in Chile, and with U.S. labor difficulties in 1967 and 1968, substantially all of those years' net income came from South America (principally Chile) and Mexico. Anaconda had tried to be a good citizen in Chile; its workers were a well-paid elite; its new company town at El Salvador was impressive (but then, so was International Petroleum Company's town at Talara in Peru). The government of Eduardo Frei Montalva (elected in September 1964) had resisted pressures to nationalize the Anaconda mines, but the Frei government would be replaced in the next election,§ and a future government might not want or be able to resist the pressures for nationalization. In September 1970 the socialist-communist-backed candidate Salvador Allende was elected—pledged to a program of nationalization of foreign mines. Anaconda could only hope the new administration would honor the com-

* When the Andes Copper Mining Company's mine at Potrerillos had been exhausted, Anaconda had searched nearby; in 1959, it initiated mining at El Salvador some fifteen miles from Potrerillos.

† Chile Exploration Company at Chuquicamata; Andes Copper Mining Company at El Salvador.

‡ Until this point, Anaconda's operations in Chile had been incorporated in the United States—a cause of much resentment among Chileans.

§ Under the Chilean constitution, Frei was ineligible to run for reelection in September 1970.

pany's agreement with the Frei government. As 1970 came to a close full expropriation seemed in prospect.[101]

The pattern of state participation in foreign mining operations spread. In Venezuela, when in 1968 U.S. Steel's wholly owned iron ore mining subsidiary embarked on the construction of a "high-iron briquette" plant, the Venezuelan government obtained an option to participate in the ownership of the plant.[102] In 1970, newspaper readers learned of a new $100 million venture in mining ferronickel in Colombia, a joint enterprise between a Colombian government agency, Chevron Petroleum Company (Standard Oil of California), and Hanna Mining. Similarly, in Guyana, in the summer of 1970, the administration of Prime Minister Forbes Burnham proposed to have not less than 51 per cent participation in the bauxite mining operations of Aluminium Ltd.'s subsidiary and the newer venture of Reynolds Metals Company.[103]

Clearly, by 1970 in Latin America, U.S. mining companies were in an entirely new position vis-à-vis host nation shareholders and governments from that of the mid-1950s. Direct host government participation seemed destined to increase. Accordingly, U.S. executives in mining companies far preferred to invest in Canada and Australia than in Latin America, although there continued to be new ventures in the nations to the south (as in the case of the new Colombian mining enterprise, described as the "biggest in the history of the Colombian mining industry").[104] Likewise, non-Latin, Latin American countries such as Jamaica and Surinam attracted large new investments in bauxite. Cuba excepted, in the 1960s, the transfers of control by U.S. direct investors in the mining industry in Latin America, had come as a result of legislation and negotiation rather than through expropriation. The actions indicated the growing economic powers of sovereign governments. Moreover, expropriations (with or without compensation) were in the future by no means unlikely.

In agriculture, host government pressures coupled with some expropriations caused retreats by U.S. investors. In 1959–1960, the U.S. sugar companies in Cuba were expropriated—a substantial acquisition on the part of that nation's government. In the early 1960s, fearing expropriation and concerned with the hostility it faced, United Fruit adopted a policy of voluntarily divesting itself of land; whenever possible it sought to purchase rather than grow bananas. Early in 1969, the Peruvian government acquired the large cattle ranches owned by the mining company Cerro de Pasco, promising compensation of over $36 million. That summer, the Peruvian government also took over W. R. Grace & Co.'s sugar plantations and mills (although it did not expropriate Grace's manufacturing facilities).[105] These expropriations and divestments, along with the earlier Mexican expropriations of agricultural properties in the 1920s and 1930s, effectively eliminated most of the principal U.S. agricultural investments in Latin America.*

As for utilities, here, too, Latin American governments expropriated properties.† Even more alarming, as governments in Latin America promoted industrialization and national requirements for electric power rose, host government agencies moved in to fill the demand. Host governments hesitated to grant foreign utilities rate increases; thus, while the private companies' costs rose with inflation, their profits fell. As a consequence of the governments' not allowing higher rates, the management of the largest U.S.-owned electric power company in Latin America— American & Foreign Power Company—resolved that investments in other sectors would be more profitable. Table XIII.4 indicates its divestments. Often the company was required by the host country to reinvest its funds in other businesses in that country. It complied, hoping to transform unproductive investments into earning assets. Much of the reinvestment was in manufacturing. In fact, by 1965, American & Foreign Power Company could no longer be considered an international utility; the major portion of its revenue came from foreign government notes (received in payment for its utilities) and from its diversified holdings in such sectors as metal products, automotives, and petrochemicals. Similarly, International Telephone and Telegraph Corporation sold most but not all of its investments in Latin American utilities, and it, too, diversified into a wide range of manufacturing and other stakes.[106]

In sum, the powers of Latin American governments grew vis-à-vis the

---

* Some remained; some new ones began; but the sum total represented a ghost of past activities.

† In 1958, an American & Foreign Power Company subsidiary was expropriated by the municipal government of Toberia in Buenos Aires Province. In 1959, the Government of Rio Grande do Sul, Brazil, expropriated another subsidiary's properties, while in Vitoria, Brazil, in 1962 a third subsidiary was expropriated. When Castro took power in Cuba, American & Foreign Power Company was embarked on a giant expansion program (its books carried its direct investment in Cuba in 1960 at $136.3 million). American & Foreign Power Company was probably the largest single loser in Castro's expropriation. The company reduced its U.S. dividends as a consequence of its Cuban loss. I.T.T. also suffered losses from expropriation. See *Annual Reports* of both companies; Legislative Reference Service, *Expropriation of American-Owned Property*, pp. 19–20.

Table XIII.4. American & Foreign Power Company's divestments in Latin America, 1958–1965

Date	Country	Company action	Terms [1]
1958	Argentina	Arranged to sell all its properties to the Argentine government.	$53.6 million over 15 years; proceeds to be reinvested in other enterprises in Argentina.
1960	Mexico	Sold properties to Nacional Financiera, S.A., a government agency.	$65 million, payable over 15 years; proceeds to be reinvested in Mexico.
1961	Colombia	Sold to the government.	$25.6 million; no requirement for reinvestment.
1963	Venezuela	Sold to a private utility.	$18.6 million; no reinvestment required.
1963	Brazil	Arranged to sell to the Brazilian government (Brazilian government of João Goulart did not make the first payment and it seemed might never pay).	$135 million, payable over 25 years.
1964	Brazil	After April 1, 1964, revolution, Castelo Branco (Brazil's new president) wanted company to continue, but company desired to stand by its initial agreement. New arrangements made.	$135 million, payable over 45 years; large portion of funds to be reinvested in *bonds* of government-owned electric power company: Petrobras.
1965	Chile	Arranged to sell to the Chilean government.	$86.5 million, payable over 30 years; proceeds to be reinvested in Chile.

Source: American & Foreign Power Company, *Annual Reports;* interviews with Henry W. Balgooyen, executive vice president, American & Foreign Power, June 18, 1964, and Silvino Rodriguez, American & Foreign Power, Rio, Sept. 18, 1964.

[1] Company received interest on its money at rates from 6 to 6¾ when payment was over time.

U.S. investor. The effects of the measures taken by the governments varied by sector. In manufacturing, in general they served to stimulate greater U.S. investments, while in toto, in other sectors, the governments' actions tended to discourage new stakes. By 1970, it was clear that the survival of all American enterprises would be under terms set by the host governments.* Indeed, at the beginning of the 1970s, the role of Latin American governments in relation to U.S. direct investment was entirely different from what it had been a decade and a half earlier.

In other less developed countries, newly sovereign governments displayed their new authority in their dealings with foreign corporations. The change in control from that of a metropolitan power (England, France, Holland, Belgium) to a national sovereign in much of Asia and Africa affected U.S. investment. To be sure, the imperial powers had not succeeded to any great extent in keeping U.S. direct investment from India, Malaya, Kenya, and Rhodesia, the French Cameroons, the Dutch East Indies, the Belgian Congo, or elsewhere. While on occasion, as noted, Americans had had to struggle to invest in European colonial territories, nonetheless, *in most cases* they had gained entry. But, in no colony did U.S. stakes exceed those of the mother country. As we have seen, generally, U.S. investors acted through companies incorporated in the imperial nation and used managers of the nationality of the imperial power. With independence, Americans went in directly and dealt with national rather than imperial sovereignties. Imperial barriers to entry were removed (although the metropolitan power in many cases retained a substantial amount of influence after independence); national barriers replaced imperial ones. On the whole, former colonial countries wanted U.S. direct investment, although some such countries imposed terms that the investors rejected.

Asian and African less developed nations desired new industries. The number of U.S. companies to invest in manufacturing and the size and degree of integration of their stakes in manufacturing were far smaller than in wealthy countries or for that matter in Latin America—areas of long interest to U.S. investors (see Table XIII.3 for comparisons and note that in *all* Asia and Africa the U.S. stake in manufacturing was less than half that in the British Isles). Part of the reason for the low investment in manufacturing lay in unfamiliarity,† part in governmental restrictions

---

* Recent revelations of correspondence of International Telephone and Telegraph Corporation indicating that the company sought to prevent Salvador Allende's government from taking power in Chile supports this statement. What is important is that I.T.T. *failed* in its efforts, and that other U.S. companies wisely refused to have anything to do with I.T.T.'s plans. See *Washington Post,* Mar. 21, 22, 1972.

† Interestingly, according to U.S. Department of Commerce figures, of all Asian and African less developed countries, U.S. direct investments in manufacturing 1955–1970

and red tape, but most important, manufacturing enterprises found only limited markets for their products in the new nations of Asia and Africa. Companies that did not benefit from economies of scale could and did establish plants to serve the small markets. On the other hand, in industries where scale-production was significant in lowering costs, the markets in most Asian and African nations were too small to warrant a U.S. company's manufacturing.[107] Nonetheless, most of the U.S. investments in manufacturing were market oriented.

In the 1960s, under friendly host government encouragement, U.S. investors made some supply-oriented investments in electronic plants in South Korea, Taiwan, and Hong Kong.* Taking advantage of low labor costs and a labor force with a high degree of dexterity, for the first time companies in the electrical industry made supply-related investments in less developed countries. The output was sent to the United States or was incorporated in finished products in a third country (generally Japan) for sale in that country, in the United States, or even in a fourth-country market.[108]

Asian and African *oil-importing* nations wanted refineries (to save foreign exchange, offer employment, and provide prestige), and they wanted low-priced oil. They often had success in encouraging U.S. companies to build refineries.[109] Their pressures were abetted by the international businesses' requirements for outlets for their abundant foreign crude oil output; American companies recognized that if they did not build refineries, others (competitors or the host government itself) might and might then turn to alternative sources of crude oil. Host governments, however, had less success in lowering the price at which foreign oil was sold. To augment their power, as in Latin America, so now in Asia and Africa, governments established state-owned companies that entered into competition with foreign oil companies in distribution (for instance, in India and Egypt),† participated in refining (for example, in the Congo—now

---

were highest in the Philippines (see *Survey of Current Business*), the Asian country "most familiar" to Americans. After independence in 1946, the Philippines embarked on an import-substitution program. See Sicat, *Philippine Economy in the 1960's*, pp. 189ff. But note also that, Japanese restrictions notwithstanding, in that *developed* nation, U.S. stakes in manufacturing in 1970 were almost three times those in the Philippines.

* These investments anticipated and were similar to the ones made on the Mexican border.

† When a public sector company went into national distribution, its share of the market generally rose rapidly. By 1967, Indian Oil Company supplied 35 per cent of

Zaire—and India), and on occasion actually replaced foreign oil companies (as in Ceylon, where after expropriating the foreign oil firms, in 1964 the state-owned Ceylon Petroleum Corporation took over the sole right to import and distribute products for the inland market).[110]

In Asia and Africa (as well as in Latin America and, for that matter, in Europe, Canada, and Australia), oil-importing countries hoped oil would be discovered in large quantities within their national borders. At first, they asked foreign companies to explore. Then, just as the governments were moving into distribution and refining, in general they took on larger roles in relation to seeking oil.* Egypt, for instance, came to urge foreign companies to explore *with the proviso* that the state would participate once oil in commercial quantities was discovered.[111] In Israel, India, Pakistan, and Ceylon, government companies looked for oil.[112] Syria established in 1964 a state monopoly to exploit its oil resources.† [113]

Because of France's balance-of-payments needs after the war, the French government's state-owned company, Bureau de Recherches de Pétrole, explored in Morocco, Algeria, and Tunisia. In 1955, it found oil in Algeria. U.S. companies then bid for concessions. By the early 1960s, Algeria (which became an independent nation on July 3, 1962) was exporting oil. The discovery of large quantities of oil in Algeria stimulated the interest of the oil enterprises in neighboring Libya (independent since 1951). Libya set conditions for exploration under its Oil Law of 1955. In 1959, Standard Oil of New Jersey's subsidiary produced the first Libyan oil; Libyan oil was first exported in 1961, and Libya soon became the leading oil exporter in Africa. Meanwhile, in 1956, oil was found in Nigeria, which nation also became an exporter.[114]

Like the oil-importing nations, host governments in the oil-exporting countries in Asia and Africa wanted refineries and *low oil prices at home;* more important, they desired *high* oil prices abroad to muster greater revenues for their fiscs.[115] These nations were familiar with events in Latin America. Yet, when in 1958 Venezuela raised its tax on the oil

---

that national market. It was given preference by the government in getting licenses for filling station land and priorities in transport. Foreign companies suffered as a consequence. *Petroleum Press Service* 34:375 (October 1967).

* Turkey was exceptional; its government had sought oil (and discovered some) from 1933 to 1954, when it decided to give exploration concessions to private enterprises. See Hartshorn, *Oil Companies and Governments*, p. 250.

† Syria became a small oil producer for the first time in the 1960s.

companies, they did not follow, hoping foreign oil companies would substitute Middle Eastern oil for Venezuelan oil. But Middle Eastern nations obtained more than 50 per cent of the actual profits, since the formula was generally based on "posted price" and crude oil was sold at 10 to 15 per cent discount. The first Libyan contracts had been based on selling prospective exports at "realized" rather than the higher "posted price"; when that country became an important exporter, the Libyan government demanded and in 1965 the oil companies conceded terms equal to those of other oil-producing nations in the Middle East.* [116] Independent U.S. and foreign oil firms new to foreign production often gave better terms to the host government than established enterprises, which added to the host state's bargaining powers with the giant companies; the host states could then obtain further revenues from the giants.† By 1970, Libya was taking the lead in seeking a greater share of oil industry profits. Its settlements in September and October 1970 in effect provided for a 75-25 profit split—in its favor. Other host governments made new demands; oil prices started to rise; and foreign companies were forced to concede new advantages to the host nations.[117]

Meanwhile, in September 1960, the major Middle Eastern oil producing nations (Iran, Iraq, Kuwait, Saudi Arabia) had joined with Venezuela to form the Organization of Petroleum Exporting Countries (O.P.E.C.).‡ This organization resolved to obtain higher, more stable oil prices, and thus to eliminate major fluctuations in oil revenues. Despite differences among O.P.E.C. members,§ the group's existence unquestionably augmented the power of the producing nations vis-à-vis the oil companies.[118]

* For certain companies the amount to be paid Libya was doubled. Hartshorn, *Oil Companies and Governments*, p. 17.

† The governments' demand for "expensing royalties"—considering royalties as an expense rather than a credit against income tax in calculating the tax—was conceded by the oil companies in the mid-1960s, which added to the states' share of the revenues.

‡ Qatar joined not long after the founding meeting; Indonesia and Libya joined in 1962; Abu Dhabi followed in 1967 and Algeria in 1969. Rouhani, *History of O.P.E.C.*, p. 80.

§ Iran has not always agreed with the Arab members. Venezuela has wanted to control supply to push up prices (Venezuela had relatively high cost production and small reserves); Libya initially was all out for expansion and was prepared to have it at the expense of other Middle Eastern exporters; by 1970, however, Libya also proposed production cutbacks to raise prices (*Petroleum Press Service* 34:362, October 1967; Penrose, *International Firm*, p. 83; *New York Times*, Sept. 3, 5, 1970). In January 1968, the Arab exporting nations, Kuwait, Libya, and Saudi Arabia, formed the Organization of Arab Petroleum Exporting Countries (O.A.P.E.C.). In 1970, Algeria, Qatar, Abu Dhabi, Bahrain, and Dubai joined. The goal was to coordinate oil policies. O.P.E.C. was, however, the more important organization.

Petroleum producing nations in the Middle East and north Africa sought not only greater revenues from existing and new concessionaires, but also more efficient oil exploitation. Under government pressures, foreign firms relinquished parts of their existing concessions, which portions were given to newcomers or to the state oil agency for development; host nations also offered concessions for offshore drilling in areas not included in the earlier grants; [119] they put pressure on the concessionaires to utilize gas that formerly had been flared (which resulted in a rapid growth of liquefied gas shipments in the late 1960s).[120]

From the mid-1950s and especially in the 1960s, host government oil companies in *oil exporting* nations multiplied.* Table XIII.5 indicates the development of such companies in the Middle East and Indonesia;

Table XIII.5. Government oil companies in major oil exporting countries in the Middle East and Indonesia, 1955–1970

Country	Principal activities involving U.S. companies	Other activities
Iran	The present National Iranian Oil Company (N.I.O.C.) was established in *1955* (successor to National Iranian Oil Company, formed in 1951 to administer the nationalized oil industry). N.I.O.C. owned the nation's oil and physical assets of the oil industry; foreign companies obtained an operating arrangement.	N.I.O.C. entered joint ventures in oil production and made agreements with Italian state-owned AGIP Mineraria (1957) and French state-owned ERAP (1966).
Indonesia	Government technically nationalized oil industry in *1960;* in 1963 signed 20 year agreements with Caltex and Stanvac (the large U.S. producers there) making these enterprises contractors rather than concessionaires (60-40 profit split). 1965: encouraged other oil companies to enter under contract.	1965: Government company moved into domestic marketing; at the end of the 1960s it purchased Stanvac's refinery, making government company sole domestic refiner.

* The Indonesian state had participated in a minor manner in the oil industry earlier (see Chapter XII, note 71). The Iranian government after the 1951 nationalization had been directly (and ineffectively) involved.

The Contemporary Scene

Table XIII.5. (continued)

Country	Principal activities involving U.S. companies	Other activities
Kuwait	Kuwait National Petroleum Company organized in *1960* (60% state owned; 40% by Kuwaiti private investors).	1961: K.N.P.C. became exclusive oil marketer in Kuwait; soon it erected its own export refinery and planned to become fully integrated oil company.
Iraq	With Law 80 (Dec. *1961*), foreign-owned Iraq Petroleum Company was ordered to relinquish about 99% of its Iraqi oil concession; negotiations followed. After the June 1967 Arab-Israeli war, the Iraq government terminated discussions and issued Law 97 (Aug. 1967), granting the government company, Iraq National Oil Company, the expropriated lands.	1967: Iraq National Oil Company announced contract with French government oil company to develop Iraq's oil lands; I.N.O.C. also went to the Soviets for aid.
Saudi Arabia	*1962:* General Petroleum and Mining Organization (Petromin) created. In the late 1960s, Petromin joined in exploration and production with two U.S. enterprises (Sinclair and Natomas) and with the Pakistani government oil company.	1967: Petromin purchased distribution facilities of ARAMCO in Saudi Arabia. 1967: Petromin began to build a refinery (75% Petromin; 25% Saudi Arab private investors).

Source: See note 115.

they participated in producing, refining, and marketing. It can be noted that in late 1965, Shell sold its facilities in Indonesia to that government, leaving U.S. enterprises the principal private producers.* The emergence of state oil corporations in the Middle East and Indonesia influ-

* But new entries in the late 1960s included other national groups (Japanese private companies, French and Italian state companies, etc.). Business International, *Doing Business in the New Indonesia*, p. 50.

enced north African leaders. After the 1967 Arab-Israeli war, Algeria nationalized the *marketing and refining* interests of Standard Oil of New Jersey and Mobil Oil in that country; Colonel Houari Boumediene (president of Algeria) pledged to liquidate U.S. and British economic interests in his nation. The French, who had not given full support to Israel during the war, were not at this time placed under similar pressure. In October 1969, Algeria acquired 51 per cent of the assets of Getty Petroleum Company and in 1970 nationalized the holdings of the other U.S. concerns producing oil in that country.*[121] In neighboring Libya where the conservative monarchy of King Idris was overthrown in September 1969 and replaced by a radical junta under Colonel Mammar el-Qaddafi, the government moved into the oil business; in July 1970 Libya nationalized the four *distributing* companies in that country. The Libyan National Oil Corporation took over all marketing of oil products in Libya. The new state agency also entered joint ventures with foreign firms. As of 1970, Libya had not nationalized the giant foreign investments in oil production, although the share of the profits of the industry going to the government had—as noted—steadily increased.[122]

The proliferation of state-owned oil companies, new to oil exporting countries in Asia and Africa, had precedent in Latin America. Mexico's nationalization of oil resources in 1938 had been in large part maintained because that nation could threaten to market its oil in Germany, Italy, and Japan. Government activities in the Middle East and north Africa were aided by state-owned companies in France and Italy; the Soviet Union also stood by to render assistance; this reduced the power of U.S., British, and British-Dutch oil enterprises in Asia and north Africa. Moreover, by the late 1960s, the government-owned oil companies in the Middle East and north Africa had begun cooperating with one another, not only in O.P.E.C., but also on a bilateral basis. In 1967, for example, the Algerian state oil company, SONATRACH, announced it would sell crude oil to the state-owned Egyptian, General Petroleum Company; Iraq and Turkey concluded a petroleum arrangement for 1968–1973; by 1969 Iraq and Algeria agreed to cooperate in developing their respective fields.[123] Cautiously, state enterprises moved further afield. The National Iranian Oil Company acquired shares in refineries in India and South Africa.[124] Clearly, government companies in oil producing nations were

* Getty Petroleum Company with its 49 per cent interest was exempted from the 1970 nationalization (*New York Times,* Nov. 28, 1970).

assuming functions previously confined to international business.[125] Yet, in 1970, in no important oil exporting nation in Asia or Africa was western capital completely excluded; the strengthening of the host country companies notwithstanding, the nations still relied on western oil enterprise (private and public sector units) to produce oil for export and to carry on abroad practically all the so-called downstream operations. But the position of the private foreign enterprises was far from what it had been in 1955; clearly, larger demands on the international oil companies from the host governments would be forthcoming.

U.S. stakes in mining in Asia and Africa were much smaller than in petroleum (see Table XIII.2). Yet the "temper of the times" had its impact on mining enterprises. In Indonesia, for example, while under Sukarno there had been no new stakes in mining, with the change in government in the fall of 1965, a friendly new government, and a liberalized investment law, U.S. mining enterprises sought copper, nickel, and bauxite.[126]

U.S. investments in mining in Africa were greater than in Asia (see Table XIII.2). In newly independent Gabon, Americans went to mine manganese and iron ore; there were new American-controlled stakes in Ghana. In some instances, U.S. mining companies went into joint ventures with government enterprise; thus, in Guinea did U.S.-controlled enterprises develop bauxite.[127] The U.S.-controlled Rhodesian Selection Trust changed its name to Roan Selection Trust, when in 1964 Northern Rhodesia became the independent Zambia. Likewise, it moved its place of incorporation from Great Britain to Zambia. The very next year, Rhodesia (formerly Southern Rhodesia) declared unilateral independence from Britain and established a state based on minority white rule. Zambia (with a black administration) depended for trade routes and coal on Rhodesia. When it sought to bypass its southern neighbor, Roan Selection Trust (R.S.T.) had to alter *its* mode of operation. Then, on August 11, 1969, Zambia decided to follow the lead of Chile and to participate directly in its nation's copper mining. Its president, Kenneth Kaunda, "invited" R.S.T. and other mining enterprises to offer the government a 51 per cent participation in their Zambian operations. On December 24, 1969, the Board of R.S.T. agreed (they actually had little choice).[128] In sum, the governments of independent African nations were beginning to take part in the development of their own mineral resources.

The few U.S. investors in agriculture in Asia and Africa also faced new state intervention. Under Sukarno, the large rubber plantations of U.S. Rubber Company and Goodyear in Indonesia were expropriated in March 1965. After the new government of Suharto was installed, in April 1966 the two American companies negotiated an agreement under which they would be paid for their properties. Then, on December 12, 1966, Indonesia's cabinet issued a decree ordering the return of all seized properties to the former owners. In the fall of 1967, U.S. Rubber repossessed its plantations, while Goodyear reacquired 36,000 of its former 56,000 acres. As for Firestone's large Liberian plantation, no efforts were made to expropriate it, although Firestone's taxes were increased.[129]

In sum, in less developed countries in Asia and Africa, just as in Latin America, action by national governments had profound impact on the course of U.S. business. The economic power of national governments in all less developed lands had risen dramatically.

5

In the late 1950s and 1960s, large areas of the world—including the Soviet Union, eastern Europe, and communist China—continued to be virtually cut off from U.S. investments. There was a thaw when, in July 1967, a Yugoslav law on foreign investment permitted joint ventures between Yugoslav and foreign firms (49 per cent foreign, 51 per cent Yugoslav). U.S. companies did not appear eager to take advantage of this legislation, although several did. Some other small U.S. investments were made in eastern Europe (Hertz and Avis Rent-a-Car, for example), but the entries were few and far between.[130]

Nonetheless, the governments of these communist countries provided challenges for U.S. investors abroad—challenges of a multinational character. Some challenges represented opportunities, others threats. For example, when the U.S. government began to ease restrictions on East-West trade, U.S. companies saw this commerce as an opportunity. As noted, often foreign affiliates of U.S. companies were in a better position to sell on behalf of the multinational enterprise than the parent company. The opportunities were for the affiliates.[131]

By contrast, Soviet oil was a threatening aspect of East-West trade. In 1961, the Soviet Union resumed second place—after the United States—in world oil production; its exports were rising. By 1961 Soviet oil supplied 35 per cent of Greek demand, 22 per cent of Italian demand, 21 per cent of Austrian, and 19 per cent of Swedish demand.[132] Western oil men became alarmed. They feared cheap (subsidized?) Russian oil. By the late 1950s and 1960s, American petroleum companies had huge stakes in foreign oil production; host country pressures notwithstanding, their main profits came from crude oil sales. Thus, they had no desire to purchase, refine, and distribute the cheap Russian oil, as they had wanted to do in the late 1920s. The contract in 1961 of Ente Nazionale Idrocarburi (the Italian state oil company) to purchase a four-year supply of Russian oil at exceptionally low prices frightened the international oil companies.* India requested U.S. oil companies to process cheap Russian crude oil, which they refused to do. Until 1967, Soviet oil exports mounted, causing apprehension among the American oil men. At the same time, the Soviets began to provide national oil companies in less developed countries with equipment and technical assistance—assistance that in earlier years these government agencies could only have received from U.S. or western European firms. As one U.S. government report put it, the Soviets exported oil, technology, and experts to seek to "displace western oil companies and weaken confidence in western methods." The position of American interests was thus threatened not only by Russian oil but by Russian aid. This was new. In 1968, Soviet oil exports to the west dropped; experts predicted that over time the Russians might need to supplement domestic resources *with imports;* the growing Russian interest in the Middle East was seen by some observers as in part a desire to obtain the region's oil. As noted, Russian influence in Iran had been an important consideration in the Iranian oil negotiations of the early 1950s. The extension of Soviet influence in the Middle East became even more a concern to western oil companies in the 1960s, and as the 1970s began. Soviet support of Nasser and Sadat in Egypt and aid to Iraq worried U.S. oil men.[133]

Russian, east European, and communist Chinese aid to less developed countries provided a challenge to private foreign investment. To be sure, American foreign aid—public sector aid—offered a similar challenge to private enterprise, but in a different manner. U.S. foreign aid generally encouraged U.S. private business activities, mainly U.S. exports; U.S. for-

---

* The American oil companies not only had to pay costs of production, but also had to obtain profits for their shareholders and pay royalties to the producing countries. The Russian state enterprise had no such obligations. E.N.I.'s contract was estimated to be at $1.15 a barrel. The companies pointed out that their royalties and other tax payments to the producing countries in the Middle East came to 80 cents a barrel, so competition at that price was impossible. Odell, *Economic Geography of Oil*, p. 54. Yet see starred note p. 386 on how low the price of western oil companies' output actually dropped.

eign aid usually went to projects that would not attract the private U.S. foreign investor. Although communist foreign aid also went, in the main, to activities unattractive to U.S. direct investors (for example U.S. private direct investors would not have invested in the Aswan dam or the railroad from Zambia through Tanzania), it also was going to certain industrial ventures. It offered both an ideological and financial challenge. If the aid proved efficiently rendered, if the *quid pro quo* was not too onerous, would countries want to attract U.S. direct investment? By 1970, the challenge was not yet a serious one, but the potentials seemed present.

Likewise, economic development in the Soviet Union and communist China—and in the 1960s communist Cuba—was taking place without U.S. capital. Cuba, especially, was closely watched in the western hemisphere. Should it provide a model for other Latin American nations, U.S. private investment would clearly be in jeopardy.

Multinational Enterprise, 1955–1970

The surge of participation by American companies in multinational operations in the late 1950s and 1960s was dramatic. By 1957, 2,800 U.S. businesses had stakes in some 10,000 direct investment enterprises abroad; forty-five companies had foreign direct investments of over $100 million. The sales of U.S.-controlled business abroad were known to exceed U.S. exports.*

In 1970, the Office of Foreign Direct Investments in the Department of Commerce collected data on 3,350 direct investors, which controlled more than 15,000 foreign business enterprises.† During the 1960s, Americans heard of individual foreign investments of more than $100 million. The dollar outflow for direct investment reached a new peak in 1970. Sales of U.S. units abroad far outdistanced U.S. exports.[1] Tables XIII.1 and XIII.2 have indicated the tremendous growth of U.S. direct investment abroad and the dollar outflows.

Yet, as noted, the American economy also expanded. It is not sufficient

* The evidence is not available to indicate when the sales of U.S. business abroad surpassed U.S. exports. There is, however, no reason to believe that this was new to the 1950s. In fact, if one tentatively hypothesizes that by sector there remains a rough direct foreign investment/sales ratio and then projects backward on that basis, by 1929 (but not by 1919), sales of U.S. business abroad had already surpassed U.S. merchandise exports. 1919 was a year of exceptionally high U.S. exports. If one looks at 1914 figures, adopting the same hypothesis, the sales of U.S. foreign branches, subsidiaries, and affiliates, excluding those in trade and finance, would surpass U.S. merchandise exports that year as well! Based on data in the present volume, data from the U.S. Dept. of Commerce, Office of Business Economics, *U.S. Business Investments in Foreign Countries,* pp. 110–111 (sales by sector), and data on exports from *Historical Statistics of the United States,* p. 537.

† There were more U.S. direct investors in 1966 than in 1969 or 1970; the number was reduced owing to mergers and consolidations in the United States. Compare Angel, *Directory of American Firms Operating in Foreign Countries,* 6th ed. (1966) and 7th ed. (1969). The number and size of operations abroad, however, rose.

to measure U.S. production abroad against U.S. exports; rather the rise of U.S. investment abroad must be related to the *overall* domestic expansion. In 1914 and 1929 the book value of U.S. direct investment abroad represented in each year a sum equal to 7.3 per cent of that year's gross national product. By 1946, the book value of U.S. direct investment abroad had dropped sharply relative to the gross national product. In subsequent years, it rose and by 1966 was once more equal to 7.3 per cent of gross national product. By 1970 it was up to 8 per cent of the current gross national product. In the years 1955–1970, U.S. direct investment abroad grew faster than the U.S. economy.[2]

2

With the exception of five isolated years (1956–1959, 1961) during the 1950s and 1960s, U.S. direct investments abroad in manufacturing held the primary position among the sectors—that is, in the book value of U.S. direct investments outside the country. This leading position was not novel and, as the reader is aware, had been maintained since the 1920s, when manufacturing replaced mining, which had held first place in 1914 and 1919.[3] Agricultural companies occasionally invested in manufacturing abroad (in making boxes, for example); mining companies manufactured brass and brass products outside the United States; public utilities, as part of their diversification program, enlarged their stakes in foreign manufacturing; petroleum companies started substantial new overseas ventures in petrochemicals. Such activities augmented the total U.S. stake in manufacturing abroad. Nonetheless, in recent years, as in the past, the bulk of U.S. interests in foreign manufacturing has been by American *manufacturing* companies in market-oriented investments. While U.S. direct investors abroad in manufacturing met new conditions at home and in foreign countries, while the sums they invested were larger than ever in history, and while their output abroad was greater than at any earlier time, the historian wants to know, what else was new?[4]

The kinds of American manufacturing enterprises that invested in plants abroad in the late 1950s and 1960s resembled closely the investors of earlier years: they were those with an advantage in technology, with unique products, with a lead in their industries in the United States, and now ever more frequently, with long histories abroad.[5] Those in the vanguard of technology in the late 1950s and 1960s were sometimes in the same (although transformed industries) of past times. Thus, the U.S. electrical industry in the 1880s *and* the 1960s had and has world leadership in many facets. So, too, in office equipment (from the early cash registers to the present-day computers), the United States has held technological superiority. These industries have retained their importance in direct foreign investments. On the other hand, only during and after World War II did the American chemical industry acquire undisputed world leadership in technology.[6] The initiative in research and development in this industry—as much as the severing (by antitrust action and wartime conflict) of the restrictive ties between the U.S. chemical companies and their British and German counterparts—has carried the American firms into new, impressive foreign expansion in recent years.* [7] On the other hand, America's technologically advanced aviation industry has been exceptionally slow in participating in direct foreign investment, although by the end of the 1960s, companies in this industry were embarking on business abroad.† Indeed, the fact that an industry was or is technologically advanced did not ipso facto guarantee large foreign direct investments, but it generally meant that leading companies in that industry would in time, after finding exports could not continue to fill foreign demand, show interest in extending their business through investments abroad.[8]

Likewise, as giant U.S. enterprises in a wide variety of industries presented unique goods to American consumers, the tendency in the late 1950s and 1960s—again as in the past—was to show such offerings in for-

---

* So much so that during the 1960s, the sales of U.S. foreign manufacturing affiliates in the chemical industry were second only to those in transportation equipment (mainly automobiles). *Survey of Current Business* (October 1970), p. 19.

† Professor Raymond Vernon attributes the airplane manufacturers' slowness to invest abroad to a desire "to play safe in matters of military security," Vernon, "International Investment and International Trade in the Product Cycle," p. 198. Rainer Hellmann suggests the reasons lie in (1) "the characteristics of production and low transport costs in the end product," (2) unlike the automobile industry, aircraft producers can sell their products in Europe without manufacturing there, (3) the need for government support in aircraft production, and (4) "The close relationship between aircraft and defense industries" means "most European governments would hardly accept foreign majority participation in aircraft building." Hellmann, *Challenge to U.S. Dominance*, p. 70. John Rae throws light on the characteristics of production: "the aircraft industry was not, except during the Second World War, a quantity producer. . . . The manufacturing operation was predominantly qualitative; the task was to manufacture a complex article to a very high standard of precision, so that each airplane was essentially a separate product." This might well add to the explanations on the slowness of plane manufacturers to invest abroad. See Rae, *Climb to Greatness*, p. 216.

eign countries, and to do so frequently involved more than simply exports: it required new foreign investments in manufacturing.[9]

Statistics reveal huge foreign commitments were made in the late 1950s and 1960s by American car manufacturers.[10] U.S. foreign manufacturing affiliates in the "transportation equipment industry" (mainly automobiles) led all other manufacturing affiliates in sales in the 1960s.[11] Once, U.S. automobile companies had world leadership in technology; once they had a truly unique product, the mass-produced cheap car; then, they had exported the vehicle and had made investments to sell (and then to assemble and to manufacture) the car abroad. In recent times, technological change in this American industry has not been dramatic; * in 1957, the United States changed from its historic position as a net exporter to a net importer of *passenger* vehicles.[12] But still U.S. automobile companies had and made substantial investments abroad. They did so to maintain their long-established position in foreign countries, to participate in filling growing foreign demand, and to meet rising foreign competition. In a sense, their business abroad reflected their continued prominent position in U.S. industry.† On the other hand, firms in the U.S. meat-packing industry, once in the top five of American industry in revenues, by the end of the 1960s were so no longer.‡ The meat packers had gone abroad before World War I.[13] By the end of 1960s, however, the leading ones were not outstanding in their foreign investment in meat packing.§ This may be seen to mirror their loss of position in U.S. industry.

* Research and development, as a per cent of sales in the transportation equipment industry (excluding aircraft), in 1961 was 2.9 per cent, compared with 24.2 per cent in aircraft and parts, 10.4 per cent in electrical equipment, 7.3 per cent in instruments, 4.6 per cent in chemicals and 4.4 per cent in machinery. Mansfield, *Economics of Technological Change*, p. 56.

† The three leading automobile companies in the United States ranked in the top dozen in U.S. industry (ranked by revenue) in 1929 and in the 1960s.

‡ Whereas in 1917, Swift & Co. ranked second and Armour & Co. ranked third in revenue among U.S. industrials, neither company ranked among the top dozen industrials in sales in 1966. See *Forbes* (Sept. 15, 1967), pp. 54, 60–61. In November 1970, Armour & Co. lost its independent existence, becoming a subsidiary of Greyhound Corporation.

§ In 1918 Swift had, as noted, placed most of its foreign operations under an independent Argentine holding company, Compania Swift Internacional, S.A.C., which company was reorganized, incorporated in Delaware, and renamed International Packers in 1950; it maintained ties with Swift interests but was not a subsidiary or affiliate of the American Swift (data from Scudder Collection, Columbia University, Swift & Co., and International Packers). Armour sold its meat-packing operations abroad to International Packers in 1958 (Armour, *Annual Report 1958*). International Packers

Yet, rank in American industry is also in itself inadequate to explain the persistence of or amount of direct foreign investment of U.S. companies in manufacturing in the late 1950s and 1960s. U.S. Steel Corporation in the late 1950s and 1960s (as in 1929 and earlier) ranked among the top dozen in sales in American industry, but its participation in foreign business in recent times has been more in mining than in manufacturing.[14] In the period of U.S. Steel's technological leadership—in the early years of the century—it had exported, set up sales outlets abroad, and even started foreign manufacturing.[15] It had not, however, built many such plants. Gradually, the U.S. steel industry—U.S. Steel included—lost its technological lead. As we have noted, by the 1920s, the industry's foreign markets were being challenged. In 1959 for the first time in the twentieth century, the United States became a net importer of steel mill products.[16] By the late 1950s and 1960s, American steel makers not only lacked technological leadership in world industry,[17] but unlike the leading U.S. automobile companies that had global direct investments, U.S. producers of steel had no network of foreign plants to provide a basis for major expansion.*

In sum, U.S. manufacturers that led in investing in manufacturing abroad in the late 1950s and 1960s—as in previous years—were those with technological advantage (generally reflected in the 1950s and 1960s in high research and development expenditures), distinctive products, leadership in American industry, and/or established overseas stakes. At least two of these attributes seem to have been a prerequisite for giant foreign investments. The sales of U.S. foreign manufacturing affiliates during most of the 1960s † were in order of industry: (1) transportation

---

changed its name to IPL Inc. in May 1968; it was acquired by Deltec International in May 1969; and in 1970, its Argentine meat-packing business was declared insolvent (*Moody's 1968* and *1969; New York Times,* Dec. 19, 1970). Wilson sold its Argentine plant to Argentine interests in 1962 (Wilson, *Annual Report 1962*). Swift & Co. did maintain market-oriented food-processing plants in Europe and Canada in the late 1950s and 1960s and embarked on new investments in Europe in chemicals (*Annual Reports,* and *Business Week,* July 13, 1963). Armour made foreign investments in the *chemical* industry.

* They did, however, begin to build some new plants abroad. U.S. Steel, for example, in the early 1960s started two production ventures in Italy, invested in a Spanish steel producer, and in 1968 acquired major interest in two Central American producers. Crucible Steel Company went to Italy, while Allegheny Ludlum Steel Corporation started producing steel in Belgium. (U.S. Steel, *Annual Reports,* and *New York Times,* Nov. 11, 1962). Such business abroad was still small vis-à-vis their U.S. stakes. The steel makers remained behind in foreign investment.

† Figures are for 1961–1965, 1967–1968.

equipment (primarily automobiles), (2) chemicals, (3) machinery (excluding electrical),* (4) food products, (5) electrical machinery,† and (6) primary and fabricated metals.[18]

The basic reason that companies invested in manufacturing outside the United States in the late 1950s and 1960s was not unlike the motive behind most earlier foreign direct investments in this sector. As in times past, companies sought extended markets. To acquire and to hold these markets, manufacturing abroad seemed a necessity. It was often impossible to obtain effective market penetration with exports from the United States.‡ There seems no satisfactory evidence to indicate in earlier years or in recent times that on an overall basis differential rates of return per se were a crucial motivation behind U.S. stakes in manufacturing abroad.[19] As in the past, some market-oriented investments were made to defend existing foreign markets. Others were aggressive new stakes designed to penetrate new overseas markets. Indeed, many of the investments of the late 1950s and 1960s fit the second category. Most U.S. investors crossed their nation's boundaries with a confidence and a sense of superiority in their product and managerial offerings, just as the U.S. pioneers in international business back in the nineteenth century had boasted of their superior products and ways of doing business.

In the late 1950s and 1960s, few novelties in *how* companies invested in manufacturing abroad emerged. Corporations started their own operations abroad, they also acquired existing foreign businesses. In a sense, takeovers abroad were part of general merger programs. In periods of high merger levels in the United States (as at the turn of the century, in the late 1920s, and in recent years), acquisitions abroad were also common.

Likewise, there were few innovations in the forms of manufacturing abroad—100 per cent versus joint ventures (which again we broadly define as ownership less than 100 per cent). U.S. manufacturers have en-

* In 1961 sales of food products exceeded those of machinery.

† One can hazard a prediction that sales of electrical machinery should rise in standing in the years ahead, since the two leading U.S. companies in that industry (General Electric and Westinghouse) have recently greatly revived interest in foreign investment, after periods of retreat.

‡ The present author agrees entirely with the statement made by Professor Robert Stobaugh to the Subcommittee on Foreign Economic Policy (1970): "Lest I be misunderstood, I am not implying that companies are interested only in making sales and not profits because such is not the case; but sales are a prerequisite of profits." (p. 876).

gaged in joint ventures in foreign countries since the earliest entries. They continued to do so, although in the years 1955–1970, U.S. companies in manufacturing seemed less apt than in the past to go into new joint ventures abroad *with one another*—for their experiences (direct or vicarious) with U.S. antitrust litigation had made them cautious of such procedures; to do so through the media of a Webb-Pomerene association was, as noted, condemned by the courts.

As in the past, to move under a "national cloak" was a frequent motive for joint ventures, and was now extended to many less developed countries. Indeed, there arose a strong element of compulsion. In all or part of these fifteen years, in Japan, India, Spain, Pakistan, and Ceylon, joint ventures in manufacturing were (with a few exceptions) a virtual requirement for doing business. In Mexico, in certain industries the government insisted that domestic ownership amount to 51 per cent. Occasionally, but not often, joint ventures have in recent times been a means of obtaining added capital for manufacturing (although in the late 1950s and 1960s, most U.S. companies going abroad had sufficient capital, or access to capital, that they did not need to enter into joint ventures to obtain financing). Quite often, joint ventures—as in the past—have provided the means to acquire skills, know-how, products, goodwill and/or existing facilities—in short, an excellent way for latecomers to enter a market, to meet competition, and occasionally to forestall competition.

For recent years, Lawrence Franko has brought forth formidable evidence to explain a manufacturing corporation's choice of joint ventures versus 100 per cent ownership.* He found that during the early stages of their overseas manufacturing involvement, most U.S. firms showed a "high tolerance" for joint ventures. This finding is highly significant, for many authors have assumed that entry into joint ventures was a sophisticated form of operation abroad. The present author's own research would substantiate the argument that joint ventures may well come early in a corporation's history abroad. Franko discovered that if after entry abroad a U.S. company diversified its product line, introducing new products for different end-use foreign markets, that company would over

* The joint ventures he studied were limited to those with *host-country corporations, individuals, and family groups.* He excluded those with widely dispersed foreign public shareholders, with third country firms, and those between two or more U.S. companies. He also excluded joint ventures in most countries where the host governments required some sort of local ownership and in Canada, where U.S. corporations formulated distinctive strategies. Franko, "Strategy Choice," pp. 29–30.

time be tolerant of joint ventures. If, on the other hand, the company concentrated on a narrow product line, it would tend over time to buy out its partners and assume control.* Spreading the risks has also been given as a reason for joint ventures by manufacturing companies, in the late 1950s and 1960s; Hugo E. R. Uyterhoeven writes that in bulk products such as heavy chemicals and aluminum, where the final product was undifferentiated, joint ventures with this motive were common.† [20]

To the present writer, the principal novelties with respect to joint ventures versus 100 per cent control of foreign manufacturing in the late 1950s and 1960s seem to lie not in the existence of joint ventures nor in the basic rationales behind them (although in some industries the sharing of risk may have been a more pronounced motive in the late 1950s and 1960s than earlier), but rather, (1) in the presence of many more joint ventures between U.S. manufacturing companies and citizens of less developed countries, some of which were clearly in response to legislation or government policies requiring or favoring this form, and (2) in the presence of a rising number of joint ventures between U.S. manufacturers and foreign government agencies, again a reflection of the enlarged role of government enterprise in the years 1955–1970.[21]

In the past, joint ventures (as we have seen) had frequently been accompanied by restrictive agreements between the U.S. parent and its foreign affiliate(s). Because of the postwar antitrust cases, it appears that in the late 1950s and 1960s most U.S. enterprises hesitated to make such agreements with their affiliates (or for that matter with independent companies),‡ although some companies apparently did retain certain restrictive arrangements.[22]

There were novelties in the late 1950s and 1960s not so much in the

---

* In addition, Franko argued that the parent company's "organizational stage" related to its tolerance for joint ventures and that organizational change typically preceded reconsideration of joint ventures. In sum, it is his contention that the parent company's product plans, organizational changes, and acceptance or rejection of joint ventures abroad were all closely interrelated.

† In the past, joint-ventures in both the chemical and aluminum industries existed. The present author had always attributed the joint ventures not so much to the sharing of risks as the fact that there were established European companies in the chemical and aluminum industries, and competitive pressures made it seem wise for corporate management to cooperate rather than compete.

‡ Agreements between wholly owned U.S. foreign subsidiaries and independent companies abroad that substantially affected U.S. commerce also became vulnerable. See *U.S. v. Watchmakers of Switzerland Information Center*, 133 F. Supp. 40 (SDNY), *reargument refused*, 134 F. Supp. 710 (SDNY), and 1963 Trade Case, Par. 70,600 (SDNY 1962), *order modified*, 1965 Trade Case, Par. 71,352 (SDNY 1965).

means of financing of U.S. direct investment abroad,* but in the motives behind the choice of methods: thus, while it was not new for companies to engage in joint ventures to raise funds for operations abroad, to reinvest foreign profits, to use depreciation allowances, to borrow from international agencies, or to borrow funds outside the United States, it was unique for U.S. subsidiaries and affiliates to borrow abroad to meet the wishes of the U.S. *government*—and to satisfy U.S. balance-of-payments requirements. For years, U.S. foreign subsidiaries and affiliates had borrowed overseas—as a hedge against devaluation of currencies, as a safeguard against blocked payments, and often as a convenience. The new element in the 1960s was the motivation. As noted, borrowing in Europe expanded tremendously.[23]

Meanwhile, innovations occurred in the administrative organization of *parent* manufacturing corporations. We noted earlier that in the 1920s, a number of U.S. manufacturing corporations with foreign business started international companies, many of which became in time international divisions. In the late 1940s and 1950s, many additional corporations started international divisions. But by the late 1950s and 1960s, for some large enterprises, the international division no longer seemed a satisfactory way to run business abroad. For various reasons, high among them growth and diversification, some giant manufacturing corporations have sought either to eliminate or to reduce the importance of the international division and to adopt what has been variously called a "worldwide," "global," or "cosmopolitan" organizational structure. In certain enterprises such a new structure involved top operating management of domestic *product* divisions in direct responsibility for international business in their specific products, generally with regional staff officials offering advice about specific areas (Europe, Latin America, and so forth). In other companies, multifunctional operating subsidiaries or affiliates (often, but not always, divided by regions) were given coequal status with operating divisions in the United States. Some reorganizations were thus on a product basis and others on a regional basis. Some companies adopted a mixed structure, with worldwide product divisions for some products and area divisions for others. A few firms used a "grid," combining product and territorial responsibilities for operating managers. Most reorganizations gave top management at headquarters greater overall

---

* Although the financial resources available to U.S. investors abroad had increased.

planning responsibility for worldwide operations. The old international division that had segregated international from domestic business to give it specialized treatment was brought by such reorganizations "out of isolation." [24]

There was nothing new in the late 1950s and 1960s in the fact that the bulk of U.S. direct foreign investment in manufacturing went to the wealthiest nations in the world—to western Europe and Canada (see Table XIII.3), for that was where the income levels were highest and the markets the greatest in recent decades as in times past.* Likewise, as we have seen, host governments did not act in an important manner to impede the investment. That after 1964, U.S. direct investments in manufacturing in Europe exceeded those in Canada is a change (although if one were to subtract the investments in paper and pulp † in Canada from the totals in the 1920s, U.S. direct investments in manufacturing in Europe would exceed those in Canada in that decade as well—compare Tables XIII.3 and III.1, including notes). In industrial countries, especially in Europe, U.S. manufacturing companies developed more integrated and diversified operations than ever before; an enterprise would not just have a plant, but might have research facilities as well; it might have numerous end products. Although the major portion of U.S. stakes in manufacturing subsidiaries and affiliates abroad was in industrial countries, clearly in the late 1950s and 1960s the figures also reflect the continuing spread of U.S. manufacturing investments—market-oriented investments—to less developed countries.[25] Here too there was over time an increasing integration and diversification. In Latin America, espe-

---

* Jack Behrman in the *Columbia Journal of World Business* in 1966, commenting on the fact that the "pulling power of manufacturing . . . investment in the developing world is something less than sensational," found three possible explanations: "(1) some companies are categorically opposed to investment in developing countries; (2) investment is made highly unpleasant or risky by the attitudes of the host government; or (3) the techniques of persuading investors to embark on such ventures are inadequate to the task." Professor Behrman found that often companies move abroad, seeking a "more secure association first—such as Canada, Europe, Australia, or Japan—before essaying a more tenuous relationship in the LDC's [less developed countries]." *Columbia Journal of World Business* 1:32 (Spring 1966). What Behrman neglects to mention is that in the developed world there is a higher per capita income and more purchasing power to buy the goods of the American manufacturing companies. The possibilities of profit are thus seen as greater. That more than any other reason, the present author would suggest, is why today as yesterday, manufacturing companies have invested to seek markets in the developed before the underdeveloped countries.

† This is legitimate, because they were atypical, supply-oriented manufacturing investments.

The Contemporary Scene

cially, full (or fuller) manufacture was replacing the assembly, bottling, and packaging plants of times past. New products were introduced. With greater knowledge, improved transportation and communication, more resources for investment, together with host government barriers to U.S. exports, the geographical scope and degree of integration and diversification of U.S. investments in manufacturing have steadily broadened. By 1970, U.S. stakes in manufacturing abroad outdistanced U.S. foreign stakes in other sectors. And since the vast bulk of U.S. interests in manufacturing were market-oriented endeavors, overall market-oriented investments of U.S. companies in foreign countries became far more important than supply-oriented stakes.

3

Only slightly less spectacular than the participation of U.S. companies in manufacturing abroad has been that of U.S. enterprises in foreign investment in petroleum. From fourth place among the sectors with the greatest U.S. direct investment in 1914, petroleum had risen by the late 1950s and 1960s typically to second place, and in 1956–1959 and again in 1961 (see Table XIII.1) to first place.* The prominent position of the petroleum is the more dramatic when one considers that the number of petroleum enterprises involved in international business has always been far fewer than the number of manufacturing companies. Likewise, while U.S. enterprises in many sectors invested in foreign manufacturing, petroleum companies have had little rivalry in the oil business abroad from other U.S. corporations (although certain U.S. mining firms have sought foreign oil, as have some diversified conglomerates and certain public utilities).†

* The speed of petroleum's ascent to second place depends on whose figures are employed. According to Cleona Lewis, in 1929 petroleum was already in second place. According to the most recently revised U.S. Department of Commerce figures on 1929, that year petroleum was in fourth place, following manufacturing, public utilities, and mining! (See Table VIII.2 above). In 1940, according to Department of Commerce figures, petroleum was in third place, following manufacturing and public utilities. Petroleum was boosted into first place in 1956–1959 by the giant outlays for leases in Venezuela in 1956–1957 (in part stimulated by the availability of new concessions there and in part by the Suez Crisis that made Americans conscious of the need for foreign oil "West of Suez") and in 1961 by the huge expenditures in Libya. *Survey of Current Business.*

† A recent example of a mining company in the oil business abroad is Natomas (a company that once dredged gold in California), which has discovered oil off the shores of Sumatra and has also embarked on exploration in Saudi Arabia. See *New York Times,* Sept. 13, 1970.

The kinds of petroleum companies that moved abroad in the late 1950s and 1960s resembled those of earlier years. Giant companies had the largest stakes; smaller firms also went abroad—perhaps more readily than in the past.* In the early years of the industry, U.S. oil companies had gone abroad *to market* their unique products.[26] Now the products were no longer unique. While the industry did introduce "new and improved" offerings, this author suggests that the innovative character of the American industry's products (excluding those in petrochemicals †and liquefied natural gas) were far less important in the late 1950s and 1960s than in times past, although there were significant *process* innovations, in refining, transporting, producing, and exploring techniques. In the late 1950s and 1960s, the U.S. oil companies exported not so much new products as improved methods. They sought to retain their prominent position worldwide. Established U.S. enterprises in oil built on their earlier activities, while the newer entries acted to spur the giant companies and to provide competition.[27]

In the free world, as the demand for oil soared, oil surpassed coal as the greatest single source of energy.[28] U.S. oil companies made large investments in marketing and to maintain their foreign markets and to satisfy growing demands they also made substantial investments in refineries in consumer nations. New refinery technology lowered costs; ‡ more important, by-products of the refineries could be used in the new petrochemical industries of the host countries. Likewise, because of transportation innovations, for sizable markets it became cheaper for U.S. firms to ship crude rather than refined oil. In 1951, the output of U.S.-owned resource refineries (those close to the source of supply) had been greater than that of U.S.-owned market refineries (those near the consumer). By 1960, the opposite was the case, and by 1965 a mere 16 per cent of the refinery capacity (outside North America and communist countries) was near the oil fields. Yet, despite the expanded sales effort, despite the new refineries in consumer countries, the major oil enterprises

* The established U.S. giant companies in the late 1960s and 1960s continued to be Jersey Standard, Mobil (the former Socony Mobil), Gulf, Texaco, and Standard Oil of California. Some twenty or thirty U.S. independents have recently gotten into the foreign oil business in an important fashion, among them Phillips, Continental Oil, Occidental, and Standard Oil of Indiana (for which this was a reentry—round two). *Petroleum Press Service* 36:253 (July 1969) lists the independents and their holdings.

† Petrochemicals were indeed innovative—but they are more properly considered as part of the chemical rather than the oil industry.

‡ Also, increased demand meant economies of scale not available earlier.

had difficulties in the 1960s in retaining their existing and capturing the expanding markets. Thus, in 1952, the seven principal oil companies * marketed more than 75 per cent of oil products outside of North America and communist countries, but by 1968 the majors obtained only slightly more than 50 per cent of such sales; their markets share had been eroded by rising competition from U.S. and foreign independents as well as from foreign state-owned oil agencies.[29]

Innovations in transportation—primarily the new huge tankers—changed the character of oil transit. When the Suez Canal was impassable from October 1956 to April 1957 (during the Suez Crisis), oil enterprises had been in a near panic.[30] When the canal closed after the six-day Arab-Israeli war of June 1967 and remained shut (it was still closed at the end of 1970), the giant tankers helped alleviate the situation, making it economical to by-pass the canal.

All during the 1960s, U.S. petroleum companies complained of over-production of crude oil. After the Suez Crisis, not only were there the giant tankers that could by-pass the canal, but oil reserves had been developed "West of Suez." Independent oil companies often produced in a helter-skelter fashion. The majors could not impose controls. The result was a vast rise in output and a decline in price.† Despite this, U.S. oil companies did not relax their search for oil, because (1) an individual company or group of companies desired to raise its *own* low-cost crude oil supplies, to safeguard its own supplies for its refining and marketing affiliates, and to keep its own costs of crude oil down (in general, it remained cheaper for a company to produce its own crude oil than to buy from others), (2) an individual company or group of companies wished to keep such crude oil out of the hands of competitors (private or government companies) and hopefully have a means of keeping production in line with demand, and (3) despite the price decline, profits for the business still lay in the sale of crude oil. In the race for oil exploration and production, the large international oil companies lost ground to independents and state-owned enterprises. Whereas in 1952, the seven major companies produced 90 per cent of the crude oil outside of North America

---

* The seven majors included the five large U.S. companies and Royal Dutch-Shell and British Petroleum.

† Professor M. A. Adelman of M.I.T. indicates that as "a rough average," prices per barrel F.O.B. Persian Gulf (including both crude and refined oil) declined from $2.10 in 1957 to $1.20 in 1969. See Adelman's "The Multinational Corporation in World Petroleum," in Kindleberger, *International Corporation*, pp. 228–229.

and communist countries, by 1968 that figure was reduced to little more than 75 per cent.[31]

In the 1960s new technology in exploration (including extensive use of aerial surveys and more sophisticated techniques in identification) and new technology in production (including new methods of offshore drilling, deeper drilling, and secondary recovery) opened possibilities of greatly raising both oil reserves and output worldwide. By the end of 1970, the price of oil began to rise; the concern with overproduction began to abate. Oilmen saw an end to the buyer's market. This would encourage even more exploration.

As for the forms of operations abroad, two of the principal joint ventures between U.S. oil companies—Stanvac and Caltex—in integrated operations have been to an important extent broken apart. In April 1962 (after a 1960 consent decree) the assets of Stanvac were divided between the parent companies, Standard Oil of New Jersey and Socony Mobil.* In 1967, Standard Oil of California and Texaco concluded their twenty-year partnership in most of Europe (excluding France, Spain, and Turkey); Caltex continued to operate East of Suez.[32] Yet joint ventures among *U.S. and western European* oil companies in marketing, refining, transporting, producing, and exploring remained in the late 1950s and 1960s— involving the majors, independents, and foreign governments. As one 1967 market survey put it, "political uncertainty is a way of life with international oil companies. There probably has not been a year since World War II when some local or major crisis has not existed." Thus, where substantial investments were required, oil companies desired to share their risks. Geographical dispersion minimized risks, and so did joint ventures. On the other hand, some joint ventures *with host country citizens or governments* were undertaken because they were mandatory or strongly advocated by host governments; the number of such ventures, especially in less developed countries, was new to the late 1950s and 1960s.[33]

Because of their joint ventures, the giant oil companies and some independents were closely associated with one another in international business. The conclusion of economist Edith Penrose, in 1968, seems valid: "It is clear from the present position and the historical record that major international [oil] Companies are, and have been, genuine competitors

* Indonesia was the key exception; as noted, Stanvac remained in Indonesia managed by Standard Oil of New Jersey.

The Contemporary Scene

(or rivals) in many fields . . . It is also clear that market-sharing and price agreements were often made." In the U.S. government suit against the leading U.S. oil firms, in 1960 Standard Oil of New Jersey and Gulf Oil and in 1963 Texaco accepted consent decrees that enjoined the signers from combinations affecting competition in the commerce of the United States. The decrees, however, left open the possibilities of strictly local foreign cartel arrangements.* Despite such an exemption, U.S. antitrust law made U.S. oil companies operate with new care in their business abroad.[34]

In financing their foreign business, oil enterprises acted in a manner similar to manufacturing corporations. They, too, raised capital overseas to meet the wishes of the U.S. government.[35]

In the 1960s, the largest U.S. international oil companies reorganized their businesses to leave the old international division (or any variant of it) behind. Socony-Mobil (now Mobil) reunified the management of its foreign operations and then decentralized its oil activities on a regional basis. By 1964, writers on management structures could declare that despite variations, "the formal division by geographic areas is a common organizational feature among the giant international oil companies." †
Moving further in this direction, in 1966, Standard Oil of New Jersey announced "a major reorganization" of its overseas business. It transferred much of its foreign operations to four regional groups (Europe, Latin America, Africa, and the Far East).‡ Michael L. Haider, Jersey Standard's board chairman, explained the move as one "toward further decentralization, whereby many of the functions once exercised by Jersey Stan-

* In 1959, before the consent decrees were accepted, under pressure from the West German government, the major oil distributors in Germany (including subsidiaries of Standard Oil of New Jersey and Socony Mobil) participated in a price-fixing cartel for the German market (Ebb, *International Business*, p. 64). In 1964–1965, the German government imposed a "voluntary" cartel on the oil companies (see Hartshorn, *Oil Companies and Governments*, p. 270). In France, the government allotted crude oil quotas (*New York Times*, Feb. 22, 1968). Note that the three U.S. consent decrees provided exceptions for acts compelled by foreign law or "pursuant to request or official pronouncement of policy of the foreign nation" wherein the acts occurred, and where noncompliance would involve loss of business (American Bar Association, *Antitrust Developments 1955–1968*, p. 54).

† The writers noted that some major oil companies had two worldwide groups, one in petroleum and one in petrochemicals. Clee and Sachtjen, "Organizing Worldwide Business," p. 64.

‡ Note that activities of Imperial Oil in Canada were exempted from the reorganization, as were those of Creole Petroleum in Venezuela, the refining company in Aruba, and ESSO's Libyan operations. *New York Times*, Feb. 25, 1966.

dard would be delegated to the regional organizations," leaving the parent company free to concentrate "on major issues, policy making, planning, and interregional coordination." [36] Thus, as large multinational manufacturing companies were reorganizing their international business, so, too were the oil enterprises—in each case to cope with greater, more diversified business abroad.

Likewise, oil companies continued to have and to place their main stakes in marketing (and market-related activities) in developed nations. The reason was the same as for the manufacturers—that was where the markets were largest. There was, in fact, in the late 1950s and 1960s, in response to the rise in demand, a phenomenal growth in investment by U.S. oil companies in distribution and refining in Europe. In Canada, American-owned marketing and refining continued to expand. In Japan, Australia, New Zealand, and South Africa, refineries (with U.S. firms participating) became ubiquitous. U.S. companies also built refineries in many less developed countries. Just as manufacturing enterprises were spreading further afield, with more integrated and diversified businesses, so were the oil companies. [37]

While in the 1960s, new investments in marketing and refining oil appear to have been larger than those in oil production, U.S. companies (majors and independents) went to find oil practically everywhere in the noncommunist world, except where they were barred by state monopolies. In 1930, 63 per cent of the world's oil output had come from the United States; by 1960 that figure was reduced to 36 per cent, and by 1969, to 24 per cent! [38] But U.S. oil companies—majors and independents—played an important role in the rise of the *foreign* oil production. By the late 1950s and 1960s, U.S. enterprises were seeking oil in Canada, now a major oil producing nation * (a new condition created in great part by the efforts of American companies). In the spring of 1968, Esso Standard Oil (Australia) Limited announced development of the "major oil and gas fields" in the Bass Straits off the coast of Victoria; Australia became a new oil producer in the 1960s. [39] Standard Oil of New Jersey, with Shell, obtained exploration rights to natural gas deposits in the Netherlands and in West Germany; Phillips Petroleum participated in the

---

* Canada ranked eighth among the world's oil producers in 1959 (after the United States, Venezuela, U.S.S.R., Kuwait, Saudi Arabia, Iran, and Iraq), and ninth in 1969 (after the United States, U.S.S.R., Venezuela, Iran, Libya, Saudi Arabia, Kuwait, and Iraq). See *Petroleum Press Service* 37:6 (January 1970).

North Sea finds in 1970. But, the bulk of U.S. interest in oil exploration and production remained in less developed countries—especially in Venezuela, and elsewhere in Latin America,* the Middle East, north Africa,† west Africa,‡ and Indonesia.[40]

5

While U.S. stakes abroad in manufacturing and oil held preeminence over those in other sectors (see Table XIII.1), it is useful to summarize briefly the shifting positions of other investments. Table XIV.1, derived

Table XIV.1. Third, fourth, and fifth place ranks of sectors involved in U.S. direct investment, 1950–1970

	Years of ranking			
Ranking	1950–1951	1952–1960	1961–1963, 1968	1964–1967, 1969–1970
3	Public utilities	Mining	Mining	Trade
4	Mining	Public utilities	Trade	Mining
5	Trade	Trade	Public utilities	Public utilities

Source: See Table XIII.1.

from Table XIII.1, indicates the changes in ranking. These are significant. Mining, which in 1914 and 1919 had headed the list in attracting U.S. direct foreign investment (see Table I.3) had by the 1950s and 1960s sunk to third or fourth place, as indicated on Table XIV.1. Although foreign investment in mining rose steadily, it failed to mount as rapidly as U.S. stakes in manufacturing.§ U.S. investments in foreign mining were made

* Ecuadorian oil showed signs of new promise in 1970.
† Libya especially, where by decade's end 88 per cent of the substantial production was by U.S.-controlled firms. Figure from *New York Times*, Feb. 22, 1971.
‡ Nigeria became an important oil producer in the 1960s.
§ The present author has puzzled on why this should be the case. As U.S. mineral resources become exhausted, one would expect greater foreign holdings to supplement domestic supplies. Synthetics have not substituted for key minerals. Why then the loss of position vis-à-vis manufacturing? The answer does not lie in foreign expropriations. Perhaps the reason lies in the distribution of product in the industry sector in the

by mining, manufacturing, and occasionally oil companies. Mining companies, as in the past, went into mining abroad when faced with shortages at home and the need to supplement domestic or world resources with cheaper sources of supply. In the past, U.S. mining firms had been innovators in mining and processing technology; in the 1950s and 1960s, they continued to innovate, using new aerial survey techniques in prospecting and developing superior methods of processing low grade ores. Manufacturing companies invested in mining abroad to obtain raw materials: bauxite (for the aluminum companies), iron ore (for the steel enterprises), and specialty metals such as manganese and chrome (required by various types of manufacturers). Oil companies moved into foreign mining as part of diversification programs.

Because of the large investments needed in mining and because of host nation requirements, in the late 1950s and 1960s investors in foreign mining often participated in joint ventures. These frequently involved other U.S. enterprises; occasionally, U.S. companies joined with western European capital, sometimes, with host nation shareholders (especially in Canada, Australia, Mexico, and Brazil), and ever more often by the end of the 1960s with foreign governments (in Chile, Colombia, and in several African nations). Joint ventures in mining were not unique to recent times, but the number was unprecedented. Most important, while there had been in less developed countries host nation participation in joint ventures with U.S. companies in the past (as in the ill-fated COSACH), it was truly atypical. By the end of the 1960s, because of host nation insistence, joint ventures with foreign governments—as we have seen—were no longer rare. U.S. antitrust law had apparently no impact whatsoever on joint ventures among mining concerns abroad.[41]

As for organizational structure, mining companies on the whole appear to have retained functional organizations, with line vice presidents for mining, sales, engineering, and so forth. Most never adopted an inter-

United States, wherein in the twentieth century the total sector has increased in the countrywide totals, but mining has declined from 6 per cent (in 1919–1928), to 5 per cent (1929), to 3 per cent (1961–1963), while manufacturing has risen from 57 per cent (in 1919–1928), to 59 per cent (1929), to 66 per cent (1961–1963), according to figures from Kuznets (*Modern Economic Growth*, p. 131). If, in *very rough* terms (as our evidence would indicate), U.S. direct foreign investment *trends* tend to mirror activities at home, these figures might help explain the great rise in U.S. manufacturing abroad vis-à-vis U.S. stakes in mining. Likewise, we have suggested elsewhere that the early U.S. direct foreign investment figures on mining may be somewhat misleading, because of the *process* of investment. Wilkins, *Emergence of Multinational Enterprise*, p. 206.

national division. Multifunctional foreign operations got supervision from functional vice presidents in the home office.[42]

In the late 1950s and 1960s a marked change occurred in the countries where U.S. companies invested in mining. In 1950, U.S. direct investment in mining in Latin America had been about double that in Canada (see Table XIII.2). In recorded history, U.S. direct investment in mining in Latin America had always been higher than in Canada. By 1960, however, U.S. stakes in mining in Canada surpassed those in the whole of Latin America.[43] This was not because of the exhaustion of Latin American mineral resources. Rather the reason lay in the conditions of doing business in Latin America that compared unfavorably with the more suitable investment climate in Canada. Likewise, in the late 1950s and 1960s, investments by U.S. firms in mining in Australia, which in earlier years had been limited, rapidly accelerated. U.S. corporations invested in lead and silver, iron ore, bauxite, nickel, and even coal. By 1970, the book value of U.S. stakes in mining in Australia for the first time was second only to that in Canada![44] Probably, the future will see greater U.S. interests in mining and smelting in Canada and Australia, where the governments are stable and the prospects look promising. Companies will go forth more modestly into Latin America (despite the obstacles), into Africa (where Americans were finding new opportunities), and into Indonesia (where in the late 1960s the investment outlook seemed excellent). Such investments would be made in keeping with the calls for resources, the need of manufacturers to integrate backward when raw material prices rise, the potentials for profit, and the general geographical diversification of international business.

The declining *relative* position of U.S. direct investments in public utilities (including transportation) abroad is clearly evident (see Table XIV.1). Total U.S. direct investments in public utilities rose, but only slightly. In Latin America, the sum dropped sharply in the 1960s as U.S. public utilities, aware of low profits and badgered by host nation pressures, sold their assets.*

Perhaps most remarkable has been the expansion of U.S. foreign investments in trade—wholesale and retail trading, excluding the oil distri-

---

* In the late 1950s and 1960s, international airlines expanded dramatically, but this was not prominently reflected in the figures on investment in "public utilities and transportation." The airlines invested abroad mainly in offices and inventories that did not involve giant sums. Some of the airline investments appear to be in the "unallocated international" category.

bution (see Table XIV.1). Direct foreign investments in trade vied with U.S. direct investments in mining for third place among the sectors attracting foreign investment in the 1960s. While still far behind manufacturing and petroleum, that investments in trade abroad should rise this high is novel. Although F. W. Woolworth, Singer, and Eastman Kodak had long histories abroad in the retail trade, most U.S. mass merchandisers had been in the past shy about international business, while small store owners would not be expected to expand abroad. The largest U.S. merchandiser in the 1960s, Sears, Roebuck, did not expand abroad dramatically until after 1942, when it opened a small store in Cuba; thereafter its business abroad grew, especially in Latin America. By the mid-1960s, it was entering the European market. In the 1960s, America's second largest merchandiser, Great Atlantic and Pacific Tea Company (A & P) still confined its foreign retail stores to Canada. Number Three, Safeway Stores, had had Canadian sales outlets since the 1920s, but only in the 1960s did Safeway invest in Europe and Australia; by 1966 it had twenty-eight stores in England, five in Germany, eleven in Australia, while in Canada it owned a full range of food processing plants, distribution centers, and warehouses, as well as 241 retail groceries. In addition, in the late 1950s and 1960s, other U.S. firms introduced the American "supermarket" concept abroad, the leader among them Rockefeller's International Basic Economy Corporation, which by 1966 had forty-three supermarkets in Venezuela, Peru, and Argentina.[45]

The Survey of Current Business in its reports on the book value of U.S. direct investments abroad no longer gives breakdowns on U.S. stakes in agriculture, finance and banking, or for the range of assorted service industries. In 1914, agriculture held third place among the sectors attracting U.S. direct foreign investments. By the late 1950s and 1960s, little new U.S. money was going into investments abroad in agriculture.* On the other hand, in the late 1950s and 1960s, new entries into direct investment abroad by U.S. banking houses proliferated. Throughout much of the noncommunist world, American banks have opened branches and acquired facilities (see Table XIV.2 on bank branches, 1955–1970). Banks have also finally turned to use Edge Act corporations.† U.S. banks have

---

* A notable exception was the new large investments by the International Basic Economy Corporation in foreign poultry operations in the late 1950s and 1960s. See Broehl, *International Basic Economy Corporation,* chap. 9.

† The Edge Act, passed in 1919, provided for the establishment of two types of corporations which could be owned by U.S. banks and would operate abroad. As noted,

Table XIV.2. Branches of U.S. banks abroad [1]
(number and distribution)

	1955	1960	1965	1970
United Kingdom and Ireland	11	13	21	44
Continental Europe	6	6	21	72
Latin America	56	55	88	223 [2]
Far East	20	23	50	79
Elsewhere	18	27	31	118 [3]
TOTAL	111	124	211	536

Source: Federal Reserve System. 1970 figures are in *Federal Reserve Bulletin*, 58:943 (October 1972).

[1] Includes only member banks.

[2] This large number did not reflect a soaring business; the assets of these 223 branches were far smaller than those of the 72 branches in Continental Europe or of the 44 branches in the United Kingdom and Ireland. It was in London and to a lesser extent on the Continent that the great expansion in business occurred.

[3] Includes 61 branches in the Bahamas.

experienced difficulties in some countries. Yet, on the whole, U.S. banks have in recent years prospered abroad—serving the needs of American businesses and also of host country residents. In Europe they have sought to take advantage of the new Eurodollar markets.[46] Credit agencies have also entered foreign business in larger numbers than in times past. Brokerage houses have established offices abroad. Investors Overseas Service sold U.S. mutual funds in Europe in the 1960s, and from the mid-1950s, the International Basic Economy Corporation introduced in Brazil, Colombia, Argentina, Chile, Thailand, and Spain the concept of mutual funds—based both on indigenous and U.S. securities.[47] Some insurance firms have looked to foreign business, although the relative scale of their international plans seems minimal when compared with the turn-of-the-century activities of the then big three in American insurance.[48]

To aid both U.S. business abroad and indigenous enterprise, there have been new foreign offices of U.S. engineering, advertising, accounting, market research, and management consultant firms. Services in for-

the Edge Act was at first used sparingly. But in the late 1950s and 1960s, Edge Act corporations multiplied—banking corporations (which could engage in commercial banking abroad) and financing corporations (which could make equity investments abroad, except in other corporations engaged in foreign banking).

eign lands by contractors (construction firms, drilling companies, and so forth) have a long history and have risen sharply. What characterizes the late 1950s and 1960s is that the range of business services provided by U.S. multinational firms has broadened. New aids to foreign travelers have proliferated. American hotel chains have spread abroad: Intercontinentals, Hiltons, and Sheraton hotels, and in the late 1960s Holiday Inn crossed the U.S. boundaries.* Howard Johnson started franchising restaurants and motor lodges in Canada and Europe as recently as 1968. Hertz and Avis † car rentals are available outside the United States. Many personal services are now offered overseas for the first time, such as Arthur Murray's dancing lessons.[49] In general, when firms in such service industries invest overseas, compared with manufacturing, oil, or mining companies, their individual stake is small. Nonetheless, the move of such businesses abroad represents an important aspect of U.S. enterprise in foreign countries in the late 1950s and 1960s. That these firms go overseas demonstrates a "cluster complex"—U.S. companies and travelers abroad attracting their traditional suppliers into new foreign stakes.

6

The massive move of U.S. business abroad in the years 1955–1970 has had both worldwide and national impacts. From the standpoint of the world economy it has contributed to the shrinking of the world's geography. Through the media of multinational enterprise goods, capital, men, management, and technology have spread internationally; unquestionably the multinational corporation contributes to a smaller world. Yet, far more significant and controversial are the *national* impacts, for this is still a world of individual nations. Such impacts have occurred both at home and abroad.

In the United States, it has been feared that direct foreign investors will (1) affect adversely this nation's balance of payments by the capital outflow, by damaging U.S. exports, and by raising U.S. imports; (2) destroy American jobs by building plants abroad and closing them at home, by reducing exports, and by increasing imports; (3) deprive the U.S. economy of technical and managerial personnel that are sent abroad with the capital and export technology to create competition from

---

* Many of the hotel-motel activities abroad were franchised operations; some involved management contracts. I.T.T. acquired Sheraton in 1968.

† Avis became a subsidiary of I.T.T. in 1965.

abroad; (4) result in tax losses to the U.S. government, owing to (a) a transfer of production abroad, (b) the inability of the United States to tax most profits earned abroad until remitted, (c) transnational intercompany pricing, and (d) the existence of foreign tax credits; (5) impair U.S. capital resources temporarily by using funds abroad rather than at home; (6) impair U.S. capital resources permanently, through commercial and political losses abroad; (7) participate in international cartels to the detriment of the American consumer; (8) develop obligations that conflict with domestic loyalties; and (9) involve the United States in foreign relationships that the nation would do well to avoid. Many of these fears are not unique to the late 1950s and 1960s.

By contrast, corporation leaders and many economists have pointed out that the impacts of U.S. direct investment abroad *on the United States* are positive rather than negative. They argue that direct investors (1) provide in net an aid to the U.S. balance of payments (historically, they correctly point out, far more money has flowed *into* the United States as a consequence of direct foreign investments than has left); (2) contribute to prosperity and employment at home by aiding nations abroad and thus enlarging American markets; in addition, U.S. subsidiaries and affiliates abroad are large purchasers of U.S. exports—components and products not made abroad, as well as capital equipment; recent data indicate that instead of exporting jobs, employment by multinational corporations in the United States has actually grown more rapidly than for corporations in general; the increase in imports that America experienced in the 1960s came more from independent foreign firms than from multinational enterprises; (3) provide an important aid to U.S. technology by opening windows to the best technological developments outside the United States; (4) do not impair U.S. tax revenues, for output abroad is supplemental to and not a substitute for U.S. production; tax evasion is not a motive for business abroad; (5) have not interfered with domestic investment, for its level has generally remained high while the large international investments have been made; likewise, there is no reason to believe that funds invested abroad would have been invested at home, had they not been invested outside the country; (6) result in additions to U.S. capital resources rather than impairment, for the losses abroad have been more than compensated by the gains from the foreign stakes; (7) create more competition worldwide rather than less; (8) aid the U.S. civilian economy and provide for U.S. defense—by virtue of control over, or of not letting others obtain a monopoly over, vital raw materials abroad, among them oil, iron ore, copper, bauxite, and uranium; and (9) can contribute to U.S. foreign policy objectives, by serving as an instrument of U.S. diplomacy; it can lower the American burden of military aid by raising economic standards abroad.[50]

While these pros and cons are debated, they do not get to the essence of the question of how vital U.S. direct foreign investment has become to the American economy. For certain U.S. companies it is clearly of vast importance, contributing significantly to their profits (see Table XIV.3). Especially in slack years in the United States, dividends from abroad can keep corporate earnings looking healthy. Yet, for the entire economy, the impact seems less profound. As noted, in 1970 U.S. direct investment abroad (*accumulated direct foreign investments—not outflows for direct foreign investment*) amounted to 8 per cent of that year's gross national

Table XIV.3. Selected U.S. companies and their foreign operations, 1960, 1965

	Percentage of net income from foreign operations	
Company	1960	1965
Burroughs	84 [1]	69
Anaconda	80	54
Colgate Palmolive	78 [2]	3
Aluminum Company of America	72	3
American Radiator & Standard Sanitary	66	57
Standard Oil of New Jersey	66	60
National Cash Register	60	47
I.T.T.	60 [2]	60
H. J. Heinz	60 [2]	65
Socony Mobil	57 [2]	52
Yale & Towne	56	3
Max Factor	53	3

Source: The Exchange 24:11–14 (January 1963), for 1960 figures; Sidney E. Rolfe, *The International Corporation* (Paris 1969), for 1965 figures.
[1] Excluding Canada.
[2] 1961 figures.
[3] Not available.

product.[51] By contrast, when Britain was *the* great investor abroad in 1914, her existing foreign investments represented more than one-and-one-half times her net national income that year! [52] *Outflow* for U.S. direct investment abroad in 1970, the peak year (see Table XIII.1), represented less than one-half of one per cent of the U.S. gross national product that year. This last figure can be compared with the foreign investment outflow from Great Britain when she was the world's great creditor nation. In the fifty years before 1914, Britain invested abroad *annually* an amount equal to roughly 4 per cent of her national income, and in the years 1905–1913 that figure rose to about 7 per cent! [53] The outflow for U.S. *direct* investments abroad has clearly never been as significant as this British (primarily portfolio) foreign investment.*

Abroad, in industrial and less developed countries alike, as noted in Chapter XIII, there existed in 1955–1970 a deep concern and ambivalence over U.S. direct investment. Recipient nations feared that U.S. investment would retard economic growth by taking large earnings out of the country and in other ways hurting the nation's balance of payments, sapping local initiative, and acting to aid the parent company's growth at the expense of the national economy. On the other hand, payments abroad by U.S. businesses were for positive contributions by the investors to the host nation's economic growth, among them, providing capital, management, technology, skills, and know-how (from production processes to product design to marketing), employment opportunities, and taxable enterprise. Primarily in less developed countries, U.S. investors have made basic infrastructure investments in transportation, housing, education, and medical care that benefited not only the U.S. enterprise but the host country. While the balance of payments effects of U.S. investment on the recipient countries vary, often the effects are positive when foreign investors' production substituted for imports and when the U.S. investors exported their output. Likewise, rather than sap local initiative, direct investors often stimulated host nation business—by demonstrating techniques that could be imitated, by training indigenous per-

---

* The reader may suggest that the comparison is not apt, that apples and oranges are being compared. Yet, we would maintain that when scholars have written about British investments, the reference has been primarily to portfolio investments, while the impact of American capital abroad has been in terms of direct foreign investment. *But* if we were to take *total* outflow for U.S. long-term private investments abroad in 1970, this sum comes to only slightly over one-half of one per cent of the 1970 gross national product.

sonnel, and by creating new activities linked with the investor's primary business. In addition, there need be no contradiction between aiding the parent company's and the host nation's growth; both can go hand in hand. In net, U.S. business abroad usually has made an important contribution to the economic growth of the host nation.

On the basis of the present author's research, it would seem that for industrial nations direct investment from abroad is and has been far more of an asset than a liability in its role in economic growth. Canada, the country with the greatest U.S. direct investment, ranks among the wealthiest nations in the world.

Likewise, in less developed countries, U.S. direct investment has aided economic growth. In the late 1950s and 1960s, foreign investors have played a significant role in the industrialization of these nations, especially in Latin America. Much of the most modern parts of the industrial sector in Latin America results from U.S. stakes. In Latin America, to repeat, manufacturing now represents the largest area for U.S. investment. In the "traditional" areas of investment, in company towns, where in the 1920s, workers' families lived in one room barracks with outhouses, some (not all) lived in the 1960s in modern private dwellings with internal plumbing. Moreover, important progress has been made to break down the isolation of the company town enclave. By the 1960s, no longer was everything company owned and run. U.S. concerns, in most instances, were actively seeking to divest themselves of "sideline activities" and to encourage autochthonic businesses. Thus, by the 1960s, local merchants traded in company towns; the company store(s) if still in existence might well be run by a local concessionaire. Movie theaters, bus lines, and laundries were in the 1960s often run by private parties, rather than by the U.S. enterprise. In some company towns, religious orders took over (at the company's request) company-built schools and hospitals. One way to eliminate the all-pervasive foreign enterprise was to have workers own their own homes rather than live in company built and owned dwellings.* Some enterprises loaned workers money to build their homes, which were located in communities where independent indigenous merchants, contractors, and doctors resided rather than in an area made up

---

* Company officials believed that there were major advantages in having a worker own his own home, for they argued a man takes better care of his own house than a company house, he develops a sense of private property, and he has a place to live when ready for retirement (with the life span of employees increasing, this became an important consideration).

exclusively of company personnel. Houses were built by private local businesses, not by the U.S. company. Such policies stimulated indigenous small business. The old barriers between the foreign enterprise and the community were lowered.

For decades, U.S.-owned smelters had encouraged local miners (buying and marketing their output), while U.S. owned fruit, rubber, and sugar companies similarly purchased from local growers. Extractive enterprises once imported all their equipment from abroad; in the 1960s, under government pressures, more purchases were made in the host nation (this was far truer in Latin America than in other developing regions); this prompted the emergence of factories to supply the enterprises. The foreign extractive or agricultural company's impact on the host nation likewise included wages paid to and the training of employees. Yet, of greatest importance in bringing the benefits of such giant enterprises to the host nations was the vastly extended ability of host governments to tax the foreign investors, providing revenues for national development programs.

In 1950, economist Hans Singer suggested that "a flow of international investment into the underdeveloped countries will contribute to their economic development only if it is absorbed into their economic system; i.e., if a good deal of complementary domestic investment is generated and the requisite domestic resources are found." This, of course, is also true of the contribution of international investment to the economic growth of industrial countries. U.S. multinational companies in the late 1950s and 1960s came to recognize the importance of this statement and to act on its argument: increasingly, they sought to stimulate this important impact.

In the late 1950s and 1960s, the contribution of U.S. investors to economic growth is what has prompted many industrial and less developed countries to want to attract U.S. direct investments.

Host nations have also feared that direct foreign investors destroy national sovereignty and create dependent relationships. Host countries are concerned about loyalties. Is a multinational corporation responsive first to the U.S. government and then to the host government, first to its parent company and then to the host nation? If the foreign investment is in an important industry or has a preeminent role in the economy, will it be able to exercise *political* power by virtue of its size? Will it be able to circumvent national goals? Can any nation retain true sovereignty if its major industry, its national defense, communications, transport, or banking activities are in foreign hands? Can foreign investors upset a national currency? Foreign investment may make a host nation dependent on outsiders, and the argument goes, for a mature nation, dependence is ipso facto not a desirable condition. To the present writer, these seem legitimate concerns, but they neglect the power of national sovereignty. Nations do have power to pass laws to control the activities of foreign investors. They have the power to make U.S. businessmen conform to national standards—the power to tax, to impose rules, and even to expropriate. Indeed, and in general, host nations have shown remarkable ability to cause foreign investors to act at their bidding. Moreover, direct foreign investment has certain advantages for a national government. Direct foreign investment can be considered free of political strings when compared with the alternative of foreign *government* capital (direct private investors have economic rather than political goals behind their investment). Likewise, economic strength and political sovereignty are linked; foreign investors that aid economic growth contribute a material basis for the enhancement of national sovereignty. In net, foreign investment does provide a challenge to national sovereignty when it reaches a certain size or when it is in a vital industry, but nations do have the power to limit foreign investors—and, in the last resort, to expropriate offenders against the national sovereignty. Japan provides an excellent example of a nation that has protected its national sovereignty, maintained economic independence, and yet has utilized effectively in its spectacular economic growth what it required of the offerings of multinational corporations. Japan provides a case where a little direct investment has served it as well, or perhaps better, than a lot would. It is fear of loss of sovereignty and dependence that has motivated many countries to impose restraints on and in some cases expropriate direct foreign investment.

A third general worry on the part of host nations is that direct foreign investors destroy the nation's culture, imposing alien cultural patterns. There is fear that giant U.S. firms—with capital, technology, and management—create structural imbalances, thereby destroying the national heritage and impairing the development process. Yet economic development, particularly industrialization, wherever it occurs, decimates old cultural patterns. The question is, does the recipient nation want to develop; if so, it must sacrifice many of the existing ways of life. There seems no choice. No nation has developed economically without some crumbling of the cake of custom.[54]

Here again, a weighing of the pros and cons of U.S. investment abroad does not bring us to answers on how vital U.S. direct foreign investment has become in foreign nations. In certain countries, the impact of U.S. business has become phenomenal. In Canada, in 1963, U.S. ownership of manufacturing industries reached 44 per cent and U.S. control 46 per cent. U.S. ownership of mining and smelting operations in the Dominion that year came to 54 per cent, and U.S. control 52 per cent. U.S. ownership of petroleum and natural gas was 54 per cent and U.S. control 62 per cent. There is, moreover, every indication that since 1963 the percentages have risen. These awesome figures are greater than in times past. Moreover, U.S. ownership and control were important in the largest firms in such vital industries as automobiles, chemicals, rubber, electrical equipment, aluminum, nickel, iron ore, and oil; in these Canadian-American industries (iron ore excepted), American leadership had been established before World War II, but in the late 1950s and 1960s control by U.S. business has increased rapidly. Never in history has an industrial nation had so much of its productive capacity in foreign hands. As Canada industrialized, instead of shedding foreign economic domination, the nation has become more dependent.[55]

While the concern about U.S. business in Europe has been pervasive, no European country has been as much affected by U.S. direct investment as Canada. Table XIV.4 gives some indication of the impact of U.S. direct investment on Great Britain in the mid-1960s. British economist John H. Dunning sees the impact as rising and estimates that in 1969, U.S. subsidiaries accounted for about 14 per cent of British production, nearly one-fifth of the fixed capital formation in manufacturing, and a quarter of British exports. He points out that the largest stakes are in such basic industries as oil refining, automobiles, chemicals, and electrical engineering.[56] In practically every industry in which Americans are important, the stakes of some participant companies go back long before the 1950s and 1960s.

On the European continent, the U.S. impact is less significant, except in one important, advanced industry—computers. In 1964, for example, 62 per cent of the new installations in the European computer market were made by one U.S. company—I.B.M.* [57] Table XIV.5 gives some in-

---

* U.S. antitrust law seems to be responsible for I.B.M.'s less important position in Britain. Back in 1908, a predecessor company of I.B.M. granted to a licensee, British Tabulating Machine Company, the exclusive rights to make and to sell tabulating machines in the British Empire (outside of Canada). Clearly, under the post–World War II interpretations of U.S. antitrust law, such exclusive privileges would be subject to

Table XIV.4. Estimated share of total production of British industries accounted for by American-controlled companies, 1966

Percentage	Industries
80 or more	Boot and shoe machinery, canned baby food, carbon black, color film, custard powder and starch, sewing machines, typewriters
60–79	Aluminum semi-manufactures, boilers, breakfast cereals, calculating machines, cigarette lighters, potato chips, razor blades and safety razors, spark plugs
50–59	Automobiles, cake mixes, canned milk, cosmetics and toilet preparations, electric shavers, electric switches, ethical drugs, foundation garments, pens and pencils, pet foods, petroleum refinery construction equipment, tractors, vacuum cleaners
40–49	Computers, locks and keys, photographic equipment, printing and typesetting machinery, rubber tires, soaps and detergents, watches and clocks
30–39	Abrasives, commercial vehicles, elevators and escalators, floor polishers, instant coffee, portable electric tools, refined petroleum products, refrigerators, washing machines
15–29	Greeting cards, industrial instruments, materials handling equipment, mining machinery, paper-back books, petro-chemicals, synthetic fibers, telephone and tele-communications equipment, toilet paper

Source: John H. Dunning, *The Role of American Investment in the British Economy,* PEP Broadsheet 507 (February 1969), p. 178, with minor modifications.

dication of the impact of U.S. stakes in France, West Germany, and Italy. Here, too, in most industries, the investments of some participating companies extend back long before the 1960s.

The U.S. impact in Europe—while larger in dollar terms than ever

---

scrutiny. In 1949, to get out of this agreement, I.B.M. contracted to give British Tabulating Machine Company a nonexclusive license, free of payment, on all existing products and on patents pending. B.T.M. obtained permission to sell worldwide, while I.B.M. could also market in what had been B.T.M.'s exclusive territory. International Computers & Tabulators, Ltd., since 1968 International Computers, successors to B.T.M. in Britain, provided formidable competition to I.B.M. I.B.M. established a new enterprise, IBM United Kingdom Ltd. to build up its own business. I.B.M., *Annual Report 1949;* Engelbourg, "International Business Machines: A Business History," pp. 285–287; *Fortune,* November 1960; *New York Times,* Mar. 14, 1971.

The Contemporary Scene

Table XIV.5. Estimated [1] U.S. share of certain industries in France, West Germany, and Italy, mid-1960s

	Industries		
Percentages	France, 1963 [2]	West Germany [3]	Italy, 1965 [4]
80 or more	Carbon black, razor blades and safety razors, synthetic rubber	Computers	Computers [5]
60 to 79	Accounting machines, computers, electric razors, sewing machines		
50 to 59			Cosmetics
40 to 49	Electronic and statistical machinery,[6] telegraph and telephone equipment	Automobiles	
30 to 39	Elevators, tires, tractors, agricultural machinery	Petroleum	Pharmaceuticals
20 to 29	Machine tools, petroleum refining, refrigerators, washing machines		Soap, petroleum
5 to 19	Automobiles	Electrical-optics-toys,[7] food, machinery-vehicles-metal products [8]	Paper, tires

Source: **Data on France and West Germany adapted from Christopher Layton,** *Trans-Atlantic Investments* **(Boulogne-sur-Seine, France: The Atlantic Institute, 1966), p. 19, with additions on France and all data on Italy from Robert Hellmann,** *The Challenge to U.S. Dominance of the International Corporation* **(New York: Dunellen, 1970), pp. 334, 100.**

[1] Other estimates vary.
[2] Turnover figures.
[3] Percentage of capital of public companies.
[4] Share in capital invested in industry (except where specified otherwise).
[5] Market share according to number of computers installed, 1969.
[6] This includes computers, which were 75 per cent.
[7] This includes computers, which were 84 per cent.
[8] This includes automobiles, which were 40 per cent.

before—is not new. When articles now point to the strength of the U.S. automobile industry in Europe, to Ford Motor Company's second place in the British market and Opel's third place in Germany,* they forget

* Opel in the late 1960s fell behind Daimler-Benz as well as Volkswagen in the German market. See figures for 1965–1968 in Hellmann, *Challenge to U.S. Dominance,*

that for a dozen years before 1924, Ford led in Great Britain, and from 1929 to World War II, the G.M.-built Opel was the bestseller in Germany. When reporters marvel at the prominent position of U.S. oil companies in Europe, they often fail to recollect that since the 1880s, American oil companies have had important direct investments in European distribution and that the role of Standard Oil Company (New Jersey) especially has been consistently substantial. Similarly, in office equipment, sewing machines, electrical supplies, and heating equipment, American industry leaders had a significant place in Europe in the past. This is not to belittle the recent flood of U.S. direct investment in Europe; it is only to point out that much of the investment has been part of a long-term process. What is truly novel is the great invasion of the chemical and electronic (as distinct from electrical) companies.[58] Likewise, the diversity of services offered is unique.

In Australia, as an expert on U.S. stakes there, Donald T. Brash pointed out in 1966, "The motor vehicle industry . . . is not only dominated by American-owned companies, it was to an important extent the *creation* of those companies." American enterprises have a principal role in oil distribution, refining, and exploration. Brash reports "that most Australians would have difficulty naming a breakfast food, a cosmetic, or a toilet article *not* produced by the local subsidiary of some American company." [59] Recently, an economist declared that the 1960s "will be known as the decade [when] Australia stopped riding on sheep back." [60] He referred to mineral exports, which were replacing wool exports; Americans were major participants in this development, whereas they had no investments in sheep or in the wool trade.

By contrast, America's impact on Japan has in recent years been more by example than by direct investors' conquests. While American cars assembled in Japan dominated the relatively small Japanese car market in 1929, when in 1966 Japan became second only to the United States in automobile production, no U.S. firms participated in the triumph. Yet the methods developed by American industry had been effectively incorporated by the Japanese. Likewise, while Americans had considerable direct interests in the fledgling electrical industry in Japan in 1929, their stakes were relatively far smaller in the late 1960s. Yet, here once again U.S. technology, carried to an extent by existing U.S. direct investors (with minority interests), was merged into Japanese practice.

p. 64. These figures are in terms of sales in Deutsche marks; in *units* sold, Opel ranked second after Volkswagen.

The Contemporary Scene

In some less developed countries, the effect of American direct invest-ment has been profound—indeed, far larger than in Europe or Australia. In Saudi Arabia, Libya, Venezuela, Chile, Surinam, and Liberia, for ex-ample, decisions of American oil, copper, iron ore, bauxite, and rubber companies to increase or decrease their investments and their production had substantial impacts on each nation's economic life. Albert Hirschman has written, "the power to interrupt commercial or financial relations with any country, considered as an attribute of national sovereignty, is the root cause of the influence or power position which a country ac-quires in other countries." In Saudi Arabia, Libya, Venezuela, Chile, Sur-inam, and Liberia, private U.S. companies had obtained that power posi-tion.* In all six nations, U.S. direct investment generated in the 1960s substantially more than 50 per cent of the nation's exports. In addition, in Saudi Arabia, oil-based revenues in the mid-1960s amounted to 88 per cent of government revenues; in Libya in mid-decade, they equaled 75 per cent of revenues; in Venezuela, 73 per cent of government revenues. In these three countries, U.S. companies contributed the bulk of these oil revenues. In Venezuela, U.S. mining companies also added to the govern-ment receipts.† U.S. direct investments have planted the seeds of social and economic change in these nations.[61] In Chile, government action in the late 1960s will sharply reduce the future impact of U.S. direct invest-ment.

U.S. investments in agriculture, far smaller in total, have tended to provide less national revenues than oil or mining. Nonetheless, before the events of 1959–1960, Cuba, with the large U.S.-owned sugar properties, would certainly have counted among the countries where U.S. business influence loomed large.‡ Elsewhere, United Fruit, by itself in 1955, contri-

* Perhaps more in theory than in fact, for if they took advantage of their power po-sition, they might well find their investments in jeopardy.

† In 1965, oil revenues from U.S. firms in Bahrain equaled 71 per cent of total reve-nues, but the sum was small (only $12 million in U.S. dollars). Oil revenues in Qatar (1964) equaled 97 per cent of national revenues, or $64 million; in Kuwait (1965–1966), 94 per cent of national revenues, or $609 million; and in Iraq (1964–1965), 53 per cent or $310 million. Copper revenues in mid-decade equaled about two-thirds of Zambia's national revenues. In these countries (Bahrain excepted), U.S. and *other foreign* com-panies shared in these contributions to government income; in none did U.S. com-panies by themselves contribute over 50 per cent of national revenues. Figures on oil companies from Cattan, *Evolution of Oil Concessions*, p. 166, and on Zambia, obtained in Zambia.

‡ But note, whereas in 1934, U.S. business controlled about 70 per cent of Cuba's sugar output, this figure was reduced to 55 per cent in 1940, 47 per cent in 1950, and 37 per cent in 1958. Cubans filled in. Guggenheim, *United States and Cuba*, p. 116,

buted in tax payments the following percentages of government revenues: 15 per cent in Costa Rica, 12 per cent in Panama, 4 per cent in Honduras, 2 per cent in Guatemala, 2 per cent in Ecuador, and .2 per cent in Colombia.[62] In the Dominican republic U.S. sugar interests dominated that small nation's most important export industry.[63]

In Mexico, Brazil, and Argentina, U.S. companies have developed modern manufacturing. Regrettably this author has not been able to locate figures on U.S. percentage ownership of Mexican, Brazilian, or Argentine manufacturing, systematic materials on shares by industry of total output, or per cent of government revenues contributed. Yet, commentators (both favorable to and opposed to the investment) agree that the involvement had become substantial in major industries.[64]

In sum, in certain countries the impact of U.S. stakes is enormous and growing, but there is nothing in the history of American business abroad to indicate the inevitability of a steady rising impact. In nations such as Russia, China, and Cuba, the impact in the past was clearly greater than in 1970.

7

If the sheer quantity of U.S. direct foreign investment in recent years is unique, if the allocation of investment by sectors and regions has changed over time, if market-oriented stakes have risen more rapidly than supply-related investments, if, with exceptions, the impact of U.S. direct investment on foreign nations has mounted in the late 1950s and 1960s, perhaps the most remarkable feature of the American multinational corporation of 1955–1970 was its position vis-à-vis European investors.

In the 1920s, American business had moved into Britain's Canada and Britain's Latin America exceeding British stakes, but total British investments abroad still surpassed total U.S. foreign investment.[65] In the early 1950s, American oil companies triumphed over British-Dutch oil interests in the Middle East. In the years 1955–1970, American investors raised their stakes in former European colonies—achieving superiority, for example, over the Italians in Libya and over the Dutch in Indonesia. But most important, by 1960, the United Kingdom's *total* private investment overseas was $26.4 billion,[66] while the book value of U.S. foreign direct

---

and Grunwald and Musgrove, *Natural Resources in Latin American Development*, pp. 348–349.

investment alone reached $31.8 billion.[67] The Organization of Economic Cooperation and Development found that for 1966, the book value of U.S. direct investments abroad was greater than the book value of direct foreign investments of all the other major free world nations combined.[68] These figures reflect a fantastic change. Not only did U.S. business's technological prowess, management skill, and effective marketing show itself worldwide, but U.S. enterprise had achieved an unprecedented financial superiority.*

This is not to say that the clash between western European and American investors had ceased. In the 1960s, the activities overseas of the French and Italian state oil companies, as well as the large British and British-Dutch oil enterprises, for example, challenged U.S. international oil firms. European manufacturing companies made direct investments in foreign lands.[69] But, and herein lies the crucial difference, it was Europeans who were now confronting Americans, rather than, as in years past, the opposite.

With U.S. investors' entry into Iran in 1954, no important Middle Eastern oil producing country remained without U.S. stakes. While it was not until 1962 that the annual inflow of private overseas investment from the United States and Canada in companies in Australia exceeded that of the United Kingdom ($A143 million v. $A125 million), between 1962 and 1968 the average annual inflow for such investments from the United States and Canada was above that from the United Kingdom.[70] U.S. investors shared in the rise of new investments in independent Asian and African states. In 1970, although many nations still existed where European stakes surpassed those of Americans, the spread and growth of U.S. multinational enterprise was serving to reduce the number of such countries.[71] The American triumph—whether lasting or not—over European investment was indeed dramatic.

* U.S. direct investment far exceeded U.S. portfolio investment abroad. In 1970, total long-term private investment of Americans abroad equaled $104.9 billion, of which $78.1 billion was direct investment. *Survey of Current Business,* October 1972, p. 21.

Six

Epilogue

In recent years a rash of theories about the course, the rationale behind and the nature of direct foreign investment have emerged in the writings of economists. Such theories have to a one acknowledged that portfolio and direct foreign investments cannot be understood using identical theoretical tools. Some of the theorists maintain that, like other international capital movements, direct foreign investment can, however, still be studied by considerations of rates of return in various countries.* Yet, these agree that more is required to understand such investments. In two recent and most useful volumes, Charles P. Kindleberger (with the aid of contributors) has summed up a variety of theories put forth by economists on direct foreign investments.[1] Among them are analyses that seek to explain direct foreign investments in terms of the parent company's financial, industrial, or monopolistic *advantages*—such advantages in different formulations include capital, strength of national currency,[2] management, technology (including patents), know-how, economies of scale, product, marketing expertise, and the like; without an advantage, the theorists argue, no direct investment abroad would be successful. Other theories try to explain direct investment in terms of "the growth of the firm" (in which category Kindleberger places those who argue that direct foreign investment is "stimulated not by profits but markets" † and theorists who see direct foreign investment as a use for surplus funds that a parent firm does not wish to distribute as dividends; other growth-of-the-firm theorists view direct investment abroad in terms of enterprise effi-

* Charles P. Kindleberger endorses this view (see his *American Business Abroad*, p. ii). Most empirical studies find little support for this contention.
† This statement seems to oversimplify such theories; rather these theorists argue that direct foreign investment is stimulated by market prospects; sales, in turn, produce profits.

Epilogue

ciencies). Then, there are those who stress direct foreign investment as essentially a response to host government restraints. These theories do not
in the main exclude one another, and many economists combine elements of all (or most). Generally, however, it is where they put their emphasis that divides them. There are those, for example, who stress the
links between industries that have a high rate of concentration and direct
foreign investment, and those who have reservations about such connections.* There are many who see great importance in the U.S. firm's having a technological advantage.† Some specifically explore the relationship between direct foreign investment and the "product-cycle" (for each
product, they argue, has a life cycle.) ‡ Few (if any) economists are
willing to accept that the availability of surplus funds in and of itself is
the principal reason behind direct foreign investment. Yet, this does not
mean they reject arguments dealing with the growth of the firm. There
has been a vast amount of evidence, from all who have undertaken empirical investigations, of the following foreign investment sequence: U.S. innovation, exposure of goods to foreign customers, foreign demand, U.S.
exports, and then U.S. direct foreign investment—the foreign investment
being made to enter or maintain foreign markets that the U.S. company
believed could not be effectively supplied by exports from the United
States.[3] In many instances, host government policy was responsible for
the inability of enterprises to fill the foreign demands through exports.[4]
"New Left" historians, from another vantage point, have argued that
American business has gone abroad because of overproduction; surpluses
have meant the need to export. These historians have assumed that
American enterprise invested abroad because of surplus capital (markets
at home were lean; there was no sense investing at home; thus, there was
the need for foreign investment).[5] To this author's knowledge, these historians have not taken the long-term figures on U.S. exports and com-

---

* Hymer was the first to make this connection. See his "The International Operations of National Firms," Ph.D. diss., M.I.T., 1960. Yet, Robert Stobaugh, studying
nine products in the petrochemical industry found that as direct foreign investment
increased, so did the number of producers making the products. See his "The Product
Life Cycle, U.S. Exports, and International Investment," DBA diss., Graduate School of
Business Administration, Harvard University, 1965.

† Raymond Vernon and Harry Johnson are among these.

‡ Raymond Vernon and his students have done important work on the product
cycle. See Vernon's "International Investment and International Trade in the Product
Cycle," *Quarterly Journal of Economics* 80:190–207 (May 1966), and his *Sovereignty at
Bay*.

pared them with the U.S. business cycle, nor have they done detailed work on U.S. foreign investments and the business cycle. Apparently, the economists who have dealt with direct foreign investments have likewise not been concerned with the relationship between such stakes and the business cycle. The valuable National Bureau of Economic Research monograph by Ilse Mintz on American exports and the business cycle [6] has to the present author's knowledge been ignored as the connections between U.S. exports and direct foreign investment have been pursued. Ilse Mintz found that "Before World War I, export cycles did not conform in a simple way to business cycles in the United States. Exports rose about as often and as much whether business in general was prosperous or depressed." This she attributed in large part to the fact that *foreign* business cycles were not synchronized with the U.S. business cycle, and thus the demand for U.S. exports varied abroad. Nonetheless, she did discern a pattern: During the business cycles in the United States 1879–1913, U.S. exports increased in the first part of the business expansion, were curtailed or fell in the second part, grew rapidly in the early part of the business contraction and then turned down in the second period. After World War I, she discovered that U.S. exports tended to grow during business expansion and drop during contraction in harmony with the U.S. business cycle. She explained this pattern in the main to the greater post–World War I coincidence between foreign and U.S. business cycles, for she concluded, "the dominant factor behind export changes . . . is foreign demand." [7] While her findings will probably give little comfort to New Left historians, they are, however, suggestive in relation to direct foreign investments. New direct foreign investments appear to rise in times of prosperity in the United States. Likewise, in general, new direct foreign investments appear highly responsive to world economic conditions.

Some theories on direct foreign investment—those emphasizing market and product—have been developed mainly from evidence on stakes by manufacturing corporations in foreign factories and some investments abroad by petroleum companies, correctly judging these to be the most significant direct foreign investments today. Yet, by such selection process, these theories, while cogent for the vast amount they cover, by themselves neglect direct foreign investments in other sectors.

Recently, labor leaders have gained publicity in arguing that U.S. business moves abroad to utilize cheap labor. Clearly, certain foreign investments have been made to take advantage of low-cost labor. When an investment is deemed desirable (either to reach markets or to gain supplies), a company studies costs, including labor costs. On occasion, labor costs have assumed major importance in the decision to invest, in particular in the recent atypical supply-oriented investments in manufacturing on the Mexican border and in Hong Kong, South Korea, and Taiwan. Usually, however, labor costs are but one of many factors considered in the decision-making process and the evidence accumulated by students of decision-making by multinational corporations seems to indicate overwhelmingly that the principal motive behind the great bulk of U.S. stakes abroad is *not* cheap labor.

The present author's research brings her squarely in agreement with those theorists who look at the dynamics of direct foreign investments and view such investments as part of a process—a process developing over time out of the requirements of the innovative business enterprise.[8] Students of direct foreign investment, she believes, have to consider both the growth of the firm and the many diverse external factors (political, economic, and military) that influence its growth. The complexity of today's U.S.-headquartered multinational corporation seems, in general, to mirror the rise of complexity of the U.S. enterprise at home. As this author has pointed out many times herein the expansion abroad cannot be isolated from the growth pattern at home.[9] Alfred D. Chandler, Jr. has documented the evolution in the United States from the single-plant, single-product enterprise to the multidivisional corporation. The expansion outside the United States seems part of the same process.[10] The present author's analysis insists on the evolutionary, cumulative, nature of direct foreign investment.

For some American enterprises the emergence of the multinational corporation began in the 1850s and for others in the 1960s. While there were direct foreign investments by American traders in the colonial period and thereafter, while in the early years of our history as a nation, U.S. investors established businesses abroad in manufacturing, mining, agriculture, banking, transportation, and other public utilities, the evolution of what is today known as the American multinational corporation owes its origins to the decade before the American Civil War.[11] The outline below seems to apply to U.S. international business, whether the company started to develop its foreign activities in the 1850s *or* in the

1960s. The timing in moving through this configuration, the size of each foreign investment, and the specific reasons why a corporation moved from one stage to the next varied greatly *among* U.S. companies— depending on such factors as (1) the company's technological, product, managerial, or marketing advantage; (2) its concern with national versus local or regional markets in the United States; (3) the actions of its customers and competitors; (4) the extent to which its resource requirements could be met at low cost through domestic investment or domestic or foreign purchases. Likewise, there failed to be uniformity in direct foreign investment activities *within* a single company, since the course of the investment depended on a multiplicity of factors, including (1) where the foreign investment was made, (2) the type of investment, (3) when the decisions were made, and (4) who made the decision.* Thus, we are in no way minimizing the vast variety in experience. Yet, we will nonetheless venture to present an overall outline.

But first one more caveat: no inevitability is implied by the growth pattern that the author is about to describe. Companies did fall by the wayside. Some started on the route to becoming multinational, but never arrived, having met with political and commercial losses, expropriation, and even bankruptcy of units abroad. Colt, the first American manufacturer that this author can verify as having had a foreign "branch" factory,† [12] in the late 1960s had no business abroad. Many corporations have not expanded outside the United States. Certain ones have retreated from investment abroad for years, only to reenter such activities under new circumstances and with new fervor. Some retreats have been partial, some quite comprehensive. Yet for every retreat in the history of American international business, there have been compensating advances, if not

---

* Some examples of the variations within a single company may add clarity: (1) A foreign investment by a U.S. manufacturing company in an industrial country *tended* to grow faster than one is a less developed country, because the market in the first country was larger. (2) A foreign investment in manufacturing would generally not be followed by social overhead expenditures, while one in mining would be, since in an urban area (where most manufacturing gravitated) social overhead facilities generally existed; elsewhere they would have to be newly installed. (3) A foreign investment made by a U.S. manufacturing company in Brazil in the first decade of the twentieth century would be apt to be in a sales outlet; one made in the late 1950s would be more apt to be in a manufacturing plant. Brazilian government policies had changed in the interim. (4) A manager with good experiences with foreign investments would be more likely to take risks than one with poor experience.

† In England in the 1850s.

by one company then another, if not in one sector then another. The following is the way the emergence and maturing of multinational enterprise seems to this author to have occurred.*

In the beginning of the growth of the American multinational enterprise, a U.S. company invested abroad with little complexity. In what we will call stage one, its approach was monocentric. The American parent company reached out to sell or to obtain and in doing so felt the necessity or saw the opportunity to cross over domestic boundaries. It might be a trader, making investments in houses in principal foreign centers. The American parent might be a manufacturer that had first exported (with no foreign investments) and then made a negligible investment in sales branches overseas—in direct marketing. It might license a manufacturer abroad and obtain a small interest in the licensee; it might buy the stock or assets of one or several foreign manufacturers to penetrate that alien market. The U.S. parent might be an oil company seeking outlets abroad for U.S. refined oil and investing overseas to market that oil, or, alternatively, it might obtain oil producing properties in another land. The American company might invest in a foreign mining property. It might establish a foreign outpost to buy bananas. Direct foreign investments, in general, began as spokes on a wheel, with the parent company at the hub. At the very start, chief executives in the parent company were generally directly involved in the establishment of the foreign units, the financing of them, and the staffing of them.

Then, in the *growth of each* branch, subsidiary, or affiliate *outside the United States,* its functions might broaden. What triggered each expansion varied, but the growth occurred.† A foreign trading establishment might integrate backward and invest in a sugar plantation. A foreign sales branch might reinvest its profits and build an assembly plant. A foreign unit that had been bottling drugs imported from the United States might start to synthesize the drugs abroad. A subsidiary that had marketed refined oil might construct its own refinery and process imported

* Having studied the history of literally hundreds of U.S. companies with foreign operations, this author finds there are probably fewer than a dozen that do not fit this pattern. Such an exceptional firm would typically start abroad, set up international business *including* American operations, and then transfer its headquarters to the United States; from that point, taking advantage of an established international enterprise the company would grow into multinational business.

† Sometimes, the growth was triggered by enterprise efficiencies, sometimes by host government pressure, sometimes by accidental events (for example, loan defaults), sometimes by a combination of factors.

crude oil. An affiliate that produced oil might erect a plant to refine that oil for its host nation market and possibly for export. A factory abroad for packing might integrate backward into making its own packing materials rather than purchasing them. A subsidiary manufacturing lead piping might buy a lead mine. A copper mining company abroad might integrate forward into refining abroad. A foreign factory acquired to serve one national market might start to sell in several countries. And all the while, as these changes were occurring *abroad,* the American parent company would probably be expanding at home and in the process establishing and acquiring abroad new and distinct units—each one of which would in time have its own history. The added functions taken on by the branches and companies abroad as well as the development of new units radiating from the United States would generally be approved or initiated by parent company executives. By this time, what exists is a growing international business. Within the parent company there would generally emerge an administrative organization to handle foreign operations.*

We now enter stage two. In effect, the initial monocentric relationship has been shattered. To be sure, new and distinct foreign units established, or acquired, by the parent company may and generally will be inaugurated as in stage one, radiating from the parent company. But what characterizes stage two is the presence of foreign units that have developed their own separate histories and their own satellite activities. In stage two, each major foreign unit of the U.S. parent continues to take on larger functions, integrating its operations and introducing new products. It might acquire other firms; it might recruit its own product planning staff; in time, it might come to do its own research; it might make its own *foreign* (third-country) investments. In its growth, the foreign unit might expand out of reinvested profits; it might borrow abroad. Within a single international enterprise, some foreign units developed at one speed, others at a different rate, while others failed and disappeared.†

* Such a structure might be the appointment of an export manager and his staff; it might involve an export company or an international company or division; it might mean the appointment of a man in charge of foreign mining and one in charge of foreign refining. The structure introduced varied by company. My research has indicated that in practically every case where an international division or international company was formed, the parent company *already* had foreign investments of some sort, although there are cases where the formation of the international division was coincident with the program of only expanding exports or of making initial foreign investments.

† By disappeared, we mean was separated from the parent enterprise, that is, went bankrupt, was sold to others, or was expropriated.

Each of those that remains takes on over time a certain autonomy and assumes its own distinct role within a foreign industry. Each operates in an economic and political environment different from its parent corporation. The management of each makes certain decisions on its own, independent of parent company direction. Other decisions, however, must have parent company approval. Still others are made exclusively in the United States. To a certain extent, the expansion abroad is analogous to domestic growth—with the relations between headquarters and field being replicated. Yet, there are profound differences. The first is geographical distance: usually, the foreign operation is farther from the home office than the domestic field office. This distance gives the foreign unit more independence. The second, and more important, is political distance: because the foreign unit is in another country, because of both the structure of and restrictions on international trade and payments, because foreign governments have different laws and regulations, because foreign nations have different languages, customs, and practices, because foreign countries have diverse industrial structures, a subsidiary abroad far more than the field office has to formulate its own unique responses. More rapidly than a domestic field office, as noted, the unit outside the United States integrates vertically and horizontally, and also diversifies.

As each foreign entity comes to possess its separate history, what evolves in stage two to replace the initial monocentric structure is a polycentric industrial relationship,[13] with heterogeneous foreign centers having varied trading, administrative, and corporate relationships with the American parent. At this point, however, the complexity has not yet reached culmination. The planets (so to speak), some with their own moons, still revolve around the parent company sun. A large chart showing lines of trade (for supply and sales), as well as lines for managerial and financial control is still possible.

Meanwhile, at home as the parent company expands geographically (deciding on new entries into foreign markets with existing products) or by diversification (increasing its line of products for the domestic, and subsequently the foreign, market),[14] if efficient, as Alfred D. Chandler, Jr. has shown, it will generally create a new administrative structure. It will frequently come to establish a central office and a multidivisional organization.[15] We have noted that between stages one and two of our model, the company that goes abroad usually develops some kind of an administrative structure to deal with foreign business. In fact, often the international company (becoming in time the international division) is among the earliest divisions established in a multidivisional company.

The third stage in the evolution of the multinational corporation may come rapidly after stage two or may be long delayed. It garbles any chart's attempt to delineate international trade and control lines. The parent company comes to have a number of foreign multifunctional centers, serving overlapping geographical areas with various products. Supply and market lines cross international boundaries in such seemingly chaotic confusion as to defy even colored pencils. Similarly, lines describing financing, personnel placement, and administrative control represent no simple configuration. The complexity of the third stage in the creation of multinational enterprise evolves from two sets of happenings, involving (1) the parent company, and (2) the existing foreign branches, subsidiaries, and affiliates.

First, as the parent company grows, it continues—as in stage one and stage two of our model—to expand abroad, starting new foreign units radiating from the parent company in its traditional products but now often further afield. Since at home it has introduced new products, these can be presented abroad and as foreign demand for them arises new foreign investments often seem wise. Likewise, the parent may require different raw materials from outside the United States. Thus, in stage three, as the parent company has new products and new needs, it accordingly continues its move abroad. The parent grows not only internally, but it may grow through foreign and domestic acquisitions. The by-now large U.S. enterprise is in a position to buy substantial foreign firms, which may already have their own international business. Likewise, such a U.S. corporation in acquiring other *domestic* enterprises may discover that these, too, have foreign operations. Thus, in the cases of both the foreign and domestic mergers, a new monocentric or polycentric *foreign* business structure is introduced. The implications become clear in the question: What is to be the relationship between (1) the established parent company's units abroad (with their ramifications developed through time); (2) the new units initiated abroad, generally covering an ever broader geographical range; (3) the new foreign units, representing new products and new raw material needs of the expanding parent; (4) companies acquired abroad through takeovers and *their* foreign subsidiaries; and (5) the existing foreign subsidiaries and affiliates obtained as a consequence of domestic mergers? In sum, there emerges abroad as an outcome of the

U.S. company's growth at home a new collection of distinct foreign units to be merged or not merged (grouped or not grouped) abroad according to corporate policy. Here, too, of course, there are analogous domestic problems: should each new field unit report back to headquarters, or should established field units assume regional authority to take in new ventures? Should established divisions or field units introduce new products, or should new divisions or field organizations be created? Should a merged company be kept separated or integrated into existing operations? If integrated, how and to what extent? The solutions of international business are not necessarily identical to those in domestic operations. In the United States, with its mass market, after a domestic merger it might make sense to retain separate organizational structures. In India, by contrast, there might be no justification for two administrators to remain totally independent of one another and to report back to different divisions within the parent company.

If the added complexity brought about through domestic growth and diversification is not sufficient, *abroad* in stage three, all the *established* foreign affiliates and subsidiaries through their own continued development contribute a further element of intricacy. For many diverse reasons —among them, increasing profits (by more efficiently using resources), U.S. tariffs or import quotas (obstacles to imports may cause a foreign subsidiary to seek third-country markets), U.S. antitrust policy (forbidding territorial divisions that affect U.S. commerce), competition from a third country (that demands new responses), foreign dollar shortages (for a U.S. company to maintain a market abroad under such circumstances may mean it will have a foreign subsidiary serve the third-country market that it can no longer handle), foreign dollar surpluses (that provide funds for expansion programs), foreign government attitudes (that encourage import substitution and export expansion), regional group policies (a plant in Germany can better serve a sales subsidiary within the common market than the U.S. company), location (it often will be more economical to supply eastern Europe from a British factory than from U.S. exports), and even the aggressiveness of management of the foreign unit— the old polycentric industrial structure (with the parent company as a sun and the subsidiaries as planets with satellite moons) breaks down. Systematically delineated market territories exist no longer. What is substituted is a formidable labyrinth. Over time, certain foreign subsidiaries and affiliates have become full-fledged, fully integrated, multiprocess, multiproduct enterprises, with engineering, product planning, and research staffs, with a continuity of employee, supplier, dealer, consumer, and banking relationships, with their own prominent role in foreign industries, with their own dealings with foreign governments, and with their own third-country investments. Such subsidiaries or affiliates become centers not of limited but of truly international trade. They can and do sell in many countries and purchase from many suppliers, not necessarily in the nation of operations or in the United States; they recruit their unskilled, skilled, and managerial personnel not only in the lands where they do business or in the United States, but in various nations. They raise money for their operations where available, irrespective of sovereignty. Some have foreign stockholders. Often, they manufacture products not made in the United States. Some specialize in particular components that will complement the components manufactured by other foreign subsidiaries or affiliates of the American parent. Some specialize in one facet of production and others in another facet. They engage in trade with other affiliates of the parent firm, often in third countries, as well as with outsiders. The American parent may be to a large extent or even completely excluded from the trading relationship. Moreover, *their* satellite operations also begin to follow the same evolution as they have followed vis-à-vis the American parent. The relatively simple polycentric industrial structure is shattered. Thus is created the conglomerate entangled structure in the present or near future of large American companies that participate in multinational business. Business abroad is no longer confined to several foreign countries, a few products, or one or two major processes but exists in numerous foreign nations and in a range of different products and production processes. Complicated, many-faceted relationships have replaced simple bilateral connections. In the process of moving from stage two to stage three the control of the operations abroad by the parent company may loosen and then retighten as managements change at home and abroad. At home, faced with the problems in stage three, U.S. businesses may again radically revise their administration to cope with and control the new complexity. Such reorganization may mean the U.S. parent will reject the old "isolated" international division and restructure its corporate administration on a worldwide basis related to product, geographical area, a combination of both, or an overlapping "grid" structure.

Most important, into the new situation in stage three is introduced an *element of choice.* As Peter Odell has written, multinational companies can decide "where the productive potential shall be worked to capacity or even extended, or, on the other hand, left partially unused." There is in the multinational corporation a unique element of flexibility.[16] Resources are dispersed. Patterns of production and trade can be altered. Financing and personnel recruitment need not be confined to one or two nations. The complete multinational corporation would probably have to have dividend payments as multinational as resources, trade, financing, and employment. In the sense that an American parent enterprise aspires to have its assets grow worldwide, it is multinational, but in that it wishes to return to the United States as high dividends and royalties as possible, it remains national. On the other hand, certain American parent companies (General Motors in the lead) have tried to sell the parent company's stock on a global basis.[17] The achievement of this on a large scale would end one significant vestige of the national enterprise (the insistence on dividends being returned to one country). But this is still for the future.*

2

Our model indicates three stages in the emergence and maturing of the multinational corporation. It emphasizes the momentum in the growth of branches, subsidiaries, and affiliates abroad that in a sense become enterprises in their own right—despite control exercised from the U.S. home offices (control that tightens and loosens and often retightens in a single company's history).

The model applies equally well to enterprises with the bulk of their foreign stakes in agriculture, public utilities, mining, trade, oil, or manufacturing. Thus, when a predecessor of United Fruit, in the 1870s, went out to trade in order to obtain bananas, it started a sequence that led to the emergence of a multinational corporation. Moving rapidly into stage two, United Fruit Company secured its sources of supply by establishing

---

*Expert on international business Paul Haenni, in conversation with this author, has noted that a survey of boards of directors of American *parent* companies would indicate there is little evidence of multinational boards. This author concedes that if U.S. companies were truly multinational, this should be reflected in the *American* company's board of directors; it is not yet reflected, although here and there recently foreigners have been placed on U.S. boards. Of course, the boards of directors of *foreign* subsidiaries and affiliates of American companies have had foreign representation for many decades.

foreign plantations in many countries and developing multifunctional overseas activities—growing, buying, shipping. Its individual foreign enterprises entered into distinct relations with host governments. When, even before World War I, such units began to sell in Europe as well as in the United States, United Fruit progressed toward stage three of our model. In the 1930s, when United Fruit invested in the Cameroons to sell in France, this was a typical action of a multinational corporation in stage three, able to choose among production sources.

United Fruit was an exceptional multinational agricultural enterprise. With its investments on four continents (North and South America, Europe, and Africa), with its geographical spread that enabled it to cope with weather, disease, commercial and political adversities, it could rearrange its production and purchasing activities as needed. It developed investments in a range of agricultural products, other than bananas. It had its own ships, its own interests in railroads, and its radio system. Yet, by the late 1950s, in part because of American antitrust actions against it and in part because of changing sentiments in the countries where it operated, United Fruit's empire abroad was dwindling. It was perhaps symbolic of the declining role of U.S. direct investments in foreign agriculture when, in the late 1960s, United Fruit lost its independent life and was absorbed into the conglomerate AMK Corporation.* [18]

In public utilities, in 1920 International Telephone and Telegraph Corporation, for example, began investing abroad in utilities, and then in foreign manufacturing (prompted by the need to supply the foreign utilities). In time, the overseas investments of I.T.T. became diverse, and their interrelationships complex. In the late 1920s and 1930s, International Telephone and Telegraph Corporation could properly be called a multinational utility—already in stage three of our model. When, after 1941, because of adversity abroad, I.T.T. began to divest itself of foreign utilities, it kept the foreign manufacturing plants and acquired additional such enterprises. It also invested anew in advanced telecommunication abroad. By 1963 I.T.T. claimed to have more people employed in foreign countries than any other single American corporation.[19] Table XV.1 indicates how its assets were divided by 1965. It was clearly no longer a multinational utility, but rather a multinational manufacturing

* Renamed United Brands Co., June 30, 1970.

Epilogue

Table XV.1. Net assets of International Telephone and
Telegraph Corporation, 1965

| Total net assets | Outside the United States | | Inside the United States | |
	Manufac-turing	Telecommunica-tions and utilities	Manufac-turing	Telecommunica-tions and utilities
$739.6	$306.7	$144.5	$230.2	$58.2

Source: I.T.T., Annual Report 1965.

corporation. I.T.T.'s various subsidiaries and affiliates abroad interacted with one another in true multinational fashion; they meet the criteria of stage three of our model.*

But what then of the multinational utility as such. American & Foreign Power (which reached stage two by the late 1920s) was also by the mid-1960s no longer a multinational utility. On April 30, 1967, the stockholders approved the merger of that company into the parent Electric Bond and Share Company, which on May 9, 1968, changed its name to Ebasco Industries, Inc. It was the end of an epoch.[20] Possibly the Communications Satellite Corporation (COMSAT), incorporated in 1963 and developing worldwide activities in telecommunication, may in time fit the criteria of a multinational utility, but with this exception, the giant, U.S.-controlled multinational utility by the mid-1960s seems to have ceased to exist—forced out of existence by host nation preferences.

As for mining companies, they fit our model, investing, diversifying, and then becoming multinational. Unlike the utilities, multinational corporations in mining do persist today. Anaconda's history abroad offers a superb example. The Anaconda mine in Montana came into production in 1882, after which the U.S. company became a giant exporter of copper. In 1899, the newly organized Amalgamated Copper Company acquired

* Note that in the 1950s and 1960s, I.T.T. sought to add to its *domestic* business, to offset its dependence on business abroad. As Harold S. Geneen, the company's enterprising chief executive, described his firm's expansion strategy, "We did not intend to withdraw from Europe. We intended to grow more rapidly in the United States to overbalance Europe and put them in better proportion [in terms of our earnings]. This is also particularly true of our South American area, which we consider even more risky." (Testimony at Antitrust Subcommittee (#5), Committee of the Judiciary, *Investigation of Conglomerate Corporations* (1969), pt. 3, p. 13.

Anaconda, and in 1900 the United Metals Selling Company was organized, serving the Amalgamated group; it had a house in London to handle U.S. exports. Thus, the first foreign investment was to aid overseas
sales. Amalgamated interests then reached out to invest in a mine in
nearby Mexico (1906). The Mexican mining company operated public
utilities as well as engaging in mining; it also participated in other businesses. It survived the Mexican revolutionary decade. Anaconda (which
in 1915 acquired all Amalgamated's properties) in 1916 invested in mining in Chile, fearing future exhaustion of U.S. supplies and hoping to develop low-cost copper. There, it established company towns (including
roads, power houses, water supply, and so forth) and thus undertook operations other than mining and ore processing. In the decade after World
War I Anaconda moved more directly into marketing in Europe (to sell
U.S. copper); it also acquired added foreign mining properties in copper
and in other metals. It started manufacturing in Canada to meet that
market's demands. By our model, it was going from stage one to stage
two. Then, with the U.S. duty on foreign copper in 1932, Anaconda
began to sell *foreign* copper in Europe. It was proceeding into stage
three. During World War II, with the demand at home for copper, Chilean copper was again directed toward the American market. Since 1941,
America has been a net importer of copper.

Over time, a few of Anaconda's foreign subsidiaries have been abandoned (the 1920s Silesian-American venture in zinc failed). Anaconda,
however, has also expanded. Its foreign units have increased capacity and
integrated their activities. Anaconda's *new* expansion has been in foreign
sales, manufacturing, and mining and processing. In the 1950s and 1960s
Anaconda opened new foreign offices to sell copper, and also zinc, lead,
and other nonferrous metals, as well as additional foreign offices to sell
mill and manufactured products. It started to manufacture in Mexico
and Brazil. In 1962, Anaconda acquired the property of Howe Sound
Company in British Columbia, its first entry into Canadian mining (producing copper, zinc, and pyrite concentrates); eight years later it had
readied for production a new open-pit copper mine in Bathurst, New
Brunswick. By 1966, it had embarked on a bauxite-mining and alumina-
producing venture in Jamaica—a complement to its new domestic expansion in aluminum. In 1968 it discovered high-grade nickel sulphate in
western Australia. Meanwhile, it expanded its existing mining operations
in Mexico and achieved new integration: For the first time in the 1950s,

Anaconda's Mexican copper output was refined there rather than in the United States. It invested giant sums in Chile, until the late 1960s, when, as we have seen, political circumstances were pushing it out of that country. It began in the late 1960s to develop a Peruvian property it had owned for years—an activity that came to an abrupt halt when at the end of 1970 the Peruvian government took over the property.

By the end of 1970, Anaconda had a marketing organization to sell its nonferrous metals with sales offices in London, Frankfurt, Milan, Paris, Buenos Aires, Tokyo, Bombay, and Calcutta. For its mill and manufactured products, it had a separate marketing organization, which included five sales offices in Canada. By that year, it was mining in Chile, Mexico, Canada, Jamaica, and Australia, refining in Chile and Mexico, producing alumina in Jamaica, and manufacturing in Canada, Mexico, and Brazil. It was indeed a multinational, multiprocess, multiproduct enterprise. Other companies in mining likewise fit the pattern of the growth of multinational enterprise; Anaconda's story is but one example. Anaconda's moves abroad were aided by its advantages—advantages in technology, know-how, management, as well as in capital.[21]

As noted, contemporary literature on international business has tended (in our estimate correctly) to concentrate on U.S. manufacturing and petroleum enterprises because of their prominence in multinational activities. Mining firms should not, however, be entirely neglected. Some of the most well-traveled men in international business have been and are in the mining community. Mining companies often lead in multinational employment policies. They buy their machinery and supplies in many countries (not necessarily the United States and only recently in less developed host countries). Throughout the 1960s,* the sales to *third-country* markets of U.S. mining affiliates abroad were greater than either their exports to the United States or their local sales—certainly a sign of the multinational character of the modern mining enterprise.† Likewise, John E. Tilton, studying international trade in certain ores and metals,‡

---

* There are figures available for 1963–1965, 1967–1968. *Survey of Current Business,* October 1970, p. 20.

† In 1968, 35 per cent of the output went to the United States, 43 per cent to third countries, and 22 per cent was sold locally. These statistics include the mining investments made by manufacturing firms as well as the mining stakes of mining companies. Had the former been excluded, third-country sales would have probably even further exceeded the exports to the United States.

‡ His data for 1960–1962 covered aluminum, bauxite, copper, lead, manganese, tin, and zinc.

found that "international ownership ties exert the greatest force shaping trade," again an indication of the significance of multinational enterprise in mining.[22] On the whole, however, most U.S. international mining companies still lack the complexity and the flexibility of oil or manufacturing corporations in stage three of the evolution. Rarely, for example, was a single mining company in the 1960s able to shift effectively from one source of production it owned abroad to another in a different foreign country, for its sources of supply usually have not been interchangeable.* This interchangeability may come, as mining companies continue to enlarge and to diversify geographically their foreign holdings.

Retail traders abroad have also moved through stages one and two of our model. The first U.S. stores abroad generally marketed U.S. goods. Quickly, it was discovered that the stores would have lower costs and better host government relations if they marketed local output. Stores encouraged local suppliers, and sometimes helped finance them.[23] They transferred abroad purchasing and marketing expertise developed in the United States.[24]

3

The major oil companies also fit our model. Examples of a single company's activities are insufficient. Instead, it is appropriate to review briefly the overall pattern, starting with the early days of the American oil industry when many of the Standard Oil companies began to export. These enterprises first sold abroad through independent agents, and then by the 1880s began to establish foreign subsidiaries and branches to market U.S. products beyond the nation's frontiers.† The United States was the world's giant producer and refiner of oil. Firms in the Standard Oil group made some early foreign investments beyond those related to marketing, but such were few and far between. In each foreign country, the marketing branches and subsidiaries began to develop an autonomy. As early as the 1880s, several foreign marketing units had built refineries since tariffs penalized the imported refined products. Some marketing subsidiaries formed to sell in one foreign country came to serve several

---

* For example, when Kennecott in the early 1960s was distressed by high Chilean taxes and did not expand there, Zambian copper output exceeded Chilean production. The paradox was that Kennecott had no investment in Zambia.

† The investment in forward integration was similar to what was occurring at home among domestic refiners, based on marketing needs.

nations. When Standard Oil acquired control of the Canadian company, Imperial Oil (in 1898), it bought a marketing and refining enterprise and also obtained a negligible amount of oil production. By the turn of the century, Standard Oil was prepared to invest in some foreign oil production. Already by 1900, the Standard Oil group had moved from stage one to stage two.

Meanwhile, there had been small U.S. investments in foreign oil production from the 1880s (mainly by individuals and not Standard Oil companies). Because America was the center of the world's petroleum industry, initially U.S. enterprises had no need to invest on any scale in foreign oil resources. The history of American oil companies outside their country is *not* the history of the British or British-Dutch oil companies in foreign lands, because America's resource base was different. Doheny's success in Mexico in 1910 was the first giant step in changing the pattern of investment.* With the identification of a major nearby oil source, American companies flocked to Mexico to take advantage of the opportunity. Some oil companies were still in stage one of our model, going abroad to obtain oil. From 1910 to 1921, U.S. direct investment in Mexican oil soared. Some of this oil was marketed in Mexico, some in the United States, some in Cuba, and some in Europe. Refineries in Mexico built to process imported Pennsylvania crude turned to refine the host nation's oil. American companies to a limited extent used their overseas marketing network to sell the Mexican output.

Before World War I some additional U.S. investments were made in foreign oil, designed *not* for the U.S. market, but for third countries' consumption. (Examples are Jersey Standard's stakes in Peru, Rumania, and the Dutch East Indies; New York Standard's concession in China and its attempts to gain properties in the Near East.) Then, with World War I the situation changed. Fears arose in the United States of oil shortages; during and especially after World War I, U.S. enterprises began to pay more attention to the search for foreign oil.

Whereas their early interest in business abroad had been primarily in seeking foreign *markets* for U.S. oil, by the 1920s and 1930s American oil companies were investing relatively large sums for exploration and production in Latin America, Russia,† the Middle East, the Dutch East In-

---

* Note that Doheny's investigations in Mexico were not to supplement American oil, but because American railroad men in Mexico wanted traffic for their lines.

† Early 1920s only.

dies, and elsewhere. The bonanzas were in Venezuela, and in 1928 Venezuela for the first time surpassed both Russia and Mexico in oil output to become second only to the United States.* While total U.S. foreign investments in oil production rose, it was not until 1939 that they exceeded the value of U.S. direct investments in marketing oil abroad.

Some U.S. oil companies—still in stage one of our model—imported their foreign oil into the United States or sold it to other oil companies for marketing. Certain firms sold their foreign oil to their own affiliates in the United States and abroad. In 1932, with the U.S. tariff on oil imports, U.S. enterprises with oil investments in Venezuela found it unprofitable to export the oil to the United States. U.S.-owned Venezuelan oil began to flow to European markets, and the established marketing channels in Europe (created to market U.S. refined products) were used for this foreign oil. By now, at least one U.S. oil company, Jersey Standard, had moved into stage three and had become truly multinational. There had been introduced into the oil business an element of choice, that is, a company could decide whether to use one foreign productive source or another for a third-country market.

The futile U.S. direct investments in Russia right after World War I and the successful ones in Middle Eastern oil production from the late 1920s were not to supply the U.S. market but to provide an economical source of supply for European and other foreign markets. Likewise, third-country sales were the goal of U.S. investors in the Dutch East Indies. U.S. oilmen were seeking the cheapest sources of supply.

Over time, American oil companies integrated their operations, starting many new foreign marketing networks and refineries, opening up new sources of production, building new pipelines and new tankers. Oil companies made foreign investments in refineries and pipelines in general *after* foreign investments in marketing or in oil production. Refineries were in the consuming and producing countries—while pipeline facilities tended to be concentrated in the producing nations. Some foreign investments failed to survive (in 1927 Spain expropriated the properties of the oil companies there; in 1937 Bolivia expropriated; in 1938 Mexico expropriated). But most did continue—the foreign units developing at different paces, taking on different functions, each expanding.

World War II meant new calls for oil, and during the war and in its

---

* A large part of this output was by Royal Dutch-Shell, not an American company.

aftermath new investments were made in all facets of the international oil business. Again, repeating the pattern, new companies entered—in stage one—making foreign investments, now often first in oil production. When after the 1952 trade agreement between Venezuela and the United States duties on U.S. oil imports were reduced, Venezuelan oil was redirected into American markets. Existing investors changed trade patterns.

After 1953, America shifted from being a net exporter to a net importer of petroleum and petroleum products. During the late 1950s, many American companies sought foreign oil for the first time. A large number of concessions were granted to them in Venezuela in 1956–1957. Most U.S. firms thought in terms of selling their Venezuelan oil on the American market. Then, in 1959, the United States introduced quotas on imports of crude oil and products, and these companies would supply third-country markets, mainly Europe.

Meanwhile, after 1948, the immense European and then the Japanese markets came in the main to be supplied from Middle Eastern oil sources. U.S. oil companies participated both in the development of the Middle Eastern oil and in the marketing and refining of that oil in Europe and Japan. In the late 1950s and 1960s, established U.S. multinational corporations and newcomers alike moved into oil production in what for them were new parts of the world—in Africa especially. In the Middle East, Canada, Indonesia, and elsewhere, U.S. businesses raised their oil output. More oil resources provided new coverage against risks and new flexibility in supply. By the end of the 1950s and in the 1960s, there seemed to be an oversupply of oil; nonetheless the search continued. By 1970, there was a concern lest there be too little oil, again stimulating exploration.

The versatility of U.S. oil companies was demonstrated in the proliferation of new refineries. In the 1960s, U.S. petroleum companies made giant investments in refining, and "market refineries" came to handle far more oil than "resource refineries." Investments in market refineries mounted in industrial countries and extended to less developed ones as well. Oil companies strengthened their distribution organizations. In fact, by the mid-1960s, American companies were spending more on marketing, market refining, and transporting than on producing oil abroad. The concentration on market-oriented investment had also existed from 1860 well into the twentieth century; the oil industry had gone a full circle. *But* the new expenditures, unlike those made in the early years of the oil industry, were mainly for selling American-owned *foreign* crude oil, rather than U.S. domestic refined oil. For many companies these investments represented stage three in the evolution of the multinational corporation.

Not only did U.S. oil companies invest in exploration, production, transportation, refining, and distribution abroad, but they diversified into foreign petrochemical plants. This was new to the 1950s and 1960s. Other diversification abroad involved oil companies in production of liquefied natural gas—gas that once had been flared and wasted. Still other diversification included new stakes in mining.

From the origin of the U.S. oil industry to the present, new companies successively have moved into business abroad. Today, we refer to the five giant American international oil companies (all of which are in stage three of our model). Of the five major companies, Standard Oil of New Jersey and the predecessors of Mobil Oil started their international investments in the 1880s; Texaco began just after the turn of the century; Gulf made its first foreign investments before World War I; while Standard Oil of California only became interested in foreign investments after World War I. In 1929, the "big three" in international investment were Standard Oil of New Jersey—and two European enterprises: Royal Dutch-Shell and Anglo-Persian. By 1939, however, one could talk of the seven large companies (including the five American enterprises). Numerous companies are now in the international oil business but are still referred to as "newcomers" compared with the "seven sisters." A few of the newcomers are in stage one, more in stage two, and a number are well on the route to multinational status.

4

Our model also applies to U.S. manufacturing corporations. American industrial leaders in technology and those with unique products began to invest abroad well before the turn of the century—some as early as the 1850s. After a preliminary use of independent foreign agents, they often established sales outlets abroad.* Some, however, faced with tariffs, patent laws, nationalism, high costs of transportation, and existing or po-

---

* They did so for marketing reasons (including the needs to keep inventories and have warehouses, to display the product, to provide service, and to grant credit). Likewise, with substantial volume, they desired the profits from the sales transaction, which otherwise went to middlemen.

tential competition, moved rapidly into manufacturing abroad to reach certain foreign markets. The first foreign stakes of U.S. manufacturers were generally made as a part of marketing strategy. At the same time, a few, exceptional manufacturers invested abroad to obtain low-cost, reliable sources of raw materials. All these stakes were in stage one—concentric investments.

Each of the foreign units (whether a *sales* outlet, a *factory* to serve foreign customers, or a *supply-related* investment) began to have its own history outside the United States and to develop business at a different pace. (Some did not grow satisfactorily and were sold off by the parent firm; expropriation during the Russian revolution eliminated others). A *sales* outlet (subsidiary or branch) might remain such for years, remitting its profits to its parent firm. Alternatively, it might reinvest some of the profits and try to cover new markets. It might expand, undertaking assembly, mixing, bottling, packaging, or a small amount of fabrication. It might continue to develop abroad for years receiving no financial aid from the parent company, and then the parent might decide that within the particular foreign country manufacturing was desirable because the market was large enough to support a plant and/or often because of trade restrictions. At this point several paths were open: (1) licensing an independent foreign firm to manufacture within the host country, (2) manufacturing through the existing foreign sales unit, or (3) purchasing a foreign manufacturing plant in the same nation. If the first course was taken, the sales subsidiary, or more likely the parent company, might acquire a small interest in the foreign licensee in exchange for the licensing arrangements; later, the U.S. business might purchase all or a greater part of the licensee's stock. If the second procedure was adopted, the foreign subsidiary or affiliate would probably not manufacture all of its parent company's products. It might make one or two, and these it might even modify, or it might produce different products suitable for the host nation market. It might build some but not all the components of the end-product (and import or buy locally the rest). If the third approach was chosen, the new plant might be combined with the existing foreign sales unit or not; it might retain its existing products or not. No matter which of the three alternatives was selected—no matter whether foreign host nation or third-country investors participated—production abroad had begun.

Meanwhile, the parent company's *established stakes in factories abroad* would become over time more integrated and diversified operations. These (along with the transformed sales outlets) would change through time. At first, foreign manufacturing subsidiaries generally had personnel consisting largely of salesmen, accountants, and production executives and depended heavily on the parent firm for technology, engineering, product plans, and added imports. In the course of growth, such subsidiaries often acquired added functions and products to provide better service to the customer, to gain lower costs, or to meet competitive pressures, or because the foreign unit was compelled to integrate and diversify since government decrees, exchange restrictions, and tariffs meant it could no longer import. In time such manufacturing facilities abroad started to assume their own identities as ever more complete enterprises. They came to train their own managerial talent in the host country. They became not simply appendages of the parent firm, but rather integrated and diversified businesses prepared to fill foreign demands. So, too, supply-related investments abroad of parent manufacturers took on their own character and their own histories.

And, all the while, the parent corporation in the act of growing at home might introduce new products, assume new functions, and participate in mergers, and these activities would in turn be reflected in international operations. Annually, also, added U.S. manufacturing firms with something distinctive to offer entered business abroad for the first time.

The process was continuous. In the 1920s, there emerged for the first time a sharp differentiation in the spread of U.S. manufacturing and petroleum firms over American borders. As we have seen, after World War I, petroleum companies became eager to invest in foreign oil. By contrast, in the 1920s, although some U.S. manufacturing companies had and made investments in their raw materials (in rubber, sisal, sugar, tobacco, bauxite, chrome, and manganese, for example), although some invested in supply-oriented manufacturing (paper and pulp mills in particular), such stakes remained far less common than those designed to meet foreign market needs. Whereas oil companies began to make their greatest investments in seeking raw materials in less developed countries, in the 1920s manufacturing enterprises continued to have their most sizable stakes in developed nations, where the market was greatest.

By the end of the 1920s, some U.S. manufacturers participating in international business were still in stage one, with their foreign investments radiating from an American center. Others, generally longer participants in business abroad, were in stage two, with the world divided into territories and foreign manufacturing affiliates to serve these areas. Some companies were approaching or in stage three, already having trade among their major foreign subsidiaries and affiliates (located in different countries), with the parent often excluded partly or totally from that trade.

The 1930s saw the slower growth of U.S. manufacturing units abroad, accompanied by a decline of interest in foreign business by many American parent manufacturing firms. When prices are low, it is frequently cheaper to buy than to own raw materials; thus manufacturers slowed their backward integration. Yet, in this decade, the process of expansion abroad did persist; some U.S. industrials entered anew into foreign manufacturing to serve markets abroad. Trade restrictions pushed certain companies toward stage three.

During the war years and the immediate postwar period, parent manufacturing enterprises felt little enthusiasm for international business. Abroad, however, most established units maintained their own momentum. Some U.S. firms made new entries into world business, while others retreated, in part owing to war losses and expropriations in eastern Europe and communist China.

After World War II, foreign dollar shortages meant that U.S. companies with overseas factories often used them to export to markets lacking dollars, which meant the expansion of the foreign subsidiary. American antitrust judgments indicated that corporations could not neatly divide the world; certain cartel relationships were destroyed. Such factors made some manufacturing enterprises more multinational. In the 1950s, underdeveloped countries demanded industrialization and imposed new restraints on trade and payments. Long-time exporters and companies new to international business alike were forced to invest to hold or to obtain markets. Soon, American manufacturers broadened their vision, looking to many new markets around the world and investing in manufacturing to reach their customers. In the late 1950s and 1960s, U.S. companies turned new attention to stakes in Europe—first to England and then to the continent, to take advantage of the opportunities offered by the common market. If their products were unique, their technology advanced, and their management efficient, they knew they would have an advantage over Europeans. In the 1950s and 1960s the lag between a corporation's eyeing a foreign market and investing in foreign production was far less than in past times; if U.S. companies were to conquer world markets, generally factories abroad were required.

With rare exceptions, most U.S. manufacturing companies in the 1950s and 1960s, as in times past, maintained their principal foreign holdings in market-oriented investments. Some corporations did integrate backward, starting new or adding to their stakes in manganese, chrome, bauxite, and now iron ore. The steel companies were, however, exceptional in their sizable supply-oriented stakes in foreign raw materials (in fact, the supply-related holdings of the steel industry appear to have been larger than their market-oriented production facilities abroad). New to the 1960s were the supply-motivated electronic plants in Hong Kong, Taiwan, South Korea, and Mexico, but these stakes were small compared with the electronic industry's market-related investments. In fact, according to the Department of Commerce, the significant rise in U.S. *imports* of goods *manufactured* by U.S.-owned foreign affiliates in recent years (8 per cent in 1968 compared with 4 per cent of their sales in 1965) was caused not primarily by these interests, but rather by the integration of the U.S. and Canadian automobile industries under the Canadian automotive agreement.[25]

In one sense, U.S. manufacturing corporations are still less multinational than mining or petroleum companies. While exports of foreign manufacturing affiliates to third countries exceeded their exports to the United States, sales by foreign manufacturing affiliates in third countries stood at only 14 per cent of their total sales in the late 1960s.* The bulk of the output of foreign manufacturing affiliates was sold in the nation where it was produced (82 per cent in 1965, 78 per cent in 1968).[26] Yet, if the multinational trade of foreign manufacturing affiliates is still relatively small,† the actual rise in sales of such affiliates has been fantastic. Moreover, while the evidence is still scant, writers are now discussing the overall importance of "within the family trading" by multinational manufacturing corporations and suggest "that multinationals are now playing a vital role in the trading activities of the major nations." [27]

While some U.S. manufacturers are still in stage one of our model, a large number have reached stage two, and some are in stage three. In recent years the speed of moving to stage three has been accelerated. Mergers at home and the rise of conglomerates, the existence abroad of full-fledged manufacturing subsidiaries and affiliates with their own histories and identities, together with political and economic conditions at home and abroad, have added complexity to multinational business. Corporate

* The figure is for 1965, 1967, and 1968.
† Relative to mining companies, for example.

diversification abroad has reflected diversification at home. Just as in the United States, so abroad a corporation adds to investment to keep its existing investments profitable.

It seems legitimate to write of *the history* of the agricultural, public utility, mining, petroleum, and manufacturing company abroad, but the reader should note that these histories overlap; companies in each sector in the past and even more so in the present cross over into other sectors in their foreign investments. Over time, with companies ever more often moving over industry lines, it will be clearly harder to separate parent companies by sectors, and it will be far more important to write of the U.S. multinational corporation as an enterprise that frequently in the process of forward and backward integration and diversification (of the domestic company *and* of its foreign subsidiaries and affiliates) participates in many sectors.

5

In summary, then, the growth of the firm's global operations has historically been an aspect of the development of its business at home. It is erroneous to assume that central direction of international activities— "management of [a common corporate] strategy at a common nerve center based on the flow of common information" is something unique to post–World War II enterprises.[28] Such a description would apply to certain U.S. corporations long before 1914.

In the worldwide expansion of American companies, it has been the innovative and aggressive ones that have moved into foreign investments, corporations that were and are technologically advanced, that had and have distinctive products, that had and have advertising and marketing expertise, and that were and are, in general, prominent at home as well as abroad. In 1901, Britisher Fred A. McKenzie noted that Americans in England dominated practically "every new industry created in the past fifteen years"; [29] in 1929, as this volume has shown, what impressed Europeans about American plants in Europe and the United States was mass production, standardization, and scientific management; in the 1960s, Europeans were remarking that America's superiority was based on technological and managerial advantage. Not only Europeans so commented; worldwide there existed a recognition of American enterprises' expertise in the United States, and also that this expertise was being exported via direct investment. Even those companies that went to seek resources in foreign countries were generally innovative in one manner or another—from introducing a new product, such as bananas, on the American market to handling low grade copper ores in Chile. So, too, U.S. investors in public utilities abroad offered new, efficient business practices.

In a sense the five aspects of the Schumpeterian entrepreneur—the development of new products, new markets, new production methods, new sources of supply, and new forms of organization—seem to have been present in the U.S. entrepreneurial enterprises that expanded over borders. In the process, U.S. corporate leaders have interrupted the continuity of economic practices *abroad* and in a true Schumpeterian sense caused economic development outside their own country. Whether it be from U.S.-owned factories or oil wells, criticism notwithstanding, American production in alien lands has served and is serving to contribute to increases in gross national product in industrialized and industrializing nations in many parts of the world.

It is clearly evident that U.S. firms, as they have spread geographically, have been influenced by numerous events external to their own operations. The experiences of American companies across their national boundaries can never be understood divorced from U.S. economic and political conditions, or from the foreign economic and political context. That the book value of U.S. direct foreign investments in 1914, 1929, and 1970 was in the range of 7 to 8 per cent of the relevant U.S. annual gross national product reveals how close has been the historical correspondence between economic circumstances at home and U.S. direct foreign investments. Many aspects of the domestic political environment have shaped U.S. international business operations.

American foreign policy has touched on the activities of U.S. global enterprises—in both positive and negative fashions. Our research indicates no exact coincidence between U.S. foreign policy and the needs of American multinational corporations. There have been many differences between the policies pursued by U.S. diplomacy and those desired by particular U.S. firms abroad. To a large extent, in the broad, overall sweep of the history of American international business, U.S. diplomatic interventions were frequently not required by U.S. enterprises operating outside the country, and when required were frequently not helpful. Since 1914, U.S. direct investments, for example, have been greater in Canada than in any other nation; yet the number of diplomatic interventions on behalf of U.S. companies there (until very recent times at least) appears to have been few and far between. When American properties were nationalized from Russia to Spain, from Mexico to Cuba, from China to Ceylon, businessmen went to their government for aid, but U.S. diplomacy failed to prevent the loss of assets—although in some but not all of these instances it did aid in obtaining compensation. In other situations, to be sure, U.S. diplomacy has helped companies to retain their properties.

In one respect, there has been a clear coincidence of U.S. business and government policies abroad and that is in the role of each vis-à-vis western European economic and political power. Throughout the history of American international corporate operations, American firms provided a challenge to European capital. In a sense the history of U.S. foreign policy has reflected the rise of America from being colonized by Europeans to becoming the greatest world power and then creating a challenge to western Europe's hegemony in world diplomacy. The growth of the U.S.-based multinational corporation and the growth of U.S. diplomacy to world leadership have occurred in tandem—and were at times mutually supportive. We are not saying here that the dollar has followed the flag, or the flag the dollar, but rather more simply that as U.S. business has succeeded in challenging European superiority in the economic sphere, American diplomacy has at the same time provided such a challenge in the political arena, and at times they have used each other in the quest for supremacy.

Economic conditions abroad have clearly been vital in influencing where U.S. companies have placed market-oriented stakes. Such U.S. enterprises have been most attracted to countries where the living standards are high and the growth potential great. In recent times, economic integration in western Europe has raised gross national products, broadened markets, and provided an excellent environment for U.S. industry to flourish. On the other hand, for investors in sugar, copper, iron ore, or bauxite, the availability of or outlook for resources far more than the standard of living in the host nation has been of crucial importance. Without these basic lures (markets or sources of supply), investment would be absent. Yet, given these attractions, in each case, in the long run far more significant has been the foreign *political* milieu. If favorable —if the host government is sympathetic to private investors (or at least not antagonistic), if the government is able to keep order, and if it acts in a manner to encourage economic development (without jeopardizing the position of U.S. producers)—then the American corporation tends to be and to remain interested in investments. This has been true of both industrial and underdeveloped lands. Nationalism, socialism, and communism have had profound impact on the path taken by U.S. international businesses. It was the burgeoning nationalism in many countries that made certain stakes necessary (stakes in manufacturing). Likewise, it has been the rise of particular political systems in the Soviet Union, mainland China, and Cuba that for years effectively barred U.S. direct investments—market and resource potentials notwithstanding. The American corporation abroad has been wooed, controlled, regulated, and rejected by foreign governments; controls and regulations have affected the amount, the type, and the form of activities U.S. firms have undertaken along with the levels of profits. That governments declare and their nations participate in war has also shaped the course of U.S. multinational enterprise, sometimes resulting in temporary fragmentation of that institution—rarely, however, completely devastating the long-term activities of international business. Since 1914, World War I, the Mexican and Russian revolutions, the Spanish civil war, World War II, the postwar anticolonial revolutions, the Korean war, and the Vietnam war, as well as the Middle Eastern conflicts, have all had impact on American companies abroad. Corporations that cross boundaries have had to make their strategies conform to diverse political and military along with commercial and industrial realities. Over time, the U.S.-controlled multinational corporation has overcome obstacles to become both giant and formidable, but, as in the past, it still must bow to the power of national sovereignties.

I. Manuscript, Record, and Oral History Collections
Includes collections consulted wherein the author obtained unpublished materials or privately printed concession agreements. (Often access to these collections was limited.)

A. *Manuscript and Record Collections in the United States.*
Boston, Mass. Baker Library, Graduate School of Business Administration, Harvard University. Thomas W. Lamont Papers.
Dearborn, Mich. Ford Motor Company Archives. Historical Records.
Detroit, Mich. Ford Motor Company. International Purchasing Records at Highland Park.
Greenville, Wilmington, Dela. Eleutherian Mills Historical Library. Jasper Crane Papers, Accession 1231.
New York. American Radiator and Standard Sanitary Corporation (American-Standard). Records of American Radiator Company, Standard Sanitary Manufacturing Company, American Radiator and Standard Sanitary Corporation, and foreign subsidiaries.
————. American Telephone and Telegraph Company. Records in Secretary's Office.
————. Columbia University Libraries. Department of Special Collections. Frank A. Vanderlip Papers.
————. ————. Graduate School of Business. Marvyn Scudder Financial Record Collection.
————. New York Life Insurance Company Archives. General Historical Records.
————. Otis Elevator Company. Records of International Division.
————. Western Electric Company Archives. General Historical Records.
Washington, D.C. National Archives. Record Group 59 (General Records of the Department of State). Record Group 76 (Records of International and Domestic Claims Commissions). Record Group 84 (Records of the Foreign Service Posts of the Department of State). Record Group 151 (Records of the Bureau of Foreign and Domestic Commerce, Department of Commerce).

B. *Record Collections in Foreign Countries.*
Data from the files of the following companies:
Caracas, Venezuela. Creole Petroleum Corporation.
Cologne, Germany. Ford-Werke A.G.
Cruz Grande, Chile. Bethlehem Chile Iron Ore Company.
Dhahran, Saudi Arabia. Arabian American Oil Company.
Limón, Costa Rica. United Fruit Company.
María Elena, Chile. Anglo-Lautaro Nitrate Corporation.
Monrovia, Liberia. Liberia Mining Company, Ltd.
Monterrey, Mexico. American Smelting and Refining Company.
Ndola, Zambia. Roan Selection Trust.
Oakville, Ontario, Canada. Ford Motor Company of Canada, Ltd.
São Paulo, Brazil. Cia. Auxiliar de Empresas Eletricas Brasileiras.
Tokyo, Japan. Mitsubishi Oil Company.
Windsor, Ontario, Canada. Ford Motor Company of Canada, Ltd.
C. *Oral History Collection.*
New York. Columbia University Libraries. Oral History Collection. Gerard
Swope Reminiscences.

II. Companies

Many corporations made available valuable information, including interviews with prominent executives in the United States and abroad, company histories (some published and some in typescript), background papers (on particular subsidiaries), and published material (prospectuses, annual reports, company and industry journals, newspaper clippings, and brochures). It is unnecessary to list each piece of information and each interview. Certain documents are cited in the notes. Executives of the following corporations (and their subsidiaries or affiliates) in the United States and/or in foreign countries provided the author with information.

Abbott Laboratories
Allied Chemical
Allis-Chalmers
Aluminium Ltd.
American & Foreign Power
American Cyanamid
American Metal Climax
American Radiator and Standard
  Sanitary
American Smelting and Refining
American Telephone and Telegraph
American Trading
Anaconda
Anderson, Clayton
Anglo-Lautaro

Armour
Arabian American Oil
Bahrain Petroleum
Bethlehem Steel
Bristol-Myers
Burroughs
California-Texas Oil
Cerro
Chesebrough-Pond's
Coca-Cola
Colgate-Palmolive
Corn Products
Deere
Du Pont (E.I.) de Nemours
Eastman Kodak

Firestone Tire and Rubber
Ford Motor
General Electric
General Motors
Goodyear Tire & Rubber
Grace (W.R.)
Guggenheim Bros.
Gulf Oil
International Business Machines
International Harvester
International Packers
International Telephone and
    Telegraph
Iraq Petroleum
Johnson and Johnson
Kennecott Copper
Kuwait Oil
Lilly (Eli)
Merck
Mitsui & Co.
Mobil Oil
National Cash Register

New York Life Insurance
Otis Elevator
Pacific Tin
Parke, Davis
Pfizer (Chas.)
Quaker Oats
Radio Corporation of America
Singer
Smith Kline and French
Société Internationale
    Forestière et Minière du
    Congo
Sperry Rand
Standard Oil (N.J.)
Standard-Vacuum Oil
Union Carbide
United Fruit
United Shoe Machinery
U.S. Rubber
Western Electric
Westinghouse Electric

III. **Government Documents (including the League of Nations,
    United Nations, and associated international organizations).**
A. *Argentina* (published in Buenos Aires).
Argentina. Ministro de Agricultura, Yacimientos Petroliferos Fiscales. *Recopila-
ción de Leyes, Decretos, y Resoluciónes sobre Materia Petrolera (1934–1937)*.
1938.
B. *Australia* (all published in Melbourne).
Australia. Committee of Economic Enquiry. *Report*. 1965.
——. Department of Trade. *The Australian Pharmaceutical Products Indus-
try*. 1960.
C. *Canada* (all published in Ottawa).
Canada. Department of Justice. Report of Commissioners, Combines Investiga-
tion Act. *Matches*. 1949.
——. Department of Labour. *Labour Organization in Canada*. 1941.
——. Department of Mines and Technical Surveys. *A Survey of the Iron Ore
Industry in Canada During 1956*. 1957.
——. ——. *A Survey of the Petroleum Industry in Canada During 1956*.
1957.
——. Department of Trade and Commerce, Dominion Bureau of Statistics.
*British and Foreign Capital Invested in Canada and Canadian Capital In-
vested Abroad 1926–1936*. 1937.
——. ——. *Foreign Owned Subsidiaries in Canada*. 1967.

Canada. Department of Trade and Commerce, Bureau of Statistics. *U.S. Direct Investments in Canada.* 1949.

———. House of Commons. *Official Report of Debates.* 1928, 1929.

———. Royal Commission on Canada's Economic Prospects. *Canada-United States Economic Relations,* by Irving Brecher and S. S. Reisman. 1957.

———. ———. *The Canadian Automotive Industry,* by Sun Life Assurance Co. 1956.

———. ———. *The Canadian Chemical Industry,* by John Davis. 1957.

———. ———. *Final Report.* 1957.

———. ———. *Mining and Mineral Processing in Canada,* by John Davis. 1957.

———. Royal Commission on the Automotive Industry. *Report.* 1961.

———. Task Force on the Structure of Canadian Industry. *Foreign Ownership and Structure of Canadian Industry.* 1968. (The Watkins Report).

D. *European Economic Community* (published in Brussels).

European Communities Commission. *L'industrie électronique des pays de la communauté et les investissements américaine.* Industrial series studies, no. 1. 1969.

E. *India* (all published in New Delhi).

India. Indian Investment Centre. *India Welcomes Foreign Investment.* 1965.

———. Ministry of Production. *Establishment of Oil Refineries, Text of Agreement with Oil Companies.* [1953]

F. *Indonesia* (no place of publication given; in English).

Indonesia. *Investment in Indonesia Today.* 1967.

G. *League of Nations and Associated International Agencies.*

International Labour Office. *Intergovernmental Commodity Control Agreements.* Montreal. 1943.

———. *Legislative Series.* Geneva. 1919+.

League of Nations. *Industrialization and Foreign Trade.* New York 1945.

———. *International Cartels,* by D. H. MacGregor. Geneva 1930.

———. *Review of the Economic Aspects of Several International Industry Agreements.* Geneva 1930.

H. *Mexico* (published in Mexico City in English).

Mexico. *Mexico's Oil.* 1940.

———. *The True Facts about the Expropriation of the Oil Companies' Properties in Mexico.* 1940.

I. *Organization for European Economic Cooperation* (published in Paris).

Organization for European Economic Cooperation. *Organization for European Economic Cooperation, History and Structure.* 1953.

———. *Private United States Investment in Europe and Overseas Territories.* 1954.

J. *United Nations and Specialized Agencies.*

International Bank for Reconstruction and Development. *Economic Development of Guatemala.* Washington, D.C. 1951.

International Monetary Fund. *Annual Report on Exchange Restrictions.* Washington, D.C. 1950+.

International Monetary Fund. *International Financial News Survey*. Washington, D.C. 1948+.

——. *International Financial Statistics*. Washington, D.C. 1948+.

——, and International Bank for Reconstruction and Development. *Finance and Development*. Washington, D.C. 1964+.

U.N. Department of Economic Affairs, Fiscal Division. *International Tax Agreements*. Vol. 3. New York 1951.

——. Department of Economic and Social Affairs. *Foreign Capital in Latin America*. New York 1955.

——. ——. Statistical Office. *Statistical Yearbook*. 1949+.

——. Economic Commission for Latin America. *Towards a Dynamic Development Policy for Latin America*, by Raul Prebisch. New York 1963.

K. *United States* (all published in Washington, D.C.).

U.S. Civilian Production Administration, Bureau of Demobilization. *Industrial Mobilization for War*. 1947.

U.S. Commission on Foreign Economic Policy. *Report to the President and the Congress*. 1954. (The Randall Report).

——. *Staff Papers*. 1954.

U.S. Congress. *Antitrust Laws with Amendments. 1890–1959*. Compiled by Gilman G. Udell. 1959.

——. House. *Report of Alien Property Custodian*. 65th Cong., 2d sess. H. Doc. 840. 1918.

——. ——. Committee on Armed Services. *Petroleum for National Defense*. Hearings before Special Committee on Petroleum. 80th Cong., 2d sess. 1948.

——. ——. Committee on Banking and Currency. *Investigation of Financial and Monetary Conditions in the United States*. Hearings before Subcommittee on Banking and Currency. 62d Cong., 2d sess. Vol. 1. 1912.

——. ——. Committee on Foreign Affairs. *Tin Investigation*. Report on H. Res. 404, 73d Cong., 2d sess., and H. Res. 71, 74th Cong., 1st sess. 1935.

——. ——. Committee on Interior and Insular Affairs. *The Defense Minerals Production Program*. Hearings before Subcommittee on Mines and Mining. 82d Cong., 1st sess. 1952.

——. ——. Committee on Interstate and Foreign Commerce. *Preliminary Report on Crude Rubber, Coffee, etc*. Report No. 555. 69th Cong., 1st sess. 1926.

——. ——. Committee on Military Affairs. *Strategic and Critical Raw Materials. Hearings*. 76th Cong., 1st sess. 1939.

——. ——. Committee on the Judiciary. *Investigation of Conglomerate Corporations*. Hearings before the Antitrust Subcommittee (Subcommittee No. 5). 91st Cong., 1st and 2d sess. 1970.

——. ——. Committee on the Judiciary. *Trust Legislation. Hearings*. 63d Cong., 2d sess. Vol. 1. 1914.

——. ——. Committee on Ways and Means. *Private Foreign Investment*. Hearings before the Subcommittee on Foreign Trade Policy. 85th Cong., 2d sess. 1958.

U.S. Congress. Joint Economic Committee. *The Euro-Dollar Market and Its Public Policy Implications.* 91st Cong., 2d sess. 1970.

————. ————. *A Foreign Economic Policy for the 1970's: The Multinational Corporation and International Investments.* Hearings before Subcommittee on Foreign Economic Policy. 91st Cong., 1st sess. 1970.

————. ————. *Foreign Government Restraints on United States Bank Operations Abroad.* 1967.

————. ————. *Private Investment in Latin America.* Hearings before Subcommittee on Inter-American Economic Relationships. 1964.

U.S. Congress. Senate. *American Branch Factories.* 71st Cong., 3d sess. Sen. Doc. 258. 1931.

————. ————. *American Branch Factories.* 73d Cong., 2d sess. Sen. Doc. 120. 1934.

————. ————. *Diplomatic Correspondence with Colombia in Connection with the Treaty of 1914 and Certain Oil Concessions.* 68th Cong., 1st sess. Sen. Doc. 64. 1924.

————. ————. *Diplomatic Protection of American Petroleum Interests in Mesopotamia, Netherlands East Indies and Mexico,* by Henry S. Fraser. 79th Cong., 1st sess. Sen. Doc. 43, 1945.

————. ————. *Mainland China in the World Economy. Report of the Joint Economic Committee.* 90th Cong., 1st sess. Sen. Report 348. 1967.

————. ————. *Oil Concessions in Foreign Countries.* 68th Cong., 1st sess. Sen. Doc. 97. 1924.

————. ————. *Oil Prospecting in Foreign Countries.* 67th Cong., 1st sess. Sen. Doc. 39. 1921.

————. ————. *Restrictions on American Petroleum Prospectors in Certain Foreign Countries.* 66th Cong., 2d sess. Sen. Doc. 272. 1920.

————. ————. Committee on Banking and Currency. *Legislative History of the Export-Import Bank of Washington.* 83d Cong., 2d sess. Sen. Doc. 85. 1954.

————. ————. Committee on Banking and Currency. *Study of Export-Import Bank and World Bank. Hearings.* 83d Cong., 2d sess. 1954.

————. ————. Committee on Finance. *Tariff Act of 1929. Hearings.* 71st Cong., 1st sess. 1929.

————. ————. Committee on Foreign Relations. *Foreign Assistance Act of 1962.* 87th Cong., 2d sess. 1962.

————. ————. Committee on Foreign Relations. *Investigation of Mexican Affairs.* Hearings and Report of Subcommittee on Foreign Relations. 66th Cong., 2d sess. Sen. Doc. 285. 2 vols. 1920 (Fall Committee).

————. ————. Committee on Foreign Relations. *Petroleum Agreement with Great Britain and Northern Ireland. Hearings.* 80th Cong., 1st sess. 1947.

————. ————. Committee on Foreign Relations. *United States-Latin American Relations.* Hearings before Subcommittee on American Republics Affairs. 86th Cong., 2d sess. 1960.

————. ————. Committee on Military Affairs. *Cartels and National Security.*

Report of the Subcommittee on War Mobilization. 78th Cong., 2d sess. 1944.

———. ———. Committee on Military Affairs. *Economic and Political Aspects of International Cartels,* by Corwin Edwards. Subcommittee on War Mobilization, Monograph no. 1. 78th Cong., 2d sess. 1944.

———. ———. Committee on Military Affairs. *Elimination of German Resources for War, Hearings.* 79th Cong., 1st sess. 1945–1946 (Kilgore Committee).

———. ———. Committee on Military Affairs. *Scientific and Technical Mobilization.* Hearings before Subcommittee on War Mobilization. 78th Cong., 1st sess. 1943 (Kilgore Committee).

———. ———. Committee on Patents. *Patents. Hearings.* 77th Cong., 2d sess. Parts 1–7. 1942 (Bone Committee).

———. ———. Committee on the Judiciary. *International Aspects of Antitrust.* Hearings before Subcommittee on Antitrust and Monopoly. 89th Cong., 2d sess. 1966 (Hart Committee).

———. ———. Committee on the Judiciary. *Petroleum, The Antitrust Laws and Government Policies.* Report of Subcommittee on Antitrust and Monopoly. 85th Cong., 1st sess. 1957.

———. ———. Committee on the Judiciary. *A Study of Antitrust Laws.* Hearings before Subcommittee on Antitrust and Monopoly. 84th Cong., 1st sess. Part 4. 1955.

———. ———. Special Committee Investigating Petroleum Resources. *American Petroleum Interests in Foreign Countries. Hearings.* 79th Cong., 1st sess. 1946 (O'Mahoney Committee).

———. ———. Special Committee Investigating the National Defense Program. *Investigation of the National Defense Program. Additional Report, Canol Project.* 78th Cong., 1st sess. Report No. 10, part 14, 1944.

———. ———. Special Committee Investigating the National Defense Program. *Investigation of the National Defense Program. Hearings.* 77th Cong., 1st sess.–79th Cong., 2d sess. 1941–1947 (Truman Committee, 1941–June 1944).

———. ———. Special Committee Investigating the National Defense Program. *Investigation of the National Defense Program. Report.* 77th Cong., 1st and 2d sess., Sen Report 480. 1941–1942.

———. ———. Special Committee Investigating the National Defense Program. *Petroleum Arrangements with Saudi Arabia. Hearings.* 80th Cong., 1st sess. 1948.

U.S. Department of Commerce. Bureau of Foreign and Domestic Commerce. *American Direct Investments in Foreign Countries,* by Paul D. Dickens. Trade Information Bulletin, no. 731. 1930.

———. ———. *American Direct Investments in Foreign Countries—1936,* by Paul D. Dickens. Economic Series, no. 1. 1938.

———. ———. *American Direct Investments in Foreign Countries—1940,* by Robert L. Sammons and Milton Abelson. Economic Series, no. 20. 1942.

———. ———. *Foreign Aid of the United States Government, 1940–1951.* 1952.

U.S. Department of Commerce. Bureau of Foreign and Domestic Commerce. *Foreign Capital Investments in Russian Industries and Commerce,* by Leonard J. Lewery. Miscellaneous Series, no. 124. 1923.

————. ————. *A New Estimate of American Investments Abroad,* by Paul D. Dickens. 1931.

————. ————. *The United States in the World Economy,* by Hal B. Lary. Economic Series, no. 23. 1943.

————. ————. Office of International Trade. *Factors Limiting U.S. Investment Abroad.* Parts 1 and 2, and Summary. 1953–1954.

————. ————. Office of International Trade. *Investment in Colombia.* 1953.

————. Bureau of Foreign Commerce. *Investment in Australia.* 1956.

————. ————. *Investment in Chile.* 1960.

————. ————. *Investment in Federation of Rhodesia and Nyasaland.* 1956.

————. ————. *Investment in India.* 1961.

————. ————. *Investment in Indonesia.* 1956.

————. ————. *Investment in Japan.* 1956.

————. ————. *Investment in Mexico.* 1955.

————. ————. *Investment in the Philippines.* 1955.

————. ————. *Investment in the Union of South Africa.* 1954.

————. ————. *Investment in Turkey.* 1956.

————. Bureau of International Commerce. *The Multinational Corporation.* Studies on U.S. Foreign Investment, Vol. 1. 1972.

————. Bureau of International Programs. *Brazil. Information for United States Businessmen.* 1961.

————. Bureau of the Census. *Historical Statistics.* 1960.

————. Commerce Committee for the Alliance for Progress. *Proposals to Improve the Flow of U.S. Private Investment to Latin America.* 1963.

————. Office of Business Economics. *Direct Private Foreign Investments of the United States—1950.* 1953.

————. ————. *Survey of Current Business.* 1921+.

————. ————. *U.S. Business Investments in Foreign Countries.* 1960.

————. ————. *U.S. Investments in the Latin American Economy.* 1957.

————. Office of Foreign Direct Investments. *Foreign Direct Investment Program.* 1971.

————. ————. *Memoranda for Direct Investors.* 1968+.

————. ————. *Press Releases.* 1968+.

U.S. Department of Commerce and Labor. Bureau of Corporations. *Report of the Commissioner of Corporations on the Petroleum Industry.* Part 3, "Foreign Trade." 1909.

U.S. Department of Interior. Bureau of Mines. *Material Resources—Copper.* 1952.

U.S. Department of State. *Assistance Rendered American Commercial Interests.* Commercial Policy Series, no. 39. 1937.

————. *A Brief History of the Relations Between the United States and Nicaragua 1909–1928.* 1928.

U.S. Department of State. *Compensation for American-Owned Lands Expropriated in Mexico.* 1939.

——. *Foreign Relations of the United States.* 1914+.

——. *List of Contracts of American Nationals with the Chinese Government.* 1925.

——. *Some Aspects of Assistance Rendered by the Department of State and Its Foreign Service to American Business.* Commercial Policy Series, no. 40. 1937.

——. *The United States Balance of Payments Problem.* Commercial Policy Series, no. 123. 1949.

——. Agency for International Development. *Aids to Business (Overseas Investment).* 1966.

——. ——. *An Introduction to the Overseas Private Investment Corporation.* 1970.

——. ——. *Press Releases.* 1961+.

U.S. Department of Treasury. Office of the Secretary. *Census of American-Owned Assets in Foreign Countries.* 1947.

U.S. Export-Import Bank. *Annual Reports.*

——. *Twenty-Fifth Anniversary Review.* 1959.

U.S. Federal Communications Commission. *Investigation of the Telephone Industry in the United States.* 1939.

U.S. Federal Reserve System. *Federal Reserve Bulletin.* 1914+.

U.S. Federal Trade Commission. *Electric Power Industry. Control of Power Companies.* 1927.

——. *Electric Power Industry. Supply of Electrical Equipment and Competitive Conditions.* 1928.

——. *Foreign Ownership in the Petroleum Industry.* 1923.

——. *Report on Cooperation in American Export Trade.* 1916.

——. *Report on International Electric Equipment Cartels.* 1948.

——. *Report on Motor Vehicle Industry.* 1939.

——. *Report on the Agricultural Implement and Machinery Industry.* 1938.

——. *Report on the Copper Industry.* 1947.

——. *Report on the Copper Industry, Summary.* 1947.

——. *Report on the Meat-Packing Industry.* Summary and part 1. 1919.

——. *Webb-Pomerene Associations.* 1967.

——. Staff Report to Senate Select Committee on Small Business. *International Petroleum Cartel.* 1952.

U.S. Foreign Claims Settlement Commission. *Decisions and Annotations.* 1968.

——. *Tenth Semi-annual Report.* 1959.

U.S. Foreign Economic Administration, *Report to Congress on Operations.* 1944.

U.S. General Service Administration. National Archives and Record Service. The National Archives. *Records of United States and Mexican Claims Commission, Preliminary Inventory #136.* 1962.

U.S. General Service Administration. National Archives and Record Service. Office of the Federal Register. *Federal Register*. 1936+.

U.S. Library of Congress. Legislative Reference Service. *Cartels and International Patent Agreements,* by Leisa G. Bronson, Public Affairs Bull. 32. 1944.

———. ———. *Expropriation of American-Owned Property by Foreign Governments in the Twentieth Century*. 88th Cong., 1st sess. 1963.

———. ———. *Problems Raised by the Soviet Oil Offensive*. 87th Cong., 2d sess. 1962.

U.S. Mixed Claims Commission, United States and Germany. *Administrative Decisions and Opinions of a General Nature*. 1933.

———. *Final Report of H. H. Martin*. 1941.

———. *First and Second Reports of Robert C. Morris*. 1923.

———. *First Report of Marshall Morgan*. 1924.

———. *First Report of Robert W. Bonynge*. 1925.

———. *Report of Robert W. Bonynge*. 1934.

U.S. President's Materials Policy Commission. *Resources for Freedom*. 5 vols. 1952 (The Paley Report).

U.S. Securities Exchange Commission. *Survey of American Listed Corporations, Showing Relationship to and Control by Parent*. 1940.

U.S. Special Assistant to the President. *Report to the President on Foreign Economic Policies*. 1950 (Gordon Grey Report).

U.S. Special Mexican Claims Commission. *Report to the Secretary of State*. 1940.

U.S. Tariff Commission. *Mining and Manufacturing Industries in Colombia*. 1949.

———. *Window Glass*. 1929.

U.S. Temporary National Economic Committee. *Investigation of Concentration of Economic Power. Hearings*. Parts 14–17, 20, 25. 1939–1940.

———. *Investigation of Concentration of Economic Power*. Monographs, no. 6, "Export Prices and Export Cartels," 1940, and no. 40, "Regulation of Economic Activity in Foreign Countries," 1941.

IV. Court Cases

General Milk Co., In re. 44 F.T.C. 1355. 1947.

U.S. v. Allied Chemical & Dye Corp. et al., Civil Action No. 14–320 (Southern District New York 1940).

U.S. v. Aluminum Company of America, 20 F. Supp. 13 (Southern District New York 1937).

U.S. v. Aluminum Company of America, Eq. No. 85–73 (Southern District New York 1940). *Brief of the Aluminum Company* and *Brief for the United States*.

U.S. v. Aluminum Company of America, U.S. Circuit Court of Appeals, 1944. *Brief for the United States*.

U.S. v. Aluminum Company of America, 148 F. 2d 416 (2d circuit court 1945).

U.S. v. Aluminum Company of America, 91 F. Supp. 222 (Southern District New York 1950).

U.S. v. Bayer Co. Civil Action No. 15–364 (Southern District New York 1941). CCH Trade Cases, pars. 56, 150–51. 1940–1943.

U.S. v. Chilean Nitrate Sales Corp. et al., Criminal Action No. 106–14 (Southern District New York 1939).

U.S. v. Electric Storage Battery Co., CCH Trade Cases, par. 57, 645. 1947.

U.S. v. Electrical Apparatus Export Association, CCH Trade Cases, par. 57, 546. 1947.

U.S. v. General Electric. Civil Action No. 1364 (District New Jersey 1941).

U.S. v. General Electric Co. 80 F. Supp. 989 (Southern District New York 1948).

U.S. v. General Electric Co., 82 F. Supp. 753 (District New Jersey 1949).

U.S. v. General Electric Co., 115 F. Supp. 835 (District New Jersey 1953).

U.S. v. Gillette Co. Civil Action No. 68-141 (District Massachusetts 1968).

U.S. v. Imperial Chemical Industries, Ltd. 100 F. Supp. 504 (Southern District New York 1951).

U.S. v. Imperial Chemical Industries, Ltd., 105 F. Supp. 215 (Southern District New York 1952).

U.S. v. Merck & Co. Civil Action No. 3159, Final Judgment (District New Jersey 1945).

U.S. v. Minnesota Mining & Manufacturing Co., 92 F. Supp. 947 (District Massachusetts 1950).

U.S. v. National Lead, 63 F. Supp. 513 (Southern District New York 1945), affirmed 332 U.S. 319 (1947).

U.S. v. Jos. Schlitz Brewing Co., 253 F. Supp. 129 (Northern District California), affirmed 385 U.S. 37 (1966).

U.S. v. Standard Oil Co. (N.J.). Civil Action No. 86-27, CCH Trade Regulation Reporter, pars. 66,075, 66,081. 1953.

U.S. v. Timken Roller Bearing Co., 83 F. Supp. 284 (Northern District Ohio 1949), modified and affirmed, 341 U.S. 593 (1951).

U.S. v. United Fruit. Civil Action No. 4560 (Federal District New Orleans 1954).

U.S. v. Watchmakers of Switzerland Information Center, 133 F. Supp. 40 (Southern District New York), reargument refused 134 F. Supp. 710 (Southern District New York) and CCH Trade Cases, par. 70,600, 1963, order modified CCH Trade Cases, par. 71,352, 1965.

V. Foreign Investment and International Business
A. *General*

Aharoni, Yair. *The Foreign Investment Process.* Boston: Division of Research, Graduate School of Business Administration, Harvard University, 1966.

Aitken, Thomas. *A Foreign Policy for American Business.* New York: Harper & Brothers, 1962.

Barlow, Edward R., and Ira T. Wender. *Foreign Investment and Taxation.* Englewood Cliffs, N.J.: Prentice-Hall, 1955.

Bauer, Raymond A.; Ithiel de Sola Pool, and Lewis Anthony Dexter. *American Businessmen and Public Policy.* New York: Atherton Press, 1963.

Behrman, Jack N. *National Interests and Multinational Enterprise, Tensions Among the North Atlantic Countries.* Englewood Cliffs, N.J.: Prentice-Hall, 1970.

———. *Some Patterns in the Rise of the Multinational Enterprise.* Chapel Hill, N.C.: Graduate School of Business, University of North Carolina, 1969.

———. *U.S. International Business and Governments.* New York: McGraw-Hill, 1971.

Blough, Roy. *International Business.* New York: McGraw-Hill, 1966.

Brewster, Kingman. *Antitrust and American Business Abroad.* New York: McGraw-Hill, 1958.

Business International. *Profit Sanctuaries and How They Work.* New York: Business International, 1960.

Clee, Gilbert H. and W. M. Sachtjen. "Organizing a Worldwide Business." *Harvard Business Review* 42 (1964):55–67.

Crosswell, Carol McCormick. *International Business Techniques.* Dobbs Ferry, N.Y.: Oceana Publications, 1963.

Dam, Kenneth W. "Background Paper on Taxation of Foreign Income." Mimeographed. Nov. 12, 1962.

Donner, Frederick G. *The World-Wide Corporation in a Modern Economy.* Address to 8th International Congress of Accountants. N.p. 1962.

Dunn, R. W. *American Foreign Investment.* New York: B. W. Huebsch and the Viking Press, 1926.

Dunning, John H., ed. *The Multinational Enterprise.* New York: Praeger, 1971.

———. *Studies in International Investment.* London: Allen & Unwin, 1970.

Dymsza, William A. *Multinational Business Strategy.* McGraw-Hill Book Co., 1972.

Ebb, Lawrence F. *Regulation and Protection of International Business.* St. Paul, Minn.: Western Publishing Co., 1964.

Eells, Richard. *Global Corporations: The Emerging System of World Economic Power.* New York: Interbook, 1972.

Ewing, John S., and Frank Meissner. *International Business Management.* Belmont, Calif.: Wadsworth Publishing Co., 1964.

Fanning, Leonard M. *Foreign Oil and the Free World.* New York: McGraw-Hill Book Co., 1954.

Fatouros, A. A. *Government Guarantees to Foreign Investors.* New York: Columbia University Press, 1962.

Fayerweather, John. *International Business Management.* New York: McGraw-Hill, 1969.

Feis, Herbert. *Europe, The World's Banker, 1870–1914.* New Haven: Yale University Press, 1930.

Fenn, Dan H., ed. *Management Guide to Overseas Operations.* New York: McGraw-Hill, 1957.

Fouraker, Lawrence E. and John M. Stopford. "Organizational Structure and Multinational Strategy." *Administrative Science Quarterly* 13 (1960):47–64.

Franko, Lawrence. "Strategy Choice and Multinational Corporate Tolerance for Joint-Ventures with Foreign Partners." D.B.A. diss., Graduate School of Business Aministration, Harvard University, 1969. Published as *Joint Venture Survival in Multinational Corporations*. New York: Praeger, 1971.

Friedman, Samy. *Expropriation in International Law*. London: Library of World Affairs, 1953.

Friedmann, Wolfgang G. *The Changing Structure of International Law*. New York: Columbia University Press, 1964.

————, and George Kalmanoff, eds. *Joint International Business Ventures*. New York: Columbia University Press, 1966.

————, and Richard C. Pugh. *Legal Aspects of Foreign Investment*. Boston: Little, Brown, 1958.

Fugate, Wilbur Lindsay. *Foreign Commerce and the Antitrust Laws*. Boston: Little, Brown, 1958.

Gabriel, Peter. *The International Transfer of Corporate Skills: Management Contracts in Less Developed Countries*. Boston: Division of Research, Graduate School of Business Administration, Harvard University, 1967.

Gaston, J. F. *Obstacles to Direct Foreign Investment*. New York: National Industrial Conference Board, 1951.

Hartshorn, J. E. *Oil Companies and Governments: An Account of the International Oil Industry and Its Political Environment*. 2d rev. ed. London: Faber, 1967.

Hellmann, Rainer. *The Challenge to U.S. Dominance of the International Corporation*. New York: Dunellen Publishing Co., 1970.

Hymer, Stephen. "The International Operations of National Firms." Ph.D. diss., Massachusetts Institute of Technology, 1960.

International Management Association. *Case Studies in Foreign Operations*. IMA Special Report No. 1. New York: International Management Association, 1957.

Kindleberger, Charles P. *American Business Abroad*. New Haven: Yale University Press, 1969.

————, ed. *The International Corporation*. Cambridge, Mass.: M.I.T. Press, 1970.

————. *Power and Money*. New York: Basic Books, 1970.

Kolde, Endel J. *International Business Enterprise*. Englewood Cliffs, N.J.: Prentice-Hall, 1968.

Krause, Lawrence B. and Kenneth W. Dam. *Federal Tax Treatment of Foreign Income*. Washington, D.C.: The Brookings Institution, 1964.

Lewis, Cleona. Assisted by Karl T. Schlotterbeck. *America's Stake in International Investments*. Washington, D.C.: The Brookings Institution, 1938.

————. *The United States and Foreign Investment Problems*. Washington, D.C.: The Brookings Institution, 1948.

Martyn, Howe. *International Business*. New York: Free Press, 1964.

————. *Multinational Business Management*. Lexington, Mass: D. C. Heath, 1970.

Meier, Gerald M. *Leading Issues in Development Economics.* Pp. 149–159. New York: Oxford University Press, 1964.

Mikesell, Raymond F., et al. *Foreign Investment in the Petroleum and Mineral Industries.* Baltimore, Md.: Johns Hopkins Press, 1971.

———, ed. *United States and Government Investment Abroad.* Eugene, Ore.: University of Oregon Press, 1962.

National Industrial Conference Board. *Costs and Competition: American Experience Abroad.* New York: National Industrial Conference Board, 1961.

Nurske, Ragnar. *Problems of Capital Formation in Underdeveloped Countries.* 1953 Reprint. New York: Oxford University Press, Galaxy Books, 1967.

———. "International Investment Today in the Light of Nineteenth Century Experience." *Economic Journal* 44 (December 1954):744–758.

Nwogugu, E. J. *The Legal Problems of Foreign Investments in Developing Countries.* Dobbs Ferry, N.Y.: Oceana Publications, 1965.

Oseas, Israel B. "Antitrust Prosecutions of International Business." *Cornell Law Review* 30 (1944):42–65.

Penrose, Edith. "Foreign Investment and the Growth of the Firm." *Economic Journal* 64 (June 1956):220–235.

———. *The Large International Firm in Developing Countries: The International Petroleum Industry.* Cambridge, Mass.: M.I.T. Press, 1968.

Phelps, Clyde William. *Foreign Expansion of American Banks.* New York: Ronald Co., 1927.

Polk, Judd, et al. *U.S. Production Abroad and the Balance of Payments.* New York: National Industrial Conference Board, 1966.

Rawles, Williams P. *The Nationality of Commercial Control of World Minerals.* New York: American Institute of Mining and Metallurgical Engineers, 1933.

Reddaway, William Brian. *Effects of U.K. Direct Investment Overseas. An Interim Report.* London: Cambridge University Press, 1967.

———. *Effects of U.K. Direct Investment Overseas. Final Report.* London: Cambridge University Press, 1968.

Robinson, Harry. *Motivation and Flow of Private Foreign Investment.* Menlo Park: Stanford Research Center, 1961.

Robinson, Richard D. *International Business Policy.* New York: Holt, Rinehart and Winston, 1967.

Rolfe, Sidney E. *The International Corporation.* Paris: International Chamber of Commerce, 1969.

———. *The Multinational Corporation.* New York: Foreign Policy Association, 1970.

———, and Walter Damm, eds. *The Multinational Corporation in the World Economy.* New York: Praeger, 1970.

Royal Institute of International Affairs. *The Problem of Foreign Investment.* London: Royal Institute of International Affairs, 1937.

Rubin, Seymour F. *Private Foreign Investment.* Baltimore: Johns Hopkins Press, 1956.

Salera, Virgil. *Multinational Business*. Boston: Houghton Mifflin, 1969.

Singer, Hans. "Distribution of Gains Between Investing and Borrowing Countries" (1950). Reprinted in Hans Singer, *International Development*, pp. 161–172. New York: McGraw-Hill, 1964.

Skinner, Wickham. *American Industry in Developing Economies: The Management of International Manufacturing*. New York: John Wiley & Sons, 1968.

Southwestern Legal Foundation. *Proceedings of the 1960 Institute on Private Investment Abroad*. Albany, N.Y.: M. Bender, 1960.

Stahl, Everett. "Branch Factories in Foreign Countries." *Harvard Business Review* 8 (1929):96–102.

Staley, Eugene W. *Raw Materials in Peace and War*. New York: Council on Foreign Relations, 1937.

———. *War and the Private Investor*. Garden City, N.Y.: Doubleday, 1935.

Stephenson, Hugh. *The Coming Clash: The Impact of the Multinational Corporation on the Nation State*. London: Weidenfeld & Nicolson, 1972.

Stobaugh, Robert B. "The Product Life Cycle, U.S. Exports, and International Investment." D.B.A. diss., Graduate School of Business Administration, Harvard University, 1968.

Stopford, John M. "Growth and Organizational Change in the Multinational Firm." D.B.A. diss., Graduate School of Business Administration, Harvard University, 1968.

———, and Louis T. Wells. *Managing the Multinational Enterprise*. New York: Basic Books, 1972.

Tanzer, Michael. *The Political Economy of International Oil and the Underdeveloped Countries*. Boston: Beacon Press, 1969.

Tugendhat, Christopher. *The Multinationals*. London: Eyre & Spottiswoode, 1971.

Turner, Louis. *Invisible Empires*. New York: Harcourt Brace Jovanovich, 1970.

University of Chicago. *Fifth Institute on Foreign Investment*. Chicago: Mimeographed, 1928.

Vaupel, James W., and Joan Curhan. *The Making of Multinational Enterprise*. Boston: Division of Research, Graduate School of Business Administration, Harvard University, 1969.

Vernon, Raymond. "Conflict and Resolution Between Foreign Direct Investors and Less Developed Countries." *Public Policy* 17 (1968):333–351.

———. *The Economic and Political Consequences of Multinational Enterprise. An Anthology*. Boston: Division of Research, Graduate School of Business Administration, Harvard University, 1972.

———. "Foreign Enterprises and Developing Nations in the Raw Materials Industries." *American Economic Review* 60 (1970):122–126.

———. "Foreign-Owned Enterprise in the Developing Countries." *Public Policy* 15 (1966):361–380.

———. "International Investment and International Trade in the Product Cycle." *Quarterly Journal of Economics* 80 (1966):190–207.

———. "Long Run Trends in Concession Contracts." *Proceedings of American*

Society of International Law, 61st Meeting, Pp. 81–89. Washington, D.C.: American Society of International Law, 1967.

————. *Manager in the International Economy.* 2d rev. ed. Englewood Cliffs, N.J.: Prentice-Hall, 1972.

————. "Multinational Enterprise and National Sovereignty." *Harvard Business Review* 45 (March-April 1967):156–172.

————. "Saints and Sinners in Foreign Investment." *Harvard Business Review* 41 (May-June, 1963):146–161.

————. *Sovereignty at Bay: The Multinational Spread of U.S. Enterprises.* New York: Basic Books, 1971.

Wells, Louis T., ed. *The Product Life Cycle and International Trade.* Boston: Division of Research, Graduate School of Business Aministration, Harvard University, 1972.

White, Gillian. *Nationalisation of Foreign Property.* London: Stevens & Sons, 1961.

Whitman, Marina von N. *Government Risk-Sharing in Foreign Investment.* Princeton: Princeton University Press, 1965.

Wilkins, Mira. *The Emergence of Multinational Enterprise: American Business Abroad from the Colonial Era to 1914.* Cambridge, Mass.: Harvard University Press, 1970.

————. "The Internationalization of the Corporation: The Case of Oil." In *The Corporation in Australian Society,* ed. K. E. Lindgren et al. Sydney, Australia: Law Book Co., forthcoming.

B. *Canada*

Aitken, Hugh G. J. *American Capital and Canadian Resources.* Cambridge, Mass.: Harvard University Press, 1961.

————. *The American Economic Impact on Canada.* Durham, N.C.: Duke University Press, 1959.

Blythe, C. D., and E. B. Carty, "Non-Resident Ownership of Canadian Industry." *Canadian Journal of Economics and Political Science* 22 (1956):449–460.

Canadian-American Committee. *Policies and Practices of United States Subsidiaries in Canada,* by John Lindeman and Donald Armstrong, Montreal (?): Canadian-American Committee, 1961.

————. *Law and United States Business in Canada,* by Kingman Brewster. Montreal (?): Canadian-American Committee, 1960.

Fayerweather, John. "Canadian Attitudes and Policy on Foreign Investment." *MSU Business Topics* 21 (1973):7–19.

Fisk, Harvey E. "The Flow of Capital: Canada." *The Annals of the American Academy of Political and Social Science* 107 (1923):170–186.

Levitt, Kari. *Silent Surrender: The Multinational Corporation in Canada.* Toronto: Macmillan of Canada, 1970.

Marshall, Herbert; Frank A. Southard, Jr., and Kenneth W. Taylor. *Canadian-American Industry.* New Haven: Yale University Press, 1936.

Moore, Elwood S. *American Influence in Canadian Mining.* Toronto: University of Toronto Press, 1941.

Porter, John. "Concentration of Economic Power." *Canadian Journal of Economics and Political Science* 22(1956):214–220.

Safarian, A. E. *Foreign Ownership of Canadian Industry*. Toronto: McGraw-Hill Co. of Canada, 1966.

Southworth, Constant. "The American-Canadian Newsprint Industry and the Tariff." *Journal of Political Economy* 30 (1922):681–697.

C. *Latin America*

Baerresen, Donald W. *The Border Industrialization Program of Mexico*. Lexington, Mass.: D. C. Heath, 1971.

Behrman, Jack N. *The Role of International Companies in Latin American Integration—Autos and Petrochemicals*. Lexington, Mass.: D. C. Heath, 1972.

Bernstein, Marvin, ed. *Foreign Investment in Latin America*. New York: Knopf, 1966.

Brandenburg, Frank. *The Development of Latin American Private Enterprise*. Washington, D.C.: National Planning Association, 1964.

Council for Latin America. *The Effects of United States and Other Foreign Investment in Latin America*. New York: Council for Latin America, 1970.

Drees, Charles W., ed. *Americans in Argentina*. Buenos Aires, 1922.

Feuerlein, Willy, and Elizabeth Hannan. *Dollars in Latin America*. New York: Council on Foreign Relations, 1941.

Furtado, Celso. *Obstacles to Development in Latin America*. Garden City, N.Y.: Doubleday, 1970.

Gaither, Roscoe B. *Expropriation in Mexico*. New York: W. Morrow, 1940.

Gordon, Lincoln, and Englebert L. Grommers. *United States Manufacturing Investment in Brazil: The Impact of Brazilian Government Policies 1946–1960*. Boston: Division of Research, Graduate School of Business Administration, Harvard University, 1962.

Gordon, Wendell C. *The Expropriation of Foreign-Owned Property in Mexico*. New York: Graduate School of Arts and Science of New York University, 1941.

Kalmanoff, George. "Joint International Business Ventures in Mexico." Mimeographed. New York: Columbia Universiry Library, 1959.

Lau, Stephen F. *The Chilean Response to Foreign Investment*. New York: Praeger, 1972.

Mamalakis, Markos. "The American Copper Companies and the Chilean Government 1920–1967." New Haven: Yale University Economic Growth Paper #37, 1967.

Marsh, Margaret Charlotte. *Bankers in Bolivia*. New York: Vanguard Press, 1928.

McMillan, Claude; Richard P. Gonzales, and Leo G. Erickson. *International Enterprise in a Developing Economy: A Study of U.S. Enterprises in Brazil*. East Lansing, Mich.: Michigan State University Press, 1964.

Meyer, Lorenzo. *Mexico y Estados Unidos en el Conflicto Petrolero (1917–1924)*. Mexico: Colegio de Mexico, 1968.

Mikesell, Raymond. *Foreign Investments in Latin America*. Washington, D.C.: Department of Economic and Social Affairs, Pan American Union, 1955.

Moore, J. R. "The Impact of Foreign Direct Investment on an Underdeveloped Economy: The Venezuelan Case." Ph. D. diss., Cornell University, 1956.

Newman, Philip C. "Joint International Business Ventures in Cuba." Mimeographed. New York: Columbia University Library, 1958.

Pan American Petroleum & Transport Company. *Mexican Petroleum.* New York: Pan American Petroleum & Transport Co., 1922.

Phelps, Dudley Maynard. *Migration of Industry to South America.* New York and London: McGraw-Hill, 1936.

Reynolds, Clark Winton. "Development Problems of an Export Economy, The Case of Chile and Copper." In *Essays on the Chilean Economy,* by Markos Mamalakis and Clark Winton Reynolds. Homewood, Ill.: Richard D. Irwin, Inc., 1965.

Rippy, J. Fred. *British Investment in Latin America 1822–1949.* Minneapolis: University of Minnesota Press, 1959.

———. *The Capitalists and Colombia.* New York: Vanguard Press, 1931.

Rottenberg, Simon. "United States Investment in Mexico." Unpub. Report Prepared for National Chamber Foundation, 1970.

Standard Oil Co. (N.J.). *Diplomatic Protection. Empty Promises. The Fine Art of Squeezing. Present Status of the Mexican Oil 'Expropriations'—1940. The Reply to Mexico.* Pamphlets on the Mexican expropriation of 1938. New York: Standard Oil Co. (N.J.), 1939–1940.

Turlington, Edgar. *Mexico and Her Foreign Creditors.* New York: Columbia University Press, 1930.

Vernon, Raymond, ed. *How Latin America Views the U.S. Investor.* New York: Praeger, 1965.

———, ed. *Public Policy and Private Enterprise in Mexico.* Cambridge, Mass.: Harvard University Press, 1964.

Winkler, Max. *Investments of United States Capital in Latin America.* Boston: World Peace Foundation, 1928.

Wright, Harry. *Foreign Enterprise in Mexico.* Chapel Hill, N.C.: University of North Carolina Press, 1971.

Wurfel, Seymour W. *Foreign Enterprise in Colombia.* Chapel Hill, N.C.: University of North Carolina Press, 1965.

Wythe, George. *Industry in Latin America.* New York: Columbia University Press, 1945.

D. *Europe*

Bertin, Gilles-Y. *L'Investissements des firmes étrangères en France.* Paris: Presses Universitaires de France, 1963.

Bonnefon-Craponne, Jean. *La Pénétration economique et financière des capitaux américaine en Europe.* Paris: Imprimerie "Labor." 1930.

Denny, Ludwell. *America Conquers Britain.* New York: Alfred A. Knopf, 1930.

Dunning, John H. *American Investment in British Manufacturing Industry.* London: Allen & Unwin, 1958.

———. *The Role of American Investment in the British Economy.* London: P. E. P. Broadsheet #507, 1969.

Gervais, J. *La France face aux investissements étrangers*. Paris: Editions de l'Entreprise Moderne, 1963.

Johnstone, Allan W. *United States Direct Investment in France. An Investigation of French Charges*. Cambridge, Mass.: M.I.T. Press, 1965.

Layton, Christopher. *Trans-Atlantic Investments*. Boulogne-sur-Seine. France: Atlantic Institute, 1966.

McCreary, Edward A. *The Americanization of Europe*. Garden City, N.Y.: Doubleday, 1964.

McKenzie, Fred A. *The American Invaders*. London: H. W. Bell, 1901.

McMillan, James, and Bernard Harris. *The American Take-Over of Britain*. New York: Hart Publishing Co., 1968.

Queen, George Sherman. "The United States and the Material Advance of Russia 1881–1906." Ph.D. diss., University of Illinois, 1941.

Servan-Schreiber, J. J. *The American Challenge*. Translated by Ronald Steel. New York: Atheneum, 1968.

Southard, Frank A., Jr. *American Industry in Europe*. Boston: Houghton-Mifflin, 1931.

Stein, Eric and Thomas L. Nicholson, eds. *American Enterprise in the European Common Market*. 2 vols. Ann Arbor: University of Michigan Press, 1960.

Sutton, Anthony C. *Western Technology and Soviet Economic Development 1917 to 1930*. Stanford, Calif.: Hoover Institute, Stanford University, 1968.

Uyterhoeven, Hugo. "Foreign Entry and Joint-Ventures: A Study of Foreign Investment Strategies in the European Chemical Industry." D.B.A. diss., Graduate School of Business Administration, Harvard University, 1963.

Williams, Francis. *The American Invasion*. New York: Crown Publishers, 1962.

E. *Asia* (excluding the Middle East)

Allen, George C., and Donnithorne, Audrey G. *Western Enterprise in Far Eastern Development*. New York: Macmillan, 1954.

———, ———. *Western Enterprise in Indonesia and Malaya*. London: G. Allen & Unwin, 1957.

Ballon, Robert J. *Joint Ventures and Japan*. Rutland, Vt.: Charles E. Tuttle, 1967.

Business International. *Doing Business in the New Indonesia*. New York: Business International, 1968.

Callis, H. G. *Foreign Capital in Southeast Asia*. New York: International Secretariat, Institute of Pacific Relations, 1942.

DeMente, Boyd. *How Business Is Done in Japan*. N.p.: Simpson-Doyle & Co., 1963.

Hou, Chi-ming. *Foreign Investment and Economic Development in China 1840–1937*. Cambridge, Mass.: Harvard University Press, 1965.

Kapoor, Ashok. *International Business Negotiations: A Study in India*. New York: New York University Press, 1970.

Kidron, Michael. *Foreign Investment in India*. London: Oxford University Press, 1965.

Kust, Matthew J. *Foreign Enterprise in India.* Chapel Hill, N.C.: University of North Carolina Press, 1964.

Remer, C. F. *Foreign Investment in China.* New York: The Macmillan Co., 1933.

Tomlinson, James W. C. *The Joint Venture Process in International Business: India and Pakistan.* Cambridge, Mass.: M.I.T. Press, 1970.

F. *Middle East*

Arabian American Oil Company. *ARAMCO Handbook.* Rev. ed. Dhahran: Arabian American Oil Company, 1968.

Cattan, Henry. *The Evolution of Oil Concessions in the Middle East and North Africa.* Dobbs Ferry, N.Y.: Oceana Publications, 1967.

Finnie, David H. *Desert Enterprise.* Cambridge, Mass.: Harvard University Press, 1958.

Hamilton, Charles W. *Americans and Oil in the Middle East.* Houston: Gulf Publishing Co., 1962.

Kuwait Oil Company. *The Story of Kuwait.* Beirut: Kuwait Oil Company, 1963.

Lebkicher, Roy, et al. *ARAMCO Handbook.* The Netherlands: Arabian American Oil Company, 1960.

Lenczowski, George. *Oil and State in the Middle East.* Ithaca: Cornell University Press, 1960.

Longrigg, Stephen Hemsley. *Oil in the Middle East, Its Discovery and Development.* 1st and 3d eds. London: Oxford University Press, 1954, 1968.

Mikdashi, Zuhayr. *A Financial Analysis of Middle Eastern Oil Concessions 1901–1965.* New York: Praeger, 1966.

Mikesell, Raymond F., and Hollis Chenery. *Arabian Oil.* Chapel Hill, N.C.: University of North Carolina Press, 1949.

Philby, H. St. J. B. *Arabian Oil Ventures.* Washington, D.C.: The Middle East Institute, 1964.

Shwadran, Benjamin. *Middle East, Oil, and the Great Powers.* New York: Praeger, 1955.

Stocking, George Ward. *Middle East Oil.* Nashville: Vanderbilt University Press, 1970.

Twitchell, Karl. *Saudi Arabia.* Princeton: Princeton University Press, 1947.

Ward, Thomas E. *Negotiations for Oil Concessions in Bahrain, El Hasa (Saudi Arabia), the Neutral Zone, Qatar, and Kuwait.* New York, privately printed, 1965.

G. *Oceania*

Brash, Donald T. *American Investment in Australian Industry.* Cambridge, Mass.: Harvard University Press, 1966.

H. *Africa*

Bostock, Mark, and Charles Harvey, eds. *Economic Independence and Zambian Copper: A Case Study of Foreign Investment.* New York: Praeger, 1972.

Carey, Jane Perry Clark, and Andrew Galbraith Carey. "Libya." *Political Science Quarterly* 26 (1961):47–68.

Chamber of Commerce of the United States. *Investment Opportunities in*

Belgian, French, and Portuguese Africa. New York: Chamber of Commerce, 1950.

Frankel, S. Herbert. *Capital Investment in Africa*. London: Oxford University Press, 1938.

Pearson, Scott R. *Petroleum and the Nigerian Economy*. Stanford: Stanford University Press, 1970.

Schätzel, L. H. *Petroleum in Nigeria*. Ibadan: Oxford University Press, 1969.

VI. Company Histories and Business Biographies (including studies of particular companies in international business)

Abbott, Lawrence F. *The Story of NYLIC*. New York: New York Life Insurance, 1930.

Ackerman, Carl. *George Eastman*. Boston and New York: Houghton Mifflin, 1930.

Adams, Frederick Upham. *Conquest of the Tropics*. Garden City, N.Y.: Doubleday, Page & Co., 1914 (United Fruit Co.).

Allen, Hugh. *The House of Goodyear*. Cleveland: Corday & Gross Co., 1943.

American & Foreign Power Company, Inc. *The Foreign Power System*. New York: American & Foreign Power Co., 1953 (booklet).

Armstrong, Theodore. *Our Company*. Dayton: National Cash Register Co., 1949.

Babcock, Glenn D. *History of United States Rubber Company*. Bloomington, Ind.: Bureau of Business Research, Graduate School of Business, Indiana University, 1966.

Baruch, Bernard M. *Baruch: My Own Story*. New York: Holt, 1957.

Belden, Thomas Graham, and Marya Robins Belden. *The Lengthening Shadow, The Life of Thomas J. Watson*. Boston: Little, Brown, 1962.

Bernfeld, Seymour S. "A Short History of American Metal Climax, Inc." In *American Metal Climax, Inc. World Atlas*, pp. 1–16. New York: n.p., n.d. [1962].

Bradley, Kenneth. *Copper Venture: The Discovery and Development of Roan Antelope and Mufulira*. London: Mufulira Copper Mines and Roan Antelope Copper Mines, 1952.

Broehl, Wayne. *The International Basic Economy Corporation*. Washington, D.C.: National Planning Association, 1968.

Buley, R. Carlyle. *The Equitable Assurance Society*. New York: Appleton-Century-Crofts, 1959.

———. *The Equitable Assurance Society of the United States 1859–1964*. 2 vols. New York: Appleton-Century-Crofts, 1967.

Burgess, Eugene W., and Frederick H. Harbison. *Casa Grace in Peru*. Washington: National Planning Association, 1954.

Carr, Charles C. *Alcoa, an American Enterprise*. New York: Rinehart, 1952.

Carr, William H. A. *The Du Ponts of Delaware*, New York: Dodd, Mead, 1964.

Chandler, Alfred D., Jr., and Stephen Salsbury. *Pierre S. Du Pont and the Making of the Modern Corporation*. New York: Harper & Row, 1971.

Clark, James. "History of Creole." Unpub. 1958.

Clark, Roscoe Collins. *Threescore Years and Ten: a Narrative of the First Seventy Years of Eli Lilly and Company 1876–1946.* Chicago: The Lakeside Press, R. R. Donnelly & Sons Co., 1946.

Cleland, Robert G. *A History of Phelps Dodge, 1834–1950.* New York: Alfred A. Knopf, 1952.

Clough, Shepard B. *A Century of American Life Insurance: A History of the Mutual Life Insurance Company of New York.* New York: Columbia University Press, 1946.

Cochran, Thomas C. *The Pabst Brewing Company.* New York: New York University Press, 1948.

——, and Reuben E. Reina. *Entrepreneurship in Argentine Culture.* Philadelphia: University of Pennsylvania Press, 1962.

Coon, Horace. *American Tel & Tel; the Story of a Great Monopoly.* New York: Longmans, Green and Co., 1939.

Croly, Herbert. *Willard Straight.* New York: Macmillan Co., 1924.

Crowther, Samuel. *John H. Patterson.* Garden City, N.Y.: Doubleday, Page & Co., 1924.

——. *The Romance and Rise of the American Tropics.* Garden City, N.Y.: Doubleday, Doran & Co., 1929 (United Fruit).

Danielian, N. R. *A. T. & T., the Story of Industrial Conquest.* New York: Vanguard Press, 1939.

Diamond Match Company. *The Diamond Years.* N.p., 1956.

Donner, Frederick. *The Worldwide Industrial Enterprise.* New York: McGraw-Hill, 1967 (General Motors).

Dorian, Max. *The Du Ponts.* Translated by Edward B. Garside. Boston: Little, Brown, 1962.

Dutton, William S. *Du Pont.* New York: Charles Scribner's Sons, 1942.

Emmet, Boris, and John C. Jenck. *Catalogues and Counters: A History of Sears, Roebuck.* Chicago: University of Chicago Press, 1950.

Englebourg, Saul. "International Business Machines. A Business History." Ph.D. dissertation, Columbia University, 1954.

European Gas and Electric Co. *Standard Oil Co. (N.J.) and Oil Production in Hungary by Maort 1931–1948.* New York: European Gas and Electric Co., 1949.

Fetherstonhaugh, R. C. *Charles Fleetford Sise, 1834–1918.* Montreal: Gazette Printing Co. for the Bell Telephone Co. of Canada, 1944.

France, Boyd. *IBM in France.* Washington, D.C.: National Planning Association, 1961.

Fritsch, William R. *Progress and Profits, The Sears, Roebuck Story in Peru.* Washington, D.C.: Action Committee for International Development, 1962.

Garwood, Ellen Clayton. *Will Clayton.* Austin: University of Texas Press, 1958.

Gauld, Charles Anderson. *The Last Titan: Percival Farquhar, American Entrepreneur in Latin America.* Stanford: University Press, 1964.

Geiger, Theodore. *The General Electric Company in Brazil.* Washington, D.C.: National Planning Association, 1961.

Getty, J. Paul. *My Life and Fortunes.* New York: Duell, Sloan and Pearce, 1963.

Gibb, George Sweet, and Evelyn H. Knowlton. *The Resurgent Years, 1911–1927.* New York: Harper, 1956.

Giddens, Paul H. *Standard Oil Company (Indiana).* New York: Appleton-Century-Crofts, 1955.

Goodyear Tire & Rubber Company. *The Story of the Tire.* Akron: Goodyear Tire & Rubber Company, 1955 (booklet).

Grace, J. Peter. *W. R. Grace and the Enterprises He Created.* New York: Newcomen Society in North America, 1953.

Gras, N. S. B., and Henrietta Larson. *Casebook in American Business History.* New York: F. S. Crofts & Co., 1939.

Gregory, Theodore. *Ernest Oppenheimer.* Cape Town: Oxford University Press, 1962.

Gulbenkian, Nubar. *Portrait in Oil.* New York: Simon and Schuster, 1965.

Hammond, John Winthrop. *Men and Volts: The Story of General Electric.* Philadelphia: J. B. Lippincott, 1941.

Hardin, Shields T. *The Colgate Story.* New York: Vantage Press, 1959.

Harrington, Fred. *God, Mammon, and the Japanese.* Madison: University of Wisconsin Press, 1944.

Harvard University, Graduate School of Business Administration. "General Electric Company." Case no. BH 81R1. Mimeographed. Boston: Graduate School of Business Administration, Harvard University, 1950.

————, ————. "United Fruit Company." Case no. ICH 150. Mimeographed. Boston: Graduate School of Business Administration, Harvard University, n.d.

Hatch, Alden. *American Express.* Garden City, N.Y.: Doubleday, 1950.

Hidy, Ralph W., and Muriel E. Hidy. *Pioneering in Big Business.* New York: Harper, 1955.

Higgins, Benjamin, et al. *Stanvac in Indonesia.* Washington, D.C.: National Planning Association, 1957.

Hiriart, Luis. *Braden: Historia de Una Mina.* Santiago, Chile: Editorial Andes, 1964.

Huck, Virginia. *Brand of the Tartan: The 3M Story.* New York: Appleton-Century-Crofts, 1955.

International Harvester Co. *A Century of Progress 1831–1933.* N.p., n.d.

Jaffrey, Robert, ed. *1825–1925, A Centennial Review of the Business Founded by Augustus Hemenway of Boston in 1825 and Now Conducted by Wessel, Duval & Co.* New York: privately printed, 1925.

James, Marquis. *The Texaco Story: The First Fifty Years 1902–1952.* New York (?): Texas Co., 1953.

Johnson, Arthur M. *Winthrop W. Aldrich.* Boston: Division of Research, Graduate School of Business Administration, Harvard University, 1968.

Josephson, Matthew. *Empire of the Air, Juan Trippe and the Struggle for World Airways*. New York: Harcourt, Brace, 1944.

———. *Sidney Hillman*. Garden City, N.Y.: Doubleday, 1952.

Kahn, E. J. *The Big Drink: The Story of Coca-Cola*. New York: Random House, 1960.

Kannappan, Subbiah, and Eugene W. Burgess. *Aluminium Limited in India*. Washington, D.C.: National Planning Association, 1961.

Kepner, Charles David, Jr., and Jay Henry Soothill. *The Banana Empire*. New York: Vanguard, 1935 (United Fruit).

———. *Social Aspects of the Banana Industry*. New York: Columbia University Press, 1936 (mainly United Fruit).

Larson, Henrietta, Evelyn Knowlton, and Charles S. Popple. *New Horizons*. New York: Harper & Row, 1971.

Lief, Alfred. *The Firestone Story*. New York: Whittlesay House, 1951.

———. *It Floats: The Story of Procter and Gamble*. New York: Rinehart, 1958.

Litchfield, P. W. *Industrial Voyage*. Garden City, N.Y.: Doubleday, 1954.

Lomask, Milton, *Seed Money: The Guggenheim Story*. New York: Farrar, Straus, 1964.

Longhurst, Henry. *Adventures in Oil: The Story of British Petroleum*. London: Sidgwick and Jackson, 1959.

Loth, D. G. *Swope of G.E.; The Story of Gerard Swope and General Electric in American Business*. New York: Simon and Schuster, 1958.

Manchester, Herbert. *Diamond Match Co., A Century of Service and Progress 1835–1935*. New York: Diamond Match Co., 1935.

Marcossen, Isaac F. *Anaconda*. New York: Dodd, Mead, 1957.

———. *Metal Magic: The Story of American Smelting and Refining Company*. New York: Farrar, Straus, 1949.

———. *Wherever Men Trade: The Romance of the Cash Register*. New York: Dodd, Mead, 1945.

Marshall, James L. *Elbridge A. Stuart: Founder of Carnation Co.* Los Angeles: Carnation Co., 1949.

May, Stacy, and Galo Plaza. *The United Fruit Company in Latin America*. Washington, D.C.: National Planning Association, 1958.

McCaffrey, E. D. *Henry J. Heinz*. New York: B. Orr Press, 1923.

Mitchell, Sidney Alexander. *S. Z. Mitchell and the Electrical Industry*. New York: Farrar, Straus & Cudahy, 1960.

Nevins, Allan, and Frank Ernest Hill *Ford*. 3 vols. New York: Scribner, 1954–1963.

———. *Study in Power, John D. Rockefeller*. 2 vols. New York: Scribner, 1953.

New York Stock Exchange Listing Statements. New York: F. E. Fitch, Inc., 1914+.

O'Connor, Harvey. *The Guggenheims*. New York: Covici, Friede, 1937.

O'Higgins, Patrick. *Madame*. New York: Viking Press, 1971 (Helene Rubinstein).

Paine, Albert Bigelow. *In One Man's Life: Being Chapters from the Personal and Business Careers of Theodore N. Vail.* New York: Harper & Brothers, 1921.

Pollan, A. A. *The United Fruit Company and Middle America.* New York, 1944 (pamphlet).

"Pond's Chronology." Typescript, n.p., n.d. [1956 or later].

Popple, Charles Sterling. *Standard Oil Company (New Jersey) in World War II.* New York: Standard Oil Company (New Jersey), 1952.

Potter, Stephen. *The Magic Number.* London: Rinehart, 1959 (Heinz).

Pound, Arthur. *The Turning Wheel: The Story of General Motors Through Twenty-Five Years.* Garden City, N.Y.: Doubleday, Doran, 1934.

Price-Hughes, H. A., comp. *B.T.H. Reminiscences, Sixty-Years of Progress.* London: British Thomson-Houston Co., 1946.

Prout, Henry G. *A Life of George Westinghouse.* New York: Scribner, 1921.

Pyle, Joseph Gilpin. *The Life of James J. Hill.* 2 vols. Garden, N.Y.: Doubleday, Page & Co., 1917.

Reader, W. J. *Imperial Chemical Industries: A History.* Vol. 1. London: Oxford University Press, 1970.

Rodgers, William. *Think: A Biography of the Watsons and IBM.* New York: Stein & Day, 1969.

Rondot, Jean. *La Compagnie Française des Pétroles.* Paris: Plon, 1962.

Scheiber, Harry. "World War I as an Entrepreneurial Opportunity: Willard Straight and the American International Corporation." *Political Science Quarterly* 84 (1969):486–511.

Sims, William Lee, II. *"150 Years . . . The Future! Colgate-Palmolive.* New York: Newcomen Society in North America, 1956.

Sloan, Alfred P. *My Years with General Motors.* Garden City, N.Y.: Doubleday, 1964.

Stehman, J. Warren. *The Financial History of the American Telephone and Telegraph Company.* Boston and New York: Houghton Mifflin Co., 1925.

Swanberg, W. A. *Citizen Hearst.* New York: Scribner, 1961.

Taylor, Wayne Chatfield. *Firestone in Liberia.* Washington, D.C.: National Planning Association, 1956.

———, and John Lindeman. *Creole Petroleum Corporation in Venezuela.* Washington, D.C.: National Planning Association, 1955.

Thompson, Craig. *Since Spindletop; A Human Story of Gulf's First Half Century.* Pittsburgh: Gulf Oil, 1951.

Thompson, John F., and Norman Beasley. *For the Years to Come: A Story of International Nickel.* New York: Putman, 1960.

Thornton, Harrison John. *The History of the Quaker Oats Company.* Chicago: University of Chicago Press, 1933.

Toshiba. *History.* Tokyo 1964 (in Japanese).

Union Carbide Corporation. *Benefit of Union Carbide's International Investment to the United States Economy.* New York: Union Carbide, 1972.

Vernon, Raymond, et al., comps. Research Reports on Business Abroad. Prepared for Multinational Business Project. Dittoed. Boston: Harvard Graduate School of Business Administration, 1965+.

Watson, Thos. J. Men—Minutes—Money. New York: International Business Machines Corporation, 1934.

Western Electric Co. The Western Electric Company and Its Place in the Bell System. New York: Western Electric Co., 1938.

Whyte, Adam Gowans. Forty Years of Electrical Progress: The Story of G.E.C. London: E. Benn, 1930.

Wiegman, Carl. Trees to News: A Chronicle of the Ontario Paper Company's Origin and Development. Toronto: McClelland & Stewart, 1953.

Wilkins, Mira, and Frank Ernest Hill. American Business Abroad: Ford on Six Continents. Detroit: Wayne State University Press, 1964.

———. "An American Enterprise Abroad: American Radiator Company in Europe 1895–1914." Business History Review 43 (1969):326–346.

Williams, Gattenby [pseud. for William Guggenheim]. William Guggenheim. New York: Lone Voice Publishing Co., 1934.

Wilson, Charles. The History of the Unilever. 3 vols. New York: Praeger, 1969.

Wilson, Charles Morrow. Empire in Green and Gold. New York: Holt, 1947.

Winkler, John K. Five and Ten: The Fabulous Life of F. K. Woolworth. New York: R. M. McBride & Co., 1940.

———. Tobacco Tycoon: The Story of James Buchanan Duke. New York: Random House, 1942.

Wood, Richardson, and Virginia Keyser. Sears Roebuck de Mexico, S.A. Washington, D.C.: National Planning Association, 1953.

Young, Desmond. Member for Mexico. A Biography of Weetman Pearson, First Viscount Cowdray. London: Cassell, 1966.

Young, Sidney. "Cananea Consolidated History." Cananea, Sonora, Mexico, 1920. Typescript. New York: Anaconda Co.

VII. Commerce and Industry

Adams, Walter, and Joel B. Dirlam. "Big Steel, Invention, and Innovation." Quarterly Journal of Economics 80 (1966):167–189.

———, ed. The Structure of American Industry. New York: Macmillan, 1950.

Adelman, M. A. The World Petroleum Market. Baltimore, Md.: Johns Hopkins Press, 1972.

Aikman, C. Howard. National Problems of Canada. The Automobile Industry in Canada. Toronto: Macmillan Co. of Canada, 1926.

Aliaga Ibar, Ignacio. La Economía de Chile y la Industria del Cobre. Santiago, Chile, 1946.

American Bar Association. Antitrust Developments 1955–1968. Chicago: American Bar Association, 1968.

Ashworth, William. A Short History of the International Economy, 1850–1950. London: Longmans, 1952.

Baer, Werner. *The Development of the Brazilian Steel Industry.* Nashville: Vanderbilt University Press, 1969.

———. *Industrialization and Economic Development in Brazil.* Homewood, Ill.: Irwin, 1965.

Bain, Harry Foster, and Thomas Thornton Read. *Ores and Industry in South America.* New York: Harper & Brothers, 1934.

———. *Ores and Industry in the Far East.* Rev. and enl. ed. New York: Council on Foreign Relations, 1933.

Bain, Joe S. *International Differences in Industrial Structure.* New Haven: Yale University Press, 1966.

Baptista, Federico G. *Historía de la Industria Petrolera en Venezuela.* Caracas: Creole Petroleum Corporation, 1961 (pamphlet).

Baranson, Jack. *Automotive Industries in Developing Countries.* Baltimore, Md.: Johns Hopkins Press, 1969.

Barber, Richard. *The American Corporation.* New York: Dutton, 1970.

Benoit, Emile. *Europe at Sixes and Sevens.* New York: Columbia University Press, 1961.

Berenson, Conrad, ed. *The Chemical Industry.* New York: Interscience Publishers, 1963.

Berge, Wendell. *Cartels: Challenge to a Free World.* Washington, D.C.: Public Affairs Press, 1944.

Berle, Adolf A., and Gardiner C. Means. *The Modern Corporation and Private Property.* Rev. ed. New York: Harcourt, Brace & World, 1968.

Bernstein, Marvin D. "The History and Economic Organization of the Mexican Mining Industry, 1890–1940." Ph.D. diss., University of Texas, 1951.

———. *The Mexican Mining Industry, 1890–1950.* Albany: State University of New York, 1965.

Berthold, Victor H. *History of the Telephone and Telegraph in Brazil 1851–1921.* New York: no publisher listed, 1922.

Betancourt, Rómulo. *Venezuela: Política y Petróleo.* Mexico: Fondo de Culture Económica, 1956.

Blainey, Geoffrey. *Mines in the Spinifex.* Sydney, Australia: Angus and Robertson, 1960.

Bonini, William, et al. *The Role of National Governments in Exploration for Mineral Resources.* Ocean City, N.J.: Littoral Press, 1964.

Bright, Arthur A. *The Electric Lamp Industry.* New York: Macmillan Co., 1949.

British Electrical and Allied Manufacturers' Association. *Combines and Trusts in the Electrical Industry.* London: British Electrical and Allied Manufacturers' Association, 1927.

Bruck, W. F. *Social and Economic History of Germany 1888–1939.* New York: Russell & Russell, 1962.

Camera de la Industria del Petróleo. *El Desarrollo de la Producción de Petróleo en la Republica Argentina 1907–1913.* Buenos Aires: Camera de la Industria del Petróleo, 1963.

Caves, Richard, E. and Richard H. Holton. *The Canadian Economy*. Cambridge, Mass.: Harvard University Press, 1959.

Centennial Seminar on the History of the Petroleum Industry. *Oil's First Century*. Boston: Harvard Graduate School of Business Administration, 1960.

Chandler, Alfred D., Jr. *Strategy and Structure*. Cambridge, Mass.: M.I.T. Press, 1962.

————. "The Beginnings of 'Big Business' in American Industry." *Business History Review* 33 (1959):1–31.

————. "The Structure of American Industry in the Twentieth Century: An Historical Overview." *Business History Review* 43 (1969):255–281.

Clayton, James L., ed. *The Economic Impact of the Cold War*. New York: Harcourt, Brace & World, 1970.

Clough, Shepard Bancroft, and Charles Woolsey Cole. *Economic History of Europe*. Boston: D. C. Heath, 1941.

Cochran, Thomas C. *The American Business System, A Historical Perspective 1900–1955*. Cambridge, Mass.: Harvard University Press, 1957.

Collie, Muriel F. *The Saga of the Abrasives Industry*. Greendale, Mass.: The Grinding Wheel Institute, 1951.

Davies, R. E. G. *A History of the World's Airlines* London: Oxford University Press, 1964.

Davis, Keith, and Robert L. Blomstrom. *Business and Its Environment*. New York: McGraw-Hill, 1966.

Day, Clive. *A History of Commerce*. Rev. and enl. ed. New York: Longmans, Green and Co., 1922.

Deane, Phyllis, and W. A. Cole. *British Economic Growth 1688–1969*. 2d ed. Cambridge, Eng.: Cambridge University Press, 1967.

Easterbrook, W. T., and Hugh G. J. Aitken. *Canadian Economic History*. Toronto: Macmillan Co. of Canada, 1956.

Edminster, Lynn Ramsay. *The Cattle Industry and the Tariff*. New York: Macmillan, 1926.

Edwards, Junius David, Francis C. Frary, and Zay Jeffries. *The Aluminum Industry*. New York: McGraw-Hill, 1930.

Elliott, William Yandel, et al. *International Control of Non-Ferrous Metals*. New York: Macmillan, 1937.

Estall, R. C., and R. Ogilvie Buchanan. *Industrial Activity and Economic Geography*. Rev. ed. London: Hutchinson University Library, 1966.

Ferrer, Aldo. *La Economía Argentina*. Mexico: Fondo de Cultura Económica, 1963.

Firestone, O. J. *Canada's Economic Development, 1867–1953*. London: Bowes & Bowes, 1958.

Forster, Colin. *Industrial Development in Australia, 1920–1930*. Camberra: Australia National University, 1964.

Fortune, editors. *The Conglomerate Commotion*. New York: Viking Press, 1970.

Friedmann, W. G., and J. F. Garner. *Government Enterprise: A Comparative Study*. New York: Columbia University Press, 1970.

Frondizi, Arturo. *Petróleo y Política*. 2d ed. Buenos Aires: Editorial Raigal, 1955.

Fryer, D. W. *World Economic Development*. New York: McGraw-Hill, 1965.

Galbraith, John Kenneth. *The New Industrial State*. Boston: Houghton Mifflin, 1967.

Gann, L. H. "The Northern Rhodesian Copper Industry and World Copper: 1923–1952." *Rhodes-Livingstone Institute Journal* 18 (1955):1–18.

Gort, Michael. *Diversification and Integration in American Industry*. Princeton: Princeton University Press, 1962.

Grunwald, Joseph, and Philip Musgrove. *Natural Resources in Latin American Development*. Baltimore, Md.: Johns Hopkins Press, 1970.

Guerra y Sanchez, Ramiro. *Sugar and Society in the Caribbean; an Economic History of Cuban Agriculture*. Trans. Marjory M. Urquidi. New Haven: Yale University Press, 1964.

Guthrie, John A. *The Economics of Pulp and Paper*. Pullman, Wash.: State College of Washington Press, 1950.

———. *The Newsprint Paper Industry*. Cambridge, Mass.: Harvard University Press, 1941.

Habakkuk, H. J., and M. Postan, eds. *The Cambridge Economic History of Europe*. Vol. 6. Cambridge, England: Cambridge University Press, 1965.

Haber, L. F. *The Chemical Industry, 1900–1930*. Oxford: Oxford University Press, 1971.

Hance, William A. *African Economic Development*. New York: Harper, 1958.

———. *The Geography of Modern Africa*. New York: Columbia University Press, 1964.

Hanson, S. G. *Argentine Meat and the British Market*. London: Oxford University Press, 1937.

———. *Economic Development in Latin America*. Washington, D.C.: Inter-American Affairs Press, 1951.

Harris, Seymour, ed. *Economic Problems of Latin America*. New York: McGraw-Hill, 1944.

Hartendorp, A. V. H. *History of Industry and Trade of the Philippines*. Manila: American Chamber of Commerce of the Philippines, 1958.

Haynes, Williams. *The American Chemical Industry*. 6 vols. New York: D. Van Nostrand Co., 1945–1954.

———. *The Stone That Burns: The Story of the American Sulphur Industry*. New York: D. Van Nostrand Co., 1942.

Henderson, W. O. *The Genesis of the Common Market*. Chicago: Quadrangle Books, 1962.

Hexner, Ervin. *International Cartels*. Chapel Hill, N.C.: University of North Carolina Press, 1945.

———. *International Steel Cartel*. Chapel Hill, N.C.: University of North Carolina Press, 1943.

Higgins, Benjamin. *Economic Development*. New York: W. W. Norton, 1959.

Hill, James J. *Highways of Progress*. New York: Doubleday, Page & Co., 1910.

Hirschman, Albert O. *National Power and the Structure of Foreign Trade.* Berkeley: University of California Press, 1945.
————. *The Strategy of Economic Development.* New Haven: Yale University Press, 1958.
Howard-White, F. B. *Nickel, an Historical Review.* London: Methuen, 1963.
Hughes, Helen. *The Australian Iron and Steel Industry 1848–1968.* Parkville, Victoria: Melbourne University Press, 1964.
Hughlett, Lloyd J., ed. *Industrialization of Latin America.* New York: McGraw-Hill, 1946.
Hunter, Alex, ed. *The Economics of Australian Industry.* Melbourne: Melbourne University Press, 1963.
Jensen, Finn B., and Ingo Walter. *The Common Market.* Philadelphia: J. B. Lippincott Co., 1965.
Jones, Joseph M. *Tariff Retaliation.* Philadelphia: University of Pennsylvania Press, 1934.
Joralemon, Ira. *Romantic Copper.* New York: D. Appleton-Century Co., 1935.
Kenen, Peter B. *International Economics.* 2d ed. Englewood Cliffs, N.J.: Prentice-Hall, 1967.
Kindleberger, Charles P. *Economic Growth in France and Britain 1851–1950.* New York: Simon and Schuster, 1964.
————. *Foreign Trade and the National Economy.* New Haven: Yale University Press, 1962.
————. *International Economics.* 4th ed. Homewood, Ill.: Irwin, 1968.
Knowles, L. C. A., and C. M. Knowles. *The Economic Development of the British Overseas Empire.* 2 vols. London: G. Routledge & Sons, 1924, 1930.
Knox, F. A., C. L. Baxter, and D. W. Slater. *The Canadian Electrical Manufacturing Industry.* Toronto, 1955.
Kranzberg, Melvin, and Carroll W. Pursell, Jr. *Technology in Western Civilization.* Vol. II. New York: Oxford University Press, 1967.
Kuchhal, S. C. *The Industrial Economy of India.* 5th ed. Allahabad, Chaitanya Pub. House, 1965.
Kuznets, Simon. *Modern Economic Growth.* New Haven: Yale University Press, 1966.
Landes, David S. *The Unbound Prometheus.* Cambridge, Eng.: Cambridge University Press, 1969.
Levin, Jonathan. *The Export Economies.* Cambridge, Mass.: Harvard University Press, 1960.
Levy, Herman. *Monopolies, Cartels, and Trusts in British Industry.* London: Macmillan, 1927.
Lewis, Howard T. *The Motion Picture Industry.* New York: D. Van Nostrand, 1933.
Lewis, W. Arthur. *Economic Survey 1919–1939.* New York: Harper & Row, Torchbook, 1969.
Lichtheim, George. *Europe and America.* London: Thames and Hudson, 1963.
Liefmann, Robert. *Cartels, Concerns and Trusts.* London: Methuen & Co., 1932.

Lieuwen, Edwin. *Petroleum in Venezuela*. Berkeley: University of California Press, 1954.

Maddison, Angus. *Economic Growth in Japan and the USSR*. New York: W. W. Norton & Co., 1969.

———. *Economic Growth in the West*. New York: The Twentieth Century Fund, 1964.

Mahoney, Tom. *The Great Merchants*. New York: Harper, 1955.

———. *The Merchants of Life; An Account of the American Pharmaceutical Industry*. New York: Harper, 1959.

Main, O. W. *The Canadian Nickel Industry*. Toronto: University of Toronto Press, 1955.

Mansfield, Edwin. *The Economics of Technological Change*. New York: W. W. Norton & Co., 1968.

Marsh, Donald Bailey. *World Trade and Investment*. New York: Harcourt, Brace, 1951.

Mason, Edward S. *Controlling World Trade; Cartels and Commodity Agreements*. New York and London: McGraw-Hill, 1946.

McDiarmid, O. J. *Commercial Policy in the Canadian Economy*. Cambridge, Mass.: Harvard University Press, 1946.

McLean, John F., and Robert W. Haigh. *The Growth of Integrated Oil Companies*. Boston: Division of Research, Graduate School of Business Administration, Harvard University, 1954.

Mikesell, Raymond F. *Public International Lending for Development*. New York: Random House, 1966.

Mintz, Ilse. *American Exports During Business Cycles 1879–1958*. New York: National Bureau of Economic Research, 1961.

Mitsubishi Economic Research Institute. *Mitsui-Mitsubishi-Sumitomo*. Tokyo: Mitsubishi Economic Research Institute, 1955.

Mitsubishi Economic Research Bureau. *Japanese Trade and Industry*. London: Macmillan, 1936.

Mouzon, Olin T. *Resources and Industries of the United States*. New York: Appleton-Century-Crofts, 1966.

Nelson, Ralph L. *Merger Movements in American Industry 1895–1956*. Princeton: Princeton University Press, 1959.

Nicholls, Wlliam H. *Price Policies in the Cigarette Industry*. Nashville, Tenn.: Vanderbilt University Press, 1951.

Odell, Peter R. *An Economic Geography of Oil*. London: Bell, 1963.

Parsons, A. B. *The Porphyry Coppers*. New York: American Institute of Mining and Metallurgical Engineers, 1933.

———, ed. *Seventy-Five Years of Progress in the Mineral Industry, 1871–1946*. New York: American Institute of Mining and Metallurgical Engineers, 1947.

Penrose, Edith. *The Economics of the International Patent System*. Baltimore: Johns Hopkins Press, 1951.

———. *The Theory of the Growth of the Firm*. New York: Wiley, 1959.

Petroleum Information Bureau (Australia). *The Age of Oil*. Melbourne: Petroleum Information Bureau (Australia), 1960.

Plummer, Alfred. *International Combines in Modern Industry.* 3d ed. London: Pitman, 1951.

Postan, M. M. *An Economic History of Western Europe 1945–1964.* London: Methuen, 1967.

Puga Vega, Mariano. *El Petróleo Chileno.* Santiago: Editorial Andres Bello, 1964.

Rae, John Bell. *Climb to Greatness; the American Aircraft Industry, 1920–1960.* Cambridge, Mass.: M.I.T. Press, 1968.

Ramirez Nova, E. *Petróleo y Revolución Nacionalista.* Lima, Peru: Ediciones "Segundo Emancipacion," 1970.

Read, Oliver, and Walter Welch. *Tin Foil to Stereo.* Indianapolis: Howard W. Sams and Bobbs-Merrill, 1959.

Reimann, Guenther. *Patents for Hitler.* New York: The Vanguard Press, 1942.

Ridgeway, George L. *Merchants of Peace.* Boston: Little, Brown, 1959.

Safarian, A. E. *The Canadian Economy in the Great Depression.* Toronto: University of Toronto Press, 1959.

Schumpeter, Joseph A. *Business Cycles.* New York: McGraw-Hill, 1939.

———. *The Theory of Economic Development.* Cambridge, Mass.: Harvard University Press, 1934.

Scott, W. R., and J. Cunnison. *The Industries of the Clyde Valley During the War.* Oxford: Clarendon Press, 1924.

Smith, Peter H. *Politics and Beef in Argentina.* New York: Columbia University Press, 1969.

Soule, George. *Prosperity Decade.* New York: Holt, Rinehart and Winston, 1964.

Southworth, Constant, and W. W. Buchanan. *Changes in Trade Restrictions Between Canada and the United States.* Washington, D.C.: Canadian-American Committee, 1960.

Spurr, Josiah Edward. *Marketing of Metals and Minerals.* New York: McGraw-Hill, 1925.

Stocking, George Ward, and Myron W. Watkins. *Cartels in Action.* New York: The Twentieth Century Fund, 1946.

———. *The Potash Industry.* New York: R. R. Smith, 1931.

Tilton, John E. "The Choice of Trading Partners." *Yale Economic Essays* 6 (1966):419–471.

Van der Haas, H. *The Enterprise in Transition: An Analysis of European and American Practice.* London: Tavistock Publications, 1967.

Vanderlip, F. A. *The American "Commercial Invasion" of Europe.* New York: Republished from Scribner's Magazine, 1902.

Vernon, Raymond. *The Dilemma of Mexico's Development.* Cambridge, Mass.: Harvard University Press, 1963.

———, ed. *The Technology Factor in International Trade.* Special Conference Series No. 22, National Bureau of Economic Research. New York: Columbia University Press, 1970.

Wallace, D. H. *Market Control in the Aluminum Industry.* Cambridge, Mass.: Harvard University Press, 1937.

Warriner, D. *Combines and Rationalization in Germany 1924–1928.* London: P. S. King & Son, 1931.

Whittlesey, Charles R. *National Interest and International Cartels.* New York: Macmillan, 1946.

Williamson, Harold F., et al. *The American Petroleum Industry 1899–1959.* Evanston, Ill.: Northwestern University Press, 1963.

Wionczek, Miguel S., ed. *Economic Cooperation in Latin America, Asia, and Africa.* Cambridge, Mass.: M.I.T. Press, 1969.

Wirth, John D. *The Politics of Brazilian Development 1930–1954.* Stanford, Calif.: Stanford University Press, 1970.

Woodruff, William. *Impact of Western Man.* New York: St. Martin's Press, 1967.

Woytinsky, W. S., and E. S. Woytinsky. *World Commerce and Government.* New York: The Twentieth Century Fund, 1955.

Yanaga, Chitoshi. *Big Business in Japanese Politics.* New Haven: Yale University Press, 1968.

Yoshino, M. Y. *Japan's Managerial System.* Cambridge, Mass.: M.I.T. Press, 1968.

Young, John Parke. *The International Economy.* 4th ed. New York: Ronald Press, 1963.

VIII. United States Diplomatic Histories

Abrahams, Paul P. "American Bankers and the Economic Tactics of Peace: 1919." *Journal of American History* 46 (1969):478–583.

Acheson, Dean. *Present at the Creation.* New York: W. W. Norton, 1969.

Anderson, Irvine H. "The Standard-Vacuum Oil Company and United States Asian Policy, 1933–1941." Ph.D. diss., University of Cincinnati, 1973.

Bailey, Thomas A. *A Diplomatic History of the United States.* 6th ed. New York: Appleton-Century-Crofts, 1958.

Bemis, Samuel Flagg. *A Diplomatic History of the United States.* 3d ed. New York: Holt, 1950.

———. *The Latin American Policy of the United States.* New York: Harcourt, Brace and Co., 1943.

Bidwell, Percy W., and William Diebold, Jr. "The United States and the International Trade Organization." *International Conciliation* 449 (1949):185–239.

Bishop, Donald G. *The Roosevelt-Litvinov Agreements.* Syracuse: Syracuse University Press, 1965.

Bisson, T. A. *America's Far Eastern Policy.* New York: International Secretariat, Institute of Pacific Relations, 1945.

Borg, Dorothy. *The United States and the Far Eastern Crisis.* Cambridge, Mass.: Harvard University Press, 1964.

Brandes, Joseph. *Herbert Hoover and Economic Diplomacy.* Pittsburgh: University of Pittsburgh Press, 1962.

Chō, Yukio. "Importing American Capital into Manchuria." In *Pearl Harbor as History: Japanese-American Relations 1931–1941,* edited by Dorothy Borg and Shumpei Okamoto. New York: Columbia University Press, 1973.

Cline, Howard F. *The United States and Mexico.* Cambridge, Mass.: Harvard University Press, 1953.

Cohen, Benjamin J., ed. *American Foreign Economic Policy.* New York: Harper & Row, 1968.

Cronon, E. David, ed. *The Cabinet Diaries of Josephus Daniels, 1913–1921.* Lincoln, Neb.: University of Nebraska Press, 1936.

————. *Josephus Daniels in Mexico.* Madison: University of Wisconsin Press, 1960.

Daniels, Josephus. *Shirt-Sleeve Diplomacy.* Chapel Hill, N.C.: University of North Carolina Press, 1947.

Davis, John. *Oil and Canadian American Relations.* N.p.: Canadian American Committee, 1959.

Dennett, Tyler. *Americans in Eastern Asia.* New York: Macmillan, 1922.

DeNovo, John A. *American Interests and Policies in the Middle East.* Minneapolis: University of Minnesota Press, 1963.

————. "The Movement for an Aggressive American Oil Policy Abroad, 1918–1920." *American Historical Review* 61 (1956):854–875.

Engler, Robert. *The Politics of Oil.* New York: Macmillan, 1961.

Feis, Herbert. *The Diplomacy of the Dollar.* Baltimore: Johns Hopkins Press, 1950.

————. *Petroleum and American Foreign Policy.* Stanford: Ford Research Institute, Stanford University, 1944.

————. *Seen from E.A.: Three International Episodes.* Bloomington: Indiana University, 1946.

Fithian, Floyd James. "Soviet-American Economic Relations, 1918–1933." Ph.D. diss, University of Nebraska, 1964.

Gardner, Lloyd C. *Economic Aspects of New Deal Diplomacy.* Madison: University of Wisconsin Press, 1964.

Gardner, Richard N. *Sterling-Dollar Diplomacy.* Rev. ed. New York: McGraw-Hill, 1969.

Gordon, David L., and Royden Dangerfield. *The Hidden Weapon. The Story of Economic Warfare.* New York: Harper, 1947.

Griswold, A. Whitney. *The Far Eastern Policy of the United States.* New York: Harcourt, Brace and Co., 1938.

Guggenheim, Harry. *The United States and Cuba.* New York: Macmillan, 1934.

Harris, Seymour E., ed. *Foreign Economic Policy for the United States.* Cambridge, Mass.: Harvard University Press, 1948.

Heymann, Hans, Jr. "Oil in Soviet-Western Relations in the Inter-War Years." *American Slavic and East European Review* 7 (1948): 303–316.

Hill, Lawrence F. *Diplomatic Relations Between the United States and Brazil.* Durham, N.C.: Duke University Press, 1932.

Hull, Cordell. *Memoirs.* 2 vols. New York: Macmillan, 1948.

Hurewitz, J. C. *Diplomacy in the Near and Middle East, A Documentary Record 1914–1956.* Vol. 2. Princeton: Princeton University Press, 1956.

Ickes, Harold L. *Secret Diary*. 3 vols. New York: Simon and Schuster, 1953–1954.

Ise, John. *The United States Oil Policy*. New Haven: Yale University Press, 1924.

Jenkins, Shirley. *American Economic Policy Toward the Philippines*. Stanford, Calif.: Stanford University Press, 1954.

Jenks, Leland. *Our Cuban Colony*. New York: Vanguard Press, 1928.

Kenen, Peter B. *Giant Among Nations, Problems in United States Foreign Economic Policy*. Chicago: Rand McNally, 1963.

Kolko, Gabriel. "American Business and Germany 1930–1941." *Western Political Quarterly* 15 (1962):713–728.

———. *The Roots of American Foreign Policy*. Boston: Beacon Press, 1969.

Kolko, Joyce, and Gabriel Kolko. *The Limits of Power*. New York: Harper & Row, 1972.

Lissitzyn, Oliver James. *International Air Transport and National Policy*. New York: Council on Foreign Relations, 1942.

Magdoff, Harry. *The Age of Imperialism: The Economics of U.S. Foreign Policy*. New York: Monthly Review Press, 1969.

Mikesell, Raymond F. *U.S. Economic Policy and International Relations*. New York: McGraw-Hill, 1952.

Munro, Dana G. *Intervention and Dollar Diplomacy in the Caribbean 1900–1921*. Princeton: Princeton University Press, 1964.

———. *United States and the Caribbean Area*. Boston: World Peace Foundation, 1934.

Nash, Gerald. *United States Oil Policy, 1890–1964*. Pittsburgh: University of Pittsburgh Press, 1968.

National Foreign Trade Council. *Position of National Foreign Trade Council with Respect to the Havana Charter for an International Trade Organization*. New York: National Foreign Trade Council, 1950.

Nixon, Edgar B., ed. *Franklin D. Roosevelt and Foreign Affairs*. 3 vols. Cambridge, Mass.: Harvard University Press, 1969.

Offutt, Milton. *Protection of Citizens Abroad by the Armed Forces of the United States*. Baltimore: Johns Hopkins Press, 1928.

Parks, E. Taylor. *Colombia and the United States*. Durham, N.C.: Duke University Press, 1935.

Parks, Wallace Judson. *U.S. Administration of Its International Economic Affairs*. Baltimore: Johns Hopkins Press, 1951.

Parrini, Carl P. *Heir to Empire: United States Economic Diplomacy 1916–1923*. Pittsburgh: University of Pittsburgh Press, 1969.

Rippy, J. Fred. *Globe and Hemisphere. Latin America's Place in the Post-War Relations of the United States*. Chicago: Regnery, 1958.

———. *The United States and Mexico*. Rev. ed. New York: F. S. Crofts & Co., 1931.

Smith, Robert F. *The United States and Cuba: Business and Diplomacy 1917–1960*. New York: Bookman Associates, 1960.

Vernon, Raymond. *America's Foreign Trade Policy and the GATT*. Princeton: Princeton University Press, 1954.

Wagner, R. Harrison. *United States Policy Toward Latin America*. Stanford, Calif.: Stanford University Press, 1970.

Wilkins, Mira. "The Role of U.S. Business." In *Pearl Harbor as History: Japanese-American Relations 1931–1941*, edited by Dorothy Borg and Shumpei Okamoto. New York: Columbia University Press, 1973.

Williams, Benjamin H. *Economic Foreign Policy of the United States*. New York: McGraw-Hill, 1929.

Williams, William Appleton. *The Shaping of American Diplomacy, Readings and Documents in American Foreign Relations*. Vol. 2. Chicago: Rand McNally, 1956.

———. *The Tragedy of American Diplomacy*. Rev. ed. New York: Dell Publishing Co., 1962.

Wilson, Henry Lane. *Diplomatic Episodes in Mexico, Belgium, and Chile*. Garden City, N.Y.: Doubleday, 1927.

Wilson, Joan Hoff. *American Business and Foreign Policy 1920–1933*. Lexington, Ky.: University Press of Kentucky, 1971.

Wood, Bryce. *The Making of the Good Neighbor Policy*. New York: Columbia University Press, 1961.

IX. General Works (for background)

Ackerman, Carl. *Mexico's Dilemma*. New York: George H. Doran Co., 1918.

Basadre, Jorge. *Historia de la Republica del Peru*. 5th ed. Lima: Ediciones "Historia," 1962.

Belgrave, James H. D. *Welcome to Bahrain*. 4th ed. Manama, Bahrain: James H. D. Belgrave, 1960.

Biesanz, John, and Mavis Biesanz. *Costa Rican Life*. New York: Columbia University Press, 1944.

Brogan, D. W. *Roosevelt and the New Deal*. London: Oxford University Press, 1952.

Brunn, Geoffrey, and Victor S. Mamatey. *The World in the Twentieth Century*. 4th ed. Boston: D. C. Heath, 1962.

Burns, James MacGregor. *Roosevelt: The Lion and the Fox*. New York: Harcourt, Brace and Co., 1956.

Cooper, Clayton Sedgwick. *Understanding South America*. New York: George H. Doran Co., 1918.

Deutsch, Karl W. *Nationalism and Social Communication*. 2d ed. Cambridge, Mass., M.I.T. Press, 1966.

Dulles, Foster Rhea. *Americans Abroad*. Ann Arbor: University of Michigan Press, 1964.

Forbes, W. Cameron. *The Philippine Islands*. 2 vols. Boston and New York: Houghton Mifflin, 1928.

Friedman, Milton, and Anna Jacobson Schwartz. *A Monetary History of the United States*. Princeton: Princeton University Press, 1963.

Graham, Frank, and Charles R. Whittlesey. *Golden Avalanche*. Princeton: Princeton University Press, 1939.

Hanna, A. J. *The Story of the Rhodesias and Nyasaland*. 2d ed. London: Faber and Faber, 1965.

Harriman, Averell. *Peace with Russia?* New York: Simon and Schuster, 1959.

Herring, Hubert. *A History of Latin America*. 2d ed. New York: Alfred A. Knopf, 1964.

Hijazi, Ahmad. "Kuwait: Development from a Semitribal, Semicolonial Society to Democracy and Sovereignty." *American Journal of Comparative Law* 13 (1964):428–438.

Hofstadter, Richard. *The Age of Reform*. New York: Random House, 1955.

Hoover, Herbert. *Memoirs*. Vol. I. New York: Macmillan, 1951.

Huntington, Samuel P. *Political Order in Changing Societies*. New Haven: Yale University Press, 1969.

Johnson, Harry G. *Economic Nationalism in Old and New States*. Chicago: University of Chicago Press, 1967.

Jones, Jesse. *Fifty Billion Dollars*. New York: Macmillan, 1958.

Laqueur, Walter. *The Struggle for the Middle East*. New York: Macmillan, 1969.

Leuchtenburg, William E. *Franklin D. Roosevelt and the New Deal*. New York: Harper & Row, 1963.

———. *The Perils of Prosperity, 1914–1932*. Chicago: University of Chicago Press, 1958.

Link, Arthur S. *Wilson: Confusion and Crises 1915–1916*. Princeton: Princeton University Press, 1964.

Longrigg, Stephen Hemsley. *Iraq 1900 to 1950*. London: Oxford University Press, 1953.

Marinas Otero, Luis. *Honduras*. Madrid: Ediciones Cultura Hispanica, 1963.

May, Stacy. *Costa Rica*. New York: Twentieth Century Fund, 1952.

Nehemkis, Peter. *Latin America*. New York: Alfred A. Knopf, 1964.

Nelson, Donald. *Arsenal of Democracy*. New York: Harcourt, Brace, 1946.

Palmer, R. R., ed. *Atlas of World History*. New York: Rand McNally, 1957.

Pelling, Henry. *A History of British Trade Unionism*. London: Macmillan, 1963.

Pinson, Koppel S. *Modern Germany*. 2d ed. New York: Macmillan, 1966.

Rippy, J. Fred. *Latin America and the Industrial Age*. 2d ed. New York: G. P. Putnam's Sons, 1947.

Royal Institute of International Affairs. *The Middle East*. 2d ed. London: Royal Institute of International Affairs, 1954.

Schlesinger, Arthur M., Jr. *The Coming of the New Deal*. Boston: Houghton Mifflin Co., 1959.

———. *The Politics of Upheaval*. Boston: Houghton Mifflin Co., 1960.

Sorensen, Theodore C. *Kennedy*. New York: Harper & Row, 1965.

Tamayo, Jorge L. *Geografía General de México*. Vol. 4. Mexico: Instituto Mexicano de Investigaciones Económicas, 1962.

Tannenbaum, Frank. *The Mexican Agrarian Revolution*. Washington, D.C.: The Brookings Institution, 1930.

Walton, Francis. *The Miracle of World War II*. New York: Macmillan, 1956.

Wilkins, Mira. "The Businessman Abroad." *The Annals of the American Academy of Political and Social Science* 368 (1966):83–94.

Wilson, Charles Morrow. *Challenge and Opportunity: Central America*. New York: Holt, 1941.

Woodward, C. Vann, ed. *The Comparative Approach to American History*. New York: Basic Books, 1968.

X. Directories, Handbooks, and Conference Proceedings

American Bankers Association. *Proceedings of a Symposium on Federal Taxation*. 1965.

American Exporter. *Export Trade Directory*. 1919–1920.

Angel, J. L. *Directory of American Firms Operating in Foreign Countries*. 6th and 7th eds. New York: World Trade Academy Press, 1966, 1969.

Annual Financial Review, Canadian, July 1929.

China Year Book 1926.

Dictionary of American Biography.

Directory of Directors. 1918–1938.

Filsinger, Ernest. *Exporting to Latin America; a Handbook for Merchants, Manufacturers and Exporters*. New York: Appleton, 1919.

The Mineral Industry. 1914–1944. New York: Engineering and Journal, 1914–1944.

Moody's Industrial Manual: American and Foreign. 1914 to date. Title varies. New York: Moody's Investors Service, 1914–date.

Moody's Public Utility Manual. Title varies. New York: Moody's Investors Service, 1914–date.

National Foreign Trade Convention. *Official Report of the National Foreign Trade Convention,* 1914–date. New York: National Foreign Trade Convention Headquarters, 1914–date.

Stewart, Charles F., and Simmons, George B. *A Bibliography of International Business*. New York: Columbia University Press, 1964.

Vernon, Raymond. "The Multinational Corporation: A Bibliography." Mimeographed. Boston: Harvard Graduate School of Business Administration, 1966.

XI. Periodicals (includes only those used in connection with this study)

American Bar Association Bulletin

American Economic Review

American Historical Review

Annals of the American Academy of Political and Social Science

Barron's

Brazilian Business

Business History Review

Business International
Business Topics (now *MSU Business Topics*)
Business Week
Canadian Mining Journal
Canadian Motor
Car Life
Columbia Journal of World Business
Comments on the Argentine Trade
Commercial and Financial Chronicle
Economic Journal
Economic Review of the Soviet Union
Economist
Engineering and Mining Journal
Explorations in Entrepreneurial History
Explorations in Entrepreneurial History, series 2
Export Trade
Far Eastern Economic Review
Financial World
Forbes
Fortune
Harvard Business Review
Inter-American Economic Affairs
Journal of Business
Journal of Economic History
London Times
Mining World
National City Bank Monthly Letter
New York Review of Books
New York Times
Oil and Gas Journal
Petroleum Press Service
Political Science Quarterly
Quarterly Journal of Economics
Vital Speeches of the Day
Wall Street Journal
Washington Post
Western Electric News
World Business (Chase Manhattan Bank)

Chapter I: World War I

1. National Foreign Trade Council, *Official Report 1914*, 5 (meetings in Washington); George L. Ridgeway, *Merchants of Peace*, Boston 1959, 21–22 (Chamber of Commerce). Mira Wilkins, *The Emergence of Multinational Enterprise: American Business Abroad from the Colonial Era to 1914*, Cambridge, Mass. 1970, esp. chap. X (participants in business abroad).

2. Wilkins, *Emergence of Multinational Enterprise, passim.*

3. *Commercial and Financial Chronicle*, Aug. 1, 1914 (European financial paralysis); Foster Rhea Dulles, *Americans Abroad*, Ann Arbor 1964, 151 (quote), 152; Herbert Hoover, *Memoirs*, New York 1951, I, 135–148; Alden Hatch, *American Express*, Garden City, N.Y. 1950, 114–116; company records; data in Scudder Collection, Columbia University; Wilkins, *Emergence of Multinational Enterprise*, 212 (stakes on both sides).

4. American Radiator Co., Minutes, Board of Directors, July 31, 1903, 1907–1914 (Woolley's warnings about war), Nov. 4, 1914 (Woolley's experiences and mobilization); *ibid.* and Nov. 4, 1915 (general military situation), all in Secretary's office files, American-Standard, New York; National Radiator Co., Ltd., Minutes, Board of Directors, June 30, 1916 (English company), and minutes of the boards of each national company in files of International Division, American-Standard; American Radiator Co., Minutes, Board of Directors, May 14, 1916 (Woolley's worry about costs); records in International Division, American-Standard (profits); Mira Wilkins, "An American Enterprise Abroad: American Radiator Company in Europe, 1895–1914," *Business History Review* 43:326–342, Autumn 1969 (background).

5. *National City Bank Letter*, October 1914, 1 (United Shoe); Carl W. Ackerman, *George Eastman*, Boston 1930, 282–291.

6. Mixed Claims Commission, United States and Germany, *Report of Robert W. Bonynge*, Washington, D.C. 1934, 152.

7. Coffin to Vanderlip, Nov. 24, 1919, Vanderlip Papers, Special Collections, Columbia University Library, and *BTH Reminiscences, Sixty Years of Progress*, comp. H. A. Price-Hughes, London 1946, 34.

8. J. K. Rice, Jr. & Co., "Singer Manufacturing Company, Ltd.," 1924, Scudder Collection, Columbia University, and W. R. Scott and J. Cunnison, *The Industries of the Clyde Valley During the War,* Oxford 1924, 208. (Singer's British plant); American Consul, London, to Secretary of State, Mar. 17, 1919, Record Group 59, 763.72112.11876, National Archives (Singer in Germany).

9. George Sweet Gibb and Evelyn H. Knowlton, *The Resurgent Years 1911–1927,* New York 1956, 676, 83, 231–235, and Mixed Claims Commission, United States and Germany, *Administrative Decisions and Opinions of a General Nature,* Washington, D.C. 1933, 877.

10. Hatch, 119.

11. Wilkins, *Emergence of Multinational Enterprise,* 121–122 (early Mexican speculations); U.S. Rubber, *Annual Reports,* 1910, 1911, 1916; Hugh Allen, *The House of Goodyear,* Cleveland 1943, 82ff, and Goodyear, *The Story of the Tire,* Akron 1955, 34; Alfred Lief, *The Firestone Story,* New York 1951, 90. Cleona Lewis, *America's Stake in International Investments,* Washington, D.C. 1938, 268–271, 590; data on Cuban companies and on Amalgamated Sugar Company, Scudder Collection, Columbia University.

12. At the outbreak of the European war there was a depression in the Argentine meat industry, but this quickly changed into a boom as the British government began purchasing. The largest U.S. investments in meat packing were made in Argentina; new stakes were also made in Uruguay and Brazil. The American companies in addition introduced canning operations in South America and Australia (Swift only). See Federal Trade Commission, *Report on the Meat-Packing Industry,* Washington, D.C. 1919, pt. 1, pp. 172–193.

13. Herbert Marshall, Frank A. Southard, Jr., and Kenneth W. Taylor, *Canadian-American Industry,* New Haven 1936, 35ff, and Constant Southworth, "The American-Canadian Newsprint Paper Industry and the Tariff," *Journal of Political Economy* 30:683 (October 1922).

14. Margaret Charlotte Marsh, *Bankers in Bolivia,* New York 1928, 49 (International Mining); Benjamin H. Williams, *Economic Foreign Policy of the U.S.,* New York 1929, 380 (direct purchasing).

15. Clayton Sedwick Cooper, *Understanding South America,* New York 1918, 221, and Williams Haynes, *The American Chemical Industry,* 6 vols., New York 1945–1954, II, 58–60 (Grace).

16. Testimony of Ryan, U.S. House, Committee of the Judiciary, Hearings on the Clayton Act, 63rd Cong., 2d sess. (1914), I, ser. 7, pt. 11, p. 441. A. B. Parsons, *Porphyry Coppers,* New York 1934, 159 (purchase and properties); Luis Hiriart, *Braden Historia de Una Mina,* Santiago 1964, 172–177 (Kennecott and Braden); Harvey O'Connor, *The Guggenheims,* New York 1937, 352–353 (Kennecott); Anaconda, *Annual Report 1916* (Anaconda); intervs. in Chile, 1964 (Bethlehem).

17. 1916 Scrapbook, Bethlehem Chile Iron Ore Co., Cruz Grande, Chile, which contains clippings from *La Opinion, El Mercurio, El Chileno, El Diario, La Nación.*

18. *U.S. v. Alcoa,* Brief of the U.S., U.S. Circuit Court of Appeals, Oct. 1944, 29–33 (Alcoa).

19. John F. Thompson and Norman Beasley, *For the Years to Come,* New York 1960, 167–169; Haynes, III, 89; Hugh G. J. Aitken et al., *The American Economic Impact on Canada,* Durham, N.C. 1959, 20.

20. Haynes, III, 77 (chrome).

21. RG 151, Folders 622: China, NA (Dept. of Comm. attempts to interest American investors); Confidential Report by Julean H. Arnold, Hankow, China, Nov. 28, 1914, *ibid.* ("take the place [of] German capital"); corresp., *ibid.,* esp. Rowe to Platt, Feb. 8, 1915 (quote), and Straight to Platt, July 2, 1915 (quote); M. F. Perkins, American Consul Changsha, to C. C. Batchelder, Jan. 27, 1920, *ibid.* (Andersen, Meyer investments); Arnold to Platt, May 18, 1915, and Perkins letter cited above, *ibid.* (Japanese influence and few investments).

22. Gibb and Knowlton, 89–91 (Canada); see Chap. II herein (Mexican situation); Dana G. Munro, *Intervention and Dollar Diplomacy in the Caribbean 1900–1921,* Princeton 1964, 430–432; *Moody's 1917: Foreign Relations of the United States 1919,* I, 866–872 (events in Costa Rica); H. F. Sinclair to the Shareholders of Sinclair Gulf, Nov. 8, 1917, Scudder Collection (Sinclair).

23. RG 59, 821.6363/39, NA, and Wilkins, *Emergence of Multinational Enterprise,* 162–163 (Standard Oil in Colombia). Gibb and Knowlton, 369 (de Mares concession); Assistant Secretary John E. Osborne to Mark J. Trazivak, Nov. 27, 1916, RG 59, 821.6363/40, NA (quote). Perhaps one could argue that there was no change, that "legitimate enterprises" were not "monopolistic concessions." But the concessionaires did in fact gain monopoly privileges, so there does seem to be a change.

24. Gibb and Knowlton, 384.

25. Wilkins, *Emergence of Multinational Enterprise,* 186; Jorge Basadre, *Historia de la Republica del Peru,* 5th ed., Lima 1962, 2816; Gibb and Knowlton, 98–105.

26. Wilkins, *Emergence of Multinational Enterprise,* 205 (agreement of Standard Oil of New York and Chinese officials); RG 59, 893.6363/9, 20, 26, 27, NA (full details of negotiations).

27. Wilkins, *Emergence of Multinational Enterprise,* 85–86, and Gibb and Knowlton, 91–92 (Dutch East Indies).

28. Sidney A. Mitchell, *S.Z. Mitchell and the Electrical Industry,* New York 1960, 106–107; Memo re: "Proposed Merger of Power Companies," Panama, Panama, May 8, 1916, and *Star & Herald* clipping, n.d. [May 8, 1916?], RG 59, 819.153/1, NA; *Moody's 1918;* RG 59, 819.6463/1, NA (EBASCO in Panama).

29. Muriel F. Collie, *The Saga of the Abrasive Industry,* Greendale, Mass. 1951, 24 (wartime needs), 212–213 (Exolon), 132 (Carborundum), 219 (International Abrasives Co. and Brebner); John Davis, *The Canadian Chemical Industry,* Ottawa 1957, 16 (Carborundum's plant was the world's largest).

30. Marshall et al., 83 (Aetna Explosives); Davis, 16 (chemical enterprises); Haynes, VI, 180–181 (Nichols).

31. *Moody's 1914*, and Alfred Lief, *It Floats*, New York 1958, 118 (Procter & Gamble); James L. Marshall, *Eldridge A. Stuart*, Los Angeles 1949, 109–110 (Carnation).

32. Marshall et al., 68 (Chrysler); C. Howard Aikman, *The Automobile Industry of Canada*, Toronto 1926, 13.

33. Marshall et al., 83 (du Pont), 64 (Ford); Gibb and Knowlton, 131, 678 (Imperial Oil).

34. Federal Trade Commission, *Report on Cooperation in American Export Trade*, Washington, D.C. 1916, II, 180, and Luis P. O'Farrell, Buenos Aires, to E. H. Hampton, Apr. 3, 1917, and Hampton, Buenos Aires, to Klingensmith, Apr. 9, 1917, Accession 140, Box 5, Ford Archives, Dearborn, Mich. (Argentine inducements). Charles W. Drees, ed., *Americans in Argentina*, Buenos Aires 1922, 110–111, 104 (cement company; Studebaker); Mira Wilkins and Frank Ernest Hill, *American Business Abroad: Ford on Six Continents*, Detroit 1964, 91 (Ford); Goodyear, *Annual Report 1915;* Glenn D. Babcock, *History of United States Rubber Company*, Bloomington, Ind. 1966, 90 (U.S. Rubber); Richard L. Humphrey to Customers of Hayden, Stone & Co., Jan. 22, 1916, Scudder Collection (Cuban cement).

35. F. A. Vanderlip letter, Nov. 27, 1915, in American International Corporation, *Annual Report 1916* (quote); Vanderlip, European Diary, Vanderlip Papers (1901 trip); Vanderlip, *American Commercial Invasion of Europe*, New York 1902, 18–19; U.S. House, Subcommittee on Banking and Currency, *Investigations of Financial and Monetary Conditions in the U.S.*, 62d Cong., 2d sess. (1912), I, 51–52, 64, 73 (testimony notes exceptional character of the loans); Vanderlip to R. W. Hardenbergh, Buenos Aires, May 29, 1912, Vanderlip Papers (representative to South America); *National City Bank Letter*, January 1914, 14, and August 1914, 1–2 (branches and the reason for them); "Report on Activities Foreign Trade Department," [July 1915?], Vanderlip Papers (this was distinct from the "Foreign Department" and was a new departure); *National City Bank Letter*, September 1914, 4 (quote).

36. Wilkins, *Emergence of Multinational Enterprise*, 107, 204 (background International Banking Corporation); Vanderlip to Stillman, Oct. 8, 1915, Vanderlip Papers; C. W. Phelps, *Foreign Expansion of American Banks*, New York 1927, 143; L[awrence] M. J[acobs], "What Shall We Do with the International Banking Corporation," typed memorandum, May 23, 1916, Vanderlip Papers.

37. Vanderlip to Stillman, Oct. 8, 1915, and Nov. 13, 1915, Vanderlip Papers (A.I.C.); *National City Bank Letter*, December 1915, 2 (50% owned by NCB stockholders); "A.I.C." Box 2, Vanderlip Papers (board members have right to subscribe); N.S.B. Gras and Henrietta M. Larson, *Casebook in American Business History*, New York 1939, 634–642 (Ogden Armour); G.E., *Annual Reports* (Coffin); Joseph Gilpin Pyle, *The Life of James J. Hill*, Garden City, N.Y. 1917, I, 298–326, II, 49–66; Eugene W. Burgess and Frederick H. Harbison, *Casa Grace in Peru*, Washington, D.C. 1954, 22, 26; Thompson and Beasley, *For the Years to Come*, 167 (Monell); Allan Nevins, *Study in Power*, New York 1953, 286 (Percy Rockefeller); Anaconda, *Annual Reports;* Henry G. Prout,

George Westinghouse, New York 1921, 262–272 (Westinghouse's European interest); Albert Bigelow Paine, *In One Man's Life,* New York 1921, 205–212, 221; *Dictionary of American Biography,* IX, 139, and data from Western Electric Archives (Vail). For the role of the bankers, see Harry Scheiber, "World War I as an Enterpreneurial Opportunity: Willard Straight and the American International Corporation," *Political Science Quarterly* 84:486–511 (September 1969), and data in Vanderlip's Papers. James B. Duke to Vanderlip, Nov. 23, 1915, Vanderlip to Duke, Dec. 9, 1915, and Cyrus McCormick to Vanderlip, Dec. 3, 1915, Vanderlip Papers (they declined to become directors). A.I.C. *Annual Reports,* 1916, 1917, 1918; correspondence in "A.I.C." Box 2, Vanderlip Papers.

38. M. D. Carrell, "Memorandum for Mr. Eldridge Regarding Commercial Work in South America," Nov. 5, 1915, Vanderlip Papers; National City Bank Memo, Feb. 3, 1917, in *ibid.,* and *Federal Reserve Bulletin* 4:944, Oct. 1, 1918 (new branches); Vanderlip to [Stillman], Mar. 23, 1917, Vanderlip Papers (Vanderlip quote); conversation with First National Bank of Boston official, Buenos Aires, 1964 (motivation First National Bank); Phelps, 145ff. In 1915 the Grace National Bank of New York was formed to carry on banking activities in Latin America that had been handled by W. R. Grace. Burgess and Harbison, 3; *National City Bank Letter,* January 1917, 2.

39. Public Law 91, 65th Cong. (HR 4960).

40. U.S. House, *Report of Alien Property Custodian,* 65th Cong., 2d sess., H. Doc. 840, Washington, D.C. 1918, 268–271 (German actions); RG 59, 763.72113A/274, 441, 447, 491, NA (State Dept. records list investments). American Radiator, Minutes, Board of Directors, May 1, 1919, Secretary's office, American-Standard (Woolley's finding); RG 59, 763.72113A/165, NA (Steinway & Sons).

41. American Consul, London, to U.S. Secretary of State, Mar. 17, 1919, RG 59, 763.72112.11876, NA (Singer circulars), RG 76, List Nos. 350 to 370 folder, NA (Singer German war claims).

42. Gibb and Knowlton, 517–518.

43. Data in RG 59, company records and histories, and Gibb and Knowlton, 203.

44. Data from International Division files, American-Standard (American Radiator); Coffin to Vanderlip, Nov. 24, 1919, Vanderlip Papers (G.E.); data in Ford Archives (Ford); J.K. Rice, Jr. & Co., "Singer Manufacturing Company, Ltd.," 1924 (Singer's British plant); Floyd James Fithian, "Soviet American Economic Relations, 1918–1933," Ph.D. diss., University of Nebraska 1964, 276–278, and Foreign Claims Settlement Commission of the U.S., *Tenth Semi-Annual Report,* Washington, D.C. 1959, 235–236 (G.E. in Russia 1917); Haynes, III, 89; Gibb and Knowlton, 678 (U.S. firms in Canada).

45. U.S. Rubber, *Annual Report 1919;* Allen, *House of Goodyear,* 82ff; Federal Trade Commission, *Report on the Meat-Packing Industry,* Washington, D.C. 1919, pt. 1 pp. 172–193. Lewis, 590 (sugar). The meat packers made new investments in Paraguay, where the first packing plants in the country were built by American capital. In 1917 the Central Products Company (a Delaware

corporation) obtained a contract with the Paraguayan government (authorized by the country's congress) to establish a slaughterhouse. It got exemption for the next 20 years on all import duties on materials and supplies for the packing house and practically all export duties on packing house products (hides excepted). International Products Company (organized in 1916 by interests connected with American International Corporation) acquired Central Products in 1917. (I.P.C also purchased a million acres of cattle land and quebracho forests in Paraguay, plus about 50,000 heads of cattle; it erected a quebracho extract plant that started production at the end of 1918; Central Product's packing house was not complete until 1919.) Armour's British sales subsidiary handled the new enterprise's foreign marketing. Swift also established itself in Paraguay and opened a canning and dried beef plant on the Paraguay River near Asuncion. "Confidential Draft on Paraguay Project," n.d. [1916?], Percival Farquhar to Stockholders, I.P.C., Sept. 3, 1918, and I.P.C., Plan of Reorganization, Nov. 23, 1925, all three in Scudder Collection, (Paraguayan activity). Compania Swift Internacional, S.A.C., *Annual Report 1919* (Swift's Paraguayan activity). Note 14 above (tungsten and tin); Haynes, II, 58–60 (Grace and du Pont in Chile); note 16 above (copper producers); National City Bank, Memo, Jan. 14, 1918, Vanderlip Papers (Cerro de Pasco). RG 59, 832.635/10; 832.635/18; 832.635/45, NA (Brazilian activities); note 18 above (Alcoa).

46. Bernard Baruch, *My Own Story*, New York 1957, 213; David E. Cronon, ed., *The Cabinet Diaries of Josephus Daniels 1913–1921*, Lincoln, Neb. 1963, 233; *Mineral Industry 1918* (oil production figures).

47. Data in Scudder Collection (Sinclair); Gibb and Knowlton, 369 (de Mares concession); RG 59, 821.6363 Barco/3, NA (price Barco concession); RG 59, 821.6363 Barco/4, NA (opposition to Barco concession); J. Fred Rippy, *The Capitalists and Colombia*, New York 1931, 251, and Leonard Fanning, *Foreign Oil and the Free World*, New York 1954, 35 (more on Barco concession). *Foreign Relations of the United States 1919*, 873–874 (oil properties in Panama Canal area; this vol. covers correspondence, 1913–1919).

48. Lawrence F. Hill, *Diplomatic Relations between the United States and Brazil*, Durham, N.C. 1932, 303. In 1918 the Argentine government granted the U.S. company a concession to lay cables between Buenos Aires and Montevideo, thus again challenging the British monopoly. See *Foreign Relations of the United States 1919*, I, 172–204, and *ibid. 1922*, I, 521, 537.

49. Drees, 128, and National Lead, *Annual Reports 1917* and *1918;* Theodore Geiger, *General Electric Company in Brazil*, Washington, D.C. 1961, 39; Burgess and Harbison, 22 (Grace).

50. Gerard Swope, *Reminiscences*, 76, 78, Oral History Collection, Columbia University. Interv. Yoshinori Iwadare, Kamakura, Japan, Oct. 1, 1965 (Nippon Electric and Mitsui; later Nippon Electric became associated with Sumitomo); Swope, *Reminiscences;* D. G. Loth, *Swope of G.E.: The Story of Gerard Swope*, New York 1958, 83; financial records from the archives of Western Electric, New York; A. Viola Smith, Report of June 13, 1928, RG 151, 623: Branch Factories, NA (Chinese expansion).

51. Smith Report, see note 50 (G.E. in China); Lewis, *America's Stake in International Investments,* 308, citing an article in the *Chronicle,* Apr. 23, 1921, 1745, writes that "General Edison" (surely General Electric) started to manufacture lamps in 1918 and in 1921 "was putting up fourteen new factories in China." (Is this a misunderstanding of the word "factories"? Were they merely warehouses?) On the other hand, RG 151, 623: China, indicates manufacture of lamps started in 1920. (See Julean Arnold to Bureau of Foreign and Domestic Commerce, Dec. 1, 1920, which refers to G.E. company's having had six months of operations.) Mitsubishi Economic Research Institute, *Mitsui-Mitsubishi-Sumitomo,* Tokyo 1955, 270, 276, 321 (joint ventures in Japan); data from Ministry of International Trade and Industry, Tokyo (percentages).

52. A.I.C., *Annual Report 1918;* C. W. Phelps, *Foreign Expansion of American Banks,* New York 1927, 142.

53. O. P. Austin, "Memo for Mr. Vanderlip," Nov. 23, 1918, Vanderlip Papers (rubber investment); Clayton Sedwick Cooper, *Understanding South America,* New York 1918, 76 (per cent output by American *oficinas*).

Chapter II: Difficulties Abroad, 1914–1920

1. The experiences of U.S. business in Mexico, 1911–1914, are given in Mira Wilkins, *The Emergence of Multinational Enterprise: American Business Abroad from the Colonial Era to 1914,* Cambridge, Mass. 1970, 125–134.

2. *Special Mexican Claims Commission,* Washington, D.C. 1940, 130, 142–143, 147–148, 161, 194, 202, 205, 266, 283, 303, 363, 481–482, 555, 560, 591, 600, 623 (examples of damages to plantations and ranches); Frank Tannenbaum, *Mexican Agrarian Revolution,* New York 1929, 171 (Jan. 6 decree); Investor's Agency Report, "American Chicle Company," Apr. 12, 1916, and A. Hicks Lawrence, "American Chicle Co.," Sept. 1919, Scudder Collection, Columbia University.

3. *Mineral Industry 1914,* 197–199; *Engineering and Mining Journal,* 100:890 (Nov. 14, 1914); *Foreign Relations of the United States 1915,* 899–900, 903, 893–894 (decrees), 915–916 (State Dept. on Carranza's decree), 927ff (Villa's demands), 935 (solution problem), 946–947 (mining companies' request), 950ff (protest on mining taxes), 963 (Lansing quote).

4. Arthur S. Link, *Wilson: Confusions and Crises 1915–1916,* Princeton 1964, 195–221, 280–318 (we have used his numbers; 17 American engineers; more than 6000 men); Samuel Flagg Bemis, *A Diplomatic History of the United States,* 3rd ed., New York 1950, 551–552 (15 American engineers; 15,000 men under Pershing); Howard Cline, *United States and Mexico,* New York 1953, 175–183 (16 American engineers; 6000 men under Pershing); American Smelting and Refining Company, *Annual Report 1916.*

5. George Sweet Gibb and Evelyn H. Knowlton, *The Resurgent Years 1911–1927,* New York 1956, 85, 87, 132 (Jersey Standard invested in a topping plant in 1914 in Mexico); *Foreign Relations of the United States 1914,* 781ff; *Special Mexican Claims Commission,* 226, 336 (Doheny's losses).

6. Tannenbaum, 518–527 (copy of Art. 27), 188–203, esp. 197–201 (discussion

of Art. 27), 204ff (Art. 123); testimony of Edward Doheny, U.S. Sen., Subcommittee on Foreign Relations, *Investigation of Mexican Affairs, Hearings,* 66th Cong., 2d sess., Washington, D.C. 1920, 259–268; henceforth cited as *Fall Committee Hearings* (controversy between government and oil companies); *Mineral Industry 1918* (comparative oil production figures); Cleona Lewis, *America's Stake in International Investments,* Washington, D.C. 1938, 588, and O. P. Austin, Memo for Vanderlip, May 16, 1919, Vanderlip Papers, Special Collections, Columbia University (size of oil investment in Mexico); Doheny testimony, *Fall Committee Hearings,* 257 (152 American companies).

7. Wilkins, 126–127 (1911 figures); Table I.3 above (1919 figures); Report of the Group on American Petroleum Interests in Foreign Countries, Oct. 15, 1945, in U.S. Sen., Special Committee Investigating Petroleum Resources, *American Petroleum Interests in Foreign Countries, Hearings,* 79th Cong., 1st sess., Washington, D.C. 1946, 238 (revenues).

8. ASARCO, *Annual Reports 1918* and *1919;* Lewis, 203, Marvin D. Bernstein, *The Mexican Mining Industry 1890–1950,* Albany 1965, 95–123 (general data on mining during the revolution); *Engineering and Mining Journal,* 108:935, Dec. 27, 1919 (compare with *ibid.,* 93:389, Feb. 24, 1912); by 1916 most of the business community and press favored intervention. National City Bank, *Monthly Letter,* August 1916, *Journal American,* July–August 1916, and W. A. Swanberg, *Citizen Hearst,* New York 1961, 296–298. David E. Cronon, ed., *The Cabinet Diaries of Josephus Daniels 1913–1921,* Lincoln, Neb. 1963, 461, 590.

9. Cables to Vanderlip, London, Jan. 31, 1919 and Feb. 3, 1919, Vanderlip Papers.

10. U.S. Sen., Subcommittee on Foreign Relations, *Investigation of Mexican Affairs, Report,* 66th Cong., 2d sess., Washington, D.C. 1920, II, 3399 (Fall Committee estimates); Bemis, *Diplomatic History,* 562, and *Records of U.S. and Mexican Claims Commission, Preliminary Inventory #136,* Washington, D.C. 1962, 28 (1931 status); *Special Mexican Claims Commission,* 4–5.

11. Between March and November 1917, G.E. made an investment in Russia and so did National City Bank. Singer had problems in Russia in this period. See *New York Times,* Oct. 11, 1917.

12. U.S. Legislative Reference Service, Library of Congress, Report for the Committee of Foreign Affairs, *Expropriation of American-Owned Property by Foreign Governments in the 20th Century,* 88th Cong., 1st sess., Washington, D.C. 1963, 8.

13. Kean, Taylor & Co., "Singer Manufacturing Company," February 1926, Scudder Collection and Lewis, 296 (Singer's $84 million loss); later Singer claimed a loss of $100 million based on bank deposits ($39 million) and properties of the subsidiary ($61 million); see Foreign Claims Settlement Commission of the United States, *Tenth Semi-Annual Report,* Washington, D.C. 1959, 263 (henceforth cited as *Foreign Claims Report*); Tom Mahoney, *The Great Merchants,* New York 1955, 69 puts Singer's loss at $115 million but gives no source. For a description of Singer's Russian properties and the difficulty in establish-

ing the amount of the loss, see Foreign Claims Settlement Commission, *Decisions and Annotations,* Washington, D.C. 1968, 350 and 347–367.

14. State of N.Y. Insurance Department, "Report of Examination—New York Life Insurance Company," Dec. 31, 1940 in New York Life Insurance Company Archives (loss of $67.3 million); see *Foreign Claims Report,* 243–244, for slightly different figures. R. Carlyle Buley, *The Equitable Life Assurance Society of the United States 1859–1964,* New York 1967, II, 952–982 (aftermath of Russian expropriation); Donald G. Bishop, *The Roosevelt-Litvinov Agreements,* Syracuse, N.Y. 1965, 143, gives Equitable's claimed loss as $10 million.

15. International Harvester, *Annual Report 1918; ibid., 1924;* later, International Harvester claimed a loss of $41.4 million; see *Foreign Claims Report,* 256.

16. *Foreign Claims Report,* 237–240.

17. *New York Times,* Oct. 17, 1928, Floyd James Fithian, "Soviet American Economic Relations 1918–1933," Ph.D. diss., University of Nebraska 1964, 288ff., and *Foreign Claims Report,* 234–236. G.E.'s initial claim of loss was $1.8 million. Bishop, 144.

18. Lewis, 296.

19. H. H. Westinghouse, Chairman, Westinghouse Air Brake Co., to Stockholders, Mar. 21, 1919, Scudder Collection. In Westinghouse's reports to stockholders, 1920, 1921, 1924, he refers to the factory in Russia and the lack of information; in 1926 there is no mention of the Russian enterprise. H. H. Westinghouse reports to shareholders, Scudder Collection; *New York Times,* Apr. 2, 1925, and *Foreign Claims Reports,* 240–243. Lewis, 296 (Parke, Davis).

20. Western Electric Financial Reports and Thayer to Swope, Nov. 4, 1918, Western Electric Company Archives (Dec. 1918: Petrograd factory carried at a mere $353,000). Records in the Western Electric Company Archives indicate that in 1921 Western Electric had an investment in "notes, advances and open accounts receivable" equal to $279,000, plus $12,000 in 29.3% of the Russian company's stock. The former figure was reduced to 0 in 1922, while the latter sum remained on the financial record until 1925. The stock in the Russian enterprise was not sold when all the other foreign properties of Western Electric went to I.T.T. in 1925.

21. Edward Prizer to Secretary of State, Oct. 27, 1918, RG 59, 763.72113A/510, NA (Vacuum Oil). Vacuum Oil later claimed a loss of $1.6 million. Bishop, 143. Other losers: Lewis, 296 (Victor Talking Machine); Carl Ackerman, *George Eastman,* Boston 1930, 288, 290–291, 295, 300, 301; U.S. Dept. of Comm., Bureau of Foreign and Domestic Commerce, *Foreign Capital Investments in Russian Industries and Commerce,* transl., Misc. Series, No. 124, Washington, D.C. 1923, 27 (Otis, Babcock & Wilcox, trading companies: Russian American Trade and Industrial Corporation, J. Black Co., and Russian-American Rato Corp.); *Ford Times,* 6:306 (April 1913), *ibid.,* 7:124 (December 1913), and *Foreign Claims Report,* 163–171 (M. S. Friede's prewar Russian investment in Ford dealerships and in general); George Sherman Queen, "The

United States and the Material Advance in Russia 1881–1906," Ph.D. diss., University of Illinois [1941], 170, 219–220 (Enoch Emery's and W. Ropes & Co. trading investment); *ibid.,* 219, 220 (mining investments). F. A. Vanderlip to Stillman, July 6, 1917, Vanderlip Papers, estimated that the National City Bank's assets in Petrograd were one hundred million rubles, or roughly $50 million at the prewar rate of exchange. The investment was "practically all in government obligations or loans secured by government obligations." It was, of course, lost. This was portfolio rather than direct investment. See also J. Allen Palmer, "Memo" n.d. [1918?], Vanderlip Papers (Russian losses).

22. The $200 million loss to *direct* investors is my own estimate. For compensation see reports of Foreign Claims Settlement Commission of the United States. Newspapers and company records indicate the business response to the Russian revolution.

23. RG 76, NA, has extensive data on the claims; see esp. RG 76, List Nos. 350 to 370 folder, NA (Singer's German war claims). See also RG 59, 763.72113A/821, NA (International Harvester's property in enemy territory) and RG 59, 462.11 Si 63, NA (detailed data connected with Singer's Rumanian claim).

24. Gibb and Knowlton, 323.

25. On the disruption and disorganization see for example, International Harvester Company, *Annual Report 1919.*

26. Wilkins, 213; Lewis, 296; Henry G. Prout, *A Life of George Westinghouse,* New York 1921, 264–266, and John H. Dunning, *American Investment in British Manufacturing Industry,* London 1958, 27.

27. Wilkins, 106–107; Walter Buckner, "Reinsurance and Transfer of Company's Business in Foreign Countries," n.d. [1928?] (quote); Buckner, Memorandum to President and Board of Directors of New York Life Insurance Co., Dec. 13, 1921; and Buckner, Executive Vice President of New York Life Insurance, Memorandum to the Board of Directors, "Final Liquidation of Company's Foreign Business," Oct. 13, 1938, all in New York Life Insurance Company Archives, New York. (These memoranda explain the difficulties in liquidating NYLIC's foreign business. In certain countries, an "enabling act" was necessary; Czechoslovakia, Hungary, Yugoslavia, Bulgaria, Austria, and Spain passed special laws permitting New York Life Insurance Company to transfer its business to a domestic company within those countries. In other countries different procedures were followed. In total, New York Life Insurance Company entered into 28 separate agreements involving the liquidation of the business; the agreements were in 20 different languages.)

28. Mixed Claims Commission, United States and Germany, *First Report of Robert Bonynge,* Washington, D.C. 1925, 250.

29. Exolon Co. stopped making aluminum oxide; International Abrasives Co. and D. A. Brebner & Co. went bankrupt. Muriel F. Collie, *The Saga of the Abrasives Industry,* Greendale, Mass. 1951, 212–213, 219, 220.

30. Mixed Claims Commission, United States and Germany, *First Report of*

Marshall Morgan, Washington, D.C. 1924, 42, and *First Report of Robert W. Bonynge,* 52.

Chapter III: The Outlook

1. Geoffrey Brunn and Victor S. Mamatey, *The World in the Twentieth Century,* 4th ed., Boston 1962, 177–180; R. R. Palmer, ed., *Atlas of World History,* New York 1957, 172ff.

2. *Antitrust Laws with Amendments,* Washington, D.C. 1959, 38–40 (copy of P. L. 126, approved Apr. 10, 1918: Webb-Pomerene Act); Federal Trade Commission, *Report on Cooperation in American Export Trade,* Washington, D.C. 1916 (background on Webb-Pomerene Act); Kenneth W. Dam, "Background Paper on Taxation of Foreign Income," Mimeographed Draft, Nov. 12, 1962, 27 (foreign tax credit: Sec. 222, Revenue Act of 1918); Paul P. Abrahams, "American Bankers and the Economic Tactics of Peace: 1919," *Journal of American History* 46:578–583, December 1969 (Edge Act). Joseph Brandes, *Herbert Hoover and Economic Diplomacy,* Pittsburgh 1962, 15 (quote from Harding).

3. For some 1919–1920 stakes in manufacturing in Europe see Cleona Lewis, *America's Stake in International Investments,* Washington, D.C. 1938, 302 (Willys-Overland in England in 1919); Coca Cola, *Annual Report 1921;* Larry Pressler, "American Machine and Foundry Company," Vernon Research Reports; RG 151, 623 Germany, NA (Lehn & Fink).

4. Harvey E. Fisk, "The Flow of Capital—Canada," *The Annals of the American Academy of Political and Social Science* 107:175 (May 1923).

5. Secretary of State Robert Lansing, quoting "the best technical authorities" declared in 1919 that the "peak of petroleum production in the United States will be practically exhausted within a measurable period." Lansing to Grey, Dec. 20, 1919, *Foreign Relations of the United States 1919,* I, 171. See also John A. De Novo, "The Movement for an Aggressive American Oil Policy Abroad, 1918–1920," *American Historical Review* 61:854–875 (July 1956).

6. See Chap. II above (Mexico); *West Coast Leader,* Apr. 20, 1918 (Peru); U.S. Sen., Special Committee Investigating Petroleum Resources, *American Petroleum Interests in Foreign Countries, Hearings,* 79th Cong., 1st sess., Washington, D.C. 1946, 70 (Rumania), and George Sweet Gibb and Evelyn H. Knowlton, *The Resurgent Years 1911–1927,* New York 1956, 105 (general); *ibid.,* 328–335, 356 (Russian oil); Lewis, 226 (others' new stakes in oil).

7. U.S. Rubber, *Annual Report 1919;* Lewis, 270 (Charles E. Hires); *New York Times,* Oct. 26, 1970 (Anaconda).

8. Harry Scheiber, "World War I as Entrepreneurial Opportunity: Willard Straight and the American International Corporation," *Political Science Quarterly* 84:486–511 (September 1969), and A.I.C., *Annual Report 1919.* Abrahams, 578–583; *Federal Reserve Bulletin* 6:449 (May 1920), 7:68 (January 1921), 7:137–138 (February 1921); C. V. Phelps, *Foreign Expansion of American Banks,* New York 1927, 25, 143, 148, and *Federal Reserve Bulletin* 42:1289 (December 1956).

9. National City Bank, *Monthly Letters 1919–1921,* and William Ashworth, *A Short History of the International Economy,* London 1959, 187ff.

10. Coca Cola, *Annual Report 1921* and *1928;* Herbert Marshall, Frank A. Southard, and Kenneth W. Taylor, *Canadian-American Industry,* New Haven 1936, 254–255 (Canadian failures).

11. U.S. Rubber, *Annual Reports 1921;* Lewis, 271–272; and Robert F. Smith, *The United States and Cuba,* New York 1960, 30 (sugar); Federal Trade Commission, *Report on Copper Industry,* Washington, D.C. 1947, 346. *New York Times,* Oct. 26, 1970.

12. American International Corporation, *Annual Report 1921; Federal Reserve Bulletin* 42:1298, December 1956 (Edge Act companies); Phelps, 144, 156 (branch bank closings).

13. Clive Day, *A History of Commerce,* New York 1922, 603.

14. Paul E. Samuelson and Everett E. Hagen, *After the War 1918–1920: Military and Economic Demobilization of the U.S.,* Washington, D.C. 1943, 2–37 (factors affecting the 1921 downturn).

15. William E. Leuchtenburg, *The Perils of Prosperity,* Chicago 1958, chap. 10; see also George Soule, *Prosperity Decade,* New York 1947; Adolf A. Berle and Gardiner Means, *The Modern Corporation and Private Property,* rev. ed., New York 1968, 42–43 (basis for corporate expansion).

16. Note 2 above (Harding); *Foreign Relations of the United States* 1927, II, 212 (Coolidge quote); Joseph Brandes, *Herbert Hoover and Economic Diplomacy,* Pittsburgh 1962, 163ff (Hoover's views); RG 151, 623: Branch Factories, NA (Domeratzky quote); W. H. Rastall, Chief Industrial Machinery Division, Memo, Sept. 2, 1925, and W. H. Rastall to Taylor, June 7, 1929; RG 151, 623: Branch Factories, NA (Westinghouse).

17. C. F. Remer, *Foreign Investment in China,* New York 1933, 323–325, 328.

18. Milton Offutt, *Protection of Citizens Abroad by the Armed Forces of the United States,* Baltimore 1928.

19. Joan Hoff Wilson, in *American Business and Foreign Policy 1920–1933,* Lexington, Ky. 1971, 156, argues that the open door policy existed for the Far East, while a closed door policy prevailed in Latin America, i.e., that the United States developed a sphere of influence in Latin America. I would suggest that the open door–closed door policies were one the same; the U.S. government wanted U.S. stakes in these areas above and beyond the stakes of Europeans. I agree entirely with Mrs. Wilson that in the 1920s aid to U.S. business in the Far East and Latin America was considered by the U.S. government as part of its duty.

Chapter IV: The Conquest of Markets

1. John H. Dunning, *American Investment in British Manufacturing Industry,* London 1958, 37 (British restrictions); W. Arthur Lewis, *Economic Survey 1919–1939,* New York 1969, 48 (lower French tariffs); William Ashworth, *A Short History of the International Economy,* London 1959, 187ff (European postwar problems); *New York Times,* Sept. 18, 1927 (quote).

2. For the theme of Canada as a fine place for foreign investment, see Herbert Marshall, Frank A. Southard, Jr. and Kenneth W. Taylor, *Canadian-American Industry*, New Haven 1936, 198ff; Royal Commission on Canada's Economic Prospects, *Final Report*, Ottawa 1957, 385; Irving Brecher and S. S. Reisman, *Canada-U.S. Economic Relations*, Ottawa 1957, 114; John Lindeman and Donald Armstrong, *Policies and Practices of United States Subsidiaries in Canada*, n.p. 1961, 2–3; Hugh G. J. Aitken et al., *The American Economic Impact on Canada*, Durham, N.C. 1959, vii; U.S. Dept. of Comm., Bureau of Foreign and Domestic Commerce, *American Direct Investments in Foreign Countries*, Trade Information Bulletin No. 731, Washington, D.C. 1930 (henceforth cited as *Dickens 1930 Report*); C. Vann Woodward, ed. *The Comparative Approaches to American History*, New York 1968, 67 (Canadians more conservative). Mira Wilkins, *The Emergence of Multinational Enterprise: American Business Abroad from the Colonial Era to 1914*, Cambridge, Mass. 1970, 145 (background). Data on market-oriented and supply-oriented stakes based on figures in Table III.1 and author's personal knowledge.

3. This pattern applied from cereals to corn products. See Frank A. Southard, Jr., *American Industry in Europe*, Boston 1931, 3 (Shredded Wheat: the American Shredded Wheat was acquired by National Biscuit in 1929). Corn Products, *Annual Report 1964* (histories of foreign companies), *Fortune*, September 1938, 55ff, and interview, Emerson Schroeder, Corn Products, New York, June 17, 1965 (Corn Products' methods of operations). By 1929, companies such as Heinz, Kraft, Royal Baking Powder (U.S. parent acquired by Standard Brands in 1929), Wrigley's, American Chicle, Sun Maid Raisins, and American Milk Products had plants in at least one European country. See Stephen Potter, *The Magic Number*, London 1959 (Heinz); Kraft, *Annual Reports 1926, 1927;* data in Scudder Collection, Columbia University (Royal Baking Powder); *Moody's 1929* (Wrigley's); Scudder Collection (American Chicle); *Moody's 1929* (Sun Maid Raisins); Temporary National Economic Committee, *Export Prices and Export Cartels*, Monograph #6, Washington, D.C. 1940, 192 (American Milk Products).

4. Swift & Co., *Annual Reports*. In 1928 Borden Co. acquired in a domestic transaction Merrell-Soule Co. (makers of KLIM), which had a sales subsidiary in England in 1926; this apparently gave Borden its first direct investment in Europe (*Moody's 1928* and Borden Co., *Annual Reports 1928, 1929*). On Borden in Canada, see *Annual Report 1930*.

5. *Moody's 1929* (Kellogg had plants in Canada and Australia); *Moody's 1928*, and Donald T. Brash, *American Investment in Australian Industry*, Cambridge, Mass. 1966, 309 (Kraft had plants in England, Canada, and Australia).

6. For example, early in 1927, American Chicle opened a new chewing gum factory in Mexico City (American Chicle, *Annual Report 1927*); Sun Maid had a repacking plant in Shanghai; the cartons were made and purchased locally (Report of A. Viola Smith, June 13, 1928, RG 151, 623: Branch Factories, National Archives). Both had operations in Europe.

7. Corn Products, *Annual Report 1964*.

8. T.N.E.C., *Export Prices and Export Cartels*, 192 (American Milk Products); Federal Trade Commission, *Report on Cooperation in American Export Trade*, Washington, D.C. 1916, and Federal Trade Commission, *Webb-Pomerene Associations*, Washington, D.C. 1967, 1–8.

9. United Fruit Company, *Annual Reports*.

10. *Dickens 1930 Report*, 40 (Commerce Dept. findings).

11. *Moody's 1929* and *Annual Reports*.

12. Matthew Josephson, *Sidney Hillman*, Garden City, N.Y. 1952, 260–266, 285, and Sidney Hillman, *The Russian-American Industrial Corporation, Report to the Board of Directors*, New York 1923.

13. *Moody's 1929*.

14. See Wilkins, *Emergence of Multinational Enterprise* (G.E.'s early history abroad). David Loth, *Swope of G.E.: The Story of Gerard Swope*, New York 1958, 93–100; Gerard Swope, *Reminiscences*, Oral History Collection, Columbia University Library; Theodore Geiger, *The General Electric Company in Brazil*, Washington, D.C. 1961, 37, and interview, W. Rogers Herod, Feb. 24 and Mar. 11, 1964 (I.G.E.C.). U.S. v. General Electric Company, 82 F. Supp. 753 (1949) at 772, 828—829; George Ward Stocking and Myron W. Watkins, *Cartels in Action*, New York 1946, 330–332 (lamp agreement).

15. International General Electric Company, *Annual Reports 1919–1929;* General Electric, *Annual Report 1923;* Canadian General Electric Company, Ltd., *Annual Reports 1919–1929;* General Electric, *Annual Reports 1893–1900;* Marshall et al., *Canadian-American Industry*, 72–73 (our telling of the story of Canadian General Electric differs from that in Marshall, et al., based on information in the annual reports).

16. I.G.E.C., *Annual Reports* (rise in investment); Swope, *Reminiscences;* Adam Gowans Whyte, *Forty Years of Electrical Progress*, London 1930, 112–113; Dunning, 40–41; Southard, 21–23, 182; *Economist*, Mar. 23, 1929; interview, Herod, Mar. 11, 1964.

17. Wilkins, 94 (A.E.G. ties); A.E.G., Prospectus on Debenture Issue, Jan. 15, 1925, Scudder Collection (A.E.G. boasted its relationship with G.E. was a "source of mutual strength to both companies"); I.G.E.C., *Annual Report 1929* (stock interests); *New York Times*, Aug. 3, 1929 (promise); Southard, 26 (Siemens and quote).

18. Interview, Herod, Feb. 24, 1964 and Federal Trade Commission, *Electrical Power Industry*, Washington, D.C. 1928, 138.

19. Federal Trade Commission, *Report on International Electrical Equipment Cartels*, Washington, D.C. 1948, 2–7 (International Notification and Compensation Agreement); Harvard Business School Case, #BH 81R1 (the present author does not agree with the case's interpretation of the I.N.C.A. as a consequence of the depression and feels it was far more the consequence of G.E.'s overall policy; a principal G.E. executive confirmed this author's feeling in this regard).

20. F.T.C., *Electric Power Industry*, 141.

21. U.S. v. General Electric Company, 82 F. Supp. 843.

22. John Winthrop Hammond, *Men and Volts: The Story of General Elec-*

tric, Philadelphia 1941, 375–377 (excellent on formation R.C.A.); *Moody's 1929* (Victor Talking Machine and Gramophone Co.); for other U.S. interests in phonograph companies see Southard, 108 (Brunswick-Balke-Callender).

23. Western Electric Financial records, Western Electric Archives, New York; interviews, Western Electric executives; F.T.C. v. General Electric, et al. Docket #1115 (investigation included A.T.T.).

24. I.T.T., *Annual Report 1925* (acquisition); I.T.T., *Annual Reports* (background); interview (description of Behn). I.T.T., *Prospectus,* Aug. 19, 1925 (Spanish activities); conversation Murray D. Kirkwood, I.T.T., Feb. 28, 1961 (Behn's hope to buy Barcelona plant); *New York Times,* Aug. 15, 1925 (press comment on I.T.T.'s acquisition). Note that this was a small sum compared with the $77 million "deal" between Anaconda and the Guggenheims—see Chap. V herein); Federal Communications Commission, *Investigation of the Telephone Industry,* Washington, D.C. 1939, 33 ($29.3 million); *Wall Street Journal,* Aug. 6, 1926, I.T.T., *Prospectus,* June 14, 1927, *Moody's 1929,* and *Annual Reports* (expansion); Southard, 50 (employment).

25. *Moody's 1930* (Kelvinator); Marshall et al., 72 (Hoover, Premier).

26. Marshall et al., 264 (68 per cent figure).

27. General Electric was associated with Mitsui; Westinghouse had licensing arrangements with Mitsubishi; I.T.T. was associated with Sumitomo. Data from companies in Japan.

28. Mira Wilkins and Frank Ernest Hill, *American Business Abroad: Ford on Six Continents,* Detroit 1964, 435 (assembly plants), 189ff (Dagenham).

29. *Ibid.,* chap. 6, and data from Ford Motor Company, Canada.

30. Wilkins and Hill, 145 (Vauxhall), 192 (G.M. acquired 80% interest in Opel); G.M., *Annual Reports 1920–1929,* and Alfred P. Sloan, *My Years with General Motors,* Garden City, N.Y. 1964, 316–327. Koppel S. Pinson, *Modern Germany,* 2d ed., New York 1966, 226, and *Car Life,* September 1967, 15 (background on Opel). Federal Trade Commission, *Report on Motor Vehicle Industry,* Washington, D.C. 1939, 454–455, 462, 479, 481. C. Howard Aikman, *The Automobile Industry of Canada,* Toronto 1926, and Sun Life Assurance Co. of Canada, *The Canadian Automobile Industry,* Ottawa 1956.

31. F.T.C., *Report on Motor Vehicle Industry,* 553, 555; Marshall et al., 68; Wilhelm R. Meisinger, a student of Chrysler's international operations, in a letter to the author, Nov. 19, 1966, indicates the Dodge truck manufacturing in England; Southard, 218 (Chrysler assembly in Germany).

32. U.S. Sen., Committee on Finance, *Tariff Act of 1929, Hearings,* 71st Cong., 1st sess., Washington, D.C. 1929, 833 (market for cars). Wilkins and Hill, 152 (Fordismus).

33. For data on European automobile producers see bibliographical essay, Wilkins and Hill, 457. The European producers Citroen and Austin had desired American financing; both approached Ford and G.M. seeking joint ventures; nothing materialized. See *ibid.,* 97 (Ford); Frederick G. Donner, *The World-Wide Industrial Enterprise,* New York 1967, 18, and Sloan, 317, 318, 320 (G.M.).

34. Harvey E. Fisk, "The Flow of Capital—Canada," *Annals of the American*

Academy of Political and Social Science 107:175–176 (May 1923); Marshall et al., 63, 264 (the 83 per cent figure is for 1932, but it seems applicable to late 1929).

35. Mitsubishi Economic Research Bureau, *Japanese Trade and Industry,* London 1936, 303.

36. Cram's Automotive Reports, Inc., "Analytic Report on the B. F. Goodrich Company," Detroit 1929, Scudder Collection (Goodrich in Great Britain; British capital participated); Hugh Allen, *The House of Goodyear,* Cleveland 1943, 263, and Southard, 106, 117 (Goodyear in England); Southard, 106, and Raymond Firestone, Speech to National Foreign Trade Council, 1964 (Firestone in Britain); Southard, 8, 106 (Goodrich in Germany; this 25 per cent investment was relinquished in 1929, but a "community of interest was continued.")

37. Marshall et al., 31–33; Allen, 221, 218–219, 223; "U.S. Rubber" folder, Scudder Collection.

38. Goodyear, *Annual Report 1929,* and Allen, 398–400; B. F. Goodrich, *Annual Report 1929,* and J. Crawford, "Memorandum on the Visit of Messrs. Caywood and Aspell of the B. F. Goodrich Rubber Co. to Mr. Ford's Office," Oct. 15, 1936, Acc. 390, Box 85, Ford Archives, Dearborn, Mich. (historical data on B. F. Goodrich's joint venture in Japan).

39. Wilkins and Hill, 204 (Briggs and Kelsey-Hayes); Southard, 5 (Ambi-Budd), 92–93 (Timken); Timken Roller Bearing Company, *Annual Reports; Moody's 1929* (Pressed Steel, Electric Autolite, Electric Storage Battery); Champion Spark Plug, *Annual Report 1958* (England, 1922; France, (1923); du Pont, *Annual Reports.* Libbey-Owens in association with Belgian financiers started in Europe in 1922. By 1929, it was manufacturing in Belgium, France, Germany, Italy, Spain, and Switzerland. In the first four countries, it had plate glass factories as well as window glass plants. See U.S. Tariff Commission, *Window Glass,* Washington, D.C. 1929, and *Moody's 1930.*

40. Aikman, 11; company *Annual Reports; Moody's 1930.*

41. Company *Annual Reports; Moody's.*

42. Theodore Armstrong, *Our Company,* Dayton, Ohio 1949, 112 (National Cash); Thomas Watson, *Men—Minutes—Money,* New York 1934, 114; Saul Englebourg, "I.B.M.," Ph. D. diss., Columbia University 1954, 287; Boyd France, *I.B.M. in France,* Washington, D.C. 1961, 23 (French company plant still for assembly). In Watson to Roosevelt, July 6, 1935, in Edgar B. Nixon, ed., *Franklin D. Roosevelt and Foreign Affairs,* Cambridge, Mass. 1969, 550, Watson says European factories established "to protect our interests abroad" in the face of trade barriers. Remington-Rand, *Annual Report 1929; Moody's 1929;* Royal Typewriter and Underwood-Elliott-Fisher Company, *Annual Reports* (sales companies). Samuel Crowther, *John H. Patterson,* Garden City, N.Y. 1929; William Rodgers, *Think,* New York 1969.

43. These are 1932 figures, but they seem to apply to 1929 as well. Marshall et al., 60.

44. Dudley M. Phelps, *Migration of Industry to South America,* New York 1936, 5 (Singer, International Harvester, National Cash in South America); see also George Wythe, *Industry in Latin America,* New York 1945, 6.

45. U.S. v. Aluminum Co. of America, *Brief of the Aluminum Co.*, Equity No. 85–73, Southern District Court-New York 1940, 601 (henceforth cited as *Alcoa Brief*). George Ward Stocking and Myron W. Watkins, *Cartels in Action*, New York 1946, 248 (for a different view of why Alcoa expanded abroad). *Alcoa Brief,* 607–609, 613, 618–620, 620–623, 638, and W. Y. Elliott et al., *International Control of Nonferrous Metals*, New York 1937, 238 (for specifics of Alcoa's expansion in Europe).

46. Aluminium Ltd., *Annual Report 1929* and *Mineral Industry 1929* (percentage of output exported).

47. U.S. Sen., Committee on Patents, *Hearings*, 77th Cong., 2d sess. (henceforth cited as *Bone Committee Hearings*), 2245 (du Pont's European manager); *U.S. v. I.C.I.*, 100 F. Supp. at 521, Southern District Court-New York 1951 (quote); Williams Haynes, *The American Chemical Industry*, 6 vols., New York 1945–1954, IV, 38, du Pont, *Annual Reports 1925–1929*, and W. J. Reader, *Imperial Chemical Industries*, London 1970, I, 396–397, 409–418 (du Pont's foreign interests); *Bone Committee Hearings*, 2278–2283, 2392–2406 (relations with I.C.I.), 2264–2265, 2268 (relations with I. G. Farben). Du Pont and I. G. Farben discussed a joint venture in the United States; du Pont insisted on control and I. G. did not approve; apparently that ended the discussions; see *ibid.*, 2252–2253, 2254–2260.

48. Union Carbide and Carbon, *Annual Reports 1919–1929;* New York Stock Exchange Listing Statement #A-7040, Feb. 16, 1926; Union Carbide and Carbon, "Union Carbide and Carbon Corp." 3d ed., New York 1929. Interviews in India.

49. Reader, 345, 462, and Wendell R. Swint to Jasper Crane, Dec. 17, 1926, in *Bone Committee Hearings, Exhibits*, 2247 (Allied's European connections). Reader, 334, Haynes, VI, 179–181, *Moody's 1929*, Stocking and Watkins, 430, and data in Scudder Collection (Allied Chemical in Canada).

50. Haynes, III, 421–422 (relations U.S. and foreign chemical industries). A number of du Pont's most important products originated from European sources, for example rayon, cellophane, ammonia, hydrogen peroxide, titanium dioxide. See J. K. Jenny to J. E. Crane, Dec 9, 1936, Jasper Crane Papers, Acc. 1231, Box 2, Eleutherian Mills Historical Library.

51. Reader, 458ff.

52. *Bone Committee Hearings, Exhibits*, 3468–3473, and George Sweet Gibb and Evelyn H. Knowlton, *The Resurgent Years, 1911–1927*, New York 1956, 546 (1927 contract); *Bone Committee Hearings, Exhibits*, 3434 (Teagle quote, Aug. 2, 1927), 3444–3445, 3451–3469 (1929 agreement); Gibb and Knowlton, 546, *Bone Committee Hearings*, pt. 7, and Centennial Seminar on the History of the Petroleum Industry, *Oil's First Century*, Cambridge, Mass. 1960 (implications).

53. Tom Mahoney, *Merchants of Life*, New York 1959, 193–195. Haynes, VI, 271. Exhibit A, "Treaty Agreement November 17, 1932," in *U.S. v. Merck & Co.*, Civil Action 3159, District Court New Jersey, reads, "The parties [Merck & Co. and E. Merck] heretofore have carried on their respective businesses under conditions of mutual cooperation."

54. Mahoney, 213–214; Corwin Edwards, *Economic and Political Aspects of*

International Cartels, Washington, D.C. 1944, 50, and *Time* (Sept. 15, 1941), 73 (Sterling Products); *Fortune* (October 1930), 43; Dunning, 42; Drug Inc., New York Stock Exchange Listing Statement,#A-7898, Mar. 5, 1928.

55. Haynes, VI, 26–27; Southard, 221; *Moody's 1930* (American Home Products).

56. Mahoney, 79.

57. Spencer Trask & Co. and Lehman Brothers, "Colgate Palmolive Peet Company as an Investment," September 1930, 6–7, Scudder Collection.

58. Charles Wilson, *The History of Unilever,* 3 vols., New York 1968, II, 344.

59. *Dickens 1930 Report,* 30.

60. Wilkins, *Emergence of Multinational Enterprise,* 61; Eastman Kodak, *Annual Reports;* Southard, 117; *Encyclopaedia Britannica,* 14th ed., London 1929, VII, 875 (research in England).

61. Wilkins, 84–86 (results of Supreme Court decision).

62. *Ibid.,* 85 (Anglo-American); Gibb and Knowlton, 187, 499, 502 (sales to Anglo-American), 563 (Agwi and continued ties with Anglo-American).

63. Gibb and Knowlton, 517–518 and Southard, 65, 69.

64. Gibb and Knowlton, 516–517 and Southard, 175.

65. Jean Rondot, *La Compagnie Française des Pétroles,* Paris 1962, 11, 35, 36; Teagle's comments at a meeting, Aug. 31, 1928, in exhibit, *Bone Committee Hearings,* 3420; Edith T. Penrose, *The Large International Firm in Developing Countries: The International Petroleum Industry,* London 1968, 135; Federal Trade Commission, *International Petroleum Cartel,* Washington, D.C. 1952, 321; Southard, 64, and Gibb and Knowlton, 510.

66. *Ibid.,* 679 (other refineries of Jersey Standard), 686 (Jersey's employment minus the 5,330 in Rumania involved in production). Southard, 216–217; Atlantic Refining Co., *Annual Report 1926; Moody's 1930; China Year Book 1926,* ii; and Craig Thompson, *Since Spindletop,* n.p. 1951, 70 (other oil companies).

67. Southard, 68–69, 64. See Gibb and Knowlton, 510 for different figures on France that do not include the numerous companies operating there.

68. *Annual Financial Review,* Canadian, July 1929; Henrietta M. Larson, Evelyn H. Knowlton, and Charles S. Popple, *New Horizons,* New York 1971, 819 (employment at Imperial Oil). Gibb and Knowlton, 503 (Imperial's leading position).

69. Marshall et al., 76; *Annual Financial Review,* Canadian, July 1929; Marquis James, *The Texaco Story,* New York (?) 1953, 66; *Moody's 1930.*

70. Gibb and Knowlton, 503 (leading position); Larson et al., 819 (Jersey Standard and its affiliates had in 1929 41,684 employees in the eastern hemisphere, a large percentage of which were in market-related activities in Europe; 20,282 in Canada; and 9,986 in Latin America, an unspecified number of which were involved in supply-related stakes).

71. Interviews, plus U.S. Dept. of Comm., Bureau of Foreign and Domestic Commerce, *Petroleum Refineries in Foreign Countries, 1930,* Washington, D.C. 1930, *passim* (no refineries based on imported crude).

72. Gibb and Knowlton, 501.

73. Nubar Gulbenkian, *Portrait in Oil,* New York 1965, 96 (oilmen are like cats); F.T.C., *International Petroleum Cartel,* 199ff (Achnacarry accord).

74. *Dickens 1930 Report,* 10 ($231 million). Cleona Lewis, *America's Stake in International Investments,* Washington, D.C. 1938, 579, 588, puts the total at $239 million, of which $219 million was said to be in "oil distribution." See Tables III.1–2 above.

75. Both the *Dickens 1930 Report,* 13, and Lewis, 588 give this figure for *all* petroleum investment by U.S. companies in Canada. Under oil distribution (p. 579), Miss Lewis gives no figures, classifying all the U.S. stake in Canadian oil under "production," under which heading she classified refining companies.

76. *Dickens 1930 Report,* 19.

77. *Ibid.,* 26.

78. *Ibid.*

79. Information from F. L. Chandler, Secretary-Treasurer, Anaconda Sales, Sept. 18, 1963 (Anaconda's sales organization in the 1920s); Anaconda, *Annual Report 1922* (Brown's Copper); Federal Trade Commission, *Report on the Copper Industry, Summary,* Washington, D.C. 1947, 12 (Copper Exporters).

Chapter V: Supply Strategies

1. Only a handful of multinational enterprises had supply-oriented stakes in three or more countries before 1914. See Mira Wilkins, *The Emergence of Multinational Enterprise: American Business Abroad from the Colonial Era to 1914,* Cambridge, Mass. 1970, 215, 216.

2. Calculations made by present author based on figures given on Table III.1. If public utilities were included, market-oriented stakes would be vastly more important.

3. Cleona Lewis, *America's Stake in International Investments,* Washington, D.C. 1938, 605.

4. Frank A. Southard, Jr., *American Industry in Europe,* Boston 1931, 89–91 (Union Carbide and Alcoa in Norway); Union Carbide and Carbon Corp.," New York Stock Exchange Listing Statement, #A-7040, Feb. 16, 1926, and Union Carbide and Carbon Corp., "Union Carbide and Carbon Corp.," 3d ed., New York 1929 (Union Carbide in Norway and Canada). American Cyanamid, *Annual Reports,* and Williams Haynes, *American Chemical Industry,* 6 vols., New York 1945–1954, IV, 21 (American Cyanamid). U.S. v. Aluminum Co. of America, *Brief of the Aluminum Co.,* Equity No. 85–73, Southern District Court-New York 1940, 103, 146 (Shawinigan Falls and Arvida facilities); *Mineral Industries 1929,* 18 (exports).

5. John A. Guthrie, *The Newsprint Industry,* Cambridge, Mass. 1941, 58–59 (major companies in 1929); Herbert Marshall, Frank A. Southard, Jr., and Kenneth W. Taylor, *Canadian-American Industry,* New Haven 1936, 35–56 (U.S. stakes in Canadian wood and paper products); *ibid.,* Table V, 24–25 (percentage of gross value of output controlled by U.S. capital in various industries,

1932; the 1929 percentages are not that different); Lewis, 595 (size of U.S. investment).

6. Armstrong Cork, *Annual Report 1929;* Lewis, 306 (sardines). U.S. Dept. of Comm., Bureau of Foreign and Domestic Commerce, *American Direct Investments in Foreign Countries,* Washington, D.C. 1930 (henceforth cited as *Dickens 1930 Report*), 20, 23, 31 (manufacturing in Cuba, Argentina, and Brazil). Cuban Atlantic Sugar Company, *Prospectus,* Apr. 9, 1946, Scudder Collection, Columbia University, and Robert F. Smith, *The United States and Cuba,* New York 1960, 54 (Hershey's refinery). *Comments on the Argentine Trade* 8:17, January 1929 (Argentine meat exports). A. V. H. Hartendorf, *History of Industry and Trade of the Philippines,* Manila 1958, 31–32, Helmut G. Callis, *Foreign Capital in Southeast Asia,* New York 1942, 15, and folder "General Foods," Scudder Collection (coconut factories); California Packing Co., *Annual Report 1929* (canning plant). The Borden Company, *Annual Report 1929,* and A. Viola Smith, Report, June 13, 1928, RG 151, 623 Branch Factories, National Archives (egg factories and pig bristles in China); R. W. Dunn, *American Foreign Investments,* New York 1926, 163 (Americans in jute). Cia. Swift Internacional, *Annual Reports* (Swift).

7. Marvin Bernstein, "The History and Economic Organization of the Mexican Mining Industry, 1890–1940," Ph.D. diss., Univ. of Texas 1951, 1050 (Peñoles's refinery); this thesis was revised and published as *The Mexican Mining Industry, 1890–1950,* Albany 1965. Isaac Marcosson, *Metal Magic,* New York 1949, 206 (ASARCO's refinery). E. S. Moore, *American Influence on Canadian Mining,* Toronto 1941, 71, and *Moody's 1930* (American Metal's participation in Ontario Refining Company).

8. George Sweet Gibb and Evelyn H. Knowlton, *The Resurgent Years,* New York 1956.

9. *Dickens 1930 Report,* 27, 45; C. F. Remer, *Foreign Investment in China,* New York 1933, 289, 327; G. C. Allen and A. G. Donnithorne, *Western Enterprise in Far Eastern Development,* London 1954, 178 (all three on American textiles in China). Dunn, 167 (embroidery in the Philippines). Breslin-Griffith Carpet Co. manufactured rugs in Turkey. *Moody's 1929.*

10. Wilkins, 190 (reasons for U.S. meat packers' initial stakes in Argentina). Peter H. Smith, *Politics and Beef in Argentina,* New York 1969, 119 (the embargo). C. E. Herring, Memo for the Secretary, May 20, 1921, RG 151, 623 China, NA.

11. Smith, *Politics and Beef,* 87–103 (Argentine attitudes toward the packers). Marcosson, 206, and data in legal files, American Smelting and Refining Co., Monterrey, Mexico. "Law for Protection of New Industries," Mar. 24, 1928, State of Nuevo León, *Periodica Oficial del Estado,* LXV. American Smelting and Refining Co., *Prospectus,* Feb. 19, 1937. On fears about Venezuela's future political instability, see S. W. Morgan, Memo, Apr. 21, 1928, RG 59, 831.6363 Lago Pe/1, NA.

12. U.S. Dept. of State, *Compensation for American-Owned Lands Expropriated in Mexico,* Washington, D.C. 1939, 3. On Mexican policies, see Hubert

Herring, *A History of Latin America*, 2d ed., New York 1961, 365, 369, and U.S. response, *Foreign Relations of the United States, 1925*, II 530–531, 552–554; *ibid., 1926*, II, 643ff.

13. Stacy May and Galo Plaza, *The United Fruit Company in Latin America*, Washington, D.C. 1958, 163 (Panama disease); interview, Michael Connolly, Boston, June 1964 (United Fruit and the generals). Samuel Crowther, *American Tropics*, Garden City, N.Y. 1929, 251 (Costa Rica). In 1964 United Fruit Company at Limón, Costa Rica, had a full archives of historical records. Some historian would find this material an excellent source; regrettably this author was only able to spend limited time with these papers; they are the source for the information that the Costa Rican president, Don Ricardo Jiménez Oreamuno, was urging the company to aid him in floating a loan in New York. He got the loan. Crowther, 321.

14. Sumner Welles to Secretary of State, June 2, 1924, RG 59, 815.00/3185, NA (Welles quote). Crowther, 262 (planks in Honduras's programs); Luis Marinas Otero, *Honduras*, Madrid 1963, 89, and Crowther, 256 (fruit companies in Honduras). Milton Offutt, *Protection of Citizens Abroad by the Armed Forces of the United States*, Baltimore 1928, 137–139, and U.S. Dept. of State, *A Brief History of the Relations Between the United States and Nicaragua 1909–1928*, Washington, D.C. 1928 (Nicaragua). See also Jefferson Caffrey, Bogotá, Colombia, to Secretary of State, Jan. 16, 1929, RG 59, 821.5045/51, NA, on conditions of operations (labor unrest) in Colombia.

15. *Dickens 1930 Report*, 18 (size of Cuban investment), 20 (integration of U.S. business); Max Winkler, *Investments of U.S. Capital in Latin America*, Boston 1928, 185–186 (lists Cuban sugar companies); Smith, *United States and Cuba*, 30–31 (Cuban sugar companies), chaps. 3 and 4 (tariff controversy), 187 (tariff levels); Lewis, 273 (sugar prices), 275 (investment peak), 276–278 (other sugar holdings). See Eugene W. Burgess and Frederick H. Harbison, *Casa Grace in Peru*, Washington, D.C. 1954, 26 (on Grace's sugar plantations). Lewis, 590 and *Dickens 1930 Report*, 18 (investments in sugar).

16. U.S Rubber, *Annual Reports 1910, 1922*, and Hugh Allen, *The House of Goodyear*, Cleveland 1943, 408 (their existing plantations); Mira Wilkins and Frank Earnest Hill, *American Business Abroad: Ford on Six Continents*, Detroit 1964, chap. 8 (Ford's activities). RG 151, 621.2, NA (activities of Dept. of Commerce).

17. *Foreign Relations of the United States 1925*, II, 367–379 (Firestone's 1924 plans); Alfred Lief, *The Firestone Story*, New York 1951, chaps. 10–11, esp. p. 153 (lease of Mount Barclay and the rest of the story); *Foreign Relations of the United States 1925*, II, 379–381 (Miller's point of view), 383 (Hines), 386 (Hughes), 403–404 (State Dept. policy in general); Wayne Chatfield Taylor, *Firestone in Liberia*, Washington, D.C. 1956, 4–7, 42–57 (excellent on Firestone's entry into Liberia); interviews with Romeo Horton, minister of commerce and industry, Charles Sherman, secretary of treasury, and President W. V. S. Tubman, Monrovia, July 15, 16, and 17, 1965; Secretary of State of Liberia, Edwin Barclay, to the American Minister (Hood), Apr. 28, 1925, *For-*

eign Relations of the United States 1925, II, 424 (reasons why Liberians wanted Firestone).

18. Allen, 408–409 (Goodyear); U.S. Rubber, *Annual Report 1927;* Lief, chaps. 10 and 11 (the problems); Goodyear and U.S. Rubber, *Annual Reports.* Lewis, 590 (estimated size U.S. stakes in rubber in Asia and Africa at $51 million in 1929). Wilkins and Hill, chap. 8 (Ford).

19. Lewis, 289 (tobacco). International Harvester, *Annual Report 1919* (indicates owns sisal plantation in Cuba; no indication when purchased); International Harvester, *Annual Report 1928.* See *Annual Financial Review, Canadian,* July 1929, for the large holdings of International Paper. Frank B. Cahn & Co., "Singer Manufacturing Co.," October 1929, Scudder Collection (Singer's holdings of Canadian timber); interviews, Central America and the Caribbean (small businessmen's holdings). Hartendorf, 31 (timber in the Philippines). International Products Corporation, *Annual Reports* (International Products Company was reorganized as International Products Corporation in 1926).

20. Dawson to Secretary of State, Dec. 28, 1922, RG 59, 811.42612/2, NA (doctors and lawyers); William Loeb, ASARCO, to Secretary of State, May 7, 1925, RG 59, 811.42612/5, NA (ASARCO); and C. M. Loeb to Secretary of State, June 24, 1925, RG 59, 811.42612/9, NA (American Metal).

21. Interviews in Mexico (Mexican doctors); Bernstein, "History," 1064 (1925 decree); *Engineering and Mining Journal* 122:26 (July 3, 1926), quoted by Bernstein, "History," 1068. American Smelting and Refining Co., *Annual Reports* (increase in investment).

22. Foster Bain and Thomas Thornton Read, *Ores and Industry in South America,* New York 1934, is excellent on U.S. stakes in mining in South America. R. P. Miller, "General Resume Guggenheim Nitrate Enterprise," n.d., Anglo-Lautaro Files, María Elena, Chile; Haynes, *American Chemical Industry,* II, 76–77 (nitrate industry); Anaconda, *Annual Report 1923,* and Harvey O'Connor, *The Guggenheims,* New York 1937, 413–414 (the transaction); Miller, "General Resume." The leaching vats at María Elena are identical in appearance to those at Chuquicamata, so exactly was there a transfer of method from the copper to the nitrate industry. *Engineering and Mining Journal* 126:824, Nov. 24, 1928 (employment in Chilean nitrates). Ignacio Aliaga Ibar, *La Economía de Chile y la Industria del Cobre,* Santiago, Chile 1946, 101 (nitrate exports).

23. Anaconda, *Annual Report 1929;* "Presentation on behalf of Chile Exploration Co. and Braden Copper Co.," May 7, 1928, in RG 59, 825.5123/27, NA (employment in copper). Aliaga Ibar, 101 (copper exports).

24. B. T. Colley, "A Sketch History of Cerro de Pasco," La Oroya, Peru; American Smelting and Refining Co., *Annual Report 1924* (N. Peru operations).

25. *Engineering and Mining Journal* 118:353 (Sept. 6, 1924), 118:663 (Oct. 15, 1924); "New South American Enterprise," *Comments on Argentine Trade* 3:17 (July 1924); National Lead, *Annual Report 1924;* Newmont Mining Corp., *Annual Report 1929.*

26. Bain and Read, 307; Haynes, III, 87 (Guggenheims and Caracoles Tin); A. J. Barnard, Memo, Oct. 30, 1925, RG 151, 622:Chile, NA (quote); Margaret Charlotte Marsh, *Bankers in Bolivia*, New York 1928, 49, lists Fabulosa Mines Consolidated, Bolivian Tin Corporation, International Mining Company (a W. R. Grace subsidiary) as other companies with U.S. interests involved.

27. Data on Bethlehem in Chile from company there (iron ore investment); Bain and Read, 336 and Charles Anderson Gauld, *The Last Titan: Percival Farquhar, American Entrepreneur in Latin America*, Stanford, Calif. 1964, 281–289 (iron ore in Brazil). Bain and Read, 337 (Grace and manganese in Chile); George Wythe, *Industry in Latin America*, New York 1945, 34 (U.S. Steel and manganese in Brazil); *Mineral Industry 1929*, 431 (manganese in Brazil). Vanadium Corporation had vanadium investments in Peru; W. R. Grace & Co. mined tungsten in Bolivia. Bain and Read, 335, 342 (on gold in Colombia and Ecuador and platinum in Colombia). On bauxite, see *ibid.*, 332, and U.S. v. Alcoa, *Brief for the United States*, U.S. Circuit Court of Appeals, 1944, 30 (Demerara Bauxite), 34 (Surinaamsche Bauxite Maatschappij). In 1929 American Cyanamid acquired the Kalbfleische Company with bauxite mines in Dutch Guiana (American Cyanamid, *Annual Report 1929*).

28. Bain and Read, 347.

29. O. W. Main, *The Canadian Nickel Industry*, Toronto 1955, 106 (90%); *Moody's 1930* (assets).

30. E. S. Moore, *American Influence on Canadian Mining*, Toronto 1941.

31. *Moody's 1929;* Anaconda, *Annual Reports 1925–1926.*

32. *New York Times,* Nov. 6, 1921, Feb. 20, 1923, Aug. 18, 1927, and *Economic Review of the Soviet Union* 3:7 (Jan. 1, 1928).

33. *London Times,* Oct. 28, 1924 (MacDonald); F. W. B. Coleman to U.S. Secretary of State, June 26, 1925, RG 59, 861.637/17, NA (reports from Soviet press); RG 59, 861.637 Harriman 1 and 861.637/37 (all the State Department information was secondhand; the State Department did not participate in the negotiations. The first contract had had a fixed royalty on exports, the second had a sliding scale). Letters to Secretary of State from Coleman, Riga, Sept. 11, 1928, RG 59, 861.637/44; J. G. Shurman, Berlin, Mar. 18, 1928, 861.637 Harriman 1; J. B. Stetson, Warsaw, June 12, 1928, 861.637 Harriman 9; L. Sussdorff, Riga, Dec. 21, 1928, 861.637 Harriman 23, and E. L. Rankin, Prague to Domeratzky, July 17, 1929, 861.637 Harriman 27 (long quote); *ibid.* (ruble crisis); Coleman letter, Sept. 11, 1928 (termination); 861.637 Harriman 18, 20 (terms); Averell Harriman, *Peace with Russia?* New York 1959, 2 (quote).

34. *Dickens 1930 Report,* 26, indicates no mining in the Philippines, but Dickens excluded Americans resident in the Philippines. American-born John W. Haussermann, for example, was mining gold in the Philippines in the 1920s, having started in 1914. H. Foster Bain, *Ores and Industry in the Far East,* rev. ed., New York 1933, 135; Fred Harvey Harrington, *God, Mammon, and the Japanese,* Madison, Wisc. 1944, 166–167 (gold mining in Korea). *Dickens 1930 Report,* 26 (no American mining in China); but see RG 59, 893.6353/5, NA, and RG 151, 623 China, NA (Pacific Development Co.); RG 59, 893.6362/6,7,8

(Andersen, Meyer); RG 59, 893.6354/23 (New York Orient Mines). The New York Orient Mines was a syndicate, headed by William Boyce Thompson, the founder of Newmont Mining Corporation. Bain, xi, and *Fortune,* October 1965, 134 (Thompson); Bain, 103, 159–160 (N.Y. Orient Mines in China).

35. Bain, 106 (N.Y. Orient); Nov. 15, 1929 letter, RG 59, 867.63/31, NA (ASARCO), and Apr. 12, 1929 letter, RG 59, 867.6352/1, NA (Newmont Mining). Data on Krebs Pigment from Dr. Richmond D. Williams, Eleutherian Mills Historical Library.

36. Interview, Albert E. Thiele, chairman of the board, Pacific Tin, New York, Apr. 26, 1965; Harvey O'Connor, *The Guggenheims,* New York 1937, 213; U.S. House, Report of the Subcommittee of the House Committee on Foreign Affairs, *Tin Investigation,* Washington, D.C. 1936, 785–786 (Earl quote).

37. Theodore Gregory, *Ernest Oppenheimer,* Capetown 1962, xvi, 85–89, and *passim.*

38. The background on American Metal's entry is given in C. P. Jenney, Memo, Dec. 28, 1949, in Roan Selection Trust Archives, Ndola, Zambia.

39. Gregory, 30, 413–415.

40. *Ibid.,* 412–413.

41. *Ibid.,* 31 (shift in the balance); H. A. Guess, vice president, American Smelting and Refining Company, Memo, Nov. 15, 1929, RG 59, 867.63/32, NA, and Gregory, 423ff (thwarting of the plans).

42. *Mineral Industry 1929,* 119–120 (British fears and Vogelstein quote).

43. Haynes, *American Chemical Industry,* VI, 290, and interview, Sir Ernest Guest, Salisbury, Rhodesia, Aug. 4, 1965 (Vanadium Corp. and Mutual Chemical).

44. Sir Ernest Guest interview ("chrome king"); *Directory of Directors,* 1918–1938 (Sir Edmund's affiliations).

45. The African Manganese Company, Ltd., "The Nsuta Story," n.d., n.p. (a booklet published by the company in the mid-1950s); *Directory of Directors,* 1910, 1918, 1924 (Sir Edmund's affiliations); interviews in Nsuta, Ghana (company looked British); Union Carbide and Carbon, *Annual Report 1925* (Norway); interviews, G. H. Parkinson, manager of the chrome company in Rhodesia, Selukwe, Rhodesia, Aug. 4–5, 1965 (Parkinson was especially helpful in re-creation of this story).

46. Bernard M. Baruch, *My Own Story,* New York 1957, 209–211; Société Internationale Forestière et Minière du Congo, *Status,* Bruxelles 1950 (details of concession); interview, Albert van de Maele (a director of *Forminière*), New York, Apr. 19, 1965. Lewis, 215, and O'Connor, 182 (Angola company); interview, Albert E. Thiele, New York, Apr. 26, 1965 (Portuguese management). On other smaller stakes by U.S. investors in Africa, see testimony of Edward J. Cornish, chairman of the board, National Lead, *Tin Investigation,* 791 (in Nigeria) and *Dickens 1930 Report,* 25 (in Algeria).

47. Jorge L. Tamayo, *Geografía General de Mexico,* Mexico 1962, IV, 437 (Mexican oil output); *Foreign Relations of the United States 1921,* II, 447ff; Pan American Petroleum & Transport Company, *Annual Report 1922;* Report

of the Group on American Petroleum Interests in Foreign Countries, Oct. 15, 1945, in U.S. Sen., Special Committee Investigating Petroleum Resources, *American Petroleum Interests in Foreign Countries, Hearings,* 79th Cong., 1st sess., Washington, D.C. 1946, 235 (salt water), 237–342, 336 (political considerations), henceforth cited as *Petroleum Hearings.* Samuel Flagg Bemis, *A Diplomatic History of the United States,* 3d ed., New York 1950, 558–561 (diplomatic problems); Pan American Petroleum & Transport Company, *Annual Report 1926; Foreign Relations of the United States,* 1920–1929 (every year the State Department devoted considerable time and energy to dealing with problems involving oil and Mexico). Gibb and Knowlton, *Resurgent Years,* 362–366 (Jersey Standard's problems).

48. Venezuelan figures from Ministerio de Minas; Mexican figures from Tamayo, 437; William Bonini et al., eds. *The Role of National Governments in Exploration for Mineral Resources,* Ocean City, N.J. 1964, 160, and Federico G. Baptista, *Historía de La Industria Petrolera en Venezuela,* Caracas 1961, 8–9 (the famous blowout).

49. U.S. Dept. of State, Division of Latin American Affairs, Memo, Feb. 6, 1924, RG 59, 831.6363/232, NA; "Report on Venezuelan Petroleum Legislation," Caracas, Feb. 24, 1940, Creole Petroleum Corporation, Caracas; C. J. Bauer, "Summary of Standard Oil Company (N.J.) Position in Venezuela as of Jan. 1, 1933," Feb. 27, 1933, Creole Petroleum Corporation, Caracas. Willis C. Cook, Caracas, to Secretary of State, June 22, 1922, RG 59, 831.6363/106, NA (the best in Latin America); James Clark, "History of Creole," 1958.

50. S. K. Hornbeck, Memo, Mar. 7, 1923, RG 59, 831.6363/233, NA (visit of Doheny interests); Paul Giddens, *Standard Oil (Indiana),* New York 1955, 254 (Lago and Aruba); S. W. Morgan, Latin American Division, Memo, Apr. 21, 1928, RG 59, 831.6363/Lago Pe/1 (Gómez can't live forever).

51. *Dickens 1930 Report,* 19 (gives the number as 39); Edwin Lieuwen, *Petroleum in Venezuela,* Berkeley 1954, 44, says 107 foreign companies, "most American," were registered and involved in oil exploration in Venezuela. Baptista indicates 73 companies were searching for oil at the end of 1929—but does not indicate how many were American. The number of U.S. companies is difficult to determine, because (1) many companies were registered but invested nothing; a holding company might be registered but might not enter into exploration or production; (2) a single company used numerous affiliates; some people in counting, count *one* company's investments, and others count the parent and each affiliate; in certain cases the parent company operated, and in the other cases, it simply functioned as a holding company; and (3) companies combined, recombined, and developed complicated relationships with one another. Max Winkler, in *Investments of U.S. Capital in Latin America,* Boston 1928, 159–173, attempted valiantly to list the American companies. One example of the complication is the following: Standard Oil of New Jersey owned majority control of Beacon Oil Company, which owned 50 per cent of Beacon Sun Oil Company (the other 50 per cent being owned by Sun Oil Company), the Venezuelan properties of which were operated by Richmond Petroleum Company, a

subsidiary of Standard Oil Company of California! See Beacon Oil Co., *Annual Report 1928*.

52. Lieuwen, 44 (rank); Wayne C. Taylor and John Lindeman, *The Creole Petroleum Corporation in Venezuela*, Washington, D.C. 1955, 12–13, 88–89; Baptista, 23–25 (Jersey in eastern Venezuela); Lieuwen, 53 (impact on Venezuela).

53. Memo from American Consul, Cartagena, Colombia, Mar. 23, 1922, RG 59, 821.6363/Barco/41, NA (Sinclair and Pure Oil); the dispute over the Barco concession is well documented in RG 59, 821.6363/Barco, NA; "The Petroleum Problem," *Comments on the Argentine Trade* 6:48, July 1927 (Argentine situation).

54. Mariano Puga Vega, *El Petróleo Chileno*, Santiago, Chile 1964, 73, 77; data from A. K. Chellew, president, ESSO-Chile, Santiago, Chile. Peter R. Odell, "The Oil Industry in Latin America," in Edith T. Penrose, *The Large International Firm in Developing Countries*, London 1968, 284, 279, indicates that Chile refused in the late 1920s to grant concessions to ESSO "on the grounds that would constitute an infringement of Chilean sovereignty."

55. See, for example, data in RG 59, 821.6363/Barco, NA, esp. Kellogg to Legation, Apr. 3, 1928, RG 59, 821.6363/Barco 87, NA (amicable adjustments).

56. Gibb and Knowlton, 366–369, and information from Standard Oil of New Jersey, New York.

57. By 1929, Jersey Standard was producing oil in Mexico, Colombia, Venezuela, Peru, Argentina, and Bolivia.

58. Data from RG 59, NA; *Moody's; Engineering and Mining Journal;* and Giddens, 240 (Standard Indiana).

59. In 1929 Canada's total oil production was only 3,070 barrels daily (an all-time record to that date); this can be compared with 1929 Rumanian daily production of 98,209 barrels and Polish production of 13,383. More oil was thus produced in Europe (excluding Soviet oil) than in Canada. *Petroleum Hearings*, 355.

60. Gibb and Knowlton, 318–358 and Southard, 56–60 (search for oil in Europe); *Foreign Relations of the United States 1922*, I, 606–608 (Sinclair and New York Standard were interested in concessions in Albania).

61. See Chap. III above.

62. Floyd James Fithian, "Soviet American Economic Relations 1918–1933, American Business in Russia During the Period of Non-recognition," Ph.D. diss., University of Nebraska 1964, 172–176, and Hans Heymann, "Oil in Soviet-Western Relations in the Interwar Years," *American Slavic and East European Review* 7:308ff (1948) (Sinclair).

63. Gibb and Knowlton, 340–358 (fascinating story about Jersey Standard and the purchase of Russian oil—to 1927); *Commercial and Financial Chronicle* 125:470, July 23, 1927 (indicates Vacuum Oil had been using Russian oil for several years); *ibid.*, 471 (Whaley quote); *New York Times*, July 31, 1927, *Economic Review of the Soviet Union*, II, Sept. 15, 1927, and *Fortune*, May 1931, 134 (New York Standard's relations with the Russians; according to *Fortune* the

1927 contract was a $25 million deal, involving the delivery to Standard Oil of New York of 7 million barrels of refined products over a five-year period).

64. Sinclair got a concession in 1923, but Sinclair's efforts came to naught; it formally withdrew in 1925. See *Foreign Relations of the United States 1923*, II, 711, and S. H. Longrigg, *Oil in the Middle East*, London 1954, 39.

65. There has been much written on Middle Eastern oil in the 1920s. The U.S. Sen., *Diplomatic Protection of American Petroleum Interests in Mesopotamia, Netherlands East Indies, and Mexico*, 79th Cong., 1st sess., Washington, D.C. 1945, is useful. More helpful are the following: John A. De Novo, *American Interests and Policies in Middle East 1900–1939*, Minneapolis 1963, 169–204 (he used State Department records extensively); Gibb and Knowlton, 279–306 (they had access to Standard Oil of New Jersey records); Longrigg, *Oil in the Middle East*, 19ff (Longrigg was an oil company executive for many years and had important experiences with the Iraq Petroleum Company); Thomas E. Ward, *Negotiations for Oil Concessions in Bahrain, El Hasa (Saudi Arabia), The Neutral Zone, Qatar, and Kuwait*, New York 1965 (Ward took part in the negotiations, kept records, and is splendid on details; pp. 268–293 contain the text of the two Gulf, Nov. 30, 1927 contracts); Charles W. Hamilton, *Americans and Oil in the Middle East*, Houston 1962 (this oil company executive had access to Gulf Oil records). When sources conflict on detail, I have relied on Ward's and Hamilton's account of *Gulf's* role. Also valuable are Federal Trade Commission, *International Petroleum Cartel*, Washington, D.C. 1952, 45ff; George Lenczowski, *Oil and State in the Middle East*, Ithaca 1960; David H. Finnie, *Desert Enterprise*, Cambridge, Mass. 1958, 25–41; Benjamin Shwadran, *The Middle East, Oil and The Great Powers*, New York 1955; Roy Lebkicher et al., *The ARAMCO Handbook*, The Netherlands 1960, 113ff; George Ward Stocking, *Middle East Oil*, Nashville, Tenn. 1970; Jean Rondot, *La Compagnie Française des Pétroles*, Paris 1962; J. C. Hurewitz, *Diplomacy in the Near and Middle East: A Documentary Record 1914–1956*, Princeton 1956, II. In addition, I have made use of the companies' annual reports and, to a small extent, State Department records in RG 59, NA. Hughes to Teagle, Dec. 22, 1922, *Foreign Relations of the United States 1922*, II, 352 (Hughes quote); see Joan Hoff Wilson, *American Business and Foreign Policy 1920–1933*, Lexington, Ky. 1971, 189, on Hughes-Hoover views 1921; Gibb and Knowlton, 292 (Sadler quote). When in 1931 Atlantic Refining Co. sold its marketing organization in Italy, a fraction of the stock it held in a German distribution company, *and* its 16⅔ interest in Near East Development Corp., it received *only* $1,433,000 for all these assets. Atlantic Refining Co., *Annual Report 1931*. For Standard Oil of California's attempt to find oil in the 1920s, see U.S. Sen., Special Committee Investigating Petroleum Resources, *American Petroleum Interests in Foreign Countries, Hearings*, 79th Cong., 1st sess., Washington, D.C. 1946, 370–375, henceforth cited as *Petroleum Hearings*.

66. *Foreign Relations of the United States 1925*, II, 701.

67. Gibb and Knowlton, 391–394, 506; Herbert Feis, *Petroleum and American Foreign Policy*, Stanford 1944, 10–11; B. Higgins et al., *Stanvac in Indone-*

sia, Washington, D.C. 1957, 21–25; Federal Trade Commission, *Report on Foreign Ownership in the Petroleum Industry,* Washington, D.C. 1923, xix; Penrose, 55. The main oil fields in the Dutch East Indies, however, remained in the hands of Royal Dutch-Shell. H. Foster Bain, *Ores and Industry in the Far East,* rev. ed., New York 1933, 138.

68. *Fortune,* March 1931, 41; data in Scudder Collection, Columbia University; Lewis, *America's Stake in International Investments,* 230.

69. *Petroleum Hearings,* 381 (Australia).

70. *Ibid.,* 354.

71. See Wolfgang Friedmann, *The Changing Structure of International Law,* New York 1964, 177, for comments on the specialized nature of such relationships.

72. These generalizations are mainly the results of visits that the present author took to 31 American company towns in Latin America in the summer of 1964; they were mining camps, oil towns, banana and sugar plantations. In the fall of 1961, the author visited a rubber plantation once owned by an America company in Brazil. Of these 32 company towns, with five exceptions all had some houses that had been built in the 1920s. Company employees described in detail the changes that had taken place since the 1920s. In addition to her own visits, the author also read accounts of travelers in the 1920s and used company histories to supplement her impressions. The quotation on dinner jackets comes from Clayton Sedgwick Cooper, *Understanding South America,* New York 1918, 224; interviews confirmed its validity.

Chapter VI: Others Abroad

1. Radio Corporation of America, *Annual Reports.*

2. *Unifruitco,* June–July 1949, 36 and Stacy May and Galo Plaza, *The United Fruit Company in Latin America,* Washington, D.C. 1958,18.

3. *Foreign Relations of the United States 1922,* II, 154, 158, 159; Western Union, *Annual Reports; Moody's 1929.*

4. R. C. Fetherstonehaugh, *Charles Fleetwood Sise,* Montreal 1944, 208 (decline in ATT interest).

5. Data in Scudder Collection, Columbia University (I.T.T.), and I.T.T., *Annual Reports.*

6. Frank A. Southard, Jr., *American Industry in Europe,* Boston 1931, 37–38.

7. Grosvenor M. Jones, Memo, Jan. 9, 1923, Record Group 151, 623:Italy, National Archives.

8. Intercontinents Power Co., *Annual Report 1929.*

9. American & Foreign Power, *Annual Reports* 1924–1929 (basic data); *ibid.,* 1924–1945 (Owen Young director); American & Foreign Power, "The Foreign Power System," (booklet), New York 1953; interviews, H. W. Balgooyen, New York, and representatives of American and Foreign Power throughout Latin America, summer 1964. Especially useful on the growth of American interests in electric power in Mexico are Miguel S. Wionczek, "Electric Power," in Raymond Vernon, ed., *Public Policy and Private Enterprise in Mexico,* Cambridge,

Mass. 1964, 34–47, and Raymond Vernon, "The Mexican View," in Raymond Vernon, ed. *How Latin America Views the U.S. Investor,* New York 1966, 106–107. *China Year Book 1926* (indicates Shanghai plant largest in China); Edwin S. Cunningham to Secretary of State, Apr. 26, 1929, RG 59, 893.6463/46, NA (U.S. consul).

10. Matthew Josephson, *Empire of the Air, Juan Trippe and the Struggle for World Airways,* New York 1944, 42–45, 49–51, 53–57, 64–75, and R. E. G. Davies, *A History of the World's Airlines,* London 1964, 141ff (excellent background on Pan Am); Oliver James Lissitzyn, *International Air Transport and National Policy,* New York 1942, 328 (Faucett).

11. Drug, Inc., New York Stock Exchange Listing Statement, #A-7898, Mar. 5, 1928. J. K. Winkler, *Five and Ten,* New York 1940, 151–161, and Southard, 109; *Moody's 1930;* Best & Co., *Annual Report 1929.*

12. RG 151, 630:Latin America; U.S. Dept. of State, *List of Contracts of American Nationals with the Chinese Government,* Washington, D.C. 1925.

13. For J. Walter Thompson's international business see, for example, advertisement in *Fortune,* January 1930, 125.

14. *Moody's 1930* (National City Bank). See also Clyde William Phelps, *Foreign Expansion of American Banks,* New York 1927, 160 (American Express), 131–153 (other bank branches). American Express became a subsidiary of Chase Securities in 1929; see Arthur M. Johnson, *Winthrop W. Aldrich,* Boston 1968, 101. See also *Federal Reserve Bulletin* for the 1920s, esp. 12:106 (February 1926), and 42:1284–1299, December 1956 (summary information).

15. William Victor Strauss, "Foreign Distribution of American Motion Pictures," *Harvard Business Review* 8:207, April 1930 (quote); Southard, 94–99 (investments).

Chapter VII: An Overview

1. Eastman Kodak, *Annual Report 1935* (there is evidence this arrangement existed in the 1920s). H. H. Westinghouse to shareholders, Apr. 1, 1921, Scudder Collection, Columbia University (Westinghouse Air Brake); see Chap. V above (Guggenheims); Coty, *Annual Reports 1925–1930,* and *Moody's 1929.*

2. Based on data in New York Stock Exchange Listing Statements, *Moody's,* company records, and company histories.

3. Sherwin-Williams, Prospectus, 1920, Scudder Collection. Ford Motor Company records, Dearborn, Mich. See Chap. V above (Jersey Standard).

4. American & Foreign Power Company, *Annual Reports 1929.* Record Group 59, 893.6463/37, National Archives, for specific British investments.

5. Data from Ford records, Dearborn, Mich., and Oakville, Ontario (Ford of Canada); interviews, Swift officials, Buenos Aires, Argentina 1964; interviews, National Cash Register officials, Johannesburg, South Africa, 1965.

6. Du Pont, *Annual Report 1926.*

7. Private interviews, including those with Singer officials, New York 1964.

8. J. K. Jenney to J. E. Crane, Dec. 9, 1936, Jasper Crane Papers, Acc. 1231, Box 2, Eleutherian Mills Historical Library.

9. See Chap. V above on sources on United Fruit, Union Carbide, Jersey Standard, and the Argentine meat packers.

10. Mira Wilkins, *The Emergence of Multinational Enterprise: American Business Abroad from the Colonial Era to 1914*, Cambridge, Mass. 1970, 216.

11. Anaconda in 1915 took over the properties of Amalgamated Copper Company.

12. Data in Scudder Collection and in *Moody's 1930*.

13. Anaconda, *Annual Report 1929;* Henrietta M. Larson, Evelyn H. Knowlton, and Charles S. Popple, *New Horizons,* New York 1971, 819 (71,952 versus 57,865 in 1929).

14. Alfred D. Chandler, Jr., in *Strategy and Structure,* Cambridge, Mass. 1962, opened my eyes to the connection between strategies and changes in organizational structure. Wilkins, 58, and G.E., *Annual Reports, 1892, 1893* (Thomson-Houston).

15. For example, in 1913 International Harvester Company had organized International Harvester Corporation to handle all its foreign business. In 1918, the two companies were reunited. (International Harvester Company, *Annual Reports*). In 1917, Singer Manufacturing Company "cast off" its British manufacturing subsidiary. As we have noted, Swift set up an international company for its foreign operations.

16. Data in Western Electric Archives, New York.

17. David Loth, *Swope of G.E.,* New York 1958, 93–100; Gerard Swope, *Reminiscences,* Oral History Collection, Columbia University Library; Theodore Geiger, *General Electric Company in Brazil,* Washington, D.C. 1961, 31; interviews W. R. Herod, Mar. 11 and Feb. 24, 1964.

18. Westinghouse Electric, *Annual Report 1919*.

19. G. M., *Annual Reports*.

20. Mira Wilkins and Frank Ernest Hill, *American Business Abroad: Ford on Six Continents,* Detroit 1964.

21. Chandler, 216 (quote), 215 (structure), 174, 202, 213 (Imperial Oil).

22. Data in Scudder Collection and *Annual Reports*.

23. Crown Cork & Seal Company, *Annual Reports, 1928* and *1929;* Crown Cork International Inc., *Annual Report 1929*.

24. Based on data in U.S. v. Alcoa, *Brief for the United States,* Eq. No. 85–73, Southern District Court-New York 1940, 683–701, 705ff, and U.S. v. Alcoa, *Brief of the Aluminum Company,* Eq. No. 85–73, SDNY 1940, 727–730, 735. Henceforth cited as *Alcoa Brief.* It is interesting that Alcoa—while decentralizing its foreign business—did not adopt a multidivisional structure for its domestic operations. Chandler, 327.

25. Company *Annual Reports,* and Chandler, 327–329.

26. Wilkins, *Emergence of Multinational Enterprise,* chap. IV.

27. Wilkins, 100 (1909 activities); U.S. v. Timken Roller Bearing Co. 83 F. Supp. 284, Northern District Court—Ohio 1949, modified and affirmed 341 U.S. 593 (1951); *Moody's 1929;* Timken Roller Bearing Co., *Annual Reports*.

28. We have made this specific point before; see Wilkins, 77.

29. Temporary National Economic Committee, *Investigation of Concentration of Economic Power, Hearings,* pt. 25 ("Cartels"), Washington, D.C. 1940, 13166–13187, and J. W. F. Rowe, *Primary Commodities in International Trade,* Cambridge, Eng. 1965, 125 (copper). See Chap. IV above on Achnacarry Accord.

30. In fact, New York Life Insurance spent much of the decade terminating its earlier foreign business. See Walter Buckner, "Reinsurance and Transfer of Company's Business in Foreign Countries," n.d. [1928?], and Buckner, Executive Vice President of New York Life Insurance, Memorandum to the Board of Directors, "Final Liquidation of Company's Foreign Business," Oct. 13, 1938, in New York Life Insurance Company Archives, New York.

31. Wilkins, 91–93 (background).

32. On the tobacco industry, we have used *Annual Reports;* Reavis Cox, *Competition in the American Tobacco Industry,* New York 1933; William H. Nichols, *Price Policies in the Cigarette Industry,* Nashville, Tenn. 1951.

33. Wilkins, 101, 177, 212.

34. Report of Commissioner Combines Investigation Act, Dept. of Justice, *Matches,* Ottawa 1949, 7–8.

35. See U.S. Steel, *Annual Reports,* 1920s; Frank A. Southard, Jr., *American Industry in Europe,* Boston 1931, 173, 219.

36. Wilkins, 70–71.

37. W. Y. Elliott et al., *International Control of Nonferrous Metals,* New York 1937, 240 (measures by Swiss and French companies taken against Alcoa); *Economist,* Mar. 23, 1929 (measures against G.E. in England). John H. Dunning, *American Investment in British Manufacturing Industry,* London 1958, 41; Southard, 181, and U.S. Sen., *American Branch Factories Abroad,* Sen. Doc. 258, 71st Cong., 3d sess., Washington, D.C. 1931, 22 (general measures to bar foreigners). Anthony C. Sutton, *Western Technology and Soviet Economic Development,* Stanford, Calif. 1968 and Floyd James Fithian, "Soviet American Economic Relations, 1918–1933, American Business in Russia During the Period of Nonrecognition," Ph.D. diss., Univ. of Nebraska 1964 (Soviet policies). Southard, 177 *(ueberfremdung);* Ludwell Denny, *America Conquers Britain,* New York 1930, 148 (French proposal). Herbert Feis, *Europe: The World's Bankers, 1870–1914,* New Haven 1930.

38. George Sweet Gibb and Evelyn H. Knowlton, *The Resurgent Years 1911–1927,* New York 1956, 519.

39. Southard, *passim;* see 225ff for bibliography of articles on American industry in Europe; J. Bonnefon-Craponne, *La Pénétration économique et financière des capitaux américains in Europe,* Paris 1930; Denny, 137ff. Southard, xiv (1300).

40. Frank A. Knox, "Excursus, Canadian Capital Movements and the Canadian Balance of International Payments, 1900–1934," in Herbert Marshall, Frank A. Southard, Jr., and Kenneth W. Taylor, *Canadian-American Industry,* New Haven 1936, 299 (U.S. and British *total* investments).

41. The best overall study of British investment in Latin America is J. Fred Rippy, *British Investments in Latin America,* Minneapolis, Minn. 1959. Rippy,

75, believes that British investment in Latin America peaked at the end of 1928 and declined in 1929. He claims that the figure given by the *South American Journal* of the "nominal total" for British investment in Latin America of £1,211,038,544 for 1928 is "probably at least £80 million too high." This would make his estimate, £1,131,038,544. The figure, he argues, went down in 1929, owing to the Guggenheim purchase of British nitrate investments and American & Foreign Power and I.T.T. purchases of British utilities in Latin America. On the basis of an exchange rate of $4.86, we can change Rippy's estimate into dollars—$5.50 billion for 1928. Cleona Lewis's estimate (Lewis, *America's Stake in International Investments,* Washington, D.C. 1938, 606) for U.S. direct and portfolio investments in Latin America *in 1929* was $5.43 billion. Thus, if there was at least a $70 million dollar drop in British investment in Latin America between 1928 and 1929, which seems to be the case, then total U.S. investment on that continent in 1929 exceeded that of the British. In certain Latin American countries, Argentina for example, British stakes to be sure still exceeded those of Americans, but the British position was being sharply challenged and no one doubted that even in Argentina, U.S. capital had a "place of great importance in the economy of the country." See Enrique Garcia Vazquez, "An Argentine View," in Raymond Vernon, ed., *How Latin America Views the U.S. Investor,* New York 1965, 50–52, and Arturo Frondizi, *Petróleo y Política,* 3d ed., Buenos Aires 1955, 139.

42. As late as 1927, American exporters were advised to sell in Liberia through European trading houses. See Clifton R. Wharton, Vice Consul to Merchant's Association of New York, Dec. 7, 1927, RG 84, American Consulate General, Monrovia, Liberia, Post Record-1927, IV 869.12, NA.

43. Eccles J. Gott (S. Essex), Canada, House of Commons Debates, *Official Report, 1929,* 1285. See also *ibid., 1928,* 966–967.

44. Royal Commission on Canada's Economic Prospects, *Final Report,* Ottawa 1957, 143 (hydro-electric power). Samuel Flagg Bemis, *A Diplomatic History of the United States,* 3d ed., New York 1950, 797–798; Lynn W. Meekins to Bureau of Foreign and Domestic Commerce, Oct. 3, 1927, RG 151, 623:Canada, NA. U.S. Sen., *American Branch Factories Abroad,* 21 (appeals to British capital); A. A. Heaps (N. Winnipeg), Canada, House of Commons Debates, *Official Report 1928,* 637 (hewers of wood and drawers of water): Cameron R. McIntosh (N. Battleford), in *ibid, 1929,* 1352 (there is "no danger of absorption by the United States . . . through the investments which have been made in this country.") See also Marshall et al., 287. *New York Times,* Jan. 11, 1966 (economic and political control).

45. U.S. Sen., *American Branch Factories Abroad,* 30; Irving Brecher and S. S. Reisman, *Canada-U.S. Economic Relations,* Ottawa 1957, 98, 100 (the figures); Hugh G. J. Aitken et al, *The American Economic Impact on Canada,* Durham, N.C. 1959 (strategic impact).

46. Richard Hofstadter, *The Age of Reform,* New York 1955, 137–138.

47. Although not confined to the 1920s nor to U.S. investment in Latin America, Marvin D. Bernstein, ed., *Foreign Investments in Latin America,*

New York 1966, has useful data on attitudes toward foreign investment. Vernon, ed., *How Latin America Views the U.S. Investor,* is even more valuable.

48. Hubert Herring, *A History of Latin America,* 2d ed., New York *1961,* 447, states "For years United Fruit has been the favorite whipping boy for fervid nationalists, who accuse it of exploiting the workers, suborning local governments and draining off exorbitant profits to the United States. In the earlier years of the twentieth century there were grounds for some of these charges, but most of the critics of the company are still leveling their fire against the United Fruit of 1910 rather than of 1960. During the past twenty-five years United Fruit has emerged as one of the most intelligent and socially alert of all U.S. companies operating outside their homeland." *Compare* this with Frederick Upham Adams, *Conquest of the Tropics,* Garden City, N.Y. *1914,* 165–166: The United Fruit has not come into "conflict with any of the many nations in which they have operated . . . Wars have been waged between these nations, strained relations have existed between some of them and the United States, revolutions have succeeded revolutions, our troops have been landed on these soils to protect American lives and property, but in all these years and amid all these happenings the United Fruit Company has continued its creative work without voicing complaint or having one made against it . . . If the Nobel Peace Prize could be awarded a corporation, the United Fruit Company would have valid claims to recognition. It has done more to pave the way for peace and prosperity in Central America and the Caribbean countries than all the statesmanship and oratory which have vainly been directed to the same purpose." Samuel Crowther, in *American Tropics,* Garden City, N.Y. *1929,* 243ff, recognized that United Fruit had been criticized, but only, he claimed, because it had been "misunderstood." He, too, explained the company's virtues. C. D. Kepner, *Social Aspects of the Banana Industry,* New York 1936, and C. D. Kepner and Jay Henry Soothill, *The Banana Empire,* New York 1935, present a very biased, negative appraisal. Unquestionably, in the present writer's mind, the company in the early years was a progressive one: The present author has seen the hospital at Quirigua and other remnants of times past; what she would like to see is an honest explanation of some of the controversies. United Fruit Company managers were human beings, who faced continual problems in operating in tropical climates. They had to deal with weak governments. One wants to know what the managers thought were their responsibilities; what their aims were; when they became concerned with the hostility and how concerned they were; how much they wanted to mix in politics and how much they wanted to *avoid* mixing in politics. Standard Oil of New Jersey and Ford Motor Company both should be congratulated for letting historians into the records and letting them write balanced historical accounts; United Fruit should do the same. Until then, historians must reserve judgment on both the praise and enmity.

49. On these policies see Chap. V above. Crowther, *American Tropics* 321, indicates the praise for United Fruit. Likewise, the president of Honduras (Dr. Miquel Paz) told Crowther, "We want more and not less American capital" (p. 323); Crowther got similar responses from the presidents of Nicaragua, El Salva-

dor, and Guatemala (see pp. 326–332). Later, Costa Rican President Ricardo Jiménez did not have kind words for United Fruit. John and Mavis Biesanz, *Costa Rican Life,* New York 1944, 142, describe the Costa Rican president's "blistering denunciations" of United Fruit.

50. Colin Forster, *Industrial Development in Australia, 1920–1930,* Canberra 1964, 19 (Australian Industries Protection League). U.S. Sen., *American Branch Factories Abroad* ("less than cordial").

51. Interviews in Japan and company records.

52. For example, in 1928, American Radiator planned a factory in Spain; all building in Spain required government approval, and approval was refused. The company went to the American ambassador in Spain. At the same time, it investigated the possibility of a joint venture with Spanish capital (with the company's main competitor in Spain); this was the alternative it finally adopted. See Henry S. Downe to Clarence Woolley, Feb. 10, 1928, Advisory Board to W. E. Kugeman, Dec. 19, 1928, Kugeman to Advisory Board, Dec. 29, 1928, in Spanish company files, International Division, American-Standard, New York, and American Radiator Co., Minutes, Board of Directors, Apr. 18, 1929, Secretary's Office, American-Standard.

53. Generalizations based on company records and interviews. See also on changes in policy that took place, Boyd France, *I.B.M. in France,* Washington, D.C. 1961, 19 (I.B.M.); testimony of A. V. Davis, *Alcoa Brief,* 601 (Alcoa); Wilkins and Hill, *American Business Abroad,* 193–194 (Ford Motor Company). I.B.M. operated in Germany in 1929 under the following names: Deutsche Hollerith Maschinen Gesellschaft, Optima-Maschinenfabrik, A.G., and Deutsche Geschaftsmachinen Gesellschaft. Its stock ownership in these companies ranged from 90 per cent in the first to 99.75 per cent in the last (New York Stock Exchange Listing Statement, Nov. 16, 1929, #A-9108). General Motors declared in its *Annual Report 1929* that it sought to make G.M. "a local institution in each country in which it is operating . . . This is accomplished by recognizing the customs of the country, and harmonizing the Corporation's procedures and policies with such customs." It added, "The Corporation's products are adapted in the fullest possible measure to local taste." Where adaptation was impossible, G.M. introduced specialized products. Thus did American enterprises become "assimilated."

54. *Foreign Relations of the United States,* and RG 59, NA provide ample evidence for these generalizations.

55. For example, John Parke Young, *The International Economy,* 4th ed., New York 1963, has large historical sections and deals with problems; in the entire book there is one footnote devoted to Canada!

56. A. B. Parsons, "William Loeb of A.S. & R Sees Improved Industrial Relations," *Engineering and Mining Journal* 126:566–567 (Oct. 13, 1928).

57. William Loeb, ASARCO, to Secretary of State, May 7, 1925, RG 59, 811.42612/5, NA.

58. W. S. Culbertson to S. W. Morgan, Oct. 2, 1928, RG 59, 825.5123/29, NA, and also RG 59, 825.5123/27, 30, NA.

59. E. C. Squire, to Bureau of Foreign and Domestic Commerce, June 14, 1928, RG 151, 623 Branch Factories, NA.

60. Company histories and data obtained from Mitsui, Mitsubishi, and Sumitomo interests in Tokyo, 1965.

61. See RG 59, 493.11 St 2/36, NA.

62. *Forbes,* Sept. 15, 1967, 56, gives the *revenues* of the top twenty U.S. industrials in 1929: 1. Standard Oil (N.J.); 2. General Motors; 3. Ford Motor; 4. U.S. Steel; 5. Swift; 6. Armour; 7. Standard Oil (Indiana); 8. General Electric; 9. Western Electric; 10. Chrysler; 11. Bethlehem Steel; 12. International Harvester; 13. Borden; 14. Anaconda; 15. National Dairy Products; 16. Gulf Oil; 17. R. J. Reynolds Tobacco ("Camel" cigarettes); 18. Goodyear Tire & Rubber; 19. Westinghouse Electric; 20. Texas. Revenues were not available for Standard Oil (New York) or American Tobacco (with its "Lucky Strike" cigarettes)—both of which may have qualified for the top twenty. The present author checked this list against her own records on direct foreign investment and found that all had foreign investments of some kind in 1929. She finds no record of foreign investments by Standard Oil of Indiana or R. J. Reynolds in 1919; National Dairy was formed in 1922 and had at formation no foreign investments.

63. U.S. Dept. of Commerce, Office of Business Economics, gives G.N.P. figures for the United States in 1929 as $103.1 billion; direct foreign investment, using Cleona Lewis's and Department of Commerce figures (see Table VIII.2 herein) equaled $7.5 billion or 7.3 per cent of G.N.P.

64. Wilkins, *Emergence of Multinational Enterprise,* 201. The actual 1914 percentage was 7.3.

Chapter VIII: Obstacles to Growth

1. International General Electric Company, *Annual Report 1930;* Hugh Allen, *The House of Goodyear,* Cleveland 1943, 263; *Comments on the Argentine Trade* 10:33, April 1931 (Firestone broke ground for the new plant in December 1930 and started to make tires May 1, 1931); information from Parke, Davis Co., Buenos Aires, Argentina. The number of new, enterprises in 1929—based on data collected at the start of 1930—is in U.S. Dept. of Comm., Bureau of Foreign and Domestic Commerce, *American Direct Investments in Foreign Countries-1936,* Washington, D.C. 1938, 47–49 (henceforth cited as *Dept. of Comm. Report 1936*). 1930 figures are in Louis Domeratzky to Representative John L. Cable, July 18, 1932, RG 151, 623:Br. Factories, National Archives. Accounts of various manufacturing companies indicate the return of funds to the United States. Balance of payments data show a sharp drop in the total *net outflow* of funds from the United States—from $602 million in 1929 to $294 million in 1930. See U.S. Dept. of Comm., Bureau of the Census, *Historical Statistics of the United States,* Washington, D.C. 1960, 564.

2. C. P. Jenney, Memorandum, Dec. 28, 1949, in Roan Selection Trust Archives, Ndola, Zambia (henceforth cited as *RST Memo*); interview, Sir Ronald Prain, Lusaka, Zambia, Aug. 10, 1965 (impracticality of offering); Theodore

Gregory, *Ernest Oppenheimer,* Capetown 1962, 436 (Sir Auckland); Roan Selection Trust, "An Introduction to RST," August 1964 (booklet).

3. Geoffrey Blainey, *Mines in the Spinifex,* Sydney, Australia 1960, 142, 144, 163, 173, 174; Isaac Marcosson, *Metal Magic,* New York 1949, 166–167.

4. American & Foreign Power, *Annual Report 1930;* International Telephone and Telegraph Corporation, *Annual Report 1930; Moody's 1931; Fortune,* December 1930, 37, 39 (I.T.T.); Samuel Insull's Middle West Utilities Company in April 1930 formed the Middle West Utilities Co. of Canada, Ltd., to own control of the Great Lakes Power Co. Ltd., the Algoma District Power Company, and the National Utilities Company. The Utilities Power & Light Corporation, which made large investments in England in 1929, in 1930 acquired the Maritime Coal, Railway, and Power Co., Ltd., Canada Electric Co., Ltd., and the Eastern Electric & Development Co., Ltd., all operating in Canada (in Nova Scotia and New Brunswick). Early in 1930, Iowa Southern Utilities organized National Light and Power Co., Ltd., to own and operate the electric light and power system purchased from the city of Moosejaw, Saskatchewan. The purchase price for the system was $2.875 million. *Moody's 1930.* Matthew Josephson, *Empire of the Air,* New York 1944, 46 (Pan Am Airway). Arthur M. Johnson, *Winthrop W. Aldrich,* Boston 1968, 117; *Federal Reserve Bulletin* 42:129 (December 1956), and Chase National Bank, *Annual Report 1935.*

5. Hubert Herring, *A History of Latin America,* 2d ed., New York 1961 (revolutions in Latin America).

6. League of Nations, *Industrialization and Foreign Trade,* New York 1945, 134.

7. Joseph M. Jones, *Tariff Retaliation,* Philadelphia 1934.

8. William Ashworth, *A Short History of the International Economy, 1850–1950,* London 1952, 157, 203ff.; W. S. Woytinsky and E. S. Woytinsky, *World Commerce and Government,* New York 1955, 42; Shepard Bancroft Clough and Charles Woolsey Cole, *Economic History of Europe,* Boston 1941, 797.

9. Geoffrey Brunn and Victor S. Mamatey, *The World in the Twentieth Century,* 4th ed., New York 1962 (general background); Herring, *passim.* (Latin American revolutions).

10. Atlantic Refining Co., *Annual Report 1932* (quote).

11. *Financial World,* Nov. 9, 1932, 439.

12. Eastman Kodak, *Annual Report 1932.*

13. E. C. Squire, Sydney, to W. H. Rastall, Nov. 23, 1932, RG 151, 623:Australia, National Archives. Oliver North, Ottawa, to Bureau Foreign and Domestic Commerce, Nov. 9, 1933. RG 151, 623 Canada, NA.

14. W. H. Rastall, Industrial Machinery Division, Bureau of Foreign and Domestic Commerce, Memo, Dec. 14, 1931, RG 151, 623:UK, NA.

15. Edgar B. Nixon, ed., *Franklin D. Roosevelt and Foreign Affairs,* 3 vols. Cambridge, Mass. 1969, III, 75–76, and Herbert Marshall, Frank A. Southard, Jr., and Kenneth W. Taylor, *Canadian-American Industry,* New Haven 1936, 71.

16. Dudley M. Phelps, *Migration of Industry to South America,* New York 1936, 289.

17. R. Grau to C. E. Sorenson, June 23, 1930, Accession 38, Box 63, Ford Archives, and interview, Humberto Monteiro, São Paulo, Nov. 8, 1961.

18. *Moody's 1932* and John K. Winkler, *Five and Ten,* New York 1940, 241.

19. *Moody's 1930, 1935,* and *1938.*

20. Drug Inc., New York Stock Exchange Listing Statement #A10037, Mar. 2, 1933, and A. H. Diebold to stockholders, July 26, 1933, Scudder Collection, Columbia University.

21. Among the U.S. companies to sell out was American Chicle, which in March 1933 closed out its wholly owned British manufacturing subsidiary. American Chicle, Standard and Poor's, *Individual Corporate Descriptions,* III, Mar. 4, 1942.

22. William L. Cooper, Commercial Attache to Frederick M. Feiker, Director, Bureau of Foreign and Domestic Commerce, Feb. 17, 1932, RG 151, 623: UK, NA; Underwood Elliott Fisher, *Annual Report 1930;* E. C. Squire to Bureau of Foreign and Domestic Commerce, Mar. 19, 1931, RG 151 623:Australia, NA; S. G. Sabine to Bureau of Foreign and Domestic Commerce, Mar. 14, 1933, RG 151, 623:Canada, NA; Constant Southworth and W. W. Buchanan, *Changes in Trade Restrictions Between Canada and the United States,* New York 1960, 1, 9 (Canadian tariffs); Louis Domeratzky to Representative John L. Cable, July 18, 1932, RG 151, 623:Br. Factories, NA; Marshall et al., 255, estimate that for every four new American factories established in Canada between 1930 and 1934, one existing plant was closed or sold to Canadians. Royal Institute of International Affairs, *The Problem of International Investments,* London 1937, 43–44 (general problems; forced investment).

23. The blue pages in *Moody's* give the losses of companies and industries. Anaconda, *Annual Report 1932.*

24. L. H. Gann, "The Northern Rhodesian Copper Industry and the World of Copper, 1923–1952," *Rhodes-Livingstone Institute Journal,* 18:7, 1955 (Bwana Mkubwa shut down); Rhodesian Selection Trust, *Annual Report 1932* (curtailment); Roan Antelope Copper Mines, Ltd., *Annual Report 1932* (Roan); William Yandell Elliott et al., *International Control of Non-Ferrous Metals,* New York 1937, 151 (indicates this sale of Canadian shares was because of American Metal's financial difficulties).

25. Ervin Hexner, *International Cartels,* Chapel Hill, N.C. 1945, 224, and *New York Times,* July 11, 1932 (Copper Exporters Inc. dissolution). Anaconda, Prospectus, Oct. 15, 1935, Scudder Collection, and Temporary National Economic Committee, *Hearings,* Pt. 25 (1940), 13537 (exhibit)—changing trade patterns.

26. R. P. Miller, "General Resume Guggenheim Nitrate Enterprises" [n.d. 1933?], in files, Anglo-Lautaro Nitrate Corporation, María Elena, Chile. Miller himself was a participant in the COSACH negotiations.

27. International Labour Office, *Intergovernmental Commodity Control Agreements,* Montreal 1943, 73 (henceforth cited as *ILO Commodity Agreement*

Report); Elliott et al., 325; J. W. F. Rowe, *Primary Commodities in International Trade,* Cambridge, England 1965, 90.

28. *ILO Commodity Agreements Report.*

29. *Financial World,* June 15, 1932; Victor Cutter to Stockholders of United Fruit, Oct. 18, 1932, Scudder Collection (revaluation); *Barron's,* Feb. 6, 1933 (write-offs); *Econostat,* Oct. 14, 1933 (reorganization).

30. Robert F. Smith, *The United States and Cuba,* New York 1960, 66–67, 70 (Cuban share of the U.S. sugar market dropped from 49.4 per cent in 1930 to 25.3 per cent in 1933); Rowe, 145–147; *Dept. of Comm. Report 1936,* 13.

31. William Hance, *African Economic Development,* New York 1958, 221 (price of rubber).

32. Temporary National Economic Committee, Investigation of Concentration of Economic Power, *Regulation of Economic Activity in Foreign Countries,* Monograph #40, 76th Cong., 3d sess., Washington 1941, 106ff (Argentine regulations), henceforth cited as *T.N.E.C. Monograph #40.* Data in files of International Packers, Buenos Aires. Simon Hanson, *Argentine Meat and the British Market,* Stanford, Calif. 1937; George Wythe, *Industry in Latin America,* New York 1945, 115–116.

33. Frederick Sears, "International Paper," unpublished report 1964, 1; Marshall et al., 39, 52 (American output).

34. American & Foreign Power, *Annual Reports,* 1930–1932.

35. *Financial World,* Apr. 5, 1933.

36. Data in Scudder Collection, and *Moody's 1933.*

37. Matthew Josephson, *Empire of the Air,* New York 1944, 46.

38. U.S. Dept. of Comm., Bureau of Census, *Historical Statistics of the United States,* Washington, D.C. 1960, 564.

39. *New York Times,* Mar. 5, 1933.

40. Milton Friedman and Anna Jacobson Schwartz, *A Monetary History of the United States,* Princeton 1963, 462ff; Cordell Hull, *Memoirs,* New York 1948, vol. I. Raymond F. Mikesell, *United States Economic Policy and International Relations,* New York 1952; D. W. Brogan, *Roosevelt and the New Deal,* London 1952; James MacGregor Burns, *Roosevelt: The Lion and The Fox,* New York 1956; Arthur Schlesinger, *The Coming of the New Deal,* Boston 1959 and *The Politics of Upheaval,* Boston 1960; William E. Leuchtenburg, *Franklin D. Roosevelt and the New Deal,* New York 1963.

41. Raymond A. Bauer et al., *American Business and Public Policy,* New York 1963, 114–115 (businessmen and liberalization of of trade); Smith, *United States and Cuba,* 161–164, George L. Ridgeway, *Merchants of Peace,* Boston 1959, 126–127.

42. Cuban Atlantic Sugar Company, Listing Application on the New York Curb Exchange, Dec. 18, 1939, amended Apr. 22, 1940, Scudder Collection; for some background on these measures, see Lloyd C. Gardner, *Economic Aspects of New Deal Diplomacy,* Madison 1964, 53–57, and Smith, *United States and Cuba,* chap. 10; *ibid.,* 187 (tariffs on Cuban raw sugar).

43. U.S. Dept. of State, *Assistance Rendered American Commercial Interests,*

Commercial Policy Series No. 39, Washington, D.C. 1937, 1–4; U.S. Dept. of State, *Some Aspects of Assistance Rendered by the Department of State and Its Foreign Service to American Business,* Commercial Policy Series No. 40, Washington, D.C. 1937. *Foreign Relations of the United States, passim.* Export-Import Bank, *Annual Reports;* U.S. Sen., Committee on Banking and Currency, *Study of Export-Import Bank, Hearings,* 83rd Cong., 2d sess., Washington, D.C. 1954, 86–92. Josephson, *passim.*

44. Curtis E. Calder in National Foreign Trade Convention, *Official Report 1941,* 24.

45. Smith, *United States and Cuba,* 157; Samuel Flagg Bemis, *Latin American Policy of the United States,* New York 1943, 334–345.

46. National Foreign Trade Convention, *Official Report 1941,* 24.

47. Mira Wilkins, "The Role of U.S. Business," in Dorothy Borg and Shumpei Okamoto, eds., *Pearl Harbor as History: Japanese-American Relations 1931–1941,* New York 1973, 359–360.

48. Interviews with U.S. businessmen who operated abroad in the 1930s, and books cited in note 40 for the specific measures.

49. *Foreign Relations of the United States 1933,* II, 928 (FDR's statement); *Foreign Relations of the United States 1935,* III, 1098 (claimant should go to local courts); National Foreign Trade Convention, *Official Report 1940,* 280. See also *ibid.,* 276. There were some businessmen who disagreed and felt the U.S. government had been helpful. See *ibid.,* 399.

50. Data on Chinese currency based on Table VIII.5 herein. Canada, Dept. of Labour, *Labour Organization in Canada 1940,* Ottawa 1941, 14 (background on Canadian labor). International Labour Office, *Legislative Series,* published in Geneva during the 1920s and 1930s provides a good source on international social legislation. Henry Pelling, *A History of British Trade Unionism,* London 1963, 211 (British unions); interview and company records (industrial relations issues). *Historical Statistics of the United States,* 564 (direct investment flows).

51. James W. Vaupel and Joan P. Curhan, *The Making of Multinational Enterprise,* Boston 1969, studied 187 companies in international business. They found (p. 123) that in 1929 these companies had 987 foreign subsidiaries (or affiliates) and in 1939 they had 1763 such subsidiaries (or affiliates). We can assume that there is a certain bias in these figures: (a) information on more recent subsidiaries is more accessible; (b) data from the Securities Exchange Commission were available for the 1930s and not for the 1920s; (c) nonoperating subsidiaries may remain on record. Nonetheless, the bias in favor of a higher 1939 figure seems insufficient to discount the substantial rise encountered. Note, however, that the *number* of subsidiaries tells us nothing about the *size* of the investment.

52. U.S. Sen., Committee on Patents, *Hearings and Exhibits,* 77th Cong., 2d sess., Washington, D.C. 1942 (subsequently cited as *Bone Committee Exhibits*), 2396 (du Pont sale); Williams Haynes, *American Chemical Industry,* 6 vols. New York 1945–1954, IV, 38 (du Pont-I.G. Farben sale); *Bone Committee Exhibits,* 2405 (du Pont quote).

53. American Radiator Company, Minutes, Board of Directors, Aug. 9, 1934, Secretary's office, American-Standard, New York and American-Standard, *Annual Report 1934*. Monsanto Chemical Company, Prospectus, July 15, 1937, Scudder Collection, Columbia University. Similarly, in 1935, Timken Roller Bearing reduced its majority interest in its British affiliate to a minority stake.

54. Mira Wilkins and Frank Ernest Hill, *American Business Abroad: Ford on Six Continents*, Detroit 1964, 261 (G.M.). Ford by contrast remained open and lost money. See *ibid.*, 261–262.

55. Nixon, *Franklin D. Roosevelt and Foreign Affairs*, III, 75–76; U.S. Steel Corporation, *Annual Report 1937*.

56. Mira Wilkins, *The Emergence of Multinational Enterprise: American Business Abroad from the Colonial Era to 1914*, Cambridge, Mass. 1970, 138.

57. Interviews in Tokyo with American and Japansese businessmen, 1965, and data from Ministry of International Trade and Industries, Tokyo.

58. U.S. Dept. of Comm., Bureau of Foreign and Domestic Commerce, *American Direct Investments in Foreign Countries-1940*, Washington, D.C. 1942, 11 (involuntary rise in investment). *Foreign Relations of the United States, 1933*, II, 418 ff (difficulties of American firms), 428 (German competitors). *Franklin D. Roosevelt and Foreign Affairs*, III, 456 (Dodd report). The Truman, Bone and Kilgore Committees, 1941–1945, scrutinized the "cartel" agreements with German firms in great detail. RG 151, 623:Germany, NA (1936 data on companies desiring to dispose of holdings in Germany). Interview, John Miller, New York 1963 (attitudes in Germany); Wilkins and Hill, 270–285. T. G. Belden and M. R. Belden, *The Lengthening Shadow; The Life of Thomas J. Watson*, Boston 1962, 195–196; *Fortune*, September 1938, 108; RG 151, 602.1 Australia, Mar. 9, 1936, NA (on G. M.'s proposal to barter wool for Opel motor car parts); Ford Motor Company, International Purchasing Records, Boxes 4 and 8, Highland Park, Detroit, Mich. (Ford and the barter of rubber for car parts).

59. The generalizations on Ford are based on a careful study of the records of Ford Motor Company and its German subsidiary—records in Dearborn, Mich., and in Cologne, Germany. National Lead, *Annual Report 1927* (its joint venture). See Chap. III above (du Pont). National Cash Register Company, *Annual Report 1934*.

60. George L. Ridgeway, *Merchants of Peace*, Boston 1959, 132–133 (the meetings in Berlin). See also Wilkins and Hill, 282ff on naive views of Ford officials. Gabriel Kolko, "American Business and Germany 1930–1941," *Western Political Quarterly* 15:713–728 (December 1962), argues that while U.S. business spoke of antagonism to nazism, U.S. businesses in Germany *acted* in pursuit of their private business interests.

61. Alfred Lief, *The Firestone Story*, New York 1951, 412–413; Hugh Allen, *The House of Goodyear*, Cleveland 1943, 263; *Bone Committee Exhibits*, 2406–2407, 2409–2410 (du Pont); Tom Mahoney, *Merchants of Life*, New York 1959, *passim* (drug industry); Abbott, Prospectus, Oct. 23, 1939; interviews in Latin America and South Africa. Phelps, *Migration of Industry*, 8; *Annual Reports*.

62. Werner Baer, *The Development of the Brazilian Steel Industry*, Nashville 1969, 72–75. Helen Hughes, *The Australian Iron and Steel Industry 1848–1968*, Melbourne 1964, 127 (ARMCO). Federal Trade Commission, *Report on the Agricultural Implement and Machinery Industry*, Washington, D.C. 1938, 982–983 (International Harvester). Hughes, 128 (other U.S. investors in Australia included: Rheem Manufacturing Company and Cleveland File Company).

63. "Historical Highlights of National Cash Register Company's Activity in Japan," from National Cash Register, Tokyo; National Cash Register Company, *Annual Reports, 1934, 1935, 1940*. U.S. v. National Lead, 63 F. Supp. 519 (1945). Interviews, I.B.M. officials, Tokyo, 1965.

64. This is evident when one compares Tables III.1 and VIII.2 above. It is also evident from the number of manufacturing companies. Vaupel and Curhan, 125, indicate that in 1919 their sample of 187 American companies had 180 foreign *manufacturing* subsidiaries and in 1929 467, an absolute increase of 287 or a rise of 159 per cent. In 1939 these 187 American companies had 715 manufacturing subsidiaries, a rise of 248 over 1929 or a 53 per cent increase.

65. Interviews in Latin America, and company *Annual Reports*.

66. Ervin Hexner, *International Cartels*, Chapel Hill, N.C. 225ff, and Temporary National Economic Committee, *Hearings*, pt. 25 (1940), 13234ff (copper agreement).

67. T.N.E.C., *Hearings*, pt. 25, 13270–13271, and *Mineral Industry 1939*, 344 (lead producers agreement); Elliott et al., *International Control of Non-Ferrous Metals*, 710, 716; *Mineral Industry 1932*, 536; *ibid., 1934*, 584; and Hexner, 249–251 (zinc agreements). Anaconda, *Annual Reports* (Silesian American).

68. R. P. Miller, "General Resume Guggenheim Nitrate Enterprises" [n.d. 1933?], in files, Anglo-Lautaro Company, María Elena, Chile. Law #5350 established the new sales corporation, see data in files of Anglo-Lautaro Company, María Elena, Chile. Interview, John A. Peeples, chairman of the board, Anglo-Lautaro Nitrate Corporation, New York, April 1965 (details on sales corporation). See also M. G. B. Whelpley, "Reorganization of the Chilean Nitrate Industry," in Haynes, *American Chemical Industry*, V, 502–503.

69. U.S. House, Report of the Subcommittee of the House Committee on Foreign Affairs, *Tin Investigation*, Washington, D. C. 1935, 807, 810.

70. Hexner, 222–276, and Eugene W. Staley, *Raw Materials in Peace and War*, New York 1937, 256–304.

71. Raymond F. Mikesell, *United States Economic Policy and International Relations*, New York 1952, 28 (FDR's commitment to restore commodity price levels); *Mineral Industry 1933*, 229–231 (copy of silver agreement); Harry Foster Bain and Thomas Thornton Read, *Ores and Industries in South America*, New York 1934, 342–343; Mikesell, 34 ff.; *ILO Commodity Agreements Report*, p. xv; Elliott, et al., 9; and Staley, 296–297 (all on silver agreement).

72. *Mineral Industry 1932*, 175 (gold output); ASARCO and Newmont, *Annual Reports;* Isaac Marcosson, *Magic Metal*, New York 1949, 167 (ASARCO in Australia and Canada), 169 (W. Africa), 173 (Saudi Arabia); Helmut G. Callis, *Foreign Capital in Southeast Asia*, New York 1942, 14 (mining became the most

important American investment sector in the Philippines; by 1936 more than 60 per cent of the total gold reserve of the Island was controlled by American investors); *Mineral Industry 1934*, 254 (Mexico); Frank Graham and Charles R. Whittlesey, *Golden Avalanche,* Princeton 1939, 33 (too much gold).

73. Hubert Herring, *A History of Latin America,* 2d ed., New York 1961, 380, *Dept. of Comm. Report 1936,* 26; Howard Cline, *The United States and Mexico,* New York 1953, 225–226, 291; *Foreign Relations of United States 1935, 1936, 1937, 1938;* Wendell C. Gordon, *The Expropriation of Foreign-Owned Property in Mexico,* Washington, D.C. 1941, 15–18, 44–46; U.S. Dept. of State, *Compensation for American-Owned Lands Expropriated in Mexico,* Washington, D.C. 1939, *passim.*

74. Stacy May and Galo Plaza, *United Fruit Company in Latin America,* Washington, D.C. 1958, 83 (sigatoka); Harvard Business School Case, "United Fruit Company," #ICR 150 (Central American governments borrowed); Charles David Kepner and Jay Henry Soothill, *The Banana Empire,* New York 1935, 213 and *Moody's 1939* (higher taxes); interviews in Boston and Central America, 1964, United Fruit Co. and others (general and IRCA); International Bank of Reconstruction and Development, *Economic Development of Guatemala,* Washington, D.C. 1951, 169ff (IRCA); May and Plaza, 11 (IRCA); Harvard Case ("under attack"); *New York Times,* Mar. 16, 1939 (contributions United Fruit); *Moody's 1939* (net income); interviews in Central America and elsewhere (attitudes).

75. Interview, Denis Brown, Compagnie des Bananes, Douala, Cameroons, July 21, 22, 1965.

76. J. W. F. Rowe, *Primary Commodities in International Trade,* Cambridge, Eng. 1965, 91 and 153 (rubber agreement). Wayne Chatfield Taylor, *Firestone Operations in Liberia,* Washington, D.C. 1956, 56 (new loan agreement); *Foreign Relations of the United States 1934,* I, 617 (Baron van Lynden); Allen, 97–98 (Goodyear in Central America); Wilkins and Hill, *American Business Abroad,* 178 (Ford).

77. Rowe, 145–148 (sugar agreements); Cuban Atlantic Sugar Company, Application for Listing on the New York Curb Exchange, Dec. 18, 1939 (amended Apr. 22, 1940), Scudder Collection. *Dept. of Comm. Report 1936,* 13, and *Dept. of Comm. Report 1940,* 12 (decline in investment).

78. *Dept. of Comm. Report 1940,* 20; U.S. Dept. of Comm., Office of Business Economics, *U.S. Business Investments in Foreign Countries,* Washington, D.C. 1960, 1 (agriculture included with "other investments").

79. *T.N.E.C. Monograph #40,* 106ff (Argentine regulations); Copy of Law 11.747; also data in files of International Packers, Ltd., Buenos Aires. Peter H. Smith, *Politics and Beef in Argentina,* New York 1969, and Simon G. Hanson, *Argentine Meat and the British Market,* Stanford, Calif. 1937 (general situation and meat packer's opposition); George Wythe, *Industry in Latin America,* New York 1945, 115-116-127, 187 (Argentine, Uruguayan, Brazilian regulations); Cia. Swift Internacional, S.A.C.; Prospectus, Jan. 16, 1947, Scudder Collection (quote re: National Meat Board; Uruguayan regulations).

80. Ellen Clayton Garwood, *Will Clayton*, Austin 1958, 15, 24, 78, 79, 93, 95, 102, 134; Morgan, Stanley, & Co., "Anderson, Clayton & Co.," New York 1951, booklet in Scudder Collection; Anderson, Clayton & Co., Prospectus, Apr. 6, 1945, Scudder Collection; *Brazilian Business* 15:300 (August 1935); interview, Tajano Pupo Neto, Anderson, Clayton, São Paulo, Brazil, September 1964.

81. American & Foreign Power, *Annual Reports 1933–1942;* H. W. Balgooyen speech, Columbia University Law School, March 2, 1963; Records of American & Foreign Power Company subsidiary in Brazil, São Paulo, Brazil; American & Foreign Power Company, "The Foreign Power System," New York 1953 (booklet); interviews with company officials in Latin America and New York; *Foreign Relations of United States 1936*, V, 330–331 (Ross-Calder Agreement), 720ff (Mexican expropriation law); Miguel S. Wionczek, "Electrical Power" in Raymond Vernon, ed., *Public Policy and Private Enterprise in Mexico*, Cambridge, Mass. 1964, 52ff (this is excellent); Nelson Johnson to Thomas Lamont, Mar. 26, 1940, Box 184, Folder 17, Lamont Papers, Harvard Business School (booming business in Shanghai).

82. I.T.T., *The Telephone in Argentina, Chile, Cuba, Mexico, Peru, Puerto Rico, and Southern States of Brazil*, New York 1939; I.T.T., *Annual Reports 1933–1940*.

83. Cleona Lewis, *America's Stake in International Investments*, Washington, D.C. 1938, 329; John H. Dunning, *American Investment in British Manufacturing Industry*, London 1948, 40; *Moody's (Public Utilities) Manual 1941*, 1698.

84. Matthew Josephson, *Empire of the Air*, New York 1944, Chaps. 8 and 9.

85. *Federal Reserve Bulletin* 41:1290 (December 1956); Dorothy Borg, *The United States and Far Eastern Crisis*, Cambridge, Mass. 1964, 130 (American-Oriental); Chase National Bank, *Annual Report 1935*,

86. U.S. v. Aluminum Company of America, 20 F. Supp. 13, S.D.N.Y. 1937. U.S. v. Chilean Nitrate Sales Corp. et al., S.D.N.Y. 1939, Crim. Act. No. 106-14. The criminal proceedings were later *nolle prossed*. A complaint was then filed U.S. v. Allied Chemical & Dye Corp. et al., S.D.N.Y. 1940, Civil Act. No. 14-320, which ended with a consent decree, May 29, 1941. On the latter, see George W. Stocking and Myron W. Watkins, *Cartels in Action*, New York 1946, 173.

87. See T.N.E.C., *Hearings*.

88. Company accounts and *Annual Reports*.

89. *Dept. of Comm. Report 1940*, 6.

90. *Ibid.*, p. v. See also, Hal B. Lary, *The United States in the World Economy* (U.S. Dept. of Comm., Bureau of Foreign and Domestic Commerce, Economic Series 23), Washington, D.C. 1943, 82.

91. *Historical Statistics*, 564.

Chapter IX: The Paradox of Oil

1. Interview, Howard Page, director of Standard Oil of New Jersey, New York, June 4, 1965.

2. Interview, Vincent Collings, former chairman of the board, Standard-Vacuum Oil Company, New York, June 10, 1965.

3. The best survey of American foreign investment in oil, covering the 1930s, is U.S. Sen., Special Committee Investigating Petroleum Resources, *American Petroleum Interests in Foreign Countries, Hearings,* 79th Cong., 1st sess., Washington, D.C. 1946 (henceforth cited as *Petroleum Hearings*), 157,165,166,171 (rise in investment).

4. The "near panic" is described in Harold Williamson et al., *The American Petroleum Industry,* Evanston 1963, II, 543; J. Paul Getty, *My Life and Fortunes,* New York 1963, 133 (wells run full blast); Atlantic Refining Company, *Annual Report 1930* (price structure). Edwin Lieuwen, *Petroleum in Venezuela,* Berkeley 1954 (general background on Venezuelan industry).

5. Data on origins of Socony-Vacuum Oil Company from the Mobil Oil Company. Background information collected from company officials in Africa, the Far East, and in the United States, as well as *Annual Reports.* Frank A. Southard, Jr., *American Industry in Europe,* Boston 1931, 61, 63 (Vacuum Oil in Europe).

6. Federal Trade Commission, *International Petroleum Cartel,* Washington, D.C. 1952, 53n, 218–220 (henceforth cited as *F.T.C. Petroleum Report*).

7. Paul Giddens, *Standard Oil Company (Indiana),* New York 1955, 461–462, 489–493; Lieuwen, 59–60; Pan American Petroleum & Transport Company, *Annual Report 1932;* Wayne C. Taylor and John Lindeman, *The Creole Petroleum Corporation in Venezuela,* National Planning Association Study, Washington, D.C. 1955, 13; C. J. Bauer, "Summary of Standard Oil Company of New Jersey Position in Venezuela as of Jan. 1, 1933," Feb. 27, 1933, in Creole Petroleum Corp. files, Caracas (SONJ acquisition); according to Giddens, 492, SONJ paid Standard of Indiana on May 27, 1932, $47.9 million in cash and 1,778,973 shares of Jersey stock. Standard-Indiana thus became Jersey Standard's largest stockholder, with a 7 per cent holding.

8. "The Pricing of Crude Oil," *World Petroleum,* November 1961.

9. For example, Standard Oil of California in the Dutch East Indies in 1931 and Saudi Arabia in 1933.

10. Chap. V, note 51 above (a joint venture in Venezuela); Gulf and the Carib Syndicate had a joint venture in Colombia. None was with host nation capital.

11. Chap. V above (Iraq).

12. Southard, 63; *F.T.C. Petroleum Report,* 321; and Chap. IV above.

13. In 1929, Associated Oil Company (later Tide Water Associated Oil Company) made the contract with Mitsubishi; it was not consummated until 1931. Contract, Nov. 5, 1929, between Mitsubishi and Associated Oil Company, Mitsubishi Oil Company Archives, Tokyo; Mitsubishi Economic Research Institute, *Mitsui-Mitsubishi-Sumitomo,* Tokyo 1955, and data in Mitsubishi Oil Company Archives (the 1931 refinery).

14. Benjamin Higgins et al., *Stanvac in Indonesia,* Washington, D.C. 1957, 33.

15. Thomas E. Ward, *Negotiations for Oil Concessions in Bahrain, El Hasa (Saudi Arabia), the Neutral Zone, Qatar, and Kuwait,* New York 1965, 179–181,

222–252; 1934 Concession Agreement, in files, Kuwait Oil Company, Kuwait; Anglo-Iranian Oil Company, *Proceedings of Annual General Meeting*, June 21, 1937; Kuwait Oil Company, *The Story of Kuwait*, n.p. 1963, 20; Gulf Oil Corp., *Annual Report 1938*; Anglo-Iranian Oil Company, *Annual General Meeting*, June 20, 1938; *ibid.*, June 26, 1939. John A. DeNovo, *American Interests and Policies in the Middle East 1900–1939*, Minneapolis 1963, 205–206; Henry Longhurst, *Adventures in Oil, the Story of British Petroleum*, London 1959, 228–233; Stephen Hemsley Longrigg, *Oil in the Middle East*, London 1954, 110–113; Charles W. Hamilton, *Americans and Oil in the Middle East*, Houston 1962; David H. Finnie, *Desert Enterprise*, Cambridge 1958; George Lenczowski, *Oil and State in the Middle East*, Ithaca 1960; B. Shwadran, *The Middle East, Oil and the Great Powers*, New York 1955, 384–390; Roy Lebkicher et al., *The ARAMCO Handbook*, The Netherlands 1960, 122–123; *F.T.C. Petroleum Report*, 129–134; Raymond Mikesell and Hollis Chenery, *Arabian Oil*, Chapel Hill, N.C. 1949, 50–57.

16. *Foreign Relations of the United States 1929*, III, 80–81, and Ward, 159–160, 164 (U.S. government pressures); Bahrain Petroleum Company, "A Short Account of Operations of the Bahrain Petroleum Company, Ltd," mimeographed, n.d. in files of Bapco, Bahrain; Bahrain Petroleum Company, Ltd. *1957 Annual Report to the Ruler of Bahrain and Its Dependencies*. The Annual Reports were given in accord with the provisions of the Mining Lease of December 29, 1934.

17. F. A. Davis, "Forward," H. St. J. B. Philby, *Arabian Oil Ventures*, Washington, D.C. 1964, pp. xi, 73–134, and Ward, 193 (background). The Saudi Arab Government and Arabian American Oil Company, "Basic Agreements and Selected Documents Pertaining Thereto," n.p. 1958, in files of Aramco, Dhahran, Saudi Arabia (contains text of original concession agreement May 29, 1933, and the letter agreement of same date)—henceforth cited as *Basic Agreements*. See also *ARAMCO Handbook*, 131ff; Longrigg, 106–110; Shwadran, 285–300; Hamilton, 145–147; Karl Twitchell, *Saudi Arabia*, Princeton 1947; *F.T.C. Petroleum Report*, 113–117; Mikesell and Chenery, 51ff.

18. Standard Oil of California, *Annual Report 1936*, and James Terry Duce in Dan H. Fenn, ed., *Management Guide to Overseas Operations*, New York 1957, 41.

19. Standard Oil of California, *Annual Report 1936* and Texas Co., *Annual Report 1936*. Ward, 185–188.

20. *Mineral Industry 1939*, 456 (Bahrain production); interviews, Awali, Bahrain, 1965.

21. Interviews, Tokyo and Nairobi, 1965, with men who participated in the Caltex organization in the Far East and Africa in the late 1930s.

22. Supplemental Concession, May 31, 1939, *Basic Agreements* (here again no mileage was specified, only boundaries); Bapco, Ltd., *1957 Annual Report* (relations with California Arabian Standard Oil Company).

23. Standard Oil of California, *Annual Report 1936*; Texas Co., *Annual Reports 1936–1940*; G. C. Allen and Audrey G. Donnithorne, *Western Enterprise*

in Indonesia and Malaya, London 1957, 178 (Caltex production); *Petroleum Hearings,* 228 (size of investment).

24. Leonard Fanning, *Foreign Oil and the Free World,* New York 1954, 35–38 (Barco concession); interviews, Latin America (Barco concession); Texas Co., *Annual Reports 1936, 1937, 1939, 1940;* Carib Syndicate, *Annual Report 1936.*

25. Gulf Oil Corp., *Annual Report 1937;* information from Mene Grande in Venezuela.

26. Ward, 169–170. Visits and interviews in Bahrain and Kuwait, 1965.

27. Mikesell and Chenery, 41, Stephen Hemsley Longrigg, *Oil in the Middle East,* 3d ed., London 1968, 58–60, and Arabian American Oil Company, *Middle Eastern Oil Developments,* 4th ed., March 1956, 22 (the dispute with Iran). Cleona Lewis, *America's Stake in International Investments,* Washington, D.C. 1938, 232; Scudder Collection file and *Moody's 1937* and *1938* (Seaboard Oil's investments; the company also obtained an abortive concession in Afghanistan).

28. The Royal Institute of International Affairs, *The Middle East,* 2d ed., London 1954, 263–265 (background on Iraq). *F.T.C. Petroleum Report,* 91–94 (royalty issue). *Middle Eastern Oil Developments,* 28; *Petroleum Hearings,* 60 (pipeline). Interviews in Iraq, 1965. Besides Iraq Petroleum, in 1932 Mosul Petroleum Co. was formed. Mosul Petroleum Co. came to be owned by the Iraq Petroleum group in 1936. In 1939 Basrah Petroleum Co. was formed—also owned by the same Iraq Petroleum Company grouping.

29. Original Concession Agreement, May 29, 1933, Art. 36, *Basic Agreements;* interviews in Saudi Arabia; materials in files of Arabian American Oil Company, Dhahran, Saudi Arabia; Fenn, ed., 41ff (excellent on impact of ARAMCO).

30. U.S. Dept. of Comm. and Labor, Bureau of Corporations, *Report of Commissioner of Corporations on Petroleum,* Washington, D.C. 1909, pt. 3, pp. 272–274.

31. Mariano Puga Vega, *El Petróleo Chileno,* Santiago 1964, 73, 77, 129; *Petroleum Hearings,* 328 ("forced to cooperate with COPEC").

32. Data from Esso Brasileira de Petroleo, S.A., indicate that Jersey Standard's exploration company, Companhia Geral de Petroles Pan-Braziliero, was formed in 1921, while John D. Wirth, *The Politics of Brazilian Development 1930–1954,* Stanford, Calif. 1970, 274n, cites a 1941 letter from T. R. Armstrong of Jersey Standard stating the company was formed in 1930. Clearly, the subsidiary obtained leases before 1931 (see *Petroleum Hearings,* 83). Wirth indicates it ceased operating after 1934, while data from Esso-Brazil indicate the exploration company functioned until the 1937 constitution took effect in Brazil. It never found oil. With the decree law 2627 (Oct. 1, 1940), under which foreign-owned exploring companies were declared illegal, the Companhia was dissolved (Wirth, 247n, and data from Esso-Brazil). Under decree law 395, April 29, 1938, Brazil established a National Petroleum Council; refining in Brazil was limited to Brazilian-born nationals. See *Brazilian Business* 18:227 (May 1938), Wirth, 148–149, and *Petroleum Hearings,* 394. On Jersey Standard's refinery in Brazil see Wirth, 139, and *Petroleum Hearings,* 205–206.

33. *Petroleum Hearings,* 82, 327, and George Wythe, *Industry in Latin America,* New York 1945, 127–128.

34. Ministro de Agricultura, Yacimientos Petroliferos Fiscales, *Recopilación de Leyes, Decretos, y Resoluciónes sobre Materia Petrolera (1934–1937)* Buenos Aires 1938, is the basic source; Camera de la Industria del Petróleo, *El Desarrollo de la Producción de Petróleo en la Republica Argentina 1907–1963,* Buenos Aires 1963, 1–2; *Petroleum Hearings,* 327; *Foreign Relations of the United States 1936,* V, 184ff; Standard Oil of New Jersey, *Annual Reports;* Arturo Frondizi, *Petróleo y Política,* 2d ed., Buenos Aires 1955, 343, 398.

35. Gulf Oil's dispute with the Colombian government over the Barco concession (noted in Chap. V) was resolved in 1931 with the Chaux-Folsom agreement between the United States and Colombia. Fanning, 36.

36. Hubert Herring, *A History of Latin America,* 2d ed., New York 1961, 514.

37. *Petroleum Hearings,* 338; Edith Penrose, *The Large International Firm in Developing Countries,* London 1968, 299n. E. Ramirez Novoa, *Petróleo y Revolucion Nacionalista,* Lima, Peru 1970, 4–5.

38. James Clark, "History of Creole," unpubl. 1958, 275 ("Sow the Petroleum"); interviews in Venezuela, 1964; Report by W. D. (?), Feb. 24, 1940, Creole Petroleum Corp. files, Caracas; Fanning, 81 (industry reaction to 1938 act); Lieuwen, 74 ff.

39. *Petroleum Hearings,* 277; interview, Caracas, 1964 (1936 labor law); Clark, 218 (Linam quote).

40. Bryce Wood, *The Making of the Good Neighbor Policy,* New York 1961, 168 (SONJ's plan to sell Bolivian property); Standard Oil of New Jersey, *Annual Report 1936* (published after the seizure); Wood, 168ff (a fascinating account of the Bolivian expropriation); *Petroleum Hearings,* 84, 248 (size of loss); Wood, 174 (Argentina and Peru), 185 (State Dept.).

41. *Mineral Industry 1939,* 450–451 (comparative figures; Mexico, Venezuela, etc.); Government of Mexico, *Mexico's Oil,* Mexico City 1940 (this 881-page government publication—in English—contains many of the basic documents on the expropriation; it will be cited as *Mexican Government Report); ibid.,* 546–548 (production figures), 593–602 (August 1937 commission report), 811, and Standard Oil of New Jersey, "The Fine Art of Squeezing," New York 1940, 12–13 (company protests); *Mexican Government Report,* 697ff (Federal Labor Board award), 807ff (companies' appeal); SONJ, "The Fine Art of Squeezing," 15 (sequence after March 1); *Oil and Gas Journal,* Mar. 17, 1938; *Mexican Government Report,* 877–879 (Cárdenas' speech); Wendell Gordon, *The Expropriation of Foreign-Owned Property in Mexico,* Washington, D.C. 1941, 95; *New York Times,* Mar. 27, 1938, and Josephus Daniels, *Shirt-Sleeve Diplomat,* Chapel Hill, N.C. 1947, 229 (bolt from the blue); Standard Oil of New Jersey, *Annual Report 1937* (published after the 1938 expropriation); *New York Times,* Mar. 30, 1938, Wood, 207, and E. David Cronon, *Josephus Daniels in Mexico,* Madison 1960, 185ff (State Department protest); *Petroleum Hearings,* 21 (Rayner); SONJ, "Diplomatic Protection," New York 1939, 13ff; Samuel Flagg Bemis, *Latin American Policy of the United States,* New York 1943, 348;

Wood, chaps. 8 and 9, and Cronon, chaps. 7–10 (both excellent on U.S. State Department and the expropriation); Daniels, 222–223, 227ff, Cronon, *passim*, and Wood, 208ff (Daniels attitudes); private interviews lead the present author to believe that others in the State Department felt more pro-Cárdenas than in favor of the oil companies; Nicholas Roosevelt, "Creative Dollars Abroad," *National Foreign Trade Convention, 1940*, 272ff (business's review of State Department action); Wood, 219–220 (on force); Standard Oil of New Jersey, "Empty Promises," New York 1940, 13 (maintains Mexico can't pay; properties should be returned); Bemis, 347–348 (different evaluations); *Petroleum Hearings*, 21–22 (settlements). The petroleum industry journals covered the Mexican expropriation in detail. There have been a number of books on the subject. See, for example, Roscoe B. Gaither, *Expropriation in Mexico*, New York 1940. Standard Oil Company of New Jersey published a series of booklets representing its point of view. The Mexican government retorted with Government of Mexico, *The True Facts about the Expropriation of the Oil Companies' Properties in Mexico*, Mexico City 1940; see also *Foreign Relations of the United States, 1936*, V, 710–730, *ibid., 1937*, V, 644–678, *ibid., 1938*, V, 720–761, *ibid., 1939*, V, 667–719 and *ibid., 1940*, V, 976–1068.

42. Wood, 255 (arguments based on principles); Mikesell and Chenery, 10 (quote—my italics).

43. Mira Wilkins, "The Role of U.S. Business," in Dorothy Borg and Shumpei Okamoto, eds., *Pearl Harbor as History: Japanese-American Relations 1931–1941*, New York 1973, 362–367. On Jersey Standard officials' statement that the State Department was helpful, see comments by W. S. Farish in *Foreign Relations of the United States, 1938*, V, 754.

44. *F.T.C. Petroleum Report*, 218–274 (international agreements; a very partisan appraisal); *Petroleum Hearings*, 325–326 (national trade agreements in Europe).

45. The *Petroleum Hearings* are especially useful in giving the oil industry's problems in Europe in the 1930s; *Annual Reports* of the companies were somewhat helpful as was *Oil and Gas Journal*.

46. *Petroleum Hearings*, 377–378; European Gas and Electric Co., *Standard Oil Co. (N.J.) and Oil Production in Hungary*, n.p. 1949, 1–2.

47. *Oil and Gas Journal*, Sept. 12, 1935, 35.

48. *Petroleum Hearings*, 391.

49. *Petroleum Hearings*, 324–327; *ibid.*, 326 (Czechoslovakia, quote).

50. Jean Rondot, *La Compagnie Française des Pétroles*, Paris 1962, 37, 63; George Sweet Gibb and Evelyn H. Knowlton, *The Resurgent Years*, New York 1956, 511 and 723; *Foreign Relations of the United States 1933*, II, 168–174; *Petroleum Hearings*, 325, 391; and *F.T.C. Petroleum Report*, 322.

51. *Petroleum Hearings*, 108–113; Penrose, 142 (date of formation AGIP); *Oil and Gas Journal*, Oct. 24, 1935, 21 (SONJ and Italy); Herbert Feis, *Seen from E.A.*, New York 1947, chap. 3 (on U.S. failure to impose sanctions).

52. *Foreign Relations of the United States, 1934*, II, 320–331 (SONJ and Germany); *National Foreign Trade Convention 1941*, 96–97 (Jersey Standard and blocked currency); *Oil and Gas Journal*, Oct. 10, 1935, 13 (final quotation).

53. *Petroleum Hearings, passim.;* data collected from oil companies in the United States and abroad.

54. *Petroleum Hearings,* 205–207 (refineries; we have modified the numbers given here to omit the refineries not U.S.-owned in 1939).

55. *Petroleum Hearings,* 355 (crude oil production statistics).

56. Fanning, 354 (Middle East oil output); Herbert Feis, *Petroleum and American Foreign Policy,* Stanford, March 1944, 35 (quote).

57. *Petroleum Hearings,* 74 (foreign oil production and percentages).

58. *Ibid.,* 191, 170, 193. In 1919–1922 and 1924, U.S.-owned oil production abroad had been temporarily and atypically greater than that of the British-Dutch group, primarily because of Mexican oil output. *Ibid.,* 190. Otherwise, from 1912 (when the first available figures exist) through 1944, the foreign crude oil output of the British-Dutch group was greater than that of the U.S. companies. *Ibid.,* and Fanning, 351.

59. Standard Oil (N.J.), *Annual Reports 1929* and *1939.*

60. Adapted from *Petroleum Hearings,* 157.

Chapter X: Before America's Entry

1. Thomas Watson's "World Peace through World Trade" was the theme of the International Chamber of Commerce meetings in Berlin in 1937. See Chap. VIII above. Gerald P. Nye had held hearings on the munitions industry in the 1930s and was convinced big businessmen were "merchants of death."

2. Companies' annual reports, 1939. U.S. Sen., Committee on Patents, *Hearings,* 77th Cong., 2d sess., 1942 (henceforth cited as *Bone Committee Hearings*), pt. 5, p. 2113–2114 (Corn Products), pt. 7, p. 4135 (Howard quote).

3. The United Kingdom imposed exchange restrictions on Sept. 3, France on Sept. 9, Finland on Oct. 26, 1939. See International Monetary Fund, *Annual Report on Exchange Restrictions 1950,* 49, 73, 72. Companies' records and annual reports.

4. Geoffrey Brunn and Victor S. Mamatey, *The World in the Twentieth Century,* 4th ed., Boston 1962, 469–470 (background). Companies' annual reports.

5. National Foreign Trade Convention, *Official Proceedings 1940,* 399.

6. Dan H. Fenn, Jr., ed., *Management Guide to Overseas Operations,* New York 1957, 72–73.

7. *Bone Committee Hearings,* pt. 9, 5123, and Charles Sterling Popple, *Standard Oil Company (New Jersey) in World War II,* New York 1952, 77.

8. Mira Wilkins and Frank Ernest Hill, *American Business Abroad: Ford on Six Continents,* Detroit 1964, 319, and data in Ford Archives (Ford conflict).

9. U.S. Sen., Special Committee Investigating the National Program, *Investigation of National Defense Program, Hearings,* 77th Cong., 1st sess., 1942 (henceforth cited as *Truman Committee Hearings*), pt. 11, p. 4361 (Farish testimony).

10. Brunn and Mamatey, 470–471, 465 (background).

11. E. W. Bliss, *Annual Reports 1939 and 1940,* plus other companies' annual reports.

12. On the Spanish situation, this author found especially useful, Roca to Kugeman, Jan. 11, 1940, and Roca to Reed, June 17, 1941, International Division files, American-Standard, New York; Merrill Lynch, Pierce, Fenner, & Beane, "International Telephone and Telegraph Company" (1947), Scudder Collection, Columbia University.

13. Matthew Josephson, *Empire of the Air,* New York 1944, 138, 139.

14. Arabian American Oil Company, *ARAMCO Handbook,* rev. ed., Dhahran, Saudi Arabia 1968, 120.

15. U.S. Sen., Special Committee Investigating the National Defense Program, *Petroleum Arrangements with Saudi Arabia, Hearings,* 80th Cong., 1st sess., 1948. pt. 41, pp. 24805 (British) and 24815 (Brewster).

16. Jesse Jones, *Fifty Billion Dollars,* New York 1951, 239.

17. U.S., Sen., Special Committee Investigating Petroleum Resources, *American Petroleum Interests in Foreign Countries, Hearings,* 79th Cong., 1st sess., 1946, 24 (henceforth cited as *Petroleum Hearings*).

18. Jones, 241–242.

19. *Petroleum Hearings,* 357 (11.8 thousand barrels daily for all of 1941).

20. National Cash Register, *Annual Report 1940.*

21. Nelson Johnson to Thomas Lamont, Mar. 26, 1940, Box 184, Folder 17, Lamont Papers, Harvard Business School.

22. Mira Wilkins, "The Role of U.S. Business" in Dorothy Borg and Shumpei Okamoto, *Pearl Harbor as History: Japanese American Relations, 1931–1941,* New York 1973, 366–367.

23. Josephson, 121, 148.

24. Alex McD. McBain, "Explanations of Objectives and Operations of Canadian Exchange Control," National Foreign Trade Convention, *Official Proceedings 1939,* 46–49.

25. File in Box 3716, Record Retention Center, Ford Motor Company of Canada, Ltd., Windsor, Ont. (Ford of Canada production); Remington-Rand, *Annual Report,* Year Ended Mar. 31, 1941; other *Annual Reports;* see also *Truman Committee Hearings,* pt. 3, 934.

26. Interviews with company officials. Oliver James Lissitzyn, *International Air Transport and National Policy,* New York 1942, 394–395.

27. See, for example, Superheater Company, *Annual Report 1939.* Electrical companies were particularly active in the trade—replacing British and German suppliers. See National Foreign Trade Convention, *Official Proceedings 1939,* 361, 371.

28. National Foreign Trade Convention, *Official Proceedings 1939,* 357–358.

29. David L. Gordon and Royden Dangerfield, *The Hidden Weapon: The Story of Economic Warfare,* New York 1947, 152.

30. Tom Mahoney, *Merchants of Life,* New York 1959, 253–257.

31. E. Merck and Merck & Co., Treaty Agreement, Nov. 17, 1932, printed in U.S. and Alien Property Custodian v. Merck & Co., Inc., Civil Action #3159, District Court of New Jersey 1943.

32. Williams Haynes, *American Chemical Industry,* New York 1949, VI, 406,

and Corwin Edwards, *Economic and Political Aspects of International Cartels,* Washington, D.C. 1944, 52, 23, 47.

33. Edwards, 67 (Weiss quote); *Fortune* 25:90 (June 1942), and *Time,* Sept. 15, 1941, 73.

34. E. R. Squibb & Sons, *Prospectus,* June 11, 1951 (interest in Latin America); American Cyanamid, *Annual Report 1940* (Lederle); American Home Products, *Prospectus,* Dec. 16, 1944 (Latin America, most important foreign market).

35. Letter to Harry Hopkins, cited in Lloyd C. Gardner, *Economic Aspects of New Deal Diplomacy,* Madison 1964, 131.

36. Josephson, 161, 165.

37. U.S. Civilian Production Administration, Bureau of Demobilization, *Industrial Mobilization for War,* Washington, D.C. 1947, xii–xiv.

38. Export-Import Bank of Washington, *Twenty-fifth Anniversary Review,* Washington, D.C. 1959, 6, and U.S. Sen., Committee on Banking and Currency, *Study of Export-Import Bank and World Bank, Hearings,* 83rd Cong., 2d sess., 1954, 95.

39. *Industrial Mobilization for War,* 125.

40. U.S. Dept. of Comm., Bureau of Foreign and Domestic Commerce, *Foreign Aid of the United States Government, 1940–1951,* Washington, D.C. 1952, 33.

41. *Industrial Mobilization for War,* 73.

42. Jesse Jones, *Fifty Billion Dollars,* New York 1951, 435–439.

43. *Ibid.,* 434 (quote); Anaconda, *Annual Report 1941;* Kennecott, *Annual Report 1941;* Cerro de Pasco, *Annual Report 1941;* American Smelting and Refining, *Annual Report 1941.*

44. *Foreign Relations of the United States 1941,* II, 811–835 (intervention in Surinam); *Mineral Industry 1941,* and Jones, 449 (dealings with Aluminum Company of Canada); *Truman Committee Hearings,* pts. 3 and 7 (1941: aluminum situation).

45. *Mineral Industry 1941,* 565 (tungsten in Bolivia); *Export-Import Bank Hearings,* 99–101 (bank's role in financing).

46. U.S. Sen., Special Committee Investigating the National Defense Program, *Investigation of National Defense Program,* Report, 77th Cong., 1st and 2d sess., Sen. Report 480, 1941–1942, pt. 7, pp. 42–50 (henceforth cited as *Truman Committee Report 480*). Herbert Feis, *Seen from E.A.,* New York 1947, 3–90.

47. Cordell Hull, *Memoirs,* 2 vols., New York 1948, II, 1142.

48. Bryce Wood, *The Making of a Good Neighbor Policy,* New York 1961, 267ff, is excellent on the State Department and Venezuela.

49. Interviews in Caracas and New York (Standard Oil of New Jersey policies); see also James Clark, "History of Creole," unpub. 1958. The international lawyer referred to in the text is identified in Henrietta Larson et. al., *New Horizions,* New York 1971, 482, as Professor Edwin M. Borchard of Yale University.

50. *Petroleum Hearings,* 355 (production).

51. Quoted in Gardner, *Economic Aspects of the New Deal,* 111.

52. Josephson, 158, 165.

53. *Ibid.*, 158, 161.

54. John W. Pehle, Address to National Foreign Trade Convention, 1941 in *Official Proceedings* (foreign exchange control); David L. Gordon and Royden Dangerfield, *The Hidden Weapon. The Story of Economic Warfare,* New York 1947, 152; Raymond Mikesell, *United States Economic Policy and International Relations,* New York 1952, 102–105; *Federal Register,* Mar. 6, 1941, 1299–1302, esp. 1300 (for Proclamation 2465); Jasper Crane to Ter Meer (I.G. Farben), Apr. 18, 1941, Jasper Crane Papers, Accession 1231, Box 4, Eleutherian Mills Historical Library; a letter from Crane to Ter Meer, Apr. 18, 1941, in *ibid.* indicates that the expression "all other obligations. . . . to remain in force" referred to licensing arrangements. U.S. Dept. of Comm., Bureau of Foreign and Domestic Commerce, *American Direct Investments in Foreign Countries,* Washington, D.C. 1942, 6 (I.T.T.; other refusals); *Truman Committee Hearings,* pt. 11, 4372–4373 (testimony of Farish-SONJ), 4517 (testimony of Edward Foley-Treasury Department).

55. Anaconda, *Annual Report 1941.*

56. *Foreign Relations of the United States,* 1941, IV, 863.

57. *Fortune* 25:90 (June 1942); *Time,* Sept. 15, 1941; Haynes, *American Chemical Industry,* VI, 408.

58. *Truman Committee Report 480,* pt. 7 (1942), 39 (Standard Oil of New Jersey's Brazilian subsidiary); *Bone Committee Hearings,* 5063–5064 and 5129–5131 (Standard Oil of New Jersey's interpretation of the Brazilian episode; Farish testimony).

59. Temporary National Economic Committee, *Investigation of Concentration of Economic Power, Hearings,* Washington, D.C. 1940. Part 25 is on "Cartels." The entire hearings are relevant. Temporary National Economic Committee, *Monographs.* See especially, Monograph #6 (1940), *Export Prices and Export Cartels.* The *Truman Committee Hearings* (cited in note 9 above) began in 1941 and went through the war. The hearings and the reports issued by the committee have a large amount on international business relationships.

Chapter XI: Global War

1. A. V. H. Hartendorp, *History of Industry and Trade of the Philippines,* Manila 1958, 64. Interviews.

2. Socony-Vacuum, *Annual Report 1941;* U.S. Sen., Committee on Patents, *Hearings,* 77th Cong., 2d sess., 1942, pt. 9, pp. 5122–5123 (henceforth cited as *Bone Committee Hearings*); Benjamin Higgins, *Stanvac in Indonesia,* Washington, D.C. 1957, 24–26.

3. Interviews; annual reports; company records. For example, an internal memo (Jan. 2, 1944) in du Pont files indicates that after 1941 the company knew nothing of its affiliates under Axis control. See Accession 1231, Box 2, Jasper Crane Papers, Eleutherian Mills Historical Library.

4. Interviews; annual reports; company records; Matthew Josephson, *Empire*

of the Air, New York 1944, 201, 169 (Pan Am); *Business Week,* July 10, 1943 (expansion of U.S. companies in Brazil).

5. *Bone Committee Hearings,* pt. 9, pp. 5044–5045.

6. U.S. Sen., Committee on Military Affairs, Subcommittee on War Mobilization, *Scientific and Technical Mobilization, Hearings,* 78th Cong., 1st sess., 1943 (henceforth cited as *Kilgore Committee Hearings*). This committee continued to meet in 1944. See U.S. Sen., Committee on Military Affairs, Report of the Subcommittee on War Mobilization, *Cartels and National Security,* pt. 16, 78th Cong., 2d sess., 1944. Corwin Edwards, *Economic and Political Aspects of International Cartels,* Washington, D.C. 1944, was issued as Monograph 1 by the U.S. Sen., Committee on Military Affairs, Subcommittee on War Mobilization, 78th Cong., 2d sess., 1944. The Truman, Bone, and Kilgore committee hearings became the raw materials for a collection of books on cartelization: these ranged from the journalistic debunking of Guenther Reimann, *Patents for Hitler,* New York 1942, to the thorough volume by Ervin Hexner, *International Cartels,* Chapel Hill 1945, to the revealing study done under the auspices of the Twentieth Century Fund, George W. Stocking and Myron W. Watkins, *Cartels in Action: Case Studies International Business Diplomacy,* New York 1946. See also Wendell Berge, *Cartels: Challenge to a Free World,* Washington, D.C. 1944 (Berge was Thurman Arnold's successor as head of the antitrust division); Edward S. Mason, *Controlling World Trade, Cartels and Commodity Agreements,* New York 1946 (a judicious treatment prepared for the Committee for Economic Development); Charles R. Whittlesey, *National Interest and International Cartels,* New York 1946; and Leisa G. Bronson, *Cartels and International Patent Agreements,* Washington, D.C. 1944. The articles in popular and academic journals are too prolix to include.

7. Israel B. Oseas, "Antitrust Prosecutions of International Business," *Cornell Law Review* 30:42–65 (1944), is excellent on the wartime court cases.

8. See Chap. IV, note 52 above (Standard Oil-I.G. Farben accords); *Bone Committee Hearings,* pt. 9, pp. 5042ff (advantages to Standard Oil of N.J.); U.S. Sen., Special Committee Investigating the National Defense Program, *Investigation of National Defense Program, Report,* 77th Cong., 1st and 2d sess., Sen. Report 480, 1941–1942, pt. 7 (1942), 28 (conclusion). This will be henceforth cited as *Truman Committee Report 480.*

9. The background comes out in testimony before and exhibits submitted to the various committees. See also *Truman Committee Report 480,* pt. 7, p. 27–42.

10. The case for Standard Oil of New Jersey was given time and again by William S. Farish, the company's president. See for example his testimony before the Truman Committee: U.S. Sen., Special Committee Investigating the National Defense Program, *Investigation of the National Defense Program,* 77th Cong., 1st sess., 1941–1942, pt. 11, pp. 4394 (not involved), *passim* (technological advantage), 4395–4398, 4770 (encouraged government to be interested), 4395 (encouraged independents), 4763 (did not discourage licensing after war broke out). These and successor hearings are henceforth cited as *Truman Com-*

mittee Hearings. Charles Sterling Popple, *Standard Oil Company (New Jersey) in World War II,* New York 1952, 18–19 (reason for signing decree). See also *Truman Committee Report 480,* pt. 7, 27–42.

11. Truman, Bone, and Kilgore committee hearings, *passim.* Mason, 66, has sharpened our thinking on the questions posed. See also Kingman Brewster, *Antitrust and American Business Abroad,* New York 1958, 11–12 (questions posed). The conclusions are our own.

12. Donald Nelson, *Arsenal of Democracy,* New York 1946, and Francis Walton, *Miracle of World War II,* New York 1956. Annual reports, newspaper articles, and magazine pieces indicate business's aid to the war effort.

13. Walton, 143 (industry executives in Washington); interviews.

14. Williams Haynes, *The American Chemical Industry,* 6 vols., New York 1945–1954, V, 64. Jesse Jones, *Fifty Billion Dollars,* New York 1951, 443, and U.S. President's Materials Policy Commission, *Resources for Freedom,* 5 vols., Washington, D.C. 1952, V, 129–131 (henceforth cited as *Paley Report*). John F. Thompson and Norman Beasley, *For the Years to Come: A Story of International Nickel of Canada,* New York 1960.

15. Nelson, 12; Jones, 441; *Paley Report,* V, 134, 132–133; Anaconda, *Annual Report 1942* and *1943.*

16. Kennecott, *Annual Report 1945.*

17. Phelps Dodge, *Annual Report 1942* and *1943.*

18. Jones, 434–435.

19. The Truman, Kilgore, and Bone committee hearings all deal with rubber supplies and the problems. Jones, 420 (17 countries). Mira Wilkins and Frank Ernest Hill, *American Business Abroad: Ford on Six Continents,* Detroit 1964, 181–182. A. A. Pollan, "The United Fruit Company and Middle America," pamphlet, January 1944, 22.

20. Interview, Romeo Horton, Monrovia, Liberia, July 15, 1965; other interviews in Liberia; Wayne Chatfield Taylor, *Firestone Operations in Liberia,* Washington, D.C. 1956, 59 (production); Jones, 420 (rubber from Latin America and Liberia), 414 (synthetic output).

21. Chase National Bank, *Annual Report 1944* (role of C.C.C. in financing Cuban crop). Robert F. Smith, *United States and Cuba,* New York 1960, 187 (duties); Cuban Atlantic Sugar Company, Prospectus, Apr. 9, 1946, Scudder Collection, Columbia University (sugar in World War II). The world market price of raw sugar rose (in cents per pound) from 1.46 (1941), to 2.65 (1942–1944), to 3.10 (1945). *Ibid.*

22. Data from United Fruit, Pollan, and *Paley Report,* V, 134–135.

23. Herbert Feis, *Petroleum and American Foreign Policy,* Stanford, 1944, 18 (western hemisphere).

24. U.S. Sen., Special Committee Investigating Petroleum Resources, *American Petroleum Interests in Foreign Countries,* 79th Cong., 1st sess., 1946, 355 (oil production). These hearings are henceforth cited as *Petroleum Hearings. Truman Committee Hearings,* pt. 22, 9658 (shelling of Aruba). Bryce Wood, *The Making of a Good Neighbor Policy,* New York 1961, 270–274, and Vene-

zuelan newspaper clippings 1942. Creole Petroleum Corp., Letters to Stockholders, Mar. 11, 31, 1943, Scudder Collection; James Clark, "History of Creole," unpub. 1958, 247 (on Linam); interviews, Caracas, 1964. Wayne C. Taylor and John Lindeman, *The Creole Petroleum Corporation in Venezuela,* Washington, D.C. 1955, 27–28, 89; Leonard Fanning, *Foreign Oil and the Free World,* New York 1954, 80–84; Edwin Lieuwen, *Petroleum in Venezuela,* Berkeley 1954, 90–99; Rómulo Betancourt, *Venezuela: Politica y Petróleo,* Mexico 1956, chap. 3; companies' annual report; Lieuwen, 108 (percentages); *Petroleum Hearings,* 355 (production).

25. Roosevelt to Ickes, Feb. 28, 1942, cited in Lloyd C. Gardner, *Economic Aspects of the New Deal Diplomacy,* Madison 1964, 206.

26. *Truman Committee Hearings,* pt. 22, p. 9603 (Patterson); Imperial Oil, *Annual Report 1932* (background on Norman Wells); *Truman Committee Hearings,* pt. 22, pp. 9287–9935 (Canol project), 9598–9599 (rationale), 9456–9457 (Imperial Oil), 9840, 9552 (the cost), 9840 (the plan), 9600 (not commercial), 9340–9341 (reason for continuing), 9840 ($105 million spent), 9549 (Gavin); *Truman Committee Report No. 10,* Washington, D.C. 1944, pt. 14, p. 461; Imperial Oil, *Annual Report 1944* (published in 1945; end of venture); *Business Week,* Mar. 10, 1945 (the finale); *Commercial and Financial Chronicle,* Apr. 19, 1945, 1760; U.S. Sen., Special Committee Investigating the National Defense Program, *Hearings,* 79th Cong., 2d sess., 1947, pt. 39, pp. 23011 (Mar. 26, 1945 letter of Admiral D. Leahy evaluating the Canol project), 23017 ("for junk"); Royal Commission on Canada's Economic Prospects, *Final Report,* Ottawa 1957, 131 (quote). *Petroleum Press Service,* 36:64, February 1969 (the search in the 1960s).

27. *Petroleum Hearings,* 355, 357 (oil production figures); data from Kuwait Oil Company (its wartime activities). U.S. Sen., Special Committee Investigating the National Defense Program, *Petroleum Arrangements with Saudi Arabia, Hearings,* 80th Cong., 1st sess., 1948, pt. 41, pp. 25385–25386 (Rodgers and Colliers' memo), 25276 (consequences). Herbert Feis, *Seen from E.A.,* New York 1947, 123ff; Cordell Hull, *Memoirs,* 2 vols., New York 1948, II, 1520; *Petroleum Arrangements with Saudi Arabia,* 25277 (U.S. government plans), 25234 (Ickes testimony); Roy Lebkicher et al. *ARAMCO Handbook,* The Netherlands 1960, 147 (conclusion; release of strategic materials); interview, J. Josephson, Awali, Bahrain, Aug. 27, 1965 (wartime expansion); Standard Oil of California, *Annual Report 1946* (Bahrain refinery capacity).

28. Feis, *Petroleum and American Foreign Policy,* Stanford 1944, 40, and Feis, *Seen from E.A.,* 140ff (pipeline plans); Hull, 1525 (quote); data from ARAMCO on later culmination.

29. *Petroleum Arrangements with Saudi Arabia,* 25430 (American interest in Iran); Hull, 1508–1509 and Feis, *Seen from E.A.,* 175ff (U.S. companies' interest in Iran); see Chaps. V and IX above on U.S. companies' interest in Iran in the 1920s and 1930s.

30. Hull, 1523 (Churchill cable and FDR retort); Feis, *Seen from E.A.,* 179 (Feis thought the treaty would "probably win the ultimate approval of Con-

gress"; he was wrong); U.S. Sen., Committee on Foreign Relations, *Petroleum Agreement with Great Britain and Northern Ireland, Hearings,* 80th Cong., 1st sess., 1947, *passim* (on the agreements).

31. U.S. Dept. of Comm., Bureau of Foreign and Domestic Commerce, *Foreign Aid of the United States Government,* Washington, D.C. 1952, 84 (total aid).

32. *Petroleum Hearings,* 26 (last quote).

33. Matthew Josephson, *Empire of the Air,* New York 1944, 162, 166, 171–184.

34. U.S. Civilian Production Administration, Bureau of Demobilization, *Industrial Mobilization for War,* Washington, D.C. 1947, pt. 3, chap. 7, and *passim;* Hull, 1154–1155 (multiplicity of agencies); U.S. Dept. of Treasury, *Census of American-Owned Assets in Foreign Countries,* Washington, D.C. 1947 (survey conducted in 1943); U.S. Sen., Committee on Banking and Currency, *Study of Export-Import Bank and World Bank, Hearings,* 83rd Cong., 2d sess., 1954, *passim* (Export-Import's wartime role); U.S. Foreign Economic Administration, *Report to Congress,* Sept. 25, 1944 (on various agencies); Geoffrey Brunn and Victor S. Mamatey, *The World in the Twentieth Century,* 4th ed., Boston 1962, 482, 477, 475, 520, 503, 525 (wartime background); Samuel Flagg Bemis, *Diplomatic History of the United States,* 3d ed., New York 1958, 757 (Bretton Woods); Hull, II, 1712 (events at San Francisco).

35. *Foreign Aid of the United States,* 33 (Lend Lease).

36. U.S. Dept. of Treasury, *Census,* 20 (2,750 companies).

37. U.S. Department of Commerce, Office of Business Economics, gives U.S. G.N.P. in 1946 as $208.5 billion.

Chapter XII: Recovery and Reconsideration, 1945–1954

1. U.S. Dept. of Comm., Bureau of Foreign and Domestic Commerce, *Foreign Aid by the United States Government 1940–1951,* Washington, D.C. 1952, 1, 6–7, 65–66. Foreign aid far exceeded direct foreign investments.

2. *Ibid.,* 6, 115. See 64 Stat. 204.

3. Joyce and Gabriel Kolko, *The Limits of Power,* New York 1972, 2.

4. Benjamin J. Cohen, ed., *American Foreign Economic Policy,* New York 1968, 283, and The Export Control Act, 63 Stat. 5.

5. 63 Stat. 5.

6. National Foreign Trade Council, *Position of National Foreign Trade Council with Respect to the Havana Charter for an International Trade Organization,* New York 1950, esp. 3–10, 99, and Percy W. Bidwell and William Diebold, Jr., "The United States and the International Trade Organization," *International Conciliation,* March 1949, 208, 188, 211. See also Raymond Vernon, *America's Foreign Trade Policy and the GATT,* Princeton, N.J. 1954, 5–6, and Richard N. Gardner, *Sterling-Dollar Diplomacy,* rev. ed., New York 1969, 348–380, esp. 371–378.

7. On GATT see *American Bar Association Bulletin,* Section on Interna-

tional and Comparative Law, July 1957, 2–6, and Vernon, *America's Foreign Trade Policy, passim.*

8. United Nations, Department of Economic Affairs, Fiscal Division, *International Tax Agreements,* New York 1951, vol. III. On treaties, see U.S. Legislative Reference Service, *Expropriation of American-Owned Property by Foreign Governments in the Twentieth Century,* Washington, D.C. 1963, 30.

9. Marina von N. Whitman, *Government Risk-Sharing in Foreign Investment,* Princeton, N.J. 1965, 73.

10. *Mining World* 13:42 (July 1951); U.S. Sen., Committee on Banking and Currency, *Study of Export-Import Bank and World Bank,* 83rd Cong., 2d sess., 1954, *passim.*

11. Raymond F. Mikesell, *United States Economic Policy and International Relations,* New York 1952, 110ff; Donald Bailey Marsh, *World Trade and Investment,* New York 1951, 343ff; Peter Kenen, *Giant Among Nations,* Chicago 1963.

12. U.S. Dept. of State, *The United States Balance of Payments Problems,* Commercial Policy Series 123, Washington, D.C. 1949, 1–2.

13. U.S. Special Assistant to the President (Gordon Grey), *Report to the President on Foreign Economic Policies,* Washington, D.C. 1950 (on overall foreign economic policy).

14. The stockpiling was done under the authority of the Strategic and Critical Materials Stockpiling Act of 1946 and the Defense Production Act of 1950. See The President's Materials Policy Commission, *Resources for Freedom,* 5 vols., Washington, D.C. 1952, V, 137, 142, 145–146, on stockpiling. This report will be henceforth cited as *Paley Report.*

15. Gerald Nash, *United States Oil Policy, 1890–1964,* Pittsburgh 1968, 195–196.

16. *Paley Report,* I, 68–73 (quotation is on p. 73).

17. 65 Stat. 644, Oct. 26, 1951.

18. U.S. Commission on Foreign Economic Policy, *Report to the President and the Congress,* Washington, D.C. 1954, 16–26, 36, 40 (The Randall Report).

19. U.S. Dept. of Comm., Bureau of Foreign and Domestic Commerce, *Factors Limiting U.S. Investment Abroad,* Washington, D.C. 1953, pt. 2, 7–8; J. Frank Gaston, *Obstacles to Direct Foreign Investment,* New York 1951, 7; E. R. Barlow and Ira T. Wender, *Foreign Investment and Taxation,* Englewood Cliffs, N.J. 1955. International Development Advisory Board, *Partners in Progress,* New York 1952.

20. The court cases, *Annual Reports* of the companies involved, interviews with corporation executives (especially general counsels), copies of relationship agreements, statements of the National Foreign Trade Council, and the International Chamber of Commerce are primary sources. See also U.S. Sen., Committee on the Judiciary, Subcommittee on Antitrust and Monopoly, *A Study of Antitrust Laws,* pt. 4, 84th Cong., 1st sess., 1955, and U.S. Sen., Committee on the Judiciary, Subcommittee on Antitrust and Monopoly, *International Aspects of Antitrust,* pts. 1 and 2, 89th Cong., 2d sess., 1966 (henceforth cited as *Hart*

Committee Hearings). Kingman Brewster, *Antitrust and American Business Abroad*, New York 1958, and W. L. Fugate, *Foreign Commerce and the Antitrust Laws*, Boston 1958, are basic books on the subject. Lawrence F. Ebb, *International Business*, New York 1964, republishes some of the cases and has useful commentary.

21. U.S. v. National Lead Company, 63 F. Supp. 513, Southern District Court New York 1945, aff'd 332 U.S. 319, 1947. National Lead, *Annual Reports 1945, 1951, 1952*. New York Stock Exchange Listing Statement, National Lead, #A-13110, Nov. 30, 1948, and Hemphill, Noyes, & Co., "National Lead," June 1953, in Scudder Collection, Columbia University. National Lead Co., *Annual Reports* 1952–1966, and data in Scudder Collection, Columbia University, on postcase responses.

22. U.S. v. Electric Storage Battery Co., 1947, CCH Trade Cases, par. 57,645. Later, Electric Storage Battery Company would renew its interest in international business. See Vernon Research Report, "Electric Storage Battery Company."

23. U.S. v. Timken Roller Bearing Co., 83 F. Supp. 284, Northern District Court Ohio 1949, modified and aff'd 341 U.S. 593, 1951; *Moody's 1929;* Timken Roller Bearing Co., *Annual Reports* 1922ff; H. E. Markley (executive vice president of Timken Roller Bearing Co.), article in *Export Trade,* Apr. 25, 1960; data in Scudder Collection.

24. U.S. v. Imperial Chemical Industries, 105 F. Supp. 215, Southern District Court New York 1952; du Pont, *Annual Reports;* interviews; *Fortune* 74:179, August 1966 (I.C.I.).

25. The first case began in 1941, was postponed during the war, renewed after the war, settled in 1949 with a decision against G.E.; in 1953, the "remedy" was ordered by the courts. U.S. v. General Electric Company, 82 F. Supp. 753, District Court New Jersey 1949, and U.S. v. General Electric Company, 115 F. Supp. 835, District Court New Jersey 1953. This litigation dealt exclusively with the lamp business. Meanwhile, on January 18, 1945, the Department of Justice brought civil suit against G.E. and I.G.E.C. in the district court of New Jersey, charging that General Electric had made agreements with foreign companies in the electrical equipment area. *New York Times,* Jan. 19, 1945. This case was apparently dropped; there is no reported decision. A third case began when the Department of Justice filed a complaint, May 16, 1945, that the Electrical Apparatus Export Association and its principal members (including G.E.) had violated the Sherman Act. G.E. was found to have participated in a cartel involving the electrical equipment industry; this ended in a consent decree. U.S. v. Electrical Apparatus Export Association, 1947, CCH Trade Cases, par. 57,546. Still a fourth case dealt specifically with G.E.'s international agreements on tungsten carbide; it involved restraints on American production and exports. It was settled against G.E. in *U.S. v. General Electric Co.,* 80 F. Supp. 989, Southern District Court of New York 1948.

26. U.S. v. General Electric Co., 115 F. Supp. 835, District Court New Jersey, 1953, Section IX of the decree.

27. General Electric, *Annual Report 1953;* interview, W. R. Herod, New York, Feb. 24, 1964 (Herod was in charge of I.G.E.); John H. Dunning, *American Investment in British Manufacturing Industry,* London 1958, 23 (repatriation of G.E.'s investment in A.E.I.); interview, P. M. Markert, Johannesburg, South Africa, Aug. 3, 1965 (on the Australian business). For the new interest in the 1960s, see Ralph J. Cordiner, "Managerial Strategy for International Business," *Vital Speeches of the Day* 27:248, 252 (Feb. 1, 1961).

28. Except for the Timken case, I have relied here on the conclusions of Brewster, 207–208. Brewster writes of the Timken case, "A minority ownership . . . acquired as a compensation for a license would not seem to offer any legal immunity for explicit exclusive or restrictive arrangements." According to the company's *Annual Report 1927,* it paid cash for its interest in the British Timken company. The interpretation of the Timken case is that of the present author.

29. In April 1970, the Department of Justice brought a complaint against Westinghouse, charging that Westinghouse was forbidding its licensed Japanese affiliate from exporting to the United States. Westinghouse responded that this was a desirable practice. *New York Times,* April 23, 1970. The Report of the Task Force on the Structure of Canadian Industry, *Foreign Ownership and the Structure of Canadian Industry,* Ottawa 1968, 98, states, "It is believed that a number of these [licensing] agreements" made by Americans with affiliated firms, "contain prohibitions on right to export." This same sentiment was expressed at the *Hart Committee Hearings,* 189, 240. In reply to a questionnaire administered in the late 1960s, one-half of the U.S. subsidiaries and affiliates in Mexico surveyed stated that their parent companies' limited their markets. Simon Rottenberg, "United States Investment in Mexico," unpub. report, 1970.

30. U.S. v. Aluminum Company of America, 148 F. 2d 416, 2nd circuit court 1945; Brewster, 73–74; U.S. v. Aluminum Company of America, 91 F. Supp. 333 at 418–419, Southern District Court New York, 1950. Judge Hand's statement ignored the national sovereignty over persons outside the United States. See American Bar Association, *Antitrust Developments 1955–1968,* Chicago 1968, 48, 55.

31. See Chap. IV above.

32. U.S. v. Electrical Apparatus Export Association, 1947, CCH Trade Cases, par. 57,546.

33. *General Milk Co.,* 44 F.T.C. 1355, 1947. Data in the Scudder Collection on Carnation Co. indicate that in 1956 it still owned 65 per cent of General Milk; New York Stock Exchange Listing Statement, Pet Milk Company, #A-2953, Apr. 8, 1949, indicates that Pet Milk retained its 35 per cent, as does data in Vernon Research Report, "Carnation Milk."

34. U.S. v. Minnesota Mining & Manufacturing Company, 92 F. Supp. 947, District Court Massachusetts 1950. Brewster, 117–118; International Management Association, *Case Studies in Foreign Operations,* IMA Special Report, No. 1, New York 1957, 108 and Virginia Huck, *Brand of the Tartan: The 3M Story,* New York 1955, 241–243 (the consequences).

35. Federal Trade Commission, *International Petroleum Cartel,* Washington, D.C. 1952; U.S. v. Standard Oil Co. (N.J.), Civil No. 86–27, 1953, CCH Trade Regulation Reporter, pars. 66,075, 66,081.

36. Brewster, 28; briefs of companies; court records; and interviews.

37. The present author would agree with this conclusion of Paul Rand Dixon, Chairman of the Federal Trade Commission. See his testimony at the *Hart Committee Hearings,* 515.

38. Annual reports of the companies; Brewster, chap. X. Professor Emile Benoit, interviewing businessmen in Europe, learned of their caution. See also in this respect the Netherlands government protest against the proposed decree in the *General Electric* case, May 3, 1951, in Ebb, 571–573. Wolfgang Friedmann, *The Changing Structure of International Law,* New York 1964, 25–26 (the heyday past).

39. This was the conclusion of the U.S. Department of Commerce study, *Factors Limiting U.S. Investment Abroad,* and Gaston's research, *Obstacles to Direct Foreign Investment.*

40. The best source on the foreign exchange restrictions is the International Monetary Fund, *Annual Report on Exchange Restrictions.* The first such annual report was issued in 1950.

41. *The Survey of Current Business,* December 1951, 13, estimated U.S. direct investments abroad in 1950 at $13.5 billion. As the *Paley Report* pointed out (V, 107), these figures included investments in expropriated property for which compensation had not been received and other properties in Germany and Japan. A 1950 census provided a basis for revised figures. The new total for 1950—taking into account wartime losses, expropriations, and write-downs— came to $11.8 billion. (See U.S. Dept. of Comm., Office of Business Economics, *Foreign Investments of the United States—1950,* Washington, D.C. 1953, 2.)

42. *Foreign Investments of the United States—1950,* 2.

43. American & Foreign Power Company, *Foreign Power System,* New York 1953; American & Foreign Power Company, *Annual Reports.* U.S. Dept. of Comm., Bureau of Foreign Commerce, *Investment in Mexico,* Washington, D.C. 1955, 57, and Miguel S. Wionczek, "Electric Power" in Raymond Vernon, ed., *Public Policy and Private Enterprise in Mexico,* Cambridge, Mass. 1964, 75ff. Speech by Henry W. Balgooyen, executive vice president, American & Foreign Power Company, Columbia University, Mar. 2, 1963, and interview, Balgooyen, June 18, 1964. Interviews, company general managers in Latin America.

44. Merrill, Lynch, Pierce, Fenner & Beane, "I.T.T.," 1944, and *ibid.,* 1947, Scudder Collection (quote). I.T.T., *Annual Reports.*

45. Interviews in Brazil, and *Mining World* 13:29 (Apr. 15, 1951) (Brazil); Republic Steel, *Annual Reports* 1945 and 1949; Jones & Laughlin, *Annual Report 1945;* interviews in Chile; Bethlehem Steel, *Annual Reports* 1932, 1933, 1945ff, and John D. Wirth, *The Politics of Brazilian Development,* Stanford, 1970, 79; U.S. Steel, *Annual Reports,* 1949, 1954; Venezuelan Central Bank, *Annual Reports,* gives iron ore and oil investments; for comparative purposes, I have used Bs. 3.33—the official rate—for conversion, although Bs. 3.09 was the

differential exchange rate applicable to dollars originated by the petroleum sector in these years.

46. J. K. Gustavson, "Labrador-Quebec Ore District," *Canadian Mining Journal,* June 1953, 64; *Engineering and Mining Journal,* Jan. 19, 1950, and John Davis, *Mining and Mineral Processing in Canada,* Ottawa 1957, 353 (Iron Ore Company of Canada); Kennecott Copper Company, *Annual Report 1948;* Canada, Dept. of Mines and Technical Surveys, "A Survey of the Iron Ore Industry in Canada during 1956," May 3, 1957 (background on U.S. Steel's activities).

47. *Paley Report,* I, 65, and II, 15 (French policy); Christie got his concession in Liberia on Aug. 27, 1945; it was approved by the Liberian Congress Jan. 22, 1946, and took effect Jan. 23, 1946; see data in files of Liberia Mining Company, Ltd., Monrovia, Liberia. Generalizations based on company *Annual Reports* and *Mining World.*

48. Mira Wilkins, *The Emergence of Multinational Enterprise: American Business Abroad from the Colonial Era to 1914,* Cambridge, Mass. 1970, 18, 136–137, 150, 151, 183, gives instances of early stakes. Leland Jenks, *Our Cuban Colony,* New York 1928, 292 (U.S. Steel's Cuban property).

49. See issues of *Mining World* and *Paley Report,* II, 34, 39, 45.

50. Seymour F. Rubin, *Private Foreign Investment,* Baltimore 1956, 43 ("nibbling expropriation"); J. Frank Gaston, *Obstacles to Direct Foreign Investment,* New York 1951, 174, 177, 248, 250 (problems of mining companies). Interviews with executives of mining companies in the United States and abroad.

51. Royal Commission on Canada's Economic Prospects, *Final Report,* Ottawa 1957, 213 (quote), 217 (new activities). See also, H. G. J. Aitken, *American Capital and Canadian Resources,* Cambridge, Mass. 1961; H. G. J. Aitken et al., *The American Economic Impact on Canada,* Durham, N.C. 1959; and Davis, *Mining and Mineral Processing in Canada.*

52. *Foreign Investments of the United States—1950,* 2 (financing manufacturing operations).

53. For background see M. M. Postan, *An Economic History of Western Europe, 1945–1964,* London 1967; David S. Landes, *The Unbound Prometheus,* Cambridge, Eng. 1969, 488–498; U.S. Legislative Reference Service, *Expropriation of American-Owned Property,* Washington, D.C. 1963, 12–15; Geoffrey Brunn and Victor S. Mamatey, *The World in the Twentieth Century,* 4th ed., Boston 1962, 639, 536–537, and chap. 5 (French and German recovery). O.E.E.C., *Organization for European Economic Cooperation, History and Structure,* Paris 1953; Emile Benoit, *Europe at Sixes and Sevens,* New York 1961; W. O. Henderson, *The Genesis of the Common Market,* London 1962, 124ff; George Lichtheim, *Europe and America,* London 1963; and Finn B. Jensen and Ingo Walter, *The Common Market,* Philadelphia 1965. Specifically on investments and obstacles see *Factors Limiting U.S. Investments Abroad,* pt. 1, pp. 44–45; Gaston, *Obstacles to Direct Foreign Investment,* 267ff; Minneapolis Honeywell, *Annual Report 1948,* and International Management Association, *Case Studies in Foreign Operations,* New York 1957, 267ff; John H. Dunning, *American Investment in British Manufacturing Industry,* London 1958,

esp. 315–316; O.E.E.C., *Private United States Investment in Europe and Over-seas Territories,* Paris 1954.

54. Quotation is from J. B. Eliason, treasurer, to J. E. Crane, vice president, E. I. du Pont, Jan. 2, 1946, Jasper Crane Papers, Accession 1231, Box 2 Eleutherian Mills Historical Library. Another American businessman typically stated in 1953, "we regard Canadian investment as fully attractive as domestic. We feel that the Canadians understand us and we understand them." See O.E.E.C., *Private United States Investment,* 23. See also Irving Brecher and S. S. Reisman, *Canada-United States Economic Relations,* Ottawa 1957. U.S. Dept. of Comm. Office of Business Economics, *U.S. Business Investments in Foreign Countries,* Washington, D.C. 1960, 93 (rise in investment in manufacturing in Canada), and *Survey of Current Business.*

55. *U.S. Business Investments in Foreign Countries,* 93, 91, and *Survey of Current Business.* United Nations, Dept. of Economic and Social Affairs, *Foreign Capital in Latin America,* New York 1955; Rafael Izquierdo, "Protectionism in Mexico," in Raymond Vernon, ed., *Public Policy and Private Enterprise in Mexico,* Cambridge, Mass. 1964, 241ff. Dept. of Commerce, Bureau of Foreign Commerce, *Investment in Mexico,* Washington, D.C. 1955, 20, 22. Lincoln Gordon, *U.S. Manufacturing in Brazil,* Boston 1962, 15–16; interviews throughout Latin America; company records; annual reports. See also *Factors Limiting U.S. Investment Abroad,* pt. 2, and Gaston, 137ff. In 1940, U.S. direct investment in mining in Latin America was more than double that in manufacturing.

56. U.S. Legislative Reference Service, *Expropriation of American-Owned Property,* 16; Law Concerning Foreign Investment, Law No. 163, May 10, 1950. Interviews in Japan; data from Japanese Ministry of International Trade and Industry.

57. *Factors Limiting U.S. Investment Abroad,* pt. 1, 132; Frederick Donner, *The World-Wide Industrial Enterprise,* New York 1967 (General Motors); Donald T. Brash, *American Investment in Australian Industry,* Cambridge, Mass. 1966, 22 and *passim.* (U.S. direct investment in Australian manufacturing rose from $48 million in 1943 to $98 million in 1950 to $201 million in 1954.)

58. U.S. Sen., Special Committee Investigating Petroleum Resources, *American Petroleum Interests in Foreign Countries, Hearings,* 79th Cong., 1st sess., Washington, D.C. 1946, 120; F.T.C., *International Petroleum Cartel;* U.S. v. Standard Oil Co. (N.J.), Civil No. 86-27, 1953, CCH Trade Reg. Rep., pars. 66,075, 66,081. Gaston, *passim.;* Annual reports of major oil companies reflect the expansion.

59. Standard Oil Company (N.J.), *Report to Annual Meeting, 1949;* J. E. Hartshorn, *Politics and World Oil Economics,* New York 1962; interviews; Standard Oil Company (N.J.), *Annual Report 1948;* Standard Oil Company (N.J.), *Report to Annual Meeting, 1952,* Socony-Vacuum, *Annual Report 1950;* Standard Oil of California and Texas Company, *Annual Reports.* Leonard Fanning, *Foreign Oil and the Free World,* New York 1954, 192–200.

60. "Report of the Petroleum Advisory Group, Nov. 1945 to June 1951," May 31, 1951 (unpub.); background data on American-Japanese relationships in the

petroleum industry from Robert Anderson (Esso), S. E. Van Nostrand, R. N. Trackwell, and E. C. Robinson (Caltex), A. H. Zinkand (Mitsubishi Oil Co.), all in Tokyo, September 1965. The joint-venture structures were very complex. Stanvac, although it owned 50 per cent of the Japanese refining company, owned 100 per cent of the marketing company and did its own distribution as before the war. On the other hand, Caltex and the independent Japanese Nippon Oil Company each owned 50 per cent of Nippon Petroleum Refining. Caltex also owned 50 per cent of Koa Oil Company. Caltex sold crude oil to Nippon Petroleum Refining, Nippon Oil, and Koa; it also sold products to Nippon Oil. The independent Nippon Oil Company did the marketing to the Japanese public.

61. Petroleum Information Bureau (Australia), *The Age of Oil*, Melbourne 1960, 99, 175–176. Caltex chose its site in 1951, poured its foundations in 1953, and began refining in Australia in 1956. Government of India, Ministry of Production, *Establishment of Oil Refineries: Text of Agreement with Oil Companies*, New Delhi, n.d. [1953]. Interviews in India. Stanvac's refinery was completed in 1954, Caltex's in 1957. See Michael Tanzer, *The Political Economy of International Oil and the Underdeveloped Countries*, Boston 1969, 168–169.

62. Royal Commission on Canada's Economic Prospects, *Final Report*, Ottawa 1957, 127–132; Imperial Oil, Ltd., *Annual Reports;* Fanning, 175–188; *Moody's Transportation Manual* (pipeline companies); Canada, Department of Mines and Technical Surveys, *A Survey of the Petroleum Industry in Canada during 1956*, Ottawa 1957 (contains background).

63. Edwin Lieuwen, *Petroleum in Venezuela*, Berkeley 1954 96–114; Fanning, 83–108; Creole Petroleum Corp., *Stenographic Report of the Annual Meeting of Stockholders*, 1948–1952; Wayne C. Taylor and John Lindeman, *Creole Petroleum Corporation in Venezuela*, Washington, D.C. 1955, 29ff.

64. Data from Latin American offices of oil companies. Camera de la Industria del Petroleo, *El Desarrollo de la Producción de Petróleo en la Republica Argentina (1907–1963)*, Buenos Aires, n.d. [1963], 1–2 and Gráfico No. II; U.S. Dept. of Comm., Office of International Trade, *Investment in Colombia*, Washington, n.d. [1953?]; Seymour W. Wurfel, *Foreign Enterprise in Colombia*, Chapel Hill, N.C. 1965, 46, 48; Hubert Herring, *A History of Latin America*, 2d ed., New York 1961, 517–518. Gaston, 185. *Factors Limiting U.S. Investments Abroad*, pt. 1, 3, 28.

65. U.S. Sen., Special Committee to Investigate the National Defense Program, Investigations of the National Defense Program, *Petroleum Arrangements with Saudi Arabia*, 80th Cong., 1st sess., 1947–1948, pt. 41, p. 24923 (Rodgers quote; Rodgers added that Standard Oil of New Jersey executives were likewise "amazed."); *ibid.*, 24903 (the price). Standard Oil of New Jersey, Standard Oil of California, Texaco and Socony-Vacuum, *Annual Reports, Prospectuses*, and *Reports to Annual Meetings*. F.T.C., *International Petroleum Cartel*, 99–107, 119–128; George Lenczowski, *Oil and State in the Middle East*, Ithaca 1960, 18–19.

66. Daniel da Cruz, "Tapline," *Aramco World,* Sept.–Oct. 1964 (background on the pipeline); "Agreement between Saudi Arab Government and Trans-Arabian Pipe Line Company, and Related Documents"; U.S. House, Special Committee on Petroleum, Committee on Armed Services, *Petroleum for National Defense, Hearings,* 80th Cong., 2d sess., 1948, 211, 9. Roy Lebkicher et al., *ARAMCO Handbook,* The Netherlands 1960, 151ff. Benjamin Shwadran, *Middle East, Oil, and the Great Powers,* New York 1955, 332–337; Geoffrey Brunn and Victor S. Mamatey, *The World in the Twentieth Century,* 4th ed., Boston 1962, 597–604 (background). "Middle Eastern Petroleum Data," booklet published by ARAMCO (petroleum production statistics).

67. Kuwait Oil Company, Ltd., *The Story of Kuwait,* Beirut 1963, 20; Fanning, 326.

68. Interviews with AMINOIL executives, Kuwait Neutral Zone, 1965. Lebkicher, 123 (AMINOIL). ARAMCO's 1933 contract had granted preference rights, and its 1939 concession had included the Neutral Zone. Article 9 of Original Concession agreement of May 29, 1933, and Article 7 of Supplemental Concession contain relinquishment provisions. Agreement of October 10, 1948 (relinquishment of its rights in Neutral Zone). All of these agreements are printed in "The Saudi Arab Government and Arabian American Company, Basic Agreements and Selected Documents Pertaining Thereto," (1958). J. Paul Getty, *My Life and Fortunes,* New York 1963, 219–229; Zuhayr Mikdashi, *A Financial Analysis of Middle Eastern Oil Concessions, 1901–1965,* New York 1966, 136 (Getty's concession).

69. Interviews; Henry Cattan, *The Evolution of Oil Concessions,* Dobbs Ferry 1967, 5; ARAMCO-Saudi Arabian Government, "Agreement of December 30, 1950"; Lebkicher, 136; Mikdashi, 135ff; *The Story of Kuwait,* 26; C. J. P. Andrews, "50-60 in Iraq," typescript, Bagdad, Iraq, Oct. 14, 1963; Shwadran, 259–263 (Iraq), 398 (Qatar), 383 (Bahrain); Cattan, 10.

70. Shwadran, 104–190; Stephen Hemsley Longrigg, *Oil in the Middle East,* 3d ed., London 1968, 159–173; Mikdashi, 154–155; Fanning, 354; interview, Howard Page, Standard Oil (New Jersey), June 4, 1965. For the U.S. government role during the Truman administration see Dean Acheson, *Present at the Creation,* New York 1969, chaps. 52 and 71.

71. U.S. Dept. of Comm., Bureau of Foreign Commerce, *Investment in Indonesia,* Washington, D.C. 1956, 40–42. By 1954, half the crude oil in Indonesia was produced by Stanvac and Caltex; the rest came from the largest producing company, a subsidiary of Royal Dutch-Shell, and from the smallest, a joint, Indonesian government–private firm. *Ibid.,* 40–41. For other data, see *Petroleum for National Defense,* 204. J. E. Hartshorn, *Oil Companies and Governments,* rev. ed., London 1967, 334 (Caltex); Benjamin Higgins et al., *Stanvac in Indonesia,* Washington, D.C. 1957.

Chapter XIII: The Environment for Multinational Business, 1955–1970

1. See, For example, Alfred D. Chandler, Jr., "The Structure of American Industry in the Twentieth Century: An Historical Overview," *Business History*

Review 43:267 (Autumn 1969); *Fortune* editors, *The Conglomerate Commotion,* New York 1970; U.S. Bureau of the Census, *Historical Statistics of the United States,* Washington, D.C. 1960, 572, and *Statistical Abstract 1968,* 487 (mergers); Edwin Mansfield, *The Economics of Technological Change,* New York 1968, 5–6, 8; Melvin Kranzberg and Carroll W. Pursell, Jr., *Technology in Western Civilization,* New York 1967; National Science Foundation publishes data on research and development expenditures; John Kenneth Galbraith, *The New Industrial State,* Boston 1967; Keith Davis and Robert L. Blomstrom, *Business and Its Environment,* New York 1966, 167–170.

2. Peter B. Kenen, *Giant Among Nations,* Chicago 1963, 164ff.

3. These treaties were by no means new to the 1955–1970 period. The Oregon Treaty of 1846 between the United States and Great Britain had such a clause. The new treaties provided for prompt payment of just compensation should properties be expropriated. Latin American countries regarded such treaties as infringements on their sovereignty and refused to enter into them; they believed they should decide how to treat property domiciled in their countries. See Legislative Reference Service, *Expropriation of American-Owned Property,* Washington, D.C. 1963, 29–31.

4. Carol McCormick Crosswell, *International Business Techniques,* Dobbs Ferry 1963, chap. 5.

5. Marina von Neumann Whitman, *Government Risk-Sharing in Foreign Investment,* Princeton 1965; Crosswell, chap. 3; Agency for International Development, *Aids to Business,* Washington, D.C. 1966, 14–24; A.I.D. Press Release, July 27, 1967; A.I.D., "An Introduction to the Overseas Private Investment Corporation," [Washington, D.C.] 1970, 3.

6. A.I.D., *Aids to Business,* 26–27.

7. *Ibid., passim.*

8. A.I.D., "An Introduction to the Overseas Private Investment Corporation," and A.I.D. Press Release, Jan. 10, 1971.

9. John S. Ewing and Frank Meissner, *International Business Management,* Belmont, Calif. 1964, 201–243; Raymond F. Mikesell, *Public International Lending for Development,* New York 1966; Crosswell, chap. 4; Miguel S. Wionczek, ed., *Economic Cooperation in Latin America, Asia, and Africa,* Cambridge, Mass. 1969, 357–480.

10. Legislative Reference Service, *Expropriation of American-Owned Property,* 27–27, 20; private interviews; see excellent article, *New York Times,* Mar. 26, 1970.

11. Business International, *Profit Sanctuaries and How They Are Used,* New York 1960; Lawrence B. Krause and Kenneth W. Dam, *Federal Tax Treatment of Foreign Income,* Washington, D.C. 1964; Arnold C. Harberger, "Tax Aspects of Foreign Economic Policy," American Bankers Association, *Proceedings of a Symposium on Federal Taxation,* Washington, D.C. 1965, 67; and Roy Blough, *International Business,* New York 1966, 257.

12. Ray R. Eppert, president of Burroughs Corporation, "Passport for World Markets," *Business Topics* 13:9 (Autumn 1965).

13. Theodore C. Sorensen, *Kennedy,* New York 1965, 459.

14. Christopher Layton, *Trans-Atlantic Investments,* Boulogne-sur-Seine, France 1966, 42–43.

15. U.S. Dept. of Comm., Press Release Dec. 6, 1965.

16. *Federal Register* 33:47–53 (Jan. 3, 1968).

17. U.S. Dept. of Comm., Press Release, June 12, 1968.

18. *Federal Register* 33:49–50, 52 (Jan. 3, 1968).

19. Based on U.S. Dept. of Comm., Office of Foreign Direct Investment, press releases.

20. This is evident from the tone of communications from the Office of Foreign Direct Investment, set up to administer the program. Some U.S. businessmen recognized the need for the restrictions but hoped they would be temporary. See testimony of Arthur K. Watson, chairman of the board of IBM World Trade Corporation, before the Joint Economic Committee, Subcommittee on Foreign Economic Policy, *A Foreign Economic Policy for the 1970's, Hearings,* 91st Cong., 1st sess., Dec. 2, 1969 (1970), pt. 1, p. 11.

21. The business position is evident from the proceedings of the National Foreign Trade Council. R. Harrison Wagner, *United States Policy Toward Latin America,* Stanford, Calif. 1970, 96–97 (quotas). Kenen, 210, gives some of the trade restrictions still remaining in the Trade Expansion Act. Richard Barber, *The American Corporation,* New York 1970, 248 (rise of protectionism). The annual reports of U.S. Steel are particularly useful on its attitudes toward foreign competition.

22. Interviews in India, 1965; see also Michael Tanzer, *The Political Economy of International Oil and the Underdeveloped Countries,* Boston 1969.

23. Based on interviews in the United States and Latin America.

24. See annual reports of leading U.S. corporations. Benjamin J. Cohen, ed., *American Foreign Economic Policy,* New York 1968, 284–285, 293–304; Barber, 245, and William A. Dymsza, "East-West Trade: Types of Business Arrangements," *MSU Business Topics* 19:23 (Winter 1971).

25. Cohen, 285. The conflict is often remarked on in the literature; for example, Charles P. Kindleberger, *American Business Abroad,* New Haven 1969, 43, 142.

26. *New York Times,* Dec. 20, 1969. On April 14, 1971, Nixon relaxed the embargo on nonstrategic exports to China. *Ibid.,* Apr. 15, 1971. On June 10, 1971, Nixon authorized the export of specified nonstrategic goods to China and eliminated all bars on imports from China. *Ibid.,* June 11, 1971.

27. *New York Times,* Jan. 6, 1967 (sanctions). With State Department approval, Ford Motor Company sold the shares in its company assemblying in Rhodesia to the Rhodesian Development Corporation. (Information from the Ford Motor Company). On the other hand, Union Carbide—the largest investor in chrome in Rhodesia—lobbied in Washington and in September 1971 was successful, when the U.S. embargo on Rhodesian chrome ore was removed.

28. Joint Economic Committee, *Mainland China in the World Economy,* Sen. Rpt. No. 348, 90th Cong., 1st sess., 1967, 24. Recently (1970) there has been talk

of oil prospects off the South Vietnam coast. Such prospects were not a cause of the war; if anything the war would tend to retard the development of such oil. It has been argued (see, for example, comments by Mary McCarthy in *New York Review of Books,* Jan. 25, 1973, 11–12) that "in a larger sense. . . . our investments and markets *are* at stake in Vietnam," since Vietnam became a "symbol of the right of US capital to flow freely throughout the globe and return home." "A Viet Cong 'takeover,' if it is allowed to happen, deals a blow to the American way of life and free-enterprise mystique. . . ." Such an analysis sees U.S. policy makers as acting for the "greater good" of U.S. business and brushes aside the evidence that in some specifics the war proved detrimental to the development of U.S. international business and that the rationale behind U.S. participation was far broader.

29. J. J. Servan-Schreiber, *The American Challenge,* New York 1968 emphasizes the American advantages in research. So, too, Raymond Vernon, *Sovereignty at Bay: The Multinational Spread of U.S. Enterprise,* New York 1971, makes the vital connection between multinational enterprise and research and development.

30. K. H. Redmond to Shareholders United Fruit, Feb. 24, 1958, Scudder Collection, Columbia University (1958 decree); Standard Oil of New Jersey, *Annual Reports;* U.S. Sen., Committee on the Judiciary, Subcommittee on Antitrust and Monopoly, *International Aspects of Antitrust, Hearings,* 89th Cong., 2d sess., 1967 (henceforth cited as *Hart Committee Hearings*) and American Bar Association, Section on Antitrust, *Antitrust Developments 1955–1968,* New York (?) 1968, 40–64. There were new developments in the 1960s, when the Department of Justice and the Federal Trade Commission for the first time attacked U.S. companies' acquisitions abroad under Section 7 of the Clayton Act. In *U.S. v. Jos. Schlitz Brewing Co.,* 253 F. Supp. 129, Northern District California, aff'd per curiam 385 U.S. 37 (1966), the Department of Justice took to court the acquisition by Schlitz of 39.3 per cent of the stock of John Labatt, Ltd., a large Canadian brewer which controlled General Brewing Co. of California. The court found in 1966 that the acquisition was a violation of the Clayton Act on the grounds that competition between Schlitz and General Brewing in the U.S. market would be substantially lessened. On Feb. 14, 1968, the Justice Department filed suit against the acquisition by Gillette Company of a German maker of electric razors (Braun A.G.). U.S. v. Gillette Co., civ. 68–141, District Massachusetts. The Justice Department sought to require Gillette to divest itself in the stock of Braun A.G. (purchased for $50 million) because the two companies "are in almost worldwide competition in the sale of shaving instruments." Braun A.G. had a licensing agreement (made in 1954) with Ronson Corporation that prohibited it from selling in the United States until 1976. (See *New York Times,* Feb. 15, 1968.) On April 11, 1969, the Federal Trade Commission started proceedings against Litton Industries' acquisition of two German firms. F.T.C., In the Matter of Litton Industries, Doc. No. 8778. The F.T.C. believed the effect "may be to substantially lessen competition . . . throughout the United States." It sought divesture of these corporations. The complaint is in-

cluded in U.S. House, Committee on the Judiciary, Antitrust Subcommittee No. 5, *Investigation of Conglomerate Corporations,* 91st Cong., 1st and 2d sess. (1970), pt. 5, pp. 122–126.

31. *Hart Committeee Hearings,* 190.

32. Arthur K. Watson, chairman of the board, IBM World Trade Corp. to the Subcommittee on Foreign Economic Policy (cited in note 20), 7.

33. Thomas Aitken, vice president of McCann-Erikson, an advertising firm, in his book, *A Foreign Policy for American Business,* New York 1962, 147.

34. Interviews. This is by no means a general view.

35. Interview with key executive of important multinational enterprise.

36. Charles P. Kindleberger, *Power and Money,* New York 1970.

37. Interviews. Seymour J. Rubin, "The International Firm and the National Jurisdiction," in Charles P. Kindleberger, ed. *The International Corporation,* Cambridge, Mass. 1970, 186–187.

38. *Survey of Current Business* (size of U.S. investment in Britain); John H. Dunning, *American Investment in British Manufacturing Industry,* London 1958, and his *The Role of American Investment in the British Economy,* London 1969. Works on U.S. investment in Europe (see note 43) include data on investment in Britain. Interviews and annual reports have also been helpful.

39. Dunning, *Role of American Investment,* 160–162.

40. Task Force on the Structure of Canadian Industry, *Foreign Ownership and the Structure of Canadian Industry,* Ottawa 1968, 378.

41. *Survey of Current Business,* November 1972, 30.

42. For background on the common market and the European Free Trade Area, see Chap. XII, note 53. The periodical *European Community* has been useful in following the course of European unity.

43. Most useful among the numerous volumes on U.S. investment in Europe have been Christopher Layton, *Trans-Atlantic Investment* (see note 14) and Servan-Schreiber, *The American Challenge* (see note 29).

44. Kindleberger, *Power and Money,* 172–173; for more details see Joint Economic Committee, *The Euro-Dollar Market and Its Public Policy Implications,* 91st Cong., 2d sess., 1970.

45. *New York Times,* Jan. 15, 1968 (blocking the takeover).

46. *Survey of Current Business,* October 1970, 28 (attractions of Germany); Belgian Consulate General, Industrial Section, *Business Memos* contain details of the offers.

47. Layton, 32.

48. *Ibid.,* 39.

49. *Ibid.,* and Allan W. Johnstone, *United States Direct Investment in France, An Investigation of French Charges,* Cambridge, Mass. 1965, 25.

50. *New York Times,* Nov. 9, 1969 (Westinghouse's plans), Dec. 6, 1969 (the veto), and Feb. 24, 1970 (general policies); Layton, 43–44; *Survey of Current Business,* October 1970, 28 (figures). See also on U.S. investments in France, Gilles-Y Bertin, *L'Investissement des Firmes Étrangères en France,* Paris 1963; J. Gervais, *La France face aux investissements étrangers,* Paris 1963; Testimony of Olivier Giscard D'Estaing before *Hart Committee Hearings,* 203–210.

51. The importance of the public sector is emphasized by M. M. Postan, *An Economic History of Western Europe 1945–1964*, London 1967, 217–228. Rainer Hellmann, *The Challenge to U.S. Dominance of the International Corporation*, New York 1970, 139, is excellent on U.S. joint ventures with government agencies in Italy.

52. Garden City, N.Y. 1964.

53. New York 1962.

54. New York 1968.

55. New York 1968.

56. This is made clear in most of the literature, especially Servan-Schreiber, *The American Challenge*. See also H. van der Haas, *The Enterprise in Transition: An Analysis of European and American Practice*, London 1967.

57. *Survey of Current Business*, October 1970, 28.

58. See Harry G. Johnson, "Economic Nationalism in Canadian Policy," in Johnson, ed., *Economic Nationalism in Old and New States*, Chicago, Ill. 1967, 85–97, and testimony of Melville H. Watkins at Joint Economic Committee, Subcommittee on Foreign Economic Policy, *A Foreign Economic Policy for the 1970's Hearings*, 91st Cong., 2d sess., July 1970, pt. 4, p. 913 ("rising nationalism"). Of most interest on U.S. impact on Canada are the reports of the Royal Commission on Canada's Economic Prospects, especially Irving Brecher and S. S. Reisman, *Canada-United States Economic Relations*, Ottawa 1957, and the Commission's *Final Report*, Ottawa 1957. See also C. D. Blythe and E. B. Carty, "Nonresident Ownership of Canadian Industry," *Canadian Journal of Economics and Political Science*, November 1956; Hugh G. J. Aitken, *The American Economic Impact on Canada*, Durham, N.C. 1959; Aitken, *American Capital and Canadian Resources*, Cambridge, Mass. 1961; A. E. Safarian, *Foreign Ownership of Canadian Industry*, Toronto 1966; Task Force on the Structure of Canadian Industry, *Foreign Ownership and the Structure of Canadian Industry*, Ottawa 1968 (henceforth cited as *Watkins Report*); and Kari Levitt, *Silent Surrender*, Toronto 1970.

59. *Watkins Report*, 383–384. See Levitt, 6–7 (banks).

60. *Watkins Report*, 383–384.

61. *New York Times*, Aug. 15, 1970 (Control Data). See Jack N. Behrman, *Some Patterns in the Rise of the Multinational Enterprise*, Chapel Hill, N.C. 1969, 19–20 (for certain Canadian subsidies in the 1960s).

62. *Watkins Report*, 320.

63. *Petroleum Press Service* 37:216 (June 1970).

64. *Watkins Report*, 385. *Hart Committee Hearings*, 495.

65. See Levitt, 13–15, on what she considers the shocking *quid pro quo*.

66. Harry Johnson, "The Ottawa-Washington Troubles" (1964), in Benjamin Cohen, ed. *American Foreign Economic Policy*, New York 1968, 265 (background on the automobile pact); *New York Times*, Jan. 22, 1965; Jack Baranson, *Automotive Industries in Developing Countries*, Baltimore, Md. 1969, 74, 75; *Survey of Current Business*, October 1970, 19. On the role of multinational corporations, interviews in Dearborn, Mich. By 1970, Washington began to have its doubts about the accord—whether Canada benefited more than the United

States. See *New York Times,* Nov. 28, 1970. On joint-industry cooperation in *oil,* see J. E. Hartshorn, *Oil Companies and Governments,* rev. ed., London 1967, 247–248.

67. Interviews at the U.S. Embassy and with executives of U.S. subsidiaries, South Africa, 1965.

68. Donald T. Brash, *American Investment in Australian Industry,* Cambridge, Mass. 1966, 2–3; Edith Penrose, "Foreign Investment and the Growth of the Firm," *Economic Journal* 64:220–235 (June 1956).

69. *Australian Financial Review,* Sydney, Sept. 17, 1969. See also Donald T. Brash, "Australia as Host to the International Corporation," in Charles P. Kindleberger, ed. *The International Corporation,* Cambridge, Mass. 1970, chap. 12.

70. Angus Maddison, *Economic Growth in Japan and the USSR,* New York 1969, chap. 5, for a record of and more reasons for the "explosive growth."

71. Interviews in Japan, 1965; see also Maddison, 62. Between 1950 and 1970, the Japanese government approved 4,811 contracts between Japanese and American firms, whereby the former purchased U.S. technology. Terutomo Ozawa, "Should the United States Restrict Technology Trade with Japan," *Business Topics,* Autumn 1972, 35.

72. Interviews and data collected in Japan, 1965, 1969. On Japanese policies extensive data are available from the Ministry of International Trade and Industry, the Ministry of Finance, the Mitsubishi Economic Research Institute, the Bank of Japan, the Industrial Bank of Japan, the Tokyo Chamber of Commerce and Industry, and the Federation of Economic Organizations (Keidanren). Some of the published materials are available in English. Information can also be obtained from the American Chamber of Commerce in Japan. For a fascinating study of the Japanese acquisition of American technology through licensing arrangements, see G. R. Hall and R. E. Johnson, "Transfers of United States Aerospace Technology to Japan," in Raymond Vernon, ed., *The Technology Factor in International Trade,* New York 1970, 305–358. On specific Japanese rules on direct foreign investment, see excellent article by M. Y. Yoshino,' " Japan as Host to the International Corporation," in Kindleberger, *International Corporation,* 345–369.

73. *Survey of Current Business,* November 1972, 30.

74. Samuel P. Huntington, *Political Order in Changing Societies,* New Haven 1968, 12.

75. Just before independence in the Congo, a group of American businessmen surveyed investment possibilities and found them superb. Data acquired in Africa.

76. Philip C. Newman, "Joint International Business Ventures in Cuba," unpubl. study, Columbia University 1958, 1.

77. Legislative Reference Service, *Expropriation of American-Owned Property,* 16.

78. By the late 1950s and 1960s, Americans had encountered such political uncertainties in Venezuela, Nicaragua, Mexico, Brazil, Colombia, and Argentina, for instance, and had in each case met with losses as a result. See Mira

Wilkins, *The Emergence of Multinational Enterprise: American Business Abroad from the Colonial Era to 1914*, Cambridge, Mass. 1970, 163–165, 25–27, 133, 188, and the present volume, for examples. Likewise, British experiences in Latin America had been unhappy. See. J. Fred Rippy, *British Investments in Latin America 1822–1949*, Minneapolis, Minn. 1959, 18, 26, 32.

79. Commerce Committee for the Alliance for Progress, *Proposals to Improve the Flow of U.S. Private Investment to Latin America*, Washington, D.C. 1963, Appendix A on the effects of currency depreciation on operations U.S. manufacturing abroad.

80. Data from Iraq Petroleum Company and Kuwait Oil Company.

81. *New York Times*, June 8, 1967.

82. *Baghdad Observer*, Baghdad, May 8, 1969.

83. *Petroleum Press Service* 36:264 (July 1969), and 37:220 (June 1970).

84. *New York Times*, Jan. 30, 1971, on the reopening.

85. *New York Times*, June 17, 1969.

86. Harry G. Johnson, "The Ideology of Economic Policy in the New States," Johnson, *Economic Nationalism*, 124–141, has much of interest on the nationalism of the emerging countries. See also Werner Baer and Mario Henrique Simonson, "American Capital and Brazilian Nationalism," in Marvin Bernstein, ed. *Foreign Investment in Latin America*, New York 1966, 271–282.

87. See Raymond Vernon, "Conflict and Resolution Between Foreign Direct Investors and Less Developed Countries," *Public Policy* 17:334–337 (Fall 1968), and Vernon, *How Latin America Views the Foreign Investor*, New York 1966.

88. The International Monetary Fund publishes an *Annual Report on Exchange Restrictions*, which is invaluable on the attitudes of host governments toward foreign investment.

89. Interviews in Latin America, 1961, 1964; Vernon, *How Latin America Views the Foreign Investor;* Lincoln Gordon and Engelbert L. Grommers, *United States Manufacturing Investment in Brazil: The Impact of Brazilian Government Policies, 1946–1960*, Boston 1962; Claude McMillan, Jr., Richard F. Gonzales, and Leo G. Erickson, *International Enterprise in a Developing Economy: A Study of U.S. Enterprises in Brazil*, East Lansing, Mich. 1964; Jack Baranson, *Automotive Industries in Developing Countries*, Baltimore 1969, chap. VI. Frank Brandenburg, *The Development of Latin American Private Enterprise*, Washington, D.C. 1964, chap. 3, is good on public sector activities. *Survey of Current Business*, October 1970, 28 (country data), 20 (local sales); *ibid.*, November 1972, 31 (1970 data).

90. This point is well made by Carlos F. Diaz Alejandro in his "Direct Foreign Investment in Latin America," in Kindleberger, *International Corporation*, 331n. The same paradox has existed elsewhere, Canada being the prime example. See Celso Furtado, *Obstacles to Development in Latin America*, Garden City, N.Y. 1970, for such concern by a Brazilian.

91. Interviews with oil company executives in Latin America and the United States, 1965. Tax levels from Creole Petroleum Corporation, Caracas, *Petroleum Press Service, passim.* P. R. Odell, "Oil Industry in Latin America," in Edith T.

Penrose, *The Large International Firm in Developing Countries: The International Petroleum Industry,* London 1968, 294–297.

92. Michael Tanzer, *The Political Economy of International Oil and the Underdeveloped Countries,* Boston 1969, 327–328; *Survey of Current Business,* August 1961, 21; *Petroleum Press Service* 36:55 (February 1969). *New York Times,* Nov. 14, 1970, Jan. 25, Feb. 18, 1971 (on profit percentages). From 1960–1966 net investment (including capital repatriation) in Venezuela was negative. See Joseph Grunwald and Philip Musgrove, *Natural Resources in Latin American Development,* Baltimore 1970, 290. The book value of U.S. stakes in Venezuelan petroleum was higher in 1966 than in 1970. *Survey of Current Business.*

93. On October 9, 1968 the military regime seized the oil fields (La Brea y Pariñas) and the Talara refinery. On February 6, 1969, the military regime completed the seizure of all other holdings of International Petroleum Company. See *New York Times,* Feb. 7, 1969 and E. Ramirez Novoa, *Petroleo y Revolucion Nacionalista,* Lima, Peru 1970, xvii.

94. *New York Times,* Mar. 27, 1956, and Sept. 27, 1960; Gulf Oil, *Annual Report 1956,* and *Petroleum Press Service* 23:265 (July 1956). *New York Times,* Oct. 31, 1969.

95. *New York Times,* Oct. 19, 1969 and Sept. 9, 1970.

96. Camera de la Industria del Petroleo, "El Desarrollo de la Produccion de Petroleo en la Republica Argentina (1907–1963)," Buenos Aires 1963, revised 1964. Odell, 288n.

97. Interviews in Venezuela, 1964; *Petroleum Press Service* 36:55 (February 1969); *International Financial News Survey* 12:334 (Oct. 9, 1970), and 12:384 (Nov. 20, 1970); *New York Times,* Nov. 14, 1970.

98. Southern Peru Copper Corporation started developing its large deposits in the 1950s and became in the 1960s the largest copper producer in Peru. See *International Financial News Survey* 21:30 (Sept. 19, 1969), and Grunwald and Musgrove, 166. On Law 11, 828, see C. W. Reynolds' contribution to Markos Mamalakis, *Essays on the Chilean Economy,* Homewood, Ill. 1965, 249, 252–254, and Grunwald and Musgrove, 169–170.

99. American Smelting and Refining Company, *Annual Reports 1963* and *1965,* and *New York Times,* June 22, 1965. Grunwald and Musgrove, 166.

100. *Business Week,* Nov. 20, 1965, and *New York Times,* Dec. 24, 1964, and Dec. 22, 1965. See Raymond F. Mikesell et al., *Foreign Investment in the Petroleum and Mineral Industries,* Baltimore, Md. 1971, 345–364, 443 (for Hanna's experience; by June 1970 the joint venture had not yet been consummated, but still seemed likely).

101. Our data on these transactions comes from the copper companies in the United States and Chile, their annual reports, 1960–1970, *El Mercurio,* Santiago, Chile, the *New York Times,* esp. Dec. 22, 1964, Jan. 22, 1968, June 24, 27, 29, and Aug. 17, 1969, Jan. 2 and Sept. 9, 1970, and Grunwald and Musgrove, 170–172. Visits to El Salvador and Talara. Other U.S. mining companies in Chile would undoubtedly be affected by Allende's plans.

102. U.S. Steel, *Annual Report 1968*. Grunwald and Musgrove, 196, indicate the Venezuelan government plans that no new iron ore mining concessions will go to 100 per cent foreign-owned firms.

103. *New York Times,* Aug. 15, 1970.

104. *Ibid.*

105. Legislative Reference Service, *Expropriation of American-Owned Property*, 17–18; interviews with United Fruit Company officials in the United States and Central America; *New York Times,* Jan. 15, 1969 (Cerro), *ibid.,* Aug. 27, 1969 and correction Aug. 28, 1969 (W. R. Grace).

106. American & Foreign Power Co. and I.T.T., *Annual Reports.*

107. Based on interviews with U.S. executives in less developed countries in Asia and Africa, 1965. After the Philippines, according to U.S. Department of Commerce figures (as published in *Survey of Current Business*), U.S. stakes in manufacturing in all less developed countries in Asia and Africa were highest in India. U.S. Dept. of Comm., Bureau of Foreign Commerce, *Investment in India,* Washington, D.C. 1961 and Michael Kidron, *Foreign Investments in India,* London 1965 are useful on conditions for investments in India. Essential are the numerous publications of the Indian Investment Centre, for example, *Investing In India,* Bombay 1962, and *India Welcomes Foreign Investment,* New Delhi 1965. For a brief survey of the varieties of legislation on foreign investment in Africa, see Alison K. Mitchel, "Foreign Investment Legislation in Africa," *Finance and Development* 7:7–11 (March 1970).

108. Interviews in Japan, 1969. It is interesting that a most articulate opponent of U.S. direct investment among labor leaders is Paul Jennings, president of the International Union of Electrical, Radio & Machine Workers. See his testimony before the Subcommittee on Foreign Economic Policy, Joint Economic Committee, *A Foreign Economic Policy for the 1970's, Hearings,* 91st Cong., 2d sess., Washington, D.C. 1970, pt. 4, pp. 813–816.

109. In 1965 alone, U.S. companies announced new refinery projects in the Malayasia, South Vietnam, Ivory Coast, Liberia, and Malagasy Republic. *Petroleum Press Service* 32:288 (August 1965). In the 1950s and 1960s, Americans built new refineries in the Philippines, India, Pakistan, Kenya, and Senegal, for example.

110. Edith Penrose, *The Large International Firm in Developing Countries,* London 1968, 222–223, 230; *Petroleum Press Service* 34:231 (June 1967).

111. Henry Cattan, *The Evolution of Oil Concessions in the Middle East and North Africa,* Dobbs Ferry, N.Y. 1967, 139–143; Penrose, 244; *International Financial News Survey* 20:289 (Aug. 30, 1968).

112. Stephen Hemsley Longrigg, *Oil in the Middle East,* 3d ed., London 1968, 331 (Israeli National Oil Co.); Penrose, 82 (India and Pakistan); *Petroleum Press Service* 34:231, June 1967 (Ceylon).

113. Cattan, 126.

114. *Annual Reports;* Jane P. C. Carey and Andrew G. Carey, "Libya," *Political Science Quarterly* 76:59–68 (March 1961); *Petroleum Press Service* documents the news of discoveries. See also L. H. Schätzel, *Petroleum in Nigeria,*

Ibadan 1969, and Scott R. Pearson, *Petroleum and the Nigerian Economy*, Stanford 1970.

115. Interviews in the Middle East and data from companies. On actions of Middle Eastern oil producing states, see Penrose, *The Large International Firm;* Cattan, *Evolution of Oil Concession;* J. E. Hartshorn, *Oil Companies and Governments*, London 1962, and rev. ed., 1967; Longrigg, *Oil in the Middle East;* George Stocking, *Middle East Oil*, Nashville, Tenn. 1970; *ARAMCO Handbook*, rev. ed., Dhahran, Saudi Arabia 1968; and Fuad Rouhani, *A History of O.P.E.C.*, New York 1971. The Cattan, Hartshorn (1967), and Rouhani volumes are useful on North Africa. On Indonesia, Rouhani; Government of Indonesia, *Investment in Indonesia Today,* Oct. 30, 1967; Business International, *Doing Business in the New Indonesia*, New York 1968; *Petroleum Press Service, passim;* and *Fortune,* August 1963, 79ff.

116. Penrose, 74 (1955 oil law), 76; Cattan, 53, Hartshorn (1967), 17–25, and *New York Times,* Dec. 5, 1965 (new Libyan Contracts).

117. See note 115, *New York Times,* Oct. 4, Nov. 25, 1970, and Jan. 29, 1971.

118. Rouhani, *passim;* Longrigg, 351–352; Penrose, 200.

119. Penrose, 75; Cattan, 14–20.

120. *Petroleum Press Service* 37:9 (January 1970).

121. *New York Times,* Aug. 31, 1967, July 22 and Nov. 13, 1970. Later the Algerians seized 51 per cent of the assets of the French enterprises operating in Algeria. See *New York Times,* Feb. 25, May 18, 1971.

122. *Ibid.,* July 6, 1970.

123. *Petroleum Press Service* 34:394 (October 1967), 35:34 (January 1968); *International Financial News Survey* 21:183 (June 13, 1969). 124.

124. Rouhani, 89.

125. As 1971 began, the countries were negotiating as a bloc with the international oil companies; since this book covers only to 1970, these negotiations will not be commented on; they are, however, a logical extension of the new cooperation of the 1960s within O.P.E.C. and the agreements just discussed.

126. *Far Eastern Economic Review,* Hong Kong, June 15–21, 1969.

127. Data collected in Africa, 1965, and *Annual Reports; International Financial News Survey* 21:335 (Oct. 17, 1969), and *New York Times,* Jan. 30, 1970.

128. Roan Selection Trust, *Annual Reports; Wall Street Journal,* Jan. 5, 1968; Roan Selection Trust, Explanatory Statement to Shareholders, June 30, 1970.

129. Letter from N. H. Gouldin, U.S. Rubber, to author, Feb. 16, 1967; James M. Sutherland, Goodyear Tire & Rubber Co., to author, Feb. 17, 1967 and Aug. 3, 1970; N. H. Gouldin, Uniroyal, to author, Aug. 13, 1970.

130. *International Financial News Survey* 21:339 (Oct. 24, 1969), and Rainer Hellmann, *The Challenge to U.S. Dominance of the International Corporation,* New York 1970, 11–12; on Hertz and Avis in eastern Europe, see U.S. House, Committee on the Judiciary, Antitrust Subcommittee #5, *Investigation of Conglomerate Corporations,* 91st Cong. (1969), pt. 3, pp. 1054, 589–590, 1244.

131. See Dymsza, "East-West Trade" and Xerox, *1970 Annual Meeting of Stockholders*.

132. United Nations, *Statistical Abstract 1966*, 203 (Soviet ranking); Walter Laqueur, *The Struggle for the Middle East*, New York 1969, 119.

133. Legislative Reference Service, *Problems Raised by the Soviet Oil Offensive*, Washington, D.C. 1962, vii. Laqueur, 121, 135–136; *Petroleum Press Service* 35:25–26 (January 1968), 36:63 (February 1969); interviews in India and the Middle East.

Chapter XIV: Multinational Enterprise, 1955–1970

1. U.S. Dept. of Comm., Office of Business Economics, *U.S. Business Investment in Foreign Countries*, Washington, D.C. 1960, 6 (1957 investments), 110 (total sales of U.S. businesses abroad $38 billion in 1957). Total U.S. exports of goods and services, according to Department of Commerce data, equaled $26 billion in 1957; merchandise exports were $19 billion. U.S. Dept. of Comm., Office of Foreign Direct Investment, *Foreign Direct Investment Program*, July 1971, 1; J. L. Angel, *Directory of American Firms Operating in Foreign Countries*, 7th ed., New York 1969; and *Survey of Current Business* (1960s and 1970 data). In 1968, for example, sales of U.S. *manufacturing* affiliates abroad alone equaled $59 billion, while U.S. merchandise exports totaled $35 billion. See *Survey of Current Business*, October 1970, 18, S-21.

2. In 1914, G.N.P. was $36.4 billion, and U.S. direct foreign investment, $2.65 billion or 7.3 per cent of G.N.P. See Mira Wilkins, *The Emergence of Multinational Enterprise: American Business Abroad from the Colonial Era to 1914*, Cambridge, Mass. 1970, 201 and 293n.14. In 1929, G.N.P. was $103.1 billion; U.S. direct foreign investment $7.5 billion or 7.3 per cent of G.N.P. See Chap. VII, note 63 above. In 1970, G.N.P. was $976 billion; U.S. direct investments abroad reached $78.18 billion or 8 per cent of G.N.P. *Survey of Current Business*, November 1972, 30.

3. See Tables I.3, III.1, VIII.2, XIII.1 herein.

4. The literature on U.S. direct investment abroad in manufacturing in the late 1950s and 1960s is enormous. The bibliography indicates some of the numerous works that the present author has found useful.

5. See William H. Gruber, Dileep Mehta, and Raymond Vernon, "The R. & D. Factor in International Trade and International Investment of United States Industries," *Journal of Political Economy* 75:30 (February 1967), for their argument that technologically advanced manufacturing firms participate in direct investments.

6. Melvin Kranzberg and Carroll W. Pursell, Jr., eds., *Technology in Western Civilization*, New York 1967, II. The change in position of the U.S. chemical industry vis-à-vis the German chemical industry is beautifully illustrated in Robert Stobaugh's study of nine petrochemical products involved in international production. Every one of these products (five in all) introduced before World War II was first introduced in Germany; every one of the remaining four products introduced during or after World War II was first introduced in

the United States. Robert B. Stobaugh, "The Product Life Cycle, U.S. Exports, and International Investment," DBA diss., Graduate School of Business Administration, Harvard University, 1968, 68.

7. On the expansion of U.S. chemical companies abroad, see Hugo E. R. Uyterhoeven, "Foreign Entry and Joint-Ventures: A Study of Foreign Investment Strategies in the European Chemical Industry," DBA diss., Graduate School of Business Administration, Harvard University, 1963. See also Conrad Berenson, *The Chemical Industry*, New York 1963, 37–38, 163–167, 227.

8. R and D expenditures as a percentage of sales is considered to be one measure of a technologically advanced industry. The highest percentages recorded for the 1960s were for the aircraft, electrical equipment, instrument, and chemical industries. See Edwin Mansfield, *The Economics of Technological Change*, New York 1968, 57.

9. Based on annual reports of numerous companies.

10. See data in *Survey of Current Business.*

11. *Ibid.*, October 1970, 19.

12. While U.S. exports exceeded U.S. imports of all transportation equipment, these are not the relevant figures. U.S. investment abroad in the transportation equipment industry was mainly in making passenger cars. Thus, one wants to look at export-import figures on passenger cars. See *Statistical Abstract, 1960*, 559, *1968*, 552, and *1969*, 800. These reveal the predominance of imports after 1957.

13. Wilkins, *Emergence of Multinational Enterprise* 189–190, 212–213.

14. U.S. Steel, *Annual Reports.* Of course one could argue that U.S. Steel's place in U.S. industry has dropped dramatically in the 1960s—from ranking fifth in sales in 1960 to twelfth in 1969! (See *Fortune*'s "500" lists).

15. Wilkins, 209, 214n.

16. Data from the U.S. Department of Commerce.

17. Walter Adams and Joel B. Dirlam, "Big Steel, Invention, and Innovation," *Quarterly Journal of Economics* 80:167–189 (May 1966).

18. *Survey of Current Business,* October 1970, 19.

19. This has been the conclusion of such students of foreign investment as S. H. Hymer, "International Operations of Foreign Firms—A Study of Direct Foreign Investment," Ph.D. diss., M.I.T., 1960; Judd Polk et al., *U.S. Production Abroad and the Balance of Payments,* New York 1966; and Raymond Vernon (see for example, his "International Investment and International Trade in Product Cycle," *Quarterly Journal of Economics* 80:190–207, May 1966). All these writers give additional detailed reasons on the foreign investment decision. See also Yair Aharoni, *Foreign Investment Decision Process,* Cambridge, Mass. 1966. Gruber, Mehta, and Vernon write, "One way of looking at overseas direct investments of U.S. producers of manufactures is that they are the final step in a process which begins with the involvement of such producers in the export trade" (p. 30).

20. On joint ventures, see Wolfgang G. Friedmann and George Kalmanoff, eds., *Joint International Business Ventures,* New York 1961; country studies on

joint ventures, Columbia University Law School and Business School libraries. Roy Blough, "Joint International Business Ventures in Less Developed Countries," in Southwestern Legal Foundation, *Proceedings of the 1960 Institute on Private Investments Abroad*, Albany, N.Y. 1960; James W. C. Tomlinson, *The Joint Venture Process in International Business: India and Pakistan*, Cambridge, Mass. 1970; Lawrence Franko, "Strategy Choice and Multinational Corporate Tolerance for Joint-Ventures with Foreign Partners," DBA diss., Graduate School of Business Administration, Harvard University, 1969. This has been published as *Joint Venture Survival in Multinational Corporations*, New York 1971. Uyterhoeven, *passim*.

21. On joint ventures with governments: U.S. chemical producers went into joint ventures with the Indian government to build petrochemical and fertilizer plants (interviews in India); in Mexico, du Pont entered into a joint venture with Petróleos Mexicanos (Pemex), the state-owned oil company, to produce tetraethyl lead in Mexico (in this case while the U.S. company held 49 per cent interest and the Mexican government agency had 51 per cent, du Pont by agreement with Pemex held management responsibility. L. A. Rossi, du Pont, to author, Feb. 16, 1967.) For other examples, see article by Carlos F. Diaz Alejandro, in Charles P. Kindleberger, ed., *The International Corporation*, Cambridge, Mass. 1970, 341. The only precedent for such ventures that the present author can think of was the joint venture started in China in 1918 by Western Electric. See note 51, Chap. XIII, on joint ventures with government agencies in Italy.

22. The extent of these arrangements is unknown. See note 29, Chapter XII above.

23. Interviews; company records; annual reports. To facilitate foreign borrowing companies formed overseas finance companies: see, for example, International Harvester Overseas Capital Corporation and the Clark Equipment Overseas Finance Corporation, prospectuses. Of course, there was much that was new in international capital markets. See Sidney E. Rolfe, *The International Corporation*, Paris 1969, 106–118.

24. Our considerations here are stimulated by the pioneer work done by Alfred D. Chandler, Jr., *Strategy and Structure*, Cambridge, Mass. 1962; interviews and data from companies; John O. Tomb and Donald B. Shackelford, "The Future Structure of International Companies" in McKinsey & Co., *International Enterprise*, New York 1962. Franko, "Strategy Choice," 116, 121. Gilbert H. Clee and W. M. Sachtjen, "Organizing a World-Wide Business," *Harvard Business Review* 42:55–67 (November–December 1964). Lawrence E. Fouraker and John M. Stopford, "Organizational Structure and Multinational Strategy," *Administrative Science Quarterly* 13:47–64 (June 1968). John M. Stopford, "Growth and Organizational Change in the Multinational Firm," DBA diss., Graduate School of Business Administration, Harvard University, 1968. Of 72 manufacturing and petroleum companies studied that once had an international division, 57 no longer had it by 1968. See Raymond Vernon, *Sovereignty at Bay*, New York 1971, 126.

25. See Table XIII.3, and James W. Vaupel and Joan P. Curhan, *The Making of Multinational Enterprise*, Boston 1969, 124.

26. Wilkins, 62–64.

27. *Petroleum Press Service* has been an invaluable source of information.

28. J. E. Hartshorn, *Politics and World Oil Economics*, New York 1962, 33.

29. Arabian American Oil Company, *ARAMCO Handbook*, rev. ed., Dhahran, Saudi Arabia 1968, 82; *Petroleum Press Service* 35:11–12 (January 1968); Edith T. Penrose, *The Large International Firm in Developing Countries*, London 1958, 82; *Petroleum Press Service* 36:458 (December 1969).

30. Bache & Co., "International Oils," March 1963 is good on the impact of Suez Crisis.

31. *Petroleum Press Service* 37:203 (June 1970) and 36:458 (December 1969).

32. Standard Oil of New Jersey, *Annual Reports;* Texaco, Press Release, Jan. 17, 1967.

33. Interviews with oil company executives. E. F. Hutton & Company, "International Oils," May 1967 (quote). There were fewer joint ventures involving U.S. companies in marketing than in any other facet of the business—presumably because (a) risks were less substantial in marketing and (b) joint ventures in marketing were more vulnerable to U.S. antitrust action. On the extensive joint ventures in Middle Eastern oil production, see *ARAMCO Handbook*, 87–103. On other joint ventures, see *Petroleum Press Service, passim*, and J. E. Hartshorn, *Oil Companies and Governments*, rev. ed., London 1967, 166–168. Allan W. Johnstone, *United States Direct Investment in France*, Cambridge, Mass. 1965, 33–34 (1959 joint venture between Caltex and the French government in refining); *Petroleum Press Service* 35:13 (January 1968), and Penrose, 82 (joint ventures in refining); Michael Tanzer, *The Political Economy of International Oil and the Underdeveloped Countries*, Boston 1969, 218, 223, 258 (joint ventures in less developed countries). In the 1960s, joint ventures between U.S. oil companies and host governments in oil producing and refining were numerous in Asia and Africa and nonexistent in Latin America. The reason is not altogether clear, although it may lie in the state of development of the oil industry in the various regions. Likewise, in the future, joint ventures in Latin America seemed in the offing.

34. Penrose, 151, diagrams the ownership links between the majors in the Middle East; *ibid.*, 150 (quote); annual reports of the oil companies, and the *Economist*, Nov. 19, Dec. 3, 1960.

35. Interviews with oil company officials.

36. Endel J. Kolde, *International Business Enterprise*, Englewood Cliffs, N.J. 1968, 251; Chandler, 233; interviews; Clee and Sachtjen, 62; *New York Times*, Feb. 25, 1966. Of the eight U.S. international petroleum companies that Stopford studied on the basis of 1966 data, two still retained international divisions, three he designated as having "mixed" area product structures, and three he felt had "grid" structures. Stopford, 38.

37. *Petroleum Press Service* is an excellent source on this dispersion.

38. Peter R. Odell, *An Economic Geography of Oil*, London 1963, 27 and *Petroleum Press Service* 37:6 (January 1970).

39. *Petroleum Press Service* 34:388 (October 1967), and *International Financial News Survey* 20:211 (June 21, 1968) (Australian ventures).

40. Rainer Hellmann, *The Challenge to U.S. Dominance of the International Corporation*, New York 1970, 57, 60 (oil companies in Europe); *Petroleum Press Service* 37:2, 6 (January 1970) (oil business in the 1960s).

41. Most of our data comes from annual reports of mining companies.

42. Chandler, *Strategy and Structure*, 326–330, supplemented by interviews and annual reports of companies.

43. Wilkins, *Emergence of Multinational Enterprise* 110, and tables herein substantiate these generalizations.

44. Companies such as American Smelting and Refining, American Metal Climax, Anaconda, and Kaiser Aluminum and Chemical (all of which had stakes in less developed countries) made giant investments in mining in Australia in the 1960s. See Donald T. Brash, *American Investment in Australian Industry*, Cambridge, Mass. 1966, 10; *International Financial New Survey* 20:94 (Mar. 22, 1968), and 20:211 (June 21, 1968); *New York Times*, Jan. 19, 1970. *Survey of Current Business*, November 1972, 30 (Australia's ranking). In Latin America *as a whole*, U.S. stakes in mining exceeded those in Australia.

45. The ranking of the three largest merchandisers is from *Fortune*, July 15, 1966, 256. Richardson Wood and Virginia Keyser, *Sears, Roebuck de Mexico, S.A.*, Washington, D.C. 1953; William R. Fritsch, *Progress and Profits, the Sears, Roebuck Story in Peru*, Washington, D.C. 1962, 3–4 (history of Sears abroad); *New York Times*, Nov. 15, 1963 (Sears in Europe); *Moody's 1966* (on all the merchandising firms). Wayne G. Broehl, *The International Basic Economy Corporation*, Washington, D.C. 1968, chap. 5, esp. p. 125. John Dunning, *The Role of American Investment in the British Economy*, P.E.P. Broadsheet #507, London 1969 (U.S. supermarkets in England).

46. On the expansion and the difficulties, see Joint Economic Committee, *Foreign Government Restraints on United States Bank Operations Abroad*, 90th Cong., 1st sess. (1967). The report concluded that Mexico, Canada, Sweden, Australia, Denmark, the Trucial States, Saudi Arabia, Senegal, and Taiwan were closed to further U.S. banking at that time (p. 30). Since then, Denmark gave Bank of America permission to open there (Hellmann, 115), while in 1970, Peru purchased control of the previously 100 per cent foreign-owned banks (*New York Times*, Sept. 3, 1970). Julien-Pierre Koszul, "American Banks in Europe," in Charles P. Kindleberger, ed., *The International Corporation*, Cambridge, Mass. 1970, 274–289, documents the very recent expansion of U.S. banks in Europe, the motivation behind them, their activities, and European reaction to them.

47. Broehl, chap. 7 (I.B.E.C.).

48. On the earlier activities, see Wilkins, 64–65, 103–107, 208–209.

49. *Business Week*, Mar. 5, 1966 (Holiday Inn); Hellmann, 106–107 (U.S. hotels in Europe). *New York Times*, July 15, 1968 (Howard Johnson). On Avis, see U.S. House, Committee on the Judiciary, Antitrust Subcommittee No. 5, *Investigation of Conglomerate Corporations*, 91st Cong. (1969), pt. 3, 583–593, 964, 975, 979–980, 983, 988, 1000–1007, 1016, 1027–1034, 1051–1054, 1072–1074,

1079, 1084, 1087, 1094–1099, 1101, 1176–1187, 1197, 1202, 1236–1249. *Business Week* and *Wall Street Journal* have carried announcements of these service enterprises abroad. Every U.S. traveler abroad is aware of this.

50. The various impacts appear in the books in the bibliography (especially under the heading international business), in such U.S. government hearings as U.S. Sen., Committee on the Judiciary, Subcommittee on Antitrust and Monopoly, *International Aspects of Antitrust*, 89th Cong., 2d sess. (1966), and Joint Economic Committee, Subcommittee on Foreign Economic Policy, *A Foreign Economic Policy for the 1970's*, 91st Cong., 2d sess. (1970), and in numerous public statements made by businessmen, government officials, and labor leaders. The best statement of labor's fear about jobs is by Paul Jenning in the hearings on *Foreign Economic Policy*, pt. 4, pp. 814ff.

51. See p. 375 above.

52. According to Phyllis Deane and W. A. Cole, *British Economic Growth 1688–1959*, 2d ed., Cambridge, Eng. 1967, 330, British national income in 1914 was £2,294,000, which translated into dollars at the then current exchange rate ($5.00 per £), equals $11.47 billion; in 1914, British foreign investments have been estimated at $18.3 billion. See W. S. Woytinsky and E. S. Woytinsky, *World Commerce and Governments*, New York 1955, 191. $18.3 billion is more than one-and-one-half times $11.5 billion.

53. Derived from figures in *Survey of Current Business* (one-half of 1 per cent); Ragnar Nurkse, "International Investments Today in the Light of Nineteenth Century Experience," *Economic Journal* 44:744–754 (December 1954) and Deane and Cole, 308 (British experience).

54. This is our own summation from the vast literature on the pros and cons of direct foreign investment to the host country. The material on traditional investments is developed from the personal experiences of the author, who in 1961, 1964, and 1965 visited forty-five U.S. company towns in Latin America, Africa, and the Middle East. Hans Singer, "The Distribution of Gains between Investing and Borrowing Countries," *American Economic Review* 11:485 (May 1950) (the quote).

55. Task Force on the Structure of Canadian Industry, *Foreign Ownership and the Structure of Canadian Industry*, Ottawa 1968, 422 (henceforth cited as *Watkins Report*); testimony of Melville H. Watkins at Joint Economic Committee hearings on Foreign Economic Policy, 1970, pt. 4, 911; Hugh G. J. Aitken et al., *The American Economic Impact on Canada*, Durham, N.C. 1959; Kari Levitt, *Silent Surrender: The Multinational Corporation in Canada*, Toronto 1970, 122.

56. Testimony of John Dunning at Joint Economic Committee hearings on Foreign Economic Policy, 1970, pt. 4, p. 796.

57. Christopher Layton, *Trans-Atlantic Investments*, Boulogne-sur-Seine, France 1966, appendix, table XVII. See also Robert Hellmann, *The Challenge to U.S. Dominance of the International Corporation*, New York 1970, 98–101, and *passim* (general impact).

58. European Communities Commission, *L'industrie électronique des pays de la Communauté et les investissements américaine*. Industrial series studies, no.

1, Brussels 1969, indicates that 100 U.S. companies at that time held interests in 196 European electronic companies—a cause for alarm.

59. Donald T. Brash, *American Investment in Australian Industry,* Cambridge, Mass. 1966, 33.

60. *New York Times,* Jan. 19, 1970.

61. The most recent general study of the impact of raw materials investments on host countries is Raymond Mikesell et al., *Foreign Investment in the Petroleum and Mineral Industries: Case Studies of Investor-Host Country Relations,* Baltimore 1971; contributions to this volume by William G. Harris and Markos Mamalakis deal with the impact of U.S. investments on Venezuela and Chile respectively. Albert O. Hirschman, *National Power and the Structure of Foreign Trade,* Berkeley 1945, 16 (quote). Data on Liberian exports obtained in Liberia. Surinam obtained 87 per cent of its foreign exchange from bauxite exports; Alcoa was the principal exporter. *New York Times,* Jan. 25, 1971. Joseph Grunwald and Philip Musgrove, *Natural Resources in Latin American Development,* Baltimore, Md. 1970, 22 (on copper as a per cent of Chilean exports). *Ibid.,* 23, is excellent on petroleum and Venezuelan exports. *International Financial Statistics* for Chilean, Libyan, and Venezuelan exports (by type). On contributions to government revenues, see Henry Cattan, *The Evolution of Oil Concessions in the Middle East and North Africa,* Dobbs Ferry, N.Y. 1967, 166; Venezuelan Central Bank, *Annual Reports,* and Venezuelan Ministry of Mines and Hydrocarbons, *Annual Reports.* Clark Winton Reynolds, "Development Problems of an Export Economy, the Case of Chile and Copper," in Markos Mamalakis and Clark Winton Reynolds, *Essays on the Chilean Economy,* Homewood, Ill. 1965, 387 (for government copper revenues as a per cent of total government expenditures 1928–1958; in 1955, these revenues peaked at 37 per cent of government expenditures). Wayne Chatfield Taylor, *Firestone in Liberia,* Washington, D.C. 1956, 90, indicates that Firestone alone accounted for nearly 39 per cent of government revenues in 1955; to this should be added revenues contributed by U.S. investors in iron ore plus customs duties paid by other U.S. investors. For other general works on the U.S. business impact, see Grunwald and Musgrove, 172–174, 184 on Chile; J. R. Moore, "The Impact of Direct Investment on an Underdeveloped Economy: The Venezuelan Case," Ph.D. diss., Cornell University 1956, and Wayne C. Taylor and John Lindeman, *Creole Petroleum Corporation in Venezuela,* Washington, D.C., 1955 (both useful but by now outdated).

62. Stacey May and Galo Plaza, *The United Fruit Company in Latin America,* Washington, D.C. 1958, 181.

63. Grunwald and Musgrove, 349, 22.

64. Council for Latin America, *The Effects of United States and Other Foreign Investment in Latin America,* New York 1970 (on favorable aspects of U.S stakes in manufacturing). For an opposite view, see Celso Furtado, *Obstacles to Development in Latin America,* Garden City, N.Y. 1970, esp. pp. 63–64. Furtado is attacking U.S. stakes in *manufacturing* rather than making the typica attack on U.S. stakes in enclave-type industries.

65. See Chapter VII.

66. William Woodruff, *Impact of Western Man*, New York 1967, 150.

67. See Table XIII.1 herein.

68. Sidney E. Rolfe, *The Multinational Corporation*, New York 1970, 28 gives O.E.C.D. 1966 figures: $35 billion direct investments abroad by non-U.S. companies; $54 billion by U.S. companies. Rolfe, 29, feels the $35 billion is a "gross underestimate" and that over $50 billion is a more realistic figure. Yet even his revised estimate gives U.S. companies the advantage. Figures include U.K., France, Germany, Italy, Holland, Belgium, Switzerland, Sweden, Canada, Japan, and Australia.

69. Stephen Hymer, testifying before the Joint Economic Committee in 1970, p. 906, predicted an expansion of European foreign investment in the near future. Rolfe, 35, agrees. See Hellmann, chap. 6, on recent European business in the United States.

70. Based on Donald T. Brash, "Australia as Host to the International Corporation" in Kindleberger, *International Corporation*, 294. The capital under the rubric "American and Canadian" was mainly U.S. capital. In earlier years, some of the U.K. investment was actually U.S. investment, since U.S. companies operated through British subsidiaries and affiliates in Australia (see Chapter VII above).

71. A new challenger of the future may be Japanese business abroad, but in the 1960s, Japan's direct foreign investments—totaling the equivalent of only $1 billion in 1966—were still relatively small.

Chapter XV: International Business in Perspective

1. Charles P. Kindleberger, *American Business Abroad*, New Haven 1969, chap. 1, and the introduction to Kindleberger, ed., *The International Corporation*, Cambridge, Mass. 1970. See in this volume, Robert Z. Aliber, "A Theory of Direct Foreign Investment" and Raymond Vernon, "Future of Multinational Enterprise."

2. This is distinctive to Aliber, "A Theory."

3. See text above and Vernon, "Future of Multinational Enterprise," 374. Part or all of this process has been pointed out in many studies, for example, E. R. Barlow and Ira T. Wender, *Foreign Investment and Taxation*, Englewood Cliffs, N.J. 1955, 127, 146; Judd Polk et al., *U.S. Production Abroad and the Balance of Payments*, New York 1966. Yair Aharoni, *The Foreign Investment Decision Process*, Boston 1966; Mira Wilkins and Frank Ernest Hill, *American Business Abroad: Ford on Six Continents*, Detroit 1964, illustrates this sequence in relationship to most direct foreign investments of Ford Motor Company. See Vernon, 374–376, notes 1–2, for a list of volumes that document this process.

4. Vernon, "Future of Multinational Enterprise," 376–377, notes the "many" defensive investments.

5. William Appleton Williams leads this group.

6. Ilse Mintz, *American Exports During Business Cycles, 1879–1958*, New York 1961.

7. *Ibid.*, 66–69.

8. In emphasizing process, the author is clearly not being original. For others who likewise do so, see note 3 above.

9. In this we find relevant the work of Edith Penrose, *The Theory of the Growth of the Firm*, New York 1959, and more specifically, her "Foreign Investment and the Growth of the Firm," *Economic Journal* 66:220–235 (June 1956). Likewise, Aliber, "A Theory," 20, has directed our attention to the work of R. H. Coase, "The Nature of the Firm," *Economica*, n.s. 4(1937):386–405, from which Aliber indicates an explanation of business abroad involving enterprise efficiencies "realised by coordinating activities that occur in several different countries." Coordination within the firm results in cost reductions—as in the multinational integrated oil company. Business abroad is seen under such an explanation as an aspect of the growth of the firm. This would mesh well with our own interpretation.

10. Alfred D. Chandler, Jr., *Strategy and Structure*, Cambridge, Mass. 1962.

11. Mira Wilkins, *The Emergence of Multinational Enterprise, American Business Abroad from the Colonial Era to 1914*, Cambridge, Mass. 1970, 30, 37ff.

12. *Ibid.*, 30.

13. The use of the words "monocentric" and "polycentric" were first suggested to the present author by an address by Hans Thorelli at the International Business Association meeting, Dec. 30, 1965. Professor Thorelli, however, used the terms to apply to *organizational* structure and not as I am using them to apply to industrial structure.

14. Chandler, 299–300.

15. *Ibid.*, 299–326.

16. Peter R. Odell, *An Economic Geography of Oil*, London 1963, 33. The present author has generalized his idea to apply to more than the multinational oil company.

17. See Frederick G. Donner, *The World-Wide Industrial Enterprise*, New York 1967, for General Motors' ideas on this. Such companies as du Pont, Eastman Kodak, Ford Motor, G.E., G.M., and Goodyear had by the late 1960s their U.S. company's stock listed on Belgian, French, Dutch, and West German stock exchanges. Sidney Rolfe, *The International Corporation*, Paris 1969, 202.

18. *Fortune* editors, *The Conglomerate Commotion*, New York 1970, 146–156; in September 1968, AMK made a large purchase of United Fruit Company stock followed several months later by a tender offer.

19. *Business Week*, May 4, 1963, 82.

20. *New York Times*, July 15, 1968.

21. Anaconda *Annual Reports* are excellent in documenting the recent expansion and contraction. Company officials have been helpful, as well. U.S.-controlled mining and smelting companies that entered into business abroad in different decades and which now are in stage one, two, or three of our model include such firms as: American Metal Climax, American Smelting and Refining, Cerro, Hanna Mining, International Mining (successor to South American

Gold & Platinum Co., an early U.S. investor in Colombia), International Nickel, Kennecott, Newmont Mining, and Phelps Dodge.

22. John E. Tilton, "The Choice of Trading Partners: An Analysis of International Trade in Aluminum, Bauxite, Copper, Lead, Manganese, Tin, and Zinc," *Yale Economic Essays* 6:419–474 (Fall 1966).

23. The data on Sears, Roebuck, for example, substantiate this point. See Chap. XIV, note 45.

24. Again, there were failures. Best & Co., with stores in Paris and London in 1929, had by 1970 gone out of business abroad *and* in the United States.

25. *Survey of Current Business,* October 1970, 19.

26. *Ibid.,* 20.

27. See Louis Turner, *Invisible Empires,* New York 1970, 70–71.

28. The assertion of this novelty often appears in the literature. The quote is from U.S. Dept. of Comm., Bureau of International Commerce, *The Multinational Corporation,* Washington, D.C. 1972, pt. 1, p. 3. See also, Christopher Tugendhat, *The Multinationals,* London 1971, 11.

29. Fred A. McKenzie, *The American Invaders,* New York 1901, 31.

* Out of print